# Family Law

CORE TEXT SERIES

# Family law

*Third Edition*

MARY WELSTEAD

Visiting Professor of Law, University of Buckingham
Visiting Fellow, Child Advocacy Program, Harvard University

SUSAN EDWARDS

Professor and Dean of Law, University of Buckingham
Barrister, Clarendon Chambers, London

*Series Editor*

NICOLA PADFIELD

Fitzwilliam College, Cambridge

OXFORD
UNIVERSITY PRESS

# OXFORD
UNIVERSITY PRESS

Great Clarendon Street, Oxford OX2 6DP

Oxford University Press is a department of the University of Oxford.
It furthers the University's objective of excellence in research, scholarship,
and education by publishing worldwide in

Oxford New York

Auckland Cape Town Dar es Salaam Hong Kong Karachi
Kuala Lumpur Madrid Melbourne Mexico City Nairobi
New Delhi Shanghai Taipei Toronto

With offices in

Argentina Austria Brazil Chile Czech Republic France Greece
Guatemala Hungary Italy Japan Poland Portugal Singapore
South Korea Switzerland Thailand Turkey Ukraine Vietnam

Oxford is a registered trade mark of Oxford University Press
in the UK and in certain other countries

Published in the United States
by Oxford University Press Inc., New York

First edition 2006
Second edition 2008

British Library Cataloguing in Publication Data

Data available

Library of Congress Cataloging in Publication Data

Data available

Typeset by Newgen Imaging Systems (P) Ltd, Chennai, India
Printed in Great Britain
on acid-free paper by
Clays Ltd, St Ives Plc

ISBN 978-0-19-958615-8

For Jeremy, Abdul Redha and our families

# Preface to third edition

We are delighted to be bringing out the third edition of *Family Law*. The new edition has allowed us to update those areas of law which have changed significantly since the second edition was published in 2008, and to bring some new insights into focus.

In the field of adult relationships, there has been a significant increase in the number of decisions relating to forced marriage partly as a consequence of the Forced Marriage (Civil Protection) Act 2007. These decisions are discussed in the context of nullity in Chapter 3, and in the context of domestic violence in Chapter 5. Death and inheritance have become an even more important part of family law since the Law Commission has commenced its major study of this topic. We have cut back on our coverage of property law because most students will study this in detail in specialized property law courses. This has allowed us to cover in more detail the problematic area of ancillary relief, including the Supreme Court's ruling in *Radmacher v Granatino (2010)* and the enforceability of nuptial agreements at the end of relationships which has so taxed the minds of the judiciary. As we write, no further developments have happened in the law relating to cohabitants. The Law Commission report of 2008 remains on the table, and the government has stated that it wishes to wait and see the effects of the recent changes in the Scottish legislation in this field. Lord Lester's private member's bill on cohabitation also failed to become law. We have, therefore, decided to continue to consider the limited rights which are given to cohabitants alongside those of spouses and civil partners rather than devoting one specific chapter to them; it allows for better comparison and avoids the repetition of material. We have also drawn attention to the lack of legal rights for those who are biologically related, or good friends, who live together platonically in the same household. These families continue to be the poor relations of family law and have been largely ignored in any discussion of family law reform.

In the field of child law, we focus in Chapter 14 on the problems relating to reliability of expert evidence, and the fair trial issues that arise with regard to the erosion of the rule relating to the self-incrimination privilege. In Chapter 15, the new developments in the law relating to significant harm and children, and the decision in *Re B (2008)*, are discussed in detail, as are the developments in the law relating to the particular aspects of evidence that arise in care proceedings.

Human rights issues have continued to pre-occupy us, and we have attempted to illustrate, throughout the chapters, the effect of the European Convention on

Human Rights 1950 (ECHR) on all aspects of family law. In particular, we draw attention to the acceptance of the fact that children have rights which take precedence over the so-called parental rights of the past. However, we recognize that the courts remain reluctant to accede to the rights of adolescents where life and death matters are concerned.

Since the second edition of *Family Law* was published in 2008, the new Supreme Court has taken over the judicial functions of the House of Lords as the final court of appeal for England and Wales, Northern Ireland, and for civil appeals from Scotland. There has also been a change of government which means that certain legislative plans have been dropped, and it is too early to know how family law might change under the new Conservative-Liberal Democrat Coalition.

As in our previous editions, we have attempted to make the complexities of family law easier to understand not only for law students but also for all those who wish to know more about the effects of family law on their own family life. We also hope that we have made family law interesting so that our readers will want to explore family law in greater depth and the fascinating stories of family life which have so often engaged us throughout the writing of the third edition.

We regard the carousel (or merry-go-round as some might prefer to call it) which has appeared on the front cover of each edition of *Family Law* as an appropriate icon for the twenty-first century family. People ride on the carousel, and some leap on and off excitedly as the carousel starts and stops; others clamber on reluctantly and ride in a state of terror that they might fall off; some change horses in mid-ride, and some return over and over again because they love the carousel so much. It all resembles the ever changing nature of the modern day family.

On a final note, we would like to thank our families for their love and for their engaging us, for the most part happily, in the everyday experiences and endeavours of family life.

*Mary Welstead*
*Susan Edwards*
31 October 2010

Mary Welstead wrote the Introduction and Chapters 1–8, Susan Edwards wrote Chapters 9–16.

# New to this edition

- An increased number of self-test questions are included to encourage further reflection and to stimulate critical thinking
- Completely revised to reflect recent key developments in this fast-paced area of law, such as the Cohabitation Bill, the law on media involvement in, and access to, family courts, the Human Fertilisation and Embryology Act 2008, and reforms to the Child Support Agency
- Includes further coverage on ancillary relief, domestic violence, private and public child law, and issues surrounding surrogacy
- Now with an accompanying Online Resource Centre, featuring web-links and updates.

# Contents

# Table of cases

# Table of statutes

# Table of statutory instruments

# 1

# Introduction to family law

## What is family law?

1.1 Family law is perhaps the most fascinating of all areas of law because it is the only one in which all of its students have been personally involved from the moment of birth. It is also of interest because of its multi-faceted nature. It includes every aspect of legal intervention into the private or domestic lives of those who are related by blood or affinity, or who have, or have had, emotional ties with each other. Those who come within its sphere of influence tend to occupy, or will have occupied, the same family home.

1.2 Over the last 150 years, family law has acquired an evolving, yet discrete, core of its own, which reflects and influences societal views of what constitutes a family, and why, and how, it should be regulated. The majority of those relationships which the State regards as benefiting society as a whole have tended to be labelled as familial. Those who participate in these familial relationships have been granted legal rights and, in return, the adult participants have had legal responsibilities imposed upon them. The State's view of familial will, of course, change over time.

1.3 Twenty-first century family lawyers require not only a knowledge of, and an expertise in, the core area of family law, they also need, *inter alia*, a knowledge of financial matters, property law (both real and personal), the law of contract and tort, criminal law, the law of wills and trusts, medical law, and the ever-increasing law relating to human rights. They must be familiar with the social and biological sciences, in particular human psychology and reproductive technology. They must also be interested in the fascinating stories of family life and the black humour which, so frequently, is to be found in them. Above all, family lawyers must remain optimists in the face of the tragedies which so regularly confront them in the material of family law.

# Legal rights and obligations or freedom of contract?

1.4 During the latter half of the twentieth century, familial relationships developed in a way which emphasized the fulfilment of individual emotional needs. The idea that the family's major role was to serve the needs of society began to be questioned. Alongside this evolution, a growing and more general respect for individual rights to self-determination and privacy also gained momentum. The philosophy behind these interrelated developments would appear to demand the freedom for adults to contract with each other, free from State control, about the terms of their relationship, and have those contracts legally enforced. The limited enforcement of some private familial contracts can be seen as a natural development of this individualism.

1.5 However, privatization of familial relationships and freedom of contract may also be viewed as out of tune with other aspects of current social thought which emphasize the importance of protection of the potentially vulnerable, the imposition of mutual responsibility, and redistributive justice, for those who commit to caring for each other which benefits society as a whole. There are potential adverse effects which may result from the enforcement of private contracts. One or more family members may be left in a vulnerable economic position and dependent on the State for legal aid, welfare benefits, and medical and psychiatric support. Contracts, which were negotiated at the beginning of a relationship at a time of romantic optimism, may fail to meet the parties' needs when it ends acrimoniously. It is not an easy task for couples, who are embarking on a committed relationship, to contemplate its future breakdown and the ensuing consequences.

1.6 A tension has developed in family law which mirrors the debate between those who espouse individualism and those whose concern is the social and economic good of society. Family law appears to vacillate between the enforcement of privately negotiated contracts and the imposition of legal rights and obligations laid down by common law or statute. Where the enforcement of private contracts alleviates State expenditure, they are more likely to be enforced. There are, of course, areas of family law where private contracts will always remain inappropriate; one obvious example is in matters which relate to the needs of children.

# Changing definitions of family

1.7 The term 'family' in family law is not a term of art; it has no independent generalized legal meaning; it changes over time, and can only be understood within the particular socio-legal context in which it is used. However, it may be helpful to consider some of the ways in which the term 'family' has been defined, and changed, over time. Historical definitions of the word family encompassed a wide group of people who shared the same household.

For instance, in *R v Inhabitants of Darlington (1792)*, Lord Kenyon CJ stated that

*In common parlance the family consists of those who live under the same roof with the pater familias: those who form...his fireside.*

Servants were included in this definition; they often lived with a family for the whole of their lives.

In *Blackwell v Bull* (1836), Lord Langdale said:

*It is evident that the word family is capable of so many applications that if any one construction were attributed to it in wills, the intention of the testators would be more frequently defeated than carried into effect. Under different circumstances it means a man's household, consisting of himself, his wife, children and servants; it may mean his wife and children, or his wife; in the absence of wife and children, it may mean his brother and sisters or his next of kin, or it may mean the genealogical stock from which he may have sprung.*

1.8 By the twentieth century, legal intervention into family life developed and definitions of the family grew narrower. The field of Rent Act legislation provides a plentiful supply of illustrations of this trend. Judicial statements, relating to the classification of a person as a member of a deceased tenant's family which would give him or her the right to continue to live in their family home, are tinged with social and moral perceptions of the legitimacy of certain kinds of familial relationships. The following decisions illustrate this approach.

In *Langdon v Horton (1951)*, the Court of Appeal refused Rent Act protection to two elderly ladies who had lived for 30 years with their cousin in a house, which she had held on a statutory tenancy prior to her death. The court held that all three had lived together for the sake of personal convenience and not because they were part of the same family.

In *Gammans v Ekins (1950)*, the Court of Appeal rejected the claim of a male cohabitant to remain in the family home on the death of his partner. Asquith LJ took the view that either the relationship was platonic and the couple were not members of each other's family, or it was not. If the relationship was platonic, Asquith LJ believed that to recognize the cohabitants as members of the same family would also require the court to accord the same status to two old cronies of the same sex innocently sharing a flat. If the relationship were not platonic, Asquith LJ thought it

*...anomalous that a person could acquire a Rent Act protected status by living or having lived in sin, even if the relationship had not been a mere casual encounter but protracted in time and conclusive in character.*

He concluded by saying that to accept a same-sex couple, masquerading as husband and wife, as members of the same family was an abuse of the English language.

Evershed MR agreed with Asquith LJ and stated that it

*...may be no bad thing that by this decision it is shown that, in the Christian society in which we live, one, at any rate, of the privileges which may be derived from marriage is not equally enjoyed by those who are living together as man and wife but who are not married.*

In *Ross v Collins (1964)*, a woman claimed the right to succeed to a statutory tenancy on the death of her partner. She had lived with the deceased for a substantial period of time. She was 40 years younger than him and had looked after him dutifully, regarding him as a sort of elder relative, partly father, partly brother. Russell LJ ruled that this platonic, familial relationship was not within the definition of family because there was no kinship between the couple. He maintained that:

*...two strangers cannot ever establish artificially a familial nexus by acting as brothers or as sisters, even if they refer to each other as such and consider their relationship to be tantamount to that. Nor can an adult man and woman who establish a platonic relationship establish a familial nexus by acting as a devoted brother and sister or father and daughter would act, even if they address each other as such and regard their association as tantamount to such. Nor would they indeed be recognised as familial links by the ordinary man.*

1.9 By 1980, the courts had begun to recognize that those living in stable heterosexual cohabiting relationships could be classified as members of each other's families in the context of landlord and tenant disputes.

In *Watson v Lucas (1980)*, it was held that a married man, who had left his wife to live with another woman in a stable and long-term relationship, was a member of her family.

1.10 A major change in the concept of family relationships occurred at the beginning of the twenty-first century.

The decision in *Fitzpatrick v Sterling Housing Association (2000)* accepted that homosexuals could be members of each other's families. Lord Slynn, in a most sensitive judgment, viewed the essential hallmarks of a familial relationship as a degree of mutual interdependence, the sharing of lives, the caring and love for each other, and the commitment and support for each other. He explained that:

*In respect of legal relationships these are presumed, though evidently they are not always present, as the family law and criminal courts know only too well. In de facto relationships these are capable, if proved, of creating membership of the family.*

In *Mendoza v Ghaidan (2004)*, the House of Lords went further and held that the term *as husband and wife* in Rent Act legislation, could be read to mean *as if they were husband and wife*. It, therefore, included a same-sex partner who had lived with the deceased in a spouse-like manner.

1.11 Since these decisions, the concepts of family, and spouse, have been further extended in two other contexts. In accordance with the Gender Recognition Act 2004 (GRA

2004), transgendered persons, who have obtained a gender recognition certificate (see Chapter 3), may marry a member of the opposite sex to that of their newly acquired gender. Prior to the Act, they were restricted to marrying members of the opposite sex to their previous biological gender. The Civil Partnership Act 2004 (CPA 2004) has also given a quasi-spousal, and familial, status to same-sex couples who register their partnerships (see Chapter 3). Family law appears to have gone almost full circle in terms of its now extensive definition of the terms family and familial.

## Excluded relationships

1.12 There remain two categories of adult relationships, which although functionally familial, have only been granted limited legal rights. The first category consists of heterosexual and same-sex cohabitants. Their relationships are often identical to those of married couples and civil partners but have simply not been formalized. The government asked the Law Commission to undertake a review of the law relating to cohabitants. Its recommendations were published in 2007 but no action has been taken. In 2008, the Labour government announced that it would wait until research was completed on the cost and effectiveness of the recently implemented Scottish legislation.

1.13 The second category of familial relationships has been largely ignored by the legislators, and there are no plans to consider bringing it within the fold of the legal family in the foreseeable future. It consists of those who live together in the same household as members of a family but who have never engaged in sexual relationships with each other. This is either because they are closely related to each other, and they do not wish to have an illegal incestuous relationship, or because they are very close friends who have personally assumed responsibility for each other, but a sexual relationship is not a desired aspect of their friendship. These relationships also perform a familial function; many of the parties are elderly and would be unable to remain in their own homes were it not for the relationship.

A prime example of one such relationship is to be found in *Joram Developments v Sharratt (1979)*:

> Lady Salter was the widow of a High Court judge who had died in 1929. In 1957, when she was aged 75, she suggested to Mr Sharratt, who was aged 24, that he should come to live with her in her flat. They shared similar interests and enjoyed each other's company for 19 years until Lady Salter died in 1976, aged 94. Mr Sharratt was with Lady Salter when she died because her family regarded him as her next of kin. Throughout, their relationship was platonic, motivated by kindness and affection.

The county court judge had concluded that:

*Lady Salter and this defendant achieved through their relationship what must surely be regarded in a popular sense, and in common sense, as a familial nexus. That is to say, a nexus as one would find only within a family. I am sure Shakespeare's [base, common and popular] man would say: 'Yes, it is stranger than fiction, but they established a familial tie'. Everyone linked to her through the blood was remote by comparison with the defendant.*

The House of Lords had no difficulty in rejecting this view and held that Mr Sharratt was not a member of Lady Salter's family.

1.14 During the passage of the CPA 2004 through Parliament, the House of Lords tabled amendments to extend the scope of the Act to this second category of familial relationships consisting of siblings, parents and adult children, carers, and other home sharers. Estimates suggest that there are 60 times more of these relationships than there are of same-sex relationships. The amendments failed; accusations were made that they had been tabled, in a rather cynical manner, in order to ensure the failure of the Bill rather than to help, and avoid discriminating against, a vulnerable category of persons who regarded themselves as enjoying familial relationships.

1.15 It would seem that to date, a sexual relationship or, at least, a potential for it, is often the triggering factor for the legal recognition of adult relationships as familial. This, of course, leaves adult sibling, and parent and adult child relationships, largely without legal protection.

The case of **Burden v UK (2008 and 2009)** in which two elderly sisters were denied the possibility of the inheritance tax relief, which is given to married and civil partners, is a perfect example of such a relationship. The majority in **Burden** remarked in a rather circular way:

*...the relationship between siblings is qualitatively of a different nature to that between married couples and homosexual civil partners under the United Kingdom's CPA 2004. The very essence of the connection between siblings is consanguinity, whereas one of the defining characteristics of a marriage or CPA 2004 union is that it is forbidden to close family members... The fact that the applicants have chosen to live together all their adult lives, as do many married and CPA 2004 couples, does not alter this essential difference between the two types of relationship.*

# Changing concerns of family law

## Children

1.16 The increasing emphasis in family law today is centred on the needs, rights, and welfare of children from their conception to adulthood. Parenthood is seen as more concerned with obligations towards children rather than rights over them, and it is no longer dependent on marital status. The definition of parenthood has evolved to cover new forms of biological and social parent/child relationships. More complex means of medically assisted reproduction present new challenges to legal concepts of parenthood. Multi-parentage, which may involve as many as six or even seven different adults in the process of conceiving, gestating, and socially parenting a child, requires innovative legal responses.

## Financial matters

1.17 In the area of law relating to adult relationships, financial and property disputes are at the forefront. A move towards equal division of a couple's assets has been suggested as a fair solution to the problem of ancillary relief when a relationship has been legally ended. In the absence of legislation relating to home sharing, the family home, which is the cornerstone of family life, continues to tax the creative ingenuity of family lawyers in establishing rights by way of informal trusts.

## The international family

1.18 The family no longer remains in one village, city, county, or country. It is a mobile institution; partners marry across international boundaries. They experience problems when the family breaks down and one partner wishes to return to his or her country of origin with the children. The courts are faced with the impossible task of determining in which country a child should live and, thereby, effectively depriving the child of a relationship with one of his, or her, parents.

1.19 Families also move from their country of origin because of unemployment, war, famine, terrorism, environmental disasters, or poverty. Society has become multicultural, and family law is faced with disputes in which family members have very different cultural expectations of how family life should be conducted from those which exist in their new society. Family law has to deal with the problem of determining when it is appropriate to take into account these differing cultural expectations and when it is not.

## Human rights

1.20 The Human Rights Act 1998 (HRA 1998) has had a significant effect on family law; it requires, *inter alia*, that family law complies with the European Convention on Human Rights 1950 (ECHR). Section 3(1), HRA 1998 provides that:

> ...*so far as is possible to do so, primary legislation and subordinate legislation must be read and given effect in a way which is compatible with the Convention Rights.*

If this not possible, HRA 1998, s 4 allows the High Court, the Court of Appeal, the Supreme Court, and the Judicial Committee of the Privy Council to make a declaration of incompatibility. If remedial action is not taken by the government after such a declaration, the case has to be dealt with by the European Court of Human Rights (ECtHR). An individual who believes that his or her human rights have been breached may take action against a public authority which acts in a way which is incompatible with any of the Convention Rights (see HRA 1998, s 7(1)).

1.21 Although the HRA 1998 cannot be used directly by individuals against each other, they may be able to use it indirectly. For instance, where one member of a family refuses to obey a court order in favour of another family member, and that refusal also breaches a Convention Right, the court may be forced to take action to ensure that the court order is obeyed in order to prevent a breach of Convention Rights.

1.22 The most important Articles of the ECHR for family lawyers are Art 6, the right to a fair trial; Art 8, the right to respect for private and family life; Art 12, the right to marry; and Art 14, the right to enjoy the Convention rights without discrimination. Protocol 12 of the ECHR provides for a self-standing right to freedom from discrimination but the UK government has not yet ratified the Protocol in spite of recommendations to do so in 2007 from the Joint Committee on Human Rights.

1.23 Art 8 is subject to the very significant proviso that:

> *...there shall be no interference by a public authority with the exercise of this right except such as is in accordance with the law and is necessary in a democratic society in the interests of national security, public safety or the economic well being of the country, for the prevention of disorder or crime, for the protection of morals, or for the protection of the rights and freedoms of others.*

The proviso is an attempt to balance the rights of the individual and the rights of the larger community but it also limits the impact of Art 8.

1.24 An additional limitation to the effectiveness of the ECHR is a feature of the ECtHR's jurisprudence known as 'the margin of appreciation'. This concept allows the Court to take into account, when considering an alleged breach of one of the Convention rights, the fact that cultural norms may vary from one Convention State to another. In certain circumstances, where there is no absolute agreement on an issue involving a Convention right, an individual State may be deemed to be in a better position to judge whether a particular law is necessary to meet its cultural needs (see ***Burden v United Kingdom (2006 and 2008)***).

1.25 Challenges and fears of challenges under the ECHR are now a constant theme throughout family case law. They have brought about dramatic changes in legislation to ensure conformity with the ECHR. The enactment of the GRA 2004 and the CPA 2004 were both products of challenges, and a fear of further challenges, under the ECHR.

## Organization of the text

1.26 The text is divided into two parts: Part I (Chapters 2–8) concerns the law relating to adult relationships and Part II (Chapters 9–16) the law relating to children. Each part is self-contained and may be read in whichever order the reader chooses.

---

**FURTHER READING**

All readers may find it helpful to look at *Family Law* on a regular basis; it is published monthly by Jordans. A selective reading of a daily newspaper should also keep you abreast of family matters, both legal and social.

Bamforth N, 'The Role of Philosophical and Constitutional Arguments in the Same-sex Marriage Debate: a Response to John Murphy' [2005] CFLQ 165

Barton C, 'Spending More Time With Their Families—The Government's Consultation Document' [1999] Fam Law 136

Barton C, 'Family Law in the Classroom' [2004] Fam Law 269

Bonne D, Fenwick H and Harris-Short S, 'Judicial Approaches to the Human Rights Act' [2003] ICLQ 549

Bridgeman J, Keating H and Lind C, *Responsibility, Law and the Family* (Jordans, 2008)

British Social Attitudes 26th Report, http://www.natcen.ac.uk/study/british-social-attitudes-26th-report/findings

Conway H, 'The Human Rights Act 1998 And Family Law—Part One' [1999] Fam Law 811

Conway H, 'The Human Rights Act 1998 And Family Law—Part Two' [2000] Fam Law 30

Coontz S, *Marriage: a History* (Viking, 2005)

Cretney S, *Family Law in the Twentieth Century: a History* (Oxford University Press, 2003)

Douglas G, *An Introduction to Family Law* (2nd edn, Oxford University Press) (2004)

Douglas G and Lowe N (Eds), *The Continuing Evolution of Family Law* (Jordans, 2009)

Government White Paper, 'Supporting Families' (1998), http://www.homeoffice.gov.uk/

Hale B, Pearl D, Cooke E and Monk D, Ch. 12, *The Family Law and Society: Cases and Materials* (6th edn, Oxford University Press, 2008)

Harris-Short S and Miles J, *Family Law: Text, Cases and Materials* (Oxford University Press, 2007)

Hunt S. (Ed), Family and Parenting Institute (FPI). Family Trends: British Families since the 1950s, Joint Committee on Human Rights Reports http://www.publications. parliament.uk

Lowe N and Douglas G, *Bromley's Family Law* (10th edn, Oxford University Press, 2007)

Probert R, 'Family Law: a Modern Concept' [2004] Fam Law 901

Scherpe J, 'The Gametes of European Family Law' [2008] IFL 98

The Rt Hon Lord Justice Thorpe, 'The Rise and Rise of International Family Law' [2008] Fam Law 105

Waller M, *The English Marriage* (John Murray, 2009)

Wasoff F, Mordaunt E and Miles J, Legal practitioners' perspectives on the cohabitation provisions of the Family Law (Scotland) Act 2006 www.crfc.ac/uk/researchprojects/r-cohabitation.html

Welstead M, 'Reshaping Marriage and the Family—The Gender Recognition Act 2004 and the Civil Partnership Act 2004', *International Survey of Family Law 2004* (Jordans)

Welstead M, 'Who Are My Family?' *International Survey of Family Law 2005* (Jordans)

## SELF-TEST QUESTIONS

1 Consider your own family relationships from birth to the present day, and the extent to which the law has involved itself in them in either a positive or negative way.

2 Read **Burden v UK (2006) and Burden v UK (2008)**; consider the approaches taken by the judges to the similarities and differences between two sisters who live together in their family home, and spouses or civil partners, who live together.

3 Do you share the view of the majority in **Burden (2006 and 2008)** that the decision to deny the sisters the possibility of exemption from inheritance tax was justified? If not, explain why you disagree.

4 How would you overcome the supposed difficulties of giving biologically related adult members of the same family who live together similar rights to those given to married couples and civil partners?

# 2

# State intervention in personal relationships

## SUMMARY

The State chooses to involve itself in personal relationships in order to promote those economic and social policies, which it believes to be beneficial for itself and for society. This intervention takes the form of giving benefits to, and imposing burdens on, those parties who enter into personal relationships which meet with State approval. Those who are unable, or unwilling, to play the familial game in accordance with State expectations remain, for the most part, exempt from specific legal responsibilities for each other, and they receive negligible legal or economic advantages.

If benefits are to be given, and responsibilities enforced, it is necessary for the State to know who has entered into one of the approved familial relationships and who has not. The law, therefore, must define what constitutes such a relationship and what determines its point of entry and exit.

In this chapter, we consider the law relating to the nature and formation of the legally approved relationships of marriage and civil partnerships and that somewhat nebulous status given to those who are engaged to be married or who have agreed to enter into a civil partnership. We also examine the nature of those informal cohabiting relationships in which the State has decided to intervene, albeit to a more limited degree. We note the minimal nature of State intervention in familial relationships involving siblings, and parent adult-child relationships.

There is an inevitable overlap in this chapter with the topics discussed in Chapter 3, and it may be helpful read these chapters in conjunction with each other.

# Form v function

2.1 In determining which familial relationships should receive the special attention of the law, the State may take a formalistic approach, often referred to as following the bright-line rule, and define with precision the nature of the relationship and the entry point into, and the departure point from, it. The purpose of this approach is to produce predictable and consistent results and leave no room for interpretation or discretion. If the parties in a relationship do not comply with the formal requirements, they will not be granted the status of an approved familial relationship.

2.2 It is equally possible for the State to take a functional approach towards the family and bring any relationship, which performs the essential functions of the family in line with the State's expectations, within both its protective and demanding legal sphere.

# A dual approach

2.3 English law takes a dual approach to familial relationships. Marriage is regarded as the ideal family model; those who marry acquire a status and are granted rights appropriate to that view. It has a fixed entry point with strict rules relating to its formation and dissolution. Those who enter into it may not, for the most part, determine the nature of the matrimonial contract for themselves; it is defined by law and, as will be seen, there is very limited opportunity to depart from it.

2.4 Since 2005, when the Civil Partnership Act 2004 (CPA 2004) came into force, State intervention has been extended to same-sex partnerships. These relationships have been granted the status of a form of quasi-marriage if the couple register a civil partnership. The rules relating to the formation and dissolution of same-sex partnerships are very similar to those relating to marriage, and civil partners are given many of the rights and duties of spouses but are not accorded the gold standard title of spouses.

2.5 An engagement, or an agreement to enter into a civil partnership, are viewed by the State as a preliminary to the formal relationship of marriage or civil partnership. Fiancés have always received some legal rights, although these rights have lessened significantly over time. Today, in the absence of formal betrothal ceremonies, it is not easy to determine what constitutes an engagement sufficient to bring the relationship within the law's sphere. Those who agree to enter into a civil partnership may also benefit from similar rights to those given to engaged couples.

2.6 The State has shown a certain amount of reluctance to intervene when a couple cohabits. The nature of informal cohabiting relationships means that it is difficult to determine with any precision when they begin and when they end. However, both heterosexual and same-sex cohabiting relationships perform some of the functions of marriage or civil partnership, and the State has given cohabitants some legal protection and imposed limited responsibilities on them. In 2007, the Law Commission proposed major reforms to the law relating to cohabitants on relationship breakdown (*Cohabitation: The Financial Consequences of Relationship Breakdown*, Law Com No 307). These proposals will be discussed in the relevant chapters throughout the text.

## Relationships exempt from legal intervention

2.7 There is one important category of familial or quasi-familial cohabiting relationship in which the State has chosen largely not to intervene, even though it fulfils many of the approved familial functions. It is the non-sexual, living together relationship which exists between adults who may be siblings; parent/adult child, or caring friends. During the passage of the Civil Partnership Bill through Parliament in 2003, concern was expressed at the state's neglect of these relationships. Lord Tebbit, a Conservative Peer, pointed out that persons in these relationships might be able to claim that the lack of provision for them is discriminatory and a breach of their human rights. He maintained that:

> *The financial and tax impact of the death of a parent who has been cared for by a son or daughter at the sacrifice of his or her own career and financial well-being is no less than that of the surviving member of a homosexual couple who may have made a similar commitment one to the other, but for perhaps a far shorter period. Daughters are made just as homeless when inheritance tax demands force the sale of their family home as those who would be members of civil partnerships under the provisions of the Bill.... when there is a relationship between a parent and a child who is particularly vulnerable, what happens then? The vulnerable child is left with an inheritance tax Bill which forces the sale of the home in which he or she has lived, and has been cared for by parents, throughout the whole of their natural life. Are these not matters which are of concern to us here and now?*
>
> *(Hansard, House of Lords, 24 June, Vol. 662 (no. 104), Col 1368-1369)*

Many would assert that Lord Tebbit's concerns were more connected with an interest in derailing the civil partnership legislation (see below). However, his comments, once again, drew attention to the feelings of those who are excluded from entering into a legally recognized familial relationship either because they are already close family members, or are caring friends, and would regard it as inappropriate to marry or enter into a civil partnership.

# The decision of the European Court of Human Rights in *Burden and Burden v UK (2006)*

2.8     In 2006, in **Burden and Burden v United Kingdom (2006)**, two elderly spinsters made an application to the European Court of Human Rights (ECtHR)and complained, under Art 14 (prohibition of discrimination), taken in conjunction with Art 1 of Protocol 1 (the protection of property), of the European Convention on Human Rights 1950 (ECHR), that UK law discriminated agains\t them by preventing them from registering a civil partnership and thereby losing the right to protection of their family home. When the first of them died, the survivor would be required to pay 40 per cent inheritance tax on her dead sister's share of their family home which she might be forced to sell to pay that tax. By contrast, the survivor of a married couple, or a homosexual relationship registered under the CPA 2004, would be exempt from paying such a tax.

The Court rejected the application by four votes to three. Its ruling centred on the wide margin of appreciation enjoyed by a State in deciding whether, and to what extent, differential treatment is justified. It maintained that States may well need to strike a balance between the need to raise revenue and the social objectives in doing so, and were generally in a better position to determine their social and economic policies than the Court. Their decisions relating to these policies will, therefore, normally be respected by the Court unless it is evident that they are without reasonable foundation and consequently unjustifiable.

In a joint dissenting judgment, Judges Bonello and Garlicki maintained that once the UK legislature decided to extend the inheritance tax exemption to civil partners as well as married couples, it had failed to establish that it had behaved reasonably, and in a non-arbitrary manner, by not granting siblings who live together a similar right. In their opinion:

*The situation of permanently cohabiting siblings is in many respects—emotional as well as economical—not entirely different from the situation of other unions, particularly as regards old or very old people. The bonds of mutual affection form the ethical basis for such unions and the bonds of mutual dependency form the social basis for them. It is very important to protect such unions, like any other union of two persons, from financial disaster resulting from the death of one of the partners....*

*...unless some compelling reasons can be shown, the legislature cannot simply ignore that such unions also exist.*

The judges also acknowledged that:

*The situation of permanently cohabiting siblings under the UK legislation has also been negatively affected by the fact that—being within the prohibited degrees of relationship—they cannot form a civil partnership. In other words, they have been deprived of the possibility of choice offered to other couples.*

In a second dissenting judgment, Judge Pavlovschi stressed that he was particularly influenced by the nature of the sisters' property which would be subject to inheritance tax:

*The case concerns the applicants' family house, in which they have spent all their lives and which they built on land inherited from their late parents. This house is not simply a piece of property—this house is something with which they have a special emotional bond, this house is their home.*

*It strikes me as absolutely awful that, once one of the two sisters dies, the surviving sister's sufferings on account of her closest relative's death should be multiplied by the risk of losing her family home because she cannot afford to pay inheritance tax in respect of the deceased sister's share of it.*

*I find such a situation fundamentally unfair and unjust. It is impossible for me to agree with the majority that, as a matter of principle, such treatment can be considered reasonable and objectively justified. I am firmly convinced that in modern society there is no 'pressing need' to cause people all this additional suffering.*

Joyce Burden on learning of the Court's decision commented:

*If we were lesbians we would have all the rights in the world. But we are sisters, and it seems we have no rights at all.*

## The decision of the Grand Chamber in *Burden v UK (2008)*

2.9    The Burden sisters did not give up and, in 2007 at their request, the Panel of the Grand Chamber of the ECtHR decided to refer their case to the Grand Chamber which refused to accept that a relationship between siblings could be seen as analogous to that of a married couple or civil partners. There was, therefore no discrimination against the Burden sisters.

In functional terms, it is difficult to see how the relationship between Joyce and Sybil Burden could properly be regarded in any way other than analogous with that of a married couple or a same-sex partner. They had chosen to live with each other in their family home in a loving, committed and stable relationship for many decades, foregoing the possibility of marriage or civil partnership with any other person, yet unable to legalize that relationship because of their consanguinity. The sisters, not surprisingly, found it difficult to understand why:

*...two single sisters in their old age, whose only crime was to choose to stay single and look after their parents and two aunts to the end, should find themselves in such a position in the UK in the 21st century. We certainly do not regret our decision to look after our family for a single moment; we were glad to repay them for the happy, good, Christian upbringing they gave us...we have been fighting for 32 years just to gain the same rights, as regards inheritance tax, as married couples and couples in civil partnerships.*

# Definitions and formation of relationships

## Engagement

2.10 Fiancés are given limited legal rights both during and at the end of their relationship. One of the problems for modern day law is the difficulty in determining precisely what constitutes an engagement. In general, the term fiancé appears to encompass a wide array of relationships. At one extreme, a couple may describe themselves as engaged where the man has formally proposed marriage to the woman (except in leap years when custom provides that a woman may propose to a man); presented her with a ring; a formal announcement has been made; the wedding date has been set, and the wedding plans are well under way. At the other extreme, a couple who cohabit and have children may refer to themselves as fiancés, yet have no intention of marrying in the near future, if ever. They may not be even be free to marry each other.

Historically, the term fiancé was more circumscribed. An engagement, or betrothal, was formally announced and an engagement ring was given to seal the promise to marry. The custom of giving an engagement ring began in 1477 when Maximilian, the Archduke of Austria, presented his fiancée Mary, Duchess of Burgundy with a diamond ring. It was possible prior to 1970 for a woman to sue for breach of promise if an engagement was broken because she had risked the loss of the possibility of marrying someone else and had potentially suffered damage to her reputation.

2.11 There appears to be no exact counterpart of an engagement for prospective civil partners although in the period immediately prior to their civil partnership, one would assume that they have agreed to enter into one.

2.12 UK immigration rules (para 290) require, *inter alia,* that a person who wishes to enter the country as a fiancé, or as a prospective civil partner, must have met his or her future spouse or civil partner, and plans to marry or enter into a civil partnership within six months of entering the country. The couple must have the capacity to legalize their relationship and intend to live together. They must also have adequate resources for their own maintenance and accommodation, as well as for that of their prospective partner and any dependants, without recourse to public funds.

## Marriage

2.13 Many people, including family lawyers, when asked to define marriage, automatically regurgitate the catechismal, definition in *Hyde v Hyde (1866)*:

> ... marriage is the voluntary union for life of one man to one woman to the exclusion of all others.

2.14  This brief statement is neither an adequate description nor an accurate reflection of what marriage is today. Marriage can hardly be said to be for life. Divorce is readily obtainable and its incidence in England and Wales is high (see Ch 6). Since the enactment of the Gender Recognition Act 2004 (GRA 2004), marriage is no longer restricted to those who were born respectively male and female.

2.15  Bigamous marriages entered into in jurisdictions which permit them may, in certain circumstances, be recognized by English law. Such marriages also appear to be socially accepted; the Queen invited the Sultan of Brunei and both his wives, as her guests, to the wedding of her youngest child in 1999.

2.16  The definition in *Hyde (1866)* gives minimal information about the nature of marriage and the legal consequences which flow from it. By virtue of the marriage ceremony, couples agree to accept the spousal status but most of them will have little advance knowledge of the matrimonial rights and duties which attach to that status. They only become aware of such matters after the marriage, and by negative means; they must look to the legislation on nullity, divorce, property, death, and domestic violence to discover the opaque terms of the contract which governs their new status. It is through the remedies (or lack of them) which the courts may (or may not) grant to them, if married life does not work out in the way they had romantically and optimistically hoped, that they learn the weighty consequences of the marriage contract.

2.17  Thorpe LJ in *Bellinger v Bellinger (2001)* explained that:

> . . . the world that engendered those classic definitions [of marriage] has long since gone. We live in a multi-racial, multi-faith society. The intervening 130 years have seen huge social and scientific changes. Adults live longer, infant mortality has been largely conquered, and effective contraception is available to men and women as is sterilisation for men and women within marriage. Illegitimacy with its stigma has been legislated away: gone is any social condemnation of cohabitation in advance of or in place of marriage. Then marriage was terminated by death: for the vast majority of the population divorce was not an option. For those within whose reach it lay, it carried a considerable social stigma that did not evaporate until relatively recent times. Now more marriages are terminated by divorce than death. Divorce could be said without undue cynicism to be available on demand. These last changes are all reflected in the statistics establishing the relative decline in marriage and consequentially in the number of children born within marriage. Marriage has become a state into which and from which people choose to enter and exit. Thus I would now redefine marriage as a contract for which the parties elect but which is regulated by the state, both in its formation and in its termination by divorce, because it affects status upon which depend a variety of entitlements, benefits and obligations.

## The right to marry

2.18  The ECHR Art 12 states that

> Men and women of marriageable age have the right to marry and to found a family, according to the national laws governing the exercise of this right.

2.19    In *R (on the application of Baiai and others) v Secretary of State for the Home Department (2008)*, the House of Lords considered the right to marry under the Asylum and Immigration (Treatment of Claimants, etc) Act 2004, s 19(3)(b). The section requires the written permission of the Secretary of State to marry if one, or both parties, to the marriage is subject to immigration control unless entry clearance had been granted specifically for the purpose of marriage in the UK (s 19(3)(a)), or the relevant party was settled in the UK within the meaning of the Immigration Rules (s 19(3)(c)). A fee of £295 is payable by the applicants (Immigration (Procedure for Marriage) Regulations 2005).

Their Lordships held that the right to marry protected by Art 12 was a strong right. However, a Convention State could impose reasonable conditions on the right of a third country national to marry in order to check whether the proposed marriage was a genuine one or one of convenience for immigration purposes, and if so, prevent it. In order to prevent a breach of Art 12, S.19 (3)(b) of the Act should be read as referring to person who

> *...has the written permission of the Secretary of State to marry in the UK, such permission not to be withheld in the case of a qualified applicant seeking to enter into a marriage which is not one of convenience, and the application for, and grant of such permission not to be subject to conditions which unreasonably inhibit exercise of the applicant's right under Art 12 of the European Convention.*

The House of Lords also held that the current fee payable under the 2005 Regulations was set at a level which could infringe the right to marry.

## Capacity to marry

2.20    The law relating to capacity to marry is laid down in the Marriage Act 1949, ss 1–3 and Sch 1 and the Matrimonial Causes Act 1973 (MCA 1973), ss 11, 12, 13.

### Male and female

2.21    The parties who wish to marry must be respectively male and female; same-sex partners may not marry. Until 2005, transgendered persons were not permitted to marry a member of the opposite sex to that of their newly acquired gender. If a transgendered person attempted to marry, the marriage was deemed to be a same-sex marriage, and, therefore, invalid (MCA 1973, s 11(c)). Thus a male to female transgendered person could only marry a female, and a female to male transgendered person could only marry a male. Such marriages were rare and, to the outsider, looked remarkably like same-sex marriages. (For a summary of the law prior to the GRA 2004, see the Court of Appeal decision in *Bellinger v Bellinger (2001)*, *Goodwin v UK (2002)*.) Transgendered persons were deemed to remain trapped in their birth gender. Unless they were found to be inter-sexed, their birth certificate could not be altered to reflect their adult-determined gender (see *W v W (nullity) (2000)*.)

2.22    In the Court of Appeal decision in *Bellinger (2001)*, Thorpe LJ in a dissenting judgment concluded that:

*To make the chromosomal factor conclusive, or even dominant, seems to me par-*
*ticularly questionable in the context of marriage. For it is an invisible feature of an*
*individual, incapable of perception or registration other than by scientific test. It*
*makes no contribution to the physiological or psychological self. Indeed in the con-*
*text of the institution of marriage as it is today it seems to me right as a matter of*
*principle and logic to give predominance to psychological factors just as it seems*
*right to carry out the essential assessment of gender at or shortly before the time of*
*marriage rather than at the time of birth.*

2.23 In 2003, the House of Lords considered Mrs Bellinger's appeal. It held that a person, whose sex had been correctly diagnosed at birth, could not later become, or come to be regarded as, a person of the opposite sex. The House of Lords maintained that it was for Parliament rather than the courts to change the law on such an important matter because there was considerable uncertainty about the circumstances in, and purposes for, which gender reassignment should be recognized and it should not be dealt with in a piecemeal fashion. However, the House of Lords formally recorded, the fact that the failure of the MCA 1973 to recognize gender reassignment for the purposes of marriage was incompatible with Art 8 (the right to private and family life) and Art 12 (the right to marry and found a family of the ECHR.

2.24 At the time of the decision in *Bellinger (2003)*, the government was already in the process of examining the law in this area because of the ECtHR's decision in *Goodwin (2002)*. The outcome of its deliberations was the enactment of the GRA 2004. Section 1 of that Act permits transgendered persons, of whom there are an estimated 5,000 in England, to apply for a gender recognition certificate from the Gender Recognition Panel (see http://www.dca.gov.uk/constitution/transsex/index.htm). The Panel was set up to determine the gender identity of both pre-operative and post-operative transgendered persons over the age of 18. The applicant for such a certificate need not have undergone gender reassignment surgery if it would be inappropriate for them to do so. The grant of a certificate allows them to acquire a new gender from that registered on their birth certificate. If the transgendered person is already married to a person who is the opposite sex to that of his or her birth gender, only an interim certificate will be issued. A full certificate will be issued after an application has been made for a decree of nullity and the decree has been granted (see Chapter 3).

2.25 Once a person has obtained a full gender recognition certificate, he or she may marry a member of the opposite sex to that of their newly acquired gender. In practice, it may be difficult to distinguish between the marriage of a pre-operative trans-gendered person, armed with a gender recognition certificate, to a member of the opposite sex to that of his or her acquired gender which will be valid, and a marriage between two people of the same sex which will be invalid.

*Age*

2.26 The parties to a marriage must be over the age of 16 and, if under the age of 18, have obtained the written consent of those who have parental responsibility. If these cannot be found, the registrar may give his consent. If those with parental responsibility refuse, the parties may apply to the court which has the power to overrule the need for parental consent (Marriage Act 1949, ss 2, 3).

*Prohibited degrees of relationship*

2.27 The Marriage Act 1949, s 1, provides that a marriage between persons related by blood or marriage within the prohibited degrees of consanguinity or affinity is void. It is also a criminal offence under the Sexual Offences Act 2003 (SOA 2003), s 64 for a person to have a sexual relationship with anyone who is within the prohibited degrees of relationship to him or her. The prohibition is based on a mixture of religious beliefs, social repugnance, genetics, and social policy. Marriage within certain prohibited degrees of relationship risks the birth of children with genetic defects. It has also been suggested that unless there is a ban on marriage between close members of families, there will be a danger of jealousy developing between them, which may create family instability.

2.28 However, not all cultures take the same approach towards this issue; some regard it as totally inappropriate to marry cousins whilst others regard it as preferable to marry a close relation. Societal rules may depend on economic factors; marrying outside the family may bring greater wealth to poorer families. For wealthier families, marriage within the kin group family may safeguard their wealth and strengthen familial bonds.

2.29 In 1839, Charles Darwin married his first cousin, Emma Wedgwood. Of their ten children one daughter died of tuberculosis, aged ten, one died at birth and one at the age of two. Five of the remaining seven children had serious illnesses or suffered some disability. Darwin expressed his concern about whether these problems were a consequence of his marrying his cousin.

2.30 In 2007, Anne Cryer, the Labour MP for Keighley, commissioned a report on marriage between cousins and proposed a ban on such marriages. The report claimed that 30 per cent of all births in the British Pakistani community had recessive gene disorders, and stated that more than 55 per cent of British Pakistanis are married to first cousins. The likelihood of unrelated couples having the same variant genes which cause recessive disorders are estimated to be 100–1. Between first cousins, the odds increase to as much as one in eight. In Bradford, more than three quarters of all Pakistani marriages are believed to be between first cousins. The city's Royal Infirmary Hospital has identified more than 140 different recessive disorders among local children, compared with the usual 20–30 (BBC, 16 November 2005).

2.31 Relationships which offend the consanguinity rule can occur by accident; a German brother and sister were separated whilst young and met and fell in love later in life. They live together and have four children. The man is currently appealing against his jail sentence for incest (*Independent*, 9 March 2007).

2.32 The Marriage Act 1949, Sch 1 (as amended) lists those relatives who may not marry. The list includes both blood relationships and relationships of affinity:

- father/daughter;
- mother/son;
- niece/uncle;
- nephew/aunt;
- brother/sister;
- grandparent/grandchild;
- half-siblings;
- adopted child/adoptive parent.

2.33 In the light of concern about the risk of destabilizing the family, it is surprising that a person may marry his or her adopted sibling. Marriage between a step-child and step-parent is also permissible if both parties are over 21 years of age and if the child, prior to the age of 18, has never been a child of the family in relation to the step-parent.

2.34 Prior to the decision in *B & L v UK (2006)*, marriages between parents-in-law and children-in-law were restricted, under the Marriage Act 1949, except in circumstances where both parties were over 21 years of age and their spouses were dead, or they had obtained a personal Act of Parliament allowing them to marry.

> B and L were a father-in-law and a daughter-in-law who wished to marry each other; he was aged 60 and was divorced from his son's mother; she was aged 40 and was divorced from his son. The couple claimed that UK law was a breach of their rights under Art 12 (the right to marry and found a family) of the ECHR. The ECHR found that although UK law pursued the legitimate aim of protecting the integrity of the family, it did not prevent relationships between parents-in-law and children-in-law from happening or even marriages from taking place if the parties were able to meet the exceptional circumstances provisions. As a result of the Court's ruling, the prohibition on such marriages was removed by the Marriage Act 1949 (Remedial) Order 2007.

2.35 Transgendered persons will also benefit from this change in the law; for example a woman who is a male-to-female transgendered person, and who has obtained a gender recognition certificate, may now marry her ex-wife's father.

*Already married or has entered into a civil partnership*

2.36 A person who is already married, or has entered into a civil partnership, may not enter into a valid marriage in England and Wales. If the parties to a bigamous marriage have the personal capacity to marry under the law of their domicile in a country in which such marriages are legally recognized, their marriage will be recognized as valid (see MCA 1973, s 11(d)). Immigration rules, however, restrict entry for family settlement in the UK to one spouse. As yet, no one has challenged the rules as an infringement of Art 8 (the right to respect for private and family life) and Art 12 (the right to marry and found a family) of the ECHR.

2.37 It is also a criminal offence to marry bigamously in England and Wales (see now OAPA 1861, s 57). Bigamy was first declared to be a crime in 1604 when the first Parliament of James 1 took action to restrain the

> ...*divers evil disposed persons who were bigamously marrying 'to the greate dishonour of God and utter undoinge of divers honest men's children and others', by ensuring that anyone found guilty would receive a sentence of death.*
>
> *(Samuel Chapman, 2001)*

*Mental capacity*

2.38 In order to marry, a person must be capable of understanding the nature of the marriage contract (MCA 1973, s 12(c), (d)). Given the absence of a document which defines with any precision the nature of marriage and its duties and responsibilities, it is difficult to know what level of mental capacity is required to enter into marriage. Judicial statements relating to mental capacity have not helped in any significant way. They tend to be a little opaque and, probably, for very good reason; there is a reluctance to limit the emotional life of mentally vulnerable persons.

2.39 In **Re SA (Vulnerable Adult with Capacity: Marriage) (2006)**, the court discussed the question of capacity to marry, and the right to self-determination under Art 8 (the right to respect for family and private life) and Art 12 (the right to marry and found a family) of the ECHR, in the context of a vulnerable adult at risk of a forced marriage.

Ms SA was an eighteen year-old deaf and mute young woman who could only communicate in British Sign language (BSL). She was partially sighted, and was assessed as having the intellectual capacity of an early teenager, and the reading age of a seven year-old. The psychologist, who evaluated her, acknowledged the problems in determining mental capacity in this context. Psychological testing uses both verbal and non-verbal communication; the former tests are inappropriate for a deaf person who is only capable of understanding non-verbal communication. He concluded that Ms SA had

> ...*a rudimentary but nevertheless clear and accurate understanding of the concept of marriage and of what a marriage contract would entail; that she has an accurate and realistic understanding of what a sexual relationship is, its effect and implications, and what would be expected within the relationship, and that she understands that a marriage can be legally ended in divorce.*

However, he drew attention to the fact that Ms SA was unable to comprehend the very real possibility that her parents might take her to Pakistan, organize her marriage, whilst she was there to a man who would not, or could not, because of immigration rules, return with her and live in the UK. If that were to happen, she would be unable to express her concerns to anyone in Pakistan or obtain help to return to the UK. She might be compelled to remain in a country where she would be unable to communicate with anyone in BSL, including the man she might have been forced to marry. Such a possibility would result in her leading an isolated existence and her mental health would suffer severely.

Munby J, reiterated what he had said in *Re E (An Alleged Patient): Sheffield City Council v E and S (2005)*. He maintained that the general rule of English law relating to capacity is to

*...understand the nature and quality of the act.*

In the context of marriage, a person wishing to enter into a valid marriage must know that he or she is taking part in a marriage ceremony and understands the words of the ceremony; he or she must also be able to appreciate the responsibilities which stem from the contract of marriage agreed to in that ceremony. According to Munby J, the marriage contract confers on the man and woman the status of husband and wife. From this status flow consequences. The parties are expected, *inter alia*, to live together, love only each other as husband and wife, and be responsible for each other's care and comfort.

2.40  Given the nebulous nature of the State-determined English marriage contract, it might be argued that Munby J's test is a very high hurdle for anyone, who is contemplating marriage, to leap and, particularly, persons as intellectually challenged as Ms SA. After all, it is not easy to appreciate the full significance of the marriage contract, which is unwritten, and can only be compiled from a reading of case law and statutes primarily relating to marital breakdown. This is not the reading matter of most couples who are about to embark on marriage, and certainly not of an adult on the borderline of learning ability with a reading age of a seven year-old.

2.41  However, Munby J did not share this view. He maintained that the contract of marriage is essentially a very simple one, and does not require a high degree of intelligence to comprehend it. He was, quite understandably, anxious to avoid discriminating against those of limited mental ability, were the test of capacity to marry to be set too high. Marriage or civil partnership remain the only legal means of establishing a stable relationship; a mentally disabled person living in a protected environment may be incapable of understanding the nature of the marriage contract (as indeed may many mentally able persons in advance of marrying) but may be capable of sustaining, and benefiting from, an emotional and loving relationship. The major argument against marriage of mentally incapacitated persons is the risk to any children born of such a marriage. However, that risk exists whether or not the couple marry; it could be taken care of by adequate preventative measures which would be overseen by those responsible for the mentally incapacitated person or persons.

2.42    In *Re SK (2008)*, a young Afghani woman aged 33, lived in residential accommodation provided by Westminster Council and only saw her mother and siblings under strictly controlled supervision. She had a severe learning disability and a mental disorder which was not controlled because she failed to take her medication. She had been pregnant a number of times by three husbands but had miscarried, had an abortion, or lost the child soon after birth. She longed to have a sexual relationship, marry again and have more children. She was vulnerable to exploitation by her family and by potential male partners.

The Local Authority successfully sought a declaration, *inter alia*, that SK lacked capacity to marry (see also *City of Westminster v IC (by his friend the official solicitor) and KC and NN (2008)*).

The question remains as to whether a vulnerable adult might be able to succeed in challenging the denial of a right to marry under the ECHR, Art 8 (the right to privacy and family life) and Art 12 (the right to marry and found a family) (see *Re MM (2009)* below).

# Formalities of marriage

2.43 The formalities of marriage are laid down in the Marriage Act 1949, Parts II–VI (as amended). They limit the ways in which a couple may choose to marry and are indicative of the values placed by the State on the serious nature of marriage. All marriages, whether civil or religious (except for Jewish and Quaker marriages), must normally take place between the hours of 8am and 6pm in a venue accessible to the public. Except in the circumstances described below, the parties must give 15 days' notice to the registrar of marriages or other appointed person. The parties' details are available to the public.

2.44 In 2002, the government produced a White Paper on changing, *inter alia*, the registration procedures for marriage and giving people more freedom to marry in the way that they wish (*Civil Registration: Vital Change* (Cm 5355, 2002)). The reforms relating to marriage have not yet been fully implemented.

## Civil ceremonies

2.45 Those who do not wish to marry in a religious place of worship must marry in a civil ceremony in a registry office or in an approved place which has been licensed by the local authority. Such a venue must be a permanent structure and not a marquee or open air location. The main use of the building must be one which would not demean marriage or bring it into disrepute, and it must be open to the public to permit them to witness any marriage and make objections prior to or during the ceremony. Celebrity figures who wish to marry away from the public gaze have, usually, been forced to marry outside the jurisdiction. In theory, the marriage of Prince Charles and the Duchess of Cornwall, in 2005, in a registry office in Windsor, was open to the public, although no one attempted to exercise the right to attend.

2.46 The building must be secular in nature and have no connection with any religion. It must also be regularly available to the public for marriage ceremonies. Prince Charles and the Duchess of Cornwall were forced to abandon their original plan to marry in Windsor Castle when it was realized that the venue would have to be made available to other couples.

2.47 Marriages whilst sky diving, swimming underwater or in other bizarre circumstances which seem to attract the interest of those who find the more acceptable forms of marriage ceremonies just a little dull, are not permissible under English law.

2.48 Whether the marriage takes place in a registry office or other licensed venue, a superintendent registrar is responsible for conducting the civil ceremony. The couple may devise their own ceremony but law forbids any religious element in it. The ceremony must include the statutory declaration using the words below, or an alternative but essentially similar version, followed by the contracting words:

> *I do solemnly declare that I know not of any lawful impediment why I,…may not be joined in matrimony to…I call upon these persons here present to witness that I…do take thee…to be my lawful wedded husband/wife.*

## Religious ceremonies

2.49 Where the parties wish to marry in a religious ceremony, different rules apply to different religious denominations. Each religious denomination has the right to refuse permission to a couple to marry in a particular place of worship.

### Marriage in the Anglican Church

2.50 Because there is no separation of the Anglican Church and the State, Anglican clergy may deal with all the preliminary matters relating to marriage including the minimum 15-day period of notice. They may conduct the ceremony and formally register it. A couple have always had the right to be married in the parish church of a parish where one or both of them are resident or entered on the electoral roll. However, since October 2008, it is possible for those who wish to marry in the parish church of a parish with which one or both of them can demonstrate a 'qualifying connection'. A person has a qualifying connection with a parish if that person:

- was baptized in the parish;

or

- had his or her confirmation entered in a church register book of a church or chapel in the parish;

or

- has at any time had his or her usual place of residence in the parish for at least six months;

or

- has at any time habitually attended public worship in the parish for at least 6 months;

or

- a parent of that person has at any time during that person's lifetime had his or her usual place of residence in the parish for at least six months or habitually attended public worship in the parish for at least six months;

or

- a parent or grandparent of that person was married in the parish.

2.51 The church may refuse to conduct a marriage where either of the parties has been divorced. The words of the marriage vows in the Anglican Church give some indication to the parties of what is expected of those who enter into a Christian marriage. In addition to the essential contracting words required by law, the couple also promise each other:

> *to have and to hold*
>
> *from this day forward;*
>
> *for better, for worse,*
>
> *for richer, for poorer,*
>
> *in sickness and in health,*
>
> *to love and to cherish,*
>
> *till death us do part.*

The Archbishop of Canterbury also has a right to grant a special licence for Anglican marriages to take place in special premises at any hour of day or night; such licences are comparatively rare.

### Quaker and Jewish marriages

2.52 Quaker and Jewish marriages are not required to follow the rules for other religious denominations. The parties must fulfil the notification requirements, although in the case of Quaker marriage, notification is given to the Quaker authorities. Quaker and Jewish couples may marry wherever, and whatever any time, they wish with the approval of their religious authorities. Approval will not be given for Jewish marriages to take place on Saturdays, the Jewish Sabbath or on Holy Days. Jewish and Quaker marriages do not have to be accessible to the public. The parties, in these religions, are regarded as performing the ceremony themselves; the ceremony, therefore, does not need to be conducted by a religious official or other approved person although such a person will be in attendance. Where that person is licensed to do so, he or she must register the marriage, if he or she does not, a civil registrar must attend the ceremony and register the marriage.

Members of the Jewish faith and Quakers have never believed that a religious building is necessary to enable them to worship. They also have had an excellent reputation for record keeping and ensuring that anyone wishing to marry has the legal capacity to do so. It would seem that these longstanding historical facts are the major reasons for members of these religions having the right to marry in accordance with their beliefs.

### Other religious marriages

2.53 Members of other religious denominations may marry in their place of worship if it has been registered for marriage ceremonies. Places of worship may be registered if the religion involves devotion to some form of deity. Many Catholic and Non-Conformist Christian religious ministers have registered their churches. Few Sikh, Hindu, or Muslim places of worship have been registered.

2.54 Notification must be given to the registrar in advance, and a superintendent registrar must be present to register the marriage unless the religious minister has been authorized to perform the marriage ceremony.

2.55 Where their place of worship has not been registered, members of a religious denomination who wish to marry religiously will have to undergo two separate ceremonies, one in a registry office or other approved place, and one in their unregistered place of worship.

### Marriages of the sick, the housebound, or prisoners

2.56 The sick, housebound and prisoners may be married in hospital, at home, or in prison, at any hour of the day or night, by licence of the Registrar General. They do not need to fulfil the requirements of notice.

## Common law marriage

2.57 The expression common law marriage is frequently used in everyday speech to describe a couple who are not legally married but who live together and believe that they will be treated in the same way as legally married partners (see Law Com No 307 (2007) *Cohabitation: The Financial Consequences of Relationship Breakdown*, discussed below). In English law, the term has had no validity since 1753. If two people live together as if husband and wife, the same legal consequences do not flow from their relationship as would flow from a legally valid marriage. Fifty-seven per cent of British people seem to believe that there is common law marriage and that it will give rise to similar rights as if they were formally married, (*National Centre for Social Research, 18th Report (2001–02)*).

In 2005, the government funded the legal advice group, Living Together, to help eliminate the phrase 'common law marriage' and publicize the fact that it has no legal meaning.

2.58 The Scottish concept known as 'marriage by habit and repute' is not accepted under English law. The concept refers to the situation where two people set up home together as a married couple and are generally accepted by the community as married, they will be regarded as married in the eyes of the law. However, if they express the view that they do not believe in marriage they will not be regarded as married.

## Presumption of marriage by cohabitation and repute

2.59 Where a marriage does not comply with the relevant formalities laid down by law, it may be rescued by the common law doctrine known as presumption of marriage by cohabitation and repute. Rayden and Jackson (1997) have explained that:

> *Where a man and woman have cohabited for such a length of time and in such circumstances, as to have acquired the reputation of being man and wife, a lawful marriage between them will be presumed [to have taken place], though there be no positive evidence of any marriage having taken place, particularly where the relevant facts have occurred outside the jurisdiction and this presumption can be rebutted only by strong and weighty evidence.*

The doctrine is based on the idea that it is conceivable that the documents recording the marriage might have been lost or indeed, the marriage may not have been documented in the first place. It is of particular importance to those who have always assumed that they were validly married outside the jurisdiction, and who would risk losing legal benefits which are only available to married persons. Caroline Bridge (2001) has suggested that:

> *It is clear that the interests of a culturally diverse population in the UK require that a long-standing marriage should not be lightly struck down for want of compliance with the formalities of local law relied on many years later.*

The following two decisions illustrate her point.

2.60   In **Pazpena De Vire v Pazpena De Vire (2001)**, a woman of German origin sought a decree of divorce. She maintained that she had been married for 35 years to an Argentinean-born man. There was no direct evidence of a marriage having taken place. The petitioner claimed that she and the respondent had used a proxy to whom they had granted a special power of attorney to contract the marriage for them in Uruguay. She had obtained an Argentinian passport on the strength of being married and had given birth to the respondent's child. The respondent denied that there was a valid marriage; he maintained that he himself had procured a fraudulent marriage certificate and that there was no other record of the marriage. His assertion was backed up by strong expert evidence that the certificate might be fraudulent.

However, the court held that there was insufficient evidence to rebut the strong presumption of marriage arising from a long period of cohabitation as husband and wife and public recognition of them as such. Even if the certificate were a forgery, that did not prove that there had been no later ceremony. The petitioner was, therefore, held to have been validly married and entitled to seek a petition of divorce.

2.61   The woman, in **A-M v A-M (2001)**, sought to divorce, or obtain a decree of nullity from, her husband. She alleged that they were validly married, although there was no evidence of such a marriage. The couple were Middle Eastern Muslims. They had undergone a ceremony of marriage in London in a private home, intending it to be a formal Islamic marriage. The wife subsequently learned that the marriage was not valid under English law. She was advised that she should seek to validate it by marrying in a country which permitted polygamy. The couple went to Sharjah but were unable to regularize their status there. They would have had to obtain an Islamic divorce first in order to marry and this would not have been permissible under Islamic law merely to enable them to marry each other again in order to satisfy the demands of an overseas jurisdiction. They returned to England, had children and regarded themselves, and were regarded by others, as married. The wife became a British citizen and acquired a British domicile prior to the breakdown of the relationship.

The court held that there was a presumption of a valid marriage on the basis of cohabitation and repute; only strong and weighty evidence to the contrary would take that presumption away. The presumption was stronger in circumstances such as here, because the marriage presumed to have taken place could have taken place with minimal formality. A valid polygamous marriage could have been contracted in an Islamic country without a public ceremony and in the absence of the wife if she had signed a power of attorney. Although there was no firm evidence that she had done so, she did frequently sign documents for her husband and it was conceivable that one of these had been a power of attorney.

2.62 The decision in *A-M v A-M (2001)* was a most liberal interpretation of the doctrine of presumption of marriage by cohabitation and repute. If it is followed, it will be difficult to displace the presumption in cases where couples, who originate from a country where the formalities of marriage and registration are less rigid than in the UK, are able to prove that they have cohabited in a traditional marriage-like manner.

2.63 The doctrine will, however, rarely be applicable to British-born residents as will be seen from the decision in *Martin v Myers (2004)*.

> In **Martin**, the inheritance rights of the daughters of a deceased couple depended on their parents' unmarried status. The inheritance rights of the remaining members of the family depended on the parents' married status. The parents had cohabited for some 50 years and had seven children. The mother was always vague about her marital status but all the family had always assumed that their parents were married until after their death when the inheritance issue arose, although on one occasion, when she was in her late 70s and ill in hospital, the mother had briefly suggested to one of her daughters that she and the daughters' father had never been married because they had been unable to afford to do so.
>
> The court held that there could be no presumption of marriage because there was no reasonable doubt that they were not married. The mother herself had cast doubt on the presumption; the register of marriages had been searched and it was unlikely that an error had been made in the register. The couple had always been poor and never travelled, and the possibility of a marriage out of the jurisdiction was remote. The court pointed out that most of the authorities on presumption of marriage either predate the system of registration of marriages or relate to parties who may have been married abroad. The absence of a certificate is strong evidence to refute the presumption, unless marriage abroad is a real possibility.

(By contrast see the decisions in *Taylor v Taylor (1961)*; *Mahadervan v Mahadervan (1964)*; *Chief Adjudication Officer v Bath (2000)*.)

## Civil partners

2.64 In 2004, the CPA 2004 was enacted to allow same-sex partners to formalize their relationships by means of a registration process. Because of the cultural and religious connotations of marriage, the government had sought to achieve a compromise between those who were opposed to same-sex marriage and those who believed that marriage should be extended to same-sex partners. Although the government has refuted strongly the idea that civil partnership is equivalent to same-sex marriage, it has been unable to give any satisfactory explanation as to how it differs from marriage; the explanations given lack any credibility. For instance the government's Women and Equality Unit explained that:

*Civil Partnership is a completely new legal relationship, exclusively for same-sex couples, distinct from marriage.*

*The Government has sought to give civil partners parity of treatment with spouses, as far as is possible, in the rights and responsibilities that flow from forming a civil partnership.*

*There are a small number of differences between civil partnership and marriage, for example, a civil partnership is formed when the second civil partner signs the relevant document, a civil marriage is formed when the couple exchange spoken words. Opposite-sex couples can opt for a religious or civil marriage ceremony as they choose, whereas formation of a civil partnership will be an exclusively civil procedure.*

*(http://www.womenandequalityunit.gov.uk/lgbt/faq.htm (2005))*

2.65　In spite of these protestations, the provisions of the CPA 2004 are remarkably similar to the law relating to married partners. Civil partnership is regularly referred to by the media and the general public as gay marriage. When the singer Elton John and his partner, David Furnish registered their civil partnership in December 2005 soon after the CPA 2004 came into force, the media referred to it as the couple's wedding. Websites and 'gay wedding' planners have come into existence to provide help for gay partners wishing to have a ceremony and reception which is as similar as possible to those available to married couples.

Somewhat surprisingly, in 2009, the Law Commission, in its Consultation Paper (No 191), *Intestacy And Family Provision Claims On Death*, also chose to use the term spouse with reference to both married couples and civil partners.

2.66　The government had hoped that by giving more or less the same rights to civil partners as those given to married couples, it would forestall any challenge under the ECHR that the restriction of marriage to opposite sex partners is a breach of Art 8 (the right to respect for private and family life) and Art 12 (the right to marry and found a family). That hope was short lived.

2.67　In *Wilkinson v Kitzinger (2006)*, Susan Wilkinson sought a declaration, under s 55 of the Family Law Act 1986, that her marriage to Celia Kitzinger which took place in Canada, where same-sex marriage is legal, was valid under English law. In the alternative, if the court found that the marriage was not valid, she sought first, a declaration that the law breached her rights under Art 8 (the right to private and family life), Art 12 (the right to marry and found a family) and Art 14 (the right to enjoy the rights of the ECHR without discrimination) of the ECHR. Second, she sought a declaration that MCA 1973, s 11(c) (marriages are not valid between persons of the same sex), and CPA 2004, s 1(1)(b), Ch 2, Pt 5 (marriages between same-sex couples outside the jurisdiction will be treated as civil partnerships under English law) are incompatible with the ECHR and that the court should make a Declaration of Incompatibility under s 4 of the Human Rights Act 1998 (HRA 1998). She was supported in her application by Celia Kitzinger.

Ms Wilkinson was fervent in her view that:

*While marriage remains open to heterosexual couples only, offering the 'consolation prize' of a civil partnership to lesbians and gay men is offensive and demeaning. Marriage is our society's fundamental social institution for recognising the couple relationship and access to this institution is an equal rights issue. To deny some people access to marriage on the basis of their sexual orientation is fundamentally unjust, just as it would be to do so on the basis of their race, ethnicity, and nationality, religion, or political beliefs.*

*... marriages and civil partnerships are clearly not equal. They are not equal symbolically, when it is marriage that is the key social institution, celebrated and recognised around the world; and they are not equal practically, when it is apparent that civil partnership is a lesser alternative, which will not be recognised around the world, or even across Europe.*

*... I feel a sense of moral outrage that, counter to my own personal experience of the importance of my marriage to Celia, this second marriage is deemed by society to be of less value than my first, simply because it is a marriage with a woman....*

*... I want my marriage, and same-sex marriages more generally, to be recognised in Britain, and elsewhere, because I want to be able to refer to Celia as my wife and have that immediately and unproblematically understood as meaning that she is my life-partner with all the connotations and social consequences that using the term 'wife' or 'husband' has for a heterosexual couple....*

The President, Sir Mark Potter, declined to grant the declarations demanded. In a very conservative judgment, he held that there was no contravention of Art 12. He merely reiterated, without further justification, the traditional view that the definition of marriage is a heterosexual relationship and the basis of the family (see also *Rees v United Kingdom (1987)*). He maintained that:

*It is apparent that the majority of people, or at least of governments, not only in England but Europe-wide, regard marriage as an age-old institution, valued and valuable, respectable and respected, as a means not only of encouraging monogamy but also the procreation of children and their development and nurture in a family unit (or 'nuclear family') in which both maternal and paternal influences are available in respect of their nurture and upbringing.*

*The belief that this form of relationship is the one which best encourages stability in a well regulated society is not a disreputable or outmoded notion based upon ideas of exclusivity, marginalisation, disapproval or discrimination against homosexuals or any other persons who by reason of their sexual orientation or for other reasons prefer to form a same-sex union.*

The President also held that there had been no breach of Art 8. In his opinion:

*By withholding from same-sex partners the actual title and status of marriage, the Government declined to alter the deep-rooted and almost universal recognition of*

*marriage as a relationship between a man and a woman, but without in any way inter-*
*fering with or failing to recognise the right of same-sex couples to respect for their*
*private or family life.... Not only does English law recognise and not interfere with the*
*right of such couples to live in a very close, loving, and monogamous relationship; it*
*accords them also the benefits of marriage in all but name.*

With respect to Art 14, Sir Mark Potter accepted that Parliament may have distinguished between same-sex couples and heterosexual couples by reserving the institution of marriage as a heterosexual union whilst, at the same time, giving same-sex couples the same rights and responsibilities as married couples. However, to the extent that the distinction discriminated against same-sex partners it had a legitimate aim, which was reasonable and proportionate, and fell within the margin of appreciation accorded to Convention States.

Ms Wilkinson has said that she does not have the financial resources to fund an appeal against the decision but has stated that she will campaign for the law to be changed.

2.68    In 2010, Sandra Davies, the head of the family law department of a major London firm of solicitors explained the concerns of same-sex partners at their exclusion from the status of marriage.

*'Marriage' conveys a sense of celebration sadly lacking from the legal construct of*
*'civil partnership'. This may in part be because those who lobbied hard for the enact-*
*ment of the Civil Partnerships Act took the view that its passage through Parliament*
*and into law would be much smoother if they steered clear of the traditional*
*vocabulary of marriage, and its religious connections. As such this 'separate but*
*equal' approach continues to stigmatise same-sex couples. Gay peoples' committed*
*relationships are often still viewed to be something less than their straight counter-*
*parts. Whether overt or covert, the suggestion remains that gay people are seen as*
*something 'other'; a community that has no place in normal society.*

*And yet, whether gay or straight, the legal recognition of a relationship affords*
*identical legal rights, responsibilities and obligations. What possible justification*
*can there be then for distinguishing between the social ceremonies by which*
*same-sex and heterosexual couples respectively formalize their relationships?*

## Capacity to register a civil partnership (CPA 2004, ss 3, 4)

### Same sex

2.69    The parties who wish to register their partnership must be of the same sex. The government refused to extend the provisions to heterosexual cohabitants. It maintained that marriage was open to this group and, therefore, civil partnership was unnecessary for them. During the passage of the Civil Partnership Bill through Parliament, attempts were made to amend the Bill to allow family members of whatever sexual persuasion, who live together in non-sexual caring relationships, to enjoy the benefits of civil partnership. These attempts were almost certainly based on a desire by those, opposed to the legislation, to prevent its enactment, and the government successfully resisted them. It argued that the amendment would create particular difficulties relating to property and inheritance between family members, and that problems relating to ancillary relief would arise if a civil partner, who later decided to marry, had first to terminate the partnership with the family member. Baroness Scotland explained:

> *Should a daughter in a civil partnership with her mother wish to marry, she would have to go through a formal court-based dissolution of the civil partnership first. If her mother had become mentally incapable, or objected to the marriage, she would have to live apart for five years. These are serious disincentives to marriage. Moreover, if she did seek a dissolution, the daughter would be entitled to a share of her mother's property, which might mean that the elderly mother would be dispossessed of her home because it would have to be sold and shared to make provision for her civil partner. So depending on the circumstances, this might require the mother to sell the family home in order to provide a settlement. I am sure that noble Lords did not have that in mind. She would also have to prove irretrievable breakdown of the relationship. That is very difficult to prove when it is with your mother. It might be that there is not an irretrievable breakdown. The mother might agree that the daughter or the son could live with the new partner in her home. How will that be dealt with?*
>
> *I regret to tell your Lordships that the amendment made a nonsense of the Bill in the form in which it was considered.*
>
> *(Hansard, House of Lords, 1 July 2004 Vol. 663 (No 109)*
> *1 Jul 2004: Column 395)*

2.70 There is nothing in the legislation which prevents same-sex heterosexual friends from registering a civil partnership and thereby obtain the associated benefits of that status but for many such a step would be disingenuous given that the legislation was clearly enacted for the protection of gay relationships.

2.71 Transgendered persons, who have obtained gender recognition certificates from the Gender Recognition Panel, may enter into a civil partnership with a member of the same sex to that of their newly acquired gender. They need not have undergone gender reassignment surgery if it would be inappropriate for them to do so. It may be difficult to distinguish between the registration of a civil partnership between a pre-operative transgendered person, armed with a gender recognition certificate, and a member of the same sex to that of his or her acquired gender, which will be valid, and one between an opposite sex couple, which will be invalid.

## Age

2.72 Civil partners must have attained the age of 16 years, and if under the age of 18, unless they have already had a previous civil partnership, have obtained the written consent of those who have parental responsibility or one of the appropriate persons responsible for the care of the child listed in CPA 2004, Sch 2.

## Prohibited degrees of relationship

2.73 It is forbidden for a person to register a civil partnership with anyone who is within the prohibited degrees of relationship to him or her. CPA 2004, Sch 1, Part 1 lists those relatives who may not register a civil partnership. It divides them into absolute prohibitions (s 1(1)) and qualified prohibitions (s 2(1), (2), (3)).

### *Absolute prohibitions*

2.74 A person may not register a civil partnership with his or her:

- adoptive child;
- adoptive parent;
- child;
- former adoptive child;
- former adoptive parent;
- grandparent;
- grandchild;
- parent;
- parent's sibling;
- sibling or half-sibling;
- sibling's or half-sibling's child.

### *Qualified prohibitions*

2.75 A person may not register a civil partnership with any of the following unless:

(a) both of them have reached 21 years of age at the time when they register as civil partners of each other, and

(b) the younger has not at any time before reaching the age of 18 been a child of the family in relation to the other (CPA 2004, Sch 1, Part 1, para 2(2) defines a child of the family as a person who (i) has lived in the same household as that other person, and (ii) has been treated by that other person as a child of his family):

- child of former civil partner;
- child of former spouse;
- former civil partner of grandparent;
- former civil partner of parent;
- former spouse of grandparent;
- former spouse of parent;
- grandchild of former civil partner;
- grandchild of former spouse.

2.76 Since same-sex couples are unable to reproduce biologically with each other, these prohibitions are entirely connected with social mores relating to familial relationships. They appear to be over-extensive and not entirely justifiable.

2.77 The absolute prohibitions reflect the determination of the government not to extend the status of civil partnerships to those who are members of each other's family of origin. Incest is not an overt concern behind the prohibitions because there is no acknowledgement in the legislation that a civil partnership involves a sexual relationship. It is almost certainly a covert reason for these prohibitions.

### Already a civil partner or married

2.78 A person who is already a civil partner or who is married may not register a civil partnership without first legally ending the existing relationship (see Chapter 6).

### Mental capacity

2.79 In order to register a civil partnership, a person must understand the nature of the relationship and its consequences. It is presumed that the decisions relating to mental capacity to marry will be equally applicable to civil partners.

## Formalities of civil partnership

2.80 The formalities are laid down in CPA 2004, ss 5–27 and are not dissimilar to those relating to marriage. Notice must be given 15 days in advance except where either party is seriously ill and may not survive. The information relating to a proposed registration must be made public in order that anyone may object on the grounds that the couple are not eligible to register a civil partnership. Gay rights groups had objected to the public nature of registration on the grounds of the right to privacy, and to prevent risks of discrimination towards, or homophobic attacks on, civil partners. These objections were discounted.

2.81 Registration must take place in offices provided by a local authority, or in premises licensed by it for the registration of civil partnerships, between the hours of 8 am and 6 pm. The original idea of registration was that it would merely involve the parties signing a document. However, many local authorities have provided for personalized ceremonies to take place at the time of registration, but the law requires that there must be no religious element to them. In March 2010, the House of Lords, in an amendment to the Equality Bill, voted in favour of lifting the ban on same-sex couples holding civil partnership ceremonies inside religious premises. The amendment was incorporated into the Equality Act 2010. Couples are, of course, free to organize their own separate religious ceremonies before or after the registration process if they wish to do so but such ceremonies will have no legal effect on the couple's status.

## Cohabitation

2.82 The final category of relationship to be considered in this chapter, heterosexual and same-sex cohabitation, has been subject to limited State intervention.

2.83 A person may cohabit within the prohibited degrees of relationship subject, of course, to the criminal law relating to under-age sexual relationships and incest.

2.84 Cohabiting partnerships do not bring about relationships of affinity; thus, a child of one cohabitant may marry his or her parent's partner although such a relationship is almost certain to cause family jealousies. An example from another jurisdiction is provided by the marriage of Woody Allen, the New York film director and actor, who was able to marry Soon Yi Previn, the adopted daughter of his long-term partner, Mia Farrow, and her ex-husband, Andre Previn.

2.85 Societal views vary on whether cohabitants should be brought within a similar legal framework to married couple and civil partners. During the passage of the Civil Partnership Bill through Parliament, the issue of according legal rights to cohabitants was debated. The government took the view that heterosexual cohabitants did not require the protection of the CPA 2004 because they already had the right to marry, and same-sex cohabitants would, as a result of the CPA 2004, be given protective rights.

2.86 This approach ignores the fact that cohabitants do not belong to a heterogeneous group. There are heterosexual cohabitants who are unable to marry because one of them is already married and unwilling or unable to divorce. A minority group of cohabitants involves couples who have married polygamously in countries where that is permissible but do not have capacity in accordance with English law to do so. Their marriages are void and the parties only have the status of cohabitants. They may not realise that that is so until legal issues relating to marital status arise. Some cohabitants do not wish to marry or enter into a civil partnership because of the social, cultural, and political significance attached to those relationships and would resent any possibility of State interference into a status which they have deliberately chosen for themselves. There are same-sex cohabitants who do not wish to enter into a civil partnership because they wish to marry, and view civil partnership as a compromise. Other cohabitants, both heterosexual and of the same-sex, may be contemplating formalizing their relationships but may not yet be ready to do so. There are also those cohabitants who simply suffer from inertia and fail to marry or register a civil partnership. All of these groups may be unaware of the problematic consequences of informal relationships until they find themselves in a situation where they are denied rights, which are solely the prerogative of married couples or civil partners. This tends to occur at the end of a relationship.

2.87 It is difficult to produce accurate figures relating to cohabitation. Census information, whilst helpful, does not give a complete picture. At what point in a relationship is a couple prepared to admit to cohabitation and convey that information on a census form? Couples vary in their perceptions of what constitutes cohabitation and when it begins. Some couples regard themselves as cohabiting although each retains a home of their own and they visit regularly. For other couples, cohabitation dates from the time one moves into the home of the other or when they acquire a new joint residence. For a further group cohabitation is determined when they have children. There are couples who claim to be married because they are indeed married but not to the person with whom they are cohabiting. Other couples do not admit to cohabiting because they wish to keep their status private, and some describe themselves as married because they actually believe that after a long period of cohabitation they have acquired the status of common law spouses; they are unaware that such a status no longer exists (see above).

2.88 In 2007, the Law Commission proposed a complex scheme of financial relief for cohabitants (*Cohabitation: The Financial Consequences of Relationship Breakdown*, Law Com No 307). It based its statistical information, *inter alia*, on the most recent decennial census information of 2001, which found that 8 per cent of the population are in cohabiting heterosexual relationships. However, it also cited more helpful figures from the office of National Statistics concerning the birth of children. In 2004, 42 per cent of all children were born outside marriage, and of these, 80 per cent were registered in the names of both parents.

The Law Commission maintained that:

> *Cohabitation is therefore already a significant social practice. It is growing, and continued growth is forecast. This is, of course, not in itself a reason for law reform. But if it is accepted that the current law is inadequate and gives rise to unwelcome consequences, the fact that these consequences potentially affect a significant and increasing proportion of the population is highly relevant. The issues considered in this paper are therefore not issues that will go away. We urge Government to take the necessary steps to provide this increasingly significant section of society with legal remedies capable of dealing fairly with the financial consequences should they separate.*

The report did not provide a draft bill and the government seems disinclined to undertake any immediate reform in this area. The Family Justice Council has deplored the government's attitude and described it as a wasted opportunity and a failure of its commitment to equality and the protection of the disadvantaged. The Law Commission's proposals will be considered, where appropriate alongside the current law in the relevant chapters which follow.

2.89 It is the second time in five years that the Law Commission has considered the issue. In 2002, it also maintained that:

> ... the current law is inadequate and gives rise to unwelcome consequences, the fact that these consequences potentially affect a significant and increasing proportion of the population is highly relevant. The issues considered in this paper are therefore not issues that will go away. We urge Government to take the necessary steps to provide this increasingly significant section of society with legal remedies capable of dealing fairly with the financial consequences should they separate.... further consideration should be given to the adoption, necessarily by legislation, of new legal approaches to personal relationships outside marriage, following the lead given by other jurisdictions (such as France, Australia and New Zealand.
>
> These approaches may include such mechanisms as the formal registration of civil partnerships, or less formally, a power for the court to adjust the legal rights and obligations of individuals who are or have been living together for a defined period or in defined circumstances.
>
> (Sharing Homes: A Discussion Paper (2002) Law Com No 278)

2.90 Not all legal commentators share this desire for reform. Ruth Deech in her 2010 Gresham Lecture stated firmly:

> My preference is for the rights of the individual, or human rights, in this instance autonomy, privacy, a sphere of thought and action that should be free from public and legal interference, namely the right to live together without having a legal structure imposed on one without consent or contract to that effect. It is better not to have legal interference in cohabitation and leave it to be dealt with by the ordinary law of the land, of agreements, wills, property and so on. Recently special laws for cohabitants, that would treat them like married couples when divorcing or on death, have been proposed by the Law Commission and by Lord Lester in a private bill of a rather different nature. But I would argue that cohabitation law retards the emancipation of women, degrades the relationship, takes away choice, is too expensive and would extend an already unsatisfactory maintenance law for married couples to another large category. I rate most highly personal autonomy and the use of agreements to settle legal boundaries with others, the respect for individuals' expectations and contributions, rather than stereotyping and fitting every couple into the traditional marriage mould.

2.91 Where one or both of the cohabitants or prospective cohabitants are considered to be vulnerable adults, the courts have considered their rights to cohabit with each other and have a sexual relationship. The approach has been taken that it is only in truly exceptional circumstances that a vulnerable adult should be denied these rights even where they have been found to lack the capacity to marry.

> In *Re MM (2009)*, a 39-year-old woman, suffered from severe mental illness. She had a very low IQ of 56 and had been involved in a 15-year relationship with KM who was also

mentally unstable. He led a nomadic life, and had been violent towards MM. The local authority applied for declarations as to MM's lack of capacity with respect, *inter alia*, as to where and with whom she should live, and preferably with very limited contact with KM. Munby J held that capacity to consent to sexual relations depended upon an understanding of the consequences of sexual intercourse per se rather than its consequences with one particular individual. Where a person does have the capacity to understand the consequences of sexual intercourse, he or she might not have the capacity to decide on the more complex issues of contact and a long-term relationship. It was then up to the court to decide whether contact between the vulnerable adult and a sexual partner was in his or her best interests. The court was entitled to intervene to protect him or her from the risk of future abuse or exploitation if there was a real possibility, of such harm. However, in doing so, the court must adopt a pragmatic, common sense and robust approach and be willing to tolerate acceptable risks. The court must be careful to ensure that it did not rescue a vulnerable adult from one type of potential abuse and expose him or her to another—treatment at the hands of the State which might affect his or her dignity, happiness or even be an infringement of his or her human rights. The local authority should make a care plan for MM which would provide for her to have regular contact with KM and facilitate her sexual relationship with him.

## FURTHER READING

Barlow A and James G, 'Regulating Marriage and Cohabitation in 21st Century Britain' [2004] CFLQ 2

Barlow A, Duncan S, James G and Park A, *Cohabitation, Marriage and the Law: Social Change and Legal Reform in the 21st Century* (Hart Publishing, 2005)

Barlow A, Burgoyne C, Clery E and Smithson J, 'Cohabitation and the Law: Myths, Money and the Media' [2008] British Social Attitudes 29

Bridge C, 'Case comment on *Pazpena de Vire v Pazpena de Vire'* [2001] Fam Law 96

Bull L, 'Cohabitation Outcomes after the Law Commission Report' [2008] Fam Law 56

Chapman S, *Polygamy, Bigamy and Human Rights Law* (Xlibris Corporation, 1991)

Civil Registration: Vital Change (Cm 5355, 2002)

Crompton L, 'Civil Partnerships Bill 2004: the Illusion of Equality' [2004] Fam Law 88

Curry-Sumner, 'European Recognition of Same-sex Relationships: We Need Action Now' [2008] IFL 102

Deech R, Gresham Lectures (2010), http://www.gresham.ac.uk

Evans S, 'Talking Shop: Two Sisters and Two Weddings' [2008] Fam Law 579

Family Justice Council, 'Cohabitation Concerns' [2009] Fam Law 567

Gaffney-Rhys R, 'Siblings and Civil Partnerships' [2007] IFLJ 84

Gaffney-Rhys R, 'The Law Relating to Marriageable Age from a National and International Perspective' [2009] IFLJ 228

Hale B (Baroness Hale of Richmond), 'Unmarried Couples in Family Law' [2004] Fam Law 419

Hammond-Sharlot R and Booth P, 'Same-sex Marriage and the Church of England' [2008] Fam Law 260

Harper M et al, *Civil Partnership: The New Law* (Jordan, 2005)

Hess E, 'The Rights of Cohabitants and How Will the Law be Reformed' [2009] Fam Law 405

House of Lords Research Paper, *The Civil Partnership Bill: Background and Debate* (7 September (2004)<http://www.parliament.uk/commons/lib/research/>; http://www.dca.gov.uk/constitution/transsex/index.htm(2005);http://www.womenandequalityunit.gov.uk/lgbt/faq.htm (2005)

Law Commission, 'Sharing Homes, A Discussion Paper' (Law Com No 278, 2002)

Law Commission, 'Cohabitation: The Financial Consequences of Relationship Breakdown' (Law Com No 307)

Law Commission Consultation Paper No. 191, Intestacy and Family Provision Claims on Death

McKnorrie K, 'What the Civil Partnership Act 2004 Does Not Do' 2005 SLT (6) 35

McK Norrie K, 'Marriage Is For Heterosexuals—May the Rest of Us be Saved From It' [2000] CFLQ 363

Murphy J, 'Same-Sex Marriage In England: a Role for Human Rights?' [2004] CFLQ 245

National Centre for Social Research, 18th Report (2001–02)

Probert R, 'Lord Hardwicke's Marriage Act: Vital Change 250 Years On' [2004] Fam Law

Probert R, Marriage, *Law and Practice in the Long Eighteenth Century* (Cambridge University Press, 2009)

Probert R, 'Why Couples still Believe in Common-law Marriage' [2007] 37 Fam Law 403

Rains R, 'Legal Recognition of Gender Change for Transsexual Persons in the United Kingdom: the Human Rights Act 1998 and Compatibility with European Human Rights Law' [2005] Georgia Journal of International and Comparative Law 333

*Rayden and Jackson's Law and Practice in Divorce and Family Matters* (17th edn, Butterworths, 1997)

Quammem D, *The Reluctant Mr Darwin* (Atlas Books, 2006)

Singer S, 'What Provision for Unmarried Couples Should the Law Make When their Relationships Break Down' [2009] Fam Law 234

Welstead M, 'Invitation to a Marriage: a Canadian Perspective' [2004] JSWFL 161

Welstead M, 'Vulnerable Adults: The Inherent Jurisdiction and the Right to Marry: Re SA (Vulnerable Adult with Capacity: Marriage)' [2007] Denning Law Journal 259

1 At the Liberal Democrat Conference in the UK in 2010, a motion was passed which called for both marriage and civil partnerships to be open to both same-sex and opposite sex sex couples.

It also called for allowing those who change their gender and obtain a Gender Recognition Certificate to be allowed to remain married or in a registered civil partnership.

Critically analyse this motion.

2 Write out a detailed contract relating to the rights and duties of spouses and civil partners, which you could give to a couple to read before they decide to marry or enter into a civil partnership. Where did you find the information to enable you to write this contract? If you find it impossible to write the contract at this stage, revisit this question when you have read the remaining chapters of the book.

3 Elisabeth and Frederick are habitually resident in the UK. They have rented out their home in Oxfordshire whilst they are working in Greece. They wish to marry in England but can only leave Greece together for one week at a time, although they will be allowed a two-week vacation away from Greece after their wedding.

Explain to them the formalities of marriage and whether they will be able to marry in England.

4 Why should civil partners be bound by a similar contract to that of married couples, determined by the State, when they have been denied the right to marry?

5 Why should relationships involving siblings, adult children and their parents, or other types of blood relationships, be excluded from the law relating to civil partnerships?

6 What recommendations would you make to the government relating to the rights of cohabitants when their relationships end? Would you incorporate the Law Commission's proposals in 'Cohabitation: The Financial Consequences of Relationship Breakdown', Law Com No 307 (2007) into your recommendations? Explain the reasons for your decision.

# 3

# Nullity and its consequences

**SUMMARY**

A couple may participate in a ceremony of marriage, or register a civil partnership, yet not acquire the status of spouse or civil partner because they failed to meet one or more of the requirements which would allow them to enter into a new status. Although their relationship is said to be a nullity, it may still have legal consequences.

In this chapter we consider the law relating to nullity and its consequences. The law divides null relationships into two categories: those which are void and those which are voidable. We examine the differences between these two categories of relationships; we also draw attention to the nebulous concept of non-marriage which falls totally outside the ambit of the law of nullity.

## Nullity: an important concept

3.1 For the majority of couples, the law relating to nullity of relationships is far less important today. Divorce has become more socially acceptable and, for the most part, both divorce and dissolution of civil partnerships may be obtained fairly easily.

There are many, including family lawyers, who regard the concept of nullity as unnecessary, and who recommend its abolition.

3.2 However, the doctrine of nullity cannot be discarded quite so readily; the most important reason for its retention for both spouses and civil partners is the contractual nature of their relationships. All contracts must satisfy certain legal requirements if they are to be valid. If the parties to a relationship are contracting with each other to enter into the new status of spouse or civil partner with responsibilities and advantages, a failure to comply with the essential contractual requirements would deny them their new status.

3.3 Whilst many partners may not care whether a purported contract is declared to be at an end by either a decree of divorce, dissolution of a civil partnership, or a decree or order of nullity, others do. There are, for instance, those who for religious, cultural or social reasons would only be able to end the relationship by way of a decree or order of nullity.

3.4 The remedy of nullity is also important for the limited few who, were it not available, might have to wait five years in order to obtain a legal dissolution of their relationship (see Chapter 6).

3.5 Most recently, nullity has proven to be a very useful remedy for those who have been forced into marriage (see below and Chapter 5).

3.6 The Law Commission reviewed the law in 1970 in *Nullity of Marriage*, Law Com No 33 and there are no further plans to reconsider the topic. Its recommendations were incorporated into the Matrimonial Causes Act 1973 (MCA 1973) which now governs the law relating to nullity. The separate categories of void and voidable relationships remain and, for the most part, no satisfactory explanations, other than historic ones, exist for the reasons why certain impediments continue to make a relationship voidable rather than void.

## Void or voidable relationships

3.7 Historically, nullity was under the jurisdiction of the ecclesiastical courts. The law in these courts was concerned with guarding the sexual morals of the nation. The judges in the ecclesiastical courts claimed to exercise their jurisdiction for the sake of the souls of the parties who came before them. Marriage had to conform to religious views about sexual relationships. It was also considered important to be able to establish the legitimacy of children for inheritance purposes and prove that they were born during a valid marriage.

3.8 If a couple were living together and were found not to be validly married because of some serious obstacle to the marriage, such as a pre-existing marriage; marriage to a relation within the prohibited degrees of kindred; lack of consent, or an inability to sexually consummate the marriage, the parties had to be separated by a decree of nullity (there was no divorce at this time). The decree declared that the marriage had never existed; it was said to be void *ab initio* (from the start). Marriages could be declared void even after the death of the parties. Children, in these circumstance, became illegitimate and risked disinheritance.

If the couple were found to be validly married, the court would order the parties to perform their respective mutual marital obligations.

3.9 Eventually, the ecclesiastical courts were forced by the common law courts to distinguish between the more serious defects which would invalidate a marriage from the time of the ceremony and those defects which were regarded as less fundamental and would make the marriage merely voidable from the date of the court's decree. Non-consummation, for example, became a ground for making a marriage voidable rather than void. Voidable marriages could not be challenged by third parties, but only by a petition from either of the spouses themselves (see the scholarly judgment of Simon P in *Padolecchia v Padolecchia (otherwise Leis) (1968)*. Neither spouse could challenge the voidability of the marriage after the death of one of them.

3.10 In *de Reneville v de Reneville (1948)*, Lord Greene MR explained:

> *So far as English law is concerned, there is a clear distinction between void and voidable marriages.... In what, for present purposes, does the distinction consist? It is argued that there is no real distinction by reason of the fact that in each case the form of the decree is the same and pronounces the marriage 'to have been and to be absolutely null and void to all intents and purposes in the law whatsoever'. It is, perhaps, unfortunate that a form of decree which was appropriate when a marriage was regarded as indissoluble and could only be got rid of by decreeing that it had never taken place is still used indiscriminately in the cases of both void and voidable marriages.... The substance, in my view, may be thus expressed. A void marriage is one that will be regarded by every court in any case in which the existence of the marriage is in issue as never having taken place and can be so treated by both parties to it without the necessity of any decree annulling it; a voidable marriage is one that will be regarded by every court as a valid subsisting marriage until a decree annulling it has been pronounced by a court of competent jurisdiction. In England only the Divorce Court has this jurisdiction. The fact that in both cases the form of the decree is the same cannot alter the fact that the two cases are in this respect quite different.*

# Void relationships

3.11 Those who enter into a purported marriage, or civil partnership do not need to go to court to obtain a decree of nullity. Their relationship never came into existence; it was void *ab initio*. Their status did not change as a result of their actions; they never became spouses or civil partners. They may enter into a new legal relationship without any further action on their part.. However, given that the void marriage or civil partnership may have been made public, they may wish to avoid any misunderstanding about their status. It is not possible for them to obtain a declaration from the court that their purported relationship was void *ab initio* under the Family Law Act 1986 (FLA 1986), s 55 which allows the court to make declarations about a person's marital status. However, it is possible for either partner to petition for a decree of nullity. This may be particularly relevant if either party wishes to marry, or enter into a civil partnership, with a new partner and does not wish to risk a public challenge, even one with no foundation in law, at the time of the ceremony.

3.12 A decree of nullity also has the additional advantage that the parties may ask the court, at the time of the petition, to make an order for ancillary relief in the same way as for those whose relationships have been legally dissolved (see **Ben Hashem v Al Shayif (2008)** where ancillary relief was granted after a bigamous marriage).

3.13 Logically, because the decree operates retrospectively, it may be obtained not only by the parties themselves, but also by any other interested party, and even after the death of either of them. For example, a third party, who stands to benefit from the deceased's estate were it not for the marriage or civil partnership of one of the other beneficiaries, might wish to challenge the validity of that beneficiary's relationship status.

# Grounds on which a marriage will be void

## MCA 1973, s 11(a) that it is not a valid marriage under the provisions of the Marriage Acts 1949–1986 in that:

### (i) the parties are within the prohibited degrees of relationship

3.14 The prohibited degrees were considered in Chapter 2.

### (ii) either party is under the age of 16

3.15 In **Pugh v Pugh (1951)**, Pearce J explained the rationale for this rule:

> [A]ccording to modern thought, it is socially and morally wrong that persons of an age at which we now believe them to be immature and provide for their education should have the stresses, responsibilities and sexual freedom of marriage and the physical strain of childbirth. Child marriages, by common consent, are believed to be bad for the participants and bad for the institution of marriage. Acts making carnal knowledge of young girls an offence are an indication of modern views on this subject. The remedy that Parliament has resolved for this mischief and defect is to make marriages void where either of the parties is under sixteen years of age.

There remain countries where under-age marriage is permitted; however, a person domiciled in England cannot evade the rule by marrying in such a country.

In the **Sussex Peerage Case (1844)**, Sir John Stuart V-C stated that:

> This incapacity is personal and, being impressed upon the persons by the law of their own country, cannot be cast off or removed by mere change of place. It is a personal quality which, according to Huber and other jurists, travels round everywhere with the persons; inseparable from them as their shadows.

The government has become increasingly concerned about under-age marriage in the context of forced marriages (see below and Chapter 5).

### (iii) the parties have intermarried in disregard of certain requirements as to the formation of marriage

3.16 Not all failures to comply with the formalities related to a marriage which takes place in England and Wales will make the marriage void. Even where the parties have not complied with those formalities which might make their marriage void, it will only actually be void if the parties deliberately ignored them.

> The parties in **Gereis v Yacoub (1977)** did precisely that. They went through a purported ceremony of marriage, at a Coptic Orthodox Church, knowing that it was not licensed for marriages under the Marriage Act 1949, which in itself would not have made the marriage void. However, they also knew that the priest who conducted the ceremony was not licensed to conduct marriages, and that notice of the marriage had not been given to the superintendent registrar. The priest had advised the couple that a civil marriage ceremony should take place, but no such ceremony was carried out. The marriage was held to be void.

## S 11(b) that at the time of the marriage, either party was already lawfully married or in a civil partnership

3.17 The parties to such a marriage may also have committed the offence of bigamy, unless they reasonably believe that the first marriage was invalid or that the other party to it is dead.

## S 11(c) that the parties are not respectively male and female

3.18 Same-sex marriages are not permitted under English law. It remains debatable whether the marriage of a same-sex couple would come within the category of a void marriage or whether it would be a non-marriage (see below).

3.19 Since the enactment of the Gender Recognition Act 2004 (GRA 2004), the rules relating to marriages of transgendered persons have changed significantly. If no gender recognition certificate has been obtained, a transgendered person remains the same gender as his or her birth gender. If such a person attempts to marry a person who is the same sex as that of his or her birth gender, the marriage will be void and will remain so even if he or she were to apply subsequently for a gender recognition certificate (see *J v C (2007)* below). Once a certificate has been granted the parties will have to marry if they wish to have their relationship validated.

3.20 If a transgendered person, who has obtained a gender recognition certificate, attempts to marry a person of the same sex as that of his or her newly acquired gender (that is to a person of the opposite sex to his or her birth gender), the marriage will be void. If no gender recognition certificate has been obtained, the marriage of a transgendered person to a member of the opposite sex to that of his or her birth gender, remains valid unless, and until, an application for a decree of nullity is made (see below).

## S 11(d) In the case of a polygamous marriage entered into outside England and Wales, that either party was, at the time of the marriage, domiciled in England and Wales

3.21 Polygamous marriages which have been celebrated abroad have become a more common occurrence in England; immigrants return to their countries of origin, where polygamous marriages are legal, and marry. However, if either party to the marriage is domiciled in England the marriage will be void (see eg *Bibi v Chief Adjudication Officer (1998)*).

## Void marriage or non-marriage

3.22 There remains uncertainty about what type of ceremony, which fails to conform to the required formalities, will permit either party to apply for a decree of nullity. Some ceremonies are considered to be so far removed from the accepted idea of a marriage ceremony that they will be regarded as a non-marriage. There is a very fine line between a marriage which is void *ab initio* and a non-marriage, yet the distinction has important consequences. A non-marriage, unlike a void marriage, means that a petition for a decree of nullity and an application for ancillary relief may not be made by either party. However, an application for a declaration of non-marriage which provides for certainty of a person's marital status may be made.

The decisions are very much dependent on the individual facts.

3.23   In *Gereis (1977)* the court emphasized the importance of whether the purported marriage had all

   *...the hallmarks of a Christian marriage; that it would be a monogamous marriage and a marriage for life.*

It found it to be void rather than a non-marriage.

3.24   In *R v Bham (1966)*, the Court of Criminal Appeal held that a private ceremony of nichan, which is a potentially polygamous marriage in accordance with Islamic law, was a non-marriage. Therefore, the defendant, a leader of a Muslim sect, who had performed the ceremony, could not be guilty of an offence under the Marriage Act 1949.

3.25   In *Gandhi v Patel (2002)*, Jawaher Gandhi, a wealthy Indian astrologer and according to Park J, a ladies' man with several mistresses, went through a Hindu ceremony of marriage with Hasmita Gandhi, after she had consulted him astrologically. She claimed to have married in good faith and, therefore, to have become his wife. The ceremony took place in an Indian restaurant in London in considerable style, and it had complied fully with the requirements and traditions of a Hindu marriage. The Brahmin priest who conducted the ceremony maintained that he was only concerned with the rituals and requirements of his own faith, and not with the requirements of English law.

Park J held, rather obtusely, that the Hindu ceremony

*...created something which was not a marriage of any kind at all, not even a marriage which was void. It might be described as a non-marriage rather than a void marriage. To draw a distinction between a non-marriage and a void marriage may seem artificial and elusive to the uninitiated—a class which until very recently included myself—but I am now convinced that the distinction exists, and that the relationship between Jawahar and Hasmita brought about by the Hindu ceremony fell into the category of non-marriages rather than void marriages...if a ceremony which takes place in England is to create a relationship which English law will recognise as a marriage, it must comply with the formal requirements of English law... The ceremony failed in multiple respects to comply with the formal requirements of the Marriage Act 1949, and therefore it was incapable of creating a marriage recognised as such under English law.*

3.26   The most recent decisions in which attempts have been made by the courts to differentiate between non-marriages and void marriages have involved ceremonies which have taken place outside England and Wales. The courts here have jurisdiction relating to these marriages in accordance with MCA 1973, s.14.

3.27   In *Jagger v Hall (unreported, 1999)*, Mick Jagger, the wealthy pop star, and Jerry Hall, a well-known model, had married in a Hindu ceremony in Bali but had failed to register the marriage in accordance with Indonesian law. When the relationship broke down nine years later, the High Court found that the ceremony did not give rise to a non-marriage. This finding allowed Jerry Hall to petition for a decree of nullity on the grounds that the marriage was void ab initio, and obtain substantial financial relief in an out of court agreement.

3.28   In *B v B (2008)*, a couple began a relationship in 1999. The woman maintained that after giving birth to two children, the man agreed with her that they would marry in California and have a blessing in church in England. In 2003, they married in California in a hot air balloon. They returned to England and the church blessing took place. When the relationship broke down, the wife accepted that the marriage was not valid under

Californian law, but maintained that she had acted in good faith at the time of the ceremony, and petitioned for a decree of nullity. The husband maintained that they had not obtained a licence in California and that the marriage was not void but a non-marriage. The court granted the wife's petition and said that was in the interests of public policy and justice to find the marriage to be void.

3.29    In *B v I (Forced marriage) (2009)*, the court rescued a 16 year-old girl from the effects of a ceremony in Bangladesh by declaring it to be a non-marriage. The girl had been taken to Bangladesh by her parents and the day before she was due to return to England, an Imam was brought to her bedroom and performed a ceremony in Bengali. The girl was instructed by her father to say 'I accept' at certain points during the ceremony. She thought that it was an engagement ceremony rather than an attempt to marry her to her absent cousin. The next day the cousin came to the girl's hotel and had sexual intercourse with her against her will. When she complained to her family, they explained that she was now married and must accept this. The girl returned to England with her family but without her cousin. It took her three years to gather together her courage to leave the family. This meant that she was time barred from pleading that the relationship was voidable for lack of consent (see below.) The court was very sympathetic to her plight and granted a declaration, under the inherent jurisdiction, that the ceremony she had undergone in Bangladesh was a non-marriage (see also *SH v NB (2009)*).

3.30    In *Hudson v Leigh (Status of non-marriage) (2009)*, an English couple who had lived together for 12 years and had had a daughter together decided to marry. The woman mainly lived in the man's second home in South Africa. She was a devout Christian and wanted to have a religious marriage ceremony, The man claimed to be a Jewish atheist and wanted a civil marriage. They agreed to have a religious ceremony in South Africa, even though it would not be legally binding. It was agreed that it would be followed soon after by a civil marriage in England. The South African ceremony took the form of a wedding; the woman wore a wedding dress, and their daughter was a bridesmaid. A wedding dinner was held at which the guests referred to the couple as having married that day. The couple returned to England, and made arrangements for the civil ceremony. They took an oath stating that they were not already married but did explain to the registrar about the South African ceremony. However, before the civil ceremony could took take place, the relationship broke down. The woman applied, *inter alia*, for a decree of nullity on the basis that the South African ceremony was void because it failed to comply with the formal requirements of South African law. The court rejected the woman's petition and used the inherent jurisdiction to make a declaration that the ceremony gave rise to a non-marriage. It maintained that it was in the public interest to do so and, thereby, create certainty. The court explained that in deciding the effect of a ceremony, the particular facts of the case should be taken into account including, whether the ceremony purported to be a lawful marriage; whether it had all or enough of the hallmarks of marriage; whether the minister, or other officiating person, and the couple believed, and intended, that the ceremony gave rise to the status of a lawful marriage, and what were the reasonable perceptions, and beliefs of those who attended the ceremony.

### Marriage by cohabitation and repute

3.31 In several decisions involving couples who have come to live in England from overseas, the courts have rescued them from the adverse consequences of non-marriages. They have found that they were validly married under the common law principle of presumption of marriage by cohabitation and repute. The principle was discussed in Chapter 2.

# Grounds on which a civil partnership will be void

3.32 The Civil Partnership Act 2004 (CPA 2004), ss 3 and 49 provide the grounds, which are very similar to those relating to void marriages, on which a civil partnership will be void:

- s 49(a): the parties are not of the same sex;
- s 49(b): either of them is already a civil partner or lawfully married;
- s 49(c): either of them is under the age of 16; or
- s 49(d): they are within the prohibited degrees of relationship.

3.33 In 2007, a married woman, Suzanne Mitchell lied about the fact that she was still married and registered a civil partnership with Caroline Beddows. The civil partnership was clearly void but Ms Mitchell was also prosecuted for giving false information to the registrar and given an eight months suspended prison sentence and 100 hours of community service. The judge refused to believe Ms Mitchell's excuse that she had not realised that she was breaking the law because she thought that she was taking part in some kind of blessing of friendship. She subsequently returned to her husband and gave birth to their sixth child. Her lawyer, in mitigation, described Ms Mitchell was a woman of limited acumen who had acted naively (*The Guardian*, 6 August 2007).

# Voidable relationships

3.34 A voidable relationship, unlike a void relationship, remains valid until either party decides to seek a decree of nullity from the court. Neither is at liberty to regard the relationship as invalid unless, and until, the court grants the decree. The decree is not retrospective. The parties are the only ones who may apply for the decree; it is not open to third parties to do so.

# Grounds on which a marriage will be voidable

## MCA 1973, s 12 provides the grounds on which a marriage will be voidable

### S12(a) that the marriage has not been consummated owing to the incapacity of either party to consummate it

3.35 Historically, the main purposes of marriage were procreation and to control sexual behaviour within society. This subsection retains as its basis those now outmoded views. It provides that a marriage will be voidable if either party is unable to have sexual intercourse with the other. The impotent party may rely on his or her own inability to consummate the marriage. Impotence requires a detailed and, for many of those who seek the decree, embarrassing examination of the parties' sexuality or, rather, lack of it. The provision is sexist in that a male is, more obviously, and easily, able to prove his inability to consummate than a female can prove hers.

3.36 The ground on which a spouse relies to annul his or her marriage must normally exist at the time of the marriage. This requirement has been liberally and sensitively interpreted. Either spouse may apply for a decree of nullity if either of them, although capable of consummation at the time of the marriage, was unable to do so after the marriage. Thus, where a spouse is injured after the marriage but prior to consummation of it, the marriage may be voidable even if the couple had had a sexual relationship prior to marriage. It is unfortunate for spouses who consummate their marriage immediately after the wedding and then suffer an injury which prevents any further sexual relationship, given that intercourse need only take place once for a marriage to be consummated. Such spouses would have to apply for a divorce if they wish to end the marriage (see Chapter 6).

3.37 According to Dr Lushington, in *D-E v A-G (1845)*, for a plea of incapacity to succeed, there must be an inability to have ordinary and complete intercourse.

3.38 The incapacity need not be a generalized sexual impotence towards the world at large but may relate only to a specific spouse.

Lord Birkenhead LC in *C (otherwise H) v C (1921)*, pointed out in a judgment very sympathetic to the male dilemma of incapacity, that it is

> *...a grave and wounding imputation that the husband is lacking, at least quoad hanc, in the power of reproducing his species, a power commonly and rightly considered*

*to be the most characteristic quality of manhood. The allegation made in the present case is not that the husband completely lacks the capacity of reproduction... it is urged that he is incapable of consummating this particular marriage with this particular woman. In general, the vitality, the animal spirits, and the resources of youth will enable a man to support intercourse with any woman of suitable years, if she be neither repulsive nor antipathetic. There are, nevertheless, instances where the absence of physical sympathy has in the first place delayed intercourse and has afterwards by an accretion of nervous apprehension rendered it impossible for a particular man and a particular woman to unite in the generative act. The relation, no doubt, in many cases and moods appeals only to the animal in man, and so long as the required standard of attractiveness, be it high or be it low, is attained by the woman, the function of coition will be as readily performed as in the case of animals.*

3.39    In *Baxter v Baxter (1948)*, it was held that sexual intercourse is complete even when contraceptives have been used and that incapacity does not extend to an inability to have children.

3.40  Either of the parties may petition for the decree of nullity based on incapacity.

In *Harthan v Harthan (1949)*, it was held that a petitioner may rely on his own inability to have a sexual relationship with his wife.

3.41  The reason for the incapacity may be physical or psychological and must be permanent and irremediable. The incapacity will be accepted as irremediable if it cannot be readily cured or would require dangerous medical intervention. Any refusal to have straightforward remedial treatment for any incapacity will be deemed to be a wilful refusal to consummate the marriage.

In *SY v SY (otherwise W) (No 2) (1963)*, the court held there was no incapacity on the part of the wife because her vaginal defect could be remedied by simple surgery.

3.42  Psychological impotence may also be permanent and irremediable but is likely to be more difficult to prove than impotence resulting from a physical condition.

In *Singh v Singh (1971)*, the parents of a Sikh girl, aged 17, arranged a marriage for her with a 21 year-old Sikh male. She met her husband for the first time at the registry office ceremony. She did not like him. She thought that he was neither as handsome nor as educated as she had been led to believe by her parents. After the civil ceremony, she returned home with her parents and refused to go ahead with the Sikh religious ceremony and have a sexual relationship with her husband. Subsequently, the wife petitioned for a decree of nullity on the grounds, *inter alia*, of her own incapacity because of an invincible repugnance, on her part, towards her husband.

The court rejected her allegation of incapacity and held she had not shown an invincible repugnance to having intercourse with the husband, because of some psychiatric or sexual aversion on her part. She merely did not wish to have a sexual relationship with him because she did not like what she had seen of him at the registry office ceremony.

3.43 The expectation of the court that a young girl can be expected to have a sexual relationship with a man whom she does not like, and whom she has never met before the arranged marriage ceremony, seems to be unnecessarily restrictive of the definition of invincible repugnance.

3.44 In **Corbett v Corbett (1971)**, a transgendered person had male-to-female gender reassignment surgery and was held to be incapable of having a sexual relationship because she had no vagina but merely a newly constructed cavity, which served as an artificial vagina.

The enactment of the GRA 2004 will now prevent such a ruling, but a petitioner who has no knowledge of his spouse's gender change at the time of the marriage will be able to obtain a decree of nullity.

3.45 A transgendered person, who has not undergone gender reassignment surgery, but has obtained a gender recognition certificate in accordance with the provisions of the GRA 2004, will be able to marry although unable to consummate the marriage. Once again the voidability of such a marriage will depend on the petitioner's knowledge at the time of the marriage.

## S 12(b) that the marriage has not been consummated owing to the wilful refusal of the respondent to consummate it

3.46 Case law illustrates the close relationship between inability to consummate and wilful refusal to do so. However, a spouse who wilfully refuses to consummate the marriage, unlike one who is incapable of doing so, may not rely on his or her own wilful refusal.

Wilful refusal, in **S v S (otherwise C) (1956)**, was held to mean a settled and definite decision, without sufficient reason, not to have a sexual relationship with one's spouse. The husband left his wife and petitioned for nullity because his wife was indecisive about undergoing the necessary surgery to correct a physical defect which prevented consummation. The court held that indecisiveness does not constitute wilful refusal.

3.47 In **Potter v Potter (1975)**, a wife successfully underwent treatment for her physical inability to have intercourse. In spite of this, her husband refused to have a sexual relationship with her. The wife petitioned for a decree of nullity on the grounds of the husband's wilful refusal to consummate. The court accepted that the husband was not wilful in his refusal but had merely lost his ardour whilst waiting for his wife's condition to be cured.

3.48    In **Ford v Ford (1987)**, the husband was convicted of armed robbery and sentenced to five years' imprisonment. During his imprisonment there were opportunities to engage in sexual relations and it was common, although against prison rules, to do so. The husband refused to have a sexual relationship with his wife in prison and told her that he did not wish to live with her on his release. He also demanded to be taken to a former girlfriend's house during parole visits. The court held that the husband's behaviour showed a determination not to consummate the marriage and granted the wife a decree of nullity.

3.49  Failure to consummate a marriage until a religious ceremony has taken place, following the civil ceremony, will not constitute wilful refusal to consummate. However, failure to organize or go through with the religious ceremony may be interpreted as wilful refusal to consummate.

> In **Kaur v Singh (1972)**, the parties, who were both Sikhs, married in a registry office on the understanding that they would not cohabit until a religious ceremony had been held in a Sikh temple. The husband refused to arrange the ceremony and was held to have wilfully refused to have a sexual relationship with his wife.

3.50    In **A v J (1989)**, the husband was prepared to arrange the religious ceremony following a civil ceremony of marriage but the wife demanded that it be postponed indefinitely. The court granted the husband a decree of nullity on the grounds of the wife's wilful refusal to consummate.

3.51  Whether one party may apply for a decree of nullity, if both have agreed prior to the marriage not to consummate their relationship, will depend on their reasons for reaching such an agreement.

> In **Brodie v Brodie (1917)**, for example, it was accepted that in the ordinary case of a young couple, any agreement not to consummate a marriage would be void as against public policy. Where there is a good reason for such an agreement, it will almost certainly be accepted as a valid defence against a petition for nullity based on wilful refusal to consummate.

3.52    It was held in **Scott v Scott (1959)** that the husband could not petition for a decree of nullity based on wilful refusal to consummate because he and his wife were not young and had agreed to a non-sexual, companionate marriage.

### S 12(c) that either party did not validly consent to it whether in consequence of duress, mistake or otherwise

#### Duress

3.53  A spouse who enters a marriage because of threats, force, or duress has not freely consented to it. The threat need not emanate from the respondent spouse but may come from another source.

In *Szechter v Szechter (1971)*, a woman was sentenced to three years' imprisonment in Poland for anti-government activities. She knew that her health would suffer and that she would have no future there after her release from prison. The man married her, having divorced his wife in order to do so, and thereby help her enter England. The woman claimed that she had married the man under duress and successfully applied for a decree of nullity in order to enable him to remarry his first wife. The court held that a spouse pleading duress must prove that their will was overborne by genuine and reasonably held fear caused by threat of immediate danger (for which the party is not himself responsible) to life, limb, or liberty, so that the constraint destroys the reality of consent to ordinary wedlock.

Sir Jocelyn Simon P explained that a yielding of the lips but not of the mind can have no legal effect.

As a postscript to the decision, it is of interest that the man divorced his first wife again and remarried the second one.

3.54 In *Buckland v Buckland (1968)*, the petitioner was falsely charged with a sexual offence against a young girl. In spite of his claim that he was innocent, he was told that he would be sent to jail for two years unless he married her. He was afraid of going to jail and did marry the girl. He proceeded to petition for a decree of nullity and was successful. Scarman LJ maintained that the fear or duress had to be objectively judged. The court also suggested that had he been justly accused of the offence, he himself would have been responsible for the threats. This would have prevented him from claiming that he had not validly consented to the marriage because of fear or duress.

3.55 The strict test in *Szechter (1971)* and *Buckland (1968)* was followed in two cases involving young immigrant girls who had been forced into marriage by their parents. In *Singh v Singh (1971)* and *Singh v Kaur (1978)*, both girls were held not to have fulfilled the requirements of this arduous objective test. Their age and cultural background, which demanded parental obedience, was not taken into account.

3.56 In *Hirani v Hirani (1983)*, however, Ormrod LJ preferred the simple subjective test in *Scott v Sebright (1866)* in which Butt J explained that:

*...the woman had been reduced by mental and bodily suffering to a state in which she was incapable of offering resistance to coercion and threats which in her normal condition she would have treated with the contempt she must have felt for the man who made use of them; and that, therefore, there never was any such consent on her part as the law requires for the making of a contract of marriage. Such being the case, I know of no consideration consistent with justice or with common sense which should induce me to hold this marriage binding.*

He maintained that the question to be asked is:

*...whether the pressure...is such as to destroy the reality of consent and overbear the will of the individual?*

*Forced marriages*

3.57 Ormrod LJ's return to the 1866 test in *Hirani (1983)* was an important step forward. It has re-emerged in recent years to play a significant role in the rescue of young adults who have been forced into marriage by their parents. Such marriages have become increasingly problematic for young second generation immigrants, both male and female—the phenomenon is not gender specific—who have been forced to marry, often by being taken to their parents' countries of origin to be married there. Whilst the government is attempting to control such practices via the joint endeavours of the Foreign Office and the Home Office (see <http://www.fco.gov.uk/>), and the Forced Marriage (Civil Protection) Act 2007 (see Chapter 5), nullity is an essential remedy for those who are unable to avoid a forced marriage because of cultural and familial pressures. In many cases, the treatment of some of these young spouses by their families, would satisfy even the stricter test laid down in *Szechter (1971)* and *Buckland (1968)*.

3.58 In *P v R (Forced Marriage: Annulment: Procedure) (2003)*, the petitioner was a 17 year-old British citizen of Pakistani origin whose parents persuaded her to attend a family funeral in Pakistan. They wished to remove her from England because she was involved in a relationship of which they disapproved. Whilst there, arrangements were made, against her will, for her to be married to a Pakistani cousin. She was terrified by her brother's threats of physical violence and also believed that if she refused to go through with the ceremony she would not be permitted to return to England. Her parents told her that her refusal to marry would bring shame on the family and that it would merit severe long-term punishment. The girl escaped to England and was granted a decree of nullity.

3.59 The judgment of Munby J, in *NS v MI (2006)*, gives a most helpful account of the doctrine of nullity in the context of forced marriage. The petitioner, a young British girl aged 17, was taken to Pakistan by her parents, ostensibly for a holiday. Her passport was taken from her by her mother and she became, in effect, a prisoner trapped in Pakistan and was then forced to marry her 17 year-old cousin. He admitted that he only wanted to marry her in order to gain admission to the UK.

The marriage was not consummated and the girl was allowed to return to the UK with her mother. She had nothing further to do with her husband and sought a decree of nullity on the grounds of duress. She maintained that her family had morally blackmailed her and threatened to commit suicide if she disobeyed their wishes *vis a vis* the marriage.

Munby J was most concerned to draw a distinction between arranged and forced marriages:

*[A]rranged marriages are to be supported as a conventional concept in many societies. And for that very reason they are, I emphasise, not merely to be supported but to be respected... We must guard against the risk of stereotyping. We must be*

*careful to ensure that our understandable concern to protect vulnerable children (or, indeed, vulnerable young adults) does not lead us to interfere inappropriately— and if inappropriately then unjustly—with families merely because they cleave, as this family does, to mores, to cultural beliefs, more or less different from what is familiar to those who view life from a purely Euro-centric perspective*

(See also Munby J's judgment in *Re K (2007)*.)

Forced marriages, however, he described as an appalling practice, a gross abuse of human rights and a form of domestic violence that dehumanises people by denying them their right to choose how to conduct their lives. He compared them to the barbarous practices of female genital mutilation and so-called 'honour killings'.

Munby J explained that there can be no consent to marriage where the person marrying is able to say

*...my tongue has sworn but my mind [that is, the mind as the seat of the mental faculties, perception, thought] is unsworn.*

(See the words of Staughton LJ in *Re T (Adult: Refusal of Treatment) (1993)* in which he quotes from Euripides' *Hippolytus*.)

Pressure put to bear by a parent or close member of the family on a young vulnerable person, according to Munby J, is extremely powerful and, particularly so, when the threats are insidious and involve subtle arguments relating to matters of personal affection, duty, religious beliefs, and social and cultural conventions. He accepted that it might be necessary in certain circumstances to allow a vulnerable petitioner to give evidence from behind a screen or via a video link in order to protect him or her from intimidation by family members

Munby J also drew attention to the problem of evidence in petitions based on duress and stated that the more serious the allegation the more convincing be the evidence required to prove it. He quoted the words of Butt J in *Sebright (1866)*:

*Public policy requires that marriages should not be lightly set aside, and there is in some cases the strongest temptation to the parties more immediately interested to act in collusion in obtaining a dissolution of the marriage tie. These reasons necessitate great care and circumspection on the part of the tribunal, but they in no wise alter the principle or the grounds on which this, like any other contract, may be avoided.*

## Mistake

3.60 Voidable marriages based on mistake are rare. The only mistakes which have been recognized to date are those relating to the identity of a spouse or to the nature of the ceremony.

In the New Zealand case of *C v C (1942)*, the wife claimed that she had married her husband in the erroneous belief that he was a famous boxer. The court held that this was not a mistake which invalidated the marriage. She had intended marrying her husband but thought that he had qualities which he did not have.

3.61　In *Valier v Valier (1925)*, the petitioner was an Italian who did not speak English. He was taken to a registry office and went through a ceremony of marriage without any realization of what was happening. It was held that he had not given a valid consent to the marriage.

3.62　In *Messina (formerly Smith Orse Vervaeke) v Smith (Messina intervening) (1971)*, the parties had undergone a sham marriage merely to allow the wife, who was a prostitute, to escape arrest by leaving Belgium and obtaining British citizenship. It was held that the marriage was valid even though the wife claimed to be mistaken as to the consequences of a sham marriage. She subsequently obtained a decree of nullity in Belgium which the English court also refused to recognize.

The decision is to be contrasted with that of *Szechter (1971)*, in which it could equally be argued that the marriage was a sham. Public policy clearly favours those who indulge in activities against an unfriendly foreign government and not those who engage in criminal activities in countries which are regarded as allies.

## Unsound mind

3.63　A marriage will be voidable if one of the parties shows that they did not understand the nature of the contract.

In *Re Park (1954)*, the test was held to be:

*Was the person capable of understanding the nature of the contract into which he was entering, or was his mental condition such that he was incapable of understanding it? To ascertain the nature of the contract of marriage a man must be mentally capable of appreciating that it involves the responsibilities normally attaching to marriage. Without that degree of mentality, it cannot be said that he understands the nature of the contract. (See also the cases on mental incapacity discussed in Chapter 2.)*

3.64　If a mentally incapacitated adult does enter into a voidable marriage, they may require the help of the inherent jurisdiction to escape from it. The inherent jurisdiction is so wide that it almost certainly gives the courts the power to help in such circumstances (see *Re SA (Vulnerable Adult with Capacity: Marriage) (2006)*); for a discussion of the inherent jurisdiction see Chapter 2). If a voidable marriage can be shown to be damaging to the best interests of such a person, it would be unacceptable to leave him or her trapped in that marriage. Without the aid of the court, vulnerable adults would find it impossible to apply for a decree of nullity against their spouse's will.

3.65　It is arguable that many of those who embark on marriage are too immature to understand the nature of the contract; they only come to understand it over time, and when faced with difficulties. Whether a court would accept general immaturity as evidence of lack of consent is debatable.

### Or otherwise

3.66 The courts have rarely discussed the meaning of the words 'or otherwise', which are included in MCA 1973, s 12(c). Perhaps, more use could be made of them where one party is totally unaware of some significant fact relating to the spouse at the time of the marriage and might not have consented had they known about it. Such facts might include the existence of a mistress or cohabitant with or without children, or that another woman is pregnant by the man at the time of the marriage, or that the spouse is suffering from a serious communicable disease which does not come within the category of venereal disease (see below).

Where a spouse marries under the influence of drink or drugs, and given the nature of the celebrations surrounding marriage, many do, it may be possible to maintain that a valid consent cannot have been given. Such circumstances could be encompassed by the general umbrella of the words of MCA 1973, s 12(c) 'or otherwise'.

### S 12(d) that at the time of the marriage, either party, although normally capable of giving a valid consent, was not able to do so because he or she was suffering from a mental disorder within the meaning of s 1 of the Mental Health Act 1983, such as to be unfitted for marriage

3.67 MCA 1973, s 1(2) defines mental disorder somewhat liberally as 'mental illness, arrested or incomplete development of mind, psychopathic disorder and any other disorder or disability of mind'. The petitioner may rely on his or her own mental disorder.

### S 12(e) that at the time of the marriage the respondent was suffering from venereal disease in a communicable form

3.68 HIV or AIDS do not come within the category of venereal disease nor do several other diseases which are equally transmitted by means of intimate contact.

### S 12(f) that at the time of the marriage, the respondent was pregnant by some other person than the petitioner

3.69 A man is presumed, in the absence of evidence to the contrary, to be the father of any child born during marriage. This subsection is based on the view that it is unjust to expect a man to bring up another man's biological child when he may have married only because he believed the child to be his.

3.70 A wife may not petition on the basis that another woman is pregnant by her husband at the time of the marriage despite the fact that this event could have a profound effect on their future together.

**S 12(g) that an interim gender recognition certificate under the GRA 2004 has after the time of the marriage been issued to either party to the marriage**

3.71 This provision is clearly based on policy, and perhaps compassion for the parties. It allows either party to marry without having to undergo divorce. It is, however, difficult to see how a change of gender, possibly undertaken many years after the marriage took place, nullifies what was a valid contract at the time of the marriage.

**S 12(h) that the respondent is a person whose gender at the time of the marriage had become the acquired gender under the GRA 2004**

3.72 This provision protects a person who marries and is unaware at the time of the ceremony that his or her spouse has acquired a gender recognition certificate under the GRA 2004. The provision appears to defeat the aims of the GRA 2004. It suggests that, although a gender recognition certificate has been issued, there remains some question over the true gender of the certificate holder. It was noted above that nullity based on mistake is rigidly interpreted; the provision under s 12(h) appears to extend the interpretation of nullity based on mistake.

# Bars to relief where a marriage is voidable

3.73 An application for a decree of nullity in the case of a voidable marriage may be barred under the MCA 1973, s 13 in order to prevent injustice to a spouse who would suffer serious disadvantages if the decree were to be granted. There are no bars to an application for a decree of nullity in the case of a void marriage.

## Knowledge of the petitioner and injustice to the respondent

3.74 The MCA 1973, s 13(1) provides that a petition will not be granted if the petitioner, with the knowledge that the marriage was voidable, had led the respondent to believe that he or she would not do so, and it would be unjust to the respondent to grant the decree. There are clearly two limbs to the section and both must be satisfied.

> In *D v D (1979)*, the parties adopted two children at a time when the husband knew that he could have the marriage annulled because of his wife's wilful refusal to consummate the marriage. He was held to have conducted himself in a way that led the wife to believe that he would not seek an annulment. However, the court considered that it would not be unjust to the respondent wife to grant the decree, partly because the wife did not object.

3.75 Where the petitioner wishes to rely on venereal disease, pregnancy by another, or that he or she has married a transgendered person in possession of a gender recognition certificate, MCA 1973, s 13(3) provides that the petitioner must be ignorant of those facts at the time of the marriage.

## Delay

3.76 MCA 1973, s 13(2) provides that any proceedings for nullity, where the petitioner is relying on grounds other than non-consummation, or the issue of an interim gender recognition certificate, must be brought within three years of the date of the marriage unless the court grants leave under MCA 1973, s 13(4). The court will only grant leave to apply out of time where the petitioner has suffered from mental disorder, and the court considers that it would be just to grant leave to apply out of time. The Mental Health Act 1983, s 1(2) defines mental disorder as 'mental illness, arrested or incomplete development of mind, psychopathic disorder and any other disorder or disability of mind'.

3.77 The GRA 2004 inserts into the MCA 1973 a new s 13(2A), which provides that where the parties are married, any application for a decree of nullity must be made within six months of the issue of an interim gender recognition certificate.

# Grounds on which a civil partnership will be voidable

3.78 CPA 2004, s 50(1) provides the grounds on which a civil partnership will be voidable:

- s 50(1)(a): either of the parties did not validly consent to its formation (whether as a result of duress, mistake, unsoundness of mind, or otherwise);

- s 50(1)(b): at the time of its formation either of them, though capable of giving a valid consent, was suffering (whether continuously or intermittently) from mental disorder of such a kind or to such an extent as to be unfitted for civil partnership;

- s 50(1)(c): at the time of its formation, the respondent was pregnant by some person other than the applicant (this will only be relevant in a case involving a gender change under the Gender Recognition Bill and is subject to s 50(6) which provides that the court may not make a nullity order if the applicant knew of the pregnancy at the time of the formation of the civil partnership);

- s 50(1)(d): an interim gender recognition certificate under the GRA 2004 has, after the time of its formation, been issued to either civil partner;

- s 50(1)(e): the respondent is a person whose gender at the time of its formation had become the acquired gender under the GRA 2004.

It is presumed that the relevant decisions relating to voidable marriages will be followed.

3.79 There is a notable absence of any provisions relating to sexual consummation of the relationship, or of the presence of venereal disease at the time the civil partnership is registered. It would seem that the legislators were unable to come to terms with the nature of sexual relations in same-sex relationships and were determined to avoid the issue completely. In November 2004, in the debate in the House of Lords on the Civil Partnership Bill, Baroness Scotland attempted to explain, with little success, that one of the major differences between marriage and civil partnership is that of consummation:

> *[I]n relation to marriage, for a marriage to be valid it has to be consummated by one man and one woman and there is a great deal of jurisprudence which tells you exactly what consummation amounts to, partial, impartial, penetration, no penetration... There is no provision for consummation in the Civil Partnerships Bill. We do not look at the nature of the sexual relationship, it is totally different in nature.*

> *(House of Lords, Hansard 17 November 2004, col 1479)*

3.80 It may be that an application could be made for a decree of nullity under the provisions for lack of valid consent in consequence of 'otherwise' (CPA 2004, s 50(1)(a)), where the respondent remained silent about either his or her intention with respect to a sexual relationship or about having a communicable sexual disease.

# Bars to relief where a civil partnership is voidable

## Knowledge of the applicant and injustice to the respondent

3.81 The applicant may not obtain a decree of nullity if the respondent satisfies the court that, according to the provisions of the CPA 2004:

- s 51(1)(a): the applicant, with knowledge that it was open to him to obtain a nullity order, conducted himself in relation to the respondent in such a way as to lead the respondent reasonably to believe that he would not seek to do so, and
- s 51(1)(b): that it would be unjust to the respondent to make the order.

3.82 There can also be no grant of a decree where the applicant was aware, at the time of the registration of the partnership, that the respondent was pregnant, or was a person whose gender had become an acquired gender under the GRA 2004.

## Delay

3.83 Except where a gender recognition certificate has been issued, CPA 2004, s 51(2)(a) provides that all applications must be made within three years of the registration of the civil partnership. In the case of a gender recognition certificate, the application must be made within six months of its issue (CPA 2004, s 51(5)).

3.84 Leave to apply after the three-year period has elapsed may be granted if the applicant has at some time during the three-year period suffered from mental disorder, and in all the circumstances of the case it would be just to grant leave for the institution of proceedings (CPA 2004, s 51(3)(4)).

# Consequences of nullity for married couples and civil partners

## Relationship status

3.85 In the case of a void relationship, either party may enter into a new marriage or civil partnership and treat the void relationship as having never existed whether or not they have sought a decree of nullity. In the case of a voidable relationship, the parties must obtain a decree of nullity from the court before their relationship can be said to have ceased to exist.

3.86 In the case of a void relationship, because it is deemed to have never existed, the provision, or denial, of any benefit will be based on the status of the parties prior to the purported marriage or civil partnership. For example, any State benefits, or dispositions in a will, dependent on marital or civil partnership status will be forfeited.

3.87 Where a person enters into a voidable relationship, they lose their former status. On the grant of a decree of nullity, they are deemed not to revert that status but are regarded as having acquired a new status.

> In **Ward v Secretary of State for Social Services (1990)**, a widow's pension was terminated when she remarried. The marriage was declared to be voidable; on the grant of the decree of nullity she was held not to revert to her status of widowhood. The decision meant that she could not reclaim her pension rights.

3.88 The decree of nullity does not normally affect the status of parenthood. However, in *J v C (2007)*, the Court of Appeal held that a transgendered female to male was not the father of children conceived by artificial insemination in 1986 and 1991 because at the time of conception his marriage was void. The GRA 2004 could not come to his aid because it does not provide for the retrospective recognition of a marriage which was entered into prior to the issue of the gender recognition certificate which the man had later obtained. Both the man and his children have lost their legal and social relationship with each other.

The man may be able to bring a claim that his right to respect for private and family life, under Art 8 of the European Convention on Human Rights 1950 (ECHR), has been breached.

## Revocation of wills

3.89 All wills are revoked on marriage or registration of a civil partnership (Wills Act 1837, s 18).

> In *Re Roberts (1978)*, it was held that this includes a marriage, which is voidable. In the case of a void marriage, the will, of course, will not be revoked.

## Ancillary relief

3.90 In the case of both void and voidable relationships, either party may apply to the court for ancillary relief at the time they make the application for the decree under the provisions of MCA 1973, Part II or under the provisions of CPA 2004, s 72 (1) and Sch 5 (see Chapter 7). It may seem strange that a party to a void relationship might be made responsible for the financial support of a partner even though that person never acquired the status of spouse or civil partner. However, policy reasons demand that those who believe that they have entered a new status which involves obligations towards each other, should not necessarily be allowed to escape from them when the relationship ends and a petition for nullity has been granted.

3.91 In determining whether to make an award, and if so, its quantification, the courts have the same task as in granting financial provision on the legal dissolution of a relationship (see Chapter 7). It is remarkable how large a part conduct has played in determining financial provision in decisions relating to nullity of marriage.

> In *Whiston v Whiston (1995)*, a man, who had lived with a woman for 15 years after they purported to marry, discovered that she already had a husband at the time of the marriage. He applied to the court for a decree of nullity and maintained that the woman should not be given financial relief because of her appalling conduct. The Court of Appeal refused the woman's claim for financial relief because to do so would allow her to assert rights directly arising from the commission of the crime of bigamy.

3.92    In *S-T (formerly J) v J (1998)*, it was held that a female-to-male transgendered person should not receive any financial provision when his 'wife' was granted a decree of nullity. He had lied about his gender to the registrar by describing himself as a bachelor. Furthermore, he was found to have misled his 'wife' as to the nature of his birth gender. In the light of the fact that the 'marriage' had endured almost 20 years; that he had kept a penile prosthesis in a drawer in the bedroom; that he always backed out of the shower, and that the couple had two children by means of reproductive technology carried out in an infertility clinic, it is surprising that the court viewed his 'wife's' lack of knowledge as entirely blameless.

3.93    By contrast, in *Rampal v Rampal (2001)*, the Court of Appeal, faced with a husband's claim for financial provision in the case of a 22-year bigamous marriage, concluded that the husband should not be denied his claim. It distinguished the decision in *Whiston (1995)*, and maintained that not all crimes of bigamy would automatically deprive a claimant of financial provision; all the facts must be considered. The court held that it was relevant that the wife had engineered the marriage with full knowledge that it would be a bigamous one.

## FURTHER READING

Bradney D, 'Duress, Family Law and the Coherent Legal System' (1994) 57 MLR 963

Brunner K, 'Nullity in Unconsummated Marriages' [2001] Fam Law 837

Gaffney-Rhys R, 'Sheffield City Council v E and Another—capacity to marry and the rights and responsibilities of married couples' [2006] CFLQ 181

Hutchinson, Hayward and Gupta, 'Forced Marriage Nullity Procedure in England and Wales' [2006] IFL 20

Ingman T and Grant B, 'Duress in the Law of Nullity' [1984] Fam Law 92

Law Commission, 'Nullity of Marriage' (Law Com No 33, 1970)

Miller G, 'When "I do" turns into "I didn't" ' [2004] NLJ 252

Probert R, 'How would Corbett v Corbett be Decided Today?' [2005] Fam Law 382

Probert R, 'When are we married? Void, non-existent and presumed marriages' (2002) 22 Legal Studies 398

Spon-Smith R, 'Civil Partnership Act' [2004] Fam Law 369

Welstead M, 'A Constitutional Solution to Royal Marital Breakdown' [1994] NLJ 144

Welstead M, 'The Virtue of Virginity' [2009] NLJ 95

## SELF-TEST QUESTIONS

1 Why do we need to categorize nullity of relationships into those which are void and those which are voidable?

2 Discuss the circumstances in which it might it be unjust to grant a decree of nullity to a spouse or civil partner.

3 Critically analyse the decision in *S-T (formerly J) v J (1998)*.

4 Jeffrey married Kate 10 years ago but was unable to consummate the marriage because he claimed that he found that he was not sexually attracted to her. At the date of the marriage, he suspected that he preferred men to women and had had several sexual relationships with men.

He has now met Karl with whom he wishes to have a permanent relationship, and register a civil partnership with him. Karl registered a civil partnership four years ago with Liam but has since discovered that Liam was married to Miranda at the time of the registration.

Advise all parties on their current statuses and what, if any action they need to take in order to enter into a new legal relationship.

5 Jonathan is a male-to-female transgendered person, who has not had gender reassignment surgery because he belongs to a humanist organization which is opposed to blood transfusion, and the reassignment surgery could well require the need for blood transfusion. He has not yet obtained a gender recognition certificate. Three years ago, when Jonathan was aged 22, his father persuaded him that it was vital for the family business, in which Jonathan worked, to marry Helena, a daughter of a well-known criminal. Jonathan was also told that if he refused he would certainly lose his job, and that he could also 'expect a rough visit from Helena's dad and friends'. The marriage took place on Jonathan's twenty-third birthday. He did not reveal to Helena that he was a transgendered person until after the marriage. Jonathan suggested to Helena that to please her father they should foster a baby boy with a view to adopting him, and Helena agreed. Last year, a three-month-old baby came to live with them; they were told that they would be able to adopt the child this year. Helena gave up work to care for the baby and was supported by Jonathan's earnings. Immediately prior to the adoption date, Jonathan was offered the opportunity to work abroad. He decided to obtain a gender recognition certificate because he regrets his marriage to Helena and wishes to live life as a female.

Advise Jonathan whether he will be able to obtain a decree of nullity.

6 Oliver, aged 24, has attention deficit disorder. His parents were most protective of him and did not want him to marry because they believed that he was not able to make a sensible decision about an appropriate partner. For the last four years he has had a romantic relationship with Penelope who was so keen to marry him that she asked Oliver's friends to help her achieve her aim. They persuaded Oliver to go to the Registry Office with them and Penelope to complete the pre-wedding formalities.

They told Oliver that the documents he must sign would allow him to be free of his parents' control. Three weeks later, Oliver and Penelope were married at the Registry Office. They went away on their honeymoon and continued with their sexual relationship which had started four years earlier.

Oliver's parents are furious and want to know whether they and Oliver can do anything to have the marriage annulled.

Advise Oliver, who is unsure about what he wants to do, and his parents.

# 4

# Acquisition and protection of rights in the family home

**SUMMARY**

The family home is important both as a secure living space and as a potentially valuable but vulnerable asset. Its loss has profound effects on the welfare of the family, and on the State which has to support those who lose their home. Since the second edition of this book was published in 2008, a significant economic down turn has taken place and its longer term effects on the family home have yet to be seen.

In this chapter, we consider the ways in which the doctrine of informal trusts; the doctrine of proprietary estoppel; the law of contract; the provisions of the FLA 1996, Part IV, and the law relating to bankruptcy have been used by family members to protect their occupation of their home and/or to receive a share in the proceeds of sale.

A certain amount of confusion surrounds this area of law because, in the absence of reforming legislation, a number of judicial efforts, at the highest possible level, have been made to bypass the rigidity of traditional property law. A new pragmatism has taken over.

The grant of orders under the FLA 1996 in the context of domestic violence is considered in Chapter 5 and the reallocation of rights in the family home on the legal dissolution of a relationship in Chapter 7.

# The family home: an overview

4.1 For many families, their home has become not only their most valuable financial asset (often in close competition with a personal pension) but it also provides them with the stability and security which is essential for their survival as a family. Without a home in which to live, and without the knowledge that they are secure from eviction, no family can thrive satisfactorily; after food and clothing, shelter is the most basic of all human needs.

4.2 It has been accepted that Art 8 (the right to respect for privacy and family life) of the European Convention 1950 (ECHR), includes respect for a person's home.

> Lord Millett in **Harrow London Borough Council v Qazi (2003)** recognized that the home is a place where a person and his family
>
> *...are entitled to be left in peace from interference by the state or agents of the state. It is an important aspect of his dignity as a human being, and it is protected as such and not as an item of property.*

4.3 Between 1920 and 2007, a significant social change relating to home ownership occurred. In 1920, only 10 per cent of property in the UK was owner-occupied; by 2007, this figure had risen to 70 per cent. Margaret Thatcher's government in the 1980s popularized the idea of a property-owning democracy which would have a stake in the economic system. Later governments, regardless of political persuasion, took a similar approach even to the extent of providing help with mortgage interest payments when family members become unemployed.

4.4 This increase in home ownership for most families has been achieved by means of heavy borrowings, normally secured by way of mortgage of their home. Many families were persuaded to take this risk because house price inflation gave them the opportunity to acquire capital. In 2007, average house prices rose by 10.9 per cent and the price of the average family home was £205,286. The home was seen as a source of wealth which could be passed on by inheritance from parent to child. It was regularly used as security for further borrowings to help finance, *inter alia*, such ventures as family businesses, university education, holidays, or to help adult offspring purchase their own family homes.

4.5 By 2009, the house inflation of previous years, and uncertainty about future inflation, alongside a global economic recession led to a slight fall in owner occupation. More people have not only found it difficult to raise money to make a down payment on a home, but they have also had to face the risk of unemployment. This has led them to rely on the increase in the supply of private sector rented property. It remains to be seen whether this trend will continue.

# Problems of home ownership

4.6 Where personal borrowings to fund the family home are exceptionally high, and when unemployment is a serious possibility, financial difficulties become common-place. Families risk having to sell their property. In some cases, where borrowers have been unable to make repayments on loans secured against the family home, lenders may attempt to repossess it, and bankruptcy may follow.

4.7 In these difficult circumstances, disputes can arise over ownership of the home, the rights of occupation in it, and the division of the beneficial interest if the property is sold. Many couples do not lead the organized lives expected of them by the complexities of land law. The legal title to the property may have been conveyed into one, or even both, of their names but they may have failed to give any thought to the precise nature of the beneficial interest in the property or may have failed to record it in writing. (For more information on the difference between legal and beneficial ownership, see any of the property law textbooks listed at the end of this chapter.)

4.8 In determining beneficial ownership where a couple has failed to clarify the matter, the law is supposedly bound by strict principles of property law. These principles have long been criticized as inappropriate in the family context. They do not reflect the informality with which many couples conduct their financial affairs. They have been particularly problematic for cohabitants who, unlike married couples or civil partners, do not have the benefit of the court's jurisdiction to redistribute their property as it thinks fit at the end of a relationship (see Chapter 7).

4.9 Various solutions have been proposed by the Law Commission but legislation has not followed. Lady Hale in the House of Lords decision in *Stack v Dowden (2007)* (see below) commented that the lack of legislation in this area means that

> *...the evolution of the law of property to take account of changing social and economic circumstances will have to come from the courts rather than Parliament.*

# The Law Commission proposals

## Home sharing

4.10 In 2002, the Law Commission produced *Sharing Homes: a Discussion Paper* (Law Com No 278). It examined the problems experienced by all those who share homes and emphasized the importance of persuading them to formalize their arrangements and declare the nature of their respective shares in the beneficial interest. The Law Commission proposed that any changes in the law should be by way of a default system which would apply only if home sharers had failed to specify the share of the beneficial interest. The report was inconclusive but took an approach which, very broadly, would take into account the partners' contributions to the property in determining their share. There has been no legislation resulting from the Commission's Report.

## Cohabitation

4.11 In 2007, the Law Commission's report, *Cohabitation: The Financial Consequences of Relationship Breakdown* (Law Com No 307) considered the problem of how to resolve disputes relating to family homes shared by the ever growing number of cohabitants. It pointed out the difficulties of using strict property law to resolve these disputes. Its recommendations are considered in more detail in Chapter 7. However, a government statement made clear that there would be no immediate action.

> *The report has been carefully considered and the Government have (sic) decided it wishes to seek research findings on the Family Law (Scotland) Act 2006, which came into effect last year. This Act has provisions which are similar in many respects to those which the Commission recommends. The Scottish Executive intend to undertake research to discover the cost of such a scheme and its efficacy in resolving the issues faced by cohabitants when their relationships end. The Government propose to await the outcome of this research and extrapolate from it the likely cost to this jurisdiction of bringing into effect the scheme proposed by the Law Commission and the likely benefits it will bring. For the time being, therefore, the Government will take no further action.*
>
> *(Hansard, 6 Mar 2008: Col 123 WS)*

# The ideal—express declaration of ownership

4.12 In a perfect world all family members who decide to live together would decide how they wish to share the beneficial interest in their family home. If it is to be a genuine joint enterprise, and they propose sharing the profits and losses equally, they would decide to register the legal title in both names. They would also tick the relevant box on the registration application form making clear that the beneficial title is to be shared equally. This would comply with the formal requirements for property transactions to be in writing (Law of Property Act 1925, ss 52, 53, Law of Property (Miscellaneous Provisions) Act 1989, s 2), and the parties' decision could not be challenged at a later date. If the property is already owned by one partner who decides to give a share of the beneficial interest to the other partner, that too would have to be made in writing.

4.13 Of course, it is possible that the parties may later change their minds about the nature of their share in the beneficial interest. If so, they would have to record that too in writing.

4.14 In making the decision about how to share the beneficial interest in their family home, the couple must also consider whether they wish to be joint tenants or tenants-in-common. Very broadly, if they decide to be joint tenants, each partner owns all the property. When one partner dies, his or her interest disappears. The surviving partner will now own all the property alone, and no share remains to be inherited under the deceased's will or on an intestacy (see Chapter 8). If the property is sold, the joint tenancy ends, and each partner is entitled to receive an equal share of the proceeds of sale.

If the partners would prefer to be tenants in common, each of them will own an agreed specific share of the beneficial interest in the property. When one of them dies, he or she may leave that share by will, or it may pass on an intestacy. If the property is sold each will receive the proportion of the proceeds of sale in accordance with their agreement.

4.15 The judiciary has regularly emphasized that disputes about family homes would disappear entirely if all couples behaved in this ideal way. Unfortunately, the judicial cry has been ignored by so many, and the decisions discussed in this chapter illustrate this.

# The real world

4.16 For those couples who have ignored the niceties of property law, and there are many of them, harsh legal reality hits when their relationship breaks down, or their partner dies, or a lender, with a secured interest in the property, takes action because loan payments have not been kept up to date. They may try to rescue themselves from complete disaster by attempting to claim rights under the doctrines of informal trusts or proprietary estoppel. They should not rely on a favourable outcome because according to Carnworth LJ, in the Court of Appeal decision in *Stack v Dowden (2005)*, the various interpretations of these doctrines are confusing:

> To the detached observer, the result may seem like a witches' brew into which various esoteric ingredients have been stirred over the years, and in which different ideas bubble to the surface at different times. They include the implied trust, constructive trust, resulting trust, presumption of advancement, proprietary estoppel, unjust enrichment and so on. These ideas are likely to mean nothing to a layman and often little more to the lawyers who use them.

4.17 One of the advantages of informal trusts of the family home is that they are not required to be in writing (Law of Property Act 1925, s 53(2)). If a partner is able to establish the existence of such a trust, he or she acquires a beneficial interest in the property and, along with it a right to occupy the family home (Trusts of Land and Appointment of Trustees Act 1996, s 12; Family Law Act 1996, Part IV); a right to ask the court for sale or delay of sale of the home (Trusts of Land and Appointment of Trustees Act 1996, s 14), and an entitlement to a share in the proceeds of sale. All these rights have the potential to prevail over the rights of third parties.

4.18 Rights in the family home acquired by way of proprietary estoppel give rise to similar benefits.

# Informal trusts

4.19 Since the decision in *Williams and Glyns Bank v Boland (1981)*, lenders and purchasers have become more cautious about the possible existence of an informal trust in the family homes of borrowers. They normally demand that any person, who might conceivably claim that such a right exists, waive their rights prior to sale, or the grant of any loan which will be secured against the property.

In *Boland*, the husband borrowed money which was secured against the family home in order to finance his business. When he could not afford to repay the loan, the bank sought to take possession. Mrs Boland maintained that she had a beneficial interest in the property which gave her a right to remain in residence (Land Registration Act 1925, s 71(g); see now Land Registration Act 2002, Sch 3). The House of Lords ruled in her favour.

As a consequence of the Boland decision, the courts have tended to become more demanding and require proof of how the beneficial interest came into existence and not a mere statement by the claimant of the interest. They also ask questions about the claimant's knowledge of the loan, and whether he or she benefitted from it (see eg *Bristol and West Building Society v Henning (1985); Abbey National v Cann (1991); Lloyds Bank v Rosset (1991)*).

4.20 Traditionally, informal trusts were categorized as resulting or constructive trusts. However, the two categories tend to overlap partly because of the way in which family homes are purchased, and partly because, increasingly, the courts have decided not to distinguish between them in any precise or helpful way. Rather, the trend appears to lean towards an elision of the two concepts and it is unusual now to find examples of a family home dispute based solely on resulting trust principles (see eg *Springette v Defoe (1992)*).

## Resulting trusts

4.21 In the familial context, the conventional view of a resulting trust is that it comes into existence in two types of situation. The first of these is where property is conveyed into the sole name of one party, and another party makes a financial contribution to the purchase price, there is a rebuttable presumption that the parties expect to share the beneficial interest in the property in proportion to their financial contributions. This presumption is based on the rather materialistic view that no one would make a financial contribution to another person's property without expecting something in return. The contribution of the person claiming a resulting trust may take the form of payments towards the overall cost of the property; the initial deposit; mortgage payments; legal fees, or the transfer of a discount, which had been granted to the claimant by the seller. The right arises at the moment of purchase.

4.22 In the second situation, where property is conveyed into the names of both parties without any explicit declaration of their respective beneficial interests, a rebuttable presumption arises that the beneficial interest follows the legal interest, and it will be held in equal shares. This right also arises at the moment of purchase.

### The presumption of advancement

4.23 The presumption of a resulting trust will be rebutted if the presumption of advancement applies. This rather archaic and paternalistic principle provides that where a husband, father or fiancé has made a contribution towards the purchase price of a property, which is conveyed into his wife's, child's or fianceé's name, he is presumed to have made a gift of the property. There will be no resulting trust in his favour. The principle does not apply to wives or fiancées who provide money towards the purchase price of their husbands' or fiancées' properties, nor does it apply to civil partners. The presumption of advancement may, of course, be rebutted by evidence to the contrary.

> In *McGrath v Wallis (1995)*, Nourse LJ stated that:
>
> *...in its application to houses acquired for joint occupation, the equitable presumption of advancement has been reclassified as a judicial instrument of last resort...For myself, I have been unable to recollect any subsequent case of this kind in which the presumption has proved to be decisive, even where one of the parties had since died.*

4.24 In 2005, Rob Marris MP, who believes that the law relating to presumption of advancement is discriminatory and in breach of the European Convention for the Protection of Human Rights and Fundamental Freedoms 1950 (ECHR), proposed a change in the legislation by way of a private members bill, the Family Law (Property and Maintenance) Bill. He was forced to withdraw the bill for lack of support.

### Gifts or loans

4.25 No resulting trust will arise where the evidence suggests that the financial contribution made to the legal owner of the property was a gift or a loan.

In *Vajpeyi v Yusaf (2003)*, Dr Vajpeyi, who had had a relationship with Mr Yusaf and had hoped that they might marry, claimed a resulting trust on the basis of monies she had given to him to purchase property. She was a divorced Hindu older woman with children and he was a young Muslim bachelor; these facts made marriage a rather unlikely possibility. In 1980, six years after their relationship began, Dr Vajpeyi gave Mr Yusaf £10,000 to purchase a house as an investment property. She had hoped that it would be a joint nest egg for their future together and she did not demand any share of the rents or profits. In 1984 Mr Yusaf entered into an arranged marriage with a Muslim woman but his relationship with Dr Vajpeyi continued. According to the judge, Dr Vajpeyi and Mr Yusaf

*...just could not let go of each other. It was like a powerful drug—in some ways, much worse. A great deal of guilt and resentment built up on one side or another. Arranged marriages are said to work just as well as the other sort. At any rate, over time Mr Yusaf seems to have developed a close relationship with his wife Tehsin, although for a long period he was torn both ways. Mr and Mrs Yusaf had a daughter on 5 November 1985 and a son on 1 February 1988.*

*It was the Claimant's evidence that she was the deceived woman: that she went along with the Defendant's marriage only because she believed it was nothing but a barren (sic) formality, entered into under extreme family pressure, and that he would in due course leave his wife for her. In my judgement the Claimant's heart wanted it to be so, and she may at times have been persuaded (or have persuaded herself) that it was so. But the Claimant had a head as well as a heart. This was no Regency novel, Dr Vajpeyi was no simple country girl and Mr Yusaf was no heartless old libertine. He loved her with a passion. She was 12 years older that he. She was a highly educated woman—a doctor with a busy family practice—and she was well acquainted with the customs of the Indian sub-continent.*

*On any conventional view neither of them behaved well. I have said that I do not propose to set out more of the circumstances than is necessary, and I shall keep to that resolution. In my judgement, it came to this. On the one side, she sought to put him under intense emotional pressure—perhaps not a difficult thing for her to do in the first place, for she was very attractive and he felt about her intensely—but she strongly worked on his feelings of guilt by performing certain acts which I refrain from describing in detail. On the other side, he told her things about his relationship with his wife that were manifestly absurd, and I do not mean the platitudes that men are traditionally supposed to utter in those situations. He said things that her heart wanted to hear but her head could not have believed. He did it because, in his own words:*

*'Dr Ravi Vajpeyi would leave me in no doubt as to the answers I must provide. Dr Ravi Vajpeyi wanted spurious comfort—I knew what Dr Ravi Vajpeyi wanted to hear; Dr Ravi Vajpeyi knew that I knew what she wanted to hear, and I would deliver the required answer...'*

Dr Vajpeyi argued, *inter alia*, that Mr Yusaf held the property on trust for both of them because the £10,000 had been an investment in that property. The court held that in the circumstances of the parties' relationship which could never have been a long-term possibility, the presumption of resulting trust was rebutted. On a common sense view of what had happened the monies advanced had been loans and they had been repaid.

### Contributions attributable to some other motive

4.26    In *Walsh v Singh (2010)*, the court refused to accept a woman's significant financial contributions as evidence of a common intention or an agreement that she should obtain a
share in the beneficial interest in her cohabitant's property. It regarded her contributions
as merely referable to her long term relationship and the parties' intention to marry.

### Quantification of shares in the beneficial interest

4.27    According to the traditional principles of resulting trusts, where the legal title is in
the names of both parties, the beneficial interest will be shared equally. Where the
legal title is in the sole name of one of the parties their respective beneficial interests
will be in accordance with their financial contributions to the purchase price (see
*Springette v Defoe (1992)*). Since judicial attempts have been made to merge the
principles of resulting trusts with those of constructive trusts, it is more likely that
the quantification of beneficial interests in the case of a resulting trust will follow
the flexible, holistic approach in the constructive trust decisions.

## Constructive trusts

### Agreements

#### *The decision in* Lloyds Bank plc v Rosset (1991)

4.28    For many years, the decision of the House of Lords in *Lloyds Bank v Rosset (1991)*
was regarded as the gold standard for establishing constructive trusts of the family
home.

> Mr Rosset had purchased a semi-derelict farmhouse using money provided by the trust-
> ees of a family trust. Before the family moved into the property, Mrs Rosset spent every
> day at the house for four months. She monitored the builders' work; went to the builders'
> merchants and organized the delivery of all the necessary materials. She helped plan all
> the renovations of the house, and carried out a substantial part of the preparations prior
> to the decoration of the interior. During this period, Mr Rosset was mainly abroad, and Mrs
> Rosset had total responsibility for the care of their children.
>
> Without his wife's knowledge, Mr Rosset obtained a bank overdraft and mortgaged the
> family home to the bank. He subsequently became unable to make the repayments. The
> bank commenced proceedings to sell the property. Mrs Rosset claimed that she had a
> beneficial share in the property which was binding on the bank.
>
> The House of Lords rejected her claim; Lord Bridge explained in some detail the principles
> of constructive trusts. In his view, there were two types of agreements which could give
> rise to a constructive trust. The first required the court to ask the question:
>
> *...whether there has, at any time prior to acquisition, or exceptionally at some
> later date, been any agreement, arrangement or understanding reached between*

*them that the property is to be shared beneficially. The finding of an agreement or arrangement to share in this sense can only, I think, be based on evidence of express discussions between the partners, however imperfectly remembered and however imprecise their terms may have been.*

*Once this agreement has been found, the person claiming a trust must show that he or she has acted to his or her detriment in reliance on the agreement or intention. The detriment in these circumstances must relate to the property in some way but need not necessarily be a financial contribution.*

The second type of agreement, according to Lord Bridge, is

*... in sharp contrast with [the first] situation is the very different one where there is no evidence to support a finding of an agreement or arrangement to share, however reasonable it might have been for the parties to reach such an arrangement if they had applied their minds to the question, and where the court must rely entirely on the conduct of the parties both as the basis from which to infer a common intention to share the property beneficially and as the conduct relied on to give rise to a constructive trust.*

He maintained that only direct financial contributions, made by the claimant, and referable to the purchase of the property, could provide the dual function of the inference of an agreement or intention and the relevant detrimental reliance on it. Nothing else would be sufficient (see **Gissing v Gissing (1971)**).

Lord Bridge acknowledged the difficulties involved in determining the intentions of the parties in familial disputes at a time when the relationship had broken down. He explained that:

*Spouses living in amity will not normally think it necessary to formulate or define their respective interests in property in any precise way. The expectation of parties to every happy marriage is that they will share the practical benefits of occupying the matrimonial home no matter who owns it. But this is something quite distinct from sharing the beneficial interest in the asset, which the matrimonial home represents. These considerations give rise to special difficulties for judges who are called on to resolve a dispute between spouses who have parted and are at arm's length as to what their common intention or understanding with respect to interests in property was at a time when they were still living as a united family and acquiring a matrimonial home in the expectation of living in it together indefinitely.*

The House of Lords maintained that in spite of the agreed joint venture to create a family home, there was insufficient evidence of the first type of agreement to share the beneficial interest. Indeed, there could have been no agreement because Mr Rosset had purchased the house and paid for its renovations from trust funds. He knew that the trustees would not have released the funds to him had they known that he was planning to share the beneficial interest with Mrs Rosset. Furthermore, there was no conduct from which the second type of agreement could be inferred because Mrs Rosset had provided no financial input for the purchase of the farmhouse.

4.29 The decision in **Rosset (1991)** limited the possibility of any future claims to a beneficial interest in the family home. Beneficial interests are not part of the everyday conversation of most couples. Even if they do discuss them, partners often fail to understand their significance and do not always make clear their agreements with each other. Inferred agreements equally elude them; women without financial resources are more likely to make non-financial contributions, often in the form of housekeeping and childcare, which enable their partners to earn the money to pay for the family home. If women do earn money, they are more disposed to use it to purchase consumable household goods. In the absence of evidence of a clear agreement, neither of these types of contributions, according to *Rosset (1991)*, permits a claim to a share in the beneficial interest of the family home. (See also *Burns v Burns (1984)* where a cohabitant in a 19-year relationship was denied any rights in the family home because there was no explicit agreement and all her financial contributions were made towards the purchase of personal property for the family and not towards the family home.)

*A different approach*

4.30 Prior to *Rosset (1991)*, the courts had begun to develop an approach which recognized that the analysis of familial relationships and the discovery of relevant agreements is not a scientific exercise. The judiciary were prepared, by a sleight of hand, to find evidence of agreements in circumstances where the partner who was the legal owner of the property had made an excuse about his motivation for purchasing the family home in his own name, thus leading the other partner to believe that he would have liked her to have a share in the property had the circumstances been slightly different.

An example of this approach can be found in *Eves v Eves (1975)* where a male cohabitant told his female partner that the only reason why the property was to be acquired in his name alone was because she was under 21 years of age; this was accepted as a relevant agreement in the context of a constructive trust. A similar approach was taken in *Grant v Edwards (1986)* where a man had told his partner that if he could not put the house in joint names because it might affect her divorce settlement. This was held to be evidence of a common intention to share the beneficial interest (see also *Hammond v Mitchell (1992)*).

4.31 Following *Rosset (1991)*, the courts continued to accept the above approach as a way to overcome Lord Bridge's seemingly rigid principles. Finally, Lord Walker, in the House of Lords decision in *Stack v Dowden (2007)* maintained that Lord Bridge's view that only financial contributions would lead to an inference of a common intention to share the beneficial interest should be questioned:

> *Whether or not Lord Bridge's observation was justified in 1991, in my opinion the law has moved on, and your Lordships should move it a little more in the same direction, while bearing in mind that the Law Commission may soon come forward with proposals which, if enacted by Parliament, may recast the law in this area.*

Baroness Hale agreed, and said that **Rosset (1991)** had set the hurdle too high for claimants seeking to show that there was an implied intention, or agreement, to share the beneficial interest.

4.32 The decision in **Stack v Dowden (2007)** was about quantification of the beneficial share, and it was not in dispute that the couple had agreed to share the beneficial interest. As yet there is no clear decision which has lowered the hurdle and inferred the relevant intention to share the beneficial interest from non-financial contributions in the context of constructive trusts, but it will surely happen.

## Detrimental reliance

4.33 In addition to the relevant intention or agreement, the claimant must also show detrimental reliance.

### Financial detriment

4.34 It has generally been accepted that where the claimant has made a significant financial contribution to the property, that will also serve as proof of both the relevant intention and the necessary detrimental reliance.

### Non-financial detriment

4.35 Where the court accepts the existence of an agreement or common intention, any conduct referable to the property has been accepted as sufficient detriment if it is found to be in reliance on the agreement or common intention of the parties.

In **Rosset (1991)**, Lord Bridge found that Mrs Rosset's conduct was insufficient. He explained that even if the Court had been prepared to find the relevant agreement or common intention, the conduct claimed as detrimental reliance was not only de minimis, but was also explicable by her desire to get her family happily installed in their new home prior to Christmas.

4.36 In **Eves v Eves (1975)**, Mrs Eves claimed that in reliance on the agreement she had

*... stripped the wallpaper in the hall; painted the woodwork in the lounge and kitchen, and the kitchen cabinets, and generally cleaned the whole house; she painted the brickwork in the front of the house; using a 14 pound sledgehammer she broke up a large area of concrete covering the whole of the front garden and carried the pieces to a skip which had been hired for the purpose; she then prepared the front garden for turfing; she did work in the back garden and helped the defendant to demolish a shed there and to put up a new one.*

The Court of Appeal was most impressed by this masculine-like behaviour and granted her a beneficial share in the property.

4.37 It remains uncertain what other conduct might be accepted by the courts as a relevant detriment. particularly if its not directly referable to the property in some form. In **Hammond v Mitchell (1992)**, a racy story of a 'bunny girl' who cohabited with a divorced man after a chance encounter in Epping Forest, and whose relationship ended after another chance encounter in an aeroplane on the tarmac at Heathrow as she was leaving to join her young Spanish barman lover, Waite LJ acknowledged the woman's general contributions to the household economy as well as her childcare as relevant detriment reliance.

## Quantification of the beneficial interest

4.38 For many years the constructive trust cases which came before the courts were primarily concerned with the issue of agreement or common intention More recent case law has centred on the quantification of the beneficial interest in circumstances where there was evidence of the relevant intention or agreement but the parties had given absolutely no thought to what their respective shares should be.

4.39 On a strict interpretation of the law, where the agreement is implied from financial contributions, the claimant's share will be quantified in proportion to the amount of his or her financial contribution to the property.

4.40 Where there is evidence of an explicit agreement or an intention that the property should be shared, the conservative view of the law is that the claimant will receive the share agreed.

### The move to pragmatism

4.41 The courts found this conventional view to quantification unsatisfactory in the family home context and have attempted to replace it with a move towards a more holistic, and pragmatic approach. The decisions below illustrate this movement.

4.42 The decision in *Midland Bank plc v Cooke (1995)*, was perhaps the first time the holistic approach was taken to quantification, although some might argue that Lord Denning's approach in *Eves v Eves (1975)* was the real starting point when he awarded Mrs Eves a one-third share in the beneficial interest in the property without any explanation why he had done so.

> Mrs Cooke and her husband had been given a wedding present of £1,000 in 1971. They had used the money as a deposit towards the purchase of their first home, which was conveyed into the sole name of the husband; he subsequently made all the mortgage payments. Waite LJ held that this initial contribution gave rise to an implied agreement at the time of purchase that the couple were to share the beneficial interest in some unspecified proportion between them. He stressed that the couple had not, and indeed could not have, at the time of purchase, formulated with any precision what their final shares would be. He was, therefore, perfectly happy to impute that for them on the basis of their relationship. Mrs Cooke's had, during a long marriage, contributed financially to the household income, and made a major contribution to every aspect of the relationship

including working on the property. Waite LJ explained that to give Mrs Cooke other than an equal share in the beneficial would be inequitable. He said:

*Equity has traditionally been a system which matches established principle to the demands of social change. The mass diffusion of home ownership has been one of the most striking social changes of our own time. The present case is typical of hundreds, perhaps even thousands, of others. When people, especially young people, agree to share their lives in joint homes, they do so on a basis of mutual trust and in the expectation that their relationship will endure. Despite the efforts that have been made by many responsible bodies to counsel prospective cohabitants as to the risks of taking shared interests in property without legal advice, it is unrealistic to expect that advice to be followed on a universal scale. For a couple embarking on a serious relationship, discussion of the terms to apply at parting is almost a contradiction of the shared hopes that have brought them together. There will inevitably be numerous couples, married or unmarried, who have no discussion about ownership and who, perhaps advisedly, make no agreement about it. It would be anomalous, against that background, to create a range of homebuyers who were beyond the pale of equity's assistance in formulating a fair presumed basis for the sharing of beneficial title, simply because they had been honest enough to admit that they never gave ownership a thought or reached any agreement about it.*

4.43    The decision in **Cox v Jones (2004)**, also illustrates this new flexibility towards quantification.

The claimant began to cohabit with the defendant in his flat in Lincoln's Inn; both of the parties were barristers. Ms Cox had a large Alsatian dog, named Bootsie; such dogs appear to play a not infrequent part in family decisions; Mrs Eves in **Eves v Eves (1975)** also had one! Mr Jones found life in the small flat with Ms Cox and the dog rather constricting and not compatible with his love of order. Ms Cox and the dog moved out, and she and Mr Jones sought a larger family home in the country. The house, known as The Mill, required extensive renovation and was purchased in Mr Jones' sole name. Ms Cox managed and coordinated the project, but Mr Jones paid for the cost of all the works.

Ms Cox also found a flat, which she wished to purchase as an investment. Mr Jones paid the greater part of the purchase price, because Ms Cox had insufficient financial resources to do so. The price of the flat was discounted; Ms Cox had astutely persuaded the vendor to allow her to buy it at a low price in order to avoid the expense of placing it on the open market. This property, like The Mill, was also registered in Mr Jones' sole name.

The relationship between the parties was tempestuous and, at times, violent. Not surprisingly, it failed to thrive, and Ms Cox claimed a beneficial interest in both the house and the flat. The court commented that although Ms Cox was a barrister

*...she did not always behave in a manner which one might expect of a lawyer, in particular on the occasions when she failed to pursue the idea, which was clearly*

*in play, that her interest in the two properties should be protected by a trust deed. However, I think that that can be put down to the fact that people with commercial and legal expertise very often do not deploy that expertise in their own personal affairs.*

Mr Jones denied that there was any agreement to share the beneficial interest in the house jointly, and also argued that Ms Cox had exaggerated her contribution to the management of the renovation. The court found that there was express evidence of an agreement, albeit one which did not provide for an exact quantification of the parties' shares. It recognized that in determining the existence of an agreement it must bear in mind

*... that at the heart of the differences between them lies the formation, continuance and breakdown of their relationship. It was, as they both admitted to me, a highly charged relationship with many ups and downs. That sort of situation is a perfect breeding ground for differences of perception and bona fide differences of recollection and emphasis. Sorting out what actually went on from time to time, and what passed between the parties, is particularly difficult. Their respective credibilities have to be seen in that light. Very often the parties will have equally reliable, or unreliable, recollections and views of what happened.*

The court awarded Ms Cox only a 25 per cent beneficial share in the house, based on her management of the project.

However with respect to the flat, the court took a more generous approach. Mr Jones maintained that he had purchased the flat as an investment for himself and denied that Ms Cox had any beneficial share in it. The court found an express agreement, made prior to the purchase of the property, that Mr Jones would hold it, as nominee, absolutely, for Ms Cox. She had acted to her detriment in reliance on that agreement by allowing Mr Jones to benefit from the discounted price, which had been secured by her negotiation skills alone, and she had managed the rental of the property afterwards. She was, therefore, held to have acquired a 100 per cent beneficial interest in the flat.

4.44    In *Oxley v Hiscock (2004)*, the Court of Appeal maintained that in circumstances where there had been no discussion of how to share the beneficial interest, the right question for the Court to ask

*... was what would be a fair share for each party having regard to the whole course of dealing between them in relation to the property.*

This would not necessarily mean an equal division.

Ms Oxley had purchased her council house in her sole name, in 1987, at the discounted price of £25,200 using money provided by Mr Hiscock, with whom she subsequently began to cohabit. Mr Hiscock had worked in Kuwait, and during the invasion by Iraqi troops in 1990, he was captured, taken to Baghdad and held as hostage. On his release, he returned home and a new property was purchased for £127,000. The funds for this property came from the proceeds of sale of the first house which amounted to £61,500, (£25,200 belonged to Mr Hiscock on the basis of his contribution, and £36,300 to Ms Oxley on the basis of the discount) £35,500 from Mr Hiscock's own savings own savings, and plus a mortgage loan of £30,000. The property was conveyed into the sole name of Mr Hiscock. Ms Oxley ignored warnings from her solicitor that she should ensure that the property it was conveyed into the couple's joint names, and she refused to do so. After the purchase, both parties contributed towards the maintenance and improvement of the property from their pooled resources in the belief that each had a beneficial interest. By 2001 the mortgage had been paid off. The relationship between the parties broke down, the property was sold and separate houses were purchased. Ms Oxley claimed that she had a 50 per cent beneficial interest in the proceeds of sale of the property. Her claim was granted.

Mr Hiscock appealed. He accepted that there was an intention that the beneficial interest should be shared but argued that it should be quantified in proportion to their respective contributions. The Court of Appeal granted his appeal, and maintained that a fair division would be 60 per cent to Mr Hiscock and 40 per cent to Ms Oxley.

### *The high point of pragmatism*—Stack v Dowden (2007)

4.45 The high point in the move away from rigidity in the context of quantification came with the decision of the House of Lords in *Stack v Dowden (2007)*. Their Lordships maintained that they wished to clarify the law relating to quantification, and stressed the importance of the holistic approach.

Mr Stack and Ms Dowden were unmarried. They had lived together with their four children for over twenty years before their relationship broke down. In 1983, Ms Dowden purchased a house for £30,000, the legal title of which was conveyed into her sole name. It had belonged to a man, whom Ms Dowden called Uncle Sidney. He had expressed the wish, before his death, that she should be allowed to buy it at a discount. She obtained a loan of £22,000 in her sole name; the remainder came from her own savings. She made all the payments on the loan and all the utility bills.

The couple both spent time altering, repairing, redecorating, and generally improving their new home, although Mr Stack did more work than Ms Dowden. In 1993, the property was sold for £90,000. After repayment of the loan and expenses related to the sale, Ms Dowden received a cheque for £66,613.

Another property was bought as the family home. This time the legal title was conveyed into the couple's joint names but they did not specify how the beneficial interest in the property should be shared. The purchase price was £190,000. Ms Dowden provided £128,813, and the remainder came from a loan to both parties from Barclay's Bank. The loan was secured by a mortgage and two endowment policies, one in their joint names and the other in Ms Dowden's sole name. The mortgage interest and joint endowment policy premiums, which eventually amounted to £33,747, were paid by Mr Stack, and, the capital was repaid by a series of lump sum payments, to which Mr Stack contributed £27,000 and Ms Dowden £38,435. Ms Dowden paid the premiums on the life policy in her name, and all the utility bills which were in her name, although Mr Stack claimed to have paid some of them. Improvements were made to the property but not on the same scale as those to the previous property. Throughout their relationship, the couple had separate bank accounts and separate investments and savings.

In 2002, the relationship broke down, and Ms Dowden remained in the family home with the children. Mr Stack wished to have the house sold and claim a 50 per cent share in the beneficial interest of the property on the ground that the legal title was in the couple's joint names. Ms Dowden maintained that she had a right to have a larger share of the beneficial interest because of her greater financial contributions to its purchase. The judge ruled in favour of Mr Stack, and Ms Dowden appealed.

The Court of Appeal allowed her appeal and awarded her a 65 per cent share of the property. Mr Stack appealed to the House of Lords and his appeal was denied. Their Lordships stated firmly that any division of the beneficial interest must be based on trust principles, and categorically rejected any possibility that judges should impose their own idea of a fair division based on the parties' long-term familial relationship, but maintained that it was important to take into account the realities of such relationships.

According to their Lordships, the starting point for quantification where the legal title is in the names of both parties is that the beneficial interest follows the legal interest. If one partner wishes to dispute the presumed equal division, he or she must produce evidence of a contrary intention. In assessing the evidence of such an intention, the House of Lords maintained that the court must take a 'holistic view' of the whole course of dealing between the parties in relationship to the property (see also *Abbott v Abbott (2008)*).

Baroness Hale who gave the leading judgment maintained that:

*In law, 'context is everything' and the domestic context is very different from the commercial world. Each case will turn on its own facts. Many more factors than financial contributions may be relevant to divining the parties' true intentions. These include: any advice or discussions at the time of the transfer which cast light upon their intentions then; the reasons why the home was acquired in their joint names ... the purpose for which the home was acquired; the nature of the parties' relationship; whether they had children for whom they both had responsibility to provide a home; how the purchase was financed, both initially and subsequently; how the parties arranged their finances, whether separately or together or a bit of both; how they discharged the outgoings on the property and their other household expenses. When a couple are joint owners of the home and jointly liable for the mortgage, the inferences to be drawn from who pays for what may be very*

*different from the inferences to be drawn when only one is owner of the home.
The arithmetical calculation of how much was paid by each is also likely to be less
important. It will be easier to draw the inference that they intended that each should
contribute as much to the household as they reasonably could and that they would
share the eventual benefit or burden equally. The parties' individual characters and
personalities may also be a factor in deciding where their true intentions lay. In the
cohabitation context, mercenary considerations may be more to the fore than they
would be in marriage, but it should not be assumed that they always take pride of
place over natural love and affection. At the end of the day, having taken all this into
account, cases in which the joint legal owners are to be taken to have intended that
their beneficial interests should be different from their legal interests will be very
unusual.*

In spite of this strong statement, and her warnings about taking an arithmetical approach,
Baroness Hale found that Ms Dowden and Mr Stack fell into that rare category of a couple
who kept their financial dealings very separate, and that, in the context of this particular
couple, their differential contributions were significant. The Court of Appeal's decision
was upheld.

4.46    The decision in *Stack (2007)* has not clarified the law for future claimants of beneficial interests. Unless they expressly make clear their intentions regarding quantification, regardless of whether the property has been conveyed into both names,
or into the sole name of one of them, claimants will be left at the mercy of the
court to impute their non-existent intentions from vague assessments of relationship conduct. How can courts do this other than in accordance with their own view
of fairness?

4.47    The only exception to the holistic approach in *Stack (2007)* is where property is purchased by family members for a purpose other than as a family home. There strict
property principles will apply (see *Laskar v Laskar (2008)*).

### The aftermath of Stack v Dowden (2007)

4.48    The problems raised by the decision in *Stack (2007)* are illustrated by the Court of
Appeal's decision in *Kernott v Jones (2010)*.

Ms Jones and Mr Kernott were an unmarried couple with two children. In 1985, the
couple bought a family home which was conveyed into their joint names for £30,000.
There was silence as to their beneficial shares in the property. Ms Jones provided £6,000
towards the purchase price and the balance came from an interest-only mortgage loan
supported by an endowment policy.

Mr Kernott gave Ms Jones £100 per week. From that and her own earnings she paid for
housekeeping, mortgage and other outgoings on the property including the premiums
on the insurance policy. Mr Kernott built an extension on the property which increased its
value by 50 per cent of the purchase price.

In 1993, the couple separated and Ms Jones assumed total responsibility for all the out-goings and for the maintenance of the children. In 1996, Mr Kernott purchased a home for himself. In 2006 he claimed a 50 per cent share in the family home.

Ms Jones accepted that the parties had an equal share in the beneficial interest at the time of their separation. She argued, however, that she had gained a larger share in the property post-separation because she took on sole responsibility for all the outgoings on the property from 1999 onwards. The judge at first instance and the High Court both accepted because the parties had contributed unequally to the property, fairness demanded that their beneficial shares should be unequal in the proportions of 10 per cent for Mr Kernott and 90 per cent for Ms Jones.

Mr Kernott appealed to the Court of Appeal. The Court of Appeal held that the passage of time between the separation of the parties and Mr Kernott's claim of a 50 per cent share, and Ms Jones payment of all the outgoings, were insufficient to displace the agreement that they held the beneficial interests in equal shares.

Wall LJ said:

*I described this case as a cautionary tale. So, in my judgment, it is. The purchase of residential accommodation is perhaps the single most important financial transaction which any individual transacts in a lifetime. It is therefore of the utmost importance, as it seems to me, that those who engage in these transactions, and those who advise them, should take the greatest care over such transactions, and must—particularly if they are unmarried or if their clients are unmarried—address their minds to the size and fate of the respective beneficial interests on acquisition, separation and thereafter. It is simply impossible for a court to analyse personal transactions over years between cohabitants, and the costs of so doing are likely to be disproportionate in any event. Cohabiting partners must, it seems to me, contemplate and address the unthinkable, namely that their relationship will break down and that they will fall out over what they do and do not own.*

*If this appellant and this respondent had truly intended that the appellant's bene-ficial interest in the property should reduce post separation, or if the property was to belong to the respondent when the appellant acquired his own house, they should have so decided and acted accordingly by adjusting their beneficial interests in the property. I cannot spell such an intention out of their actions.*

Mr Kernott's appeal was granted and his share in the beneficial interest quantified at 50 per cent of the value of the property.

4.49  The search for fairness in the quantification of beneficial interests in the constructive cases is very reminiscent of the House of Lords' search for fairness in its approach to property division on divorce (see *Miller v Miller; McFarlane v McFarlane (2006)*, Chapter 7). In the light of the decision in *Stack (2007)*, it seems possible that the pragmatism applied to quantification will seep into the inferring of agreements or common intention, and to detrimental reliance. Their Lordships stressed the importance of the principles of trust law but it is difficult to ascertain with any certainty what these principles are now. Readers who may feel, justifiably, that the decisions in this area of law are somewhat confusing may be consoled by the words of Peter Gibson LJ in *Drake v Whipp (1996)* when he said in the context of informal trusts of the family home:

> *...it is not easy to reconcile every judicial utterance in this well-travelled area of law.*

# Proprietary estoppel

4.50 Proprietary estoppel is based on the principle that it is inequitable for the legal owner to deny a right to anyone, who has acted to his or her detriment, in reliance on the legal owner's implied or explicit representation relating to the grant of rights in or over the property.

4.51 The doctrine of proprietary estoppel and that of the constructive trust bear a remarkable resemblance to each other; the latter has its roots in the former, and the two doctrines are often pleaded in the alternative. In all cases of a successful claim of a constructive trust of a beneficial interest in property, a claim based on proprietary estoppel would also succeed (see *Q v Q (2008)*). The reverse is not so. Judicial statements have been made to the effect that the two doctrines overlap or are even identical (see eg *Turner v Jacob (2006)*; *Oxley v Hiscock (2004)*; *Grant v Edwards (1986)*). This is clearly incorrect, as Lord Walker emphasized in *Stack v Dowden (2007)*. There is a risk that if the constant attempts to merge the doctrines are successful the current requirements to ground an estoppel will be replaced by those of the constructive trust, and even if the holistic approach in *Stack (2007)* continues to prevail, the greater flexibility of proprietary estoppel will be lost.

## Nature of the representation

### Explicit representations

4.52 There are few decisions where the claimant has relied on an explicit representation.

> In *Pascoe v Turner (1979)*, Mrs Turner had been Mr Pascoe's housekeeper and subsequently cohabited with him. After ten years of living together, he eventually informed her that he was leaving her to move in with a new woman. Mrs Turner was very distressed, but became somewhat consoled when Mr Pascoe informed her clearly, in front of witnesses, that the house and everything in it was hers. The court found that the explicit representation, albeit made in emotional circumstances, gave rise to an estoppel based right.

4.53    Similarly in **S v S (2006)**, the court accepted that the husband had made an explicit representation to his wife which allowed her to claim an estoppel based right. He maintained that he would relinquish his charge on the family home, leaving her with the entire beneficial interest in the property which he had been granted during the divorce proceedings, in return for his wife's promise to give up all claims to past outstanding maintenance payments as well foregoing any future claim for maintenance.

## Implied representations

4.54 Most representations will not be quite so clear; family relationships tend to involve more hazy and imprecise arrangements which the parties may find difficult to recall during the bitter arguments which tend to accompany estoppel claims. They may be able to persuade the court that a representation may be inferred from all the circumstances of the case, taking into account a range of factors including, *inter alia*, the extent of the claimant's detriment, the nature of the parties' relationship, and their respective housing needs.

4.55    In **Turner v Jacob (2000)**, for example, Kim Jacob was Mrs Turner's only child. She was born with severe hearing problems and was described by counsel as having intellectual limits. She was not financially astute. Her mother was described as

> *...a strong minded and outgoing person with a large circle of friends. She had a very successful career as a stunt artiste and appeared in eight James Bond films as well as the films of Batman, Superman and Robin Hood. She was by all accounts an expert horsewoman who obviously had little or no fear. Many of her stunts involved high falls, chases on horseback and spectacular car accidents. Mr Turner [her husband] said that her job as a stunt woman made her very resolute and that she was able to compete and succeed in what was a very male dominated industry.*

Prior to her death, Mrs Turner had had a very close and protective relationship with Kim. When Kim married a man who mistreated her, her mother rescued her and bought a house and renovated it to enable her daughter to escape from her marriage. All she told Kim was that she had bought a house for her. The daughter spent around £2,000 on further renovations. After Mrs Turner's death, her husband, Kim's stepfather, inherited the property left to him in Mrs Turner's will which had been hastily executed one month before her death.

The court found that Kim had not been led to expect that the house was to be hers and that there was nothing in the circumstances which would make it inequitable or unconscionable for her claim to be denied (see also **Walsh v Singh (2010)**).

The decision was made against a background of complex property dealings involving the mother and the daughter, minimal detriment on the daughter's part, and adequate provision for her in her mother's will.

Patten J stated:

*The most that I am prepared to accept is that in early 2003 Mrs Turner said to Kim [the daughter] (and perhaps others) that she had bought a house for her.... It seems to me that...a mother's friendly and concerned gesture towards her daughter has been given a significance out of all proportion to what it can properly bear.*

4.56    In **Warnes v Hedley (1984)**, Mrs Warnes had purchased a property and allowed her son and daughter-in-law to live in it prior to the birth of their first baby. The couple substantially renovated the property. Mrs Hedley admired the renovations but remained silent about the basis on which they were occupying the property.

The couple's relationship broke down and the daughter-in-law brought a claim based on proprietary estoppel. The Court of Appeal rejected her claim. By the time it came before the court, the couple's marriage had broken down and the mother-in-law was in financially straitened circumstances. She needed the house for her own occupation. The court suggested that the house

*...was bought as a family home for a young married couple by a generous mother on the one hand, mother-in-law on the other, knowing that Mrs Hedley was pregnant with her first child. I am in no way surprised, in those circumstances, that Mr and Mrs Hedley did work on the house not only to provide nursery accommodation for young Jonathan when he arrived, but also to redecorate the premises and to modernise the kitchen. There was in fact very little direct evidence about what Mr and Mrs Hedley believed or understood about their interest in the premises. What I think one can say on the evidence is that the work, which they ordered, was just as consistent with a belief that they had a licence from Mrs Warnes, a belief that the house was bought for them to occupy as licensees.*

## Detriment

4.57    The detriment in estoppel claims, whether financial or otherwise, need not be referable to the property but must be capable of financial quantification (see **Stallion v Albert Stallion Holdings (Great Britain) Ltd (2010)**). It may well be at a level which would be insufficient to satisfy the requirement in the context of a constructive trust even after **Stack v Dowden (2007)**. Mrs Turner in **Pascoe v Turner (1979)**, for example, spent very little on her improvements to the property and Cumming Bruce LJ recognized that this expenditure could not have given rise to a constructive trust of the property but he was prepared to grant an estoppel right.

4.58    The courts have accepted a very wide range of activities as evidence of detriment in the estoppel context; these include work on the property, care of the representor, working without wages, expenses of relocating to another country, and a disadvantage suffered by a close partner of the claimant.

4.59    In **Re Basham (deceased) (1987)**, the claimant was the step-daughter of the deceased. She had worked for him over a 30-year period helping to run a number of public houses and a garage. She had received no payment for this work. The claimant, her husband and their children all had a very close relationship with the deceased. On several occasions when the claimant and her husband considered moving away from the area because the husband had been offered good employment elsewhere, the deceased had dissuaded them from doing so. After the death of the claimant's mother, the claimant had cared for the deceased in his retirement. He told her that she would receive his cottage on his death in return for all her help. The court accepted that the claimant had acted to her detriment.

4.60 Detriment is not to be judged simply at the time of the representation because often the claimant is actually receiving a benefit at that point. It is only at the moment when the representor reneges on the representation that the conduct, which took place when the representation was made, may be viewed as detrimental.

## Reliance

4.61 In familial situations, it is often the case that detriment can be viewed as related to a family obligation rather than specifically in reliance on any representations made to the claimant. The courts have recognized the dual nature of family behaviour and have tended to be liberal in their interpretation of reliance. They have accepted that once a claimant has acted to his or her detriment, it will be assumed that it was in reliance on the representation, and it is for the legal owner to prove otherwise.

4.62 In **Greasley v Cooke (1980)**, Miss Cooke was the cohabitant of Mr Greasley who ran a butcher's shop. She had looked after the household for some 40 years, having arrived there aged 16 years. She had cared for Mr Greasley's mentally ill sister, Clarice, and helped in the shop. She was never paid for her services. He and his brother assured he that she would always have a home in the family property. After Mr Greasley's death, the family attempted to evict her.

Lord Denning maintained that the representations made to her

*...were calculated to influence her, so as to put her mind at rest, so that she should not worry about being turned out. No one can say what she would have done if Kenneth and Hedley had not made those statements. It is quite possible that she would have said to herself: 'I am not married to Kenneth. I am on my own. What will happen to me if anything happens to him? I had better look out for another job now rather than stay here where I have no security'. So, instead of looking for another job, she stayed on in the house looking after Kenneth and Clarice. There is a presumption that she did so relying on the assurances given to her by Kenneth and Hedley. The burden is not on her but on them to prove that she did not rely on their assurances.*

4.63 Similarly, in **Griffiths v Williams (1978)**, Mrs Williams looked after her elderly sick mother, who had repeatedly assured her that she would be allowed to live in the house for the rest of her life. She spent £2,000 on improvements, which consisted of putting in a bathroom and an indoor lavatory, rewiring the house, and undertaking external renovations to the property.

The Court of Appeal recognized that there were inevitably dual motives in these types of situations:

> *It was clear that Mrs Williams—and I think this would apply to most sensitive people in her position—was reluctant to admit, even to herself, that in spending her own money on housekeeping and house improvement, she was thinking predominantly of her own inheritance rather than the care and comfort of her mother. What she did say, however, was that had it occurred to her that her enjoyment and benefit of these improvements, or rather of the house as improved (a house that she had always regarded as her home) would be limited to her mother's life span, she would have had to think whether she was not obliged to look more closely to her own future... It was equally clear, however, that none of this occurred to her at the time, or perhaps even not until it was put to her in this court.*

## Wide range of remedies

4.64 One of the greatest advantages of a successful claim based on proprietary estoppel is the ability of the court to grant whatever remedy it thinks fit (see ***Plimmer v Wellington Corporation (1884)***). It is a particularly appropriate approach in family situations. Although the courts look at the nature of the representation in deciding on a remedy, they have accepted that the only feasible, and appropriate remedy based on all the circumstances of the parties, may be to grant the claimant an alternative remedy from that which he or she had been led to expect.

### Fee simple

4.65 The grant of a fee simple is the most valuable of all the remedies available in the context of proprietary estoppel.

> In ***Pascoe v Turner (1979)***, the court granted Mrs Turner the fee simple of the property when Mr Pascoe and his 'heavies' attempted to evict her. Cumming Bruce LJ took the view that:
>
> *... the equity cannot here be satisfied without granting a remedy which assures to the defendant security of tenure, quiet enjoyment and freedom of action in respect of repairs and improvements without interference from the plaintiff. The history of the conduct of the plaintiff in relation to these proceedings leads to an irresistible inference that he is determined to pursue his purpose of evicting her from the house by any legal means at his disposal with a ruthless disregard of the obligations binding on conscience. The court must grant a remedy effective to protect her against the future manifestations of his ruthlessness. It was conceded that if she is granted a licence, such a licence cannot be registered as a land charge, so that she may find herself ousted by a purchaser for value without notice. If she has in the future to do further and more expensive repairs she may only be able to finance them by a loan,*

*but as a licensee she cannot charge the house. The plaintiff as legal owner may well find excuse for entry in order to do what he may plausibly represent as necessary works and so contrive to derogate from her enjoyment of the licence in ways that make it difficult or impossible for the court to give her effective protection.*

## An estoppel licence

4.66  Where the court believes it appropriate to grant a right limited to the lifetime of the estoppel claimant, it may grant a licence.

> In **Matharu v Matharu (1994)**, Mrs Matharu believed that she and her late husband had acquired the fee simple of the property from her father-in-law. The court gave her a licence to occupy the property for the rest of her life. It was accepted that the prime obligation of the father-in-law had been to his son, implying that had the claim been his, he might have been granted the fee simple. Now he was dead, it was more appropriate to simply protect Mrs Matharu for her lifetime.

## Compensation

4.67  Family relationships, which begin happily, often end miserably, and it may be unreasonable to expect the parties to continue to live together, even if that is what was envisaged by the original representation.

> In **Dodsworth v Dodsworth (1973)**, a sister persuaded her brother and his wife to live with her in her bungalow on their return from Australia. The couple spent money on improvements to the bungalow, encouraged by the sister to believe that they would be able to share it with her as their home for as long as they wished to do so. Eventually, the relationship between the parties broke down. The sister became anxious to sell the bungalow and buy a smaller and less expensive one for herself. She could not do this if her brother and his wife were entitled to stay in the bungalow rent-free. She would there-fore have to continue sharing her home for the rest of her life with the couple, with whom she was at loggerheads. The couple maintained that even if their expenditure was reim-bursed, it would be insufficient to allow them to purchase a new home because property prices had appreciated since they first went to live in the bungalow.
>
> The Court of Appeal was reluctant to grant the couple a licence as a remedy, even though the sister had died by the time the case reached the court. To allow the couple to remain in the bungalow, alone, would give them more than they had been led to expect from the original representation. They were awarded monetary compensation to the extent of their expenditure on the property, including an amount for their time and labour.

# A problematic remedy

4.68  Although the flexible nature of proprietary estoppel makes it eminently suitable in the resolution of disputes in the family home, there are some disadvantages to it. Because the purpose of proprietary estoppel is to compensate the claimant for the detriment suffered, the doctrine can only be pleaded once the representation has been withdrawn. This means that the claimant has no certainty, prior to the withdrawal, what the rights, in or over the property, are. The claimant is dependent on either the goodwill of the legal owner to continue to honour the representation, or if it is withdrawn, on the court's generosity once the claim is brought before it. A claimant may be fortunate and enjoy the court's grant of a fee simple, but may be unlucky and be given minimal compensation. Where the remedy is a licence, it is personal to the claimant and is not transferable to a third party which limits the possibilities for a claimant to move elsewhere and make a new start.

# Matrimonial Proceedings and Property Act 1970, s 37

4.69 This little used provision allows married or engaged couples, either of whom have a beneficial interest in property, to acquire an enhanced share in that property if they have contributed substantially in money or money's worth to the improvement of the property without having to prove an agreement or representation. The provision is subject to the existence of any agreement between the couple to the contrary.

4.70 What constitutes an engagement is left undefined. The status, as we noted in Chapter 2, is somewhat problematic; it is often a euphemism for long-term cohabitation.

4.71 In **Laethem v Brooker (2005)**, the court rejected the woman's claim that she was engaged to the defendant as 'wishful thinking' in spite of the existence of a diamond and sapphire ring. The parties had cohabited over a long period of time and the defendant had subsequently married another woman. In the event, the non-existent engagement was irrelevant because the court granted the woman a beneficial share in the disputed properties based on a constructive trust.

# Civil Partnership Act 2004, s 65

4.72 The Civil Partnership Act 2004 (CPA 2004), s 65 makes similar provisions for civil partners, as those available to married partners in the Matrimonial Property and Proceedings Act 1970.

# The Law Reform (Miscellaneous Provisions) Act 1970, ss 2, 3; Civil Partnership Act 2004, s 74(5)

4.73 The Law Reform (Miscellaneous Provisions) Act 1970, s 2 makes provision for a couple who are engaged to be married but terminate their engagement to resolve their property ownership in accordance with any of the statutory provisions available to married couples. Section 3 provides that gifts exchanged on condition that the couple marry must be returned to the donor. However, engagement rings are presumed to be non-returnable unless there is evidence to the contrary.

4.74 The question of engagement rings played a significant role in the parties' stormy relationship in *Cox v Jones (2004)*. Mr Jones gave Ms Cox an engagement ring, worth at least £10,000 or more. Mr Jones maintained that when he gave Ms Cox the ring, he made clear that if the engagement came to an end, he would be entitled to its return. The ring was flung out of windows, locked in glove compartment, supposedly borrowed by Ms Cox after the engagement was over for sentimental reasons, and, finally, was turned into a pendant by Ms Cox which disappeared mysteriously before the court hearing. The judge rejected Mr Jones version of events:

> *I have little difficulty in rejecting Mr Jones's version of events. His case on this point contains inconsistencies and implausibilities. First, I find the initial discussion implausible. It is common ground that the trip at the end of 1997 was a romantic one which both parties enjoyed very much. They were talking about marriage. Having heard the evidence, I reject as implausible the unromantic express remark which Mr Jones says that he made. I find it hard to accept that it would have been said in the context in which it was said to have been uttered.*

4.75 The CPA 2004 s 74 makes similar provisions for civil partners with respect to property ownership but makes no mention of engagement rings.

## Implied contracts

4.76 Decisions involving implied contracts relating to occupation of the family home are rare. The following two decisions show two different approaches of the courts in dealing with implied contracts.

4.77 In *Tanner v Tanner (1975)*, a young woman, Miss McDermott (who called herself Mrs Tanner) gave birth to twins after a relationship with Mr Tanner, a married man with children. He was a milkman by day and a croupier by night. Mr Tanner purchased a house, which he divided into flats. He allowed Miss McDermott to live with the twins in one, and he leased the other. Miss McDermott collected the rent for him from the tenant. It seemed that Mr Tanner became easily bored with the women who entered his life. He left Miss McDermott, divorced his wife and went to live with a married woman whom he subsequently married. He wanted to remove Miss McDermott from the house so that he could live there with his new wife who was pregnant with his child.

Lord Denning maintained that:

*This man had a moral duty to provide for the babies of whom he was the father. I would go further. I think he had a legal duty towards them. Not only towards the babies but also towards their mother. She was looking after them and bringing them up. In order to fulfil his duty towards the babies, he was under a duty to provide for the mother too. She had given up her flat where she was protected by the Rent Acts—at least in regard to rent and it may be in regard also to security of tenure. She had given it up at his instance so as to be able the better to bring up the children. It is impossible to suppose that in that situation she and the babies were bare licensees whom he could turn out at a moment's notice. He recognised this when he offered to pay her £4,000 to get her out.*

He held that from an inference of all the circumstances, Miss McDermott had an implied contractual licence to live in the house with the children for as long as they were of school age and the home was reasonably needed by her and the children. By the time the case came before the Court of Appeal Mr Tanner had forced Miss McDermott to leave the property. Therefore the court decided to compensate her for the loss of her licence. The decision appears to be closely related to those based proprietary estoppel.

4.78    One year later, in **Horrocks v Forray (1976)**, the Court of Appeal was far less sympathetic. The defendant was the mistress of a wealthy, married man who died very suddenly in a car accident. The couple had a daughter together and the man had a son by his wife. During the relationship, the mistress was married very briefly to another man and had a child by him. The mistress eventually moved into a house purchased by her lover in his sole name. He told his solicitor that he was buying it to give his mistress and child some security. He contemplated transferring the house into his mistress' name but decided against it because of the high cost of stamp duty and capital gains tax. He also considered creating a trust for the benefit of his daughter, but again for tax reasons, he decided not to.

The wife did not learn of the existence of her husband's mistress and the house until after the husband's death. The executors wanted the property to be sold because, as a result of the husband's generosity towards his mistress, his estate would otherwise be insolvent.

The mistress maintained that, from all the circumstances surrounding her relationship with her lover, a contract should be inferred. She had subordinated her life, and choice of place to live, to that of her lover in return for his implied agreement that he would maintain her and the children and provide them all with a permanent home. She maintained that this implied contract gave rise to a licence, the terms of which were that she could remain in the house either for her life, or for the period of her daughter's full-time education, or for as long as she and the daughter reasonably required to be housed.

The Court of Appeal ruled in favour of the executors and granted possession. It held that:

*In order to establish a contract, whether it be an express contract or a contract implied by law, there has to be shown a meeting of the minds of the parties, with a definition of the contractual terms reasonably clearly made out, with an intention to affect the legal relationship: that is that the agreement that is made is one which is properly to be regarded as being enforceable by the court if one or the other fails to comply with it; and it still remains a part of the law of this country, though many people think that it is time that it was changed to some other criterion, that there must be consideration moving in order to establish a contract. In the circumstances no contractual licence, either inferred or express, could be inferred from the conduct of the couple. There was no meeting of minds or any definition of the terms of the contract.*

Scarman LJ accepted that it was not contrary to public policy for a couple who had had a child born out of marriage to reach an agreement for the maintenance of the mother and child. But it did not follow automatically that, in all such cases, an agreement would be inferred. He attempted to distinguish the case of *Tanner v Tanner (1976)* as one in which the parties' relationship had broken down and the implied agreement was made for the future of the children. In the present case:

*...right up to the death of the man there was a continuing, warm relationship of man and mistress. He was maintaining his mistress in luxurious, even, so the judge thought, extravagant, style, and, we now know, in a style beyond his means; his estate is now at risk of being insolvent... whatever relationship did exist between these two could as well be referable to the continuance of natural love and affection as to an intention to enter into an agreement, which they intended to have legal effect.*

Scarman LJ maintained that:

*Here was a generous provision made for a woman who was still the mistress and for the child of that relationship. It was generous beyond what one would reasonably expect the man to accept a legally binding obligation to provide. It was generous, not because he was bound, or was binding himself, to be generous, but because he chose to be generous to the woman for whom there was a big place in his heart.*

It must be questioned why a woman should be penalized and lose her family home on the death of her lover because the court interpreted a man's generosity as incompatible with the finding of a contract.

# Family Law Act 1996, Part IV

## Statutory right of occupation for spouses and civil partners

4.79 Where a spouse or civil partner has a beneficial estate or interest in, or contract to occupy, their family home, the Family Law Act 1996 (FLA 1996), s 30 provides the other spouse or civil partner, who does not possess any of these rights, with a statutory 'home right' This right which might be broadly termed a right of occupation includes a right not to be evicted from the home except by court order, and a right, with a court order, to re-enter the home if they have been excluded from it.

4.80 The right is personal to the spouse or civil partner and may not be transferred to a third party. It comes to an end on divorce; dissolution of a civil partnership; annulment of a marriage or civil partnership, death of a spouse or civil partner, or where it is formally terminated by agreement between the partners, usually when the home is sold. The right cannot be translated into money which limits the potential for a spouse or civil partner to leave the family home and purchase an alternative residence.

4.81 Where a spouse or civil partner, who has a home right, applies for an order under FLA 1996, s 33, the court will exercise its discretion in accordance with the broad provisions of s 33(6), (7). These provisions are considered in detail in Chapter 5.

## The family home

4.82 A family home, for the purposes of the FLA 1996, is a property, or properties in which the spouses or civil partners have lived together. They may have two or more family homes, and the definition of family home includes not only apartments and houses, but also caravans and boats, indeed any structure in which two people may live together as a family. An interesting example of the Canadian court's approach to the definition of a family home is to be found in the following case.

> In **Clark v Clark (1984)**, the Ontario Supreme Court gave the wife a right to occupy the family yacht because the parties had used it as an alternative matrimonial home during holidays. The court explained that it could see no reason why the fact that the alternative home was a mobile one should prove to be problematic. The judge said:
>
> *I frankly see no reason why the extra home or cottage should therefore be restricted to a question of evaluation of accommodation or mobility, once the principle of an alternative home has been established. The fact that that alternate home moves in some way, and that it may be difficult to locate under some circumstances, or that it may have some restrictions of accommodation, I think is not necessarily relevant, as long as it is shown that the general use of the property or thing has been by the family as an alternative residence while the family was on vacation.*
>
> The court accepted that it could make no precise order relating to the timing of the wife's occupation of the matrimonial home given the vagaries of weather at sea. She should simply return the yacht on the date given, and at whatever time the tides made it possible to enter the harbour.

## Effect of the statutory right on third parties

4.83 One of the most important attributes of the home right is that, once it has come into existence, it acts as a charge on a spouse or civil partner's estate or interest in the home, and it has the potential to bind third parties who acquire the property (FLA 1996, s 31). The charge must, however, be registered under the Land Registration Act 2002, s 31(10) (or, in unregistered land, under the Land Charges Act 1972, s 2(7), as a class F land charge), if it is to be enforceable against third parties. Only one right can be registered even if there is more than one family home. Once the right is registered it will normally be protected against a subsequent third party who obtains an estate or interest in it. However, FLA 1996, s 34(1)(a) provides that such a third party is in the same position as the spouse or civil partner from whom he acquired the property. Thus, the court may exercise its discretion under FLA 1996, s 35(6) and determine the competing rights of the spouse or civil partner who has registered the family home right, and the third party. Such decisions are rare (see eg *Kaur v Gill (1988)*).

## Potential for manipulation

4.84 Where the family home is to be sold, the spouse or civil partner who has registered a home right will normally agree to arrange to remove it from the register prior to completion of the sale, because a failure to do so will almost certainly prevent sale. Often another family home is to be purchased and a home right will be subsequently registered against it. Spouses have, however, attempted to register a right or refused to have a registration removed because they wished to use it as a bargaining tool.

4.85 In *Barnett v Hassett (1981)*, a man exchanged contracts for the purchase of a house intended to be his future matrimonial home. Before the sale was completed, he married and moved into his wife's house on a temporary basis. Soon after, the marriage broke down and he moved out. He was unable to complete the purchase of what was to have been the future matrimonial home and was forced to forfeit his deposit. The husband believed that, as the wife had agreed to purchase their proposed matrimonial home jointly with him and had only reneged on the agreement when their relationship broke down, she should share in his financial loss. The wife decided to sell her own property, at which point the husband registered an occupation right against it. The wife applied to the court to have the registration set aside.

The court agreed to her request on the basis that the purpose of the right was to protect occupation. The husband did not wish to occupy the house. He was merely registering the charge to put pressure on his wife to share the financial loss he had incurred.

# Bankruptcy

4.86 The family home is often used to secure loans, which means that the family's occupation is put at risk in the event of bankruptcy. Even where a bankrupt's partner has a beneficial interest in the property which is binding on the trustee in bankruptcy, the latter may apply for an order for sale of the bankrupt's property under the Trusts of Land and Appointment of Trustees Act 1996, s 14. The trustee in bankruptcy may only take the bankrupt's share of the property on sale, leaving the partner's share intact. However, that share will more often than not be insufficient to purchase another family home.

4.87 Where a spouse or a civil partner has a right of occupation under the FLA 1996, Part IV which is a charge on the bankrupt's property, the trustee in bankruptcy may make an application under FLA 1996, s 33.

4.88 In applications for a sale of the family home under the Trusts of Land and Appointment of Trustees Act 1996, s 14 or under FLA 1996, s 33 the Insolvency Act 1986, ss 335A and 336 apply respectively. Both sections provide that in determining whether to order sale or not, the court must take into account the interests of the creditors, the conduct of the non-bankrupt partner relating to the bankruptcy, the needs of this partner, the needs of any children, and all the circumstances of the case other than the bankrupt's needs. In addition if the application for sale is made after the end of one year after the bankrupt's property is in the hands of the trustee in bankruptcy, the court must assume that the creditors take precedent unless the circumstances are exceptional.

## Exceptional circumstances

4.89 In *Barca v Mears (2004)*, the court questioned whether the narrow approach to exceptional circumstances as laid down in *Re Citro (1991)* was consistent with Art 8 (the right to respect for private and family) of the ECHR (see also *The Official Receiver for Northern Ireland v Rooney and Paulson (2008)*).

The court held that in the general run of cases, the creditors' interests would prevail. However, it must be left open to the court to define what was exceptional in any given circumstances. Exceptional circumstances would not be limited to those cases where the consequences were unusual in the sense of going beyond the usual consequences of bankruptcy.

4.90 In *Hosking v Michaelides (2004)*, it was argued that the meaning given to the concept of exceptional circumstances in the past had been too restrictive and was incompatible with Art 8 of the ECHR. The court rejected this view and held that to be exceptional the circumstances need not be unique, unprecedented, or very rare; but they cannot be ones that are routinely or normally encountered.

The exceptional circumstances relied upon by Mrs Michaelides concerned her physical and mental health. She had overdosed on drugs; was an alcoholic; emotionally unstable, and had a tendency to act impulsively. Her psychiatrist gave evidence that Mrs Michaelides was unable to cope with any stress and trauma and that she reacted in a way which was dissimilar to that of an ordinary person faced with similar circumstances. The sale of her family home would exacerbate her emotional difficulties, which would be dangerous for both her and her children.

The court, somewhat hesitantly, found that these were exceptional circumstances and deferred sale, but only for six months. It regarded its decision as generous; the creditors' needs should prevail over those of Mrs Michaelides and her children.

4.91    In *Re Bremner (A Bankrupt) (1999)*, the trustee in bankruptcy applied for an order for sale of the bankrupt's home and an order terminating the wife's right of occupation in the property. The wife was aged 74 years; she was looking after her husband who was 79 years old. He had suffered a stroke and had inoperable cancer. The wife accepted that the court could not take into account the needs of her bankrupt husband but argued that her desire to care for him in the last few months of his life was a separate need of her own. She had offered to agree to an order for sale on condition that the marketing and sale of the property did not begin until three months after the bankrupt's death, which was expected within six months.

The court held that the circumstances here were exceptional. The fact that the wife was caring for her dying husband, and that the sale of their home would make that care impossible or more difficult, justified deferring sale in spite of the creditors' needs. The deferral of sale was likely to be short. With good Jesuitical reasoning, the court accepted that its recognition of the wife's overwhelming desire to care for her husband did not amount to taking the bankrupt's own needs into account. It had only considered the bankrupt's state of health to the extent that it was relevant to the distinct needs of his wife in satisfying her wish to look after her dying husband. According to the court

*Mrs Bremner is performing in extremely difficult circumstances one of the most compelling human and moral obligations that a person can have.*

4.92    The circumstances in *Re Haghighat (A Bankrupt) (2009)* were extremely tragic. The court recognized this and deferred an order for possession of the family home, requested by the trustee in bankruptcy, against a bankrupt husband. The conditions in which the bankrupt lived with his wife and three adult children were severely overcrowded. The eldest child had congenital quadriplegic cerebral palsy, severe learning disabilities and, epilepsy. He was doubly incontinent, could not speak, used a wheelchair, and had to be carried between his bed, his chair, and the shower. The wife slept in the same room as him and gave him 24 hours a day care.

The husband applied to the court, under s 33 of the Family Law Act 1996, and asked that the possession order not be granted because the circumstances were exceptional within s 336(5) for his wife, and s 337(6) for himself. The trustee maintained that the possession order should be made but deferred for a period of 3 or 6 months. The local authority would then have to re-house the family because it would be homeless. The trustee accepted that this would cause considerable disruption to the family in the short term.

The court deferred the order for possession for 3 years, or 3 months if the disabled child ceased to live permanently in the family home. The court accepted that these were exceptional circumstances and not merely the normal

*... melancholy consequences of debt and improvidence.*

Even if the property were to be sold, there would still be a substantial shortfall to pay the bankrupt's debts. The wife had no income or capital of her own, and lived on state benefits; she had not contributed to the bankruptcy in any way.

The deferred order would give the local authority time to make provision for the eldest child and for the wife to be re-housed in suitable accommodation, and was the best possible just and reasonable balance between the competing interests of all those concerned.

## FURTHER READING

Barlow A et al, 'Just a Piece of Paper? Marriage and Cohabitation', in A Park et al, *British Social Attitudes: Public Policy, Social Ties. The 18th Report* (2001), 29–57

Bray J, 'The financial rights of cohabiting couples' [2009] Fam Law 1151

Burrows D and Orr N, *Stack v Dowden: Co-Ownership of Property by Unmarried Parties: A Special Bulletin* (Jordans, 2007)

Chandler A, 'Quantifying Shares in Jointly Owned Property: Stack v Dowden and Kernott v Jones' [2010] Fam Law 835

Douglas G, Pearce J and Woodward H, 'Dealing with Property Issues on Cohabitation Breakdown' [2007] Fam Law 36

Gray K, and Gray S, *Elements of Land Law* (5th edn, Oxford University Press, 2009)

Hess E, 'The Rights of Cohabitants: When and How Will the Law be Reformed?' [2009] Fam Law 405

Law Commission, Sharing Homes: a Discussion Paper (Law Com No 278, 2002)

The Law Commission, Cohabitation: The Financial Consequences of Relationship Breakdown (Law Com No 307, 2007)

Pawlowski M, 'Ownership—True Intentions' [2010] Fam Law 17

Pawlowski M, 'Resulting Trusts, Joint Borrowers and Beneficial Shares' [2010] Fam Law 654

Ralton A, 'Establishing a beneficial share: *Rosset* revisited' [2008] Fam Law 424

Soni B, 'Insolvency and the Matrimonial Home' [2004] Fam Law 596

Tattersall M, 'Stack v Dowden: Imputing and intention' [2008] Fam Law 249

Thompson M, *Modern Land Law* (4th edn, Oxford University Press, 2009)

Welstead M, 'Domestic Contribution and Constructive Trusts: the Canadian Perspective' (1987) Denning LJ 151

Welstead M, 'Proprietary Estoppel: a Flexible Familial Equity' (1995) Conveyancer 61

Welstead M, 'The Deserted Bank and the Spousal Equity' [1999] Denning LJ 113

## SELF-TEST QUESTIONS

1   What advice would you give to an unmarried couple who wish to purchase a family home for the first time?

2   Will the decision in **Dowden v Stack (2007)** help a cohabitant like Mrs Burns in **Burns v Burns (1984)** to obtain rights in her family home?

3   William and Xavier are a same-sex couple who are not registered civil partners. In 1990, they purchased a property and registered the legal title in both their names; they had no discussions as to how the beneficial interest should be shared. Xavier borrowed 75 per cent of the purchase price from his employer and William used a legacy from his parents to fund the remainder of the purchase price. After they moved into the property, William gave up his job as an investment banker and took responsibility for planning, planting and maintaining the couple's large garden. In 2005, Xavier died. In his will he left all his property to his parents.

   Advise William what right he has to remain in the property, or what rights he has to a share in the proceeds of sale if the property is sold. Would your answer be any different if William and Xavier had entered into a registered civil partnership?

4   Critically analyse the decision in **Cox v Jones (2004)**.

5   Lalla and her mother, Maria, purchased a house and registered the legal title in both their names. They failed to specify how they would share the beneficial interest in the property. Lalla provided 40 per cent of the purchase price and her mother 30 per cent. The remaining 30 per cent was provided by a loan by way of mortgage to Lalla who was responsible for all the re-payments. The property was to be let to a tenant but would ultimately provide a home for Lalla when she returned from working abroad.

   Lalla and Maria had an argument and as a consequence, Lalla decided that she wanted the property to be sold. Maria agreed on condition that she received a 50 per cent share of the proceeds of sale. Lalla objected and maintained that Maria should only receive a 30 per cent share.

   Advise Maria.

6   James, a merchant banker, was the owner of a flat in London. Kate, a legal secretary and James' long-term girlfriend, lived in a flat leased to her on an annual basis. In 1993, in order to give Kate some security, James purchased her flat for her. They continued to live separately until 1995 when James invited Kate to live with him in a farmhouse, also owned by him. She accordingly quit her job and moved to the farmhouse. Kate did not seek new employment, but spent her time supervising the renovation work on the farmhouse, overseeing the building work, and carrying out the decorating herself. James was unable to do this himself owing to his commitments in London on weekdays. In 2003, Kate and James both sold their flats in London and pooled the proceeds to purchase a terraced house. The house was registered in Kate's name alone because James thought that she should have some security if he were to die before her, but Kate insisted that everything they own should be shared by both of them. James used the house whilst he was working in London, and Kate very rarely visited it; she considered the farmhouse to be her real home. In 2004 Kate and James had a baby. Shortly after the birth she discovered that Laura had moved into the house in London to live with James, and that James proposed selling the farmhouse. Kate would like to stay in the farmhouse with Mariella, their daughter.

Advise Kate what rights, if any, she might have in respect of both the farmhouse and the terraced house in London.

# 5

# Domestic violence

## SUMMARY

In this chapter we consider the incidence, nature, and causes of violence between those who are in, or who have had, familial or other close emotional relationships with each other. We examine the criminal and civil remedies which have been developed to combat what is commonly referred to as, domestic violence. We question whether a separate law is required to combat such violence. We consider forced marriage as a specific form of domestic violence and we examine the proposals which have been put forward to end all forms of violence within familial or emotional relationships.

5.1 Like many other writers, Lasch, in *Haven in a Heartless World: the Family Besieged* (1977), viewed the family home as a place of safety from the harsh world outside its walls. For many family members, Lasch's description is happily an accurate one. However, for those who regularly experience the particular form of violence which takes place behind the closed doors of the family home, Lasch's statement might appear to be merely a sentimentalized and inaccurate view.

## Incidence of domestic violence

5.2 In 2009, the Home Office Consultation paper on domestic violence reported that one in five of all violent crimes reported are related to domestic abuse, and in one in six of all murders in the UK, the victim had had a close relationship with the murderer. On a daily basis, newspapers report numerous incidents of serious violence both inside and outside the home where the victim has had an emotional relationship with the perpetrator of the violence. This form of violent crime has major economic consequences for society in terms of medical treatment, child welfare, prevention efforts, unemployment, and incarceration of perpetrators.

# Nature of domestic violence

5.3 Domestic violence tends to be defined as a repeated pattern of behaviour, which takes place primarily within the family home and includes physical, psychological, emotional, and sexual abuse.

The victims of domestic violence are predominantly women, and particularly pregnant women. who face more attacks, and from the same perpetrator, than victims of any other type of crime (see http://www.crimereduction.gov.uk/domesticviolence/domesticviolence). Women become frightened prisoners in their own homes from where escape is difficult. The perpetrators are primarily male, although a report in 2010 from Parity, an equal rights organization, based on Home Office statistics and the British Crime Survey, maintained that four out of ten victims are men. It also claimed that men who are attacked at home are often ignored by the police and the courts. It criticized the latest guidelines published by the Judicial Studies Board, which has responsibility for the training of judges, because its manual stresses that domestic violence is mainly a male crime against women.

Hester, in 2009, maintained that men are less likely to report incidents of domestic violence because they feel embarrassed to do so. She has also suggested that where victims are male, the attack is more likely to be from another male.

5.4 It is debatable whether violence which takes place between members of the family in the home should be referred to as 'domestic violence'. The word 'domestic' appears to play down the gravity of violent behaviour and suggests a certain inevitability and acceptability of the conduct. It is important to remember that those who are violent in the home may also be violent outside of the home. In *R v Bretton (2010)*, the Court of Appeal drew attention to the fact that the defendant, an alcoholic and drug addict was not only violent in the home towards his partner but was also violent in other areas of his life. The Court sentenced him, *inter alia*, to imprisonment for public protection (IPP) under s 225 of the Criminal Justice Act 2003.

5.5 Susan Edwards has argued that the term 'domestic violence'

> *...serves to neutralise the full horror, viciousness and habituation of the violence, concealing the imprisonment of its sufferers, neutralising the seriousness and the dangerousness of the aggressor, thereby rendering its victims a different and lesser*

*standard of response from the justice system and ultimately a lesser standard of protection.*

*(Sex and Gender in the Legal Process (1996))*

5.6 However, a failure to distinguish violence between familial members and other types of violence may prevent the finding of satisfactory solutions to the problem. Unlike in other cases of violence, victims and their attackers who have or have had a familial relationship with each other, are all too often forced to remain in close contact with each other because they have children or other family members, property, finances and geographical location in common. They often find it difficult to admit to the outside world what is going on behind closed doors because of embarrassment or confused emotions. As Byron James (2008) has so aptly put it:

*Being in love with someone who is violent towards you presents a tragic and impossible circumstance. The balance between emotional and physical pain is a difficult one to judge. The overtly optimistic faith in change may be akin to a life sentence of suffering. Rarely is it the case that such a victim is desirous of retribution or compensation. Most of the time, they just want it to stop.*

# Causes of domestic violence

5.7 Whatever, name is given to familial violence in or outside the home, its causes and consequences need first to be understood before it can be satisfactorily addressed. They are complex, and include psychological, emotional, sociological, cultural, in addition to legal explanations. Attitudes towards what is acceptable behaviour in close familial relationships have varied over time and between cultures. In 1627, the Lord Chief Justice of England, Sir Edward Coke, was not averse to committing serious acts of violence against his wife and 14 year old daughter (Waller, 2009).

5.8 A spate of mis-called honour killings in the UK has drawn attention to an extreme example of the relationship between culture and familial violence. Young women from immigrant backgrounds have been murdered by their families because they chose to adopt Western lifestyles and sexual values. Their families regard their conduct as bringing dishonour on them and maintain that it has to be avenged (see Welstead and Edwards, 1999).

5.9 In 2010, David Winnick MP made the forceful point that:

*'Honour-based' violence of course is a very odd description for outright thuggery and indeed murder, so 'honour' is very much in quotes. It is not honour; it is dishonour, totally, from beginning to last and it is a disgusting and evil practice.*

*(Follow up to the Committee's Report on Domestic Violence, Forced Marriage and Honour-Based Violence—Home Affairs Committee http://www.publications.parliament.uk)*

5.10 The following decisions confirm this view.

> In *R v Dosanjh (2005)*, a father procured a number of men to kill his daughter, her boy-friend, and a man he believed to be the father of the boyfriend. He wanted to avenge what he viewed as the dishonour the daughter had brought upon the family by living with her boyfriend without marrying him. The plot was unsuccessful but the decision illustrates the intensity of familial conflicts where cultures clash.

> In *R v Haq (2005)*, two brothers were convicted for killing their sister Sharifan Bibi and her lover Hashmat Ali. The sister had been brought up in England, and entered into an arranged marriage in Pakistan. She returned to England whilst her husband awaited immigration formalities. In the meantime, she met Hashmat Ali and went to cohabit with him. Her father persuaded her to return to the family home, which was nearby, and she remained there for a very brief time before returning to Hashmat Ali. She disappeared soon after and it was accepted that the likelihood was that she had been lured away and killed along with Hashmat Ali, by her brothers. No bodies were found, but there was evidence of decomposing flesh buried in her brother's house and evidence of bodies being re-excavated at a later date and burned.

5.11 Patel (2009) has drawn attention to domestic violence in some Asian communities in the form of dowry abuse. Where a woman is deemed not to have brought sufficient money or goods into the relationship as her dowry, her husband's family may use physical abuse in an attempt to extract what it deems to be appropriate from her family.

# Further examples of domestic violence

5.12 One woman's account of her imprisonment at home describes how her jealous husband, who, throughout their marriage, could not bear the possibility of his wife talking to another man, locked her up, much of the time, in a coal shed every time he went out, subjecting her to a 50-year ordeal of cruelty. The woman's secret emerged when, at the age of 74, she was taken to hospital with an illness and confided in a nurse. She thought that her experience was normal, refused help, and subsequently returned to live with her husband (*Daily Mail*, 8 February 1992).

5.13 In 2010, a chef was jailed for life for murdering his wife with a griddle pan whilst she was asleep. He had hidden the body in a freezer in the garden shed for three years before placing it in the dustbin when he left the country with his new girlfriend. It was discovered when, the dustmen refused to take the bin from in front of the house because it was too heavy. The husband told the victim's family and friends that she had died of a brain aneurism. He arranged a memorial service after filling an urn with ashes from wood which he had burnt on a barbecue. He maintained that they were his wife's ashes. He placed his wedding ring with her name on the urn. (*The Guardian,* 4 June 2010).

5.14　A particularly horrific example of murder is to be found in *R v Tabbenor (2007)*. The defendant had had a five-year relationship with his victim, Lynda Groudis. When she attempted to end the relationship, the defendant went to a 24-hour petrol station and bought a petrol can and petrol. He walked back to Lynda's home, and while she was asleep in bed poured petrol over her. She awoke and tried to run from the house. The defendant followed her and set fire to her with a cigarette lighter. The flames engulfed her and she was severely burned. Following five operations, some of which lasted in excess of six hours, Lynda's life support machine was switched off. The cause of death was multiple organ failure and sepsis caused by the fire. The defendant stated that he had intended to kill Lynda because he loved her so much that he did not want anyone else to have her. He claimed that he had wanted to kill himself at the same time.

# Criminal remedies

5.15　Many victims, their attackers and, at times in the past, even the police have failed to make the connection that familial violence is as serious a crime as any other form of violence. The police have often been accused of treating it as a private matter for the perpetrator and victim. Where, as is generally the case, the police do acknowledge that many forms of domestic violence fall within the definition of serious criminal behaviour (see http://www.met.police.uk/enoughis-enough), they have often been frustrated in their efforts. Perpetrators have been arrested but their victims have been unwilling to give evidence against them because of fear of further violence, or the loss of their home and financial support and the resultant effect on their children. They can, of course, be compelled to give evidence but that in itself may prove to be more of a punishment to them.

## Offences against the Person Act 1861

5.16　Physical violence in the domestic context has always been a crime. It has also been accepted that psychological violence is a crime too.

For example, in *R v Ireland and Burstow (1998)*, it was held that the offence of inflicting grievous bodily harm, contrary to Offences against the Person Act 1861, s 20, included the making of harassing telephone calls, writing menacing letters, visiting the victim's house, and distributing insulting cards. Although no physical violence was involved, the victim had been psychiatrically injured as demonstrated by her severe depression.

5.17    However, severe limitations were placed on the meaning of psychological violence by the Court of Appeal in *R v D (2006)*. A wife had committed suicide after many years of psychological abuse. It was held that in order to bring about a successful prosecution under s 20, there had to be evidence of a psychiatric illness resulting from the psychological damage. According to the Court, psychological damage was seen to be

*...an illusive concept, potentially unspecific, which did not amount to bodily harm for the purpose of the 1861 Act.*

The Court cited the words of Lord Steyn in *Ireland (1998)*:

*...recognisable psychiatric injury could amount to bodily harm, but of themselves, 'states of mind' could not...*

It is unfortunate that the Court felt able to make the distinction between emotionally distressed states which it accepted as normal, and a definable psychiatric illness which it thought constituted an abnormal condition. The dividing line is very fine indeed, and particularly so where a victim of sustained psychological abuse commits suicide.

## Protection from Harassment Act 1997

5.18    Whilst the Protection from Harassment Act 1997 was not specifically introduced to deal with domestic violence, it has been used for that purpose. Its main function was to deal with the problem of stalking; the term was popularized by the press to describe the way in which celebrities were harassed by their fans. It covers all conduct where an obsessive individual, with whom the victim may or may not have had a relationship, repeatedly engages in conduct, causing psychological fear even if there is no actual physical violence. Sections 2 and 4 of the Act create two criminal offences: first, harassment; and secondly, putting people in fear of violence. Both offences are punishable with custodial sentences. The Act also makes provision for the grant of civil injunctions (see below).

5.19    In order to be convicted of an offence, the person accused must have pursued a course of conduct and not merely committed one act of harassment. The harm which the Act was intended to prevent was that of persons from being put in a state of alarm or distress by the perpetrator's repeated conduct. Whether acts constitute a course of conduct does not depend upon a mathematical calculation but on the facts of the situation.

In *Kelly v Director of Public Prosecutions (2002)*, the court accepted that three phone calls in five minutes, in the middle of the night, from a man to a woman with whom he had had a relationship could be viewed as a course of conduct.

5.20    The widespread use of the internet and mobile phones has increased the potential for harassment.

In *R v P (2004)*, the defendant was divorced from his wife. She had obtained a restraining order under the Protection from Harassment Act 1997, s 5 which prevented the defendant from making any direct or indirect contact with her or their children except through solicitors. The defendant repeatedly sent text messages and made silent calls from his mobile phone to his ex-wife and children and was found guilty of breaching the order (see also *Lomas v Parle (2004)*).

## Breach of the peace

5.21   Incidents of domestic violence may be held to cause a breach of the peace, as was explained in *Foulkes v Chief Constable of the Merseyside Police (1998)*. A husband called the police after his wife had locked him out of their jointly owned family home. The police explained to him that his wife and children did not want him to re-enter the house and suggested that he leave until tempers had calmed down. The husband refused to do so and insisted that he be allowed to re-enter his home. The police then arrested him because they feared that if he were to remain outside the house or managed to re-enter, an argument or violence would ensue, thus occasioning a breach of the peace. He was taken to the police station and remained in custody overnight He was released after his wife withdrew her statement that she wished him to be bound over to keep the peace.

The husband commenced proceedings against the Chief Constable claiming damages for wrongful arrest and false imprisonment. The Court of Appeal held that the common law power of a police constable to arrest where no actual breach of the peace had occurred, but where he feared that one might be caused by apparently lawful conduct, was exceptional. It should be exercised only in the clearest of circumstances and when the police constable was satisfied on reasonable grounds that a breach of the peace was imminent. There had to be a sufficiently real and present threat to the peace to justify the extreme step of depriving of his liberty a citizen who was not at the time acting unlawfully. Here the circumstances were not such as to justify the arrest.

## Domestic Violence, Crime and Victims Act 2004

5.22   Domestic violence legislation has often been described as a hotchpotch of enactments involving both criminal and civil law. A recent attempt has been made to bridge the gap between the criminal and civil law in the form of the Domestic Violence, Crime and Victims Act 2004. It amends the Family Law 1996 (FLA 1996) and, in particular, inserts a new s 42A which makes it a criminal offence to flout civil non-molestation orders (see below). This provision will enable longer sentences, of up to five years' imprisonment, to be made than is possible in civil proceedings for contempt of court for breach of a civil order. The Act makes common assault an arrestable offence; provides greater protection to victims during court hearings; improves sentencing of those convicted; establishes multi-agency reviews after familial killings to learn how they might have been avoided; creates a register of offenders; and aims to ensure that criminal and civil courts dealing with domestic violence liaise with each other.

5.23 As yet, it is unknown how effective the Act is. Many victims do not want to see perpetrators criminalized and are reluctant to give evidence against them (Platt, Hester, Westmarland, Pearce, and Williamson, 2008).

## Criminal Injuries Compensation Scheme

5.24 Where a family member has been injured in a domestic violence incident, it may be possible for a claim to be made for compensation from the Criminal Injuries Compensation Board. However, there are two major requirements which must be met; the perpetrator of the violence must have been prosecuted unless there were good reasons not to do so, and the parties must have ceased to live together in the same household. This latter condition is clearly to prevent the violator from benefiting from his crime (see eg *R v CICB ex parte D K Mattison (1997)*).

# Civil remedies

5.25 Some victims of domestic violence may have little choice other than to turn to the civil law for protection. Others may prefer to take that route. It can prove to be more beneficial to the victim in that it places the responsibility for action under his or her control. It can raise the victim's awareness and empower him or her to escape from both the violence and from the status as a victim who must simply endure what is happening or rely on others for rescue from the situation,

## Family Law Act 1996, Part IV: occupation rights

5.26 The FLA 1996, Part IV is a very complex and convoluted piece of legislation in its provisions relating to occupation rights in the family home. It is underpinned by the value judgement that the protection of property rights is of overriding importance.

The Act was the result of a compromise by the government, after it was forced to withdraw its Domestic Violence Bill in 1995 which would have granted both married and unmarried partners similar rights to apply for occupation rights in the family home. A major successful press campaign against the Bill, proclaimed that the government's abandonment of

*...the live-in lovers bill was a happy outcome for those who care about the survival of the institution of marriage.*

5.27 The FLA 1996 provides for certain categories of family members to apply to the court for an order relating to the occupation of their family home; the family home includes any type of property which can reasonably be occupied in a domestic manner. In order to secure the Act's passage through Parliament, it was deemed necessary to differentiate between those family members who have statutory home rights proprietary rights; contractual rights, or other statutory rights in the family home, and those family members who have none of these rights (see Chapter 4 for a discussion of rights in the family home).

5.28 The first category of family members is referred to, as 'entitled' and the second category, as 'non-entitled'. These non-entitled persons, in spite of their bizarre designation, do have some rights under the FLA 1996. A third category of family members has no rights of occupation whatsoever but merely rights to apply for non-molestation orders which are discussed below.

## Entitled persons

5.29 The FLA 1996, s 33(1) provides that spouses or civil partners, who have a statutory home right (see Chapter 4) to occupy their family home under s 30 of the Act, may apply for one of the orders outlined in s 33(3). Prior to the Civil Partnership Act 2004 (CPA), these rights were referred to as matrimonial home rights.

5.30 Associated persons, who have a proprietary interest or contractual or statutory right relating to their family home, may also apply for a s 33(1) order. If they have none of these pre-existing rights, they remain outside the ambit of the FLA 1996 for the purposes of occupation orders.

Section 62(3) of the Act defines associated persons as:

- spouses or civil partners;
- former spouses or former civil partners;
- cohabitants or former cohabitants including same-sex cohabitants;
- those who live or who have lived in the same household provided the relationship was not one of employee/employer, landlord/tenant, lodger or boarder;
- relatives, including those related by marriage;
- fiancés or former fiancés;
- those who agreed to become civil partners even if they have terminated the agreement;
- those who have or have had an intimate personal relationship with each other which is or was of significant duration. Although the term suggests

a sexual element, it is not defined and arguably could include close celibate relationships;

- those who are related in relationship to a child either as parents or persons with parental responsibility;
- those who are parties to the same family law proceedings, eg adoptive parents and biological parents.

*Types of occupation orders for entitled persons*

5.31 The court may make regulatory or declaratory orders under FLA 1996, s 33(3). Regulatory orders are wide ranging and permit the applicant, *inter alia*, to return to the home and remain in it or part of it; state when and at what times the parties may occupy the home; prohibit, suspend or restrict the right to occupy it; demand that one party leaves the home or part of it; exclude one party from part of the home or the area in which the home is situated.

Declaratory orders state that the applicant has a right to occupy the family home which the court may enforce and exclude the other entitled person.

5.32 The court may also make orders under FLA 1996, s 40 requiring either party to make payments relating to the family home such as rent, mortgage payments, and renovation costs.

*Exercise of the court's discretion for entitled persons*

5.33 In deciding whether to grant an occupation order, the court must first apply the significant harm test in FLA 1996, s 33(7). It is worded in a rather long-winded manner and requires the court to balance the potential harm. It must first consider whether the applicant or any relevant child would be likely to suffer significant harm, which must be attributable to the conduct of the respondent, if the occupation order were not made. If the answer is yes, the court must make the order unless the respondent or any relevant child would suffer as great or greater harm than the applicant or child as a result of the order.

5.34 If the answer is no, then the court has a discretion to grant an order based on a wide range of factors, set out in FLA 1996, s 33(6) which might affect the rights of either party. These include housing needs, financial resources, the likely effect of any order, or any decision by the court not to exercise its discretion on the wellbeing of the parties and any relevant child, and the conduct of either of the parties. The child need not be a child of either of the parties but any child who might be affected by the decision. The conduct need not be conduct towards the other party but conduct towards another relevant person which might indicate to the court the possible future violent behaviour of the applicant or the respondent.

5.35 The courts are most reluctant to award occupation orders unless the circumstances are exceptional. Where both parties have proprietary rights in the family home, the courts have viewed the grant of an order as a draconian remedy because it interferes with proprietary rights which have generally been regarded as sacrosanct.

5.36 The harm claimed to have been suffered must result from the respondent's conduct and be more than mere inconvenience, as is shown in the following three decisions.

> In *Chalmers v Johns (1999)*, a mother and father had lived together for 25 years, occupying the family home as joint tenants. Their relationship was extremely tempestuous. The police were called regularly to investigate assaults by the mother on the father, and vice versa. The mother was a recovering alcoholic and eventually decided to leave home with their seven year-old daughter and move into temporary council accommodation. It was further away from the daughter's school than the family home. The court refused to grant the mother an occupation order; neither the mother nor the child was likely to suffer significant harm, attributable to the conduct of the father if the order were not made. There was no real risk of violence or any other harm to the child but merely inconvenience because of the child's longer journey to school.

5.37 In *Re Y (Children) (Occupation Order) (2000)*, a very dysfunctional family lived in separate parts of the family home. The wife lived with the pregnant 16 year-old daughter; the husband lived with the 13 year-old son. The husband, who was a diabetic, applied for an occupation order. The daughter was at war with the father but there was no evidence of violence by the mother towards her husband but only of his violence towards her. Harm to the husband, if any, resulted from his illness and not from his wife's conduct towards him. The court proceeded to determine occupation of the home using the discretionary factors in s 33(6). The pregnant daughter needed to be securely housed and the family home was held to be large enough to accommodate all the parties separately.

5.38 In *B v B (1999)*, the husband and wife were tenants of the family home. They lived there with their baby daughter and a child, aged six, from the husband's previous marriage. The wife left home with the baby because of her husband's violence towards her; the husband and his six year-old remained in the home. The council re-housed her in unsuitable temporary bed and breakfast accommodation and she applied to the court for, *inter alia*, an occupation order. The Court of Appeal held, after weighing the potential harm to the respective parties, that the husband's child would suffer more harm if an occupation order were made than the wife and baby would, if it were not; the position of the parties would simply be reversed. The husband and his child would be placed in accommodation similar to the unsuitable temporary accommodation which the wife and baby were already occupying. The child would have to change schools or be taken into the care of social services. The mother, on the other hand, would soon be re-housed by the council in more suitable permanent accommodation; she had, therefore, failed to satisfy the significant harm test.

### *Duration of occupation orders for entitled persons*

5.39 Because the order may be granted for an unlimited period of time under FLA 1996, s 33(10), courts are wary of granting them too easily. Judges are also aware that once an order has been granted, that status quo may prevail in any later ancillary proceedings related to a spouse's divorce, judicial separation or annulment, or to the dissolution, or grant of a separation or nullity order for a civil partner.

## Non-entitled persons

5.40 Under FLA 1996, s 35 applications may be made by for orders relating to occupation of the family home by former spouses or former civil partners. Section 36 of the Act makes provision for applications by heterosexual or same-sex cohabitants or former cohabitants who are living in, or who have lived in, a relationship as if a spouse or civil partner. All these persons are defined as non-entitled if they have no statutory home right, proprietary, contractual, or other statutory rights to occupy their family or former family home.

### *Types of occupation orders for non-entitled persons*

5.41 The orders for which non-entitled persons may apply are very similar to those applicable to entitled persons except that, if the court decides to make an order, it has the additional power to grant the applicant the right not to be evicted or the right to enter the property for the duration of the order (see FLA 1996, ss 35(3), (4), 36(3), (4)). The reason for this is self-evident in that the non-entitled person would be unable to benefit from an order without first of all being allowed to remain in, or enter into, the property. Entitled persons already have this right by way of a family home right or by way of property law.

## Exercise of the court's discretion for former spouses or civil partners

5.42 Those applicants whose marriage or civil partnership has ended receive more preferential treatment than cohabitants but less preferential treatment than married applicants. FLA 1996, s 35(6) requires the court to consider, in addition to all the factors relating to entitled applicants, the length of time the parties have been apart, the length of time since the marriage or civil partnership formally ended, and the existence of certain proceedings between the parties relating to children, finances, or property.

5.43 In *S v F (Occupation Order) (2000)*, the parents were divorced and their two children, a boy and a girl, aged 17 and 15, stayed with their mother in the former matrimonial home in London. Both parents had remarried and acquired new families. The mother eventually announced that she was moving to the country. Both children, who were at a critical stage in their education, were opposed to the move, in particular the son who indicated that he would not agree to it. The father applied for an occupation order which would permit him to move back with his new family into the matrimonial home and provide a home for his son there.

The court considered, *inter alia*, the housing needs and resources of the parties and all their children; the effect on the health and wellbeing of the parties if the order was made; the conduct of the parties; and the length of the parties' separation. The father's financial position was far weaker, at least in the short term, than the mother's. The grant of an occupation order might lead to some financial inconvenience for the mother, whereas it would provide essential security for the son and the rest of the family. As regards the conduct of the parties, the mother's sudden change of plan for her children and her failure to consult the father made her partly responsible at least for the son's implacable refusal to move. Although the parties had been separated for a long time each of them had a continuing parental responsibility for the children.

The court, after balancing all the factors, granted an occupation order to the father which would permit him to return to the property for six months or until the ancillary relief proceedings between the parties were resolved. He was also ordered to undertake to make the mortgage payments.

5.44 FLA 1996, s 35(8) provides that if the court decides to make an order and it appears that the applicant or a child might suffer significant harm, it must then proceed to balance the harm which might result to the parties before determining the precise nature of the order. This differs from the provisions for entitled persons where, if there is evidence of significant harm, the balance of harm test is carried out first. It is only when the court rejects the evidence of significant harm that it proceeds to consider other relevant factors.

### Duration of orders for former spouses or civil partners

5.45 FLA 1996, s 35(10) provides that an order may be granted for up to six months and may be renewed for further periods of six months.

### Exercise of the court's discretion for cohabitants and former cohabitants

5.46 Both cohabitants and former cohabitants are treated slightly differently from former spouses or civil partners, and it is questionable why this is so. They are the family members who are more likely to be at risk, and they have no other legal rights, such as financial maintenance, to help them if they need to find alternative accommodation.

5.47 FLA 1996, s 36(6) provides a list of factors which the court must take into account in determining any order. They include the nature of the parties' relationship and in particular the level of commitment involved in it, the length of time they were together, whether they have joint children or children for whom they have joint responsibility, and the length of time that has gone by since they ceased to live together.

5.48 The balance of harm test for cohabitants is part of the court's overall discretion and is not looked at as a separate issue.

### Duration of orders for cohabitants and former cohabitants

5.49 In keeping with the general approach that this category should be treated less generously than entitled persons or non-entitled former spouses or civil partners, any occupation order is limited to six months in the first instance and may be renewed for a further six months but for no longer.

### Circumstances where neither of the spouses, civil partners, former spouses, former civil partners, or cohabitants have rights to occupy the property

5.50 It will be rare to find a situation where none of these persons have rights to occupy the property which they are or have been occupying as their family home; it is likely to be limited to those who are squatting or who have bare licences. FLA 1996, s 37 provides for such an eventuality and allows orders of very limited effect to be made in favour of such applicants.

### Enforcement of occupation orders for both entitled and non-entitled persons

5.51 The court may attach a power of arrest to an order. FLA 1996, s 47(2) makes such an attachment mandatory if there has been violence or threats of violence towards the victim, unless the court is satisfied that it is not necessary to do so. Where the respondent is in breach of an order, he will be in contempt of court and may receive a custodial sentence.

## Family Law Act 1996, Part IV: non-molestation orders

### Molestation

5.52 The word is not defined in the FLA 1996, but it has been accepted that it includes a wide variety of threatening conduct such as physical violence, serious pestering, and psychological harassment.

> Sir Stephen Brown in *C v C (Non-molestation Order: Jurisdiction) (1998)* explained that:
>
> *...there is no legal definition of 'molestation'...It is a matter which has to be considered in relation to the particular facts of particular cases. It implies some*

*quite deliberate conduct which is aimed at a high degree of harassment of the applicant.*

He declined to grant an order against a wife who had given a tabloid newspaper information about the applicant's conduct towards her and two former wives. He maintained that the conduct was insufficient and was merely an attempt by the applicant to impose a gagging order to prevent press publication. In his view, the applicant was more concerned with damage to his reputation than with any concern to protect himself from molestation.

5.53 Ormerod LJ in **Horner v Horner (1982)** maintained that:

*I have no doubt that the word 'molesting'...does not imply necessarily either violence or threats of violence. It applies to any conduct which can properly be regarded as such a degree of harassment as to call for the intervention of the court.*

He accepted that a husband had molested his wife when he telephoned the school, where his wife was a teacher, to make unpleasant accusations against her. The husband had also placed posters making crude comments about his wife outside the school to draw the attention of parents who were collecting their children.

5.54 In **C v C (2001)**, the court considered whether the making of allegations by a husband to third parties about his wife's sexual activities was molestation or mere freedom of speech. The court ruled that it was conduct engaged in, in order to cause alarm and distress to his wife and children.

(For further examples of molestation see also **Vaughan v Vaughan (1973)**—the husband continually called at his wife's home and workplace after their relationship was over; **George v George (1986)**—the husband, whose wife had left him for a lesbian relationship, wrote angry letters to her and screamed abuse in an obscene manner when she collected the children; **Spencer v Camacho (1983)**—the searching of a partner's personal property was held to be a form of harassment; **Johnson v Walton (1990)**—a man sent private photographs picturing his partner in semi-nude poses to a newspaper.)

## Who may apply

5.55 FLA 1996, s 42(2)(a) takes a more generous approach towards applications for non-molestation orders. All associated persons may apply, and as was seen above, the definition of such persons in FLA 1996, s 62(3) includes a wide range of familial relationships. There still remains one group of persons omitted from the list and that is persons who have had a non-cohabiting relationship with each other, which cannot be described as intimate because there was no sexual relationship, but nevertheless there was a familial or emotional element to it. Should such persons experience molestation, they will be forced to seek alternative remedies under the Protection from Harassment Act 1997 (see below).

## The court's discretion

5.56  FLA 1996, s 42(5) gives the court discretion to take into account all the circumstances of the case, including the need to safeguard the health, safety, and wellbeing of the applicant or relevant child, in determining whether to exercise its powers and if so, how. It is a future-directed provision, which is aimed at protecting the applicant from violence, rather than a past-centred one which punishes the perpetrator for having already molested the victim. Of course, past conduct may be of relevance in that it might be indicative of the risk of further violence to come.

5.57  An order will not be made against a person if he or she is unable to control his or her behaviour.

> In *Banks v Banks (1999)*, a husband was refused an order because his wife's conduct was caused by her mental illness; she could do nothing to change it.

## Nature of the order

5.58  The order may be expressed in general terms forbidding molestation in any form or it may be specifically worded to suit the particular behaviour complained of by the applicant. The court may accept an undertaking by the perpetrator of the violence rather than imposing an order on him.

## Duration

5.59  Non-molestation orders may be made for a fixed period or an indefinite one depending on the nature of the requirements which will prevent harm to the applicant.

## Enforcement

5.60  Those who have experienced molestation need to know that non-molestation orders will protect them from further similar behaviour or worse. Waving a non-molestation order when faced with domestic violence gives little comfort to the victim and may only serve to enrage the perpetrator.

5.61  Since the enactment of the Domestic Violence, Crime and Victims Act 2004, there is no longer the possibility of a court attaching a power of arrest to an order. However, those who breach such orders may now be dealt with under the criminal procedure provided for in the new s 42A of the 1996 Act. Hill (2005) has suggested that the criminalization of breaches of non-molestation orders is preferred by the police and is an admission by Parliament of the failure of the power of arrest.

5.62  Those who disregard non-molestation orders may also be imprisoned for the offence of contempt of court. However, Hale LJ, in *Hale v Tanner (2000)*, maintained that a custodial sentence should not be automatic. She accepted that when relationships break down, non-molestation orders might be thoughtlessly disregarded in the resulting emotionally charged situation. She held that courts should take into account all the circumstances before resorting to imprisoning offenders and reduced a six-month prison sentence to 28 days. The respondent in this case, a woman, in breach of an injunction, had continued to make threatening telephone calls to her ex-boyfriend and his new girlfriend.

## Protection from Harassment Act 1997

5.63 The Protection from Harassment Act 1997 (discussed above) also provides for civil remedies for harassment. Prior to the enactment of the Domestic Violence, Crime and Victims Act 2004, the 1997 Act tended to be used to fill the gaps in the FLA 1996. It is now likely that the Protection from Harassment Act 1997 will, for the most part, revert to its original purpose, which was to protect from molestation those who are not in any type of familial relationship with their attacker. It may, however, continue to serve a purpose in protecting those who are, or have been, in close, quasi-familial, non-cohabiting, non-sexual relationships with the person who has been harassing them.

5.64 Sections 1 and 3 of the Act provide that any person who is the victim of harassment may seek an injunction or damages. Any breach of the injunction is a criminal offence. Harassment is not defined in the Act but must involve a course of conduct which is perceived objectively as harassment. The behaviour complained of must, therefore, take place on more than one occasion. Mental illness is no defence.

## Injunctions in other civil proceedings

5.65 Where the parties are involved in other civil proceedings, the Supreme Court Act 1981, s 37 allows the court to grant an injunction against molestation.

> In *Burris v Azadani (1996)*, for example, the Court of Appeal held that it had the power to grant an injunction in divorce or other proceedings to prevent the respondent from coming within 50 yards of the applicant's home.

# Domestic violence and human rights

5.66 The Human Rights Act 1998 (HRA 1998) has implications for the treatment of victims of domestic violence and also for those investigating it. The European Convention on Human Rights 1950 (ECHR) provides for the right to life (Art 2); the right not to be subjected to torture, inhuman or degrading treatment (Art 3);

the right to liberty (Art 5); the right to respect for private and family life (Art 8), and the right to enjoy Convention rights without discrimination (Art 14).

5.67 There are positive obligations placed on all public bodies to offer protection from violence. In all incidents of domestic violence, the police must take appropriate action, including, where permissible, the arrest of the perpetrator. Where there is no power of arrest the police should provide information about support services and refer victims to appropriate agencies (see http://www.thamesvalley.police.uk/).

# Asylum and domestic violence

5.68 Those who fear persecution in their home countries for reasons, *inter alia*, of membership of a particular social group may seek asylum in the UK. Women suffering from domestic violence abroad have had serious difficulties in having this form of persecution accepted as a ground for seeking asylum in the UK. The following decision did, however, accept it as a relevant ground.

> In *Burris v Azadani (1996)*, two Pakistani women who had been forced to leave their homes by their husbands and risked being falsely accused of adultery in Pakistan, sought asylum. They maintained that the state would not protect them and that they would face the risk of criminal proceedings for sexual immorality if they were forced to return to Pakistan. They claimed that they were refugees since they had a well-founded fear of persecution for reasons of 'membership of a particular social group' within the meaning of the Convention Relating to the Status of Refugees 1951, Art 1A(2).
>
> The House of Lords granted their appeal and allowed them asylum. It held that on its true construction, Art 1A(2) applied to whatever groups might be regarded as coming within the Convention's anti-discriminatory objectives, namely those groups whose members shared a common unchangeable characteristic and were discriminated against in matters of fundamental human rights. Women could claim to be members of such a group if they lived in a society, such as Pakistan, which discriminated against them on the grounds of sex, and it was irrelevant that certain women might be able to avoid the impact of persecution. Furthermore, the persecution they feared was caused by their membership of a social group since the Pakistani State denied them protection from violence which it would have given to men.

# Forced marriage and domestic violence

5.69 Recent concerns about domestic violence have centred on the issue of forced marriage. A forced marriage is one where one, or both, of the parties entered into it under duress. The force used may be either emotional or physical, or both. The majority of these marriages involve young people, primarily female, under the age of 18, whose parents are immigrants from countries which support the practice. The smaller number of males who appear to be affected by forced marriage may be because men who have been forced to marry accept the situation and find alternate means of coping silently. Providing they appear to conform outwardly with parental wishes, they are more likely than women to have the freedom to continue to lead lives of their own choosing including indulging in extra-marital affairs. There are instances of parents forcing a male child to marry if they suspect that he is gay.

5.70 Forced marriages may take place in England and Wales or in the country of the victims' parental origin. In some cases, victims have been tricked into travelling abroad, on the pretext that a holiday, or a family gathering, has been arranged. On their arrival, they are told that they are to be married. It is very difficult for a young person to rebel when he or she is in a strange place without financial resources or a passport (often confiscated by the parents on arrival in the country). There is no one to whom he or she may turn for help; the community is likely to support the parents.

5.71 Munby J in **NS v MI (2007)** stated firmly that there is a distinct difference between arranged marriages, where parents seek spouses for their children from their cultural community and allow their children a right of veto, and forced marriages. He maintained that arranged marriage which is a conventional concept in many immigrant cultures can be advantageous and should be respected and supported.

5.72 However, the dividing line between forced marriages and arranged marriages can be a rather fine one. Young people who have been brought up to respect and obey their parents' wishes may find it difficult to object to an arranged marriage even where there are no threats of violence or overt emotional pressure. Their cultural beliefs may prevent them from even recognizing the covert emotional force which is a feature of some arranged marriages.

## The extent of the problem

5.73 It is not easy to state with confidence how prevalent forced marriage is. Many of the victims, quite understandably, do not discuss it openly; they are too afraid to do so. Government statistics do not reveal forced marriages; they are often hidden within crime statistics where they will be reported as incidences of domestic violence, rape, assault or murder. Others will be hidden in statistics relating to annulment of marriage.

5.74 One important, albeit limited, source of information comes from the Forced Marriage Unit. This Unit was set up, and funded, as a joint venture by the Foreign

Office and Home Office in 2005, to deal with the problem (http://www.fco.gov.uk/en/travel-and-living-abroad/when-things-go-wrong/forced-marriage). In 2009 the Unit gave advice or support to 1,682 cases; 86 per cent of these cases involved females and 14 per cent involved males; calls and emails from males had increased by 65 per cent from the previous year involved males. Since its inauguration, the Unit has helped to rescue many victims; its youngest aged 11, was flown back to England from Dhaka, Bangladesh, after her parents had agreed to marry her to a Bangladeshi (see ***SB v RB (2008)***).

5.75 A government funded study in 2008 revealed that the incidence of forced marriage is almost certainly much greater than had been previously thought. The study which centred on Luton, a town with a high immigrant population found that more than 300 forced marriages were reported to various authorities, including the police and women's aid organizations, in one year alone. Nazia Khanum, who was responsible for the study suggested that the real number of forced marriages in the UK is likely to be closer to 4,000. The Luton report's victims were primarily Muslim women from families of Pakistani and Bangladeshi origin.

## Explanations of forced marriage

5.76 The cultural norms, within sub-groups of certain immigrant communities lead parents to maintain that their greater age, wisdom and experience give them a better understanding of their children's long-term welfare than the children have themselves. They claim that their right to assert their authority and give their children a good start in married life is sanctioned by custom, religion and common sense, and their children's resistance merely proves their immaturity.

5.77 Forcing ones children to marry may be seen as a form of bullying behaviour and like many other types of physical or emotional bullying conduct, is motivated, to a great extent, by fear. Members of these sub groups remain fiercely attached to the cultural values which were inculcated in them during their own upbringing in their countries of origin. They are fearful of losing their cultural identity as a consequence of coming to live in the UK. There is a cultural expectation that daughters will live at home, and be taken care of, until they marry. They may be seen as an economic burden to the family, a burden which will be relieved only by marriage. Parents fear that their children will accept the values which they are subjected to at school and, in particular, that their daughters will be at risk of finding unsuitable boy friends, and indulging in pre-marital sex, which might ruin any possibility of a marriage within the cultural community. The sooner after puberty their daughters are married, the less chance there will be of this happening.

5.78 Some parents attempt to organize marriages abroad for their mentally handicapped children who would lack capacity to marry in the UK (see Chapter 2; see also *City of Westminster v IC (by his friend the official solicitor) and KC and NN (2008)*).

5.79 Those who engage in the practice of forced marriage tend to live in tight knit communities which consist, primarily, of families from similar cultural backgrounds. The community is an important source of help and stability and a reminder of the 'home' which they have left behind. Parents would rather make their children conform than risk criticism and rejection by the community. Who will then care for them in their old age if their children marry outside of their community?

5.80 There are also economic explanations of forced marriage. It can be seen as a medium of exchange which may be used to amass, or retain, wealth, particularly so when the marriage is between members of the same extended family. Marriages may also be used to create, or redeem debts between families. They permit access to British nationality for potential migrants from the parents' home country. This has a high financial value and may be a very valuable bargaining tool in family wealth creation.

## Consequences of forced marriage

5.81 In 2004, the Home Secretary, David Blunkett, stated:

*Forced marriage is simply an abuse of human rights. It is a form of domestic violence that dehumanises people by denying them their right to choose how to live their lives. Valuing individual citizens, their dignity and the contribution they have to make to society in their own right is a central part of our drive for strong, active communities. The appalling practice of forced marriage represents the opposite extreme and that is why Government is taking tough action to eradicate it.*

*(Press release announcing the launch of the Forced Marriage Unit in 2005)*

5.82 Forced marriages have very serious consequences for their victims. By their very nature, they involve rape, as well as emotional violence. Physical violence and other forms of sexual abuse are common. Where the forced marriage is with an older man, young women, who lack any education relating to sexually transmitted disease, are at risk of infection. They are reluctant to ask questions about the man's previous sexual history.

5.83 Victims become isolated from their school peer group and friends. Their education is disrupted because they are removed from school to be married abroad. They are more likely to have children soon after marriage and are less likely to seek medical care or help from social services. They become economically dependent on their spouse, and his family with whom the couple will live, if the family is resident in the UK. This makes it even more difficult for young women to leave an unsatisfactory marriage. They risk being ill treated by the extended family.

5.84 Where a woman is particularly recalcitrant and tries to escape from a forced marriage, severe physical brutality, and even murder is not unknown. Many victims are abducted and become prisoners of their families.

> In 2008, an NHS doctor, Dr Humayra Abedin, received a telephone call informing her that her mother was seriously ill. She returned to Bangladesh but on her arrival realized that the call was a ruse to lure her home and force her to marry a Bangladeshi man. She alerted friends in England, and a Bangladeshi human rights organization, Ain O Salish Kendra (ASK), sent a representative to look for her at the family home. Prior to their arrival, her family arranged for her to be removed. Humayra's hands were tied behind her back and her head was covered with a cloth. She was bundled into an ambulance and was afraid that she would be killed. She arrived at a psychiatric hospital where she was injected daily with psychiatric drugs for two months. The Bangladeshi court acting on a Forced Marriage Act order (see below), issued by the English court, ordered her release and she returned to England (unreported High Court, December 2008).

5.85 Many young women, who are no longer virgins, either because they are sexually experienced or because their hymen has been damaged for other reasons, are terrified of a forced marriage. They are afraid that their lack of virginity will be discovered and this will lead to further punishment. To avoid sanctions, such women may seek hymenoplasty, more commonly known as re-virginization surgery.

## The Forced Marriage (Civil Protection) Act 2007

5.86 The Act illustrates what can be done to reduce domestic violence when the government is seriously committed to doing so. Not only does it provide legal remedies for victims, or prospective victims, of forced marriage, the rapidity with which it passed through Parliament, and came into force, has drawn attention to the importance of the problem. England has led the way in its determination to eradicate forced marriage, and the Act has been supported by a concerted campaign in schools and in the communities where forced marriage is likely to occur.

5.87 The Act amends the FLA 1996 and inserts a new Part 4A. It provides for applications for a Forced Marriage Protection Order (FMPO) not only by victims of forced marriages and those at risk of a forced marriage, but also by third parties who are concerned that a forced marriage has been planned, An FMPO may be made not only against the person or persons who are forcing someone to marry but also against anyone who associated with the coercion. The orders may contain a power of arrest.

5.88 Orders may relate to conduct which is about to take place, or has already taken place, in the UK or abroad. They are open ended and dependent on the circumstances;

The courts may, *inter alia*, seize the respondent's passport; require the respondent to reveal the whereabouts of the victim; order the respondent not to contact the victim; allow the victim to assume a new identity; order that a marriage may not take place; order the respondent that the victim may not be taken out of the country, and grant the victim a personal protection order.

5.89 Critics of the Act have argued that it lacks teeth because it fails to make forced marriage a crime. Nevertheless, the Act has drawn attention to the problem, and may deter some perpetrators from attempting to force a person into marriage because their behaviour will become publicized by means of court hearings. The Act may also persuade victims to come forward in the knowledge that their action will not result in a criminal prosecution of their parents. Dr Abedin (see above) made clear that she did not wish to see her parents punished.

## Other remedies aimed at the prevention of forced marriage

### Immigration controls

5.90 In November 2008 the minimum age for visas for anyone coming from abroad to marry, or because they have married, a British citizen was increased from 18 to 21 years. This is of limited help because it will do nothing to help victims forced to marry older men, but it has sent a clear message to parents contemplating marrying their children to other young people living abroad.

5.91 A new Code of Practice was published in March 2009 setting out how an application for a marriage visa or leave to remain in the United Kingdom as a husband or wife will be decided if someone is identified as vulnerable to a forced marriage. Indefinite leave to remain will be revoked which means the foreign national who is a party to the marriage will be liable to expulsion from the country.

5.92 Further plans are afoot to introduce a requirement for British citizens and permanent residents who are seeking to sponsor a spouse to come to the UK to declare their intention before leaving the UK and marrying abroad.

### The inherent jurisdiction

5.93    In *Re SK (An Adult) (Forced Marriage: Appropriate Relief) (2004)*, a young adult woman resident in England was reported to be in Bangladesh, the country from where her parents had emigrated to England. She was thought to be being kept there against her will and possibly forced to marry. An application was made on her behalf, and without her knowledge, by her litigation friend, to the High Court which held that it was within the court's inherent jurisdiction to make an order requiring members of the woman's family to arrange for her to be seen by an appropriate official at the High Commission in

Dhaka to ascertain what her true wishes were. Singer J also stated that other members of the woman's family in this country might be encouraged to give information about the woman's whereabouts as a result of the orders. The woman was interviewed and asked for the order to be withdrawn because she was not in need of the court's protection.

The judgment ended with a strong condemnation of forced marriage. Singer J maintained:

*Although therefore in this particular case it seems that the anxieties giving rise to the proceedings may have been ill-founded, their utility has been to clarify to this family (if clarification may have been needed) the importance these courts place on the right of the individual to exercise choice in this most intimate area of decision-making. There can be no doubt that a very significant number of young persons find themselves coerced into marriage each year, or subject to that threat. The count was 105 during the past year through the Islamabad High Commission alone, of whom about 20% of those seeking assistance were male teenagers or young men. It seems reasonable to suppose that these known cases may constitute a representative sample only.*

## Wardship

5.94    Where a person under the age of 18, who is British, is at risk of a forced marriage, a court may make him or her a ward of court regardless of where he or she lives. In *Re B; RB v FB and MA (2008)*, a father who was British returned to Pakistan to live there. He died in Pakistan, and his wife tried to force their daughter into marriage. The daughter who had never lived outside Pakistan sought help from the British High Commission in Islamabad. She was made a ward of court and went to Scotland to join her half-brother who lived there.

## Nullity

5.95  The remedy of nullity has become of increasing importance in the battle against forced marriage (see Chapter 3). More young people have begun to realize that they do not have to remain in a marriage to which they did not consent.

In *NS v MI (2006)*, Munby J reviewed the law relating to nullity of marriage in the context of a forced marriage. The petitioner, a young British girl, had lived in the UK all her life. When she was aged 16, she was taken to Pakistan by her mother under the pretext that she was going for a holiday. Her parents reassured her before they left the UK that she would not be married whilst she was there. The young girl rapidly realized that she had been lied to, and repeatedly asked to be allowed to return home to the UK. Her mother told her that she must remain in Pakistan until her father arrived for a holiday, and confiscated her daughter's passport. After her father's arrival, she was told that her parents would kill themselves if she did not marry her first cousin, a young Pakistani aged seventeen, whom she had never met before. She was also told that she would never return to the UK unless she went ahead with the marriage. The cousin told her that the marriage was merely a ploy to allow him to enter the UK. The marriage went ahead but it was not consummated and the girl eventually and after much pleading returned to the UK with her mother, and had no further contact with her husband. Four years later she sought a decree of nullity and maintained that her family had morally blackmailed her and pressurized her into marriage. Her family, by this stage, had accepted that the marriage was a mistake. They supported the daughter in her application to have her marriage annulled. The Pakistani husband did not object.

Munby J acknowledged that parental influences may be very subtle and reiterated his own words in *Re SA (Vulnerable Adult with Capacity: Marriage) (2006)*:

*... where the influence is that of a parent or other close and dominating relative, and where the arguments and persuasion are based upon personal affection or duty, religious beliefs, powerful social or cultural conventions, or asserted social, familial or domestic obligations, the influence may, as Butler-Sloss LJ put it in Re T (Adult: Refusal of Treatment), be subtle, insidious, pervasive and powerful. In such cases, moreover, very little pressure may suffice to bring about the desired result.*

He also stressed that:

*We must guard against the risk of stereotyping. We must be careful to ensure that our understandable concern to protect vulnerable children (or, indeed, vulnerable young adults) does not lead us to interfere inappropriately—and if inappropriately then unjustly—with families merely because they cleave, as this family does, to mores, to cultural beliefs, more or less different from what is familiar to those who view life from a purely Euro-centric perspective.*

Munby J was concerned that a sensitive understanding should be shown to petitioners with respect to the requirement that annulment cases should be held in open court. He explained that there might be circumstances where a petitioner might be reluctant to give evidence if certain people, such as those responsible for the duress, were to be present in court; she might be placed at risk. In those cases it would be possible for the petitioner's evidence to be give behind a screen or via a video link.

## Inter-country cooperation

5.96 Government representatives hold regular consultations with their counterparts in, and the judiciary of, those countries where forced marriages of British citizens are likely to take place.

# A critique of current approaches to domestic violence—the way forward

5.97 In 2005, the UK government declared its commitment to continue to develop programmes devoted to the eradication of domestic violence. It budgeted £14 million to fund a multi-agency approach aimed at prevention, protection, and justice and support for the victims. Specialist domestic violence courts have been introduced, which have the remit to coordinate both civil and criminal responses to domestic violence have been introduced. Yet, it is disappointing to learn that the vast incidence of domestic violence continues.

5.98 In 2008, a Home Affairs Select Committee concluded, rather depressingly, that the government had failed in significant areas to fulfil its promise. In particular, it criticized the fact that the approach was disproportionately focused on a criminal based solution rather than on effective prevention which it thought should begin in school. More resources were needed to help deal with victims of domestic violence problem, including additional refuges and other forms of emergency housing. It also found that more needed to be done in the area of forced marriages. Rather more worrying was the Committee's conclusion that the police were issuing cautions as an alternative to a charge under the Domestic Violence, Crime and Victims Act 2004.

5.99 Conway (2004) has suggested that what is needed is a serious effort to alter the approach, which continues to prevail, that domestic violence is a private problem, difficult to eradicate, and by implication, culturally acceptable. He has argued that if the problem is to be solved funding must be provided for educational programmes in schools and refuge places. Courts should be encouraged to remove offenders from the areas in which their victims live instead of expecting the victims to flee. He regrets that even more women will have to die before lessons are learned that could perhaps have been learned by listening to the victims who sit in court waiting rooms on a daily basis.

5.100 In 2009, the Home Office consultation, *Together We Can End Violence Against Women and Girls Strategy*, ended. An advisory group then started work on how to educate young people. A joined up approach to the problem, alongside the sharing of information amongst all those whose professions are likely to bring them into contact with women, would seem to be a way forward.

5.101 The General Election in May 2010 saw a change of government, and promises of cuts in public spending. It is therefore unknown what funds will be available for the improvement of the lives of those who suffer from the effects of domestic violence.

5.102 In the meantime the existing remedies in criminal and civil law will have to be used to protect victims of domestic violence. Victims must be encouraged, not merely, to say that they want their attackers to change, but to be prepared to take civil action or give evidence in criminal prosecutions. Far too many victims continue to protect their attackers; they do not want them to go to prison. This is partly because they fear the loss of household income during the period of incarceration of their attacker, but also because they remain emotionally attached to, and in dysfunctional relationships with, violent partners. Perpetrators of violence must be helped to find new ways of expressing their frustrations in a non-violent manner, and victims must be helped to avoid relationships with violent partners, and learn how to walk away from any relationship which turns out to be violent.

## FURTHER READING

Addison N and Lawson-Cruttenden T, *Harassment Law and Practice* (Blackstone Press, 1999)

Barran D, 'Developments in Protecting Victims of Domestic Abuse' [2009] Fam Law 416

The Communities, Equalities and People Committee, Report 9, *The Implementation and Effect of the Forced Marriage (Civil Protection) Act 2007* (11 March 2010)

Conneely S, 'Domestic Violence and the Right to Asylum' [1998] Fam Law 761

Conway H, 'The Domestic Violence, Crime and Victims Bill' [2004] Fam Law 132

Crumley B, 'The Dilemma of 'Virginity' Restoration' *The Times*, 13 July 2008

Domestic Violence, Forced Marriage and 'Honour' Based Violence (HC 263-1 (2008))

Edwards S, *Policing Domestic Violence: Women, Law and the State* (Sage, 1991)

Edwards S, *Sex and Gender in the Legal Process* (Oxford University Press, 1996)

Edwards S, 'Descent into Murder: Provocation's Stricture—The Prognosis for Women Who Kill Men Who Abuse Them' [2007] JOCL 71 342

Edwards S and Welstead M, 'Death Before Familial Dishonour' (1999) NLJ 149

Gillen, 'Domestic Violence—In What Direction?' [2005] IFLJ (194)

Grand A, 'Allegations Of Violence: Prove It' [2009] Fam Law 522

Heaton C, McCullum L, Jogi R, *Forced Marriage* (Family Law 2009)

Hester M, 'Who Does What to Whom? Gender and Domestic Violence Perpetrators' http://www.nr-foundation.org.uk

Hester M, Westmarland N, Pearce J and Williamson E, Early evaluation of the Domestic Violence, Crime and Victims Act 2004 (Ministry of Justice Research Series 14/08 August 2008)

Hill R, 'The Domestic Violence, Crime and Victims Act 2004' [2005] Fam Law 35 (281) (474)

Home Office, Domestic Violence Delivery Plan Progress Report 2008–2009 http://www.homeoffice.gov.uk

House of Commons Domestic Violence Inquiry 2008 Home Affairs 6th Report May 2008 http://www.publications.parliament.uk

James B, 'Prosecuting Domestic Violence' [2008] Fam Law 456

Kaganas F, 'Occupation Orders under the Family Law Act 1996' [1999] CFLQ 193

Khanum N, Forced Marriage, Family Cohesion and Community Engagement: National Learning Through a Case study of Luton (2008) (Select Committee on Home Affairs Sixth Report www. Parliament.uk)

Lasch C, *Haven in a Heartless World: the Family Besieged* (Basic Books, 1977)

Lawson-Cruttenden T, 'Domestic Violence and Harassment: a Consideration of Part IV of the Family Law Act 1996 and the Protection from Harassment Act 1997' [1998] Fam Law 542

Lockton D and Ward R, *Domestic Violence* (Cavendish Publishing, 1997)

Logan M, 'Imprisonment for Domestic Violence' [2004] Fam Law 747

McCulloch J, 'A Curate's Egg? The Domestic Violence Bill' [2004] NLJ 5

McEwan I, *Enduring Love* (Vintage, 1998)

McGee C, *Childhood Experiences of Domestic Violence* (Jessica Kingsley Publishers, 2000)

Metropolitan Police, Review of MPS implementation of Forced Marriage (Civil Protection) Act 2007 (2010) http://www.mpa.gov.uk

Parkinson P and Humphreys C, 'Children who Witness Domestic Violence: the Implications for Child Protection' [1998] CFLQ 147

Patel H, 'Dowry Abuse' [2009] Fam Law 1092

Peacock G, 'Domestic Abuse Research' [1998] Fam Law 628

Phillips A, Dustin M, 'UK initiatives on forced marriage: Regulation, dialogue and exit' [2004] Political Studies 52(3) 531

Pizzey E and Forbes A, *Scream Quietly or the Neighbours will Hear* (Penguin, 1974)

Platt J, 'The Domestic Violence, Crime and Victims Act 2004 Part I: Is it Working?' [2008] Fam Law 642

Sanghera J, *Daughters of Shame* (Hodder 2009)

Segal M, 'The Ouster dilemma' [2009] Fam Law 297

Taylor-Browne J (Ed), *What Works in Reducing Domestic Violence?* (Whiting and Birch, 2001)

Tilbury N, 'Domestic Violence: Times are a 'Changing' [2001] NLJ 1796

Waller M, '*The English Marriage, Tales of Love, Money and Adultery* (John Murray) (2009)

Welstead M, 'Forced Marriage—Bifurcated Values in the UK' [2009] Denning Law Journal 49

Yarwood D, 'Domestic Abuse Research' [1999] Fam Law 114

## SELF-TEST QUESTIONS

1  Is it necessary to have a special law for victims of domestic violence?

2  Is there anyone who remains legally unprotected from domestic violence whom you might want to see protected?

3 Why do you think the legislators decided on different significant harm tests in the FLA 1996 for the determination of occupation orders for entitled persons and non-entitled persons?

4 Adam and Bella are married. They live in a two-bedroom cottage, title to which is registered in the name of Bella. They have a son, Christopher, aged two. Bella is pregnant and expects to give birth in three months' time. Adam is an alcoholic and, whilst charming and reasonable when sober, he resorts to extreme forms of behaviour when drunk. Earlier this year, Adam returned home drunk with Demelza and her two young sons, aged four and six. He told Bella that he had rescued Demelza from her violent lesbian lover Elspeth, and that from now on Demelza would be living in the cottage with him and her two sons.

Demelza had been living with Elspeth in a house registered in the sole name of Elspeth. When Bella protested, Adam screamed at her and waved an antique rifle in her face and told her to get out of the cottage. Although Bella knew the rifle was incapable of being fired, she was afraid and left the cottage. She took Christopher with her and they spent two weeks in a friend's house whilst he was out of the country on holiday. On the friend's return, Bella had nowhere to live and wanted to return home but only if Adam, Demelza and the latter's two children moved out. Demelza was prepared to leave on condition that Elspeth would allow her and Adam and her two sons to live in Elspeth's house. Demelza wanted Adam there to protect her from Elspeth. Elspeth refused to agree to Demelza's proposal and Demelza and Adam have nowhere else to go.

Advise Adam.

5 In 1999, Jeffrey and Karen married. Jeffrey moved into Karen's house which was registered in her sole name. In 2003, their twins were born and Jeffrey was unable to cope with the change in lifestyle. He was an artist and needed space and time to paint. He became increasingly irritated with the chaos in the house and moved out into a studio owned by Marigold who was married to Jeffrey's good friend, Leo. After living in the studio for several weeks, Jeffrey decided that he would like to have a long-term homosexual relationship with Leo. Marigold evicted Jeffrey from the studio and told Leo to leave the family home, which was also registered in her sole name. Leo had always looked after the two children of the marriage and refused to leave them with Marigold. Jeffrey invited Leo and the two children to move into Karen's house with him. On their arrival, Karen became hysterical and threw a bottle of wine at Leo's head. Leo received stitches at the local hospital. Jeffrey now does not believe that Karen is fit to care for the twins and wishes her to leave the house. He wants to return to the house and live there with Leo, and his children. Leo has volunteered to take care of all four children.

Advise Jeffrey.

6 Oliver and Peter are former civil partners who obtained a legal dissolution of their relationship three months ago. Since then they have been living separately. Oliver remained in the family home which was registered in his sole name, and it has been put up for sale. Peter has been working abroad until recently when he returned to

England at the end of his contract. When Peter returned to the family home, he found Oliver had moved his new lover, Quentin, and Quentin's elderly mother, into the house. Peter was very angry and jealous. He began an argument with Oliver which resulted in Oliver stabbing Peter with a carving knife. Peter is temporarily unable to work and has no money to re-house himself. He would like to return to the family home for a period of one year until he has recuperated and is able to find a new job and home. He is not prepared for Quentin and his mother to remain in the property but is prepared to accept that Oliver can live there on condition he keeps to his own suite of rooms and brings no new lovers back to the house during the next year.

Advise Peter whether a court would be likely to grant him what he wants.

# 6

# Ending relationships

**SUMMARY**

It appears now to be one of the accepted values of the developed world that many relationships will not last the lifetime of the parties and that, if a relationship has become unworkable, it is better for the parties to end it and minimize the potential bitterness and hostility between them. In this chapter we consider the ways in which the State controls the process of legally ending the relationships of marriage and civil partnerships.

Because cohabiting relationships come into existence without any formal legal process, there are no legal means by which they may be formally ended.

## Divorce

6.1 Spouses may not end their marriage on demand; just as they must meet certain legal requirements to enter into the relationship, they must also meet certain legal requirements to exit from it and revert to single status. The requirements for divorce present few major obstacles for most couples.

Once divorced, either one of them becomes free to enter into a subsequent marriage with a new partner, or even remarry a previous partner, if he or so wishes. The film stars Elizabeth Taylor and Richard Burton divorced each other after ten years of marriage and remarried one year later, only to divorce again nine months after their second marriage.

6.2 A decree of divorce releases the parties from all the rights and obligations of marriage. However, it also grants new post-marital rights and imposes new post-marital obligations on the divorced couple. These rights and obligations relate primarily to children, finances and property and may mean that many couples will remain locked into a relationship with each other for many years after they have divorced. These rights and duties will be considered in Chapter 7 and Chapter 16.

6.3 For the majority of couples, divorce is both emotionally and practically unpleasant. It is not what they had hoped for when they embarked, with optimism, on marriage. It is one of the more stress-inducing experiences of life which may be exacerbated by the primarily fault-based nature of the divorce process.

## Statistical evidence of divorce

6.4 In 2010, the Office for National Statistics reported that the divorce rate in England and Wales, as measured in 2008, was 11.2 divorcing people per 1,000 married population. The figure shows a fall of a little over 5 per cent from 2007. The last time the divorce rate was as low as this was in 1979. The 2008 statistics reveal that there were 22.8 divorces per 1,000 married men aged 25 to 29, and 26.0 divorces per 1,000 married women aged 25 to 29. This compared with 16.5 divorces per 1,000 married men aged 45 to 49 and 14.5 divorces per 1,000 married women aged 45 to 49. One in five men and women who obtained a divorce in 2008 had been divorced before, and 67 per cent of divorces were granted to female petitioners.

## Reasons for divorce and its consequences

6.5 Although there has been a fall in the divorce rate, it is still high. There has been considerable speculation over the reasons for this and the consequences for the institution of marriage and the effect on society. Social explanations for divorce include increased life expectancy; social changes in the nature of family life; higher expectations about marriage; a decrease in the birth rate; financial independence of women, and the fact that many marriages are based, unrealistically, on a romantic and idealized concept of love. Given these factors, it would be surprising if a significant number of marriages did not break down. Deech (1990), however, has argued that it is the divorce legislation itself which affects the divorce rate. She maintains that divorce increases whenever new divorce legislation, which makes divorce easier, comes into force.

6.6 Whatever explanations are given, it is generally acknowledged that divorce is inevitable and may even be beneficial in the long term for the individuals involved. However, divorce does have serious consequences for society. Children are regarded as the most likely victims, but the health and welfare of the couple at the time of the divorce is also likely to be at risk. For the State, divorce has serious economic consequences in terms of medical treatment for stress and depression experienced by the couple, and because of the level of welfare benefits which are necessary to enable many divorced families to cope financially.

# The divorce process—the special procedure

6.7 For those spouses who have mutually concluded that their marriage is at an end, the divorce procedure is comparatively straightforward. It is a quasi-administrative process, rather than a judicial process which is referred to as the 'special procedure'. The spouses do not normally need to appear in court. One of the spouses, referred to as the petitioner, will complete a standard set of forms which will be sent to the other spouse who is referred to as the respondent. These will be examined by a district judge who, if satisfied that all is in order, will grant the divorce decree.

In *R v Nottingham County Court, ex parte Byers (1985)*, it was held that:

*The objectives of the special procedure are simplicity, speed and economy. This does not mean that the essentials of the petition and proof of its contents should not be satisfied. They must be. It does mean...that there should be no room for over-meticulousness and over-technicality in approach. For example, provided that the essentials are satisfied, what does it matter if there is something in the petition or affidavit evidence which is unnecessary and so surplus?*

In *Bhaiji v Chauhan (2003)*, five married couples were all young people of Indian ethnicity. One of the parties to each marriage was a UK citizen and a long-standing resident of the UK. The other party to each marriage was an Indian citizen who had recently come to the UK and had used the marriage as a means of securing indefinite leave to remain in the UK. The couples, none of whom had children, were now attempting to divorce. Wilson J explained that:

*At the time of the presentation of a petition it is the duty of court staff to take a preliminary look at it and at the accompanying documents with a view to establishing that there is no obvious flaw in it, such as presentation within the first year of marriage. The staff at the family desk in the Bolton County Court began to sense that there were curious similarities in the form of some of the petitions presented there. Thus it was that these five suits were ultimately collected together, compared and, via a circuit judge of that court, referred to the Queen's Proctor. The only similarity of form between each of the five petitions is that the particulars of unreasonable behaviour, set out in either seven, eight or nine paragraphs, are clearly the product of the same type of word-processor. But there is a much more significant similarity between each of the petitions other than the fourth. It relates to the phraseology of the allegations....*

*This hearing may serve to bring to public attention the opportunity which exists for serious abuse both of our immigration rules and of our divorce laws; and inevitably one wonders whether the abuse is more widespread than reflected in this handful of five petitions presented in the county court in Bolton. The opportunity for abuse of our immigration rules is the opportunity for a spouse married to a UK citizen to secure indefinite leave to reside in the UK on the basis of a joint false representation that they intend to live permanently with each other. The opportunity for abuse of our divorce laws is the opportunity to procure an immediate divorce by the inclusion of false allegations of unreasonable behaviour in a petition presented once the marriage has been successfully used in securing indefinite leave. I am well aware that, after 2 years of separation, one spouse can, with the other's consent, lawfully obtain a divorce. Indeed it was submitted to me that there is no point in my dismissing the petitions because the parties to all the marriages will within the next year have become separated for 2 years and will thus be entitled to a divorce by consent. With respect, that argument entirely misses the point. In England and Wales divorce is not yet available simply upon joint demand immediately following separation. This unusual hearing has exposed a concerted attempt to bypass the requirements of the present law and, by use of bogus allegations of behaviour, to secure the immediate dissolution of marriages which have outlived their perceived usefulness.*

## Contested petitions

6.8 In the rare case that a respondent spouse does not wish to be divorced and decides to contest the petition, the 'special procedure' may not be used and there will be a full hearing of the petitioner's claim and the respondent's defence. Less than 3 per cent of all petitions are contested; to do so is costly and, in any event, is unlikely to succeed. The adversarial nature of contesting the petition may well result in a respondent making statements which, in themselves, contradict and defeat the respondent's attempts to claim that the marriage has not irretrievably broken down.

In *Hadjimilitis (Tsavliris) v Tsavliris (2003)*, the husband contested his wife's petition for divorce and argued that his wife was unhappy not because of his behaviour but, rather, because of her own. The judge found that the husband

*...despite the fact that he accepted that the wife had been unhappy at times, and in particular in the year or so before the petition was filed, he was unable to see that anything about the marital relationship had caused or contributed to this. He cited his alleged financial difficulties and the wife's materialistic approach as a cause, he cited the possibility that she had had affairs and he blamed her for being provocative by reason of her domestic, maternal and general character faults. He relied on her alleged depressive nature and above all he relied on the fact that the wife had planned and manipulated the divorce from the earliest days of the relationship for monetary gain. I formed the view that the husband was a man of limited emotional insight so that he could not recognise that his behaviour had anything to do with his wife's unhappiness...*

*I also take the view that the allegation by the husband that the marriage was effectively a charade by the wife from first to last is an allegation which so undermines the matrimonial relationship that no person could live with a person who made such an*

*allegation, thereby making it unreasonable for the wife to live with the husband and well-nigh impossible for there to be any possibility of reconciliation.*

6.9 A decree of divorce will be refused only when the respondent is able to prove that the petitioner's factual statement is incorrect and/or evidence that the marriage remains viable.

## A two-part process

6.10 The divorce decree is divided into two parts. The first part, the decree nisi, is pronounced in open court, normally without the attendance of either party. The second part, the decree absolute, is granted after a period of six weeks has elapsed. If there are no objections, the petitioner, or the respondent with the consent of the court, may apply for the decree absolute and it is only when this final decree has been made that the parties are free to marry again or enter into a civil partnership.

Before the court grants the decree, it must be satisfied that appropriate arrangements have been made for any children under the Matrimonial Causes Act 1973 (MCA 1973), s 41. If the court is not satisfied, it may delay the grant of the decree absolute.

# The requirements for divorce

6.11 It may seem rather obvious but the most important of all the requirements for divorce is that the spouses must have been validly married (see Chapter 3).

> In *Islam v Islam (2003)*, the marriage took place between a man named Nurul Islam, and a woman Panna Begum. The woman subsequently petitioned for divorce. The man named in the divorce petition as her husband denied that he had taken part in the marriage ceremony but eventually accepted that he was the father of the woman's child. The woman's main supporting witness was a friend who provided written evidence that she had been a witness at the marriage, was named as such on the marriage certificate, and had attended the celebratory lunch party after the wedding. She produced a photograph of the participants. However, on the second day of the divorce hearing, she withdrew her evidence. The wife, therefore, consented to her petition being dismissed. The court accepted that the 'husband's' signature was probably a forgery and granted him a declaration that he was not married. The court gave leave to the Treasury Solicitor to disclose the necessary papers to the proper authority to determine whether there should be a prosecution for perjury and/or conspiracy to pervert the course of justice.

6.12 The law does not allow a spouse to petition for divorce until one year has elapsed from the date on which the marriage took place. The reason for this is to encourage couples to take marriage seriously and not to give up on their relationship too soon.

This rule can be harsh for a spouse living in a very difficult relationship without any hope of improvement or reconciliation. Even if a spouse is violent, has lied about important matters which affect the marriage, such as his or her sexual orientation, or the existence of children from a previous relationship, or a life- threatening illness, the one year rule applies. There are no exceptions. After one year, a spouse may petition for divorce relying on events which took place in the first twelve months of marriage.

6.13 In order to divorce in England and Wales (the jusisdiction) a spouse must meet the requirements of domicile and habitual residence. These are:

- Both spouses, must be habitually resident or domiciled in the jurisdiction;

or

- both spouses were jointly habitually resident in the jurisdiction and one of them is still habitually resident in it;

or

- the petitioner or applicant has been habitually resident in the jurisdiction for the last 12 months;

or

- the respondent is habitually resident in the jurisdiction;

or

- the petitioner, or applicant, is domiciled and habitually resident in the jurisdiction and has resided in it for at least the last six months.

For the majority of couples, these requirements will be irrelevant because they have always lived in the jurisdiction. However, there are an increasing number of spouses in international relationships who will have to prove habitual residence or domicile. For instance, each spouse may have a different country of origin, may have married in a third country, and may live and/or work in a fourth country. A spouse may want to start legal proceedings here partly because he or she believes (and usually quite rightly so) that there are financial advantages to be gained from doing so.

It is easier to prove that one is habitually resident in the jurisdiction than it is to prove that one is domiciled in it. Habitual residence relates to the practical matter of where a person usually lives. It automatically changes if one moves to a new jurisdiction.

Domicile relates more to the intention a person has to be permanently resident in the jurisdiction. A person can remain domiciled in the jurisdiction even if they leave providing they retain sufficient links with it which prove that he or she does not intend to leave permanently (see *Kearley v Kearley (2010)*; *Z v Z (2010)*; *(Munro v Munro (2007))*).

# The ground for obtaining a divorce

6.14 The MCA 1973, s 1(1) provides that there is only one ground for divorce and that is that the marriage has irretrievably broken down. It is not sufficient for a spouse who wishes to divorce to merely state that the marriage has irretrievably broken down. The petitioner must also establish one of the five facts in MCA 1973, s 1(2), even where it is self-evident that the marriage is over has no future. For most spouses, the five facts will not present any major obstacles, other than the expenditure of a rather large amount of emotional energy and, in some cases significant legal costs.

6.15 In **Buffery v Buffery (1988)**, it was undeniable that the marriage had irretrievably broken down; the parties were totally unable to communicate with one another. The Court of Appeal found no evidence of any one of the five facts and could not, therefore, grant the petitioner a decree.

## The five facts—MCA 1973, s 1(2)

6.16 Three of the five facts listed in MCA 1973, s 1(2) are fault-based and perpetuate the idea that divorce involves an aggressor and a victim. The reality is that it is often difficult to determine which partner can be said to be at fault.

6.17 The fact relied on by the petitioner need not be the cause of the irretrievable breakdown of the marriage. Indeed, it may even prove to be a symptom rather than a cause of the breakdown.

6.18 Once the petitioner has provided a statement of any one of the five facts, the court must grant a decree of divorce unless it remains unconvinced that the marriage has irretrievably broken down.

6.19 In the light of the 'special procedure', the court will hardly ever have cause to consider the five facts in any detail, and it is rare to find a new decision involving any of the five facts. It is, nevertheless, necessary to understand the case law relating to them because a petitioner may fail to obtain a decree, or the petition may have to be re-submitted and the decree delayed, if the fact relied on is not stated accurately and truthfully, and the matter is referred to the court (see **Bhaji v Chauhan (2003)** above).

### Adultery and intolerability (MCA 1973, s 1(2)(a))

6.20 More than 25 per cent of all divorce petitions rely on this fact, and a petitioner can obtain a decree easily and rapidly. Allegations have been made that s 1(2)(a) leads spouses to collude with each other and may even encourage adultery.

6.21 It is not necessary for the petitioner to know the identity of the person with whom the respondent has committed adultery (the co-respondent). If it is known, he or she may be named in the divorce petition if the petitioner wishes.

6.22 Unless the respondent denies the adultery, the petitioner's word will be accepted by the court without further proof or investigation. If the respondent does deny the allegation, evidence will be necessary. A wife's conception of a child at a time when the petitioner was absent, or DNA evidence which proves that a child cannot be the biological child of the petitioner will be sufficient proof of adultery. DNA evidence which suggests that the respondent might be the father of another woman's child will also be evidence of adultery. Statistics suggest that at least 10 per cent of children are not the biological children of the men who believe themselves to be their fathers (Jackson 2004).

6.23 Although a spouse may not rely on his or her own adultery, that adultery will not prevent him or her from petitioning for divorce if the respondent spouse has also committed adultery.

### Definition of adultery

6.24 To petition for divorce using this fact, the respondent must have had voluntary penetrative sexual intercourse with a member of the opposite sex.

6.25 Sex which falls short of this definition is not adultery. President Clinton's famous statement that he had not committed adultery with Monica Lewinsky was strictly speaking correct even though he admitted to having engaged in oral sex.

> A couple, who met in an internet chat room and married, reinvented themselves in the virtual world known as Second Life. The husband began an adulterous virtual relationship with the virtual persona created by a woman online in America. His wife protested and petitioned for divorce. Because virtual adultery is not adultery for the purposes of divorce, she was forced to claim that this was behaviour which she could not reasonably be expected to live with. (*Daily Telegraph,* 14 November 2008).

6.26 There can be no allegation of adultery where the respondent was raped or where sexual intercourse took place within a valid polygamous marriage.

6.27 There are jurisdictions which have widened the definition of adultery to include same-sex sexual conduct.

> In *SEP v DDP (2005)*, the British Columbia Supreme Court granted a petition for divorce where the petitioner's husband had had a homosexual relationship during the marriage.

### *Intolerability*

6.28 Adultery itself is not evidence of marital breakdown; many relationships recover from spousal infidelity. However, the wording of s 1(2)(a) provides that a petitioner, in addition to maintaining that the respondent has committed adultery, must also be able to state that he or she finds it intolerable to live with the respondent. It would seem logical that the betrayed spouse should be able to seek a divorce stating that he or she finds it intolerable, as a result of the adultery, to continue living with the respondent. However, the courts have made clear that there need be no connection whatsoever between the adultery and the petitioner's claim of intolerability.

In *Cleary v Cleary (1974)*, it was held that it is sufficient, once adultery has been established, that the petitioner finds it intolerable to live with the respondent for whatever reason, however trivial. The test is subjective but requires more than a mere assertion; the petitioner must explain why it is that he finds it intolerable to live with the respondent. In Cleary (1974), Lord Denning explained:

*As a matter of interpretation, I think the two facts... are independent and should be so treated. Take this very case. The husband proves that the wife committed adultery and that he forgave her and took her back. That is one fact. He then proves that, after she comes back, she behaves in a way that makes it quite intolerable to live with her. She corresponds with the other man and goes out at night and finally leaves her husband, taking the children with her. That is another fact. It is in consequence of that second fact that he finds it intolerable—not in consequence of the previous adultery. On that evidence, it is quite plain that the marriage has broken down irretrievably. He complies with [the section]... by proving (a) her adultery which was forgiven; and (b) her subsequent conduct (not adultery), which makes it intolerable to live with her.*

*I would say one word more. In Rayden on Divorce it is suggested (referring to an extra-judicial lecture by Sir Jocelyn Simon) '... it may even be his own adultery which leads him to find it intolerable to live with the respondent'. I cannot accept that suggestion. Suppose a wife committed adultery five years ago. The husband forgives her and takes her back. He then falls in love with another woman and commits adultery with her. He may say that he finds it intolerable to live with his wife, but that is palpably untrue. It was quite tolerable for five years: and it is not rendered intolerable by his love for another woman. That illustration shows that the judges in such cases as these should not accept the man's bare assertion that he finds it intolerable. In particular, what conduct on the part of the wife has made it intolerable? It may be her previous adultery. It may be something else. But whatever it is, the judge must be satisfied that the husband finds it intolerable to live with her.*

In *Roper v Roper (1972)*, it was accepted that once a single act of adultery had taken place, a wife who found it intolerable to live with her husband because he blew his nose too frequently had fulfilled the two requirements. The court granted her petition.

## *Continuing cohabitation*

6.29 Where the petitioner lives with the respondent for six months or more after learning of the adultery, he or she may not rely on MCA 1973, s 1(2)(a). It is assumed that he or she has not satisfied the test that it is intolerable to live with the respondent. If the spouses cohabit for a lesser period of time, the respondent may rely on the earlier adultery. The provision allows spouses to resume cohabitation after adultery has taken place and make an effort to repair their marriage but leaves open the option of divorce if their efforts fail.

## Behaviour (MCA 1973, s (1)(2)(b))

6.30 Behaviour is the fact which is most commonly relied on to prove irretrievable breakdown of the marriage. Although this fact is commonly referred to as 'unreasonable behaviour', it is not the respondent's behaviour itself which must be unreasonable. It is the expectation that the petitioner should continue to live with the respondent's behaviour which must be seen as an unreasonable one (see *Bannister v Bannister (1980)*). The behaviour may be active or passive.

6.31 In *Livingstone-Stallard v Livingstone-Stallard (1974)*, Dunn LJ suggested that the correct question to ask was:

> ...would any right-thinking person come to the conclusion that this husband has behaved in such a way that this wife cannot reasonably be expected to live with him, taking into account the whole of the circumstances and the characters and personalities of the parties?

Dunn LJ accepted that:

> ...her husband was...a critical and non-loving man who treated her from the very first not as a wife but as a rather stupid child. She said that even on their honeymoon, when they spent a week at the Cumberland Hotel, her husband was abusive to her. It is quite plain from the evidence of the husband himself that even at that stage there were difficulties between them. The wife had referred to a holiday with a female cousin the previous summer; the husband objected to this; and I accept the wife's evidence that the result was to make him rude, boorish and critical of her during the honeymoon.
>
> ...
>
> from the time that they started married life together the husband criticised her behaviour, her friends, her way of life, her cooking and even her dancing. 'They were all petty little things,' she said, 'but my life was not my own. I dreaded hearing his latch key in the door'. The husband agreed that he did criticise her, but said that he was quite justified in so doing because she was what he called a very constructive person. I had some difficulty in understanding what he meant by that or how it could be said to justify his criticism. But it appeared at the end, after he had been cross-examined, that he formed the opinion that she was worthy of criticism, because she was a person who potentially did things well and by his criticism would be able to do things even better.
>
> ...
>
> On one occasion, she said, in the course of an argument he spat at her. The husband denies this and I do not accept his denial. I found his evidence evasive on this issue. The wife also told me that when he was angry he called her names and she described them. In the witness box the husband spoke in a quiet carefully modulated voice; I do

*not believe that it was his real voice, particularly when he was angry. This was a man who was capable of controlled anger and I accept the wife's evidence that he called her names when he was angry. The only name he would admit to having called her was a bastard. No doubt he called her that and many other names as well.*

*The wife also told me that on one occasion the husband tried to kick her out of bed. His explanation was that he was a restless sleeper and that he jumped and jerked about in his sleep. He denied that he ever kicked his wife intentionally. I do not accept his explanation and I do not believe that the wife made it up. I am satisfied that on that occasion the husband did try to knock the wife out of bed because, as she said, he was bad tempered.*

*... The wife also complained about another incident which was, perhaps, the most illuminating incident so far as the husband's character was concerned. They had, naturally, had some photographs taken at their wedding, and not very long afterwards the photographer came round with the wedding album. The husband was out and the wife, exercising what one would imagine was normal courtesy and hospitality, offered the photographer a glass of sherry which he accepted and she had a glass of sherry too to keep him company. When the husband came home he went to his cocktail cabinet, took out the sherry bottle and said, 'You have drunk half a bottle of sherry. Don't you ever go to my cocktail cabinet again.' He asked her who she had been drinking with and she told him what had happened. He forbade her to 'give refreshment to trades people again'. He was naturally cross-examined about his attitude and it appeared to be that if his wife took a glass of sherry with a trades-man—and he apparently classed the photographer as a tradesman—then the glass of sherry might, as he put it, impair her faculties, so that the tradesman might make some kind of indecent approach to her; and that was the justification of his conduct on that occasion. To my mind, it is typical of the man.*

*Not very long after that the wife left. She left as the result of one of the few scenes of violence which took place during the marriage. I have no doubt that the wife was right when she said the husband came back in bad temper, and, although there is a dispute between the two of them as to the details of what happened, there is no doubt whatever that the husband took hold of the wife, bundled her out of the house on a cold February evening and locked the door so that she could not get back in again. She was exceedingly upset, and, being a young woman of spirit, she broke a pane of glass to try and get in again. The husband, in order to prevent her getting in, got a bowl of water and threw it through the broken glass.*

6.32 Although it has been said that the test is objective, the reference by Dunn LJ to *this husband* and *this wife* clearly implies a subjective element. The court must look at the qualities of the particular spouses in judging whether it is reasonable to expect them to live with each other, given the behaviour complained of by the petitioner, and not some elusive, and almost certainly non-existent, supposedly normal spouses.

6.33 It was suggested, rather bizarrely and almost certainly incorrectly, in *Ash v Ash (1972)* that:

*...a violent petitioner can reasonably be expected to live with a violent respond-ent; a petitioner who is addicted to drink can reasonably be expected to live with a respondent similarly addicted; a taciturn and morose spouse can reasonably be*

*expected to live with a taciturn and morose partner; a flirtatious husband can rea-*
*sonably be expected to live with a wife who is equally susceptible to the attractions*
*of the opposite sex; and if each is equally bad, at any rate in similar respects, each*
*can reasonably be expected to live with the other.*

This approach is punitive and fails to contemplate the possibility that a right-thinking person could perfectly sensibly conclude that this particular petitioner, although difficult, could not reasonably be expected to live with the behaviour of an equally difficult spouse. The spouses may have different coping mechanisms which make one of them less able to cope with the behaviour of the other.

6.34 It is readily understandable why the behaviour fact is so frequently relied on in divorce petitions. The very nature of living in an intimate relationship almost certainly gives rise to irritating behaviour. It is arguable that the majority of spouses could point to examples of behaviour which they could not reasonably be expected to tolerate.

6.35 In *O'Neill v O'Neill (1975)*, the respondent, who had no experience of building work, embarked on an extensive and prolonged renovation of the family home. He took up floorboards and left them up, removed large quantities of rubble and deposited them in the derelict garden. He mixed cement on the floors throughout the house; he left the bathroom door off for eight months, which distressed the petitioner and their teenage daughter. The court accepted that this was behaviour which the wife could not be expected to live with.

6.36 In *Hadjimilitis (Tsavliris) v Tsavliris (2003)*, the respondent, a wealthy ship-owner, was found to have treated his wife with 'criticism and low warmth, controlling and undermining behaviour, public humiliation and lack of respect, insight, sensitivity, understanding and sympathy' which resulted in her becoming depressed and stressed. His reaction to her depression was to demand that she pull herself together. He gave her no money of her own but insisted that she ask either him or his secretary whenever she required money. He refused to have his own key to the family home so that at whatever time of night, however late, his wife would have to come downstairs and let him in. By doing so, he could control her movements and ensure she remained at home in his absence.

Furthermore, the husband's behaviour whilst defending the divorce was also held to fall into the behaviour category. He alleged that his wife had been unfaithful to him, had merely married him for financial reasons, had not supported him either emotionally or practically, was a bad mother, and a drug taker. The court held that such accusations so undermined the matrimonial relationship that no person could be expected to live with a person who made such allegations.

6.37 Where the respondent is mentally ill and behaves in a manner to which clearly no blame can be attached, his actions may nevertheless constitute relevant behaviour.

In *Katz v Katz (1972)*, the husband suffered from a manic-depressive illness accompanied by paranoid or schizophrenic features. He was treated with heavy sedation drugs. He behaved in a very disturbed manner. He sent letters to various public figures seeking to put right the troubles of the world, and devoted his time and energy to tape-recorders in an obsessive manner. He would sit glued to the television and he would go about with a transistor radio constantly to his ear.

In determining whether the petitioner can reasonably be expected to live with the behaviour of a mentally disturbed spouse, the court held that it must take into full account the normal ups and downs of married life with which the spouses are assumed to be able to deal. These have been said to include the obligation to care for each other in times of illness or injury. The court must also consider the petitioner's personal capability, the efforts made to cope with the stress resulting from the respondent's behaviour, the duration of the behaviour, and the effects on the petitioner's health. The wife was suffering from serious stress as a result of her husband's behaviour and had attempted suicide. She was granted a decree of divorce (see also *Thurlow v Thurlow (1976)*).

6.38 Inaction may also satisfy the *Livingstone-Stallard* test.

In *Carter-Fea v Carter-Fea (1987)*, the husband remained silent and refused to discuss his inability to act and resolve his financial difficulties. He left bills unpaid and ignored financial demands which resulted in the arrival of bailiffs at the family home.

6.39 It remains uncertain what approach the court would take if the respondent was incapable of behaviour. Permanent sexual impotency, or a persistent vegetative state resulting from an accident, might challenge the court's current definitions of behaviour. It would seem likely that they would take a similar approach as with blameless behaviour and take into account the ability of the petitioner to cope with the blameless inaction.

6.40 A spouse may claim that it is unreasonable to expect him or her to live with behaviour which is a response to his or her own misconduct.

In *Luong v Luong (1997)*, the husband's petition, which was based on the behaviour fact, was refused. The judge at first instance explained that the wife's violent response to her husband was

*...because of the affair that the Petitioner was then having with Miss Wong which caused the Petitioner to be emotionally affected so that she assaulted him, hitting him with a metal bar and scratching him, particularly scratching his eye so that he had to receive medical treatment. One can never commend any violence between the parties but one can understand somebody who behaves in this way, particularly the mother of young children, if her husband has betrayed her and particularly if he has shortly after they had sexual intercourse announced to her that he has another*

*woman. This was a single occasion of violence and it was brought about by the extreme circumstances which I have related.*

6.41    By contrast, in 2002 in an unreported decision, a husband's petition for divorce which was based on the behaviour fact succeeded in circumstances where his wife of 50 years had reacted publicly and violently towards the news that he had a long-term mistress and child. The 75 year-old husband had led a double life for more than 10 years. For part of the week he lived with his 74 year-old wife and for the other part of the week, he lived with his 46 year-old mistress and their child. He told his wife that he was working away on business every week. The wife, on discovering the affair, had made malicious phone calls, contacted the press and spread rumours about her husband.

The judge said:

*I am satisfied that the respondent has been so overwhelmed by her hurt and outrage at the deception that she went over on to the attack in order to destroy the petitioner and his second family unit. [However, no legitimate anger can reasonably lead to the conduct of the kind committed by the respondent. I am completely satisfied that the respondent's attitude was one of aggressive retaliation. The husband ruptured the marriage but the respondent, by her behaviour and attitude, caused the irretrievable breakdown. The question I have to ask myself is: would any right-thinking person come to the conclusion that this wife has behaved in such a way that this husband cannot be reasonably expected to live with her. To me the answer is undoubtedly yes. Apart from her family and close friends, there was no need for anyone to know about the family tragedy and certainly there was no need for her to spread the news...unless her aim was to wound and humiliate.*

*(The Times, 1 September 2000)*

### Continuing cohabitation

6.42    A spouse may not rely on MCA 1973, s 1(2)(b) if he or she has lived with the respondent for a period or periods exceeding six months after the final occurrence of the behaviour on which the petition for divorce is based (MCA 1973, s 2(3)). He or she will be deemed to be able to cope with the respondent's conduct. However, the court may exercise its discretion in the petitioner's favour.

For example, in **Bradley v Bradley (1973)**, the Court of Appeal recognized that a spouse pleading the behaviour fact might have no practical choice other than to continue to live with the respondent; there may be nowhere else for him or her to go.

Where the behaviour is ongoing, s 1(2)(b) will clearly be irrelevant.

### Desertion (MCA 1973, s 1(2)(c))

6.43    Divorce petitions based on desertion are rare. The petitioner must be able to prove that the respondent has not lived in the same household as him or her for two years, has no justifiable reason for living apart, and had the intention to remain permanently apart from him or her throughout that period.

6.44 The respondent may be found to have deserted the petitioner even if they continue to live under the same roof. They would have to prove that they are living totally separate lives in completely independent households—not an easy task to achieve and most difficult to prove.

> In **Le Brocq v Le Brocq (1964)**, the husband and wife did not share a bedroom. She continued to cook for him and receive money from him but never allowed him to take meals with her or their daughter. There was no other communication between them. The court refused to find that the husband was in desertion and stated
>
> ...*separation of bedrooms, separation of hearts, separation of speaking: but one household was carried on.*

6.45 The respondent will not be held to be in desertion if the petitioner has behaved in a manner which justifies the respondent's departure or if the respondent, because of mental illness, is deluded into believing that the petitioner has behaved in such a way (see **Perry v Perry (1964)**).

Adultery or conduct on the part of the petitioner, which would come within the behaviour fact, or mental or physical illness, might be sufficient justification for the respondent to leave the petitioner without being held to be in desertion. Indeed, in these circumstances, the petitioner herself may be held to be in constructive desertion of the respondent.

6.46 The respondent will not be held to be in desertion if the petitioner has agreed to the separation.

6.47 There must be an intention to desert. Spouses may be physically apart from each other without intending to be in desertion. Work, illness, or imprisonment may all lead to separation. However, if one party changes his mind and decides not to return, desertion will commence from that moment even if circumstances, in any event, would prevent him from returning. The intention to desert need not be communicated. This makes desertion difficult to prove and it will have to be inferred from the circumstances.

6.48 A mentally capable respondent may form an intention to desert the petitioner but subsequently become mentally incapable of intending to remain apart from her before the period of two years has ended. If, on the available evidence, the court is able to infer that but for the mental incapability, the desertion would have continued for the requisite period of time, the decree will be granted (MCA 1973, s 2(4)). It is difficult to foresee what evidence would be acceptable to a court.

6.49 Where the respondent volunteers to return to the petitioner before the two years has elapsed and the petitioner refuses, without good reason, to resume living together, she will be held to be in desertion if the separation lasts for a further two years.

*Resumption of cohabitation*

6.50 The petitioner may resume living with the respondent for a period or periods not exceeding six months without losing his or her right to rely on the respondent's desertion. However, in any subsequent petition for divorce, this period of cohabitation will not count towards the requisite two-year period (MCA 1973, s 2(5)).

## Two years living apart and consent to the decree (MCA 1973, s 1(2)(d))

6.51 This fact is most commonly pleaded where both parties wish to divorce, and in a non-acrimonious and private manner; it involves no publicity about the private lives of the spouses and is not fault-based. It is significant that all the royal divorces of the last century have been brought using this fact.

6.52 As with desertion, the parties may live under the same roof during the two-year period provided that they conduct separate households (MCA 1973, s 2(6)). This is obviously easier to achieve in a royal residence than in the homes of most potential divorcees. The case law has not always taken into account the realities of everyday life. During times of economic recession, and where the divorcing couple have children, it can be difficult to maintain two separate households, yet the spouses may well be living separate lives in every other way.

> In *Mouncer v Mouncer (1972)*, whilst waiting to divorce, the spouses remained in the family home which had two bedrooms. The wife continued to cook and clean for all the family, including her husband. The couple slept in separate bedrooms. The husband maintained that he remained in the house and ate with his wife and children because he wished to care for his children and share in their life. The court refused to accept that they were living apart.

6.53 By contrast, in *Fuller v Fuller (1973)*, the wife lived with another man but allowed her husband, who was ill, to come and live with them as a lodger. They all ate together and the wife took care of the husband. The court accepted that the spouses were living apart.

*Resumption of cohabitation*

6.54 The petitioner may resume living with the respondent for a period or periods not exceeding six months without losing her right to rely on two years' living apart. However, in any subsequent petition for divorce, this period of cohabitation will not count towards the requisite two-year period (MCA 1973, s 2(5)).

*Recognition that the marriage is at an end*

6.55 The 'special procedure' requires the petitioner to state the date and reason for the separation, and the date and circumstances in which the petitioner concluded that the marriage was at an end. However, the courts have rather controversially imported an additional requirement which is not in the Act.

> In *Santos v Santos (1972)*, for example, it was held that living apart only begins when one spouse recognizes that the marriage is at an end, although it was not considered necessary for the spouse to communicate that recognition to the other spouse.

The decision, although not strictly followed by the courts, could mean that parties who had separated without any firm conviction that the marriage was at an end would be unable to petition for divorce until one of them recognized that the marriage was over, a recognition which was followed by a two year period living apart. This approach fails to recognize the imprecise nature of human relationships. Spouses who have decided to live apart may continue to harbour faint hopes of reuniting, until one party meets a new partner whom he or she wishes to marry.

6.56 At the very least, the parties must form an intention to live apart at the beginning of the two-year period and continue to do so until they sign the consent to the grant of the decree at the end of the two years.

*Rescinding a decree nisi or declining to make it absolute (MCA 1973, s 10)*

6.57 This section gives the court discretion to rescind a decree nisi, but not a decree absolute, if the petitioner misleads the respondent, even unintentionally, about any matter which the respondent took into account in deciding to give consent. The section also allows the court, at the request of the respondent, to decline to make the decree absolute if it is not satisfied with the financial arrangements for the respondent.

### Five years living apart (MCA 1973, s 1(2)(e))

6.58 The spouses must have lived apart for five years and there is no requirement that the respondent must consent to the decree. For the petitioner who pleads this fact, it is usually a case of last resort; all other possibilities have normally been exhausted. In spite of the comment that this fact provides a *Casanova's charter* for men wishing to divorce their innocent wives unilaterally (Deech, 1990), the majority of petitioners relying on this fact are women.

*The defence of grave hardship (MCA 1973, s 5)*

6.59 MCA 1973, s 1(2)(e) is considered controversial because it permits the so-called innocent spouse to be divorced against his or her will. For that reason, where a petitioner alleges five years' living apart, MCA 1973, s 5 allows the respondent to plead that the dissolution of the marriage will result in grave financial or other hardship to him or her, and that it would in all the circumstances be wrong to dissolve the marriage. The court will take into account all the circumstances, including the conduct of the parties to the marriage, their interests and those of any children, or other persons concerned, in determining whether to grant the decree.

6.60 Grave hardship of both an emotional and a financial nature will almost always occur on marital breakdown. This type of hardship will be insufficient to permit a s 5 defence because the hardship must flow from the divorce itself rather than the marital breakdown. Case law illustrates how difficult it is for respondents to prove the relevant connection. However, the defence may prove a useful bargaining tool and a respondent may agree not to claim grave hardship in return for a larger financial settlement from the party who wants to divorce.

> In *Parker v Parker (1972)*, the respondent spouse risked losing a pension if she were to be divorced. Grave financial hardship was averted, and the decree was granted, because her husband was able to purchase an annuity which would provide her with sufficient income.

> In *Lee v Lee (1973)*, a wife succeeded in preventing the divorce because her husband's offer to give her a share in the proceeds of sale of the family home was insufficient to provide her with a home for herself and her disabled son.

6.61 Where there is a possible alternative source of income for the respondent spouse, he or she will not be able to plead grave hardship.

> In *Reiterbund v Reiterbund (1975)*, the respondent wife was entitled to social security payments which would ameliorate any financial hardship.

> Similarly in *Archer v Archer (1999)*, the court held that a wife was expected to use her own capital to prevent her suffering financial hardship on divorce.

6.62 Legislation relating to pension sharing on divorce has significantly reduced the possibility of grave financial hardship to spouses on divorce (see Chapter 7).

6.63 No respondent who has pleaded non-financial grave hardship has ever succeeded.

> The decision in *Banik v Banik (1973)*, illustrates the courts' approach. The respondent wife was a devout Hindu and claimed that she would be ostracized both religiously and socially if she were to be divorced. She maintained that:

> *My husband knows and knew when he married me that I was a devout believer in the Hindu religion. A Hindu woman looks to the spiritual aspect of dying as a married woman rather than for any material benefit. A Hindu woman will be destitute as a divorcee. If I am divorced, I will, by virtue of the society in which we live and the social attitudes and conventions existing in it, become a social outcast...I and the other members of the community in which we live regard the divorce as anathema on religious and moral as well as social grounds. My husband knows the humiliation and degradation I will suffer spiritually and socially if the court grants a decree.*

> The court was most unsympathetic to her dilemma and said rather obtusely that a respondent must

*...satisfy the court that it would be a real hardship to her if the marriage was dissolved, not just something which made her unhappy or distressed her, or which she regarded personally as immoral or contrary to the rules of her community.*

### *Wrong in all the circumstances to dissolve the marriage*

6.64 Even where a spouse clears the difficult hurdle of proving grave hardship, the court retains a discretion whether or not to grant the decree after it has considered all the circumstances of the case. The court must balance out the hardship to the respondent if the decree were to be granted against the injustice to the petitioner if it were to be refused.

> In **Brickell v Brickell (1974)**, the respondent caused chaos by visiting her husband's nursing home late at night and disturbing the geriatric patients to such an extent that the husband had to give up the nursing home. The court held that this was conduct of such a serious nature that it would not be wrong to grant the husband a divorce.

> The decision in **Julian v Julian (1972)** is one of the rare cases in which the court refused to grant the decree. It held that it would not be wrong to prevent the petitioner, who was unwell, from the possibility of remarrying by declining to grant the decree. His wife, who also suffered from bad health, was found to be more in need of protection from financial hardship because she would lose both maintenance payments and a pension were the decree to be granted.

### *The court's discretion and the decree absolute (MCA 1973, s 10)*

6.65 Where the petitioner relies on living apart for five years, the court has a discretion to decline to make the decree absolute, at the request of the respondent, if it finds that the financial arrangements are unsatisfactory (see eg *Garcia v Garcia (1992)*). The discretion is rarely used but may be used as a bargaining power by a respondent to ensure an acceptable financial settlement.

# Reconciliation

6.66 The current divorce legislation pays lip service to the possibility of the spouses becoming reconciled during the divorce process. Solicitors must state whether they have discussed reconciliation with their divorcing clients and whether they have given them relevant information about agencies who may be able to give them advice (MCA 1973, s 6(1)). The court may also adjourn a divorce hearing if it believes reconciliation to be possible (s 6(2)). The provisions are regarded as ineffectual, paternalistic, and unlikely to increase spousal reconciliation in any significant numbers.

# Consequences of divorce

6.67 Once the decree absolute has been granted the spouses are free to lead separate lives free from the legal responsibilities, and without the legal advantages, of marriage. They may marry a new partner or enter into a civil partnership should they so wish. However, for many divorced couples, their lives will remain intertwined both financially and with respect to their children.

6.68 When a divorce takes place there are many other additional matters which will need to be resolved, such as the future of the family home and financial arrangements between the spouses. These issues are considered in Chapter 7 and Chapter 16.

# Critique of current law

6.69 For many years, there has been considerable despair over, and criticism of, the law relating to divorce (see eg Report of the Matrimonial Causes Procedure Committee (1985); *The Ground for Divorce* (Law Com No 192); *Looking to the Future, Mediation and the Ground for Divorce: the Government's Proposals* (Cm 2799, 1995).

6.70 Critics have suggested that the existing law with its single ground of irretrievable breakdown is confusing, misleading, outdated, and excessively legalistic. It fails to save marriages and falls short of allowing the civilized burial of dead relationships where there is no clear reason or fault for their breakdown.

6.71 Non-lawyers, and indeed many lawyers, have difficulty in understanding that although a marriage has broken down, divorce is not available for at least one year after the marriage, no matter how difficult the circumstances, and without further proof of one of the five facts. They may also find it strange that they do not have to show that the fact pleaded caused the breakdown of their marriage.

6.72 The law may be seen as over-rigid in an area of personal relationships which do not lend themselves readily to categorization. Couples who want a rapid and easy route out of marriage are more likely to rely on the fault-based facts of adultery and behaviour, often with collusion, if not actual perjury, and with little thought given to the consequences. Allegations of fault lead to bitterness and hostility which may lead to difficulties for the children of the marriage.

6.73 Finally, a spouse who wants a divorce can be held to ransom by the other party, who may make unfair demands in return for agreeing to a divorce or insist on the long wait of five years.

# Reform

## Family Law Act 1996

6.74 In 1996, the Family Law Act, after a difficult passage through Parliament and considerable compromise, received the Royal Assent. However, five years later, in 2001, the Lord Chancellor announced that Part II of the Act relating to divorce reform would not be brought into force and that Parliament would be asked to repeal it.

6.75 The divorce provisions in the FLA 1996 Part II had a two-fold aim, to strengthen marriage yet allow dead, empty shell marriages to be ended in a dignified, thoughtful manner with minimum distress and humiliation to the parties. Irretrievable breakdown was retained as the sole ground for divorce. However, it would be evidenced not by allegations of fault, but by either spouse filing a statement of matrimonial breakdown at least three months after attending an information meeting. The spouse would then have to undertake a period of reflection of nine months to allow time for ancillary matters, relating to finances, property, and children, to be organized, and possibly even for reconciliation to take place. This period would be extended for a further six months where there were children under the age of 16 or where non-molestation and occupation orders were in force. At the end of the period, the spouse would apply to the court for a divorce order stating that all ancillary matters had been arranged and that the marriage could not be saved. Where substantial hardship would result to a spouse or a child, the court would have the power to refuse the divorce order.

6.76 The major reason the divorce provisions of the FLA 1996 failed to come into force was the problematic nature of the information meetings. These meetings had been tested for two years in pilot schemes. The government had seen these meetings as an essential part of the divorce process. They would provide spouses with detailed informative material which would help them to consider the consequences of divorce; how to seek help by way of counselling; whether to divorce and, if so, how to arrange all ancillary matters. The government proved to be mistaken in its hope that spouses would use the less costly process of mediation in resolving ancillary matters, rather than recourse to lawyers. Although those involved in the pilot studies felt that modifications could be made to the rather rigid, complex model which they had used, others criticized the meetings as ineffective in helping couples to save their marriage. The government was almost certainly concerned about the costs of providing information meetings.

6.77 It is generally acknowledged now that divorce law is in an unfortunate state of limbo. The current law is accepted to be unsatisfactory but, as yet, there are no new plans to reform it. Resolution, which is an association of family law solicitors, is continuing to press for the introduction of a non-fault-based divorce law.

# Judicial separation

6.78 In a limited number of cases, either or both spouses may not wish to obtain a decree of divorce but nevertheless desire formal legal recognition that they have separated. Some may have cultural or religious objections to divorce; others may not have been married for the one-year period which is an essential requirement before divorce proceedings can be started; whilst yet a third group may be psychologically unready to divorce at the time of the breakdown of their relationship, although they may decide to do so at a later date.

## Grounds for the decree

6.79 Either spouse must prove one of the same five facts as are necessary for the decree of divorce. However, it is not necessary to prove that the marriage has irretrievably broken down (MCA 1973, s 17(2)).

## Decree and its consequences

6.80 There is no decree nisi of judicial separation; once one of the five facts is proven, the court will pronounce a decree absolute unless it has reason to believe that satisfactory arrangements have not been made for the children.

6.81 The parties are relieved from the rather nebulous obligations of the marriage contract but they may not remarry. They may use the evidence presented for the decree of judicial separation to obtain a decree of divorce at some time in the future should they wish to do so. One of the major advantages of seeking the decree is that the spouses may seek court orders to resolve their financial affairs and make arrangements for their children's future.

# Civil partnerships

## Dissolution (CPA 2004)

6.82 CPA 2004, ss 44–48 provide for the dissolution of a civil partnership in a very similar way, and with very similar consequences, to divorce. Although the process is referred to as dissolution rather than divorce, the provisions in the CPA 2004 mirror those relating to divorce, except for the notable omission of adultery as one of the five facts. The government took the approach that adultery, as defined, cannot apply to same-sex partnerships. It declined to include extra-civil partnership same-sex sexual conduct as one of the facts which would be viewed in a similar light as adultery. It seems certain that a same-sex partner will be able to plead the behaviour fact where such conduct occurs.

6.83 In the light of the government's decision not to allow same-sex partners to marry, it must be questioned why the government did not take the opportunity to take a different approach to the dissolution of civil partnerships rather than base it on the current divorce law.

6.84 The Office of National Statistics reported that 166 dissolutions of civil partnership took place in 2008. More female civil partners than males have formally ended their civil partnership.

## Separation orders (CPA 2004, ss 56, 57)

6.85 A civil partner may apply for a separation order in the same way as a spouse may apply for a decree of judicial separation. Similar consequences result in that the separated civil partners may live apart free from the obligations and rights of civil partnership but not enter into a new civil partnership or marriage.

**FURTHER READING**

Cretney S, 'Breaking the Shackles of Culture and Religion in the Field of Divorce' [2005] IFLJ 19

Deech R, 'Divorce and Empirical Studies' [1990] LQR 229

Deech R, 'Divorce a Disaster' [2009] Fam Law 1049

Gibb F, 'Judge Blames Wife for Divorce' *The Times*, 1 September 2000

Hale B, 'The Family Law Act 1996: Dead Duck or Golden Goose' in Cretney S (Ed), *Family Law: Essays for the New Millennium* (Blackwell Synergy, 2000)

Hasson E, 'Setting a Standard or Reflecting Reality' [2003] Intl J Law, Policy and the Family 338

Jackson E, 'Donor Anonymity and Rights', 23 January 2004, BioNews

Langdon-Down G, 'Divorce Law Reform: Doing the Splits' (2006) LS Gaz 20

Law Commission, The Ground for Divorce (Law Com No 192, 1990)

Law Commission, Looking to the Future, Mediation and the Ground for Divorce: the Government's Proposals (Cm 2799, 1995)

Richards M, 'Private Worlds and Public intentions: the Role of the State in Divorce' in Bainham A, Pearl D, and Pickford R (eds), *Frontiers of Family Law* (John Wiley and Sons, 1995) http://www.statistics.gov.uk/

Shepherd N, 'Ending the Blame Game: Getting No Fault Divorce Back on the Agenda' [2009] Fam Law 122

Tyler C, 'Relate and the Judge Speak Out' [2008] Fam Law 660

## SELF-TEST QUESTIONS

1   If marriage and civil partnerships are contracts, why should they not be able to be brought to an immediate end by mutual agreement?

2   What is the rationale for a fault-based divorce law?

3   Arabella has been flirting in an Internet correspondence with Boris for the last two years. Her husband Charles discovered the messages and was very distressed. He felt that Arabella had committed 'Internet adultery'. Charles would like to divorce Arabella, who does not regard her marriage as having broken down. She maintains that she simply thought that she was having fun.

    Advise both Arabella and Charles.

4   Julian is a perfectionist and likes to live in a well organized environment. He and Katrina have been married for five years. Katrina is the exact opposite to Julian and is happy to live in what she regards as a happy muddle. Julian checks the dishwasher when he arrives home in the evening because he cannot bear to see it packed other than in an orderly manner. If necessary, he will restack it according to his idea of what constitutes orderly.

    Katrina has met a rather messy artist Leonardo and would like to divorce Julian to enable her to do so. Julian loves Katrina and does not want her to leave but simply to learn how to organize the house in accordance with his wishes.

    Advise Katrina and Julian.

5   Critically evaluate the law relating to the dissolution of civil partnerships.

6   David and Edward entered into a civil partnership one year ago. David has decided that he is a bi-sexual and has been having a sexual relationship with Fenella for the last six months; they now wish to marry. Fenella has been married to George for four years. Edward wishes to enter into a new civil partnership with Harry. George wishes to marry Imogen who has never been married.

    Advise David, Edward, Fenella and George how they may legally enter into their desired new relationships.

7   Part II of the Family Law Act 1996, which has never been brought into force, would have permitted no fault divorce. After reading Part II (http://www.parliament.uk/briefingpapers/commons/lib/research/briefings/snha-01409.pdf), draft your own legislation for both spouses and civil partners which would allow them to legally end their relationships without any allegation of fault.

# 7

# Financial consequences of relationships

## SUMMARY

When relationships end, financial difficulties and property disputes inevitably follow, regardless of a couple's legal status. Financial arrangements whilst a relationship is ongoing are normally inappropriate when the relationship breaks down and a couple parts.

In this chapter, which is divided into two interrelated sections, we consider first the law relating to the ownership of personal property and rights to maintenance during familial relationships, albeit ones which may be in the final stages of breakdown. Second, we consider the law relating to the redistribution of both real and personal property, and the rights to maintenance after a relationship has been legally ended or, in the case of fiancés and their civil partnership equivalent, and cohabitants, when the couple parts. This area of law has been severely criticized by the judiciary, lawyers, academic commentators, as well as those who have been personally affected by it. However, the regular calls for reform have remained unheeded by the government and as a consequence, the judiciary has felt forced to indulge in judicial reform.

Financial matters relating to children are considered in Chapter 16.

# Part I Ownership of personal property and rights to maintenance during the relationship

## Personal property

7.1 When a relationship is working, neither partner is likely to be too concerned about the precise legal ownership of specific items. When items are purchased for the home, couples tend not to ask questions about who owns what. More often than not, they pool their resources in a rather haphazard manner, and purchases are paid for in accordance with the division of labour within the relationship, or the state of the bank balance of either partner. The person who is primarily responsible for the home and children tends to pay for food, clothes and general housekeeping items, and, even in a post-feminist world, it is more likely to be the woman who takes care of such matters. More expensive capital items tend to be funded by the highest earner in the family whether or not they are for that person's individual use. It is only when problems arise in the relationship, or a third party wishes to dispute one of the couple's rights over a specific item of property, that the question of ownership becomes an issue.

7.2 Whether a couple is married; in a registered civil partnership; cohabiting, or simply engaged to be married or planning a civil partnership, each person retains the right to his or her own personal property during the currency of the relationship. English law does not provide for community of property; strict property principles apply in determining to whom the property belongs. However, the nature of a couple's relationship may be of evidential importance in any proceedings to determine ownership of a specific item.

7.3 The law relating to ownership of personal property can only be described as a hotchpotch; it consists of outdated statutory provisions, and the judiciary's liberal, or not so liberal, interpretation of equitable remedies or contracts.

### Statutory provisions

**Married Women's Property Act 1882, s 17;**
**Civil Partnership Act 2004, s 66**

7.4 Either spouse or former spouse may apply to the court for determination of the ownership of disputed property under the Married Women's Property Act 1882 (MWPA 1882), s 17. The section is merely procedural; it provides for a rapid resolution of disputes but does not provide for the redistribution of property between spouses (see *Pettitt v Pettitt (1970)*). It is a rarely used provision. The Civil Partnership Act 2004 (CPA 2004), s 66 allows civil partners the same right.

7.5 Engaged couples and their civil partnership equivalents may only take advantage of one of these Acts if they terminate their agreement to marry or their agreement to enter into a civil partnership (see below).

7.6 There are no similar statutory rights for cohabitants.

## Married Women's Property Act 1964, s 1

7.7 Where a husband gives his wife a housekeeping allowance, the Married Women's Property Act 1964 (MWPA 1964), s 1 provides that any items purchased out of that allowance, or any savings made from it, are to be treated as belonging equally to both parties, unless they have agreed otherwise. Where one spouse purchases an item, which is obviously for his or her sole use, an agreement will normally be implied that it belongs to the person using the item.

7.8 The provision is gender-biased, paternalistic, and out of date with the reality of twenty-first century life. It does not apply where a wife gives her husband an allowance, nor does it apply to civil partners or cohabitants. Thus a husband, civil partner, or cohabitant, who receives an allowance from a partner, and purchases a lottery ticket from that allowance, will be able to retain the winnings, unless they have agreed otherwise. A wife in similar circumstances will only be allowed to retain 50 per cent of any winnings.

7.9 As long ago as 1985, the Law Commission recommended the abolition of the Act (*Matrimonial Property* (Law Com No 175, 1985)), but the recommendation was not followed. A private member's bill was introduced in 2005 by Rob Marris MP; it would have extended the provision of the 1964 Act to husbands and civil partners. It was withdrawn for lack of support in 2006.

7.10 In spite of the discriminatory effects of the Act, human rights legislation is unlikely to be of help to those affected by it. Protocol 12 to the European Convention on Human Rights 1950 (ECHR) was designed to be a freestanding provision which would prevent discrimination beyond the limited provision of Art 14 of the ECHR. Art 14 merely protects discrimination with respect to the enjoyment of any of the other Convention rights. The UK government has declined to sign Protocol 12 because it is concerned about its far-reaching effects and wishes to take a more cautious approach to the issue of discrimination. The Joint Committee on Human Rights, *inter alia*, has criticized the government's failure to sign. In its 17th Report (2005) it stated that:

> *We do not believe that such a cautious approach is warranted, or consonant with the Government's aspirations to international leadership in the development of equality*

*laws. In previous reports, we have recommended that the Government should ratify Protocol 12 ECHR, and include it within the rights protected in the Human Rights Act, in order to provide protection in domestic law equivalent to the equality rights which bind the UK internationally,...The rights enshrined in Protocol 12 are rights which the Government has accepted through its international commitments to human rights instruments. These commitments should in our view be given reality in national law through a free standing right of non-discrimination.*

# Trusts

## Express trusts

7.11 Unlike express trusts of real property which are required to be in writing (see Chapter 4), words alone may be sufficient to ground an express trust of personal property.

In *Paul v Constance (1977)*, Mr Constance, who was separated from his wife, began to cohabit with Mrs Paul. He received £950 as damages for personal injuries, which he deposited in a bank account in his sole name. He told Mrs Paul on many occasions that the money was as much hers as his, and that she was free to draw on the account with his signed agreement. The couple deposited further monies, including their joint bingo winnings, into the account. Mr Constance died intestate and his wife wished to claim the contents of the bank account.

The Court of Appeal held that to establish the existence of an express trust it had to be shown that there was clear evidence from what had been said or done of an intention to create a trust. Scarman LJ accepted that the words need not be in stilted lawyers' language; the couple were

*...simple people, unaware of the subtleties of equity, but understanding very well indeed their own domestic situation.*

The words used by Mr Constance on many occasions to indicate that the money in the deposit account was as much Mrs Paul's as his, were held to be sufficient to constitute an express declaration of trust.

In *Rowe v Prance (1999)*, the Court of Appeal also found an express trust of personal property based on informal words. Mr Prance was a married man who had had a relationship with Mrs Rowe for 14 years. They agreed that Mr Prance would buy a boat in his name, which they would share, and realize their dreams that he would leave his wife and sail around the world together. Mrs Rowe sold her own home and stored her furniture. In frequent discussions, Mr Prance referred to the boat as 'ours' or 'our boat'. He reassured Mrs Rowe that the boat would provide financial security for her. However, as is so often the case, he could not bring himself to leave his wife, and Mrs Rowe succeeded in her demand to have the boat sold and receive half the proceeds of sale.

### Informal trusts

7.12  Where there is insufficient evidence for the court to find that there was an express trust of personal property, it may be prepared to accept that a resulting or constructive trust has come into existence. The requirements to ground informal trusts of real property were considered in detail in Chapter 4. Similar principles apply to informal trusts of personal property.

7.13  In *Re Bishop (deceased) (1965)*, Stamp J explained that where a couple pools their resources and each deposits funds into a bank account which is either in joint names, or in the name of one but with joint rights to withdraw funds, each spouse will have an equal share in those funds. However, if either partner purchases personal property out of the funds, that property, in the absence of any alternative agreement, will belong to the person who purchased it.

In *Re Young (1885)*, Colonel and Mrs Young opened a joint account at the County of Gloucester Bank, Cheltenham; each had power to withdraw money. The funds in the account came primarily from Mrs Young's own income. Most of the household expenses were paid for out of the joint account and Colonel Young withdrew funds from it for his own private expenses, which included investments made in his own name. The court held that the investments were his property.

Pearson J explained that:

*Colonel and Mrs Young seem to have lived for many years a married life such as married people ought to live, on terms of affection and mutual confidence, and I can well understand that the lady, with a delicacy that I hope is not uncommon, felt that it would be unpleasant for her husband to be reminded from day to day that he was living to a great extent upon and drawing a large share of the money required for household expenses from his wife, and for that reason this joint account seems to me to have been opened, which was used to a great extent for household expenses. That being so, the inference I draw is that it was simply intended that the account should be joint, and the lady intended to sink all idea of separate character in order that her husband should be able to draw. The husband did draw, and, as I must hold, with the consent of his wife has invested from time to time a large portion of the sums drawn in his own name. There is no dispute as to such investments that they must be treated as his property.*

The decision reflects a nineteenth century approach to the delicacy of male feelings and the inferences to be drawn from the prevailing culture at that time.

7.14  By contrast, in *Hoddinott v Hoddinott (1949)*, a wife claimed a share in furniture, which had been purchased by her husband from the proceeds of bets placed on football pools. The monies had been placed in an account in the husband's name but, for the sake of convenience, the wife had a power to draw on the account.

The court held that the furniture was the husband's property. He had not made a gift of the winnings to the wife and there was no contract to share them. The fact that the wife had a right to draw on the account was merely to help the husband because he found it difficult to get to the bank because of his work.

### Contract

7.15 It is unusual for couples to contract expressly with each other about the ownership of personal property. If they have a clear, shared, intention to create a legally binding contract, and there is appropriate consideration, a court will give effect to it, provided it is not contrary to public policy.

# Rights to maintenance during the relationship

## A wife's right to be maintained at common law

7.16 At common law, a husband had a duty to maintain his wife by providing her with accommodation, food, and other necessities. It is questionable whether this right was of any real value. She could not demand that her husband provide her with an allowance; she could merely attempt to pledge his credit to tradesmen and depend on their goodwill to provide her with her essential needs. This was known as the agency of necessity, and was abolished by the Matrimonial Proceedings and Property Act 1970 (MPPA 1970). Although the Act appears to have left the common law right to maintenance intact, the right is of little use today; statutes allowing spouses to make claims for maintenance against each other have superseded it. The Family Law (Property and Maintenance) Bill (2005) proposed the abolition of a husband's duty to maintain his wife. The bill was withdrawn for lack of support.

## Contract for maintenance

7.17 The courts have been most reluctant to find contracts for maintenance during an ongoing relationship; they do not see their role as policing personal relations. They have taken a very conservative approach and have tended to find both a lack of an intention to create legal relations and an absence of consideration.

> In *Balfour v Balfour (1919)*, a wife, who was ill, remained in England when her husband returned to Ceylon (now Sri Lanka) to work for the government. She claimed that he had agreed that he would pay her maintenance of £30 a month on condition that she made no further demands for financial support.
>
> The Court of Appeal held that whilst contracts between married couples living together amicably were a possibility, it was not prepared to find one here. It explained that a contract

*...can only be determined either by proving that it was made in express terms, or that there is a necessary implication from the circumstances of the parties, and the transaction generally, that such a contract was made. It is quite plain that no such contract was made in express terms, and there was no bargain on the part of the wife at all. All that took place was this: the husband and wife met in a friendly way and discussed what would be necessary for her support while she was detained in England, the husband being in Ceylon, and they came to the conclusion that £30 a month would be about right, but there is no evidence of any express bargain by the wife that she would in all the circumstances treat that as in satisfaction of the obligation of the husband to maintain her. Can we find a contract from the position of the parties? It seems to me it is quite impossible. If we were to imply such a contract in this case we should be implying on the part of the wife that whatever happened and whatever might be the change of circumstances while the husband was away she should be content with this £30 a month, and bind herself by an obligation in law not to require him to pay anything more; and on the other hand we should be implying on the part of the husband a bargain to pay £30 a month for some indefinite period whatever might be his circumstances. Then again it seems to me that it would be impossible to make any such implication. The matter really reduces itself to an absurdity when one considers it, because if we were to hold that there was a contract in this case we should have to hold that with regard to all the more or less trivial concerns of life where a wife, at the request of her husband, makes a promise to him, that is a promise which can be enforced in law. All I can say is that there is no such contract here. These two people never intended to make a bargain which could be enforced in law. The husband expressed his intention to make this payment, and he promised to make it, and was bound in honour to continue it so long as he was in a position to do so. The wife on the other hand, so far as I can see, made no bargain at all.*

## Statutory rights to maintenance

### Matrimonial Causes Act 1973, s 27

7.18 Either spouse may apply for an order for maintenance under the Matrimonial Causes Act 1973 (MCA 1973), s 27, on the ground that the respondent spouse has failed to provide reasonable maintenance. The court determines whether there has been a failure to maintain and, if so, what award to make having considered all the circumstances of the case. Orders may be made for secured or unsecured periodical payments, or unlimited lump sums. Payments secured against a capital sum or against property may continue to be paid in the event of the death or bankruptcy of the payer. All orders terminate if the payee remarries or dies. Applications under the Act are rare; it is a more expensive procedure than an application to the magistrates' court.

### Civil Partnership Act 2004, Sch 5, Part 9

7.19 The Civil Partnership Act 2004 (CPA 2004), Sch 5, Part 9, has extended to civil partners all of the statutory provisions relating to maintenance rights for married partners under MCA 1973, s 27.

## Domestic Proceedings and Magistrates' Courts Act 1978

7.20 Spouses who require maintenance are more likely to take advantage of the Domestic Proceedings and Magistrates' Courts Act 1978 (DPMCA 1978). It is less costly to make an application under this Act than under the provisions of the MCA 1973, s 27, and the magistrates' courts are easily accessible to most couples throughout the country; there is such a court in all towns.

7.21 The grounds of application under the DPMCA 1978, s 1 are: failure to provide reasonable maintenance for the applicant or a child of the family, behaviour of such a nature that the applicant cannot reasonably be expected to live with the spouse, or desertion. It must be questioned why there is not simply one single ground—a failure to provide reasonable maintenance. Behaviour and desertion are the obsolete, leftover remnants of the old fault-based legislation which allowed the magistrates to make separation orders for those partners who were not prepared to seek a divorce, and grant a maintenance orders at the same time.

7.22 The DPMCA 1978 has been described as 'poor person's justice' because its provisions limit the magistrates' powers to the award of unsecured periodical payments, or lump sums up to £1,000 (s 2). The court may also ratify consent orders agreed by the parties, or make an order reflecting payments which have already been made on a voluntary basis (ss 6, 7). Unlike an order under MCA 1973, s 27, any order made under the DPMCA 1978 will end if the parties continue to live with each other for longer than six months from the date of the order (s 25(1)). All orders end if the payee becomes bankrupt, remarries, or dies (s 4(2)). It will also end if the payer dies.

### *The courts' discretion*

7.23 In determining whether to make an order, and if so, the amount and type of order, the court must have regard to all the matters laid down in DPMCA 1978, s 3. The wide-ranging list is analogous to MCA 1973, s 25 (see below). It includes the parties' financial resources and needs, their earning capacity, their standard of living, their ages, any disabilities which either of them may have, the contribution of either of them, in the past or the future, to the welfare of the family, and the conduct of the parties if the court thinks it would be inequitable to disregard it.

### *Conduct*

7.24 The courts have tended to ignore negative conduct, unless it is very grave, when determining an order. It is, therefore, somewhat surprising that the wife's maintenance in the following case was reduced.

> In *Robinson v Robinson (Conduct) (1983)*, a young wife refused to join her husband, a soldier, with their baby in Belize, where he had been posted. She had been very homesick in an earlier overseas posting and decided to stay with her parents. When her husband

returned she refused to return to the matrimonial home. The husband declined to pay his wife maintenance but agreed to support their child. The wife made an application under the DPMCA 1978. The magistrates reduced her maintenance from £45 per week to £15 per week because of her conduct, and limited it to a period of five years. They believed the husband to be totally blameless.

The Court of Appeal refused the wife's appeal. Slade LJ explained that:

*The guidelines, if I have understood them correctly, essentially amount to this: the past conduct of a wife should cause the court, in the exercise of its statutory discretion, to reduce or eliminate the amount of maintenance which it would otherwise have awarded to her only if it has been shown to be such that it would offend a reasonable person's sense of justice to disregard such conduct. Save in such an exceptional case, the court should not take past conduct into account; to do so would be repugnant to the principles of the relevant legislation, which does not contemplate that there will ordinarily be a minute investigation into the shares of responsibility for the breakdown of a marriage.*

The decision seems unusually harsh on a young wife, particularly when it is very rare for other types of, arguably, infinitely more heinous behaviour to be taken into account in analogous decisions under the provisions of MCA 1973, s 25 (see below). It would be most unlikely for a wife in Mrs Robinson's position to be penalized in this way today.

## Civil Partnership Act 2004, Sch 6

7.25 Under the CPA 2004, Sch 6, civil partners have been given all the same rights to maintenance as those of spouses under the provisions of the DPMCA 1978.

# State benefits

7.26 All partners who are not being maintained by each other may have little alternative other than to apply for State benefits. The State is concerned to reduce the amount of its liability to pay these benefits and has enacted legislation to ensure that, wherever possible, partners will be forced to maintain each other. Whilst a complete account of State benefits is outside the scope of this book, two important rules will be considered which affect claimants of means-tested State benefits.

## Liable relative rule

7.27 The Social Security Administration Act 1992, ss 78 and 105 provide that the Benefits Agency may recover social security benefits paid to a claimant if there is a person who is legally liable to support him or her. Spouses and civil partners are under a duty to support each other and their children. It is an offence under s 105 of the Act not to support a relative for whom one is liable where the relative has made a claim for social security benefits. Wikely (2008) has argued that the rule is in demise particularly with respect to elderly partners who are in care homes.

7.28 The rule does not apply to cohabitants.

### Cohabitation rule

7.29 The effects of the Social Security Contributions and Benefits Act 1992, s 134 and of the Jobseekers Act 1995, s 35 mean that where a couple, whether spouses, civil partners, or cohabitants, are living together in the same household as husband or wife, their income will be aggregated for the purposes of assessing a claim for means-tested benefits. It is assumed that the partner who applies for such benefits has the income of the other as an available resource. This, of course, may not necessarily be so. A partner who is not being maintained may be forced to end the relationship in order to make a claim for benefits.

7.30 The rule might be conceivably justifiable for spouses or civil partners because they have recourse to statutory rights to obtain maintenance from their partners. Cohabitants, however, have no such rights. Adjudication officers who deal with claims have been given guidelines to determine whether a cohabitant who wishes to make a claim is living with another person as husband or wife. The guidelines are:

- whether the parties are living in the same household;
- the stability of their relationship;
- financial support for each other;
- the existence of a sexual relationship between them;
- joint children;
- public acknowledgment of their relationship as that of husband and wife.

(See the Social Security Contributions and Benefits Act 1992, s 137; *Crake v Supplementary Benefits Commission; Butterworth v Supplementary Benefits Commission (1981)*.)

> In *Re J (Income Support: Cohabitation) (1995)*, it was said that the guidelines are not definitive; the totality of the relationship has to be considered.

7.31 Since the enactment of the CPA 2004, the cohabitation rule has been extended to same-sex couples who are living as if civil partners. As yet, it is difficult to know precisely what it means to live as if a civil partner. New guidelines will be required to determine claims. In particular, the guideline relating to a sexual relationship will have to be reconsidered since the legislation relating to civil partners does not acknowledge sexuality as a factor in these relationships. Baroness Scotland, when asked by Lord Tebbit for a clear explanation of the distinction between civil partnerships and marriage, replied:

> *One of the differences is consummation. In relation to marriage, for a marriage to be valid it has to be consummated by one man and one woman and there is a great deal*

*of jurisprudence which tells you exactly what consummation amounts to, partial, impartial, penetration, no penetration. If you wish me to give a dissertation on family law I would be happy to do so. There is no provision for consummation in the Civil Partnerships Bill. We do not look at the nature of the sexual relationship; it is totally different in nature.*

*(House of Lords, Hansard, 17 November 2004, Col 1479)*

7.32 It has been suggested that the enactment of the CPA 2004 may have the side effect of bringing same-sex couples who are not civil partners within the cohabitation rule. In 2005, OutRage!, a gay rights group, maintained that:

> All cohabiting same-sex couples will experience a reduction in state benefits as a side effect of the new Civil Partnership Act. . . . Even couples who don't want a civil partnership and have not registered their relationship will face cuts. In addition, same-sex friends or ex-lovers who live together will have to prove that they are not in a relationship—otherwise they, too, will lose out financially. . . . The pensions and benefits agencies will assume that all cohabitees are partners and cut their benefits accordingly.

> *(http://www.buddybuddy.com)*

7.33 The cohabitation rule is a contentious rule and has been viewed as unfair and a breach of individual privacy. It may also lead to instability in relationships because cohabitants may leave their partners rather than risk the loss of benefits. The justification for the rule is that without it, cohabitants would be treated more favourably than married couples. Whilst the rule appears to breach Art 8 (right to respect for private and family life) of the ECHR, it is likely that in any claim on the part of a cohabitant, the UK government will argue that there is a reasonable proportionality between the effect of the rule and its aim not to discriminate against married couples and civil partners.

# Part II Financial consequences of ending the relationship

## Recurring themes

7.34 Whether a relationship ends by a decree or order of nullity; a decree of divorce or dissolution order; a decree of judicial separation or a separation order, or by the decision of either or both of the parties in the case of cohabitants or engaged couples or their civil partner counterparts, there is a tension in the law relating to the re-ordering of the parties' financial affairs. This tension has been dominated by three recurring themes:

- First, private negotiation versus judicial determination.

- Second, the imposition of a clean break versus financial orders which ensure the continuation of the couple's financial relationship.
- Third, equal division of assets based on fairness versus unequal division based on needs.

7.35 Modern legal policy favours private negotiated settlements for spouses and civil partners, rather than the costly legal settlements imposed by the court after the exercise of its extensive discretion under the provisions of the MCA 1973. Couples are encouraged to consult mediators or lawyers to help them reach agreement. If they reach a satisfactory agreement with each other, the agreement may be incorporated into a court order known as a consent order once it has been reviewed by a judge.

7.36 Cohabitants have little choice other than to negotiate a private agreement; there are no statutory provisions to enable a court to redistribute their property at the end of a relationship.

7.37 Engaged couples, or couples who have agreed to enter into a civil partnership, have the minimal statutory provision of the Law Reform (Miscellaneous Provisions) Act 1970 but for the most part, they too have no alternative other than to rely on privately negotiated agreements.

7.38 There remains, however, a reluctance on the part of the State, which is both paternalistic and self-serving, to allow spouses and civil partners to have complete freedom of bargaining and make pre-nuptial agreements (see *Radmacher (2010)* below). An uneasy compromise has been reached.

7.39 Although the reported case law is dominated by accounts of the court's resolution of the disputes of the divorcing rich, it must be stressed that, in practice, most couples will attempt to reach an agreement with each other and ask the court to confirm it as a consent order. All too often their resources are so limited that they are rarely sufficient to provide satisfactorily for both of them and concessions on both sides are inevitable.

# Ancillary relief on dissolution of a civil partnership, divorce, judicial separation or nullity

## CPA 2004, s 72(1) and Sch 5

7.40 CPA 2004, s 72(1) and Sch 5, which correspond with the provisions of the MCA 1973 for married couples, provide that civil partners may ask for a redistribution of their assets, a process known as an application for ancillary relief, when they apply for a legal order to end their relationship. As yet, there are no decisions on ancillary relief for civil partners. It is assumed that the existing matrimonial case law which is discussed below, will be used as guidelines, by the court, where appropriate, when determining orders for civil partners.

# MCA 1973, Part II

7.41 All spousal applications for ancillary relief are governed by the provisions of MCA 1973, Part II. The MCA 1973, which is gender neutral, gives very wide powers to the court to deal with the parties' resources, and reallocate them as it thinks fit. This process of redistribution has two purposes; it compensates the partners for the past in terms of contribution to the marriage, and it provides maintenance, where necessary, for their future needs. This dual approach is not always made explicit in the case law; the two strands often appear entangled and confused.

7.42 The legislation has been subjected to heavy criticism, primarily for its lack of an overall objective, its discretionary nature, and its unpredictability, which may lead to high legal costs and perceptions of unfairness. The concept of fairness plays a leading role in recent decisions.

7.43 Once an application for ancillary relief has been made, both spouses risk the loss of that absolute control which they had over their individual finances and property during their marriage.

> In *Hanlon v Law Society (1981)*, Lord Denning described the court's task in language which is strongly reminiscent of a quasi-lucky dip; all the spousal property is placed in a large bag and mixed up together
>
> *The court then takes out the pieces and hands them to the two parties–some to one party and some to the other–so that each can provide for the future with the pieces allotted to him or to her. The court hands them out without paying any too nice a regard to their legal or equitable rights but simply according to what is the fairest provision for the future, for mother, and father and the children.*

### The statutory charge (Access to Justice Act 1999, s 10)

7.44 Where a spouse has received legal aid from the State in order to make an application for ancillary relief, any resources he or she succeeds in recovering, or preserving, will be clawed back to repay the legal aid. The first £3,000 is exempt from repayment. Repayment of the remainder may be deferred if the resources awarded include the family home, or the spouse uses them to purchase a family home or subsequently replaces it with a new family home. A charge will be placed on the property which will secure the repayment of legal aid at a later date (see *Hanlon v Law Society (1981)*).

# Orders available to the court

7.45 The orders available to the court fall into three categories:

- financial provision orders;
- property adjustment orders;
- pension orders.

## Financial provision orders

*Maintenance prior to decree (MCA 1973, s 22)*

7.46 Many spouses, particularly women whose relationships have broken down, will have little financial resources of their own. In any application for a decree of nullity, divorce or judicial separation, they may apply for an order for maintenance before the decree has been granted and all financial and property matters have been finalized.

*Secured or unsecured periodical payments (MCA 1973, s 23)*

7.47 Provided that a former spouse has not re-married, he or she may make an application for periodical payments. A former spouse who cohabits rather than re-marrying remains eligible to apply. However, the cohabitation may be one of the factors the court will take into account in deciding whether to grant the application (see eg *Grey v Grey (2009)*).

7.48 The payments are made to a payee at regular intervals, either for maintenance or, increasingly, where there is insufficient capital available at the time of the divorce, as compensation for past contribution to the marriage. The order for payments may be nominal where the payer has insufficient income; this leaves open the possibility of an application to vary the order for payments if the payer acquires income or capital in the future. The order for payments may be long-term or limited to a specific period of time with the expectation that the payee will become self-sufficient.

7.49 In ***Parlour v Parlour (2004)***, the Arsenal footballer, Ray Parlour was ordered to pay his ex-wife substantial periodical payments of £444,000 a year for four years, after which they would be reviewed. The award represented one-third of his future earnings. Mr Parlour had been a heavy drinker during the marriage. Mrs Parlour had realized that this problem was almost certain to ruin his career chances, and she endeavoured to help him to change his lifestyle. Mr Parlour publicly praised her for her care and encouragement to overcome the problem, and he subsequently played for England and received the ultimate footballer's accolade of an English cap on ten different occasions.

The court accepted that there was insufficient capital to compensate Mrs Parlour adequately at the time of the divorce. However, Mr Parlour's earnings were exceptionally high, and well in excess of what was required for the reasonable needs of both parties. It was only fair that Mrs Parlour should receive a significant share of them; her husband's earnings would decline fairly rapidly, as he grew older and became unable to continue to play competitive football. The high award was not only for Mrs Parlour's current maintenance but also to allow her to save and provide for her future and become financially independent as soon as possible.

7.50 All periodical payments are a high-risk solution for payees because they end automatically on their remarriage or, if not secured, on the bankruptcy of the payer, or on the death of the payer or payee (MCA 1973, s 28). This provision ignores the fact that the payments may have been awarded as compensation for a spouse's contribution to the marriage. Payees who re-marry unfairly lose that compensation and s 28 may well be viewed as a serious disincentive to re-marriage, particularly if the court does not place a time limit on the payments. Payees who die lose the possibility of leaving what they had rightfully gained for their contribution during a marriage to their children or other beneficiaries.

In either of these circumstances, the payer, or his or her estate, gains an unfair benefit.

The payee's cohabitation with a new partner does not necessarily end periodical payments but a payer may return to court and ask for a variation of them.

### Variation of periodical payments

7.51 If the parties' circumstances change after any award of periodical payments, either of them may apply to the court for a variation, discharge, or suspension of the payments, or a replacement of them with a capital order (MCA 1973, s 31).

> In *I v I (2008)*, the spouses had agreed a consent order at a time when the husband had a draft contract for new employment which would give him a higher income. He failed to tell his wife about this matter. When he later began the new employment, the wife applied for the consent order to be set aside. The court held that the husband had been in breach of his duty to make full and frank disclosure of his circumstances. However, in deciding whether to set aside the order, the court had to consider what it would have done at the time of the original consent order had it had the information which the husband had withheld. Because the new employment was only a possibility at the time the consent order was made, the court would not have acted differently. The wife's application was refused.

7.52 A payee who wishes to remarry, and whose periodical payments were compensatory rather than needs related, may be well advised to apply for an order of variation and for the periodical payments to be replaced with a capital order where possible. The capital order may be paid in instalments which, unlike periodical payments, may continue after a new marriage.

7.53  If the payee cohabits with a new partner, the court may take into account any actual or implied contribution of the payee's new partner.

> In *Fleming v Fleming (2004)*, a consent order was made which gave the wife, who was cohabiting with a new partner at that time, payments of £1,000 per month for four years. There was no provision in the order to prevent an application to extend the payments beyond that time. Shortly before the expiry date, the wife returned to court and asked for a variation of the order. The court held that cohabitation could not be treated in the same way as marriage which would automatically bring to an end the periodical payments. Nevertheless, the court should have regard to the cohabitation, including its financial consequences and its duration. Quite reasonably, the husband had an expectation that the payments would end four years after the order was made, and only in exceptional circumstances should that expectation be frustrated. The wife and her cohabitant had sufficient resources between them for their needs. The wife's application was refused.
>
> In *W v W (2009)*, a former wife who was cohabiting with a new partner, returned to court five years after her divorce when she learned that her former husband had sold his business. She asked for an increase in maintenance payments and a capitalization of them. The court held that the fact that she was cohabiting was not to be held against her and was only one of the factors to be taken into account. She was awarded an increase.
>
> In *North v North (2007)*, the couple had divorced in 1977, and the wife was given a nominal order of periodical payments at the rate of five pence per annum during their joint lives, or until remarriage, or until a further order was made. She also received a generous capital award and further generous gifts from her husband. In 2000, the wife moved to Australia, where she chose to live in an expensive part of Sydney, and failed to earn a living. Her investments failed, whilst her husband's wealth increased. She sought a variation of the nominal order, which was granted by the judge, and the husband appealed. The Court of Appeal held that the husband should not be responsible for the consequences of the wife's choices which had left her in need but he might be responsible for losses which were outside of her control. The Court invited the parties to make further arguments for and against an increase in payments by the husband.
>
> In *Vaughan v Vaughan (2010)*, the former husband of a 71 year-old woman, who had been divorced since 1986, applied for a termination of the periodical payments he had been making to her. The judge ruled in his favour on the basis that he had remarried and his support of his new wife reduced the income available for his first wife. The Court of Appeal refused to accept that either wife took priority but that it must simply use its discretion in accordance with MCA 1973 s.25. It allowed the first wife's appeal and ordered the husband to make a capital payment of £342,000. (See also *Hvorostovsky v Hvorostovsky (2009); Lauder v Lauder (2007); VB v JP (2008); Mc Farlane v McFarlane (2009).*)

## Capital orders (MCA 1973, s 23)

7.54 Where there is sufficient capital, a payee spouse is likely to prefer an order which allows complete freedom of control over future finances. A capital order, in the form of an outright transfer of a lump sum or shares, will permit that control. The court may order sale of any spousal property to allow a capital order to be made (see MCA 1973, s 24A). Capital payments may be ordered to be paid in instalments which overcomes the problems associated with periodical payments; the instalments will survive the remarriage of a payee, and may survive the death of a payer as a charge against his or her estate.

## Property adjustment orders (MCA 1973, s 24)

7.55 MCA 1973, s 24 gives the court wide powers to redistribute spousal property. This includes all personal and real property, any pre- or post-nuptial settlements made for the benefit of the spouses and their family which include life insurance policies as well a trusts of personal and real of property, and pensions.

7.56 For most spouses, the family home will be their most important resource. Where it is of sufficient value, the court may order sale of the house and divide the proceeds between the two parties to enable them to purchase individual properties. However, in many cases, the family home will not yield sufficient capital to allow for this. Alternative orders, which will allow one party to remain in the family home without doing too great an injustice to the other spouse, will be necessary.

### *Transfer of property*

7.57 Where one spouse has sufficient capital, the other spouse may be awarded a lump sum in return for the transfer of the family home. If there is insufficient capital to pay for such a transfer, a spouse may be given the family home in return for renouncing any claim for periodical payments, or a spouse may accept a reduction in periodical payments.

### *Mesher orders*

7.58 The court may make what is known as a Mesher order (see ***Mesher v Mesher (1980)***). These orders, which go in and out of favour with the court, tend only to be used where there is insufficient capital to provide homes for both parties. The order provides for sale of the property at a specified point in the future such as when the children reach the age of 18 or complete their education.

7.59 One of the major drawbacks to Mesher orders is that they leave the spouse who remains in the family home, usually the woman, with a false sense of security and delay her from facing the reality of the future and seeking gainful employment. When the house is sold, she will have to re-house herself at a time when she may not have the financial resources or career potential to enable her to do so in the foreseeable future.

> In ***Dorney-Kingdom v Dorney-Kingdom (2000)***, Thorpe LJ recognized that Mesher orders could produce
>
> *...a harsh situation in which the primary carer having discharged her responsibility to the children is then left in a position when she is unable to re-house herself as an independent person probably at a relatively vulnerable stage of life.*
>
> However, he decided to grant the order because the family home was of sufficient value that the woman could be re-housed and the man could be adequately compensated when the property was sold in the future at a time when the children would no longer need to be housed.
>
> In ***B v B (Mesher Order) (2003)***, the court declined to grant a Mesher order. It held that it was not appropriate to do so because the woman would make a significant contribution in the future by bringing up the child who was very young at the time of the court hearing. Her own income and future career opportunities would be severely affected. The man would very rapidly be able to recoup the cost to him of an outright transfer of the property to his ex-wife.

### *Martin orders*

7.60 Martin orders, named after the decision in ***Martin v Martin (1978)***, are not dissimilar to Mesher orders and were devised to overcome the problems of Mesher orders. A Martin order allows the spouse to remain in the family home for as long as he or she wishes or until the occurrence of an event, such as remarriage, cohabitation, or death, when the property will be sold and the proceeds distributed in accordance with the court order. In *Martin*, the husband was housed in council accommodation. The wife was allowed to remain in occupation of the family home. A deferred sale under a Mesher order would not have given her sufficient money to purchase a new home for herself. She too would have required to be re-housed by the local authority.

7.61 One of the problems with both Mesher and Martin orders is that they keep the parties trapped into a financial relationship with each other which appears to conflict with the 'clean break principle' discussed below.

## Pension orders (MCA 1973, s 24(b),(c),(d))

7.62 After the family home, pensions are usually the next most valuable asset. Prior to 1996, the court had no power to directly re-allocate pension benefits. It could merely attempt to compensate a spouse who risked the loss of pension benefits if there were sufficient resources to do so. The award of a lump sum payment, property settlement, or additional periodical payments could be used to offset the loss. Since 1996, through a succession of Acts, the courts have the power to deal more directly with pension benefits, although offsetting, of course, continues to remain a possibility.

7.63 The Pensions Act 1995 gave the courts power to make earmarking orders, now known as attachment orders, which set aside a portion of the pension for the benefit of an ex-spouse, when the pension came on stream on the husband's retirement. These orders have proven to be unpopular and problematic. The ex-spouse has no control over a beneficiary who decides to delay the commencement of the pension after the proposed date of retirement. If the ex-spouse remarries, he or she will lose the right to the income part of the pension, and he or she may also lose the lump sum portion of the pension because the court has the power to vary it prior the pension holder's retirement If the beneficiary dies prior to retirement, the benefits to the ex-spouse will be reduced.

7.64 In an attempt to deal with these problems, the Welfare Reform and Pensions Act 1999 introduced pension-sharing orders. At the time of the divorce the pension will be valued and a transfer of a proportion of it made to the ex-spouse. He or she may then add to that portion and build up a pension fund in his or her own right and under his or her own control.

### Variation of capital orders and orders relating to the family home (MCA 1973, s 31)

7.65 Where an order was made on judicial separation, and the parties subsequently divorce, the parties' financial situation will be considered afresh, and a new order may be made.

7.66 Where a capital order or orders relating to the family home were made in divorce or nullity proceedings, they must normally be regarded as final unless exceptional circumstances arise. If this were not so couples might be left with the permanent yet uncertain hope that, in the event of a dramatic change of fortune in the affairs of one of the spouses, an application could be made to vary the original order. The courts have shown themselves most reluctant to vary orders. Their concern has been, insofar as is possible, to allow couples that certainty which will enable them to reorganize their lives as individuals and move forward.

7.67 Where the capital payments are ordered to be made by instalments, an application for variation is possible whilst any of the instalments remain outstanding (see *Myerson v Myerson No 2 (2009)* below).

*Leave to appeal*

7.68 A spouse who wishes to appeal must first obtain the leave of the court. Secondly, if leave to appeal is granted, the court must take into account all the new facts before it in determining whether to vary the order and, if so, what the new order should be.

7.69     In *Barder v Barder (1988)*, the House of Lords laid down four conditions for a successful application for leave to appeal:

- There must have been a change of circumstances which occurred after the grant of the order; and which invalidated the basis on which it was made.
- The event must have occurred soon after the making of the original order.
- The application for leave should be made promptly.
- Third parties must not be prejudiced by the grant of leave to appeal an original order.

In the decisions relating to leave to appeal, the courts have exercised their discretion on a case by case basis. The decisions are not easy to reconcile; they appear to contain elements of a generalized, and often, unarticulated view of fairness.

7.70     The following decisions illustrate the differing approaches of the courts in determining whether to grant leave to appeal.

> In *Barder (1988)*, a consent order had been made, under which the husband was to transfer his share in the family home to his wife in order to end all further obligations between them. Five weeks later, the wife killed their two children and committed suicide. She left a will naming her mother as the beneficiary. The House of Lords held that the consent order had been based on the basic assumption that the wife and children would require a home for a substantial period of time, and that that assumption had been totally negated by their deaths. The husband's application for leave to appeal the original order was allowed.

> In *Livesey v Jenkins (1985)*, by a consent order, the husband transferred his half-share in the matrimonial home to the wife on the basis that she would live there and provide a home for herself and the children. She would also take over responsibility for the mortgage payments. Immediately prior to the making of the order, the wife became engaged and actually married two days after the family home was transferred to her. On hearing the news of her marriage, the husband successfully applied for leave to appeal the consent order. The House of Lords held that the court could not properly exercise its discretion under the MCA 1973 without adequate information on all the matters which it was required to consider. Each spouse owed a duty to each other and to the court to disclose any relevant facts; an intention to marry was one of them (see also *Bokor-Ingram v Boker-Ingram (2009)*; cf *Dixon v Marchant (2008)*).

> In *Cornick v Cornick (1994)*, the wife was awarded a lump sum payment which was equivalent to 50 per cent of the value of her husband's assets (she also obtained an order for periodical payments). Soon after the divorce, the husband's shares rose substantially in value. The court refused the wife's application for leave to appeal to set aside the

original order. There had been no mistake made in the calculation of the shares and their sudden ascent was a fortuitous event. This did not constitute a sufficient change to invalidate the basis of the original order.

By contrast, in **Thompson v Thompson (1991)**, the wife was granted leave to appeal an order, which awarded her the family home in return for her payment of £7,500 to the husband. Soon after the order was made, the husband sold his business for £45,000. There had been some confusion over the valuation of the business at the time the order was made. Prior to the order, it had been valued at £45,000 but the award to the wife had been based on a later valuation of £20,000. The court held that the sale of the business at £45,000 could be viewed as a new event which changed the situation radically. It was irrelevant that it was not some entirely new matter. Both parties had acted reasonably, and without fraud, on the assumption that the business was worth only £20,000.

## Looking afresh

7.71 Once leave to appeal has been granted, the courts have stressed that in determining whether to grant a variation or not, although the matter is looked at afresh, the basis on which leave to appeal was granted is of prime importance. The following decisions illustrate the courts' approach.

In *Smith v Smith (Smith and others intervening) (1992)*, the wife was given a capital order of £54,000 which represented 50 per cent of the couple's capital. However, the wife committed suicide within six months of the order. Her daughter was the sole beneficiary of her estate. The husband, who was unwell and without huge financial resources, appealed the original order. His appeal was allowed on the basis that the original capital order was for the wife's needs and these were no longer relevant. He was awarded an additional £25,000; the daughter retained the remaining £29,000 from the wife's award.

The husband, in **Vicary v Vicary (1992)**, had a substantial income and shares in his own company. On divorce there was a consent order which gave the wife a lump sum of £250,000 and an end to all obligations between the parties. Later, the wife discovered that, at the time of the order, the husband had not revealed that negotiations were taking place for the sale of the company. The sale was completed shortly after the order was made; this resulted in an increase in the value of the shares to £2.8 million. When the wife discovered this, she succeeded in her application to have the consent order set aside.

In **Cook v Cook (1988)**, by a consent order, an absolute interest in the family home was transferred to the wife. Prior to the divorce, she and her husband had swapped partners with a neighbouring couple. However, at the time of the divorce, the wife had maintained that her relationship with her new partner had cooled. Shortly after the order was made, the husband discovered that this information was untrue and appealed to have the consent order set aside. His appeal was rejected. The court held that the husband had been fully aware of his wife's relationship at the time of the original consent order, even if he had not known the precise nature of it. There was no significant change in the circumstances (see also *S v S (2009)*).

The economic downturn led the husband in *Myerson v Myerson (No 2) (2009)*, to ask for a variation of a consent order. He and his wife had agreed that she should receive £11 million (43 per cent of the total assets) to be paid partly in instalments and partly in property transfer, and he would retain £14.5 million (57 per cent of the total assets).

The assets to be retained by Mr Myerson were primarily shares in his company plus various properties. When the global economy collapsed, his company's share price collapsed with it. This meant that his share of the assets dropped to 14 per cent and his wife's to 86 per cent.

The Court of Appeal gave Mr Myerson leave to appeal but refused to grant the appeal. By the time the appeal was heard the share prices had deteriorated still further, and the consent order would have left the husband with almost nothing. He argued that the fall in share prices meant that the consent order was unfair and unworkable, and that the relevant events were sufficiently dramatic to constitute new events as in *Barder (1988)*. The Court of Appeal held that the natural processes of price fluctuations, however dramatic, were insufficient to allow the husband's appeal. He had agreed an order leaving him in control of both profits and losses of his shares which was speculative, and there was no justification to relieve him of the consequences of his agreement. The husband continued to enjoy control of the opportunities that went with the speculation (see also *Walkden v Walkden (2009)*; *B v B (2008)*).

# The statutory guidelines (MCA 1973, s 25)

## A lack of overarching objective

7.72 In Part I of this chapter, it was noted that there is no community of property during marriage; each spouse has total freedom to deal with his or her own financial resources. It is not, therefore, surprising that many spouses resent the power given to the court, under the provisions of MCA 1973, s 25, to redistribute property which has up to that point belonged solely to one of them. Furthermore, they have no means of knowing in advance what the outcome might be; the court has total discretion over the reallocation process.

7.73 A certain sympathy should also be expressed for the judiciary who have had to deal with the cases relating to ancillary relief. They have wrestled with all the factors in MCA 1973, s 25 in order to determine the nature and amount of any award.

The section has been heavily criticized for its lack of an overall guiding objective which might enable the judiciary to arrive at orders which are viewed as fair and predictable.

> In *Cowan v Cowan (2001)*, Thorpe LJ acknowledged that couples seeking advice from solicitors were often told that the order would all depend on the judge on the day. If the law was in such a state, how could sensible couples plan their future and reach agreements? He defended the fact that, in the absence of reform by Parliament, the judiciary had been forced to develop various mechanisms, which had no statutory basis, in order to help them reach decisions.

7.74    In *White v White (2001)*, the House of Lords, and in *Lambert v Lambert (2003)*, the Court of Appeal, stressed the concept of fairness as the guiding principle in the reallocation of property on divorce but emphasized that all the factors in s 25 should be considered in order to reach a fair outcome for the parties. In particular both courts maintained that there should be no discrimination between the contributions made by a husband and wife in their respective roles. Any proposed award should be checked against the yardstick of equality. Where appropriate, this could lead to an equal division of the assets.

The decisions led to confusion and debate about the circumstances in which equal division of assets would be a fair outcome.

## Judicial efforts to resolve the confusion

### *Miller v Miller; McFarlane v McFarlane (2006)*

7.75    The House of Lords, in the conjoined decisions of *Miller v Miller; McFarlane v McFarlane (2006)*, attempted to resolve the muddle brought about by the lack of clarity of the earlier decisions and, in the absence of Parliament's willingness to reform the law, indulged in judicial law making. By putting a gloss on MCA 1973, s 25, their Lordships elucidated principles, which they claimed were based on consistency, practicality and fairness. They maintained that these principles would serve as clear guidelines in determining the reallocation of spousal assets. Baroness Hale stressed the importance of finding a way forward in order to secure

> *...that so far as possible like cases are treated alike but also to enable and encourage the parties to negotiate their own solutions as quickly and cheaply as possible.*

### *The facts in* **Miller and McFarlane (2006)**

7.76    Mr and Mrs Miller, who were both in their thirties, divorced after a short childless marriage of less than three years. The wife had modified her career plans, and reduced her income, in order to marry her husband. At the time of the marriage, the husband was a successful fund manager with an annual income in excess of £1 million, and also had shares worth £20 million. After the couple's marriage, the husband joined a new company and acquired £200,000 of shares which, by the time of the divorce hearing, had increased in value to around £15 million.

The Court of Appeal upheld the lower court's award of £5 million to Mrs Miller which, including the matrimonial home, represented a little less than 1/6 of Mr Miller's total worth. The Appeal Court justified this significant award, in the context of such a short marriage, partly on the ground that the husband was responsible for the breakdown of the marriage; he had had an affair with another woman whom he subsequently married and with whom he had a child. The Court of Appeal, rather confusingly, stated that this was not conduct which should be taken into account under MCA 1973, s 25(2)(g). Mr Miller appealed; the House of Lords, whilst accepting that the award to Mrs Miller was at the upper limit in the light of a short marriage, dismissed his appeal.

Mr and Mrs McFarlane had three children and had been married for 16 years. The wife had practised as a solicitor with Freshfields, a high-ranking London law firm. She gave up her career to enable her to care for the family and to help her husband advance his career as an accountant. On divorce, the husband earned an annual salary of £750,000. The couple agreed to divide the total capital of £3 million equally between them; it consisted primarily of three family homes. In the context of the husband's high earnings and the wife's sacrifice of her own career, this was not sufficient to compensate her. She applied for, and was given periodical payments of £250,000 per annum. The Court of Appeal restricted these to a five-year period; Mrs McFarlane appealed against this restriction. The House of Lords granted her appeal.

### *The decision in* **Miller and McFarlane (2006)**

7.77  Lord Nicholls and Baroness Hale gave the two leading judgments. Their Lordships clarified the confusion relating to the issue of conduct, and the purpose of periodical payments. They reiterated that negative conduct should not be taken into account in assessing the size of an award unless it is of an extreme nature which was not the case in the Miller's marriage. Positive conduct, on the other hand, could be taken into account. They also acknowledged that periodical payments are not merely limited to maintenance.

Baroness Hale stated that the overall aim of the court should be to set the parties on the road to independent living, and, in agreement with Lord Nicholls, centred her judgment on the concept of fairness. They both maintained that it should be the overarching principle in the determination of any award. According to Lord Nicholls, the concept of fairness is elusive:

*. . . it is an instinctive response to a given set of facts. Ultimately is grounded in social and moral values. These values, or attitudes, can be stated. But they cannot be justified, or refuted, by any objective process of logical reasoning. Moreover, they change from one generation to the next. It is not surprising therefore that in the present context there can be different views on the requirements of fairness in any particular case.*

Given this acceptance of the relativist nature of fairness, it is interesting to note that Lord Nicholls had little difficulty in expounding, with Baroness Hale's agreement, the three elements of fairness:

- First, fairness requires that the needs of the spouses and their children, generated by the relationship, should be satisfied and for most couples there are insufficient resources to do more than that.

- Second, fairness requires compensation to redress any future economic imbalance between the spouses as a result of the way in which they conducted their marriage. For instance, a husband's income earning capacity may have been increased because of his wife's supportive role in caring for the family. On divorce, the wife's earning capacity will almost certainly be less than had she worked throughout the marriage. She also loses the possibility of sharing in her husband's increased income, a possibility which may have been envisaged if and when she gave up work to help him in his career ambitions.

- Third, fairness requires an equal sharing of the assets acquired during the marriage unless there is good reason to do otherwise. This was a natural conclusion from the fact that marriage is an equal partnership. Special and exceptional contributions should not be taken into account unless it would be inequitable to ignore them.

All three elements, according to Lord Nicholls:

*...are linked to the parties' relationship, either causally or temporally, and not to extrinsic, unrelated factors, such as a disability arising after the marriage has ended.*

Lord Nicholl's view had changed dramatically since his judgment in **White v White (2000)** where he stated that:

*...s 25 of the 1973 Act makes no mention of an equal sharing of the parties' assets, even their marriage-related assets. A presumption of equal division would be an impermissible judicial gloss on the statutory provision. That would be so, even though the presumption would be rebuttable. Whether there should be such a presumption in England and Wales, and in respect of what assets, is a matter for Parliament.*

Perhaps the most important and complex part of the judgment was their Lordships' approach to the categorization, and subsequent division, of a couple's assets into matrimonial and non-matrimonial assets. The fact that the concept of matrimonial assets does not exist in English law did not deter their Lordships. Lord Nicholls defined matrimonial property as the family home, however and whenever it was obtained, even one owned prior to marriage. He also included all other assets, which had been acquired during the marriage, other than gifts or inherited property. Property acquired prior to the marriage was excluded from his definition.

Baroness Hale added the spouses' earning capacity to Lord Nicholls list of matrimonial assets and excluded business or investment assets which had been solely or mainly acquired by the efforts of one of the spouses. She believed that it was difficult to prove that these latter assets had been created with the help of the spouse who stayed at home, even if that support was a valuable contribution to the welfare and happiness of the family. She viewed these assets as speculative and risky; the spouse to whom they did not belong may not have shared in that risk.

Lord Nicholls and Baroness Hale agreed that matrimonial assets, but not non-matrimonial assets, should normally be divided equally. Non-matrimonial assets might also be subject to reallocation depending on all the circumstances of the case. A short marriage would be a good reason not to redistribute them between the spouses. Lord Nicholls had

*...an instinctive feeling that parties will generally have less call upon each other on the breakdown of a short marriage.*

Baroness Hale believed that there was

*...a perception that the size of the non-business partner's share should be linked to the length of the marriage.*

7.78 The decision in *Miller and McFarlane (2006)* left certain issues unresolved and in particular the difference between matrimonial property and non-matrimonial property. One year later, the Court of Appeal attempted to resolve the confusion in *Charman v Charman (No 4) (2007)*. It remains doubtful whether the Court of Appeal achieved its aim.

## The decision in *Charman v Charman (No 4) (2007)*

7.79 Mr and Mrs Charman met and married when they were very young and had no assets. At first, the wife worked as a civil servant until she became pregnant with the first of the couple's two children. The husband started his career as a junior clerk at Lloyds, and enjoyed a dramatic rise in the insurance industry. After 28 years of marriage, the couple decided to divorce. By this time their assets were valued at £131 million. Mrs Charman accepted that her husband had made a special contribution to the creation of this wealth and asked for 45 per cent of the assets. Her husband offered her £20 million (a little over 15 per cent of the assets). The judge accepted that the husband's special contribution, and the level of risk he would face relating to the assets which he might retain necessitated a departure from equality. He awarded Mrs Charman £48 million (36.5 per cent of the assets).

The husband appealed; he maintained that the judge had made insufficient allowance for his special contribution, that he should have first considered the factors in s 25 of the MCA 1973 before determining the percentage division, and that he should have not included for division the £68 million of assets held in an offshore discretionary trust.

The Court of Appeal dismissed the husband's appeal and explained the correct approach in determining ancillary relief in the light of *Miller and McFarlane (2006)* and explained that:

- The starting point must be the financial position of the parties. First an assessment of the resources must be made and then distribution must be decided upon. The likely future income must always be assessed, even in a clean-break case, because it might well be relevant to a fair division of property.

- Where it is clear that the resources would provide adequately for the needs of the parties, the court may begin with an assumption of equal sharing of the assets and then consider the matters contained in MCA (1973), s25 (2) to decide whether there is a good reason to depart from it.

- In cases where it is not clear that the resources are sufficient for equal sharing to be an appropriate division, s25(2) may be the starting point.

- Equal sharing may be departed from both 'within' and 'from' the equal sharing principle.

- Departures from equal sharing 'within' the principle may well depend on the source of the assets and the time they were acquired. The court is more likely to depart from equal sharing if the property can be categorized as non-matrimonial. Where one party has produced assets by their own exceptional personal contribution it may be fair to depart from equal sharing 'within' the principle. This may be inferred from the size of the assets but the Court of Appeal refused to put a figure on the size of the assets which would lead to such an inference. If a reduction in equal sharing was to be made it should be limited to approximately 55 per cent/45 per cent at its lowest or 66 per cent/33 per cent at its highest.

- A departure 'from' the principle of equal sharing may be made where the need to compensate a partner, provide for their needs, recognise conduct, or secure a clean break overrides the equal sharing principle.

- Prima facie, all property should be open to equal sharing. The concept of 'unilateral assets', discussed by Baroness Hale in *Miller and McFarlane (2006)* was intended to apply to short or dual-career marriages. Its application to Mrs Charman's situation would be deeply discriminatory and gravely undermining of the sharing principle.

- Each of the three principles of need, compensation and sharing are contained within s 25 of the MCA 1973: the principle of need requires consideration of the financial needs, obligations and responsibilities of the parties, the standard of living enjoyed by the family, the age of the parties and any physical or mental disability of either; the principle of compensation relates to any prospective financial disadvantage which one party faces upon divorce as a result of decisions taken for the benefit of the family during the marriage; and the principle of sharing relates to the contributions of each party to the welfare of the family, to the length of the marriage and, in an exceptional case, to the conduct, either positive or negative, of either party.

- Where there is conflict between the three principles of need, compensation and sharing, the criterion of fairness rules the outcome. If the principle of needs suggests an award of property greater than that suggested by the sharing principle, the former principle should prevail. If the needs principle would give rise to a lesser award than that which would be given under the sharing principle, the latter principle should prevail.

- Where it is likely that trustees would advance the trust assets to one of the spouses, those assets may be viewed as the property of that spouse and available for redistribution.

Finally, the Court of Appeal stressed, yet again, the need for review of the law relating to ancillary relief. In its view, the extent of social change affecting the marital relationship, the increasing impact of globalization and London's role as the 'divorce capital of the world', and the drive towards harmonisation of the law within Europe make this review long overdue.

7.80 Commentators have rejoiced that the decision in *Charman (2007)* was in the form of a single judgment. However, obfuscation appears to be a feature of the Court of Appeal's decision, and it would not be too unfair to suggest that there are moments in the judgment which bear a certain resemblance to erudite discussions about the number of angels dancing on the head of a pin. The Court of Appeal's approach to which resources may be redistributed seems at odds with that of the House of Lords in *Miller and McFarlane (2006)* even though the outcome of following one approach, rather than the other, may not be very different.

7.81 Subsequent cases, as is to be expected, have attempted to revisit the issues discussed in *Charman (2007)*. For example, in *B v B (Ancillary Relief) (2008))*, the Court of Appeal considered the appeal of a wife where the assets, although not vast, exceeded the spouses' needs. The wife had inherited assets before she married and, after the marriage, they were primarily used to buy a car wash business which was built up by her husband who had had no assets of his own. The marriage lasted 12 years. The trial judge ordered an equal division of the assets which included an order that the business be transferred to the husband. The Court of Appeal resorted to the yardstick of equality as a check to determine what would be a fair division rather than the principle of equal sharing. It concluded that an unfair division in the wife's favour would be more appropriate, given that the assets on divorce all resulted from the wife's pre-marital assets.

Moylan J justified this revisitation of the issues in ancillary relief cases in *P v P (2010)*:

*At present we are engaged in an incremental search for a consistent pattern in the application of the principles identified by the House of Lords. This is unlikely to happen quickly. It needs to be incremental because if the risk of broad statements about the application of those principles can overlook the effect in different factual situations not then before the court... In this search there is a well recognized tension between predictability and flexibility in approach and outcome.*

## The guidelines (MCA 1973, s 25)

7.82 The overlapping guidelines provided in MCA 1973, s 25 will continue to be of relevance as an essential part of the court's discretionary exercise in determining ancillary relief applications. However, many of the pre-*Miller and MacFarlane (2006)* decisions must now be read in the light of that decision and that of *Charman (2007)*.

## Duty of the court (MCA 1973, 25(1))

7.83 The duty of the court when making any award is to take into account all the circumstances of the case but, in so doing, its primary task, but not its paramount one, is to consider the welfare of any minor child of the family under the age of 18.

## The 'clean break' principle (MCA 1973, s 25A)

7.84 In *Minton v Minton (1978)*, Lord Scarman explained the problematic principle of the 'clean break' principle in applications for ancillary relief:

> *The law now encourages spouses to avoid bitterness after family breakdown and to settle their money and property problems. An object of the modern law is to encourage each to put the past behind them and to begin a new life which is not overshadowed by the relationship which has broken down.*

Although the principle had its origins in judicial policy, it is now in statutory form. MCA 1973, s 25A specifically directs the court to consider whether it is possible to end all obligations between the spouses, either at the time of the hearing or at a specified date in the future. If all obligations are terminated, the 'clean break' principle is normally extended to exclude any future application for provision from a deceased ex-spouse's estate under the Inheritance (Provision for Family and Dependants) Act 1976 (see Chapter 8).

7.85 The 'clean break' principle has its limitations. It only applies to spouses; it cannot extend to ending financial provision for any children of the family. The principle reflects the fact that, in theory, the decrees of divorce, nullity, and judicial separation (albeit partially) all end the spousal status. In practice, however, these decrees do not necessarily end the spousal relationship. Marriage generates financial responsibilities which may need to continue even after it has ended. Where the available financial resources are insufficient to provide a capital sum to compensate for past contribution or future maintenance, ongoing periodical payments may be the only solution for wives who have taken care of the family and home and supported their husbands' earning capacity. They may experience problems in re-entering paid employment and be unable to attain self-sufficiency. These spouses will remain locked into a financial connection with each other because it would be unfair to permit them to do otherwise.

## MCA 1973, s 25(2)(a)

7.86 S 25(2)(a) provides for the court to take into account the income, earning capacity, property and other financial resources which each of the parties to the marriage has or is likely to have in the foreseeable future, including in the case of earning capacity any increase in that capacity which it would in the opinion of the court be reasonable to expect a party to the marriage to take steps to acquire.

7.87 The spouses must be absolutely honest about their available resources, and limitations are placed on how information about those resources may be obtained. In *Tchenguiz and others v Imerman (2010)*, the Court of Appeal condemned the manner in which information was illegally obtained from the husband's computer even though it might prove the existence of resources which he was hiding to defeat his wife's application for ancillary relief (see also *FZ v SZ (2010)*).

### Pre-marital assets

7.88 The existence of pre-marital assets may lead the court to depart from the equal sharing principle unless the needs of the parties cannot be otherwise satisfied. If they have been used to purchase a family home or include a house which is subsequently used as the family home, there will be little question about the fairness of their division (see eg *L v L (2008)*).

### Gifted assets

7.89 In *N V N (2010)*, the husband had been given significant assets by his family. Charles J was reluctant to make the husband part with all these assets even though the marriage had been a long one and had produced four children. He held that a departure from equal division would be fair. The assets had been in the husband's family since the end of the eighteenth century and Charles J thought that it was reasonable that they should be preserved to be handed on to the next generation. Furthermore, the wife had always understood that the standard of living she had enjoyed during the marriage could not have continued, had she remained married, after her husband's retirement. A settlement of £5.3 million which represented a 32 per cent share of the total assets was seen as an adequate provision for her.

### Post-separation assets

7.90 There has been considerable debate about post-separation assets.

Jackson (2002) attempted to justify the exclusion of such assets:

*Whatever the length of the marriage, a claim may fail if it is left dormant for too long, in which case one factor may be that the husband's assets have been built up with another woman. It has been said that after a long lapse of time a party to a marriage should be entitled to take the view that there would be no revival or initiation of financial claims against him; the longer the lapse of time the more secure he should feel in the rearrangement of his financial affairs and the less should any claim be encouraged or entertained.*

7.91    A good example of the difficulties brought about by delay is the decision of Booth J in *D v W (1984)* in which she stated:

*There are certain detrimental consequences of delay. The first is that delay engenders bitterness and hostility between the parties which is detrimental to the whole fairly and, In particular, to any children of the family. The husband in this case is aggrieved at the attack that is now made upon the home in which he has been living for the past 10 years. The wife, on the other hand, feels deprived of her money and the right to live there. The delay inevitably increases costs. It leads to a multiplicity of affidavits which are filed in order to deal with the ever-changing position of each of the parties. Inevitably, it lead to an exchange of correspondence over a protracted period between solicitors and, no doubt, also leads to attendance of the parties upon the solicitors. And all those matters add up in costs.*

*Further, with the change in property values and with inflation as it is in our present economic situation, as well as with the changes in the parties' own situation and the commitments they take upon themselves, the whole case can be materially altered, and the ability of the parties to cope with any orders that the court might otherwise properly have made upon the merits of a case may be put in jeopardy. Indeed, delay can put the court in the simple position of not being able to do justice between the parties according to the merits of each case. Unless it can be clearly shown that one party bears the greater responsibility for the delay that does the other, the court may be left with no alternative but to make an order which does not reflect the merits of the case.*

7.92    In *Rossi v Rossi (2006)*, the court maintained that property acquired, or created, by the sole efforts of one of the spouses (and without the use of any matrimonial property) after separation unless it is a bonus or other earned income which relates to the period prior to separation, should only be subject to reallocation in limited circumstances such as:

- if the parties' resources are so small that the court has little choice;

- if the marriage was so long that it is difficult to disentangle the matrimonial property and non-matrimonial property;

- if the applicant spouse did not delay in making a claim;

- if the spouse who owns the non-matrimonial property has treated the applicant spouse badly;

- if the spouse who owns the after acquired asset is capable of making more money in the future from which the applicant spouse will not benefit.

7.93    In *B v B (2010)*, the spouses separated in 2007 after an 11-year marriage. On their divorce in 2009, the husband maintained that his post separation bonuses should not be available for redistribution. Moylan J held that in the absence of needs or compensation, fairness demands that sharing of assets should end at the point of separation. On the basis of fairness and an assessment of the wife's needs, he awarded the wife a sum which included a 40 per cent portion of the post separation assets.

7.94    In 2009, a wife was awarded £220,000 22 years after separating from her husband. She and her husband had been married for four years prior to their separation but they did not divorce at that time. The wife learned that her husband had inherited £120,000 which he had invested in property and sold it for approximately £1.1 million, and decided to obtain a divorce and apply for ancillary relief. She maintained that she had brought the child of the marriage up on her own and without any support from her husband. She claimed that she needed money to provide her with long-term security to house herself and provide a pension. The court maintained that the award was fair and would leave her husband with sufficient to house and maintain himself (*The Times,* 13 June 2009).

## Increase in earning capacity

7.95  In determining available resources, the court may take into account any potential increase in the earning capacity of either spouse. The courts rarely do so and where they have, have tended to have higher expectations of husbands than wives.

In *Hardy v Hardy (1981)*, the husband worked for his father, who was an extremely rich man, in his racing stables. His salary was artificially low at £70 a week. It could not possibly have supported the high standard of living which he enjoyed. The court held that the husband could be expected to earn substantially more by working for an independent employer and took this into account in its award to the wife.

In *A v A (Financial Provision) (1998)*, the husband and wife had been married for 13 years and had one son, aged eight, whom the husband adored. The husband, aged 64, was very wealthy; he had assets of over £200 million and an annual income of £1 million. The wife, aged 40, had an engineering degree but had never worked. The court awarded her a lump sum of £4.4 million because she bore the major responsibility for childcare. Singer J took into account that:

*...her role as mother to the husband's most treasured success, the son, would survive the marriage, continuing until she was over 50 years old'. It would not be reasonable, therefore, to expect her to seek full-time employment and increase her income unless she chose to do so.*

## Third party assets

7.96  Where a spouse has other resources which, although belonging to a third party, are available for his or her needs, those resources may be taken into account in determining any award. The court, of course, has no jurisdiction to make an award against the third party.

> In *X v X (Y and Z intervening) (2002)*, the wife apparently had no financial resources of her own, but had an extremely wealthy family who maintained her prodigiously. The court ordered her to pay her husband £500,000 from funds promised to her by her brother.

7.97 The rule can be a source of acrimony for third parties, who marry or cohabit with an ex-spouse payee. Many perceive it as an indirect use of their financial resources to maintain a person for whom they have no legal responsibility. However, to ignore these financial resources may be equally unfair to any ex-spouse payer. His or her payment would, in reality, be supporting the cohabitant, albeit indirectly.

> In *MH v MH (1982)*, the husband, a wealthy man, provided a number of properties for his ex-wife in which she lived with her cohabitant. The husband also made generous provision for the children of the marriage by paying for holidays, outgoings, and domestic help. The wife had income from her own investments and her farming activities. Her cohabitant, an unemployed chartered accountant, made no financial contribution; he had proposed marriage to the wife but she had refused. He subsequently decided that it would be against his principles to marry anyone whom he was unable to support. The wife maintained that she could not marry again and, in any event, not her cohabitant who was 16 years younger than her. She was prepared to be physically and emotionally dependent upon him, but not financially.
>
> The husband applied to have his maintenance payments to his wife reduced on the basis that he had been indirectly subsidizing the cohabitant for a considerable period of time, and that it was only fair that the cohabitant should now make a contribution to the support of the wife.
>
> The court took a broad approach; it did not undertake a serious financial enquiry into the wife's and her cohabitant's financial affairs but felt that it was only fair to reduce her periodical payments to take into account the amount which her cohabitant could reasonably earn.

## MCA 1973, s 25(2)(b) the financial needs, obligations and responsibilities which each of the parties to the marriage has or is likely to have in the foreseeable future

7.98 In many cases, the resources will not be sufficient for the needs of both parties and a compromise will be necessary.

> In *Piglowski v Piglowski (1999)*, the husband and wife were Polish. On divorce, the husband remarried. His ex-spouse wished to remain in the matrimonial home which was

worth £100,000; the husband wanted it to be sold, and to be given half of the total assets of £127,400, in order to buy a property for himself and his new wife. The ex-spouse was granted her wish on condition she allowed the husband to have 30 per cent of the total assets which would not, of course, be sufficient to satisfy her or her husband's need to be housed.

The House of Lords accepted that the judge had legitimately taken into account the wife's major financial contribution to the family by working as a cleaner in order to pay for household expenses and school fees. She had also taken care of the home and the two children of the marriage and was continuing to do so. It would be unfair to put the wife out of her home. Thirty per cent of the assets represented fair compensation to the husband even if insufficient for his needs.

7.99 If the resources are sufficient, needs will be largely irrelevant.

7.100 Obligations and responsibilities must be ones which have been reasonably assumed. They include those related to the creation of a new family.

In *Slater v Slater (1982)*, the husband had remarried. He lived with his second wife in a house in the country in Kent. They had significant expenses for cars and petrol to allow them to work in London. The wife lived with the three children of the marriage. The court accepted that it was the husband's choice to live in the country. His excess of expenditure over income of £1,298 a year was brought about by his extravagant and unreasonable expenditure on petrol and car maintenance. The court was not prepared to take them into account as essential items expenditure, in determining the amount of the wife's award.

## MCA 1973, s 25(2)(c): the standard of living enjoyed by the family before the breakdown of the marriage

7.101 This provision will, of course, only be applicable if there are sufficient resources to take it into account, and it is likely that in many cases it will be subsumed in the sharing principle.

In *F v F (Ancillary Relief: Substantial Assets) (1995)*, Thorpe J held that in determining the reasonable needs of a wife after a marriage to a very wealthy husband, it was important as a matter of principle that the court should use the standard of living of the ultra-rich and not the scales that would seem generous to ordinary people. He concluded that:

*... it would be wrong in principle to determine the application on some broad conclusion that if the wife cannot manage at the rate of a quarter of a million a year, she ought to be able to. I think that it is necessary to establish a yardstick that more nearly reflects the standard of living which has been the norm for the wife ever since marriage and for the husband for considerably longer.*

The wife was judged to need a home worth £1.9 million; £300,000 to purchase a London flat; a chalet in Switzerland in which the wife would have a life interest; £685,000 to furnish the properties. The husband had already ceded chattels worth approximately £100,000, and the wife had been given jewellery worth £300,000. She would also need a maintenance fund of £5 million. The total cost to the husband would therefore be in the region of £9 million.

Thorpe J criticized the claim of £4,000 for the labrador and said:

*After all, from the dog's point of view, there is not a lot of difference in being owned by a very rich family or simply a comfortably off family and I find it hard to see how a dog can cost as much as £4,000 per year.*

## MCA 1973, s 25(2)(d): the age of each party to the marriage and the duration of the marriage

7.102    In *C v C (Financial Relief: Short Marriage) (1997)*, Ward LJ explained the interrelationship between all the various factors listed in s 25(2) when considering the level of award after a short marriage. He thought that the circumstances and needs of the wife, who was aged 40, were exceptional enough to justify the award of a lump sum of £195,000 and periodical payments of £19,500 per annum. She had met her husband when she was working as a high-class prostitute. They soon had a child and parted nine months after they were married.

The judge in the lower court had been overtly impressed by the wife and her efforts at dealing with the numerous adverse events of her life; these included a husband who harassed her, redundancy, dyslexia, low self-esteem, and a lack of self-confidence, a nervous breakdown, dental problems, a road accident, and a very sick child. Her career success as a prostitute was her only redeeming endeavour. He had described her as

*...an attractive lady, to whom her appearance is of critical importance. As will be seen, she has a fragile personality, and is vulnerable to emotional reverses, resulting in depression and loss of confidence and self-respect... in my view it is essential to her sense of self-worth and indeed to her effective functioning that she should present herself as attractively as possible. It is important to her to be well dressed and groomed, and thus she buys designer clothes, and spends considerable sums on hairdressing, fitness, make-up etc. I have no doubt that during the early and happier part of the cohabitation, the husband was pleased to indulge this expenditure, but as the quality of the parties' relationship quickly deteriorated, he began to resent and cavil at the cost, and for that reason reduced the wife's allowance. Nevertheless, I am satisfied that the parties enjoyed a very comfortable life-style during their cohabitation.*

This section would not be complete without mentioning the high profile case of *Mills v McCartney (2008)* which involved an application for ancillary relief after a short marriage. Ms Mills was awarded £24.3 million based on her needs, and not a half share of her husband's £400 million fortune which had been primarily generated long before he met Ms Mills. Her response to the judgment was to empty a jug of cold water over her husband's lawyer.

## MCA 1973, s 25(2)(e): any physical or mental disability, of either of the parties to the marriage

7.103   This provision is related to the idea that marriage was traditionally considered as a long-term commitment 'for better, for worse', an idea which is surely negated by the very fact of divorce. Whether a spouse should have the responsibility of supporting a partner who is disabled, particularly if the disability arose after the marriage ended, or through the applicant's own fault, remains questionable.

> In *Seaton v Seaton (1986)*, the husband, aged 42, and the wife, aged 36, had been married for 14 years. They had no children. The wife was a teacher whose resources were limited. The husband had lost his job following criminal proceedings, and had a propensity to drink excessively. His wife had financially supported him. After the divorce, the husband suffered a major stroke, which severely incapacitated him. He could watch television and go out with friends but could do little else. His parents took care of him.
>
> The court found that the husband's needs were very limited because of his illness; to make any order for the wife to contribute to his care would not enhance his life. His basic needs were already reasonably satisfied. It dismissed the husband's application for periodical payments, and ordered a clean break settlement.

## MCA 1973, s 25(2)(f): the contribution which either of the parties has made or is likely in the foreseeable future to make to the welfare of the family, including any contributions by looking after the home or caring for the family

7.104   The decisions in *White v White (2000)* and *Lambert v Lambert* (2003) emphasized that contribution should be judged in a non-sexist manner.

> In *White (2000)*, Lord Nicholls stated:
>
> *There should be no bias in favour of the money-earner and against the homemaker and the child-carer.*
>
> In *Lambert (2003)*, Mr Lambert pleaded that he had made a stellar contribution to the acquisition of the assets and maintained that his wife's contribution had been merely ornamental.
>
> Thorpe LJ said that:
>
> *... special contribution remains a legitimate possibility but only in exceptional circumstances. It would be both futile and dangerous to even attempt to speculate*

*on the boundaries of the exceptional. In the course of argument I suggested that it might more readily be found in the generating force behind the fortune rather than in the mere product itself. A number of hypothetical examples were canvassed ranging from the creative artist via the superstar footballer to the inventive genius, who not only creates but also develops some universal aid or prescription. All that seems to me to be more safely left to future case by case exploration.*

## MCA, 1973, s 25(2)(g): the conduct of each of the parties, if that conduct is such that it would in the opinion of the court be inequitable to disregard it

7.105   It will be rare for any court to take into account negative conduct. The following decisions illustrate the type of negative conduct which has affected financial awards.

In *J v S-T (formerly J) (Transsexual: Ancillary Relief) (1997)*, a decision on financial relief following a decree of nullity, the court accepted the wife's view that her transsexual husband had deceived her as to his gender over a period of 14 years. He had used a sexual prosthesis, which he kept in his bedside table; always backed out of the shower, and had agreed to his wife having donor insemination to conceive their two children. In spite of this evidence, the wife maintained she had no knowledge of his true sexual identity. The husband was denied any financial relief because of his supposed deception.

In *Kyte v Kyte (1988)*, the court reduced the wife's lump sum from £14,000 to £5,000. The husband suffered from depression and was suicidal. At first, the wife attempted to rescue him. After meeting a new lover, she changed her mind and decided to accede to her husband's demands to help him die. She took alcohol and drugs to him and, when she learned of his failure to die, telephoned him and said:

'I know you had no guts'.

It is not clear how the court determined the quantum of the reduction on the basis of the wife's conduct.

In 2010, the Court of Appeal in *K v L* upheld the trial judge's decision to order the wife to provide only minimally for her husband's needs because he had been imprisoned for sexually assaulting two of her grandchildren from a previous marriage.

In *FZ v SZ and others (Ancillary Relief: Conduct) (2010)*, Mostyn J regarded the individual conduct of each of the spouses as equally heinous and held that it cancelled out any effect it might otherwise have had on his final order.

The wife had made a false report to the police about her husband with respect to a breach of ouster orders, and the husband had reported his wife's parents to the tax authorities in their country of origin. Although the wife had taken documents belonging to her husband which concealed evidence of his assets, Mostyn J did not regard this as relevant conduct.

Had she decided to breach locks on her husband's property or to open his post then she would have being found guilty of conduct which would reduce the order made.

7.106 Conduct can, however, also be positive. It may be taken into account but only if it is exceptional.

In **Kokosinski v Kokosinski (1980)**, the wife had faithfully, and lovingly, helped her husband to build up a family business and care for the home. The marriage was comparatively short but had been preceded by a 20-year period of cohabitation, because the husband could not divorce his previous wife. The court centred its decision on the wife's positive conduct rather than on the brevity of the marriage in order to achieve a fair outcome. She was awarded £8,000.

## MCA 1973, s 25(2)(h): in the case of proceedings for divorce or nullity of marriage, the value to each of the parties to the marriage of any benefit which, by reason of the dissolution or annulment of the marriage, that party will lose the chance of acquiring

7.107 In **S v S (2007)**, the court refused to take into account a wife's potential inheritance rights from her parents on the basis that there was no certainty that she would receive them; a will may be revised until the moment of death.

## Pre-nuptial and post-nuptial agreements

7.108 Given that such a high percentage of marriages today end in divorce, it is readily understandable that couples, particularly wealthy ones and/or those marrying for a second time, might wish to make agreements before they marry, or during the marriage, which would take effect in the event of their divorce. By doing so, they hope that they might avoid the court's involvement in the discretionary reallocation of their assets.

### Problematic nature of agreements

7.109 The enforcement of agreements has been seen as problematic. Pre-nuptial agreements have been viewed as contrary to public policy in that they may be the price for entering into a marriage. Post-nuptial agreements made by deed still risk falling foul of MCA 1973, s 34 which provides that a couple may not agree to oust the jurisdiction of the court in matters relating to ancillary relief, or s 35 which allows a court to vary agreements. Those in favour of enforcing agreements have argued that it is only fair that adults should not be patronized and that their agreements should be upheld by the court on divorce. Those opposed to agreements maintain, *inter alia,* that an agreement which appears reasonable at the time it was made, may be totally inappropriate on divorce if a couple has acquired children, joint financial assets and joint financial responsibilities, and/or one of them has sacrificed a career in order to take care of the family. Although they recognize that these events might have been predictable at the time of the agreement, they maintain that the eventual reality may be ill matched with what was originally foreseen. The decisions illustrate how frequently one of the spouses regrets having signed an agreement when the consequences of doing so becomes starkly clear at the time of the divorce. Accusations of unfairness abound.

## The Home Office statement 1998

7.110 In 1998 the Home Office published a consultation document, *Supporting Families.* It proposed that if legislation were to be introduced to make nuptial agreements legally binding on divorce, six safeguards would have to be met. The agreements would not be legally enforceable in the following circumstances:

- where there is a child of the family;
- where under the general law of contract the agreement would be unenforceable;
- where one or both of the couple did not receive independent legal advice before entering into the agreement;
- where the court considers that the enforcement of the agreement would be unfair for one or both of the couple or a child;
- where one or both of the couple failed to disclose the extent of their assets and property to each other before the agreement was made;
- where the agreement was made less than 21 days prior to the marriage.

7.111 Although, there was widespread approval of the proposals, the government has taken no further action. The Law Commission is currently examining agreements and its final report is expected in 2012.

## The judicial approach to agreements

### Agreements made on relationship breakdown

7.112 A couple whose relationship has broken down may negotiate with each other and make an agreement about their financial affairs, this agreement will be regarded as a maintenance agreement under MCA 1973, s 34. Any clause purporting to oust the jurisdiction of the court will be unenforceable but the remainder of the agreement may be enforced. Such agreements will often be ratified by the court as a consent order.

> In *Kelley v Corston (1998)*, Butler-Sloss LJ explained that prior to making a consent order, the court may examine the spouses' agreement and
>
> *check, within the limited information made available, whether there are other matters which require the court to make enquiries. The court has the power to refuse to make the order although the parties have agreed it. The fact of the agreement will, of course, be likely to be an important consideration but would not necessarily be determinative. The court is not a rubber stamp.*

7.113 Maintenance orders may be varied either under the provisions of MCA 1973, ss 34–36 or, where a consent order has been ratified by the court, in the same way as any other court order (see above).

7.114 If a court sets aside a maintenance order because of the circumstances in which it was obtained, it is then free to consider any application for ancillary relief in accordance with MCA 1973, s 25.

> In *B v B (Consent Order: Variation) (1995)*, the wife was very depressed at the time she agreed to a consent order. The court agreed to discount the agreement and vary the order. It accepted that the wife had been ill, and that her legal advisers had given her bad advice at the time the agreement was drawn up.

7.115 By contrast in *X v X (Y and Z intervening) (2002)*, the court held that a wife could not renege on an agreement. The husband and wife were both practising Jews. When their relationship broke down, an agreement was reached that, in return for £500,000 provided by the wife's brother, the husband would petition for divorce using the adultery fact but would allow his wife to petition in reliance on the behaviour fact. The husband also agreed to grant the wife a get, which would allow her to remarry in accordance with Jewish law, and he would remain silent about the events surrounding the divorce.

> The husband signed the get, and the decree of divorce was granted, at which point, the wife refused to take any action to obtain the £500,000 from her brother and pay it to the husband.

> The court upheld the agreement and stated that it would not lightly allow parties to depart from a formal agreement, properly and fairly arrived at, after serious legal advice, unless there were good grounds for concluding that an injustice would be done. The wife had failed to establish any unconscionability, unfairness, inequality of bargaining power, or exploitation by the husband. In fact it was the husband who would suffer injustice if the wife succeeded in her claim that she should not be held to the agreement.

7.116   In **NA v MA (2006)**, the wife had an affair with her husband's best friend. She and her husband decided to try and salvage the relationship but the husband was only prepared to do so if the wife signed an agreement, drawn up by him, which was to take effect if their efforts were unsuccessful. In the agreement, the wife was to receive £3.3 million plus £252,000 per year for their joint lives or until remarriage. The husband had assets of about £40 million. The wife, who was in a state of severe stress, agreed to sign the agreement against the advice of her lawyer. The court overturned the agreement and awarded the wife a little over £9 million on the grounds that she had been put under emotional pressure by a very powerful husband so that she could not be held to have signed the agreement willingly.

## Other post-nuptial agreements

7.117 For many years the courts differentiated between post-nuptial agreements made prior to a breakdown in the couple's relationship and pre-nuptial agreements.

In **MacLeod v MacLeod (2008)**, the Privy Council summed up the law relating to pos-nuptial agreements and maintained that, unlike pre-nuptials, post nuptial agreements are enforceable. In determining the weight to be given to a post-nuptial agreement if one of the signatories to the agreement subsequently applies for ancillary relief, the statutory provisions governing the variation of maintenance agreements under MCA 1973, ss 34–36 must be the starting point. The Privy Council then proceeded to widen the grounds for the court's departure from enforcing the terms of the agreement if there has been:

- a change in circumstances which would produce manifest injustice;
- a failure to make proper provision for children;
- an attempt to improperly make the family rely on State support;
- unfair pressure on a signatory of the agreement.

## Pre-nuptial agreements

7.118 Until the decision in **Radmacher v Granatino (2010)**, the history of the enforceability of pre-nuptial agreements made in anticipation of the possibility of separation or divorce was somewhat chequered.

As recently as 1996, Thorpe J (as he then was), in **F v F (Ancillary Relief: Substantial Assets) (1996)**, stated that although such agreements were commonplace in the society from which the couple came, he did not attach any significant weight to it when the wife applied for ancillary relief. He said:

*The rights and responsibilities of those whose financial affairs are regulated by statute cannot be much influenced by contractual terms which were devised for the control and limitation of standards that are intended to be of universal application throughout our society.*

His comment is in sharp contrast with his description of a pre-nuptial agreement 12 years later in *Crossley v Crossley (2007)*, as:

> *...a factor of magnetic importance.*

7.119 In both *K v K (Ancillary Relief: Prenuptial Agreement) (2003)* and *M v M (Prenuptial Agreement) (2002)*, the court took a pre-nuptial agreement into account as part of its consideration of all the circumstances of the case under MCA 1973, s 25.

## *The decision in* Radmacher (2010)

7.120 This latest decision is worthy of a detailed reading, and not merely because of the media attention to it, in which exaggerated claims were made. These suggested that the Supreme Court decided that pre-nuptial agreements are enforceable, and that signatories to them would no longer be able to seek ancillary relief. That view is certainly not supported by the Court's ruling. However, the case is also of interest because it provides a complete history of nuptial agreements, and an interesting commentary on marriage and ancillary relief.

## *The facts in* Radmacher

7.121 Katrin Radmacher and Nicolas Granatino met in November 1997 whilst they were both living in London where Nicolas was working for JP Morgan. She came from a very rich German family and he from a well-off French family. At the time of their marriage, in 1998, Nicolas was earning about £120,000 per annum. Prior to the marriage, Katrin suggested that they should enter into a pre-nuptial agreement because not only did she want Nicolas to love her for herself and not her wealth, but also because of her father's insistence. Katrin's family arranged for the agreement to be drawn up in Germany by the family notary, Dr Magis. It was somewhat draconian and provided that Nicolas would not benefit from Katrin's wealth either directly, or indirectly through any future children, nor she from his were he to acquire assets. The agreement did not mention the value of the couple's respective assets because Katrin had told the notary that she and Nicolas preferred to give each other this information separately. The notary insisted that the document should be translated and that Nicolas should have sufficient time to take advice and fully understand the implications of what he was signing. When the time came to sign, the notary was angry when he learned that the document had not been translated. He considered that he might postpone the execution of the agreement but, when told that the parties were unlikely to be in Germany again prior to the marriage, he was persuaded to continue. Speaking in English because Nicolas' German was not adequate, the notary explained the terms of the agreement in detail but did not give a verbatim translation of the document. The couple signed the agreement, which was binding under both German and French law, and soon after married in London.

In 2000, Nicolas' employer sent him to work in New York and the family relocated there. Katrin did not like it and they returned to London one year later.

In 2003, after the birth of two children, Nicolas decided to change career and embarked on a doctoral degree in biotechnology at Oxford University. Three years later, the couple separated and began proceedings for divorce in London. At that time, Katrin had assets of £54 million and an income of £2 million per annum. Nicolas earned £30,000 per annum as an academic researcher and had debts of £800,000. In spite of having signed the pre-nuptial agreement, Nicolas made an application for ancillary relief.

## *The decision of the trial judge in* **Radmacher (2008)**

7.122    Baron J held that the pre-nuptial agreement was not enforceable as a valid contract under English law. She considered all the circumstances of the case under MCA 1973, s 25, and accepted that in assessing Nicolas' needs she would take into account the fact that he had signed the pre-nuptial agreement. She concluded that:

> *...he understood the underlying premise that he was not entitled to anything if the parties divorced. In essence, he accepted that he was expected to be self-sufficient. As a man of the world that was abundantly clear. His decision to enter into the agreement must therefore affect the award.*

Baron J found that the agreement was, *prima facie*, unfair because it did not meet the Home Office safeguards. In particular, the couple had two children; the preparation of the agreement had been very one-sided and no negotiations between the couple had taken place; it was obviously not neutral; it attempted to deprive Nicolas of any financial help even if he was in need, and neither he nor Katrin had disclosed the extent of their assets. As a consequence of these findings, Baron J awarded Nicolas £700,000 towards his debts of £800,000; £25,000 to buy a car, £2.5million to buy a home of his own in London, and €630,000 to buy a home in Germany. The children were living with Katrin in Germany and Nicolas needed a place where he could have the children to stay with him for visits. This latter home would remain in Katrin's ownership. He was also awarded a £2.335 million capital fund which would give him an annual income for life of £100,000. His own earning capacity had been reduced to £30,000 as a consequence of his change of career. Further periodical payments of £35,000 were awarded for each of his two daughters until they ended their full time education.

Baron J failed to explain with any precision how she had taken into account the existence of the pre-nuptial agreement in her calculation of the award, and Katrin appealed.

## *The decision of the Court of Appeal in* **Radmacher (2009)**

7.123    The Court of Appeal granted the appeal on the grounds that Baron J had barely given any weight to the pre-nuptial agreement and certainly not the decisive weight it deserved in her calculation of the award. She had not explained what effect the agreement had had on the award. The Court maintained that Nicolas should receive an award which would allow him to fulfill his role as the father of his and Katrin's children and not for his own long term needs, the £2.5 million fund for housing should be held by him only for the period that his daughters were in his care, and the capital fund should be reduced to provide for his needs only until the younger daughter's 22nd birthday. Nicolas appealed to the Supreme Court.

## *The decision of the Supreme Court in* **Radmacher (2010)**

7.124    The Supreme Court refused to differentiate between pre-nuptial and post-nuptial agreements and maintained with great clarity that the MCA 1973, s 25 governs all applications for ancillary relief. It is for the courts to exercise their discretion and determine an appropriate award and not a couple's agreement. However, there should be a presumption, or a starting point, in that discretionary process, that an agreement should be accorded weight under certain circumstances. Thus, a gloss was put on s 25, and Nicolas Granatino's appeal was denied.

The Supreme Court outlined the principles, which the courts should apply when considering the weight that should be attached to nuptial agreements along the lines of the 1998 Home Office proposals (see above). It maintained that:

- duress, fraud or misrepresentation, or undue pressure, present at the time of the agreement would reduce the importance of the agreement, and what would have happened had these circumstances been absent;

- the couple's personal circumstances at the time of the agreement would be relevant. These would include such matters as their age and maturity, whether either or both had been married or been in long-term relationships before;

- the enforceability of the agreement in the couple's own home countries if it was drawn up there might be relevant;

- fairness would be an important factor.

In spite of the Court's acknowledgement of the problem inherent in the concept of fairness and that it is fact dependent, it stated that it might be unfair to give effect to the agreement where:

- there were children;

- one of the couple had real needs or required to be compensated for looking after the family to allow the other to acquire wealth;

- the agreement addressed uncertain future circumstances which changed over time or could not be envisaged at the time of the agreement; the longer the marriage had lasted the more likely that might be the case.

The Court accepted that it might be fair to attach greater weight to the agreement where:

- the couple had given a well thought out approach to their finances which addressed their existing circumstances and not merely the contingencies of an uncertain future;

- the couple wished to exclude non-matrimonial property such as property owned prior to the relationship or acquired by one of them from a third party during the relationship.

The Supreme Court summarized its view succinctly:

*The court should give effect to a nuptial agreement that is freely entered into by each party with a full appreciation of its implications unless in the circumstances prevailing it would not be fair to hold the parties to their agreement.*

In Katrin and Nicolas' situation, the Supreme Court maintained that Nicolas' earning ability had not been incapacitated during the marriage. He was able; it was his decision to give up a lucrative career. There was no need to compensate him. His needs were satisfied, and he would benefit from the award made to support his daughters whilst they were living with him until they reached an age of independence.

7.125    It is arguable that the Supreme Court's decision is sexist in that it viewed Nicolas' decision to change careers and earn less money as entirely his decision and that the financial consequences should be born by him. No credit was given to him for agreeing to relocate to London when Katrin felt unhappy about living in New York, a decision which might have affected his career prospects. It must also be remembered that he was married to a very wealthy woman who did not object to the career change at the time it was made. Would the Supreme Court have taken the same approach to a woman, married to a wealthy man, who gave up a lucrative career to follow her own personal dreams. Little attention seems to have been paid to the circumstances surrounding the signing of the agreement. Nicolas was considered to be a man of the world; would a woman have been treated in the same way had she signed an untranslated agreement drawn up at the behest of her husband's parents?

What effect will the decision have on Nicolas and Katrin's children when they realize that their mother would not share even 10 per cent of her considerable fortune with their father?

The decision in *Radmacher* is totally fact dependent, and although nuptial agreements have been given a potential greater significance in any application for ancillary relief, it remains the case that the courts' general discretion under MCA 1973 s 25 will prevail in many situations rather than the nuptial agreement. Those couples who make them will have to continue to live with uncertainty.

## Lady Hale's dissent in *Radmacher (2010)*

7.126    In an interesting and detailed dissenting judgment, Lady Hale began by stressing the fact that marriage ( and civil partnerships) involve both contract and status. The law determines, to a certain extent, the nature of the contract into which a couple enters; they are not entirely free to decide the legal consequences of the contract for themselves. One of the consequences of the contract is that it imposes on the couple a duty of support for each other, and for their children and allows them to have recourse to law if the relationship ends.

Lady Hale acknowledged that the law relating to ancillary relief in general, and nuptial agreements in particular, is in urgent need of reform but felt that it should be left to the legislature to do so and not the judiciary:

*There is some enthusiasm for reform within the judiciary and the profession, and in the media, and one can well understand why. But that does not mean that it is right. This is a complicated subject upon which there is a large literature and knowledgeable and thoughtful people may legitimately hold differing views. Some may regard freedom of contract as the prevailing principle in all circumstances; others may regard that as a 19th century concept which has since been severely modified, particularly in the case of continuing relationships typically (though not invariably) characterised by imbalance of bargaining power (such as landlord and tenant, employer and employee). Some may regard people who are about to marry as in all respects fully autonomous beings; others may wonder whether people who are typically (although not invariably) in love can be expected to make rational choices in the same way that businessmen can. Some may regard the recognition of these factual differences as patronising or paternalistic; others may regard them as sensible and realistic. Some may think that to accord a greater legal status to these agreements will produce greater certainty and lesser costs should the couple divorce; others may question whether this will in fact be achieved, save at the price of inflexibility and injustice. Some may believe that giving greater force to marital agreements will encourage more people to marry; others may wonder whether they will encourage more people to divorce. Perhaps above all, some may think it permissible to contract out of the guiding principles of equality and non-discrimination within marriage; others may think this a retrograde step likely only to benefit the strong at the expense of the weak.*

*These difficult issues cannot be resolved in an individual case, in particular a case with such very unusual features as this one. Different people will naturally react to this particular human story in different ways, depending upon their values and experience of life.*

Although Lady Hale accepted that courts must take into account nuptial agreements as part of the discretionary exercise required by MCA 1973, s 25, she felt that the majority decision of the Supreme Court placed an impermissible gloss on the section by giving agreements precedence. She regarded the majority view as inconsistent with the importance attached to the status of marriage in English law because it failed to differentiate between those in legal relationships and those who chose to simply cohabit. Lady Hale summarized her position in a slightly different way from that of the majority:

*Did each party freely enter into an agreement, intending it to have legal effect and with a full appreciation of its implications? If so, in the circumstances as they now are, would it be fair to hold them to their agreement?*

Lady Hale concluded that she would have varied Byron J's order so that Nicolas Granatino would be allowed to enjoy his English home, or any home bought to replace it, for life. She also suggested that Nicolas' decision to leave his career in banking and study at Oxford was not as completely selfish as some may have thought it to be with the implication that he deserved some capital provision. After all Katrin had agreed to the decision:

*And why should she not? The couple were rich enough each to be able to pursue their own dreams. She had not been happy in New York and perhaps she understood why her husband was no longer happy in banking. If the decision was taken for the good of the family as a whole, this would have been for the benefit of the children as well as their parents. Happy parents make for happy children. Discontented parents make for discontented children.*

## Cohabitants

7.127 There is a debate which is currently being conducted between those who believe that cohabitants should be treated in a similar way to spouses or civil partners when their relationships end, and those who believe that cohabitants should be free to decide their own affairs without any State intervention at the end of their relationships. This debate has gained momentum since the Law Commission made its recommendations on cohabitation in 2007 (see below). Ruth Deech, in her 2009–2010 Gresham College Lectures has vociferously expressed the view that:

> Cohabitation is gradually gaining more recognition in English law, without any debate until very recently about the rights and wrongs of it. I can only echo what I said in my second lecture on maintenance, that women do not need and ought not to require to be kept by men after their relationship has come to an end. My preference is for the rights of the individual, or human rights, in this instance autonomy, privacy, a sphere of thought and action that should be free from public and legal interference, namely the right to live together without having a legal structure imposed on one without consent or contract to that effect. It is better not to have legal interference in cohabitation and leave it to be dealt with by the ordinary law of the land, of agreements, wills, property and so on.... But I would argue that cohabitation law retards the emancipation of women, degrades the relationship, takes away choice, is too expensive and would extend an already unsatisfactory maintenance law for married couples to another large category. I rate most highly personal autonomy and the use of agreements to settle legal boundaries with others—the respect for individuals' expectations and contribution rather than stereotyping and fitting every couple into the traditional marriage mould.

7.128 At present there are no statutory provisions for re-allocating property between cohabitants at the end of a relationship; they must resort to the principles of resulting or constructive trusts, proprietary estoppel (see Chapter 4), or contract.

## Contract

7.129 Cohabitants who draw up a legally binding cohabitation contract, by deed, or accompanied by consideration, are comparatively rare. Tennant, Taylor and Lewis, in their research on cohabitation in 2006, found that none of the couples studied had drawn up formal agreements.

Under contract law, cohabitation agreements may be enforceable on relationship breakdown if the couple are able to establish that:

- they intended to create a legally enforceable contractual relationship with each other;
- they had both put their minds to the terms of the agreement and agreed them without pressure from either of each other or a third party;
- the terms were expressed with precision and were not contrary to public policy;
- the consideration, if the contract was not made by deed, was not illegal.

7.130 In *Sutton v Mishcon de Reya and Gawor & Co (2004)*, the court considered a most unusual and rather bizarre contract between two male cohabitants, Sutton, an airline steward and a male prostitute, and Staal, a wealthy businessman. Staal was to become Sutton's sexual slave and give him all his financial assets. Not surprisingly the relationship broke down. Sutton unsuccessfully sued two firms of solicitors for negligence. Both had warned that the agreement was likely to be unenforceable at law.

What is of interest to the family lawyer in Hart J's judgment, in this hardly typical situation, are his comments on the enforceability of cohabitation contracts. He maintained that a property contract between two people who were having a sexual relationship and cohabited with each other could be valid. There must be no undue influence in obtaining the consent of either party, and the sexual relationship must involve no criminal conduct. A contract for payment for sexual services would not be valid.

## Indirect maintenance

7.131 Although a cohabitant may not claim maintenance from a partner at the end of a relationship, the courts have made awards for children and thereby indirectly contributed to the maintenance of the cohabitant who is caring for them.

In *Re P (A Child) (Financial Provision) (2003)*, an unmarried mother separated from a very wealthy man; she applied for maintenance for their child. Thorpe LJ explained that the mother had no personal entitlement but merely an allowance as the child's primary carer. He acknowledged that distinguishing between these two factors could be difficult but her allowance should not be diminished by the absence of any direct claim in law. The court:

*...must recognise the responsibility, and often the sacrifice, of the unmarried parent (generally the mother) who is to be the primary carer for the child, perhaps the exclusive carer if the absent parent disassociates from the child. In order to discharge this responsibility the carer must have control of a budget that reflects her position and the position of the father, both social and financial.*

Thorpe LJ took a broad-brush approach based on principles similar to those used on determining ancillary relief on divorce. He awarded the mother £1 million to purchase a house which would revert to the father at the end of the child's education, £100,000 for furnishings and periodical payments of £70,000 per annum. However, he explained that the mother should not be able to save from this allowance to provide a pension for her future but should spend it all on an annual basis, and account to the father for her expenditure.

7.132 In spite of the seemingly generous nature of the award in *Re P (2003)*, it does not resolve the issue of what a mother, who has devoted her life and sacrificed her career to caring for a child, does when the child becomes independent. Provision for a child should include compensation for the parent who undertakes the role of primary carer and, thereby, frees the other parent to pursue a career. The decision draws attention to the difficulties for unmarried partners who are left without means of financial support when their child-rearing role ends. Where there are no children of the relationship, a former cohabitant in need of maintenance because she has no resources of her own and is unable to work will be forced to rely on State benefits.

## Cohabitation: The Financial Consequences of Relationship Breakdown (Law Com No 307) (2007)

7.133 The Law Commission considered the financial problems facing heterosexual and same-sex cohabitants when their relationships came to an end. It made recommendations based on two years of research and consultation. It was not asked to draft a bill, and as already mentioned in Chapter 1, it is unknown whether or when the government will act upon the Law Commission's recommendations.

7.134 The Commission found that many cohabitants suffered hardship at the end of a relationship which had serious consequences not just for them but also for their children, and led to greater reliance on State benefits. The Commission found that a substantial majority of people believed that cohabitants should have the right to apply for financial relief from their partner at the end of a relationship; whilst a minority felt that cohabitants should be given information about the current law and decide on the basis of this whether to marry or enter into a civil partnership, and thereby receive protection. According to the Commission neither of these options was acceptable because some cohabitants are in relationships which are not as committed as marriage and they have deliberately chosen that route. They would be reluctant to have legal responsibilities thrust upon them, and are prepared to accept that they have no rights. At the other extreme there are those cohabitants who are not free to legalize their relationships, or who live with partners who refuse to do; it would be counterproductive to deny them rights.

7.135 The Commission, therefore, recommended that cohabitants should be given rights to financial relief at the end of a relationship in order to

> *...provide economically vulnerable members of society with the private means to rebuild their lives and to ensure a fairer division of assets on relationship breakdown and to ensure that the pluses and minuses of the relationship were fairly shared between the couple.*

7.136 The Law Commission's proposed scheme would not apply to all cohabitants but only to those who could bring themselves within the following rules:

- The couple had not agreed to opt out of the scheme.
- The applicant had made contributions to the relationship, which gave rise to consequences which were ongoing at the end of the relationship, either in the form of a benefit to the respondent or an economic disadvantage to the applicant.
- The cohabitants must have had a child together or had lived together for a specified number of years. The Commission made no specific recommendation about time but suggested a period between two and five years might be regarded as appropriate.
- The decision and amount of any financial award would be at the court's discretion.

Certain aspects of the scheme resemble closely the concept of proprietary estoppel, or the Canadian concept of constructive trusts based on unjust enrichment (see eg *Peter v Beblow (1993)*).

## Fiancées and prospective civil partners

7.137 Historically, the term fiancé/fiancée was used to describe an unmarried man or woman who was formally engaged to be married. The man would offer a ring to the woman as a sign of their commitment to marry. The purpose of the engagement was to allow a period of time to prepare for the wedding and for any objections to be raised to the proposed marriage. If a man terminated the engagement, he could be sued for breach of promise because of the potential damage to a woman's reputation. This was based on the assumption that a woman may have agreed to have a sexual relationship with a man because she expected to marry him. A woman could not be sued for breaking the engagement. All actions for breach of promise ended in England with the enactment of the Law Reform (Miscellaneous Provisions) Act 1970, s 1.

7.138  There is no precise legal definition of the term fiancé/fiancée. More recently, the term has become a quasi-respectable title used in the tabloid press to describe partners who are cohabiting, and who may have little intention of marrying in the future, and may not even be free to do so.

For immigration purposes, a person claiming entry as a fiancé/fiancée, or a prospective civil partner, is expected to marry within six months.

7.139  If an engaged couple, or prospective civil partners, end a relationship, they may have to rely on contract law or on the principles of constructive or resulting trusts or proprietary estoppel (see Chapter 4) to resolve any disputes relating to ownership of property acquired during their engagement.

7.140  In addition, the Law Reform (Miscellaneous Provisions) Act 1970, and the equivalent provisions of the CPA 2004 s 74 for civil partners, provides some, albeit limited, specific legal redress for the resolution of property disputes, but not the redistribution of property, when an engagement or prospective civil partnership is terminated. The policy behind the law is the recognition that a couple may acquire possessions in advance of the marriage, either as presents or because they have purchased them themselves for their future life together. They may apply to the court to determine disputes between them over property in which either or both had an interest during their relationship. The court may not re-allocate the property between the parties but merely determine to whom it belongs. It remains uncertain who may bring themselves within the ambit of the provisions. For instance, could those who have cohabited for 10 years with a person who is not free to marry or enter into a civil partnership be permitted to apply under the Act if they maintain that they plan to formalize their relationship in the future?

7.141  The symbol of any committed relationship is often a ring. Although an engagement ring is normally a gift given in contemplation of marriage, s 3(2) of the 1970 Act provides that it may only be recovered by the donor if it was made on the express or implied condition that it must be returned if the engagement is ended by either party. There is no equivalent provision relating to rings exchanged by prospective civil partners.

In *Cox v Jones (2004)*, Mr Jones and Miss Cox became engaged in 1998. Mr Jones gave her a ring valued at around £10,000. He claimed that he told Miss Cox that, if their engagement came to an end, she must return the ring to him. After the engagement ended, Miss Cox requested a jeweller to set the stone from the ring into a new pendant which was valued at £18,000. The court had little difficulty in rejecting Mr Jones' version of events. It found it implausible that any fiancé could express such an unromantic remark; Miss Cox could retain the pendant.

## FURTHER READING

Allen N and Williams H, 'The Law and Financial Provision on the Dissolution of Civil Partnerships' [2009] Fam Law 836

Arthur S, Lewis J, Maclean M, Finch S and Fitzgerald R, 'Settling Up: Making Financial Arrangements After Divorce or Separation' (National Centre for Social Research, 2002)

Bailey-Harris R, 'Towards the Recognition of Marriage as a Partnership of Equals' [2003] Fam Law 417

Bray J, 'The Financial Rights of Cohabiting Couples' [2009] Fam Law 1151

Bridge S, 'Money, Marriage and Cohabitation' [2006] Fam Law 641

Burgess P, 'Trusts and Divorce: When is a Settlement Nuptial?' [2008] Fam Law 131

Clark S, 'Should Greater Prominence be Given to Pre-Nuptial Contracts in the Law of Ancillary Relief?' [2004] CFLQ 399

Cooke E, 'Miller/McFarlane: Law in Search of Discrimination', [2006] Fam Law 753

Deech R, 'What's a Woman Worth' (Gresham College Lecture) [2009] Fam Law 1140

Deech R, 'Cohabitation' [2010] Fam Law 39

Douglas G, Pearce J and Woodward H, 'Dealing with Property Issues on Cohabitation Breakdown' [2007] Fam Law 36

Douglas G, Pearce J and Woodward H, 'The Law Commission's Cohabitation Proposals: Applying them in Practice' [2008] Fam Law 351

Edwards S, 'Division of Assets and Fairness: "Brick Lane"—Gender, Culture and Ancillary Relief on Divorce' [2004] Fam Law 809

Eekelaar J, 'Property and Financial Settlement on Divorce—Sharing and Compensating' [2007] IFLJ 18

Eekelaar J, ' Financial and Property Settlement: A Standard Deal?' [2010] Fam Law 359

Francis N and Fisher M, 'Departure from Equality: Inherited Property' [2005] Fam Law 218

Francis N and Bennett N, *Prenuptial and Cohabitation Agreements* (Jordans, 2009)

George R, Harris P and Herring J, ' Pre-nuptial Agreements: For Better Or For Worse' [2009] Fam Law 934

Government White Paper, 'Supporting Families' (1998)

Hatwood M, 'Maintenance: Where are we now?' [2010] Fam Law 636

Hess E, 'The Rights of Cohabitants: When and How Will the Law be Reformed?' [2009] Fam Law 405

Hood H, 'The Role of Conduct in Divorce Suits and Claims for Ancillary Relief' [2009] Fam Law 948

Jackson, *Matrimonial Finance and Taxation* (7th edn, Butterworths, 2002)

Kingdom E, 'Cohabitation Contracts and the Democratisation of Personal Relations' (2000) 8(1) Feminist Legal Studies 5

Law Commission, *Cohabitation: The Financial Consequences of Relationship Breakdown* (Law Com No 307, 2007)

Law Commission, *First Report on Family Property—A New Approach* (Law Com No 52, 1973)

Law Commission, *Matrimonial Property* (Law Com No 175, 1985)

Law Commission, *Transfer of Money between Spouses* (Law Com No 90, 1985)

Lewis M, 'What is the Difference Between Income and Capital?' [2009] Fam Law 1146

Maclean M and Eekelaar J, 'When Cohabiting Parents Separate: Law and Expectations' [2002] Fam Law 37

Meehan A, 'Analyse this: Radmacher v Granatino' [2009] Fam Law 816

Miles J and Probert R (Eds), *Sharing Lives, Dividing Assets-An Inter-disciplinary Study* (Hart 2009)

Miles J, 'Charman v Charman (No 4)—Making Sense of Need, Compensation and Equal Sharing After Miller/McFarlane' [2008] CFLQ 378

Morley J, 'Enforceable Prenuptial Agreements: Their Time has Come' [2006] Fam Law 768

Morris B and Keehan M, 'Hey Big Spender! Add Backs and Reckless Spending' [2010] Fam Law 714

Scherpe J, 'A Comparative View of Pre-Nuptial Agreements Features' [2006] Fam Law 768

Singer S, 'What Provision For Unmarried Couples Should the Law Make When Their Relationships Breakdown?' [2009] Fam Law 234

Solicitors' Family Law Association, A More Certain Future: Recognition of Pre-marital Agreements in England and Wales (2004)

Symes P, 'Indissolubility and the Clean Break' (1985) 48 MLR 44

The Rt Hon Lord Justice Thorpe, 'London—The Divorce Capital of the World' [2009] Fam Law 21

Todd, 'The Inevitable Triumph of the Ante-Nuptial Contract' [2006] Fam Law 539

The Rt Hon Lord Justice Ward, 'Have the House of Lords abused Cinderella? Their Contribution to Divorce Law' (lecture at King's College, London, 23 November 2004)

Welstead M, 'Judicial Reform or an Increase in Discretion—the Decision in Miller v Miller; McFarlane v McFarlane', Chapter 3 in *International Survey of Family Law* (Jordans, 2008)

Wikeley N, 'The Strange Death of the Liable Relative Rule' [2008] Journal of Social Welfare and Family Law 339

1   Write a critique of the Court of Appeal judgment in *Charman v Charman No 4 (2007)*; how does it differ from that of the House of Lords in *Miller v Miller; McFarlane v McFarlane (2006)?*

2   Sir Nicholas Mostyn, a High Court judge, described the postscript to the judgment in *Charman No 4 (2007)*, as the judicial equivalent of Sir Richard Mottram's outburst about the problems at the Department of Transport in 2002: 'We're all f***ed. I'm f***ed. You're f***ed. The whole department's f***ed' [2007] Fam Law 573. What did Sir Nicholas mean? What would you advise to resolve the problems which so clearly concerned him?

3   Andrew and Brigitte are a married. Andrew is an explorer and spends long periods of time in remote places. He wants to be sure that Brigitte has access to sufficient funds for her maintenance whilst he is away. However, he does not want her to have access to his bank account because she is an alcoholic and he fears that she may overdraw to fund her alcoholism. He agreed to transfer £1,000 per month to Brigitte's own bank account for every month he is absent from England. Whilst Andrew was in South America, he decided to stay there and use all his available financial resources to fund an anthropological study of a remote tribe. He wrote to Brigitte to inform her that he would be unable to continue to make her monthly maintenance. Brigitte was very distressed, as she had been using the money to obtain treatment for her alcoholism.

Advise Brigitte whether she can enforce the agreement.

4   Charles and Daphne have cohabited for the last 10 years. They agreed to buy a dog. Charles wanted an Alsatian and Daphne a golden retriever. Because they could not agree, they purchased one of each using funds deposited by both of them in an account set up for pet purchase and any related subsequent expenditure. Charles worked long hours and had no time to take care of either dog; Daphne, therefore, took on sole responsibility for all the subsequent care of both animals. Daphne decided to move to the country and wished to take both dogs to live with her. Charles wished to remain in the city and keep the Alsatian with him. He had persuaded a dog-loving friend that she should take care of it during the working day. Advise Charles, who maintains that the Alsatian is his, and Daphne, who maintains that there was an implied agreement that both dogs belonged to her because she cared for them.

5   Kate and Liz are a same-sex couple who each live in separate houses during the week because they work in different places 200 miles apart. They spend most weekends together, alternating between each house. They also spend six weeks together on holiday in a friend's house in France. Recently, Kate has become unemployed and wishes to claim State means-tested benefits.

Advise Kate whether the cohabitation rule will apply to her.

6   Marietta and Nathan married 15 years ago and have three children. When they married Nathan had shares in his parents' business worth £25 million. Nathan was a

heart surgeon in both private and national health hospitals, and earned £300,000 per annum. Marietta was a lawyer earning £250,000 per annum with an international law firm. Nathan owned a house worth £1 million at the time of the marriage which became the family home.

The couple signed a pre-nuptial agreement in which they agreed that Nathan's shares would remain his in the event of a divorce, and that Marietta would make no claim for ancillary relief. Seven years ago Mariettta was tired with travelling around the world for work, and was concerned about leaving the children in the care of nannies. She agreed with Nathan that she would give up her position and go to art school to pursue her interest in painting. Since then, she has not worked

The couple have now decided that their relationship is over and wish to divorce. Marietta has no resources of her own and wants to apply for ancillary relief. Nathan has told her that she will not succeed because everyone knows that pre-nuptial agreements are now enforceable.

Advise Marietta.

# 8

# Death and its consequences

**SUMMARY**

Death is an inevitable and, in most cases, an involuntary event in family life. Death happens to everyone and the legal, emotional, practical, social and financial consequences for the family are far reaching. No discussion of family law can ignore the subject of death. Death will often alter the status of family members; it allows surviving spouses or civil partners to enter into new legal relationships with new statuses attached to them. A regrouping of the family may take place and new associated familial relationships may come into existence.

In this chapter, we consider the effects of death on the status and ensuing rights of the deceased's surviving spouse, civil partner, cohabitant or other family member.

## Presumption of death

8.1 In *Le Colonel Chabert* (Balzac, 1832), a French colonel, who was presumed to have died fighting in Napoleon's Russian campaign, arrived back in Paris to find that his wife had taken his fortune and married an aristocrat. This excerpt from Balzac's novel illustrates graphically the horror experienced when a person who has been presumed to be dead, returns to find that his family and property are not as they were.

Colonel Chabert explains:

*I had no money, but I was well, and my feet were on the good stones of Paris. With what delight and haste did I make my way to the Rue du Mont-Blanc, where my wife should be living in a house belonging to me! Bah! the Rue du Mont-Blanc was now the Rue de la Chausee d'Antin; I could not find my house; it had been sold and pulled down. Speculators had built several houses over my gardens. Not knowing that my wife had married M. Ferraud, I could obtain no information. At last I went to the house of an old lawyer who had been in charge of my affairs. This worthy man was dead, after selling his connection to a younger man. This gentleman informed me, to my great surprise, of the administration of my estate, the settlement of the moneys, of my wife's marriage, and the birth of her two children. When I told him that I was Colonel Chabert, he laughed so heartily that I left him without saying another word....knowing where my wife lived, I went to her house, my heart high with hope....When I called under an assumed name I was not admitted, and on the day when I used my own I was turned out of doors. To see the Countess come home from a ball or the play in the early morning, I have sat whole nights through, crouching close to the wall of her gateway. My eyes pierced the depths of the carriage, which flashed past me with the swiftness of lightning, and I caught a glimpse of the woman who is my wife and no longer mine. Oh, from that day I have lived for vengeance!...She knows that I am alive; since my return she has had two letters written with my own hand. She loves me no more! I know not whether I love or hate her. I long for her and curse her by turns. To me she owes all her fortune, all her happiness; well, she has not sent me the very smallest pittance. Sometimes I do not know what will become of me!*

8.2  Each year, significant numbers of people disappear without trace, leaving behind them great uncertainty about their fate, some as a result of personal stress and others because of natural disasters.

The tsunami in South East Asia in December 2004, in which 220,000 died, left many believing that their partners and other family members were dead but without the satisfaction of any certainty that this was so.

Where no identifiable body has been found, none of the surviving family members will be unable to obtain a death certificate. In such circumstances, it may be possible to apply for a legal declaration of presumption of death which will permit the deceased's estate to be distributed.

In 1974, Lord Lucan, a well-known English aristocrat, disappeared from his family home in London after the murder of the family nanny. He was legally presumed dead in 1992.

## Common law

8.3  At common law, a declaration of presumption of death can be made after a person has been absent for seven years. There must have been no communication between the missing person and those with whom he or she would have been expected to make contact. The person applying for the declaration must have made enquiries about the missing person and there must be no evidence that he or she is still alive.

8.4 A declaration of presumption of death at common law did not terminate a marriage. Therefore, if a spouse remarried after a declaration of presumption of death, and the person who had been presumed dead re-appeared, the new marriage would be held to be void.

8.5 The seven-year rule and the risk of an invalid marriage caused great hardship to surviving spouses who were left in limbo. It led to a change in the law to enable spouses and civil partners to apply for a statutory presumption of death.

## Matrimonial Causes Act 1973

8.6 The Matrimonial Causes Act 1973 (MCA 1973), s 19(1) provides that a spouse may make an application to a court for a decree of presumption of death and for the marriage to be dissolved where there are reasonable grounds on which to base the presumption. Proof that a person was travelling on an aeroplane which crashed, leaving no trace of survivors, would almost certainly be accepted as reasonable grounds for the presumption of death.

8.7 Where there are no reasonable grounds for the presumption, MCA 1973, s 19(3) provides that a continuous absence for a period of seven years, where the petitioner has no reason to believe that the missing person has been living during that time, will be accepted as evidence of presumed death, unless the contrary can be proven.

8.8 The decree of presumption of death is divided into two parts, a decree nisi and a decree absolute. If the missing person returns before the decree absolute has been made, the decree will be rescinded. Once the decree has been made absolute, the marriage or civil partnership will have been dissolved irrevocably even if the missing person returns.

## Civil Partnership Act 2004

8.9 Civil partners may apply under the Civil Partnership Act 2004 (CPA 2004), s 55 for a presumption of death order in the same way as married couples.

## Cohabitants and other family members

8.10 Cohabitants along with other family members may only apply under the common law rules and will have to wait for the full seven-year period to elapse. This may cause financial difficulties where a cohabitant or family members are beneficiaries under the deceased's will or, where there is no will, would inherit under the law relating to intestate succession (see below).

8.11 The disappearance of so many British citizens in the Tsunami disaster in south-east Asia in 2004 led Foreign Office Minister, Douglas Alexander, to make the following statement:

> *It is a sad and tragic reality that, in time, it will become clear that some bodies will not be found or identified.... In normal circumstances the Foreign Office would not issue death certificates in the absences of a body or local death certificate. We have been working to resolve this issue since the week of the Tsunami. We have agreed, as a response to the exceptional circumstances we face, that the Foreign Office, at the request of families, will issue death certificates for missing British nationals, where no body has been found based on evidence provided by the British police. To reach this conclusion, it has been agreed that the police will apply four tests:*
>
> - *Evidence exists beyond reasonable doubt that the person travelled to the affected region;*
>
> - *On the balance of probability the person was in the affected areas at the time the Tsunami struck;*
>
> - *There was no reasonable evidence of life since the 26th December;*
>
> - *There was no reason, again on the balance of probability that the person would want to disappear.*
>
> *(Written Statement to Parliament—British Tsunami Victims*
> *(Death Registration) 24 January 2005)*

To date five families have taken advantage of this temporary modification of the common law. It is reasonable to assume that the modification will be extended to those affected by similar disasters in the future.

## Funeral arrangements

### Right to burial and cremation certificates

8.12 When a person dies, a doctor will issue a cause of death certificate, unless the death is unexpected when the matter will be referred to a coroner. The medical certificate must be taken to the local registrar of births and deaths within five days of its issue. The registrar will provide a death certificate and a certificate for burial or cremation of the body. The certificate allows the person who obtains it to arrange for the body to be buried or cremated.

8.13 Provided there is no dispute, the certificate will normally be given to the person who registers the death. In many cases, this will be a friend or relative of the deceased. However, from a strict legal standpoint, the deceased's executors or, in the case of an intestacy, the deceased's personal representatives such as a spouse, civil partner or other relative, are the only persons who have the right, and indeed the duty, to deal with the body. Where there is a dispute about the validity of a will and therefore, the identity of the executors, the person in possession of the body may have the right to deal with the body (see *University Hospital Lewisham NHS Trust v Hamuth (2006)*).

8.14 In *Borrows v HM Coroner for Preston (2008)*, a 15 year old boy had committed suicide whilst in a Young Offenders Institution. He had lived with his uncle and family for some time before his incarceration because of his mother's drug addiction. He had re-established contact with his mother just before he was sentenced. The uncle planned to cremate the body because that was the boy's wish but his mother wanted to bury it.

The court held that the best person to be appointed as administrator of the boy's estate was set out in the order of priority in Rule 22 of the Non-Contentious Probate Rules (SI 1987/2024):

- the surviving spouse;
- the children or their issue (if the children have pre-deceased the deceased);
- the parents;
- the siblings;
- the half siblings;
- the grandparents;
- the uncles and aunts.

8.15 If there is a dispute over priority, s 116 of the Supreme Court Act 1981 applies and the court must consider whether there are any special circumstances to vary the order of priority, and exercise its discretion. Art 8 of the European Convention on Human Rights 1950 (ECHR) and the jurisprudence of the European Court of Human Rights (ECtHR) require the deceased's wishes to be taken into account. The mother in *Borrows* was found to be incapable of making the funeral arrangements. The uncle and his family were the deceased's psychological family and the deceased had a strong connection with the area in which they lived. The uncle, therefore, was given the right to arrange his deceased nephew's cremation.

8.16 In *Hartshorne v Gardner (2008)*, the deceased died intestate at the age of 44 in a car accident. His divorced parents both wished to arrange the funeral for their son. The mother wished to have him cremated and the father wished to have him buried at some distance from the mother's home but close to where the son had lived. The mother maintained that it would be difficult for her to visit the grave because of its distance from her home. The coroner refused to release the body until the parents had reached agreement or the court had decided which of them should take precedence.

The court held that both parents had equal rights and chose to exercise its discretion in favour of the father because he had had a close relationship with the deceased compared with the mother. Furthermore, the deceased's fiancée and siblings all supported the father's wishes relating to the funeral arrangements (see also *Buchanan v Milton (1999); Fessi v Whitmore (1999)*).

## Cohabitants

8.17 Unless a cohabitant has been appointed an executor of his or her deceased partner's estate, he or she will have no right to arrange for the burial or cremation of a partner.

In *Holtham v Arnold (1986)*, a husband, who had left his wife in order to cohabit with the plaintiff, died intestate. The cohabitant made arrangements for the deceased's burial. The deceased's wife objected and ordered the hospital not to release the body until an agreement had been reached or a court order was obtained. The cohabitant asked that the body be handed over to her for burial either by a direction of the court or by appointment as administrator of the deceased's estate solely for the purpose of arranging the burial.

The court held that the deceased's wife, on the intestacy, was entitled to letters of administration of her husband's estate and, therefore, had the right to dispose of the body. Had the deceased left a will, his executors would have had the right to arrange the funeral.

8.18 In 1995, the deceased's wife and his cohabitant were forced to take a different approach. The court had urged them to go away and settle their differences or it would rule in favour of the wife and allow her to arrange the funeral. They each had two children by the deceased and had incurred substantial legal costs arguing about the funeral arrangements. They decided to reach a compromise and both participated in the funeral service, accompanied by their respective children, seated on separate sides of the crematorium, singing hymns chosen by each of them (*Guardian*, 18 July 1995).

8.19 Cohabitants may be able to argue that their rights, under Art 8 (the right to respect for private and family life) of the ECHR, are infringed where they are denied the right to bury or cremate a deceased partner. Even if the deceased is survived by a spouse or a civil partner, it is arguable that a cohabitant has a greater right to respect for the family life he or she had with the deceased, prior to death, than the right of a long-term estranged spouse or civil partner.

## Testate succession

8.20 Freedom of testation means that all sane adults have the right to make a will which will ensure that their property will be distributed after their death in whatever way they have specified. There is no obligation to make provision for a spouse, civil partner, cohabitant, other family member, or a friend who was maintained by the deceased during his or her lifetime.

If the deceased fails to provide for any of these persons, an application for limited provision from the deceased's estate may be made under the Inheritance (Provision for Family and Dependants) Act 1975 (Inheritance Act 1975) which is discussed below.

8.21 The Wills Act 1837, ss 18, 18B provide that every will is revoked by a valid marriage or civil partnership. However, if the will was made by the testator with the assumption that marriage or civil partnership to a specific person was in his or her mind, and that the will should not be revoked by the marriage or civil partnership, it will be enforceable.

> In *Court v Despallieres; Re Ikin (Deceased) (2009)*, Peter Ikin, a wealthy music entrepreneur left all his property to be divided between his nephew and various charities in accordance with his will. He subsequently entered into a civil partnership in London with Alexandre Despallieres, a Frenchman, and died very soon after. Alexandre produced a photocopy of a purported new will, which he maintained had been made before the civil partnership, making him the sole beneficiary. Alexandre argued that this new will had not been revoked by the civil partnership because it had been made with just such an event in mind. The court rejected this argument and held that the new will had been revoked. Although the new will contained a general statement that it should survive a civil partnership, there was nothing in it to show that the deceased had expected to enter into one with Alexandre or any other person at the date he signed it. Alexandre subsequently reached an out of court settlement with the executors of the earlier will, and was later arrested by the French police on suspicion of the murder of Peter and forgery of the will.

8.22 A decree of divorce or judicial separation granted to a spouse, or a dissolution or separation order granted to a civil partner, does not automatically revoke a will. However, the Wills Act 1837, ss 18A, 18C provide that in either of these events, or where a decree or order of nullity has been granted, or where a marriage or civil partnership is void *ab initio*, any bequest to a spouse or civil partner, or the appointment of a spouse or civil partner as an executor or trustee, is revoked.

# Intestate succession: Administration of Estates Act 1925, s 46

8.23 Intestate succession will take place where the deceased leaves no will or where the will is invalid. The National Consumer Council (NCC) in 2007, reported that more than 27 million adults in England and Wales do not have a will, and that almost one quarter of 55–64-year-olds have personal experience of the problems which arise as a result of intestacy.

8.24 In 2008, the Law Commission carried out statistical work with the Probate Service and HM Revenue & Customs (HMRC). It found that the less property a person owns the more likely he or she will die without making a will. The median value of an intestate estate, according to Law Commission figures, is £56,000. Where there is a will it is £160,000, and almost a third of intestate estates are valued at less than £25,000.

8.25 If a spouse or civil partner dies intestate, the property will be distributed in accordance with the Administration of Estates Act 1925. Section 46(2A) of the Act provides that a spouse or civil partner must survive for 28 days after the death of a partner to come within the intestacy rules. If he or she dies within that period, the property of the person who dies first will be distributed as if there is no surviving spouse or civil partner.

8.26 If the parties are divorced or judicially separated, or the civil partnership has been dissolved, or a separation order has been granted, or if a decree or order of nullity has been granted, or the marriage or civil partnership was void *ab initio*, they will receive nothing on an intestacy.

8.27 The Administration of Estates Act 1925, s 46 provides that a surviving spouse or civil partner takes all the personal chattels unless they have to be sold to pay the intestate's debts.

Section 55(1)(x) defines personal chattels in a rather quaint manner:

> Carriages, horses, stable furniture and effects (not used for business purposes), motor cars and accessories (not used for business purposes), garden effects, domestic animals, plate, plated articles, linen, china, glass, books, pictures, prints, furniture, jewellery, articles of household or personal use or ornament, musical and scientific instruments and apparatus, wines, liquors and consumable stores, but they do not include any chattels used at the death of the intestate for business purposes nor money or securities for money.

The remainder of the surviving spouse or civil partner's interest after he or she has received the chattels depends on which other relatives survive the deceased.

## Where there is a spouse or civil partner and children or other direct descendants

8.28 The surviving spouse or civil partner has a right to a statutory legacy of £250,000 (provided the deceased's estate is sufficient) and a life interest in half the remainder.

Whatever remains is held on trust in equal shares for the deceased's direct descendants who are alive at the time of his or her death.

8.29 A surviving spouse or civil partner has a right to demand the deceased's share in the family home to satisfy all or part of their intestate succession. If there are insufficient funds in the intestate's estate for the demand to be met, the spouse or civil partner may have to pay the deceased's personal representatives to acquire the deceased's share.

## Where there is a spouse or civil partner and no direct descendants

8.30 The surviving spouse's or civil partner's statutory legacy is increased to £450,000 and an absolute interest in half the remainder. Whatever remains is inherited first by the parents in equal shares, secondly, by the deceased's brothers and sisters in equal shares, and thirdly, by the latter's direct descendants in equal shares. If there are none of these relatives in existence, the surviving spouse or civil partner will receive all the property.

## Where there is no spouse or civil partner

8.31 The deceased's estate is inherited in the following order of precedent:

- First, by the direct descendants.
- Secondly, by the parents.
- Thirdly, by the deceased's brothers or sisters or their direct descendants.
- Fourthly, by the deceased's half brothers and sisters.
- Fifthly, by the grandparents.
- Sixthly, by the deceased's aunts and uncles.

If any of these have died before the deceased but have living children, the children will take their parent's share.

### *Bona vacantia*

8.32 The Administration of Estates Act 1925, s 46(1) provides that if there are none of the relatives, listed above, surviving at the time of the deceased's death, the estate goes as *bona vacantia* to the Crown. It is believed that the Crown acquires several million pounds each year by way of *bona vacantia*.

8.33 The Treasury Solicitor may make an *ex gratia* payment to anyone who makes an application on the ground that the deceased could reasonably have been expected to make provision for them. The process is very informal; applications by email are possible. The Treasury Solicitor has complete discretion to make a decision (see http://www.bonavacantia.gov.uk). The factors which will be taken into account include:

(a) the size and nature of the deceased's estate;

(b) the length and nature of the relationship between the deceased and the applicant;

(c) any legal or moral obligations which the deceased had towards the applicant;

(d) the way in which the applicant behaved towards the deceased, including the contribution (if any) made by the applicant to the welfare of the deceased; and

(e) any other matter which, in the particular circumstances, the Treasury Solicitor considers relevant.

8.34 No application will be considered if the person is eligible to make a claim under the Inheritance Act 1975. This rule excludes the possibility of many claims to the Treasury Solicitor because there will be few applicants eligible to claim an *ex gratia* payment who would not have a right to apply under the Inheritance Act 1975. Possible applicants might include immediate relatives or close friends, who were not being maintained by the deceased prior to death but were owed some form of moral obligation, and do not, therefore, come within the ambit of the 1975 Act.

## Claims under the Inheritance (Provision for Family and Dependants) Act 1975

8.35 This complex and rather convoluted Act was considered to be a revolutionary development at the time of its enactment. During its passage through Parliament, it was referred to as the *Mistresses' Charter* (Hansard HC Deb 16 July 1975 vol 895). The Act has the potential to provide financial maintenance for a wide range of family members, and other dependants including mistresses and cohabitants, who have received no reasonable financial provision from the deceased's estate either by will or because of the rules relating to intestacy. It has been said repeatedly that the Act does not allow the court to rewrite the deceased's will or modify the intestacy rules. However, in reality, any order made under the Act will have to be met out of the legacies intended by the testator, or where there is an intestacy, out of the statutory legacies.

8.36 Where a surviving family member is ineligible to make an application under the Act or is unsuccessful in obtaining an award from the court, a claim under the doctrine of constructive trusts or proprietary estoppel may be possible, these doctrines are discussed in Chapter 4.

### Time bar

8.37 According to s 4 of the Act, any application must be made within six months of the valid grant of probate, or from the date when letters of administration are first taken out because any award will affect the rights of other beneficiaries. The period may be extended at the court's discretion.

### Applicants

8.38 Section 1(1) of the Act defines the categories of those who may apply:

(a) Spouses or civil partners: included in this category are judicially separated spouses or civil partners, parties to a voidable marriage or civil partnership which has not been annulled prior to the deceased's death. Parties who have entered into a void marriage or civil partnership in good faith, and who have not applied for the relationship to be annulled (see Ch.3), are also included provided they have not remarried or entered into a new civil partnership.

(b) Former spouses or civil partners who have not remarried or entered into a new civil partnership and have not been barred from applying under the terms of the divorce settlement or the civil partnership dissolution settlement.

(c) Children, including adopted children.

(d) Any person who is not a child of the deceased but who was treated as a child of the deceased in relation to a marriage to which the deceased was a party.

(e) Any other person who immediately before the death of the deceased was being maintained, either partly or wholly, by the deceased.

Section 1(1A), (1B) of the Act provides that any person living in the same household as the deceased, as a spouse or civil partner of the deceased, during the two years immediately preceding the death of the deceased may make an application. Prior to the insertion of these sections (see Law Reform (Succession) Act 1995, s 2(3), CPA 2004, s 71, Sch 4, Pt 2, para 15(1), (5)), heterosexual or same-sex cohabitants had to apply under s1 (1)(e) with all the attendant problems of proving dependency. The task of such couples has been made significantly easier by ss 1(1A), (B).

## Living together in the same household as if a spouse or civil partner (ss 1(1A)(a)(b), (1B)(a)(b))

8.39 Courts continue to struggle with the meaning of living together in the same household as if a spouse or a civil partner. House and household do not have the same meaning, although, it is implicit in several of the decisions that the courts have tended to confuse the two concepts. Whether a person is living in the same household as another depends on the particular facts of the case (see *Kotke v Saffarini (2005)* below) where the issue was considered in the context of a claim under the Fatal Accidents Act 1976). Applicants have been more likely to succeed where they meet the judiciary's fairly conservative expectations that they were fulfilling one of the traditional roles associated with marriage and were living in the same house as the deceased, and had had a sexual relationship with the deceased.

8.40 In *Re Watson (deceased) (1999)*, the applicant and the deceased had had a relationship for 30 years. For the first 20 years, they did not live together because they had elderly parents to care for. When they were eventually free to live together, the applicant retained her house but left it unoccupied. She declined to marry the deceased; she preferred her freedom, although she only took advantage of it to meet her female friends. She cooked and cleaned for the deceased in his relatively primitive house, and contributed towards half the cost of the outgoings. The couple lived companionably together, having abandoned their sexual relationship prior to moving in together, until the deceased went into hospital where he died intestate. He left no surviving relatives. The deceased's estate consequently passed to the Crown as *bona vacantia*. The Treasury Solicitor maintained that the applicant's relationship with the deceased was merely a house-sharing arrangement. He had centred his argument on the applicant's refusal to marry, her lack of sexual relations with the deceased once they began living together, her retention of her own home, and her sharing of the outgoings on the deceased's house.

The court rejected these arguments and maintained it should determine the matter by asking whether, in the opinion of a reasonable person with normal perceptions, it could be said that the two people in question were living together as husband and wife. In so doing, it acknowledged the multifarious nature of marital relationships. The court suggested that:

> ...it cannot be doubted that it is not unusual for a happily married husband and wife in their mid-fifties (which was the age of the parties when they started living together in the present case) not merely to have separate bedrooms, but to abstain from sexual relations. Mr Watson and Miss Griffiths lived alone together for over 10 years in a house where they shared the bathroom and the living rooms. He went out to work and earned the bulk of the household's income, while she did the housekeeping...the shopping, the washing, the cooking and the gardening. No doubt, they ate together every day and that they enjoyed the living rooms jointly.

The court held that the nature and character of the relationship, including the deceased's assumption of responsibility for the applicant, the sexual nature of their relationship prior to living together, and the fact that they had lived together for 10 years, led to the conclusion that the applicant had lived as if she were the wife of the deceased.

8.41 In *Churchill v Roach (2004)*, a middle-aged couple, who were lovers for many years, finally purchased adjoining houses and subsequently combined them into one house in which they lived together. The man died before they had lived together in the house for the requisite two years. The court refused to accept that the couple had lived together for the requisite period under s.1 (1)(A). It maintained that the relationship lacked the following features which it thought to be indicative of living together as if a husband or wife:

(a) elements of permanence;

(b) frequency and intimacy of contact;

(c) an element of mutual support;

(d) a degree of voluntary restraint upon personal freedom;

(e) an element of community of resources.

The court did however permit the woman to claim under s 1(1)(e) of the Act on the basis that the deceased had been maintaining her immediately before his death.

(See also *Lindop v Agus; Bass and Hedley (2010)*.)

8.42 It will be interesting to see how the approach of the court might develop in applications by those claiming to be living in the same household as if civil partners. As yet there is no cultural model of a civil partnership to which the court may refer when faced with such claims.

8.43 In *Baynes v Hedger (2008)*, Lewison J took a fairly conservative approach to s 1(1)(b) and implicitly drew an analogy with heterosexual cohabiting relationships. He maintained that a lesbian couple, who had had a relationship for 40 years, were not living in the same household as if civil partners at the time of death because they each owned a separate home, and did not hold themselves out to the world as having a lesbian relationship. The fact that they visited regularly and had had a bedroom in each other's house was seen as negating the deceased partner's claim that she and the deceased were living together immediately preceding the deceased's death.

8.44 Although a claimant must have lived in the same household as the deceased for two years preceding death, an application will not fail if there is good reason not to do so. One obvious example is where a person is hospitalized immediately before death; he or she clearly remains part of a partner's household (see eg *Re Watson (deceased) (1999)*).

In *Gully v Dix (2004)*, the applicant had left the deceased three months prior to his death for a trial separation because he had a drink problem, but the relationship had not ended. The court accepted that the parties had been living together in the same household immediately prior to death. In Ward LJ's words

*... so the steadfastness of a commitment to live together may wax and wane, but so long as it is not extinguished it survives.*

## Proof of maintenance (s.1 (3)) and assumption of responsibility (s3 (3)(4))—threshold requirements

8.45 Section 1(3) of the Inheritance Act provides that applicants who make a claim under s 1(1)(e) will be treated as being maintained by the deceased, if the deceased, other than for full valuable consideration, was making a substantial contribution in money or money's worth towards their needs. The provision was intended, partly, to prevent employees who lived with the deceased from making a claim.

8.46 In *Jelley v Iliffe (1981)*, Stephenson LJ explained his interpretation of s 1(3):

*The court has to balance what [the deceased] was contributing against what [the applicant] was contributing, and if there is any doubt about the balance tipping in favour of [the deceased's] being the greater contribution, the matter must go to trial. If, however, the balance is bound to come down in favour of the [applicant's] being the greater contribution, or if the contributions are equal, there is no dependency.*

This approach to maintenance could mean an applicant who has made a significant contribution in terms of care of the deceased for little reward would appear to lose out. The lazier an applicant has been, the more likely they could be considered to have received more than they have given and be rewarded under the Act.

However, Stephenson LJ suggested that a balance must be struck and

*... the court must use common sense and remember that the object of Parliament in creating this extra class of person who may claim benefit from an estate was to provide relief for persons of whom it could be said that they were wholly or partially dependent on the deceased. It cannot be an exact exercise of evaluating services in pounds and pence.*

Rather strangely, he did suggest that companionship could be evaluated as valuable consideration. What price one puts on such an imponderable remains a mystery.

8.47 In *Re B (deceased) (2000)*, a mother and her severely disabled daughter lived in a property which was purchased using 25 per cent of the mother's money and 75 per cent of the damages which had been awarded to the daughter for severe mental and physical disabilities sustained at birth. Her father had left home when she was born and played no part in her life; her affairs were dealt with by the Court of Protection which made regular payments to the mother for the daughter's maintenance but no specific allowance for herself.

When the daughter died intestate, the estate passed to the mother and father in equal shares. The mother successfully applied for reasonable provision from her daughter's estate. She argued that her daughter had maintained her. The Court of Appeal maintained that it would have been obvious to the Court of Protection that the payments to the daughter were also being used to meet her mother's financial and material needs to enable her to look after her daughter's needs. The Court of Protection could be seen as acting as the conscience of a patient and making provision for those to whom the patient would have felt a moral obligation if mentally capable of doing so.

8.48    In *Baynes v Hedges (2008)*, Lewison J held that the gift of a house made by the deceased to her partner 30 years before her death was not maintenance immediately before death. Furthermore, he held a trust fund set up by the deceased during her lifetime for her partner's support to be maintenance which came from the settlement and not from the deceased.

8.49 Sections 3(3)(4) of the Act requires the court to take into account the extent to which, and the basis on which, the deceased assumed responsibility for an applicant's maintenance.

In *Jelley v Iliffe (1981)*, Stephenson LJ took a fairly liberal approach to the assumption of responsibility and stated that where one person had made a substantial contribution to another person's needs, it raised an inference of an assumption of responsibility and dependency.

8.50    In *Baynes v Hedger (2009)*, the Court of Appeal stressed the threshold nature of the question of whether the deceased had assumed responsibility for the applicant's maintenance.

In the deceased's will she had left her house, worth £2 million to the Landmark Trust, £2,500 to the child of the partner, who was also her goddaughter, and the residuary estate of £400,000 to her partner for life and then to the children, excluding the goddaughter.

The goddaughter applied under the Inheritance Act 1975 and maintained that the deceased's will failed to make reasonable financial provision for her. She had debts which exceeded £400,000, and she asked the court for £800,000 to help her avoid bankruptcy.

The deceased, a well-known wealthy sculptor who valued her privacy, had had a very private lesbian relationship with the goddaughter's mother for 40 years. She had been very involved with her partner's children and made gifts during her lifetime to them. She had been exceptionally generous towards her goddaughter. She had bought her a flat and had provided her with financial help. The goddaughter would also benefit as the remainderman of a trust which the deceased had set up to provide for her partner during her lifetime. The goddaughter was always in debt and had repeatedly asked the deceased for further help. In the 4 years before the deceased's death, she had received in total £171,000 expressed to be a loan, but with no real expectation on the part of the deceased that she would be repaid. Not satisfied, the goddaughter had attempted to obtain further financial help by telling the deceased that she knew the nature of her relationship with her mother.

In the High Court hearing (2008), Lewison J accepted that the goddaughter was eligible to make a claim under s 1(1)(e) but refused to make an order in her favour. He considered s 3(4) of the 1975 Act and held that the deceased wanted to pay off her goddaughter's debts to make her financially independent and had not assumed a responsibility or an obligation for her ongoing maintenance.

8.51 The goddaughter appealed and the Court of Appeal dismissed her appeal. It also emphasised that the first question a court must address is whether an applicant, to whom s 3(3) or (4) applies is eligible to make a claim. Lewison J had failed to do so; he had accepted the goddaughter's eligibility to apply and then concluded that the deceased had not assumed responsibility for the maintenance of her goddaughter. Given this conclusion, he should have held that she was ineligible to apply for mainten-ance in the first place.

## Reasonable financial provision

8.52 Applicants must be able to show that the effect of the deceased's will or the rules relating to intestacy mean that they have not received reasonable financial provi-sion from the deceased's estate. Reasonable financial provision is defined in s 1(2) of the Act.

8.53 For the surviving spouse or civil partner, it means such financial provision as it would be reasonable in all the circumstances of the case for them to receive, whether or not it was required for their maintenance (see eg *Moore v Holdsworth (2010)*). This standard may be extended to a surviving spouse or civil partner whose legal separation took place not more than 12 months before the death of the deceased. It may also be extended to a former spouse or civil partner who has not entered into a new legal relationship and whose divorce, or dissolution of the civil partnership, was granted not more than 12 months prior to the deceased's death.

8.54 For all other applicants, reasonable financial provision means such financial provi-sion as it would be reasonable in all the circumstances of the case for the applicant to receive for his or her maintenance.

8.55　　In *Espinosa v Bourke (1999)*, the Court of Appeal declined to define the exact meaning of the term maintenance but suggested that:

> ...*it connotes only payments which, directly or indirectly, enable the applicant in the future to discharge the cost of his daily living at whatever standard of living is appropriate to him. The provision that is to be made is to meet recurring expenses, being expenses of living of an income nature. This does not mean that the provision need be by way of income payments. The provision can be by way of lump sum, for example, to buy a house in which the applicant can be housed, thereby relieving him pro tanto of income expenditure... there may be cases in which payment of existing debts may be as appropriate as a maintenance payment; for example, to pay the debts of an applicant in order to enable him to continue to carry on a profit-making business or profession.*

8.56　　In *Witkowska v Kaminski (2006)*, the applicant originated from Poland, and had lived with the deceased in England prior to his death and continued to do so afterwards. The court assessed her claim under ss 1(1A) and s 1(1)(e) of the Act on the basis of the amount of maintenance she would require to live in Poland. It took the approach that £50 per week would be sufficient to maintain her in Poland. The court held that the deceased had assumed responsibility for the claimant during his lifetime on the assumption that were he to pre-decease her, she would probably have to return to Poland. She did not speak English, her family ties were in Poland, and at the time of the deceased's death she had no right to stay in England for more than six months, and no right to seek employment. The decision preceded Poland's entry into the European Union.

8.57　The decision in *Negus v Bahouse (2008)* illustrates the approach of the court towards reasonable provision for maintenance in a claim by a cohabitant where the estate was worth £2.2 million.

> The deceased, Mr Bahouse, had been divorced twice, and had one son. He had asked Ms Negus, who was aged 50 at the time of her application for maintenance, to live with him and give up her work as a receptionist. This she had agreed to do. He had treated her generously paying for all her needs in addition to giving her a small allowance of £250 a month. They had enjoyed dining in expensive restaurants and having luxurious holidays. Mr Bahouse had purchased a home for them. Eventually, after the couple had lived together for over seven years, his health declined. He became very depressed and committed suicide while Ms Negus was away for a weekend visiting her mother. Mr Bahouse had left a will leaving his estate mainly to his son, but with legacies of £75,000 each to his three siblings. Ms Negus was not mentioned in the will but had acquired a half share of Mr Bahouse's pension policy worth £459,000, and a half share of a property in Spain worth £200,000; the remaining half shares belonged to his son.
>
> In assessing what would be an appropriate amount for maintenance for Ms Negus, Judge Kaye QC referred to the Canadian decision in *Re Duranceau (1952)* where

*...in somewhat poetic language, the court said that the question is: 'Is the provision sufficient to enable the dependant to live neither luxuriously nor miserably, but decently and comfortably according to his or her station in life?'*

*What is proper maintenance must in all cases depend upon all the facts and circumstances of the particular case being considered at the time, but I think it is clear on the one hand that one must not put too limited a meaning on it; it does not mean just enough to enable a person to get by; on the other hand, it does not mean anything which may be regarded as reasonably desirable for his general benefit or welfare.*

He took into account Ms Negus' age, the length of her relationship with Mr Bahouse, his generosity to her and their lifestyle during his lifetime, and his promises to her to ensure her long-term security. It would be unjust to assume that Ms Negus would find employment at her age and with her lack of recent experience. The court awarded her the English home free of mortgage, plus £240,000 on the basis that this, together with her share of the pension fund and the Spanish property, would give her an adequate income to meet her estimated needs of around £39,000 a year (see also *Webster v Webster (2008)*).

## Factors to be considered by the court

8.58 Once an applicant has proven eligibility to apply for an award from the deceased's estate, the court must have regard to a number of factors laid down in s 3(1) of the Act. The section is remarkably similar to the discretionary factors to which the court must have regard under MCA 1973, s 25 (see Chapter 7), in making ancillary awards on divorce. The factors are:

(a) the applicant's financial needs and resources;

(b) other applicants' financial needs and resources;

(c) any beneficiaries' financial needs and resources;

(d) any obligation or responsibility which the deceased had towards the applicant or any beneficiary;

(e) the size and nature of the estate;

(f) any physical or mental disability of the applicant or beneficiary;

(g) any other matter, including the conduct of the applicant or any other person, which the court considers to be relevant.

8.59 Section 3(2)–(5) expands on these factors; s 3(2) is of particular interest. It provides, *inter alia*, that, in the case of married applicants, the court shall have regard to

*...the provision which the applicant might reasonably have expected to receive if on the day on which the deceased died the marriage, instead of being terminated by death had been terminated by a decree of divorce.*

This provision was considered by the Court of Appeal in *Cunliffe v Fielden (2006)*. Mrs Cunliffe was aged 48 when she married the deceased in 2001; her husband died one year later and left an estate of £1.3 million. Mrs Cunliffe was named in the will as a beneficiary under a discretionary trust. The trustees offered her a £200,000 lump sum, which she rejected, and applied for provision under the Inheritance Act 1975. The judge at first instance awarded her £800,000.

The executors appealed. The Court of Appeal granted the appeal and in doing so, Wall LJ drew attention to the problematic nature of the Inheritance Act 1975, s 3(2). He explained that:

*...there is self-evidently a profound difference between a marriage which ends through the death of one of the spouses, and a marriage which ends through divorce.... A marriage dissolved by divorce involves a conscious decision by one or both of the spouses to bring the marriage to an end. That process leaves two living former spouses, each of whom has resources, needs and responsibilities. In such a case the length of the marriage and the parties' respective contributions to it assume a particular importance when the court is striving to reach a fair financial outcome. However, where the marriage, as here, is dissolved by death, a widow is entitled to say that she entered into it on the basis that it would be of indefinite duration, and in the expectation that she would devote the remainder of the parties' joint lives to being his wife and caring for him. The fact that the marriage has been prematurely terminated by death after a short period may therefore render the length of the marriage a less critical factor than it would be in the case of a divorce.*

Wall LJ, acknowledged that Mrs Cunliffe had married on the basis that her husband was considerably older than she was and that she might well have expected to spend time caring for her husband in his old age. She was entitled to assume that she need not revert to her position as a single woman when her husband died and that she would be financially secure for the rest of her life.

In spite of these comments, Wall LJ thought that, in the light of a short marriage, it would be inappropriate for Mrs Cunliffe to expect to be maintained at the same level she had enjoyed during the marriage. He proceeded to look at what he perceived to be Mrs Cunliffe's reasonable needs, in spite of the fact that s 1(2) of the Act provides that in the case of a married applicant the court may make an award whether or not it is required for maintenance. He stated that she had a need for a home at a lesser value that the former matrimonial home, and income providing her with reasonable maintenance. He judged that to be £600,000 (see also *Baker v Baker (2008)*).

Since the decision in *Miller and McFarlane (2006)* (see Chapter 7), it is questionable whether the decisions in *Cunliffe (2006)* and *Baker (2008)* are correct. Both widows would almost certainly have received a higher award had they become divorcees rather than widows.

8.60    In *Malone v Harrison (1979)*, the applicant had been the mistress of the deceased for 12 years. The deceased had enjoyed multiple relationships with women. The mistress was one of a long line; there was also a wife from whom he was separated, and a cohabitant with whom he lived. The deceased had met the applicant when she was in her early 20s and persuaded her to give up her work and to travel abroad from time to time with him. He paid all her living expenses and provided her with flats in England and Malta, a car, and a hairdressing business which was unsuccessful. He gave her many expensive presents. The deceased had told the applicant that if he were free to marry, he would marry her. He constantly reassured her about her future security. The deceased told her that he would make no provision for her in his will, but, in Janus-like manner, sent her a newspaper cutting giving details of the Inheritance Act 1975.

The court found that the deceased had monopolized the applicant's life for 12 years and had

*...discouraged her from seeking gainful employment. He taught her to rely upon him for all her financial needs, but it must be said she became an apt pupil and was not slow in asking for what she wanted. This does not mean that the deceased through his estate, as it were, should be punished, but as he was generous to her in her lifetime, so within the limits set by the statute should the court be in deciding what if any order to make.*

8.61     In *Re Snoek (deceased) (1983)*, the court considered all the factors in s 3 of the Act, but particularly the applicant's conduct. The applicant was the deceased's widow and had behaved appallingly during the relationship. Wood J found:

*...the following examples of her behaviour occurred: on the 10th July 1976, she threw a pot of water over the deceased on three occasions. On the 26th July, in the same year, she drove her car at him, struck him over the head with a milk bottle damaged the windows of a van outside his place of business and bit him in the arm. On the 10th August she struck him with a rolling pin. On the 13th September she struck him with an umbrella causing a cut to his nose and bruising to his cheek and eye. On the 21st July and the 13th September, that same year, she deliberately punctured the tyres of his car. She told me in evidence that 'it was just for the experience.'...She wrote many offensive and abusive letters and notes to business colleagues and friends of the deceased and persistently telephoned at all hours.*

*...*

*The health of the deceased had been deteriorating and for some while it was known that he was suffering from a terminal disease...the applicant visited the deceased at his office. She attacked him and his secretary, ripped out the telephone, tore up papers on his desk and did other damage. She struck him, kicked him and bit him and was only controlled by the timely assistance of a workman from outside. I am satisfied that on this occasion the deceased was seriously at risk.*

Nevertheless, the court held the widow had made a contribution to the welfare of the family during the earlier part of the marriage which was not cancelled out by her later atrocious conduct.

8.62     In *Re Land (deceased) (2007)*, the applicant pleaded guilty to, and was convicted of, the manslaughter of his deceased mother and was, therefore, disentitled to inherit from her will. The court held that this did not prevent him from making a claim under the Inheritance Act 1975.

The facts of the case were both horrendous and tragic. The applicant was an inadequate only child who had always lived at home. He was a loner who had left school at 15. Throughout his life he worked as a labourer until he gave up his job to care for his sick and elderly mother. He did all the housework, shopping and cooking, and helped his mother with her personal care. They rarely went out. His mother was a stubborn, domineering woman, who hated any type of 'officialdom' including doctors and home helps. One Christmas, she fell out of her bed and complained when the applicant tried to put her back. He left her on the floor where she ate her Christmas dinner and drank her whisky. The applicant eventually called an ambulance on the following day because his mother was on the verge of unconsciousness.

When admitted to hospital, she was found to be

*...suffering from severe bed sores on her whole body, particularly an area from her shoulders to her legs. She had an horrendous sore at the base of her back measuring approximately three or four inches deep through which the sacrum was visible, described by the police surgeon as being 'capable of taking two fists inside'. It was clear she was suffering from breast cancer. Her wounds were consistent with her having been lying in one place for a period of time in her own excrement and urine, the net effect of which was to create a cocktail of chemicals which had infected her flesh. She was unconscious and so remained until her death two days later.*

The court balanced the factors listed in s 3 of the 1975 Act and decided to make an award to the son on the basis that:

(a) he had no capital, had given up his modest job to look after his mother, would face employment difficulties in view of his age, his and his criminal record, and would be dependent on State benefits;

(b) his main need was to have the long term security of his family home;

(c) no other person entitled on intestacy had applied to the court;

(d) he was the deceased's only son (he had very recently discovered that he was adopted), who had lived with his mother throughout his life and had tried to care for her. The mother had recognised an obligation to him by leaving him her entire estate;

(e) the estate consisted of the house in which the mother and son lived (now valued at some £120,000), two life policies with a combined value of about £10,500, and some £5,000 in a bank account;

(f) his conduct towards his mother which (although in the last two months of her life became culpable and blameworthy) was essentially that of one who had discharged his obligation for a considerable period of time.

# Adult children

8.63  Claims by adult children have proved to be problematic, and the courts have tended to take a very restrictive approach towards such applications.

> For instance, in **Re Jennings (1994)**, Nourse LJ maintained that, although the Act made provision for applications by adult children, such applications would only be successful where there were special circumstances. The applicant was a 50 year-old son, whose father had never provided for him during his lifetime. The court took the approach that because the deceased had not taken on any obligations or responsibilities towards his son during his lifetime, in accordance with s 3(1)(d) of the Act, it should not make provision for him now.

8.64  More recently, the courts have turned their attention to s 3 of the Act and stressed the need to balance all the factors outlined in that section but applicants have not been any more successful.

> In **H v J's Personal Representatives, Blue Cross, RSPB and RSPCA (2009)**, King J explicitly rejected the view that in order for an adult child to succeed in an application under the Inheritance Act 1975, he or she had to prove a moral obligation on the part of the deceased towards him or her, although it could, of course, be one of the balancing factors.

> The daughter in **H v J** had been brought up solely by her mother; her father had died before she was born. At the age of 17, she left home to live with a man of whom her mother disapproved. From then onwards, she had minimal contact with her mother. She later married the man and had five children by him. The mother and daughter never became reconciled in spite of various attempts to do so. The mother made a will leaving everything to various animal charities and told her daughter that she had excluded her from the will because of her behaviour. The daughter made clear that she understood her mother's wishes. When the mother died, her estate amounted to £486,000. The daughter was living primarily on State benefits in low-cost rented housing. She decided to make an application under the Inheritance Act 1975 claiming that her mother's will failed to make reasonable provision for her.

> The District Judge granted the daughter's application and ordered that she should receive £50,000 from her mother's estate. The daughter appealed, maintaining that the amount was insufficient for her maintenance. The animal charities cross-appealed on the ground that the mother's failure to provide for the daughter was a reasonable provision for her.

> The High Court dismissed the daughter's appeal and allowed the cross appeal. King J emphasized the principle of freedom of testation, and concluded that the District Judge in his generous treatment of the daughter had asked himself the wrong question. He

may have thought that the mother was unreasonable in preferring to leave her property to charities in which she had shown no interest during her lifetime because she could not forgive her daughter's behaviour. However, the question he should have asked is not whether the mother acted unreasonably but whether, after an objective balancing of all the factors in s 3 of the Act, the provision for the daughter, or the lack of it, was unreasonable.

According to King J the most relevant factors were that the mother and daughter had never become reconciled, and the daughter's circumstances resulted from her lifestyle choice to have five children and stay at home and live with a husband who only worked part-time. Following the decision in *Espinosa v Bourke (1999)*, an adult child capable of earning a living must identify some weighty factor to succeed in any claim that there has been a failure to make reasonable provision for him or her. King J declined to accept the view of the District Judge that the daughter's financial position and the normally accepted family obligations of a mother towards a child was such a factor.

8.65    A similar approach was taken by the court in *Garland v Morris (2007)*. Here, the parents of two sisters separated and the mother subsequently committed suicide. Prior to her death, she had had regular contact with the younger sister and had made a will in which she left her entire estate to that daughter. As a consequence, the father decided to leave £300,000 to the elder sister and nothing to the younger one. When he died the younger sister applied for provision from his estate under the Inheritance Act 1975. She had minimal career prospects and had a young child; she was in financial difficulties. All her inheritance from her mother had been spent on a house which required extensive renovations. Prior to her father's death, she had had nothing to do with him. Her elder sister had a good relationship with her father who had helped her financially during his lifetime. He wanted that help to continue after his death. He did ask her not to let her younger sister starve after he had died, and on his death, the elder sister gave her £6,000.

The court refused to grant the younger sister's claim. It held that there is no need for a child of a deceased parent to prove that there was a moral obligation to provide for him or her, but merely to show that taking into account all the facts, and the factors in s3 of the Act, it was unreasonable for a parent to exclude him or her from the will. Here, the failure to provide was not unreasonable; the father and his younger daughter had not had a relationship for a long time, and she had already benefited substantially from her mother's will.

8.66    John Wilson and Rebecca Bailey-Harris (2004) have suggested that the courts' approach in successful claims by adult children is one of satisfying disappointed reasonable expectation in a manner analogous to that of proprietary estoppel. The decisions below seem to confirm their view.

8.67    In *Hanbury v Hanbury (1999)*, the court took into account, as a major factor, the failure of the deceased during his lifetime to fulfil the reasonable expectation that he had a moral obligation towards his physically and mentally disabled daughter. He had offered minimal financial support and had deliberately arranged his financial affairs to avoid her being able to make any claim on his death. The daughter, through her mother, applied for provision from his estate and the court ordered a discretionary trust of £35,000 to be set up in her name, using monies which the deceased had transferred to his second wife to avoid a claim by the daughter. The income from the trust would help pay for the daughter's residential care.

8.68    In *Espinosa v Bourke (1999)*, the deceased's adult daughter succeeded in her application in spite of reneging on her agreement with the deceased to care for him in her home. Her elderly father paid for household expenses, improvements to her house and the mortgage payments on it. The daughter subsequently abandoned him to be cared for by her son and a cleaner, and went to live in Spain. She returned briefly for a few months prior to her father's death.

In his will the deceased had left a significant sum of money, including shares he had inherited from his wife, to his grandson. The father stated in the will that he had made no provision for his daughter, because she had been adequately provided for during his lifetime, and she had also shown, in his view, a degree of irresponsibility in her personal life. He disapproved of his daughter's lifestyle, in particular that she brought men, usually younger men, to sleep with her in the small three-bedroom family home. She had subsequently married a Spanish fisherman, who was 20 years younger than her; he was one of a series of husbands.

The Court of Appeal stressed the need to consider all the relevant factors in s 3. The court took into account the father's wish not to provide for her; his payments towards the property and household bills; the daughter's lifestyle; her failure to adjust to the presence of her elderly father (and indeed of her teenage son) in the house; and her neglect of the father for most of the last seven months of his life, in spite of her agreement to care for him. However, balanced out against these factors was the promise to his late wife to give their daughter a proportion of the shares which he had inherited from her. She had a reasonable expectation that her father would keep to this promise, The daughter was in debt and financially in need, it might be difficult for her to find work, and the estate was large enough not to damage the other beneficiary, the grandson. She received £60,000.

8.69    In *Re Goodchild (1997)*, the court also made provision for an adult child from his deceased father's estate for the sum of £185,000. The father had remarried after the death of the son's mother, and left all his property to his new wife, who had subsequently remarried. There had been an assumption by the mother when she made her will, which left all her property to the father, that in the event of his death, their son would receive the property. The son's income was very low. According to the court, the father was guilty of a breach of moral obligation owed by a parent towards his son, leaving him in straitened financial circumstances.

8.70      In *Re Pearce (1998)*, the applicant had worked on the family sheep farm without pay from the age of six until 16, when he left home to earn money because his father could not afford to pay him. He returned whenever he could to continue to help out. His father had repeatedly promised him that he would leave the farm to him but ultimately made a will in favour of a woman who had previously lived with him. At the time of his father's death, the applicant had acquired a small business and lived with his wife and five children in a home badly in need of improvement on an income of £8,000 a year. It was held that the deceased had been under a moral obligation to his son created by the promises he had made to him to leave him the farm, in return for which he had undertaken substantial work without pay. He received £85,000 for his maintenance.

## Reform

8.71  In 2008, the Law Commission embarked on a major review of the law relating to intestacy and the operation of the Inheritance Act 1975. In its view the changes in family structures and in property ownership since the Inheritance Act 1975 came into existence are sufficiently great to justify the review. The initial consultation period has ended and a report and draft Bill are expected in late 2011; it is to be hoped that these will address the over-complex nature of the 1975 Act.

# Fatal Accidents Act 1976

8.72  A spouse, civil partner or cohabitant who was dependent on the deceased may make an application for compensation from the defendant under s 1 of the Act, where the deceased suffered wrongful death which was attributable to the defendant.

8.73  Section 1(3)(b) of the Act defines a cohabitant as any person who:

    (i) was living with the deceased in the same household immediately before the date of the death;

and

    (ii) had been living with the deceased in the same household for at least two years before that date;

and

    (iii) was living during the whole of that period as the husband or wife or civil partner of the deceased.

8.74      The decision in *Kotke v Saffarini (2005)* provides an example of the difficulties facing cohabitants who wish to make claims.

Ms Kotke, the claimant, was walking across a bridge in Bath with the deceased one evening in March 2000, when they were struck by an out-of-control car and were thrown over the parapet wall of the bridge into the river below. The deceased was killed. Ms Kotke was severely injured but managed to swim to a barge in the river and was rescued. They had an 11 month-old child who was not with them at the time of the accident.

Ms Kotke maintained that she had lived with the deceased as his wife for two years prior to his death. Her relationship with the deceased had begun five years earlier in 1995. They each owned their own house. The claimant was 10 years older than the deceased and she did not wish to marry him. They both wanted to have a committed relationship with each other. They spent as much time as possible together, including every weekend, mainly in the claimant's house but sometimes in the deceased's house. The deceased paid money into the claimant's bank account for living expenses. The deceased's work involved considerable travel and he stayed in his own house prior to travelling because it was closer to the station. They discussed selling the deceased's house but decided to wait because of the negative equity in the property.

In 1998, the claimant became pregnant. When the baby was born in May 1999, the deceased registered the child and gave the address as that of his own house. Six months before he died, the deceased rented out his own house and when not travelling lived entirely with the claimant.

The judge rejected Ms Kotke's claim that she had lived in the same household with the deceased for two years prior to his death, but recognized that she was doing so at the time of the death. Ms Kotke appealed unsuccessfully. The Court of Appeal considered the meaning of the word 'household' and stated that the term

*... embodies a concept somewhat elusive of definition, combining as it does both the physical connotation of a place, i.e. a particular house or home and personal connotations of association, i.e. the family or household resident within it. Both aspects are covered by the various dictionary definitions available.*

The court accepted that the term 'household' has an abstract meaning and refers to people held together by a particular tie even if temporarily housed apart. However, it took the view of the lower court that Ms Kotke and the deceased were not living together in the same household until, at the earliest, the time at which the claimant became pregnant, which was only 20 months prior to the death of her cohabitant. Before that date, they may have wanted to live together, planned to live together but had not actually achieved it.

8.75 The decision illustrates a very restrictive view of what constitutes living together in the same household as husband and wife. The judicial model, in spite of statements to the effect that modern lifestyles were to be taken into account in interpreting the statute, fails to recognize the independent nature of many twenty-first century spousal relationships. They may involve two partners with two careers and two homes, possibly in two countries or even two continents. It is conceivable that a couple can live together as husband and wife in the same household, albeit in separate homes for part of the time.

8.76 Judye Hess and Padma Cartell, Professors at the California Institute of Integral Studies, believe that living apart is an option that could prevent the trauma of relationship breakdown. They found that couples who have chosen to live separately often believe that their choice is partly responsible for the success of their relationship

> We are confronted every day with people who are dealing with relationship problems. It seems that many people are trying to fit themselves into a very narrow model for long-term relationship... We believe that the increase in divorce rates indicates a problem with the way we are choosing to relate as couples in committed relationships. Perhaps if there were more options available for long-term relationships, and these options were considered healthy and desirable, some people could be spared the trauma of divorce or break up of their relationships.
>
> We question society's prejudice that people who love each other and want to be life partners should live together...
>
> What we are proposing is an alternative form of relationship, one in which each member of the couple chooses to retain their own separate domicile while still being in a committed, monogamous and loving relationship....
>
> In our society in general, the commonly held belief is that if two people are a 'couple', whether it be heterosexual or homosexual, they eventually will want to live together. That if they do not, it indicates some type of problem, often labeled as 'fear of intimacy'... rather than a legitimate life style option. This is coupled with the implication that living together, in a family situation, reflects a more advanced developmental stage. Hence, all around us there is pressure from mainstream society for us to be 'coupled', and to do this in a narrowly defined way....
>
> Couples who have chosen to live separately often believe that this choice is at least partially responsible for the harmony within their relationships. They have been able to maintain their friendships, their passion and their even-tempered good will toward each other to a greater extent than many couples who live together.
>
> *(Journal of Couples Therapy (2001))*

8.77 The German poet, Rilke, took a similar, if rather more poetically expressed, view

> The point of marriage is not to create a quick commonality by tearing down all boundaries; on the contrary, a good marriage is one in which each partner appoints the other to be the guardian of his solitude, and thus they show each other the greatest possible trust. A merging of two people is an impossibility, and where it seems to exist, it is a hemming-in, a mutual consent that robs one party or both parties of their fullest freedom and development. But once the realization is accepted that even between the closest people infinite distances exist, a marvelous living side-by-side can grow up for them, if they succeed in loving the expanse between them, which gives them the possibility of always seeing each other as a whole and before an immense sky. (Rilke, 1903)

# Family life after death

8.78    In *Re Blagdon Cemetery (2002)*, the appellants' son had died in an industrial accident in 1978 whilst living some distance from their home. They arranged for his body to be buried in consecrated ground in Somerset close to where they were living at the time of his death. They subsequently moved home several times and finally retired to Suffolk. They wished to exhume their son's body and have it reburied near to their new home in a family burial plot which they had purchased for the benefit of themselves and their son. They wished to honour the memory of their son and visit his grave in its intended new location and, eventually, join him there.

Requests for exhumation and reburial of bodies from consecrated ground are made by petition to the Consistory Court of the Anglican Church under ecclesiastical law. The Court's Chancellor declined the parents' request.

The parents appealed to the Arches Court in Canterbury which allowed the appeal. It held that there was a presumption that Christian burial was permanent; that bodily remains should not be portable, and a faculty for exhumation would only be granted in rare circumstances. It cited a paper written by the Bishop of Stafford (2001) which explained that:

*The permanent burial of the physical body/the burial of cremated remains should be seen as a symbol of our entrusting the person to God for resurrection. We are commending the person to God, saying farewell to them (for their 'journey'), entrusting them in peace for their ultimate destination, with us, the heavenly Jerusalem. This commending, entrusting, resting in peace does not sit easily with 'portable remains', which suggests the opposite: reclaiming, possession, and restlessness; a holding onto the 'symbol' of a human life rather than a giving back to God.*

The Arches Court held that it was for the parents to show their circumstances were special. Old age, poor health and a move to a new area were not sufficient reasons in themselves. However, the Court accepted as exceptional circumstances the son had died suddenly at an age when it might be expected that he had no view about where he might be buried, and there was no link between him, or his parents, and the community in the place in which he was buried. It was simply the most convenient place at the time. The Court granted the parents' request. In so doing, it made some interesting observations on family life, albeit family life post death:

*The concept of a family grave is, of course, of long standing. In a less mobile society in the past, when generations of a family continued to live in the same community, it was accepted practice for several members of a family to be buried in one grave. Headstones give a vivid picture of family relationships and there are frequent examples of one or more children predeceasing their parents due to childhood illnesses, which were incurable. Burials in double or treble depth graves continue to take place at the present time. They are to be encouraged. They express family unity and they are environmentally friendly in demonstrating an economical use of land for burials.*

## FURTHER READING

Balzac H, *Le Colonel Chabert* (1832)

Borkowski A, 'Re Hancock (Deceased) and Espinosa v Bourke: Moral Obligation and Family Provision' [1999] CFLQ 305

Brooker S, Finding the Will––A Report on Will-writing Behaviour in England and Wales National Consumer Council (NCC) 2007

Conway H, 'Dead, but not Buried: Bodies, Burial and Family Conflicts' [2004] Legal Studies 23

Hale B, 'The Quest for Equal Treatment' [2005] PL 571

Intestacy and Surviving Kin: Law Commission Research

Haskey J, 'Intestacy and Surviving Kin: Law Commission Research' [2010] Fam Law 964

Hess J and Catell P, 'Dual Dwelling Duos: an Alternative for Long-Term Relationships' (2001) 10(3/4) Journal of Couples Therapy 1

Hill C, 'Theology of Burial' (September 2001)

Maguire J, 'Til Death Do Us Part: Inheritance Claims and the Short Marriage' [2006] Fam Law 36 (374)

Law Commission, Intestacy and Family Provision Claims on Death, Overview http://www.lawcom.gov.uk

Piggott J and Windram M, 'Cohabitants and the Inheritance Act: Extending the Boundaries' [2004] Fam Law 82

Rilke RM, 'On Love and Other Difficulties' in JJL Mood (Trans.), *Translations and Considerations of Rainer Maria Rilke* (W.W. Norton & Co, 1975)

Ross S, *Inheritance Act Claims: Law and Practice* (Sweet and Maxwell, 2005)

Sloane B, 'Testamentary Freedom and Caring Adult Offspring in England & Wales and Ireland', in *The Future of Family Property in Europe: Proceedings of the 4th Conference of the Commission on European Family Law* (Boele-Woelki K, Miles J and Scherpe JM (Eds)) (Intersentia, 2010)

Welstead M, 'Truly a Charter for Mistresses' [1990] Denning Law Journal 117

Wilson J and Bailey-Harris R, 'Family Provision: the Adult Child and Moral Obligation Family Law' [2005] Fam Law 35 (555)

Wintemute R, 'Same-Sex Partners, "Living as Husband and Wife", and Section 3 of the Human Rights Act 1998' [2003] PL 621

## SELF-TEST QUESTIONS

1   What does the law relating to intestate succession in England and Wales reveal about the meaning of family?

2 The provisions of the Inheritance (Provision for Family and Dependants) Act 1975, particularly ss 1, 2, and 3, are very complex.

Could they be simplified? Attempt to redraft these three sections.

3 The law does not permit spouses or civil partners to avoid their financial responsibilities towards each other on the legal ending of their relationships but does so on death.

How would you ensure that partners whose relationships end by death are not in a worse financial situation than they would be if their relationships were to end during their lifetime?

4 Having read this chapter, what advice would you give to anyone in a familial relationship who wishes to ensure that their wishes are carried out on their death?

5 Henrietta lived with Inigo for the last 10 years prior to his death last week. His widow, Jane, has lived in an institution because she has been mentally ill for the last 12 years. Inigo did not divorce her because he felt that to do so would make her condition worse. Inigo and Jane had three children who are all adults.

Inigo's children disliked their father intensely because they believed that he was the cause of their mother's illness. They also hate Henrietta because they believe that their father might have eventually rescued their mother from the institution if he had not gone to live with Henrietta. They wish to oppose Henrietta's wishes about the organization of Inigo's funeral, to show the strength of their feelings against her. They want the undertaker to arrange the cremation of their father and dispose of the ashes for them; they do not wish to attend the cremation and have ordered the undertaker not to arrange any funeral service. Henrietta would like to organize Inigo's burial in the churchyard of the small village in Oxfordshire in which they had lived together.

Advise Henrietta.

6 Charles and Desmond, a same-sex couple, were both career diplomats. They did not enter into a civil partnership because they felt that, in certain countries, it would not be acceptable, and they preferred to keep their relationship private. They lived in different countries because at the career level they had reached, there were no openings for both of them. They visited each other whenever possible and went on holiday together. They each kept an apartment in London for their separate and vast collections of books. When they were both in London, they lived in either apartment depending on how they felt at the time. Charles was blown up in an attack on his embassy and died. His only relatives are a mother, a brother and a grandmother. Charles did not make a will.

Advise Desmond, who would like to know whether he can make a claim under the Fatal Accidents Act 1976 and/or under the Inheritance (Provision for Family and Dependants) Act 1975.

# 9

# Parents and family: rights and responsibilities

## SUMMARY

In this chapter we consider firstly, how the law defines the role of a parent. We explore how the relationship between parent and child has changed over the last century from a position where the parent—the biological father—had exclusive 'rights' over his child, to the current position where a parent—both father and mother, biological and acquired—have 'responsibilities' for a child. Within this consideration we explore firstly, the continuing importance of the biological relationship, and also the psychological and social attachment both as to its meaning and importance for the parties and also the construction of these relationships within the law. We consider secondly, the centrality of parental responsibility to this relationship and what this means and who in law has parental responsibility and how those who do not might acquire it. We consider the adults whom the law recognizes as having parental responsibilities, including, for example, birth mothers and fathers, step-parents, adoptive parents, and foster parents, and detail their responsibilities towards the child in their care. Thirdly, we consider how the law both reflects and authorizes social convention and practice. So, in the nineteenth century, the law was driven by social convention, and it was the father and not the mother who was legally recognized as the lawful parent with rights over 'his' children. Whilst, in the twenty-first century it is the mother who automatically acquires parental responsibility and the father if married to the mother. In addition, same-sex relationship families and the transgendered family has equal legal status. These changes have been driven by the right to equality and to family life for all (Art 8, European Convention on Human Rights). In the twentieth and twenty-first century children live with, and are cared for by, parents and other adults, where cultural, social and religious factors play a significant role in shaping the contemporary family and are considerations which the law must heed.

With regard to the law's framing of legal parenting, there have been three significant developments over the last 150 years. First, there has been a shift in thinking from a time when the father and not the mother had full parenting 'rights' in law, to the present time, where both father and mother, whether married or otherwise cohabiting (and where the father is named on the child's birth certificate), have an equal legal parenting role. Second, during this historical time frame, we consider the way in which 'rights' over children gradually diminished and dwindled, being replaced by the legal requirement of 'parental responsibility' for the child. Finally, in considering the displacement of the exclusive rights of the father over 'his' child we consider the residuality of the parental right and consider its resuscitation through the role played by the European Convention of Human Rights (ECHR) in accordance with Article 8, in the harnessing of a new concept of 'family rights.'

# Who is a parent in fact?

9.1 What defines a parent? Is it the biological relationship or the psychological relationship binding parent and child which defines a parent in law? Baroness Hale in *Re G (Children) (Residence: Same-Sex Partner) (2006)* identifies three types of parenting: genetic, gestational, social and psychological. She says this:

> [33] *There are at least three ways in which a person may be or become a natural parent of a child, each of which may be a very significant factor in the child's welfare, depending upon the circumstances of the particular case. The first is genetic parenthood: the provision of the gametes which produce the child.... [34] The second is gestational parenthood: the conceiving and bearing of the child. [35] The third is social and psychological parenthood: the relationship which develops through the child demanding and the parent providing for the child's needs, initially at the most basic level of feeding, nurturing, comforting and loving, and later at the more sophisticated level of guiding, socialising, educating and protecting.*

And, in considering this parent-child relationship, is it a relationship which is defined through the eyes of a parent or through the eyes of a child? In *Re G (Parental Responsibility Order) (2006)*, an application to suspend a parental responsibility order, Hedley J said of the judge who had made the original order, 'What he did, in acknowledging the fact that the order he was proposing to make might appear rather unjust to the father, was try to look at the case through the eyes of the child...' However, historically, parenthood and childhood have been constructed by and through a male/paternal frame of reference, a construction challenged only very recently, with the result that each parent has an equal legal standing and the centrality of the child in family law is now recognized through the legal requirement to apply the test of 'welfare of the child as paramount' (Children Act (CA) 1989, s 1) in matters relating to care and upbringing.

In very recent times, the law has yielded to social reality in recognizing the existence of a range of other adult/child relationships and has authorized these particular arrangements as legally valid families. And so the heterosexual/monogamous template of idealized parenting within family life may be displaced when considering how best the welfare of the child might be served (CA 1989, s 1) and at the same time mindful of the right, for example, of same-sex couples to a family life (Art 8).

9.2. Notwithstanding the new developments with regard to family life the preferred family template has been (and may still be to some extent) monogamous and heterosexual. And the distribution of power within the family may albeit to a lesser extent echo Frederick Engels' nineteenth century observation of family form. In *The Origin of the Family, Private Property and the State*, he said:

> The first division of labour is that between man and woman for the propagation of children. And today I can add: the first class opposition that appears in history coincides with the development of the antagonism between man and woman in monogamous marriage, and the first class oppression coincides with that of the female sex by the male.
>
> *(Engels 1884, 1986, 96).*

9.3 Whilst the biological family is the basic reproductive unit in all societies, Simone de Beauvoir, the celebrated philosopher and feminist, cogently analysed how society and history actually imposed itself upon, and shaped, that basic arrangement:

> The theory of historical materialism has brought to light some important truths. Humanity is not an animal species, it is a historical reality. Human society is an antithesis—in a sense it is against nature; it does not passively submit to the presence of nature but rather takes over the control of nature on its own behalf. This arrogation is not an inward, subjective operation; it is accomplished objectively in practical action.
>
> *(de Beauvior, 1949, 84).*

More recently, MA Glendon (1987) considers how the family has what he calls an 'expressive function' and asserted:

> in addition to all other things it [the family] ..., tells stories about the culture that helped to shape it and which in turn it helps to shape: stories about who we are, where we came from and where we are going.

## Biological parents—natural parent presumption to natural parent consideration

9.4 The law has traditionally approached the question of parentage by considering the biological link between adult and child within a heterosexual arrangement as preferable, and unless another arrangement better serves the welfare of the child, will rarely interfere with the authority of the biological parent. And even today that remains a significant consideration in deciding matters relating to care and upbringing. The 'natural parent presumption' remains a weighty consideration, although in recent cases it is more of a consideration for the courts. Lord Templeman articulated this presumption in *Re KD (A Minor) (Ward: Termination of Access) (1988)*:

> *The best person to bring up a child is the natural parent. It matters not whether the parent is wise or foolish, rich or poor, educated or illiterate, provided the child's moral and physical health are not endangered.*

This view has continued to exert an influence on court decision making. In *Re M (Child's Upbringing) (1996)* (see Chapters 10, 11) a Zulu boy (P) and his mother were living with a white family in Transvaal, South Africa. The boy's natural parents were Zulus both coming from an area of the Transvaal known as Leboa. Lord Justice Neil summarised the facts of the case, the relevant features of this case are summarized below:

> *The appellant is a white South African of Afrikaner descent. She came to England in 1969 when she was about 23 years of age. In 1973 she married an Englishman and acquired British nationality... The family (the husband having died) returned to the United Kingdom bringing the boy with them with the consent of his natural/ biological parents. The natural parents had worked as housekeeper and nanny to the appellants children. The natural mother made plans to send P back to the village from which she came when the white family moved to rented accommodation near Johannesburg. The appellant, who had become attached to P, offered to take responsibility for him in a way that would enable him to remain as a member of the household because of the increasing instability in South Africa. The appellant together with her daughters and P arrived in the United Kingdom on 16 March 1992. The appellant told the immigration authorities that she wished to adopt P and P was given leave to remain for three months. After some time she issued an application for an adoption order and residence order. On 29 September 1994, P became a ward of court. P's natural parents objected to the applications and wanted him returned to them.*

The court concluded that he should be returned to his natural parents even though the boy had clearly expressed the wish to remain with the appellant whom he clearly regarded as the psychological parent and with whom a strong attachment had been formed. Thorpe J, in the court of first instance, based his decision to return the child on Lord Templeman's reasoning in *Re KD* (above):

> *The starting-point for a court in wardship was the strong supposition, other things being equal, that it was in the interests of a child that he should be brought up by his natural parents... and not, as the judge had suggested, either the biological or the psychological parents according to the circumstances. The judge had concluded that the child's development must be Zulu development and not Afrikaans or English development, and in order to expedite this the proper course was to order the boy's return to South Africa.*

Neil and Ward LJJ, in the Court of Appeal, insisted that the boy be returned to his natural parents (albeit against the expressed wishes of the child). If one focuses on the outcome of this case it would appear that the natural parent presumption was a determining factor, if not, an overriding factor. Neill, LJ cites the following extracts from the expert's evidence which seem to run contrary to the decision of the court:

*If you take him away now from the [appellant's] family against his will, then the risk is that he will go downhill emotionally, he will go downhill psychologically, he will pine for [the appellant] and [her girls], he will get grumpy and disagreeable, he will not quickly grasp Ndelele and Afrikaans, he will be a bit of an outsider with the group when he gets there and everything may go horribly wrong ...*

Dr Cameron in his evidence recognized the benefits and losses on both sides of the arguement and said:

*For [P] to have the gain of education in England carries with it the weakening of his Zulu identity, his knowledge of the Zulu language and culture and so on and there are gains and losses. If he is brought up in the Zulu culture, he has the gain of identity with his family of origin and the loss of being a citizen of the larger world.*

Other factors no doubt weighed heavily on the conscience of the court in its application of the welfare of the child as paramount principle (CA 1989, s 1(1)). What might they have been?

Since the last decade of the twentieth century, considerations of 'race', 'culture', and 'linguistics' have become mandatory factors to consider when placing children in care, in foster placements, and when matching children with adoptive parents, and are considerations specifically embodied in the statutory requirements with regard to care proceedings and adoption. When, in the case of *J v C* (discussed below) in 1970, the court was alerted to, and cognizant of, the need for children to be conversant in the language of his natural parents, the court did not go any further in stressing, for example, any need for the child to be familiar with Spanish culture (the background of his parents) in any broader sense. So what else was so pressing in *Re M* which resulted in sending the child back to South Africa? Significantly, by the mid-1980s, Anglo-American jurisdictions were being reminded of their past conduct against particular communities. For example, in Australia, during the twentieth century aboriginal children had been removed from their natural parents and forcibly adopted into white families. Indeed, in February 2010 Kevin Rudd, Australia's Prime Minister publicly apologized to the Australian Aborigines for the history of colonialism in Australia, and specifically for the removal of Aboriginal children from their families, which had been government policy for many years during the 19th and 20th centuries. (See http://www.guardian.co.uk/commentisfree/2010/feb/14/australia-aboriginals-apology-disadvantaged, see also O'Hallaran). And, in the UK political debate was raging over intra-racial adoption which whilst encouraged in the 1970's as a positive move towards multi-culturalism, particularly from Labour controlled councils, was considered by the 1990s to be a potentially harmful practice which denied children the full possibility of realizing and living in and with their own cultural heritage and right to cultural identity. Critics of this practice saw intra-racial adoption not as a step towards multi-culturalism but as assimilation. It was this discourse which provided the context and background to the courts thinking in *Re M*.

However, in considering the natural parent presumption and in balancing it with the principle of the welfare of the child as paramount a range of other factors have to be taken into consideration on a case by case basis as each case may involve markedly different facts.

In *Re D (Care: Natural Parent Presumption) (1999)*, the local authority applied for care orders in respect of three children. Their care plan was that the two eldest children be cared for by the maternal grandmother and her husband, and that their half-brother, A, should be cared for by his father. The grandmother opposed the care plan, contending that A should be placed with her in order that the children could be raised together. The judge did not rule out that the father would be able to care adequately for A but concluded that it was better to place him with the grandmother and his siblings. The father appealed, contending that the judge had failed to give sufficient weight to the presumption in favour of a natural parent. The appeal was allowed on the basis that 'only compelling factors could override the right of a child to be reared by a natural parent'.

In *Re G (Children) (Residence: Same-Sex Partner) (2006)*, a case where children of a same-sex couple (G and W), who were conceived by the natural mother via artificial insemination, and where that relationship had broken down, the court held that it had been wrong of the courts, having regard to the Children Act 1989, s 1(1)(a), under which the child's welfare was to be the court's paramount consideration, to attach no significance whatever to the fact that she was the children's mother. Further, the judge had allowed herself to be distracted, by her disapproval of G (the mother) and her behaviour, from a full consideration of the evidence relating to the children's welfare, which would have led her to a different conclusion. In particular, when concluding that she had no confidence that the mother would not seek to marginalize W in the future, she had given no weight to the fact that regular and good quality contact had been continuing since it had been re-established after the move. As Lord Nicholls stated:

*In reaching its decision the court should always have in mind that in the ordinary way the rearing of a child by his or her biological parent can be expected to be in the child's best interests, both in the short term and also, and importantly, in the longer term. I decry any tendency to diminish the significance of this factor. A child should not be removed from the primary care of his or her biological parents without compelling reason.*

Further, in *Re B (A Child) (Residence Order) (2009)*, where the parents separated before the child was born both parents agreed that it was best for the child to be reared by the grandmother. However, at a later stage the father changed his mind and objected to a residence order being made in favour of the maternal grandmother. The deputy judge of the Family Division felt he was bound by the case of **G** (2006) (cited above) and made an order in favour of the (natural parent) the father. An appeal was made to the Supreme Court which allowed the appeal and found that:

*The child had lived virtually all of his life with his grandmother, he had naturally formed a strong bond with her and there was reason to apprehend that, if that bond was broken, his current stability would be threatened (see [19], [20], [38] and [41] of the judgment).*

## Statutory exceptions to the natural parent presumption

9.5 There are two automatic statutory exceptions to this 'natural parent presumption': first, where a child is adopted (Adoption Act 1976, s 39) and second, where reproduction and childbirth follows from sperm or egg donation (Human Fertilisation and Embryology Act 1990, ss 27, 28, see also Human Fertilisation and Embryology Act 2008). In the first exception, adoption terminates the legal responsibility (parental responsibility) of natural parents or legal parents (see Chapter 10). In the second exception, where a person donates genetic material (eggs, sperm, embryos), she or he relinquishes any rights to biological parentage in relation to any child that may be born as a result. In *Re D (Contact and Parental Responsibility: Lesbian Mothers and Known Father) (2006)* (discussed again later in this chapter) where a voluntary arrangement was made by a male and a lesbian woman by which she was impregnated and had a child Black J concluded:

*There is no doubt that Mr B is committed to D and that there is an attachment between them, even though from D's point of view, the degree of it is moderated by the relative infrequency of her contact with Mr B. Mr B has a real importance in her life, both in practical terms through her contact with him and because of the simple and incontrovertible but less tangible fact that he is her father. It is imperative that they continue to have contact and that a positive relationship should be fostered between them, allowing her to know that he loves her unquestioningly and wants what is best for her and to understand and appreciate his role originally in her conception and now in her life. D will also benefit from getting to see another world through him and his extended family.*

### Competing claims

In addition, where there are competing claims to parenthood this natural parent presumption may be displaced. In *Singh v Entry Clearance Officer New Delhi (2004)*, in recognizing family life and the role of adoptive parents for the purposes of Art 8 (in the context of an immigration appeal), Dyson LJ said:

*21. These close personal ties will be presumed to exist as between children and their natural parents, but exceptionally the presumption may be displaced. The notion of family life is not, however, confined to families based on marriage, and may encompass other relationships.*

## Psychological parents and the importance of attachment

9.6 Good parenting (biological or acquired) depends on bonding, that is, forming an emotional relationship and a psychological bond with the child. Attachment is at the core of the parent/child relationship and the presence and degree of attachment of parent to child and child to parent is considered an important indicator of the stability and strength of a relationship. Attachment, or lack of attachment is regarded as the key indicator of the ability of a parent to care adequately for a child and the absence of adequate attachment may trigger intervention by the local authority to place a child in care or may be the deciding factor in a finding that a local authority placement for a child with a foster carer is unsuccessful. Where attachment is poor, a child may be considered to be at risk of emotional harm and neglect (CA 1989, s 31). (The importance of attachment is considered in some detail in Chapter 15 where we consider the role of residential assessments as a mechanism by which attachment can be observed, see eg *Re W and M (Children) (2009)*).

9.7 The psychological relationship was taken into consideration in determining the question 'with whom should a child live?' in the following cases where an application for residence was made. In *Re M (Child's Upbringing) (1996)* (above), Thorpe LJ recognized, 'this case is further complicated by the fact that this boy has two psychological parents and they are both psychological mothers' (see Chapters 10 and 11). In *Re G (Children: Contact) (2002)*, the court recognized 'the adoptive parents are effectively the psychological parents and the only ones that C and T know'. And in *Re G (Adoption: Ordinary Residence) (2003)*, the court observed 'LA and FD are undoubtedly the girls' psychological parents. They are, I believe, entirely devoted to the girls' welfare and will treat them as their daughters for the remainder of their lives'.

Under certain circumstances, the biological relationship may be subordinated and yield to the psychological relationship when for example there are rival claims for residence. In *Re H (A Child) (Residence) (2002)* it was asserted:

*in cases where the child had been for a long time in the settled care of a non-parent, that non-parent would effectively have become the child's psychological parent. When weighing the rival claims of the biological parent over the psychological parent, the court had to arrive at its choice on the application of the welfare test, and while the court had properly to pay regard to parental rights, such considerations had to be qualified by what was best for the welfare of the child.*

Where children bond with the mother's partner, acting in the role of the father, this person is often described as the 'psychological father'. For example in *Re G (A Child) (Parental Responsibility) (2006)*, where the child had been conceived as a result of a 'one night stand', the child had grown up with another person acting in the role of the father and for all intents and purposes he was the psychological father of the child. In *Re P (A Minor) (Residence Order: Child's Welfare) (2000)*, the psychological tie was considered to outweigh the blood tie. The natural parents appealed and the Court of Appeal in dismissing the appeal of the parents held:

> that on an application to vary a residence order there was no presumption that a child's natural parents were to be preferred to his foster parents, and the court's primary consideration under section 1(1) of the Children Act 1989 was the child's welfare; that although, in assessing the child's welfare, the court was required under section 1(3)(d) of the Act of 1989 to have regard to the child's background, including his cultural and religious heritage, that was only one factor to be weighed in the balance and was not a paramount consideration; that, given N's exceptional attachment to her foster parents and the grave risk of long-term harm if she were moved from them, her need for an uninterrupted settled life outweighed the need for a religious life; and that, accordingly, N's welfare dictated that she should not be moved from her foster parents.

## The social reality of parenting

9.8 During the last 50 years especially, the family has undergone substantial change with respect to the regard given both in public perception and consideration, and also in the law to:

- socially acquired parentage;
- genetics and parentage.
- sexual orientation, gender reassignment and parentage;

These three aspects and the impact they have had on the law and its development is considered below.

### Socially acquired parents

9.9 With regard to this first aspect, the number of divorce decrees nisi on dissolution of marriage (numbering some 170,966 in 2002, 167,992 in 2003, 166,042 in 2004, 150,668 in 2005 (figures as published in the respective years of Judicial Statistics) and 145,242 in 2006, 143,153, and 120,868, petitions filed in 2007,2008 (figures as published in the respective years of Judicial and Court Statistics), together with remarriage, and newly formed partnerships creating second, third, or even fourth families, has resulted in children being reared by a step-mother or step-father. In addition to the changes brought about by divorce and remarriage, children are increasingly born outside marriage and reared in one-parent/single headed families. There are an estimated 1.75 million single parents caring for nearly 3 million children accounting for one-quarter of all families (Douglas and Moorhead, 2005). Baroness Howe of Idlicote, in the Lords debate on the 'Role of marriage in securing the well-being of the nation's children and their parents in 21st century Britain', charts these changes in the social demography of the family:

> We seem to have moved from an almost total marriage convention—sustained by fairly draconian divorce laws—to a situation where far fewer young people actually marry; 13 per cent of women between 18 and 49 were cohabiting in 1998—up from 8 per cent 10 years previously. If they do decide to marry it will be considerably later—most probably only at the long delayed moment in their thirties and sometimes their forties when they decide to start a family. Even for those who do marry, divorce—with or without remarriage—is increasingly common, as we have already heard—and, all too often while their children are still young. Like it or not, the trend towards cohabitation and more frequent divorce is here to stay. Almost 30 per cent of children experience divorced parents by the time they reach 16 years.

> *(17 March 2004, col 286 Hansard)*

The social demography described above reflects a pattern of family life far removed from Fletcher's description of family life in the 1950s where marriage was the norm and family size was 2.2 children per family (Fletcher, 1966). How should the law keep pace with social change? Echoing Baroness Hale in *Re G (2006)* (above), Dey and Wasoff (2006) write:

> Family law requires reform in many jurisdictions in response to change in family forms and relationships...Many 'family practices'...no longer conform to the norms embodied in family law. The growth in lone parent families, the prevalence of divorce and remarriage, and alternative ways of managing intimate relationships (such as cohabitation and 'living apart together') have eroded the normative purchase of marriage and the nuclear family.

These relationships will be considered later in this chapter when the question of 'who has parental responsibility?' is considered.

## Genetics and parentage

9.10 For children who are born as a result of new methods of reproduction achieved via IVF and sperm or egg donation, or through surrogacy arrangements the question of 'who is the parent'? will inevitably arise. This section will consider first, the position of parties donating eggs or sperm, second the position of those carrying a foetus and giving birth to a child, and third those involved in rearing the child, and finally the right of the child to discover his or her genetic heritage.

# Who is the parent?—reproductive technology

9.11 Under the Human Fertilisation and Embryology Act 1990 (HFEA 1990), where a person has donated sperm or eggs then he or she relinquishes any rights over that 'genetic material'. The donor is no longer the legal parent. The HFEA determines the legal parents in respect of a child born as the result of IVF treatment in accordance with rules laid down by the HFE Authority.

HFEA 1990 s 27 (2008 Act s 33(1) defines a 'mother' as '(1) The woman who is carrying or has carried a child as a result of the placing in her of an embryo or of sperm and eggs'. Section 28 (2008 Act s 35(1)) defines a 'father' as being married to the woman 'at the time of the placing in her of the embryo or the sperm or the eggs or of her insemination' unless it is shown that he did not consent to the placing in her of the embryo, sperm, or eggs or to her insemination. Section 28(3) (2008 Act s 35(1)) of the Act deals with unmarried couples and provides:

> *If no man is treated, by virtue of subsection (2) above, as the father of the child but (a) the embryo or the sperm and eggs were placed in the woman, or she was artificially inseminated, in the course of treatment services provided for her and a man together by a person to whom a licence applies, and (b) the creation of the embryo carried by her was not brought about with the sperm of that man, then, subject to subsection (5) below, that man shall be treated as the father of the child.*

## Consent then separate

9.12 What is the legal position with regard to parentage where the parties who initially consented to the placement of genetic material in the woman subsequently separate? This issue fell to be decided in the case below.

> In ***Re R (A Child) (IVF: Paternity of Child) (2003)*** the mother, D, and her partner, B, were unmarried, and sought IVF treatment which involved the fertilization of D's eggs with sperm from a donor. In accordance with IVF procedure, B signed a form acknowledging that he would be the father of any child born in consequence. But D and B had already separated when implantation in D had taken place, about which B had no knowledge. On an application by B, the judge declared, under HFEA 1990 s 28(3), that B was the legal father of the resulting child. The Court of Appeal allowed D's appeal. B then appealed this decision to the House of Lords. The House of Lords in ***R (IVF: Paternity of Child) (Also Known as Re D) (2005)***, dismissed the ruling of the Court of Appeal, holding that s 28(3) should apply only to cases falling clearly within it and most importantly that the legal determination of who is the parent should not be based on a fiction, especially where deception was involved; that the embryo had to have been placed in the woman when treatment services were provided for her and the man together; and that, although they had originally been so provided for D and B, they had not been when implantation had taken place.

But the ruling that the determination of parenthood should not be based on a fiction, in cases of artificial insemination, was not followed in **Leeds Teaching Hospitals NHS Trust v Mr and Mrs A and others (2003)**. In this case, a married (white) couple were undergoing IVF treatment and gave birth to twins of mixed race parentage, as a result of a sperm donor mix up, with the result that in law Mr A was not the legal father of his wife's children according to the rules.

Dame Elizabeth Butler-Sloss, President, ruled that the black sperm donor was to be the legal father, although the twins would actually live with their white mother and her white husband as a family. This apparently bizarre outcome, and one seemingly contrary to the ruling in **Re R** (above), perpetuated a fiction, albeit that the HFEA rules had been correctly applied, since parental status could not be conferred on a husband whose wife had given birth after IVF treatment because he had neither consented to the placing in his wife of the embryo which was actually placed in error nor had the couple undergone 'treatment together' within the meaning of the HFEA 1990. The solution was proposed that the parents adopt the two children who are twins.

Sperm donor mix ups are certainly rare but at the time of writing a legal suit is ongoing in Northern Ireland against the Regional Fertility Centre at Belfast's Royal Victoria Hospital where a white woman gave birth to mixed race children 'the Williamses are suing the Belfast Health and Social Care Trust (formerly the Royal Group of Hospitals Trust) for damages for their mental distress, social discredit and breach of contract under the Supply of Goods and Services Act 1982. http://www.dailymail.co.uk/news/article-1192717/Why-I-dark-daddy-The-white-couple-mixed-race-children-IVF-blunder.html#ixzz13qcbaqpT, accessed 30 October 2010.

There is also a legal suit ongoing in Canada where a fertility clinic in Ottawa is being sued over a similar mix up where a woman ' Trudy Moore found that her daughter, Samantha, conceived using her husband's sperm and her sister as a surrogate, was not a genetic match to her husband... she confronted her doctor, who suggested in e-mails to Ms. Moore that he may have contaminated her husband's sample—possibly with 3168', http://www.theglobeandmail.com/news/national/sperm-donor-mix-up-where-do-these-two-girls-come-from/article1725123/, accessed 30 October 2010.

## Who is the parent when transsexual IVF relationships break down?

9.13    In **J v C (Void Marriage: status of children) J v C and another (2007)**, the applicant had been born female, but lived as a male. In 1977, he purported to marry the respondent, without informing her that he was a transsexual. Two children were conceived by donor insemination. The marriage was subsequently declared void and the question for determination was whether the purported husband was a parent of the children. The court held:

*that since the 1989 Act did not define the term 'parent' used in section 10(4)(a) it was necessary to look elsewhere for an applicable statutory definition; that, in the context of artificial insemination by donor, parenthood was defined by both the Family Law Reform Act 1987 and the Human Fertilisation and Embryology Act 1990 and it was necessary to determine which statute applied; that it was clear from sections 28(2) and 49(3) of the 1990 Act that the Act did not apply if the artificial insemination had taken place before section 28 had commenced, and it was immaterial that the embryo resulting from the insemination had been carried by the mother after its commencement; that, therefore, since the artificial insemination of the respondent which led to the birth of the younger child had taken place before the commencement of section 28 of the 1990 Act, that Act did not apply and the case was governed by the 1987 Act (post, paras 17–19, 21–22, 26).*

This meant that the applicant who wished to be recognized in law as the father was not legally the father and changes in the law recognizing his reassignment could not change the legal position that pertained at the time of insemination. This decision demonstrates how the law flies in the face of fact.

Clearly, what and who is a parent reflects the social, historical and cultural context.

## Consent issues and embryo usage at a later date

9.14     Consider *Evans v United Kingdom (2006)*. The applicant and her then partner, J, were told in 2000 that the applicant had pre-cancerous tumours in both ovaries, and that her ovaries would have to be removed. Prior to the operation, a number of eggs were extracted for (IVF) treatment and it was explained to the applicant and J that each of them would have to sign a form consenting to such treatment. In 2002, the relationship broke down, and J withdrew his consent to further use of the embryos. The applicant commenced proceedings seeking an injunction requiring J to restore his consent to the storage and use of the embryos. That claim was dismissed; and that decision upheld on appeal and by the European Court of Human Rights. The 2008 Act introduces more rigid conditions called 'agreed fatherhood conditions' (HFEA 2008, ss 37, 38).

There are also issues with regard to posthumous parents (see the case of *R v Ex p Blood (1997)*). The Human Fertilisation and Embryology (Deceased Fathers) Act 2003 provides at (5A). If—

*(a) a child has been carried by a woman as the result of the placing in her of an embryo or of sperm and eggs or her artificial insemination,*

*both homosexual and heterosexual, may bring up children together. One or both may have children from another relationship: this is not at all uncommon in lesbian relationships and the court may grant then a shared residence order so that they may share parental responsibility.*

In *Re D (Contact and Parental Responsibility: Lesbian Mothers and Known Father) (2006)*, Black J stated the legal position in a case where A and C, the first and second respondents, were a lesbian couple who advertised for a man to father a child. The applicant, B responded and as a result D was born. Both A, as the biological mother, and C had parental responsibility because of a joint residence order. B, the biological father, sought parental responsibility to which A and C objected. The court granted parental responsibility to B with conditions that he did not contact any health professional or the school without the consent of A or C. A and C were perfectly happy for B to be recognized as D's father but they opposed any order that would recognize him as the 'parent'.

Black J said:

*This application falls to be decided at a time of considerable change in the law affecting same sex couples. It is now possible for a same sex couple to register their relationship as a civil partnership under the Civil Partnership Act 2004, the material provisions of which came into force on 5 December 2005. Civil partnerships are enduring relationships, which end only on death, dissolution or annulment. In many ways, the law applicable to civil partners is aligned with the law relating to married couples, for instance the provision for financial relief corresponds to the provision made for financial relief in connection with marriages. With the commencement of the Adoption and Children Act 2002, it will be possible for a same sex couple to adopt a child, provided they are living together as partners in an enduring family relationship.*

In addition, the court praised the invaluable report by the expert in this case which interrogated the linguistic limitations placed on attempts to describe family relationships:

*Dr Sturges (in her report) refers to the deficiencies of our language in the present context, pointing out that there is 'a range of difficulties that the present terminology does not cover', including whether two women can be 'parents', whether children's psychological thinking can accommodate three' parents', and what the biological father should be called if not a 'parent'. 'Mummy' and 'Daddy' and the variants on these names are readily recognisable but there is no recognised name for the woman or man in a same sex relationship who stands in the position of a parent but does not have a biological relationship to the child of the family (57).*

Finally, in *T v B (2010)*, a lesbian couple had a child together via IVF. They had a joint application. They had separated and the child stayed with the birth mother and her new partner whilst the former partner applied for residence and contact, the couple were awarded joint residence. The birth mother then applied for financial support from her former partner, the court held that the former partner was a parent in the social and psychological sense but not in legal sense (see chapter on Civil Partnership).

## Transgendered parents

9.17   In *X, Y and Z v United Kingdom (1997)*, a female to male transsexual (who lived with a female partner who conceived following IVF and gave birth to Y and Z ) wanted to be recognized as the father of the children. The ECtHR said (para 36):

*When deciding whether a relationship can be said to amount to 'family life', a number of factors may be relevant, including whether the couple live together, the length of their relationship and whether they have demonstrated their commitment to each other by having children together or by any other means.*

(See also *Rees* in 1987, *Cossey* in 1991, and *Sheffield and Horsham* in 1998, the court was not yet prepared to take the step it finally took in *Goodwin (2002)*—which via *Bellinger v Bellinger (2003)*—led to the Gender Recognition Act 2004.) The Act recognized that provided a person had a Gender Recognition certificate he or she could be known for all intents and purposes in his or her preferred gender. The implications for family life and parenthood means that the applicant in *X,Y,Z* finally succeeded in being recognized as the legal father to his children.

# Who is a legal parent? The current law

9.18   Within the law a parent is a person who is either the biological parent, or the legal carer of the child. Parents, whether biological or not, may or may not have what we call 'parental responsibility' for a child. Parental responsibility means 'all the rights, duties, powers, responsibilities and authority which by law a parent of a child has in relation to the child and his property' (CA 1989), s 3). Legal parenthood carries the right and responsibility to register a child's name within six weeks of birth and apply for a residence or contact order. Legal parenthood carries the right to make an application for example for a specific issue order (CA 1989, s 8), to change a child's name or to apply for a prohibited steps order to prevent a child being removed from the country.

9.19   A parent is the natural or biological mother or father of a child. Not all biological fathers have parental responsibility for their children (see *Re D (2006)* above), but a biological father with or without parental responsibility has the right to make private law applications without requiring the leave of the court (CA 1989, s 10 (4)(a)). In addition, other parties may also have parental responsibility for the child. Other parties who may have some biological connection to the child, for example, grandparents, aunts, or siblings may acquire parental responsibility where a residence order is made in their favour. In addition, the local authority may have parental responsibility for a child where a care order has been made (CA 1989, s 31). More than one person can have parental responsibility for a child (CA 1989, s 2(5)).

Where other parties have parental responsibility for the child, this responsibility only lasts for the duration of the order which is made in their favour; that is to say, where a relative or a foster parent is granted a residence order and the child is living with them, when that residence order ceases so too does their parental responsibility for the child.

## Parental responsibility: what is it?

9.20   Perhaps the most important achievement of the CA 1989 was to pave the way for a new approach and way of thinking about parenting and the relationship of parents (biological and non-biological) to children. The law wished to mark the change in real terms by providing a new nomenclature in the term 'parental responsibility'. The new thinking also reflected the recognition that rearing a child involved a parent taking responsibility for that child.

# Meaning of parental responsibility

9.21   It is beyond the scope of this chapter to detail all the ways in which parental responsibility may arise. Some of the more salient aspects are noted below.

## Responsibility to care for the child

9.22   This means the responsibility to determine the place and manner of the upbringing of the child. Conflict frequently arises over upbringing between parents who are unmarried, or who have been married and later separate or divorce, (see Chapter 12) or where there is a third party, such as where the local authority becomes involved (see Chapters 14 and 15) . A failure or inability to adequately care will result in loss of residence or else an order for defined contact, or else where there is significant harm a child will be taken into care or may be adopted.

## Responsibility to ensure the child's education

9.23   Parents have a responsibility and duty to ensure that the child receives an education, whether by going to school or else in other ways, for example, by being educated at home. If the local education authority is not satisfied that the child is attending school and no provision is made elsewhere, they can make a school attendance order. A parent who disobeys a school attendance order is guilty of an offence (see *R (on the application of R) v Leeds Magistrates and others (2005)*). Where school attendance is so infrequent as to be capable of potentially harming the child, a care order under the CA 1989 may be made (see *Re O (A Minor) (Care Proceedings: Education) (1992)*). See further the debate in the following cases about parental responsibility including ensuring attendance of the child at school: *Re K (A Child) (Secure Accommodation Order: Right to Liberty) (2001)*; *R v Carmarthenshire County Council, ex parte White (2000)*.

## Responsibility for the child's religion?

9.24 In the past bringing up a child within a religion was a key aspect of a parent's role. Today, parents have no legal responsibility to bring up a child in any particular faith. Indeed, religious upbringing is considered by many to be of little relevance, religious belief being subordinated to wider principles of love, and respect, which are principles central to all religions and to humanity itself. However, for some communities and families religious upbringing remains central to their moral role of guidance. And, for some families faith is particularly precious and rather than an adjunct to their life is intricately part of it. Thus faith is perhaps more complex in its relevance and meaning in a multi-faith and secular society. Mixed faith marriages can create tension and sometimes conflict with respect to how each parent perceives the appropriate religious upbringing of a child within these families. (See *Agar-Ellis*, discussed below where there were differences of religion between the parties who were Anglican and Roman Catholic, and *J v C (1970)*, below, where there were differences of religion between the natural and the foster parents who were Roman Catholic and Anglican). The court will need to be sensitive to issues of faith in all its dealings with the child and the relevance of faith to the child (see Munby J in *Singh*, above).

## Right/responsibility to inflict reasonable corporal punishment and otherwise to discipline the child?

9.25 In the past a parent had the right to chastise a child. Under the common law, it was chastisement with little restraint although it was held that it must not be for the 'gratification of passion': *R v Hopley (1860)*. There is no right today to chastise a child. And hitting a child is not today considered a solution to discipline. However, a child who is considered 'out of control' may be considered to beyond the care and control of its parents and therefore the parents will be deemed unable to adequately care for a child which may result in a child being taken into care (CA 1989, s 31). Judicially ordered punishment has been held to be degrading (see *Tyrer v United Kingdom (1978–79)*) and corporal punishment is prohibited in State schools by the Education (No 2) Act 1986, s 47. The United Nations Convention on the Rights of the Child (UNCRC) (1989) also imposes obligations on member states in respect of protecting children from domestic violence. The Convention contains several articles of importance. Art 2(2) provides protection from discrimination or punishment.

In *Re H (Minors) (Wardship: Cultural Background) (1987)*, the parents came from a different cultural background, but the court found that this was no defence to physical punishment.

*there was a complaint that C, then 3 years old, had been put out in the snow, naked from the waist down, as a punishment. The mother in her evidence does not deny that fact, but gave the explanation that she was running a bath and that the boy escaped outside semi-dressed. This incident has to be seen in the context of all the other incidents. There are constant reports of the children being left unattended. It happened on 9 March 1982, when the two youngest were found totally alone. In mitigation from the mother's point of view, she had a difficult pregnancy at that time and gave birth to a child 2 days later which died.*

*In May of the same year of 1982 further bruising was found on P when he was hit with a stick, and the mother on that occasion was offered a day nursery place for C, which was refused.*

*In June 1983 the NSPCC was again called by neighbours for beating C with a stick to the extent that he was found to have scratches and bruising across his face and head.*

*There was a further incident in August of 1983, the hitting of C across the face with a flip-flop. Again, the duty officer was called and C was put in care for one week. He was later offered a place at the local free school group, which was refused by the mother. there were thereafter continued reports of the children being left alone. In particular, L, on 8 November 1983, was found alone in the morning of that day when she was only 2½ years old.*

The court held:

*Where the court in the discharge of its parental duties was dealing with children of foreign ethnic origins and culture it must consider the situation against the reasonable objective standards of that culture so long as they did not conflict with minimal acceptable standards of child care in England, and always provided that the one criterion on which its decision was based was the welfare and best interests of the children concerned.*

(See for further discussion Barton, 2008.)

In *Williamson Regina (Williamson and others) v Secretary of State for Education and Employment (2005)*, the claimants who were teachers and parents wished to exercise their right as Christians to hold and manifest their belief in mild corporal punishment of pupils. The court held that their right was not absolute and that the interference with their religious right, to hold and manifest their belief which included, they argued, a right to use mild corporal punishment, was justified under Art 9(2) and necessary in a democratic society for the protection of the rights and freedoms of others, namely, children (see Chapter 14).

## Right/responsibility to consent to medical treatment

9.26 Parental responsibility to care for the child also includes ensuring that medical treatment is provided. Failure to do so may result in criminal liability. CA 1989, s 3(5) introduced a further possible proxy, a person who:

*(a) does not have parental responsibility for a particular child; but*

*(b) has care of the child*

*may, subject to the provisions of the CA 1989, do what is reasonable in all the circumstances of the case for the purpose of safeguarding or promoting the child's welfare.*

9.27 Another proxy decision-maker would be the court itself in wardship (see CA 1989, s 8 and CA 1981, s 41 for the wardship jurisdiction). See also *Re C (A Minor) (Wardship: Medical Treatment) (1989)*. The person exercising parental responsibility will be expected to consent to treatment. The parents will give consent for their children unless the child is of the age where he or she may give consent (see '*Gillick* competent' above). Although such a finding will not exclude the parental right to consent or withhold consent. Failure to provide medical care for a child may also result in a child being taken into care if significant harm to a child is found as a result of lack of adequate medical attention. Under such circumstances the court may refuse an application for residence or make a defined order for contact.

## Right /responsibility to withhold consent from a proposed marriage

9.28 Parents have the right to withhold consent from a proposed marriage where the minor is 16 or 17 years of age.

## Right /responsibility to administer the child's property and to enter into certain contracts with the child

9.29 Parents have the right to administer the child's property. See the Child Support Act 1991 in Chapter 16, Financial provision for children.

## Right/responsibility to act for the child in legal proceedings

9.30 Rules of civil litigation insist that someone else acts on the child's behalf. This is important in care proceedings where the court will appoint a children's guardian, to represent the child. Where a child has sufficient understanding (see Chapter 11,

Adolescent rights: autonomy and participation) he or she may apply for leave to apply for an order under CA 1989.

## Parental responsibility: who is entitled?

9.31 In accordance with CA 1989, s 2, more than one person may have parental responsibility for the same child at the same time (s 2(5)). Thus, parental responsibility is shared in the case of a married couple and is shared where parents are separated or divorced.

To summarize:

- the mother has automatic and permanent parental responsibility (whether a child is born outside or within marriage);
- the married father has automatic parental responsibility;
- the unmarried father has automatic parental responsibility if ACA 2002, s 111(2)(a)(b)(c) applies;
- the unmarried father has parental responsibility if he is granted a court order under CA 1989, s 4;
- the adoptive parents of an adopted child have parental responsibility;
- if a child is a ward of court the court stands in the position of the parents and a court in wardship has parental responsibility until further order;
- a guardian appointed by a parent, by deed or will, has parental responsibility after the parent's death;
- a local authority in whose favour a care order has been made has parental responsibility until further order;
- the CA 1975 created the institution of custodianship repealed in CA 1989, under which many parental rights are given to the foster parent but some rights remain with the natural parent;
- step-parents under CA 1989, s 4(a) have parental responsibility; and
- special guardians have parental responsibility.

### Mothers

9.32 The law confers automatic parentage (parental rights and responsibilities) on the mother. This, as we shall explore later in this chapter, represents a complete volte-face when compared with the lack of legal status of mothers in the nineteenth and first half of the twentieth century and the absolute right of the biological father over his child. The CA 1989, s 2(4) abolished the old patriarchal rule stating:

'The rule of law that a father is the natural guardian of his legitimate child is abolished.'

## Fathers

9.33 The biological father (where the father is married to the mother) is automatically the legal parent. And, where the man is married to the mother there is a rebuttable presumption that he is the father. Where the parties are not married, but the father's name is registered on the certificate of birth, he becomes the legal parent and acquires parental responsibility. This follows the provision in the ACA 2002, s 111:

> (1) Section 4 of the 1989 Act (acquisition of responsibility by the father of a child who is not married to the child's mother) is amended as follows.
>
> (2) In subsection (1) (cases where parental responsibility is acquired), for the words after 'birth' there is substituted 'the father shall acquire parental responsibility for the child if (a) he becomes registered as the child's father under any of the enactments specified in subsection (1A); (b) he and the child's mother make an agreement (a "parental responsibility agreement") providing for him to have parental responsibility for the child; or (c) the court, on his application, orders that he shall have parental responsibility for the child.'

## Unmarried fathers

9.34 If the unmarried father's name is not on the certificate of birth, he may apply to the court for parental responsibility either by s 2(b) or (c) above.

## Applying to the court for parental responsibility

9.35 Where the conditions under CA 1989, s 4(1)(a) and (b) are not present the father may apply to the court for parental responsibility in accordance with s 4(1)(c). The decision of the court is governed by the degree of commitment and attachment of the applicant to the child and the application of the welfare principle.

> In *Blunkett v Quinn (2005)*, the biological father wished to establish whether he was, in fact, the father, and if he was the father, then to establish his parental responsibility in law under s (4)(1)(c) and to exercise his rights and responsibilities as the child's lawful parent. David Blunkett, the then Home Secretary, applied to the court for a contact order in respect of the son of Kimberly Quinn. This was not the wish of Kimberly Quinn. The two year-old child lived with the respondent mother and her husband. The applicant, who described himself as the child's father in the application, sought a parental responsibility order and a contact order. The mother denied that the applicant was the child's father. A conciliation appointment was listed. The mother applied to vacate the appointment and to adjourn the proceedings for a number of months. The senior district judge heard and

refused the application to adjourn. He vacated the conciliation appointment and listed the proceedings for further directions on a later date. He found, *inter alia*, that while he accepted the medical evidence in respect of the risk to the mother's health, there was no necessary link between that evidence and the continuation of the proceedings, and that it was in the child's interest to have his parentage determined at the earliest opportunity. The mother appealed. She contended that she was entitled to a fair trial which she could not obtain as, *inter alia*, there was a serious risk to her physical and mental health, that any risk of harm to her would prejudice the child, and that there was no prejudice in an adjournment for a finite and temporary period. In particular, there was no benefit to the child in an earlier resolution and no detriment in a later resolution. She opposed the applicant's invitation for the judgment to be given in public. The applicant contended, *inter alia*, that delay would be damaging to the relationship between him and the child and that from the papers filed on her behalf, the mother had been able to give instructions and to take an active part in the out of court debate. The issues which arose for determination concerned the rights arising under Art 6 (the right to a fair trial), Art 8 (the right to respect for private and family life) and Art 10 (freedom of expression) of the ECHR. Following paternity testing, it was discovered that David Blunkett was indeed the father of the child.

In ***Re X (Parental Responsibility Agreement: Children in Care) (2000)*** the mother entered into an agreement with the father that he should have parental responsibility this was upheld by the court (see also 'Parental responsibility and shared residence orders: parliamentary intentions and judicial interpretations'—(2010) CFLQ 151).

Ed Miliband the leader of the Labour party is not named on the birth certificate of his 15-month-old son, Daniel as per September 2010, nor is he married to the mother, therefore it might be wise if he makes an application for parental responsibility.

## Putting parentage to proof for the purpose of parental responsibility

9.36   In cases where the identity of the biological father is unknown, uncertain or contested and the mother wishes to establish parentage for the child, or the father wishes to establish parentage or a party undertaking the role of the father wishes to dispute parentage, an order for a declaration of paternity (under the Family Law Act 1986, s 55A, as amended by the Child Support, Pensions and Social Security Act 2000, s 83(2)) may be made. The Family Law Reform Act 1969 (FLRA 1969), s 20 provides that applications are only permitted in the course of other applications and do not stand alone. The Family Law Reform Act provides that a sample will only be taken with the consent of the person concerned, although the court will draw inferences from a refusal (see *Re A (1994)*).

9.37 However, blood testing will only be ordered if it is considered to be in the child's best interests (see Wallbank, 2004). Consider the two cases below.

> In *Re O; Re J (Children) (Blood Tests: Constraint)* (2000), two separate cases, brought together before the court because they both turned on the same issue, a male applicant, had obtained an order under FLRA 1969, s 20(1) for obtaining blood tests in order to determine the paternity of a child who was the subject of the proceedings. In each case, the mother, whose consent is required under FLRA 1969, s 21(3), refused to consent to the child's blood being tested. The court held that as the law stood, the person with the care and control of a child had been given the absolute right to refuse to allow a sample of blood to be taken from the child it was therefore a matter for the mother to grant or with-hold consent. Per Wall J (per curiam):

> *Knowledge of a child's paternity is increasingly regarded not only as a matter of prime importance to a child, but as being both his right and in his interests. If a direction for blood tests cannot be enforced, the court and the child concerned are deprived of the means of acquiring that knowledge, and the court is thrown back on the unsatisfactory and blunt instrument of drawing an inference against the person with the care and control of the child. In these circumstances, it is anticipated that reform may need to be achieved when the Human Rights Act 1998 comes into force, by the point being taken that Pt III of the 1969 Act is not human rights' compliant.*

> In *Re H and A (Children)* (2002), the applicant sought an order for testing the children's blood to determine paternity; the mother opposed the application. Under FLRA 1969, s 21(3):

> *A blood sample may be taken from a person under the age of sixteen years, not being such a person as is referred to in sub-section (4) of this section—*
> *(a) if the person who has the care and control of him consents; or*
> *(b) where that person does not consent, if the court considers that it would be in his best interests for the sample to be taken.*

> Mr and Mrs R had been married. Some 22 years later Mrs R gave birth to twin girls. Mrs R had been having a relationship with Mr B. Mrs R had told Mr B that he was the father whilst Mr R had no suspicion that the twins were anybody else's than his own. Mrs R and Mr B had an argument and as a result Mr B issued an application for contact and parental responsibility. Mr R appealed. (The decision of Wall J in *Re O; Re J* above, where the court had ruled that a parent with care and control could refuse consent, was no longer good law.) Mr R had said:

> *If there was any chance, if there was only a 1% chance that Mr B is the father of these children it would impair everybody's lives, including my own. I couldn't act—if it is true then that Mr B is the father of G and L then I don't—well, I'm almost certain that I couldn't cope with that at all and I would have to let the family unit go because I couldn't look after somebody else's children, if you like...I don't think I could cope.*

The Court of Appeal concluded that the appeal should be allowed and the application remitted for retrial.

9.38 This issue of a child's right to know has engaged the European Court of Human Rights in a succession of cases. In *Mizzi v Malta (2006)*, the husband sought to dispute the paternity of the child. Maltese law permitted this but within time limits. The husband was outside the time limit. The Maltese court found this was a breach of the husband's Art 8 right, which was overturned on appeal. The ECHR held there had been a breach of Arts 6(1) and 8, and held that whilst time limits could be in the interests of children, such limits should not altogether prohibit the use of the legal remedy (see also *Rozanski v Poland (2006)*; *Paulik v Slovakia (2006)*; *Tavli v Turkey (2007)*). Tavli held that the right to know is not to prevail over 'effective respect for family life'. Where the child opposes blood testing as in *Re D (Paternity) (2006)*, the court decided that although it was in the child's best interests to know the truth the mother was not to be pressed if a sample was taken to be used in the future.

## Step-mothers and step-fathers

9.39 Where a parent remarries, the new spouse becomes the step-parent of any children of the previously married partner. Under the ACA 2002, amending CA 1989, s 4A(1):

> *Where a child's parent ('parent A') who has parental responsibility for the child is married to a person who is not the child's parent ('the step-parent') (a) parent A or, if the other parent of the child also has parental responsibility for the child, both parents may by agreement with the step-parent provide for the step-parent to have parental responsibility for the child; or (b) the court may, on the application of the step-parent, order that the step-parent shall have parental responsibility for the child.*

9.40 The Civil Partnership Act 2004 (CPA 2004), provides that civil partners are eligible to apply for parental responsibility on the same basis as step-parents under CPA 2004, s 246(1). CA 1989, s 10(5) is amended so that any civil partner in a civil partnership (whether or not subsisting) may make an application for a residence order or contact order in respect of a child who is a child of the family.

## Adoptive parents

9.41 An order of the court placing a child for adoption establishes the adoptive parent as the legal parent. ACA 2002, s 46(1), states:

> *(1) An adoption order is an order made by the court on an application under section 50 or 51 giving parental responsibility for a child to the adopters or adopter.*

(2) *The making of an adoption order operates to extinguish (a) the parental responsibility which any person other than the adopters or adopter has for the adopted child immediately before the making of the order.*

## Foster parents

9.42 When a child is being cared for by foster parents and a residence order is made in their favour parental responsibility is conferred upon them by virtue of the CA 1989. The foster carer(s) may be a single adult or an adult couple in a family arrangement. Foster parents also care for children when a care order has been made by the courts. In these circumstances the local authority has parental responsibility. There are more than 78,000 children in the care of local authority on any day, 50,000 of whom live with 38,000 foster families (2004 figures at http://www.fostering. net/news_campaigns/news/article/4042701_). 30th September 2006, there were an estimated 510,000 http://www.childwelfare.gov/pubs/factsheets/foster.cfm#key.

# Historical legacy: paternal rights to parental responsibilities

9.43 If today the mother is considered the child's natural guardian, this was not always the case. Over the last century law's pendulum, with regard to parentage, has swung from a position where the rights of the father have presided, to a position where the rights of both parents have been recognized, to a position where parental rights, both mother's and father's, have been displaced and reframed as duties and responsibilities. In addition, the rights of the child are on the ascendance.

## The history: the biological father as legal parent

9.44 The common law eschewed the biological, psychological, and social reality of the centrality of the mother in the parenting function excluding her from legal recognition, instead, enshrining the father in law as the legal parent. 'His' rights over 'his' children were absolute. He had the right to custody and control even in the face of his lack of attachment or bonding with his children, or his bad behaviour towards their mother or towards his children or even his cruelty. There were two trajectories, one which reflected the diminution of the paternal right and the second which recognized the development of children's rights.

> In *R v de Mannerville (1804)*, a father forcibly abducted his eight month-old baby who was still being breastfed by the mother. In *R v Greenhill (1836)*, the court ordered

Mrs Greenhill to hand over to the father their three daughters (all under six years of age), notwithstanding the fact that he had been guilty of cruelty to both his wife and the children.

9.45 The Custody of Infants Act 1839 made a significant inroad into paternal hegemony, empowering the courts to make an order granting custody to the mother of any child up to the age of seven and to make orders giving her access to her children until they reached the age of majority. However, the judges in interpreting the statute took a restrictive view of what Parliament had intended (see eg *R v Halliday (1853)*; *Shillito (1860)*; and *Re Winscom (1865)*). And many judges harboured a fanciful perception of women's position under the law. The Custody of Infants Act 1873 extended the mother's right to custody of her children from seven years until they reached 16 years of age.

## History: the biological father's rights as sacred

9.46 The father, on the other hand, could do no wrong. His rights to his children were sacred, and there was really nothing that he could do that would deprive him of the custody of his children. His absolute authority is demonstrated in the case of *Re Agar-Ellis (1883)*:

Mr Agar-Ellis, a Protestant-Anglican, married a Roman Catholic woman and made a promise to her that the children of the marriage would be raised as Roman Catholics. Soon after the birth of their first child, he changed his mind. The wife however continued to take the children to Roman Catholic services and Mr Agar-Ellis obtained an injunction restraining her from doing so and took their daughter, Harriet (along with their other children) away from the mother and arranged for them to be looked after by clergymen and others. When Harriet was 16 years of age she asked to be allowed to spend her holidays with her mother. An application was made to the court seeking such permission. The court refused on the grounds that it had no jurisdiction to interfere with a father's legal right. Malins VC, in pronouncing judgment, said:

*This is perhaps the strongest case that has ever occurred showing the misery that ensues from mixed marriages...The authority of a father to guide and govern the education of his child is a very sacred thing, bestowed by the Almighty, and to be sustained to the uttermost by human law. It is not to be abrogated or abridged, without the most coercive reason. For the parent and the child alike, its maintenance is essential, that their reciprocal relations may be fruitful of happiness and virtue; and no disturbing intervention should be allowed between them, whilst those relations are pure and wholesome and conducive to their mutual benefit (contra Munby J in Singh).*

Sir Baliol Brett MR asserted in this case, as if by way of a religious decree, 'The rights of a father are sacred rights because his duties are sacred duties'.

9.47 Indeed, the father also ruled from the grave. In 1871, a father was treated as having a right, which the law was bound to recognize and enforce (unless he had by misconduct of some kind forfeited the right), to dictate the religion of his child. In *Hawksworth v Hawksworth (1861–73)*, a Roman Catholic father married a Protestant woman and died leaving an only child by her of six months old who had been baptised when one week old in a Roman Catholic church. The child was subsequently brought up by the mother in the principles of the Church of England up to the age of eight and a half years. The court declared that when dealing with a child the strictest regard to the religion of the father was to be had and directed that the child be brought up in the father's faith.

9.48 The shadow of *Agar-Ellis* and the absolute right of the father was cast indelibly on the law for the next 80 years although by 1925 the Guardianship of Infants Act, provides by s 1:

> Where in any proceeding before any court...the custody or upbringing of an infant...is in question, the court, in deciding that question, shall regard the welfare of the infant as the first and paramount consideration, and shall not take into consideration whether from any other point of view the claim of the father, or any right at common law possessed by the father, in respect of such custody [or] upbringing...is superior to that of the mother, or the claim of the mother is superior to that of the father.

## Demise of paternal authority

9.49 It took nearly a century after *Agar-Ellis* for the absolute authority of the father to be challenged and finally derailed, when the House of Lords re-inscribed the meaning of 'in the custody of the parent' (see *Hewer* below) and decided in favour of non-biological over natural parents (see *J v C* below), and of mothers over fathers (see *Re K* below) in accordance with what best served the welfare of the child.

### Iterating the meaning of 'in the custody of the parent'

9.50 In *Hewer v Bryant (1970)*, a boy was seriously injured in a motor accident at work. The farmer (by whom he was employed at the time of the accident) went bankrupt. The parents thought their son had a good prospect of making a full recovery and made no claim. That was not to be. He had been mentally injured by the accident and his memory was impaired. The parents applied for leave to bring an action out of time under the Limitation Act 1963, but leave was refused. And so the question arose as to whether he was within the care and control of his parents. The boy argued that he was under the disability of infants and not within the care and control of his parents; if his argument succeeded it would allow him to bring an action against his employers which was not time barred. The court held that the question of custody was a question of fact and not a state of law, and that a person is only in the custody of his parents if he is in their effective care and control at the time when the action actually accrued to him.

Lord Denning's challenge to the presumption of paternal 'rights' could not be more emphatic, in consigning the rule in **Agar-Ellis** to the pages of history.

In a landmark ruling he said:

*I would utterly reject the notion that an infant is, by law, in the custody of his father until he is 21. These words 'in the custody of the parent' were first used in a Statute of Limitations in the year 1939. During the next year youngsters fought the Battle of Britain. Was each of them at that time still in the custody of his father? The next use of the words was in the Statute of 1954, since which time pop-singers of 19 have made thousands of pounds a week, and revolutionaries of 18 have broken up universities. Is each of them in the custody of his father? Of course not, neither in law nor in fact...I would get rid of the rule in re Agar Ellis 24 Ch D 317 and of the suggested exceptions to it. That case was decided in the year 1883. It reflects the attitude of the Victorian parent towards his children. He expected unquestioning obedience to his commands. If a son disobeyed, his father would cut him off without a shilling. If his daughter had an illegitimate child, he would turn her out of the house. His power only ceased when the child became 21. I decline to accept a view so much out of date....the legal right of a parent to the custody of a child ends at the 18th birthday; and even up till then, it is a dwindling right which the courts will hesitate to enforce against the wishes of the child, and the more so the older he is. It starts with a right of control and ends with little more than advice.*

## Deciding in favour of non-biological over natural parents

9.51    In **JvC(1970)**, theHouseofLordsconsideredanothercasewhichturneduptheparental 'right', this time in the context of adoption. Here, the court considered whether the interests of a child would best be served by being returned to his biological parents (who, over the years had demonstrated an inability to care adequately for him) or remaining with foster parents who had demonstrated an ability to care very well for the child. The background to this case is, protracted, and difficult. The boy was taken into care at four days old in 1958 and placed in the care of foster parents acting on behalf of the local authority, as his birth mother became ill with tuberculosis and consequently was unable to care for him adequately. In 1960, his natural parents returned to Spain and took the child, now aged two years, with them. In 1961, when the boy was three he was returned to England into the care of his foster parents as his mother sadly became once again unable to care for him. In 1963, his natural parents asked for his return to Spain and in order to resolve what had now become a long-term volleying of a child between two sets of carers and two countries, he was made a ward of court. The court ruled that he should remain with the foster parents in England, subject to their rearing the child in the Roman Catholic faith and also ensuring that the child knew and understood his cultural language, Spanish. Circumstances changed for the foster parents and in 1967 they returned to court over the issue of whether the child could attend a Church of England choir school at which he had won a place. The parents objected and issued a summons for care and control. The court of first instance, in considering the long-term interests of the child, held that the welfare of the child would be best served by the child remaining with the foster parents. This decision was upheld by the Court of Appeal, and also by the House of Lords, who dismissed the appeal of the parents.

Lord Donovan said:

*although the claim of natural parents to the custody and upbringing of their own children is obviously a most weighty factor to be taken into consideration in deciding what is in the best interests of the infant, yet the legislature recognised that this might not always be the determining factor, whether the parents were impeachable or not.*

Lord MacDermott said:

*While there is no rule of law that the rights and wishes of unimpeachable parents must prevail over other considerations, such rights and wishes, recognised as they are by nature and society, can be capable of ministering to the total welfare of the child in a special way, and must therefore preponderate in many cases. The parents rights, however, remain qualified and not absolute for the purposes of the investigation, the broad nature of which is still described in the four principles enunciated by FitzGibbon LJ in Re O'Hara (1900) 2 IR 232 at 240 (ie the court should act cautiously, and in opposition to the parent only when judicially satisfied that the welfare of the child requires it).*

## Mothers over fathers?

9.52 The case of ***Re K (Minors) (Children: Care and Control) (1977)*** demonstrated that paternal authority did not prevail even where the mother had been adulterous as had been the former position.

The parents were married in 1969, a boy was born in 1971 and a girl in 1974. The father was an Anglican clergyman. By March 1975, the wife had begun an adulterous relationship. The father refused to grant the mother a divorce, the mother continued to live in the matrimonial home because she wanted to be with her children. She applied to the magistrates' court for custody whilst the father applied to have the children made wards of court and for custody. The judge in the wardship proceedings found that the mother was an excellent mother; he ordered that the children should remain wards of court until they reached the age of majority and concluded that, until further order, custody of the children should be given to the mother on the ground that she was the 'natural guardian and protector of very young children'. The father appealed and the court held that in considering the care and control of a minor, the welfare of the minor was the first and paramount consideration and the court should not balance the welfare of the minor against the wishes of an unimpeachable parent or against the justice of the case as between the parents.

9.53 The question of paternal rights fell once again to be determined in a case which turned on the all too familiar facts of the abduction of children by parents.

In **Re D (1984)**, the defendant was convicted of kidnapping his five year-old daughter. Such conduct was, and is, not uncommon where cohabitation or marriage breaks down. Prior to 1984, it was not considered contrary to the law. The defendant, not unsurprisingly, appealed the conviction which the Court of Appeal quashed. Watkins LJ, Mustill and Skinner JJ, certified that two points of law of general importance were involved in the decision, but refused the Crown leave to appeal to the House of Lords. The two points of law, so certified, were as follows:

(a) *whether the common law offence of kidnapping exists in the case of a child victim under the age of fourteen years, and*

(b) *whether in any circumstances a parent may be convicted of such an offence where the child victim is unmarried and under the age of majority.*

These points were considered by the judicial committee of the House of Lords. The House of Lords reversed the decision of the Court of Appeal. Lord Brandon in his judgment, said:

*Since the nineteenth century, however, the generally accepted social conventions relating to the paramountcy of a father's position in the family have been progressively whittled away, until now, in the second half of the twentieth century, they can be regarded as having disappeared altogether. Parents are treated as equals in at least most respects, and certainly in relation to their authority over their children. English law, both common law and statute law, has recognised this fundamental change in the position of a father in the family.*

Following this case, in 1984, the Child Abduction Act 1984 was given Royal Assent and from that point forwards neither in family law nor in criminal law did a father, or indeed a mother, have a right to the physical possession of their children.

9.54 These and other cases continued to underscore the developing and changing historical social and legal reality. The paternal authority of the father was no longer omnipotent, nor indeed the authority of either parent. The law had embarked on a new chapter reframing the subject position of parents, reframing their role as one of duties and responsibilities rather than as one of rights, placing the welfare of the child at the epicentre of the modern law, and the rights of the child alongside.

## The child's right over the parental right

9.55 As paternal authority dwindled in its significance in legal decision-making regarding children, law's family empire began increasingly to reflect not only the significance of the welfare of the child in decisions taken about a child's upbringing but also the importance to be attached to the child's wishes in the matter under consideration.

> In *Gillick v West Norfolk and Wisbech Health Authority (1986)* (discussed in detail in Chapter 11), 'the most significant twentieth century decision' (Bainham, 2005), the House of Lords ruled that a child's right to determine her own treatment (in this case contraceptive treatment in the form of the oral contraceptive pill) where she was considered competent, prevailed over and above the parental right to determine the issue on her behalf. Lord Scarman in Gillick points out that although parental rights are of 'diminishing importance' they clearly do exist and do not wholly disappear until the child is 18. He considered the concept of parental authority 'horrendous'. He said:
>
> *There is much in the earlier case law which this house must discard—almost everything I would say but its principle. For example, the horrendous Agar-Ellis decisions, 10 Ch.D. 49; 24 Ch.D. 317 of the late 19th century asserting the power of the father over his child were rightly remaindered to the history books by the Court of Appeal in Hewer v Bryant.*

## More than just nomenclature: from rights to responsibilities

9.56 Whilst the trajectory of the developing law was moving towards embracing children's rights at the epicentre, in the same moment the idea of parental rights was being challenged and overthrown. The new era of the legal approach to childhood abolished once and for all the notion of proprietary rights over a child evident in the decision in *Agar-Ellis*, requiring now that the principal legal position of parenting was vested in a parent's responsibility towards a child. This paradigm shift can be observed both in case law prior to the CA 1989 and is also embodied and reflected in the Act itself.

9.57 The CA 1989 establishes a new nomenclature enshrining throughout the Act the responsibilities of parents, local authority, and the courts towards children. A nomenclature of 'responsibilities' for children, a new language was designed to cast aside the former notion of parental rights over a child.

9.58 The person in the role of the parent, whether natural parent, step-parent, adoptive parent or grandparent (who has parental responsibility with a residence order), no longer has rights but legal responsibilities towards children.

9.59 In 2004, 10,522 parental responsibility orders were granted and 214 orders refused. In 2005, 8,835 orders were made and 194 refused (figures as published in the respective years of Judicial Statistics); in 2006, 8,702 orders were made and 148 refused (figures as published in Judicial and Court Statistics 2006). More recently, in 2008, 7,072 and in 2009, 7,650 orders were made.

# Culture, faith and family

9.60 Patterns of immigration over the past 50 years have resulted in the arrival of families from countries outside the UK.

The court, in considering the welfare of the child, has in its deliberations applied either what is called the 'best interests' test or the test of 'welfare of the child as paramount' depending on what is required by law. So, for example, in any matter being decided under the Children Act 1989, the test which the courts must apply is the 'welfare paramount test' as established in s 1(1). But in matters relating to wardship, for example, the 'best interest' test is the test that is applied. Both of these tests will be discussed throughout the chapters relating to children: what is being suggested at this juncture is that the courts are likely to approach these two considerations from a particular vantage point. The court will of course approach the matter objectively but it may be that in trying to determine 'best interests' or 'welfare as paramount' such a consideration will be deliberated upon in a context of what the dominant culture considers 'best interests' or 'welfare'. Conflict may arise when 'best interests' and 'welfare' might be decided by ignoring other perceptions of welfare and best interests. The test is certainly not as objective as it claims to be. One only has to consider the lessons of history where, for example, in the nineteenth century the best interests of the child were served, said the courts, by being raised by a father. And in the twentieth century the 'best interests' were served by not being reared by a homosexual parent. In a multi-cultural society it may be that the court will need to acknowledge its own cultural subject position in deciding child matters and will need also to take into consideration the cultural subject position of the parties involved.

9.61 Many families in Britain have their own traditional customs and practices which mark the uniqueness of their way of life and their identity. In the past, there has been an unwillingness to accommodate difference and family law has reflected an assimilationist rather than multi-cultural approach. The treatment of the Roma (known previously in Britain as 'gypsies') is a case in point. Their nomadic lifestyle, not wishing to settle in any locality, unwillingness to conform to the requirement to send their children to local schools, for example, led to much prejudice. However, by 2005, 'gypsies' were renamed 'travellers' and retrospective planning applications made by travellers for travellers' sites were being granted (see *Smith v First Secretary of State and another (2005)*) in an attempt to embrace multi-culture.

9.62 The migration of families from the Caribbean and from South Asia—India, Bangladesh, and Pakistan, provide just two examples of how culture and traditions shape family arrangements and influence parenting. In a multi-cultural society, these differences will assume supreme importance for the families concerned and are matters to which the court must have regard in legal decisions affecting children.

9.63 The role of the grandmother in the Carribean family is perhaps not well understood. Yet, the Caribbean family pattern has evolved out of the historical reality and experience of slavery, where men were forcibly removed from families, leaving women, mothers and grandmothers to rear children. This reality bequeaths a legacy. And so grandmothers especially played, and continue to play, a centrifugal role as 'the' parent in the black 'matriarchal' family, whilst fatherhood for many Caribbean men is transitory (See b hooks). As Patricia Williams explains, 'the insignificance of family connection was consistently achieved through the suppression of any image of blacks as capable either of being part of the family of white men or having family of their own' (Williams, 1991, 162). The case of *Dred Scott v Sandford (1857)*, demonstrates how the legal form of traditional marriage was effectively denied to black families through and by the law, thereby effecting through law the 'black' family form. The court said:

> *Since slaves, as chattels, could not make contracts, marriages between them were not legally binding…Their condition was compatible only with a form of concubinage, voluntary on the part of slaves, and permissive on that of the master. In law, there was no such thing as fornication or adultery between slaves; nor were there bastards, for, as a Kentucky judge noted, the father of the slave was 'unknown to the law'. No slave legislature ever seriously entertained the thought of encroaching upon the master's rights by legalizing slave marriages.*

*(Stampp, 1956, 198)*

9.64 The South Asian diaspora, as our second example, has contributed to the migration of many communities from different regions including India, Pakistan, Bangladesh, introducing a variety of very different faiths, Hinduism, Sikhism, and Islam, all characterized by extended patriarchal kinship structures where uncles and grandfathers have a central place with regard to the quasi-legal parenting role, although day-to-day care is the province of mothers and grandmothers. The question of the legitimacy of children is central to the Asian family and becomes an important consideration when, for example, understanding the reluctance of Asian families to offer themselves as adoptive parents (see *Re S Newcastle City Council v Z (2007)* in Chapter 10). The relevance of status and caste is reflected in the significance of arranged marriages, and the close-knit family ties of property and inheritance are further reinforced in the organization of family assets and finance and become important factors for a court deciding matters of family assets (see, e.g. Edwards, 2004 see also Jivraj and Herman, 2007).

9.65 Furthermore, it is important to understand the role of the wider kinship members in the Asian family with regard to parental responsibility for example. In *R (on the application of Begum) v Headteacher and Governors of Denbigh High School (2006)* the brother, who was very much involved in supporting his sister (the claimant), was considered by some to be engineering the litigation. However, since the respondent's father had died in 1992 and her mother spoke little English and also subsequently died during the course of the proceedings it is not uncommon especially in Asian families for male relatives to become involved in this way (see Edwards, 2007; Edwards, 2010).

9.66 Munby J in **Singh v Entry Clearance Officer New Dehli (2004)**, provides a radical departure from entrenched notions of the idealized family and sets a new vision of how the law should reflect and embrace the diversity of contemporary families in the interests of the welfare of children living in them from a position of multi-culturalism:

> *(63)... in our multi-cultural and pluralistic society the family takes many forms. Indeed, in contemporary Britain the family takes an almost infinite variety of forms. Many marry according to the rites of non-Christian faiths. There may be one, two, three or more generations living together under the same roof. Some people choose to live on their own. People live together as couples, married or not, and with partners who may not always be of the opposite sex. Children live in households where their parents may be married or unmarried. They may be the children of polygamous marriages. They may be brought up by a single parent. Their parents may or may not be their natural parents. Their siblings may be only half siblings or step siblings. Some children are brought up by a single parent. Some children are brought up by parents of the same sex. Some children are conceived by artificial donor insemination. Some are the result of surrogacy arrangements. The fact is that many adults and children, whether through choice or circumstance, live in families more or less removed from what until comparatively recently would have been recognised as the typical nuclear family.*

9.67 Munby J, again in *Singh,* powerfully articulates the need to move away from arrogating any one faith above any other embracing the multi-dimensionality of faith.

> *(67) Although historically this country is part of the Christian west, and although it has an established church which is Christian, we sit as secular judges serving a multi-cultural community of many faiths in which all of us can now take pride. We are sworn to do justice 'to all manner of people'. Religion- whatever the particular believer's faith-is no doubt something to be encouraged but it is not the business of government or of the secular courts, though the courts will, of course, pay every respect and given great weight to a family's religious principles. Art 9 of the Convention, after all, demands no less. So the starting point of the law is a tolerant indulgence to cultural and religious diversity and an essentially agnostic view of religious beliefs. A secular judge must be wary of straying across the well-recognised divide between church and state.*

# Family rights—Article 8 'family life'

9.68 In all family matters, Art 8 Right to Respect for Private and Family Life ,ECHR, is engaged. Art 8 states:

1. *Everyone has the right to respect for his private and family life, his home and his correspondence.*

2. *There shall be no interference by a public authority with the exercise of this right except such as is in accordance with the law and is necessary in a democratic society in the interests of national security, public safety or the economic well-being of the country, for the prevention of disorder or crime, for the protection of health or morals, or for the protection of the rights and freedoms of others.*

However, Art 8 might not always be the panacea. In *Re L v M H*, Thorpe LJ warned of the 'wariness of the terminology of rights.'

9.69 We have limited our discussion of the construct of family life to family law, but in other areas of law, for example immigration law, the existence of a family life and how that is construed is central to decision making. What is clear from the case law is that a different meaning of family life resides in these decisions and a clear conflict is exposed in different areas of law which have a different objective.

> In *R (on the application of Ajoh) v Secretary of State for the Home Department (2007)*, the mother, a Jamaican national, arrived in the UK in February 1999 on a temporary visitor's visa with her three children and was later granted temporary leave to remain as a student. That leave was extended; but at the end of the extension she overstayed in the UK. On 20 February 2002, she made a fraudulent application for asylum which was refused. She eventually withdrew an appeal against that refusal. In April 1999, she had met her future husband, Mr A, a British citizen, whom she married on 11 April 2003. She had been living with him since about December 2002 and applied to be allowed to stay in the UK as his wife. After a delay of 23 months, during which time she had given birth to twins, the Secretary of State refused her application and ordered her to return to Jamaica with her children. In judicial review proceedings the judge, Collins J, quashed the Secretary of State's decision, holding that it would not be proportionate to remove A and that it was in breach of her rights under Art 8 of the ECHR and that 'family life' after 23 months had become established in the UK. He said:
>
> *There is no good reason why the Home Office should take nearly two years to decide upon an application; and Mr Patel has submitted that there is no additional prejudice as a result of the delay because the situation, so far as the claimant is concerned, has not changed. That, in my view, is a submission which lacks merit. It certainly lacks humanity. It must be obvious that the longer the husband and wife and their family are able to remain in this country and put down roots in this country, the more hard it will be for them to be uprooted and for the family life to be interfered with in the way that is suggested.*

The Secretary of State appealed. The appeal was allowed. The Court of Appeal (Sir Igor Judge P, Lord Justice May, and Lord Justice Moore-Bick) held that a balance had to be struck between Art 8 rights and the need for a consistent and fair immigration policy. The court placed a very high threshold on delay, and held that delay must be 'extreme' to the point of 'national disgrace' before it would be inequitable to enforce the rules. The requirement to return to Jamaica, said the court, would not have breached the family's Art 8 rights (Walsh explores this further in her article 'Unhappy Families and use of Article 8 for Failed Asylum Seekers', 2009).

9.70 We started this chapter with considering the wisdom of Baroness Hale in articulating the need to recognize different types of family form as families. We end with the way in which her thinking has also exercised an effect on constructing the meaning of family life in the context of immigration:

> *[8] In the case of Beoku-Betts v Secretary of State for the Home Dept [2008] UKHL 39, [2008] 4 All ER 1146, [2008] 3 WLR 166, the House has decided that the effect on other family members with a right to respect for their family life with the appellant must also be taken into account in an appeal to the Asylum and Immigration Tribunal on human rights grounds. Even if it would not be disproportionate to expect a husband to endure a few months' separation from his wife, it must be disproportionate to expect a four-year-old girl, who was born and has lived all her life here, either to be separated from her mother for some months or to travel with her mother to endure the 'harsh and unpalatable' conditions in Zimbabwe simply in order to enforce the entry clearance procedures.*

It is clear that the law in the area of parenting , parental responsibilities and the family form is both shaped by social reality, social convention, and also by the law.

## FURTHER READING

Barton C , 'British Minority Ethnics, Religion and Family Law(yers)' (2008) Fam Law 1217

Bainham A, *Children: The Modern Law* (Family Law, 2005)

Blackstone, *Blackstone's Commentaries on the Laws of England* (1765, Clarendon Press, 1857)

de Beauvoir S, *The Second Sex* (1974 edn Penguin Harmondsworth)

Dey I, and Wasoff F, 'Mixed Messages: Parental Responsibilities, Public Opinion and the Reforms of Family Law' (2006) International Journal of Law, Policy and the Family 20

Douglas G and Moorhead R, 'Providing Advice for Lone Parents: from Parent to Citizen?' (2005) 17 (1) CFLQ 55

Edwards S, 'Division of Assets and Fairness: "Brick Lane"—Gender, Culture and Ancillary Relief on Divorce' (2004) Fam Law 34

Edwards S, 'Imagining Islam...of meaning and metaphor symbolising the jilbab—*R (Begum) v Heateacher and Governors of Denbigh High School'* (2007) CFLQ 19 (2)

Edwards S, 'Defacing Muslim Women: Dialectical Meanings of Dress in the Body Politic' in Banakar R (Ed.), *Rights in Context* (Ashgate, 2010)

Engels F, The *Origin of the Family, Private Property, and the State* (1884, Penguin 1986)

Fletcher R, *The Family and Marriage in Britain* (Penguin, 1966)

Glendon M, *Abortion and Divorce in Western Law* (Harvard University Press, 1987),

Hooks B, *We Real Cool Black Men and Masculinity* (Routledge, 2003)

Jivraj S and Herman D, 'It is Difficult for a White Judge to Understand: Orientalism, Racialisation, and Christianity in English Child Welfare Cases' [2009] CFLQ 283

Judicial Statistics 2004 Cm 6565 TSO London

Judicial Statistics 2005 Cm 6903 TSO London

Judicial and Court Statistics 2006 Cm 7273 HMSO London

Law Commission, 'Non Accidental Death or Serious Injury' (Law Com No 282, 2003)

Mcguinness S and Alghrani A, 'Gender and Parenthood: The Case for Realignment' (2008) Med Law Rev 16 261

Narayan R K, *The Grandmother's Tale and Selected Stories* (,Ecco, 1999)

O'Halloran K, *The Politics of Adoption: International Perspectives on Law, Policy and Practice* (2nd edn, Springer, 2009)

Scherpe J, 'The Gametes of a European Family Law' (2008) IFL 109

Smith L ,'Clashing Symbols? Reconciling Support for Fathers and Fatherless Families After the Human Fertilisation and Embryology Act 2008' [2010] CFLQ 46

Stampp K, *The Peculiar Institution: Slavery in the Ante-Bellum South* (Knopf, 1956)

Wallbank J, 'The Role of Rights and Utility in Instituting a Child's Right to Know her Genetic History' (2004) 13(2) Social and Legal Studies 245

Walsh C, 'Unhappy Families and Use of Article 8 for Failed Asylum Seekers

Welstead M, Chikwamba v Secretary of State for the Home Department' (2008) UKHL 40, Denning Law Journal

Williams A, *The Alchemy of Race and Rights* (Harvard University Press, 1991)

## SELF-TEST QUESTIONS

1  What evidence is there to indicate that in recent times the courts have rejected the reasoning in *Agar-Ellis*?

2  'The modern conception of parental power is one of responsibilities rather than rights' (Cretney S, Masson J, *Principles of Family Law* (Sweet and Maxwell, 2003)). Discuss.

3   Who in law might have parental responsibility and with regard to what particular matters might they be required or permitted to exercise it?

4   How might an unmarried father whose name is not on the child's birth certificate acquire parental responsibility, and what factors will the court take into consideration?

5   Consider from your experience and the experience of those around you how culture may be an important consideration for the courts when considering legal decisions affecting the child.

6   What factors do you consider influenced the court in *Re M* in its decision to send P back to the Transvaal?

# 10

# From clean break to open adoption

## SUMMARY

In this chapter we consider adoption, its history, and the statutory frame-work regulating adoption following the Adoption and Children Act 2002, the Children and Adoption Act 2006 and the Children Act 2007. We consider the importance of race, religion, and cultural identity, which are now statutory requirements when considering placing a child with prospective adoptive parents. The 'welfare of the child as paramount' test, which lies at the heart of the Children Act s 1 1989, since 2002, is now the test applied in considering adoption. In this regard, we consider to what extent this overarching principle of 'welfare of the child as paramount' will allow the adoption services and the courts to dispense with parental consent to adoption where the welfare of the child requires it.

The paramountcy of the welfare test and the power to dispense with parental consent raises questions of parental human rights and is open to human rights Art 8 challenges, especially as dispensing with parental consent, from the parents' vantage point, is regarded as an attack on their civil rights and presents as a draconian measure. The chapter considers both domestic and international adoptions and concludes with an overview of the move from adoption as a secretive enterprise to 'open' adoption which includes the preservation of links through contact between birth family members and the child placed for adoption—a development which recognizes the importance of maintaining attachment in psychological and personal development.

# History of UK adoption

10.1 The essence of adoption, as Barbara Tizard (1977) wrote, 'is that a child not born to you is incorporated into your family as though he were your own. Adoption is, in many ways, an anomaly. It terminates once and for all the parental responsibility of the natural parent'.

When a person wishes to adopt, adoption can only be effected through a court order (Adoption and Children Act 2002 (ACA 2002), s 46(1), re-enacting the Adoption Act 1976, s 12(1)). Adoption has until very recently been described as a 'legal transplant' or a 'clean break'. This is because adoption traditionally completely severs the child's legal connection with the birth family and was surrounded in secrecy. Perhaps, then, the most striking development of recent adoption law post 2002 has been the shift from this complete severing of legal and social links with the birth family to a new form of 'open' adoption where contact, if appropriate, may be maintained between the child and the birth family, including siblings, grandparents and even birth parents. In addition, court orders other than adoption orders, if appropriate, are encouraged, for example, in the provision of 'special guardianship orders' (see Children and Adoption Act 2006) and the child's right to know and to contact his birth parents is formalized provided that they agree to such contact.

10.2 Legal adoption was first introduced by the Adoption Act 1926. Children available for adoption had been abandoned, orphaned or born as a result of an unwanted pregnancy. With the absence of adequate contraception and the overwhelming stigma attached to pregnancy outside marriage, both to the pregnant mother and to her born child, social mores as well as hardship forced women to give up their babies at birth, providing a pool of children dislocated from their birth mothers and available for adoption. This socially forcible removal of babies from their single unmarried mothers, which today seems an act of unbelievable cruelty to the mother, was accepted practice. Gender discrimination against women and bourgeois attitudes to sex outside marriage resulted in a climate of shame around sex before marriage and shame around such pregnancies and children born in consequence. These negative attitudes to single unmarried mothers persisted well into the 1970s and poverty, single unmarried parenthood and social stigma continued to wrest children from mothers.

Clare Short, formerly Labour MP for Ladywood, Birmingham, and a former government Minister, gave up her son for adoption when he was six weeks old. As a public figure, she was very publicly reunited with him in 1999. (http://www.guardian.co.uk/politics/1996/oct/17/labour.uk). By 1999, the number of newly born babies placed for adoption had fallen to about 50 per year. This reflected social change and the fact that single unmarried women were no longer required to give up their babies. Women are now rearing children on their own, in extended families or with the help of a new partner. The 50 newly born children placed for adoption were so placed either because of illness of the parent or because the child had a disability and the parent was unable to cope.

The adoption business in the early years was something of a meat market, adoption societies only accepting 'healthy white babies' (Houghton Report, paras 22–26). This meant that the adoptive family was engineered, as attitudes to the idealised form of 'family life' and 'children dictated these negotiations. These attitudes were further influenced by race and by cultural perceptions.

## Adoption not practised

10.3 Adoption is not a common practice across the world and each country has its own arrangements. In some countries, adoption is unacceptable, for cultural or religious reasons.

> The mother in *Re S Newcastle City Council v Z (2007)* (decided 11 July 2005), who was of the Muslim faith opposed the adoption of her child, largely on the ground that adoption, she claimed, was prohibited by Islam. The court was required to consider whether they should dispense with her consent to adoption. (This issue is considered later in some detail). Munby J said:
>
> *I accept that the mother's religious beliefs are reasonable. But that is not the question. The question is whether the mother is being reasonable or unreasonable in affording to her religious views, however reasonable in themselves they may be, the pre-eminence she plainly does when deciding to withhold her consent to S's adoption.*
>
> Munby J does not demur from the complexity of this case:
>
> *There have been enormous changes in the social and religious life of our country. We live in a secular and pluralistic society. But we also live in a multicultural community of many faiths. Our society includes men and women from every corner of the globe and of every creed and colour under the sun. We live in a society which on many social, ethical and religious topics no longer either thinks or speaks with one voice. These are topics on which men and woman of different faiths or no faith at all hold starkly differing views. All of those views are entitled to the greatest respect but it is not for a judge to choose between them. The days are past when the business of the judges was the enforcement of morals or religious belief, for we live, or strive to live, in a tolerant society increasingly alive to the need to guard against the tyranny which majority opinion may impose on those who, for whatever reason, comprise a weak or voiceless minority. And although historically this country is part of the Christian west, and although it has an established church which is Christian, we sit as secular*

*judges serving a multicultural community of many faiths in which all of us can now take pride. We are sworn to do justice 'to all manner of people'. Religion—whatever the particular believer's faith—is no doubt something to be encouraged but it is not the business of government or of the secular courts, though the courts will, of course, pay every respect and give great weight to a family's religious principles. Article 9 of the European Convention, after all, demands no less. So the starting point of the law is a tolerant indulgence to cultural and religious diversity and an essentially agnostic view of religious beliefs. A secular judge must be wary of straying across the well recognised divide between church and state. It is not for a judge to weigh one religion against another. The court recognises no religious distinctions and generally speaking passes no judgment on religious beliefs or on the tenets, doctrines or rules of any particular section of society. All are entitled to equal respect, whether in times of peace or, as at present, amidst the clash of arms.*

(See Singh, Chapter 9 and see also Jivraj and Herman, 2007).

10.4 In EU member states, very few children are accommodated by the local authority and there are very few adoptions. In some other countries, where adoption is practised it is unregulated.

## Statistics

10.5 There is no data recording the number of adoptions prior to 1930. During the 1950s there were about 13,000 adoptions annually. By 1968, 25,000 orders for adoption were made. This was partly the result of an increase in sex outside marriage and the rise of unintended pregnancies. In 1970, the rate of pregnancy of 15 to 19 year-olds stood at 82.4 per 1,000, which has now fallen in 1996 to 63.0 and in 1999 also at 63.0 (see Teenage conception rates: by age at conception and outcome: Social Trends 32). This exponential rise in adoption in the 1970s led to directives being introduced following the Adoption Act 1976, requiring the courts to give consideration to alternative legal solutions, such as custodianship or residence. By 1980, the number of adoption orders had fallen dramatically to 8,026, falling further to 6,288 orders in 1988. By 1994, 7,336 orders were made, declining further in 1999 to 3,962, stabilizing in 2003 at 4,870 orders and in 2004, 4,539 orders, in 2005, 4,004 orders. Following the ACA 2002, special guardianship orders were introduced giving the special guardian parental responsibility for the child without removing parental responsibility from the child's birth parents. This may explain the 12% decrease in adoption orders in 2005 as compared with 2004. The BAAF statistics show 5,680 adoption orders during 2002; 4,818 in 2003; 5,562 in 2004; 5,558 in 2005; 4,979 in 2006; 4,637 in 2007. There were 4,939 children entered into the Adopted Children Register following court orders made in 2008. This was 207 more than in 2007, representing an increase of 4.4 per cent. This is the first year that

**Table 10.1** Adoption of children: summary of proceedings (2005)

| Nature of proceedings | Family Proceedings courts | County courts | High Court | Total |
|---|---|---|---|---|
| Applications | | | | |
| By step-parents | 534 | 440 | 0 | 974 |
| By others | 1119 | 2671 | 3 | 3793 |
| Total | 1653 | 3111 | 3 | 4767 |
| Orders made | | | | |
| To step-parents | 446 | 416 | 4 | 866 |
| To others | 812 | 2276 | 50 | 3138 |
| Total | 1258 | 2692 | 54 | 4004 |

Source: *Judicial Statistics* (2005) 71, Table 5.4.

an increase in adoption numbers has been seen since 2004. The number of adoptions is 7 per cent greater that in 1998 and is at the highest level since 2005, http://www.statistics.gov.uk/cci/nugget.asp?id=592, Office for National Statistics, 2009.

# Who adopts today?

10.6    In 2009, the average age at adoption was three years nine months, 2 per cent (80) of children adopted during the year ending 31 March 2009 were under one year old, 72 per cent (2,300) were aged between 1 and 4 years old, 23 per cent (760) were aged between five and nine years old , 3 per cent (80) were aged between 10 and 15 years old—BAAF (accessed from http://www.baaf.org.uk/info/stats/england.shtml#afc on 28 June 2010). This compares with 2003–2004, when 58 per cent of those adopted were between one and four years of age, 30 per cent were between five and nine, 6 per cent were between 10 and 15, and 6 per cent were under one year.

## Adoption by step-parents

10.7    The ACA 2002, s 39 provides for adoption by partners of the child's natural parents. About one-half of the 7,326 adoption orders made in 1994 resulted from applications made by step-parents. In 1999, this number was 1,614 in 2003, 1,172 and in 2005 it fell to less than one fifth of all adoption orders granted—at 866. The following case demonstrates the complex and difficult issues for the natural parents posed by a step-parent wanting to adopt the child.

> In *Re B (Adoption: Father's Objections) (1999)*, the natural father had abducted the child on three occasions and received a sentence of imprisonment. The mother remarried and the step-father wanted to adopt. The natural father objected. The judge concluded that the welfare of the child demanded an adoption order and he then went on to dispense with the consent of the father on the basis that the refusal of the father to give his agreement was unreasonable. The father appealed. The court dismissed the appeal.

The new array of orders, parental responsibility and special guardianship could avoid such situations.

## Parental responsibility orders for step-parents

10.8  It is expected that the number of step-parents being granted adoption orders will further decline as step-parents acquire parental responsibility instead through a parental responsibility order obviating the need for adoption which was clearly not good practice in cases simply where the parent with care remarried. The new parental responsibility order which can now be made in favour of a step-parent (ACA, s112) will go some way to addressing the acrimony between natural parents, since the non-resident spouse no longer loses their parental status or their legal relationship with the child. A step-parent may make an agreement to obtain parental responsibility for his or her step-child providing all those with parental responsibility agree.

Special guardianship orders are discussed separately later in this chapter.

## Adoption by relatives

10.9  There has been a reluctance, at least until recently, to grant adoption orders to relatives. Adoption by family members was considered to be a risk since the child would retain contact with the natural parents, and this was regarded as potentially disruptive to the stability of the relationship between the new adoptive parent and the child. The review of adoption law in 1993 considered that there would be few situations where adoption by relatives would be desirable.

## Adoption by foster parents

10.10  Although adoption from care is the main route this aspect is discussed in more detail later. The main constituency of persons who adopt is in fact the foster parent.

10.11 The central objective of adoption in 2010 has been transformed from the earlier years of its inception. It is now aimed at providing a stable and permanent future in a family for children who are being cared for by the local authority and is now regarded and delivered as a 'service' for children. In *Freete v France (2003)* the ECtHR asserted adoption means 'giving a family to a child and not the child to a family' [42].

10.12 Perhaps the most important development is that current adoption law places the welfare of the child as paramount (ACA 2002, s 1(2)), with the result that the court must apply this test when considering whether to make an adoption order or indeed any order. Also, in this regard, the court can dispense with the consent of the natural parents if the welfare of the child requires it since child welfare is paramount. In considering welfare, the welfare checklist in the ACA 2002, s 1(4) applies. This is discussed in detail in Chapter 12.

10.13 The 2002 Act also recognizes the psychopolitics of family life—that for many children, maintaining contact with birth relatives is not simply to be desired by them but is quintessential to their development and well being. (See eg the findings of Triseliotis.) With 'maintaining contact' in mind, s 1(4)(f) requires the court to consider:

> the relationship the child has with relatives, and with any other person in relation to whom the court or agency considers the relationship to be relevant, including:
>
> (i) the likelihood of any such relationship continuing and the value to the child of its doing so;
>
> (ii) the ability and willingness of any of the child's relatives, or of any such person, to provide the child with a secure environment in which the child can develop, and otherwise to meet the child's needs;
>
> (iii) the wishes and feelings of any of the child's relatives, or of any such person, regarding the child.

10.14 ACA 2002, s 1(5) requires that in placing the child for adoption, the agency must give due consideration to the child's 'religious persuasion, racial origin and cultural and linguistic background'. This, is a significant departure from earlier adoption legislation, which had placed an emphasis on religion only, see the Adoption Act 1976, s 6. This earlier exclusive emphasis on religion reflected not only the central place religious beliefs have held for centuries in British society (remember *Agar-Ellis (1884)* and *J v C (1970)* discussed in Chapter 9) but also a society whose demography consisted largely of an indigenous people, where differences within the Christian faith and between denominations presented as the main source of potential conflict (see also eg *Re Collins (An Infant) (1950)*—a case involving the religious upbringing of a child of a deceased Roman Catholic father and deceased protestant mother and a conflict between the paternal and maternal grandparents). It is to be remembered as Malins VC said of *Agar-Ellis* when referring to marriage between a Roman Catholic wife and a Protestant husband:

> *This is perhaps the strongest case that has ever occurred shewing the misery that ensues from mixed marriages.*

10.15 Contemporary sociography demonstrates very diverse cultural, ethnic, and faith society, factors,all of which have equal importance and relevance in the development of a child's identity, all of which are central to the well being of a developing child. Whilst courts struggle to interpret these several competing considerations, it is to be noted that considerations of 'religious persuasion, racial origin and cultural and linguistic background' are not entirely new being also found in the Children Act 1989 (CA 1989), s 22(5)(c), as factors to be taken into account by the local authority when looking after children. Factors enunciated by Munby J in *Singh* (see Chapter 9) and *in Re S Newcastle City Council v Z (2007)* above.

10.16 Whilst working towards acquiring the consent of the natural parents to adoption remains a priority (ACA 2002, s 19(1)), dispensing with their consent has now been simplified and is permitted if the welfare of the child requires it, or if the natural parents cannot be found or are incapable of giving consent (s 52). The ACA 2002 abolishes the freeing order and introduces a placement order (s 21), which can only be made if the parents have consented or if their consent may be dispensed with.

10.17 Furthermore, the ACA 2002 recognizes that the contemporary family of the twenty-first century may not be monogamous or heterosexual. As Bamforth writes.

> *The CPA 2004 also allows for the same assessment criteria for adoption to apply to married, unmarried, partnered and un-partnered couples. Courts tended until comparatively recently to be troubled by the presence of lesbians or gay men as would-be adopters. However, the Adoption and Children Act 2002 allowed for adoption orders to be applied for on the same basis by same-sex and opposite-sex couples living together in 'enduring family relationships', and the CPA 2004 includes civil partners within that Act.*

The legislation, however, recognizes as of paramount importance in considering the suitability of adopters, the stability and permanence in a relationship. Unmarried couples can now adopt provided there is evidence of stability and permanence. This includes homosexual couples.

> *However, single persons can also adopt and whilst that includes homosexuals, the reasoning in Frette v France (2003) suggests that the single homosexual may not be as successful as the single heterosexual in securing an adoption. In this case, a*

*single homosexual man applied for prior authorization to adopt; his sexual orientation was a decisive factor in the court's refusal.*

The court took the view that the applicant's choice of lifestyle did not appear to be such as to provide sufficient guarantees that he would be able to provide a suitable home for a child. The applicant sought judicial review.

The court held that:

*the Convention did not guarantee the right to adopt as such. Therefore, if account was taken of the broad margin of appreciation left to states in this matter and the need to protect children's best interests to achieve the desired balance, the refusal to authorise adoption did not infringe the principle of proportionality. It followed that the difference in treatment the applicant complained of was not discriminatory for the purposes of Article 14 taken in conjunction with Article 8.*

10.18 ACA 2002, s 1(6) stipulates that the court must consider the range of powers and orders under this Act and the CA 1989, and must not make any order unless making an order would be better for the child than not making an order.

10.19 The new status of 'special guardianship', means that total severance from the birth family may not be required and the possibility of contact with natural parents for mainly older children and young people in care who may accept that they can not live with their birth parents, but do not wish all legal ties with their family to be broken, under special guardianship arrangements may not need to do so. Such orders are particularly appropriate where older children are involved, who may wish to retain some legal ties with their birth family; and also may be appropriate in the case of unaccompanied asylum-seeking children who need a secure, permanent home in the UK, but have strong attachments to their biological family abroad. Prospective carers from minority ethnic groups who may wish to offer a child a permanent family, but have religious or cultural difficulties with adoption or where members of the extended family may not want to adopt the child, but wish to care permanently for a child are provided through these new orders with security and clarity about day-to-day decision making, which assists both the carers and the children concerned.

## Adoption procedure

### Adoption is final

10.20 Once an adoption order is made, adoption is final,adoption terminates, once and for all, the parental responsibility of the natural parent (ACA 2002, s 46(2)(a)), which is one reason why arrangements such as special guardianship orders may be preferred.

This finality and irreversibility is nowhere more starkly demonstrated than in the case of *Re B (Adoption: Setting Aside) (1985)*.

Here, the applicant, who was adopted when a young child, made an application to set aside the adoption order after he discovered that his birth culture, religion, and ethnicity were fundamentally different from the religion and ethnicity he had acquired from his adoptive parents and, being so different, led him to be considered a spy when he applied to emigrate to Israel. The applicant, B, was born in 1959 to an English mother and a Kuwaiti Muslim father. The couple were not married. Three weeks after B was born, his mother put him up for adoption. The adoptive parents, who were Jewish, knew that the father of B was from the Gulf and assumed he also was a Jew. In 1968, the adoptive parents discovered that B's natural mother was not Jewish, nevertheless, the boy was received into the Jewish faith. When B was 27 years of age he intended to emigrate to Israel. On his arrival in Israel, the authorities suspected him of being an Arab spy, and refused him entry. B then made enquiries as to the background of his natural parents, discovering that his mother was English and his father a Kuwaiti. Consequently, he was rejected from Jewish culture. In an effort to resolve these issues of cultural identity and rejection, he made an application to have the original adoption order set aside. The judge said that as the order had been made in accordance with correct procedure, there was no jurisdiction to have the order set aside. B appealed. Swinton-Thomas LJ explained:

*In my judgment, a mistake or misapprehension as to the race, ethnic origin or parental religion of the natural parents could not amount to a circumstance which would vitiate a consent otherwise freely given...*

Here, law flies in the face of fact and procedural niceties are paramount.

## Not so final!

10.21 However, the mistake in the case below led to an adoption order being set aside.

In *Re M (Minors) (Adoption) (1991)*, the adoption orders made in respect of two girls were set aside. In this case the natural father agreed to the adoption by the step-father of his two daughters, aged 11 and 12 years. The natural mother, unbeknown to the father, had terminal cancer and died within three months of the adoption order being made. The step-father was subsequently unable to care for the girls who then went to reside with the paternal grandparents. Subsequently the natural father, who had settled in America with a new wife, wanted the care and custody of the two children. All parties involved agreed that this was in the best interests of the girls. The natural father appealed on the grounds that the decision had been made in the absence of the knowledge of his wife's terminal illness.

Glidewell LJ said, per curiam:

*I should say, as a postscript, that this is, if not unique, at the very least a wholly exceptional case. I say that because I do not want the setting aside of this adoption*

*order in these circumstances to be thought of as being some precedent for any
related set of facts in some other cases.*

Given that children have been adopted as a result of false conclusions drawn from
the presence of subdural haematoma and retinal haemorrhaging wrongly attributed,
in some cases, to non-accidental injury it may well be that some adoptions orders
granted in these circumstances will need to be set aside (see Chapters 14 and 15).

> In *Re K (Children) (Adoption: Freeing Order) (2004)* freeing orders were set aside on
> the application of an Indian mother who argued that she had been coerced by her hus-
> band and his family into silence in care and freeing proceedings relating to her elder child
> who had undoubtedly suffered non-accidental injuries.
>
> What happens when the original findings on which the adoption order was made are
> flawed? Is it open to the court in 2011 to set aside adoption orders? This question was
> considered in *Webster and another v Norfolk County Council (2009)*. In this case
> freeing orders for adoption were made dispensing with consent in respect of a child and
> two siblings.
>
> Following an appeal and fresh evidence which was disputed. The court considered
> whether it was appropriate to dispense with the adoption orders and concluded that it
> was not. However, Wall LJ said this:
>
> *The four children concerned, namely Brandon, his sister and his two brothers, have
> been denied the opportunity to argue that they should grow up together with their
> parents as a family. That is deeply worrying, and, on the face of it, a clear breach of
> their rights to respect for their family life under art 8(1) of the European Convention
> for the Protection of Human Rights and Fundamental Freedoms 1950 (as set out in
> Sch 1 to the Human Rights Act 1998) (ECHR).*
>
> *[3] For Mr and Mrs Webster, the parents of the children concerned, the case has
> been a disaster, quite apart from any breach of their rights under the ECHR. From
> their perspective, they have been wrongly accused of physically abusing one of
> their children, and three of their children have been removed wrongly and per-
> manently from their care. The only mitigation, from their point of view is the local
> authority's belated recognition that they are fit and able to care for Brandon.*

Clearly this was a miscarriage of justice not just an error.

# Adoption services

10.22   Under ACA 2002, s 3, only the local authority or a registered adoption society can
provide adoption services. The latter must be registered under the National Care
Standards Commission (see further, Overseas Adoption Helpline, renamed the
Intercountry Adoption Centre, British Association for Adoption and Fostering,

Catholic Children's Society). Every local authority is under a duty to maintain a service within their area.

10.23 Under ACA 2002, s 4(1), 'adoption agencies', that is, the local authority or a registered service, for example, the Catholic adoption services, have responsibility for selecting and assessing adopters and placing children for adoption. This includes the provision of support services (this is discussed in detail below). In accordance with s 5, local authorities must prepare a clear adoption plan for the provision of services with regard to the adoption of a child. Section 109 requires the court to draw up a plan with a view to determining applications, which avoids delay for a placement order or adoption order. And adoption services must abide by the law. The Catholic Children's Society, which provides an adoption service for prospective adopters, has up until now opted out from offering gay couples children for adoption. The Equality Act, in effect in England, Wales and Scotland since April 2007, prohibits discrimination in the provision of goods, facilities and services on the basis of sexual orientation. This means that Catholic adoption agencies may be forced to comply. See *Father Hudson's Society v Charity Commission (2009)* (charity which did not provide adoption services to homosexuals for religious reasons could not continue not to provide services to a person on grounds of sexual orientation); *Catholic Care (Diocese of Leeds) v The Charity Commission for England and Wales (2010).* (see also the Equality Act 2010.)

## Care plans

10.24 Where the local authority wishes to place a child for adoption, it is the duty of the local authority in all care cases to file a care plan (see *Manchester City Council v F (Note) (1993)*). The care plan sets out the local authority's plans for the child's future. The local authority may take the view that adoption is the preferred option. The Circular, 'Adoption: Achieving the Right Balance' (LAC (98) 20) which sets out the principles and the Protocol for Judicial Case Management in Public Law Children Act Cases (2003), has put in place measures for tighter care and case management.

> In *Re D and K (Care Plan: Twin Track Planning) (1999)*, Bracewell J highlighted the problems which arise for the court in cases where the local authority recognizes from an early stage that its care plan presents options of rehabilitation within the natural family or permanency outside the family, but fails to address the option of an adoptive placement until shortly before the substantive court hearing. Likewise the cases of *Re S (Minors) (Care Order: Implementation of Care Plan); Re W (Minors) (Care Order: Adequacy of Care Plan) (2002)* discussed in Chapter 14, considered as wrong the departure from the care plan for interim care orders and the decision of the judge for adoption.

## Overseas adoptions

10.25 There are clear rules and procedures, which govern the adoption of children from outside the UK (see the Adoption (Intercountry Aspects) Act 1999 SI 2005 No 392,The Adoptions with a Foreign Element Regulations 2005; see also Hague Convention below). Anyone wishing to adopt a child from outside the jurisdiction has to apply for an 'eligibility certificate' from a casework team at the Department for Education. Government figures show that in 2003, 286 children were adopted from outside the jurisdiction.

Adoption of a child, especially from developing countries and countries torn apart by war and natural disaster, is often motivated by humanitarian reasons. As Douglas (2003) writes:

> *Within the UK, more than 10,000 unaccompanied children are living with friends, relatives or strangers, having made their way here or having been sent here from abroad. Some will end up in de facto adoptions.*

## The Hague Convention

10.26 Inter-country adoption is regulated by international conventions. The Hague Convention on the Protection of Children and Co-Operation in respect of Inter-country Adoption 1973 governs such adoptions. At the heart of the Hague Convention resides the 'best interests' test. The Adoption (Intercountry Aspects) Act 1999 amends adoption legislation to include inter-country adoption, including the amendment of certain provisions for example, s 11: six months residence required for certain intercountry adoptions; s 12: registration of certain inter-country adoptions; and s 14: restriction on bringing children into the UK for adoption.

This figure had risen to 356 applications in 2008 (applications received by the inter-country adoption casework team 1 January 2003 until 31 December 2008 ).

**Table 10.2** Number of adoption applications (home study assessment reports) received by the Department of Health (year ending 31 March)

| Year | 1996 | 1997 | 1998 | 1990 | 2000 | 2001 | 2002 | 2003 | 2004 |
|------|------|------|------|------|------|------|------|------|------|
| No of applications | 162 | 331 | 212 | 264 | 312 | 326 | 329 | 286 | 326 |

# Conflicting principles: welfare v best interests

10.27 Inter-country adoption is governed not by the principle of child welfare as paramount (UK child law principle) but by the principle of what is in the best interests
of the child. But there is the problem that in inter-country matters, it becomes
impossible to set a common uniform standard applying to all countries with regard
to what is in the best interests of the child. There is no uniform international family
law or child law standard of what is best for children in a multi-cultural, multi-faith
world. Herein lies the paradox and the dilemma that inter-country 'humanitarian'
adoption may, in its rescue mode, gloss over subliminal assumptions about preferring one culture over another.

> In *Re R (No 1) (Inter-Country Adoption) (1999)*, Bracewell J considered just this
> dilemma. In 1993, the wife visited Romania, intending to adopt a child. In July 1994, R's
> natural parents, who had 13 children, agreed that R, who was five years old, suffered with
> a severe squint and was withdrawn, could go with the wife on a visit to the UK. Formal
> consent to a visit for medical treatment was given before a public notary, and the wife
> gave an undertaking to return R to Romania within three months. In September 1994, R
> was registered at a local school, and the husband and wife has begun to set in motion
> an application for adoption of R. The husband and wife made an adoption application on
> the basis of parental consent although they did not have such consent. When that lack of
> consent became apparent the husband and wife amended their application making an
> application to dispense with consent. The natural parents then made an application for R
> to be returned to them under a wardship summons. The husband and wife then subse-
> quently made an application in wardship with care and control to them and they accepted
> the need for R to have contact with the natural family. In deciding the case, that R should
> be a ward of court with care and control to the husband and wife and contact with the
> natural family, Bracewell J applied the welfare test and the welfare checklist, applying CA
> 1989, s 1 and said:
>
> *When considering the placement of AM, the welfare test demands that her parents
> are only displaced if they are unable to provide an adequate quality and standard of
> parenting for her particular needs now and in the future. The case is not a contest
> between a middle-class lifestyle in Wales with all the comforts and advantages,
> and on the other hand poverty and deprivation in Bucharest. Natural parents are
> prima facie the best people to bring up their daughter, whatever their position in life,
> whether they are rich or poor, wise or foolish, intellectual or illiterate. In respect of
> placement, the welfare checklist, s 1 of the Children Act 1989, applies and I propose
> to consider the list.*

(See also *Re K (a Minor) (Adoption: Child Born Outside the Jurisdiction) (1997)*.)

10.28 At the Parliamentary Assembly of the Council of Europe on 26 January (recommendation 1443 (2000)), the Assembly affirmed, 'The purpose of international

adoption must be to provide children with a mother and father in a way that respects their rights, not to enable foreign parents to satisfy their wish for a child at any price' (cited at para 87 in *Singh* referred to in Chapter 9).

## Trafficking in children

10.29  What has become known as 'child trafficking' is now an international problem on a large scale. It is beyond the scope of this chapter to deal with this issue in detail but readers may wish to consult, for example, the UNICEF campaign to end child exploitation (http://www.endchildexploitation.org.uk/).

> In *Haringey London Borough Council v C (E, E, F and High Commissioner of Republic of Kenya Intervening) (2007)*, following the decision in *Haringey London Borough Council v C, E and another (2005)*, the child concerned was placed for adoption, the local authority plan approved and a freeing order made dispensing with parental consent. In this case, the child was the victim of child trafficking and the woman acting in the capacity of the child's mother believed that she had given birth to the child in a miracle birth. At the time of the application the woman believed she was experiencing another spiritual pregnancy. The child, however, was well cared for by the woman and her partner and there was a bond between them. But it was not in the interests of the child to remain in this environment where the adult carers both deluded themselves and continued to do so with regard to the child's origins.

10.30  The Children (Contact) and Adoption Act 2005 considers inter-country adoptions and provides that the Secretary of State can impose restrictions on inter-country adoptions from the country concerned because of practices in a particular country (such as the trafficking of children or the removal of children from their parents without consent) and extends the provision in the earlier Adoption (Intercountry Aspects) Act 1999. Section 84 of the Adoption and Children Act 2002 (ACA 2002) does, however, facilitate the lawful removal of children from the UK for the purpose of adoption overseas, and provides for the making of an order granting parental responsibility to prospective adoptive parents and extinguishing it in every other person.

## Domestic adoptions: who can be adopted and who can adopt?

10.31  A person can only be adopted if he or she is under 19 years of age, although the application must be made before the person is 18 years old. In practice, where a child is 12 years or older then adoption which includes removal from natural parents or foster parents may not be in the best interests of the child and the local authority will look to other alternatives. Of children adopted, only 6 per cent of children are 10 to 15 years of age (see below). Of course, there are exceptions, as in the case below:

> In *Re S and J (Adoption: Non-patrials) (2004)*, the applicants, who were married, returned to the UK with two boys of 12 and 10 years. The applicants said they had found them begging on the streets of Bangladesh. The boys were in fact the half-nephews of the male applicant. Upon discovery, the couple were charged with immigration offences and the authorities intended to deport the boys but the departmental files were lost. Meanwhile, the couple applied for residence and an interim residence order was made. Later, they issued adoption proceedings with the consent of the boys' mothers—the fathers could not be found. The boys wanted to be adopted. The Home Office, at the end of the six-year legal process, opposed adoption and so did the children's guardian. At the time of the hearing the elder boy was nearly 18 years of age, his brother nearly 16 years. The Home Office said the boys could stay in the UK until they were 18 years old and then they would be deported. The court granted applications for adoption, taking the view that although the applicants had misled the authorities, which was conduct to be deprecated, they genuinely sought the psychological advantages for the boys of having a real family and, indeed, this was the only family the boys knew. Those psychological links could best be preserved by adoption, which, unlike residence, was for life.

10.32 Because adoption is not the favoured option where children are older an option is presented in the 'special guardianship' order as this order allows for removal of the child from the natural parents but also retains the child's link with the natural parents and also retains the natural parents 'parental responsibility' for the child.

10.33 The new rules under ACA 2002, s 50, provide that a heterosexual (married or unmarried couple) or homosexual couple may adopt provided that there is sufficient permanency in their relationship—'living as partners in an enduring family relationship' (s 144(4)). (Adoption by a homosexual couple is new, as is adoption by an unmarried heterosexual couple.)

10.34 Under the old law, the courts ingeniously circumvented the statutory restrictions on couples living together by allowing one member of a heterosexual couple to proceed with an adoption application (see eg *Re AB (Adoption: Joint Residence) (1996)*). In this case, Cazalet J made an adoption order in favour of the foster father of a five year-old child together with a joint residence order in favour of both foster parents. Case law also reflects the already changing attitudes towards parenting and suitability based on sexual preference. In *Re W (Adoption: Homosexual Adopter) (1997)*, Singer J held that there was nothing in the Adoption Regulations to prevent a homosexual adopting a child. In this particular case, a 49 year-old lesbian woman in a stable relationship was allowed to adopt a child (cited in Chapter 9).

10.35 Whether heterosexual, homosexual, a married or unmarried couple, or a single person, the prospective adopter must be 21 years old.

## Suitability: who is suitable?

10.36 ACA 2002, s 45 specifies two grounds in assessing the suitability of adopters (see the Adoption Agencies Regulations 2005, SI 2005/389, under s 9). In assessing suitability, the Act specifies:

- *stability and permanence of a relationship (s 45(2));*
- *religious persuasion, racial origin and cultural and linguistic background (s 1(5)).*

The previous adoption law specified only religion (Adoption Act 1976, s 6).

10.37 In addition to the statutory grounds, the adoption agency (local authority or private) may have their own criteria. Under the old law, adoption agencies developed their own views of relevant criteria and excluded certain types of persons, for example, those with children of their own, those who held certain religious views or indeed those with no religious belief, and those who were considered health risks, including smokers and those who were considered to be overweight. Local authorities also put an age limit on prospective adoptive parents, it was set for women, at 35 years, and for men, at 40 years.

> Consider, for example, the situation prevailing in *Re S (A Minor) (Blood Transfusion: Adoption Order Condition) (1994)* where the adoptive parents had to give an undertaking.
>
> Here, the child was five, her mother had committed suicide and the father was no longer around. In 1990, the child was made a ward of court and placed with foster parents. The child was placed with prospective adopters who were Jehovah's witnesses. The prospective adopters gave an undertaking that they would not impede blood transfusion if required by the child. The adopters felt that they made the undertaking under duress and appealed. The court (Staughton LJ) allowed the appeal, on grounds that it was better to leave the child with the family than put her up again for adoption.
>
> The undertaking was rescinded.

Such ad hoc views on suitability have been subject to much criticism. Baroness O'Cathain during the debate on the Adoption and Children Bill preceding the Adoption and Children Act 2002 said:

> *Prior to the Prime Minister's intervention, over 90% of the would be adopters were either turned down or gave up on the process because they had such dreadful experiences of the immensely long drawn out process... Those who were turned*

> *down were sometimes given reasons such as: you are too rich; you are too poor;*
> *you are too fat; you live in too big a house; you have too many books; you go to*
> *church.*

> *(Hansard, Lords Debates, vol 639, col 882, 16 October 2002)*

However by 2010 agencies are much more flexible, less prescriptive, focusing on the quality of care prospective adopters can give a child.

10.38 Any person wishing to proceed with an adoption application must undergo a process of assessment. A home study is carried out by the adoption agency in which the suitability of the prospective adopters is assessed. In *Haringey London Borough Council v MA, JN, IA (2008)*, the court held:

> The home environment did not have to be in England and Wales for the purposes of
> either s 84(4) or s 42(7)(a); there was a valid distinction between cases in which a child
> in the care of the local authority was placed for adoption abroad by that local author-
> ity, and other placements relating to a foreign adoption.

# Matching parents to children and children to parents

10.39 ACA 2002, s 1(5) requires consideration to be given to 'religious persuasion, racial origin and cultural and linguistic background' in the process of matching prospective adoptive parents to children placed for adoption. In *Re C (Adoption: Religious Observance) (2002)*, a child of a mixed background with Jewish, Irish Roman Catholic, and Turkish-Cypriot Muslim elements was placed for adoption with a Jewish couple. The guardian for the child issued proceedings for judicial review of the local authority's decision to place the child with the Jewish couple, arguing that the couple were unsuitable, on the basis that they were 'too Jewish' and that C should be placed in an essentially secular home. The court held that where a child's heritage was very mixed, it would rarely be possible for it all to be reflected in the identity of the adoptive home. Wilson J explained:

> As society becomes increasingly complex with children often having diverse ethnicity
> and cultures in their background, it is even more important that social workers should
> avoid 'labelling' a child and ignoring some elements of his background. Children of
> mixed origin should be helped to understand and take pride in all elements in their
> racial heritage and feel comfortable about their origins.

## Race/ethnicity

10.40 What becomes the paramount factor to be matched where race, ethnicity, culture, and linguistic background are all required considerations is impossible to predict.

Political correctness has driven and shaped previous adoption practice. In the 1970s, for example, white couples adopted black and mixed race children. The Association of Black Social Workers (ABSW) in the 1980s claimed that 'trans-racial placements are a way of perpetuating racist ideology'. Such ideological positions were informed also by the experience of Britain's colonialist history and the efforts of the colonizer to destroy the identity of the colonized. (See F Fanon, *Black Skins, White Masks* (1967) for an analysis of the psychological and psychiatric problems that present as a result of assimilation policies.) Perhaps the problem lies more with the macro and micri implications of assimilationist policies rather than trans-racial adoption per se. Certainly the resistance to trans-racial placement is a viable reaction to colonialism.

10.41 By the 1990s, Paul Boateng (a black African himself), when Labour's Parliamentary Under Secretary of State for Health,, stressed that the welfare and the right to a family life of the black child should transcend arguments about race and the correctness of race matching in adoptive placements. Mr Boateng said:

> *Some local authorities still refuse to place children for adoption because one of the prospective parents is 40-plus, or is deemed the wrong colour, or smokes, or because of the belief that the family must be kept together, no matter what, even at the expense of the child's best interest.*

Of course such placements could work within a spirit of multi-culturalism rather than assimilation.

10.42 The inter-racial adoption debate was to have its effect on courtroom decision-making. In ***Re N (A Minor) (Adoption) (1990)***, a child was born in 1984 of Nigerian parents. The mother placed the child with white foster parents and then went to the USA. The unmarried father also lived in the USA and sought to have contact with the child. In 1987, the foster parents agreed to adopt and to dispense with the mother's agreement. The father applied for care and control. Bush J said:

> *in my view the emphasis on colour rather than cultural upbringing can be mischievous and highly dangerous when you are dealing in practical terms with the welfare of children.*

> ***Re M (Child's Upbringing) (1996)*** (see Chapters 9 and 11): we have already considered separate aspects of this case notably psychological v biological parents in a previous chapters and we revisit it once again in the context of adoption and cultural considerations. In Re B (Adoption: Child's Welfare) (1995), B was born in the Gambia and both the parents were from that country. B came to live with the applicants in England as part of an informal fostering/adoption arrangement. B's parents travelled to England and sought to take her back to the Gambia. The applicants made an application to adopt B. The court, in dismissing the application, held that the test on an adoption application was not the same as that on an application for an order under the CA 1989 in private law proceedings.

Since adoption had the effect of extinguishing parental responsibility, it was right that consideration of an adoption should take into account concepts other than welfare. Of course, this has now changed and welfare is paramount.

10.43 But the importance of these considerations cannot be understated and may, if insufficiently considered or brushed aside, form the basis of an action in damages.

In *Mensah v Islington Council and another (2000)*, an action for damages was brought. Mr Mensah sought damages from the respondents, Islington Council and East Sussex County Council, for psychological damage and an apology from the local authority. In 1966, Mr Mensah, the child of a Nigerian mother and a Ghanaian father, was placed with white foster parents. Mr Mensah's case was that as a result he suffered personality and identity problems. his action failed,.

# Religion: faith

10.44 Religion has always been an important consideration in the matching exercise. Under the Adoption Act 1976, s 6, religion was an important aspect, which is stipulated as a consideration in statute important in (*Agar-Ellis (1883)* and *J v C (1970)*—Chapter 9 above), religious considerations, today, embrace a much wider range of religions and the Christian faith is not arrogated above as more important. But religion must not displace welfare, and its relevance is determined by the meaning it has for the child now and in the future (remember Munby J in *Re S: Newcastle City Council v Z (2007)* cited above).

In *Re P (A Child) (Residence Order: Child's Welfare) (1999)*, a Down's Syndrome child of orthodox Jewish parents was accommodated by the local authority, the parents having accepted that they could not adequately care for her, and since a suitable Jewish family could not be found the child was placed with Catholic foster parents, in a short-term placement. After three years, the court made a residence order to the foster parents and the parents sought the child's return to them. After a further four years, the parents applied for a variation of the residence order and return of the child. The court made a further order restricting future applications without leave of court under CA 1989, s 91(14). The parents appealed contending (i) that a child had a presumptive right to be brought up by its own parents and in its own religion and that the judge had failed to give sufficient weight to N's religious and cultural heritage; (ii) that the judge had erred in principle in his approach to contact; and (iii) that the judge should not have made an order under s 91(14). The court said:

*In considering the relevance and importance of the religious element in this appeal, I agree with Mr Ryder that s 1(3)(d) of the 1989 Act, which requires a court to have regard to the background of a child, includes a child's religious and cultural heritage. It is a relevant consideration, the weight of which will vary according to the facts of each case. In the present case, it is an important factor. No one would wish to deprive a Jewish child of her right to her Jewish heritage. If she had remained with a Jewish family it would be almost unthinkable, other than in an emergency, to remove her from it. I have no doubt, like the judge, that the orthodox Jewish religion provides a deeply satisfying way of life for its members and that this child, like other Down's syndrome children, would have flowered and prospered in her Jewish family and surroundings if she had continued to live with them. But in the unusual circumstances of this case her parents were not able to accommodate her within her community. The combination of the family illness and difficulties together with N's real medical problems as a young child made it impossible for her to be cared for within her family circle and it was then, not now, that she was deprived of her opportunity to grow up within the Jewish community. The uncontradicted evidence of the way Down's syndrome children are cared for in the orthodox Jewish community, which I do not doubt for a moment, is not relevant to the issue whether N can move.*

*The judge, faced with contradictory evidence about N's capacity to understand and appreciate the Jewish religion, rejected the partisan evidence of Professor Feuerstein, and accepted the evidence of Professor Sacks as to her limited ability. With enormous care he considered all the evidence and the advantages to N of a return to her family culture and his carefully reasoned conclusion on the first issue cannot, in my judgment, be attacked. This court cannot go behind his findings. The undoubted importance for an orthodox Jew of his religion which provides in itself a way of life which permeates all activities, is a factor to be put in the balancing exercise, particularly in considering the welfare of the daughter of a rabbi. But N's religious and cultural heritage cannot be the overwhelming factor in this case for the reasons set out by the judge nor can it displace other weighty welfare factors.*

10.45 Of course there is not a uniform solution to resolving religion, race, culture, and linguistic issues in adoption cases. The age and intellectual capacity of the child is an important consideration. To a very young child religion will be less of a consideration, however clearly some aspects of a child's identity are more enduring.

## Review of suitability decisions

10.46 ACA 2002, s 45 provides for the regulation of agency decisions in respect of suitability. A system of review introduced by the ACA 2002 ensures that what are called 'qualifying determinations', which are decisions which conclude that a prospective applicant is unsuitable, are subject to an independent review. In addition, there is a formal complaints mechanism and prospective adopters can make a complaint to the local authority.

10.47 Research has shown that objections are grouped around three main subject areas; these related to the prospective adopter's health, their parenting capacity or as a result of information supplied by referees.

10.48 Judicial review of the decision of adoption agencies is available where prospective adopters are considered unsuitable. However, judicial review is limited.

> In *R v Lancashire County Council (1992)* the foster parents sought to challenge the local authority, which had removed the child from their care following the implementation of a new policy which was to prevent children for adoption being placed with prospective adopters from a different cultural background from the natural parents. The foster parents were refused leave to bring the case for judicial review as they had failed to establish that the local authority was behaving unreasonably. *In R (W) v Leicestershire County Council (2003)*, twins were placed with the short-term foster mother. She was single and had one child of a similar age. The foster mother wanted to adopt. The local authority found that the foster mother could not meet the children's long-term needs because she did not get on with social workers or with teachers; she had bonded well with the boy but not especially with the girl; the ambivalent attitude of the father of her own child to the twins; and her uncertain handling of sexual abuse disclosures by the twins. The local authority removed the twins under the Adoption Act 1976, s 30(1) before those powers were superseded by the foster mother's issue of an application for an adoption order. (The foster mother was refused leave for judicial review.)

## Court orders

10.49 The two orders the court can make with regard to adoption are:

- a placement order, and
- an adoption order.

## Placement order

10.50 A placement order (ACA 2002, s 21) is an order authorizing a local authority to place a child for adoption which can only be made where the child is subject to a care order (s 21(2)(a)). In addition, a placement order can only be made either where there is parental consent, or if there is no parental consent then the court has already deemed that the circumstances are such (the welfare test is met) that parental consent can be dispensed with or else the parents cannot be found or where there is no parent or guardian. Without a placement order or the consent of the parents a child cannot be placed for adoption (s 18(1)). In *Re S–H (A Child) Placement Order (2008)*, here, the court held, per Wilson LJ:

> *1. This unusual case demonstrates that it will occasionally be proper for the court to grant a parent leave to apply to revoke a placement order under s.24(2)(a) of the*

*Adoption and Children Act 2002 ('the Act') notwithstanding the absence at present of any real prospect that a court would find it to be in the interests of the child to return to live with the parent.*

## The consent issue

10.51 The aspiration in adoption law is that the birth parents should give their consent before an order for placement or adoption is made. In reality however, parents rarely willingly give their consent, although they may acknowledge that it is in the child's best interests for adoption to take place and they may also accept that they are not able to care for their child adequately. Where parents consent and accede, ACA 2002, s 19 provides for placing the child. It is intended that parental consent will be witnessed by an officer of the Children and Family Court Advisory and Support Service (CAFCASS) to ensure that the parents are truly consenting. Where there is consent, this allows placement without a court order. What is true consent?

10.52 Consent is required of all those with parental responsibility. Where the unmarried father has parental responsibility (see CA 1989, s 4(1); ACA 2002, s 111) then his agreement is also required. However, the difference under the current law is that fewer unmarried fathers will not have parental responsibility than was hitherto the case, this is because ACA 2002, s 111 now provides that if the father's name is on the birth certificate then the father acquires parental responsibility automatically. Fewer fathers will now have to apply for parental responsibility orders and also more unmarried fathers will need to be approached for their consent before that consent can be dispensed with. Although the unmarried father's right is not absolute, nor is any other party's since consent is dispensed with if the welfare of the child requires it.

10.53 ACA 2002, s 52 also provides for dispensing with consent where the parent or guardian cannot be found or is incapable of giving consent. However, the right of the absent father is not absolute as the case below demonstrates:

> In *Re J (Adoption: Contacting Father) (2003)*, an unmarried 17 year-old became pregnant. She had never cohabited with the father. The father left the area and the mother did not tell him that she was pregnant. After the child's birth, she put the child up for adoption. The child had cystic fibrosis, as did the father's brother's child. The social worker pressurized the mother to reveal the name of the child's father. She assured the mother that the information would only be revealed if and when the child required it as an adult; the father would not be told. The mother reluctantly agreed to give the information. Immediately, the local authority sought declarations under Art 8 that it was in the child's best interests for the father to be informed of his existence, and that it was lawful for it to inform the father,

notwithstanding the mother's objection. The court was concerned to protect the mother from any possible abusive conduct and held that Art 8 was not engaged because her relationship with the child's father had been transitory and insubstantial.

## Dispensing with consent?

10.54 The court can dispense with the consent of parents if the welfare of the child requires it, but it must be in accordance with one of the two statutory grounds. The first ground (s 52(2)(a)) is where the parent or guardian cannot be found or is incapable of giving consent. The second ground (s 52(2)(b)) is where the welfare of the child requires the consent to be dispensed with. However, this seems to be insufficiently clear since a simple welfare test is too broad and vague and may be very disadvantageous to natural parents.

10.55 Courts have historically moved through three positions on this issue. First, consent could be dispensed with if it was considered that the refusal by the parent was ' unreasonable'. Second, consent could be dispensed with where the welfare of the child required it. Third, there is a swinging back of the pendulum where the right of the natural parent is now given more weight with the application of Art 8 ECHR but does not trump rights of adoptive parents as in *Oxfordshire County Council v X,Y and J (2010)*.

### The case law on 'unreasonableness'

10.56 There is a considerable body of case law on the point with regard to whether the refusal of consent is reasonable or not. This includes: *Re W (An Infant) (1971)*; *Re L (An infant) (1962)*; *Re P (An Infant) (Adoption: Parental; Consent) (1977)*; *Re H (Infants) (Adoption: Parental Consent) (1977)*; *Re M (Minors) (Adoption Parental Agreement) (1985)*; *Re H, Re W (Adoption Parental Agreement) (1983)*; *Re F (A Minor) (Adoption Parental Consent) (1982)*; *and Re V (A Minor) (1987)*. In Re W *(1971)* (above) where the mother withdrew her consent, her appeal to the Court of Appeal was upheld on the ground that her conduct had not been culpable or blame-worthy. A finding overturned by the House of Lords, per Lord Hailsham:

> Section 16.2.b. lays down a test of reasonableness. It does not lay down a test of culpability or self-indulgent indifference or failure or probable failure of paren-tal duty. It is not for the courts to embellish, alter, subtract from, or add to the words which, for once at least;...Parliament has employed without any ambigu-ity at all.... The test...is reasonableness not culpability..."From this it is clear that the test is reasonableness and not anything else. It is not culpability. It is not indifference. It is not failure to discharge parental duties. It is reasonable-ness and reasonableness in the context of the totality of the circumstances. But although welfare per se is not the test, the fact that a reasonable parent does pay regard to the welfare of his child must enter into the question of reasonableness

*as a relevant factor. It is relevant in all cases if and to the extent that a reasonable parent would take it into account. It is decisive in those cases where a reasonable parent must so regard it.*

The construct of reasonable and unreasonable in these cases was hugely subjective and elusive although welfare was considered as a part of this. Bainham (2005, 292) noted that 'after *Re W* the courts have attached more significance to the welfare of the child and to dispense with consent more readily'.

> In *Re B (A Minor) (Adoption: Parental Agreement) (1990)*, Butler-Sloss LJ held:
>
> *. . . the question then arises as to whether this court should substitute its own discretion upon the facts before us . . . In our judgment, a reasonable parent in the position of the mother would recognise the overwhelming force of the negative points and the unreasonableness of refusing to agree to the freeing for adoption. We therefore, hold that the mother has unreasonably withheld her agreement under s 16.2.*
>
> Again in *Re AB (A Minor) (Adoption: Parental Consent) (1996)*, where the mother refused consent to adoption the court said the test was actually objective:
>
> *I bear in mind that the test to be applied is an objective one in the light of the facts of each individual case 'what would a reasonable parent in the position of this mother consider to be appropriate' it follows therefore that in deciding whether refusal is unreasonable, all the circumstances which would weigh with a reasonable parent are to be considered. Including the child's prospects if adopted as compared with those if not adopted.*

10.57 These earlier cases continue to inform the reasoning of the courts when considering whether to dispense with consent under s 52(1)(b) of the Adoption and Children Act 2002 where the central question is no longer the elusive reasonable/unreasonable parent but whether the welfare of the child requires consent to be dispensed with. For example, in ***Down Lisburn Health and Social Services Trust v H and another (2007)*** the mother was an alcoholic and unable to care adequately for her youngest child who was four. The child was put up for adoption and the parents' consent dispensed with. The judge agreed that the child should have contact three or four times a year with her natural parents. The Court of Appeal agreed that the parents' consent should be dispensed with. The parents appealed to the House of Lords that their withholding of agreement to adoption was not unreasonable when it had not been known whether post-adoption contact arrangements could be made.

> The court held that when deciding to dispense with a parent's refusal to consent, the standard to be applied was an objective standard of reasonableness. Baroness Hale said:
>
> *I recognise, of course, that just as there is a band of reasonable parental decisions each of which may be reasonable in any given case, there is a band of reasonable judicial decisions, each of which may be reasonable in any given case. Just as a*

*judge should be careful not to substitute his own view for another view which a reasonable parent could take, an appellate judge must be careful not to substitute her own view for one which a reasonable judge could take. I pay tribute to the care with which the judge approached his anxious and difficult task and to the very important shift in attitudes which his interventions produced. But in my view he placed considerable weight upon an irrelevant consideration when deciding that the parents were unreasonably withholding their agreement at that stage. Perhaps because of the beneficial movement he had secured, he did not take into account the other legal options available in seeking to achieve the best possible outcome for this little girl. I do not, of course, suggest that post-freeing and post-adoption contact are appropriate in every case or that uncertainty about whether contact will be possible is always a good reason for withholding consent. But they are often important factors both for the parents and for the judge to consider.*

*I myself would allow the appeal and set aside the freeing order.*

(**See also** *Re P (Children) (Adoption: Parental Consent) (2008)* in this case the father appealed against placement orders and the appeal was dismissed, and *R (W) v Brent London Borough Council (2010)*.)

## Adoption order

10.58 Under ACA 2002, s 46, an adoption order is made by the court on an application under s 50 or s 51 which gives parental responsibility for the child to adopter(s). An adoption order can be made by the High Court, county court or magistrates' court. The application must be made at the court in the district where the child lives.

10.59 No order can be made without the child attending the hearing, unless there are special circumstances.

10.60 An adoption order gives parental responsibility to the adopters. Each parent or guardian must be 'joined' as a party ('respondents') as well as the adoption agency whether local authority or voluntary organization which has care of the child. Adoption documents are confidential. If the adoption is refused, the child must be returned to the adoption agency within seven days of the order. The agency will then try to find another suitable placement.

10.61 The court can also make a short-term order, which gives the applicants parental responsibility for a period of not more than two years.

10.62 The court can attach conditions to the adoption order, such as allowing the natural parent to have contact with the child (see *A Local Authority V Y, Z and others (2006)*), or attaching conditions with regard to, say, the child's religious upbringing. This development of permitting contact with birth relatives is of recent origin.

## No order for adoption, or alternatives

10.63 The ACA 2002, like the CA 1989, requires the court to be satisfied that the order it makes is better than an alternative order or better than making no order at all (s 1(6)). Therefore, in adoption the court is required to consider all alternatives and, given the new philosophy towards open adoption, will now be looking to maintain links between the child and the natural family (s 1(4)). The court must always consider all the options.

Consider the case below.

> In *Re K (Children) (Adoption: Freeing Order) (2004)*, the parents were married in India, in 2001 when the mother was 18 years old. The mother came to England to live with the father in his parents' household. They had two children, A and M. In 2003, A was admitted to hospital, where medical staff concluded that she had suffered non-accidental injuries. The mother alleged that she did not know how the injuries had been caused.... A care order was made in relation to A and she was freed for adoption. By that time, M had been born and had been removed from her mother under an interim care order. The court then made a full care order in relation to M and an order freeing her for adoption. The mother subsequently left her husband and took up residence in a refuge. She made statements alleging that the grandmother had been violent and cruel towards her and suggesting that the grandmother had shaken A. The mother appealed against the freeing orders made in relation to both children and sought the replacement of the full care orders by interim care orders pending a reconsideration of the question of the perpetrator of the injuries to A. The court held that it was in the public interest for those who caused serious non-accidental injuries to children to be identified, wherever such identification was possible. It was paradigmatic of such cases that the perpetrator denied responsibility and that those close to, or emotionally engaged with, the perpetrator likewise denied any knowledge of how the injuries occurred. Accordingly, having regard to the circumstances of the case, the orders freeing both children for adoption would be set aside and the children would be made the subject of interim care orders in favour of the local authority. The question of the identity of the perpetrator of the non-accidental injuries to A would be remitted to a judge at first instance for further investigation and reconsideration. Accordingly, the appeal was allowed.

## Special guardianship as an alternative

10.64 Special guardianship was to provide for children who could not return home. As Mitchell (2007) observes, 'Special guardianship is less intrusive on the family life of the birth family than adoption'. The Department for Education and Skills 2005 issued some regulations, 'Special Custodianship Guidance' where special guardianship can be an outcome of care proceedings where the child is to stay with extended family. Natural parents can apply for a variation but only with the leave of the court and where there are exceptional circumstances. (CA 1989, ss 14A–F were inserted by ACA 2002, s 115(1) and came fully into effect on 30 December 2005, see also the consequential Special Guardianship Regulations 2005 (SI 2005/1109).

> In *A Local Authority v Y, Z and others (2006)*, for example, special guardianship orders were made in respect of three children. The Deputy High Court Judge said:
>
> *Special guardianship, therefore, operates as follows. It creates parental responsibility—the bundle of rights and duties a parent has in respect of a child—in the special guardian or guardians. The parental responsibility already vested in others—in this case the mother—is not extinguished. However, whereas parental responsibility is normally a matter for exercise in partnership between those holding it, under a special guardianship it is exercised exclusively by the special guardian or guardians. That principle is subject to limitations. One of these is that the order may be varied or discharged. However, before a parent may obtain the exercise of the court's power in this respect, he or she must obtain permission of the court to bring an application. Moreover, as there are no relevant amendments to ss 8 or 10 of the 1989 Act, another limitation appears to be that the parent may continue to apply for a s 8 order in respect of a child without seeking leave, notwithstanding that the child is subject to a special guardianship order. This was debated during submissions and all counsel suggested that this was the case. I agree this appears to be so and any special guardianship order is certainly made 'subject to any order in force with respect to the child under this Act'* (see s 14C (1)(b) 44).

The special guardianship order has been subject to several appeals (see *Re R (A Child) (Special Guardianship Order) (2007)*; *Re J (Special Guardianship) (2007)*; *Re M-J (Special Guardianship Order) (2007)*. Special guardians are entitled to financial support. This issue was the point of appeal in the following case: *B v Kirklees Metropolitan Council (2010)*.

### Leave to discharge

10.65 In *Re G (A Child) (Special Guardianship Order: Leave to Discharge) (2010)*, the matter of an application made by the mother for leave to discharge a special guardianship order in favour of the maternal grandmother, the application was refused but later allowed on the basis of evidence of change in the mother's circumstances and behaviour. See also Hall, 2008.

10.66 In fact, about one-quarter of all original applications for adoption fail and a residence order under CA 1989, ss 8(3), 10(1) may be made instead. The CA 1975 provided alternative orders including joint custody or custodianship and courts were required to make these orders when they were considered to be better for the child than making an adoption order. Following the Adoption Act 1975 there was a decline in adoption orders which affected step-parents although the CA 1989 repealed the restriction.

10.67 The ACA 2002 has reverted to provision of a variety of alternative orders. This is because the pendulum has swung in favour of retaining links with the natural family, also permitting the retention of parental responsibility by the natural family, and facilitating and maintaining links with other relatives (see the report by J Masson, D Norbury, and SG Chatterton, *Mine, Yours or Ours: a Study of Step Parent Adoption* (HMSO, 1983): the issue may well have been that the child in the past lost all links with natural grandparents). The question of Art 8, the right to family life, is more pressing.

# Human rights—adoption and the family

10.68 Adoption has historically been considered as a course of very last resort, as the case below demonstrates. However, it will be suggested later in this chapter that this may no longer be the case.

> In *Re H (A Minor) (Care or Residence Order) (1994)*, there were two children, K, who was three years of age and G, who was two. There was a third child who was born in 1985 and who had been made the subject of a care order in 1986. He had been placed for adoption following a failed rehabilitation with the mother. Following K's birth, the local authority commenced care proceedings because of the mother's drug abuse and related offending. In July 1992, the mother was committed to prison. G was looked after by her father and K was cared for by her maternal great-grandparents. The children were later placed with a maternal aunt. In May 1993, the mother was released from prison and the children were returned to her care. The care plan of the local authority was for adoption. The magistrates granted a care order to the local authority regarding G, K already being subject to a care order. In January 1994, leave was given to the children to appeal against the order through their guardian ad litem (now children's guardian). The court allowed the appeal:
>
> *There was no evidence before the magistrates upon which they could come to the conclusion that neither of the grandparents could meet the severe demands of parenting the children. The witness-box in a court of law was not the best place in which to assess people, and the magistrates had not given convincing reasons for disagreeing with the guardian ad litem. The magistrates had not appeared to carry out any balancing exercise. They concentrated on the demerits of the grandparents, but did not mention anywhere the risks of attempting to place the children for adoption. Adoption was in reality a course of last resort.*

(See also *Re H (Freeing Orders: Publicity) (2006)*; *Re C (Care Proceedings: Disclosure of Local Authority's Decision-Making Process) (2002)*.)

# Back to back care to adoption: local authority

10.69 Adoption of children already in care is the main route into adoption. Figures published by British Association for Adoption & Fostering 3,300 children were adopted from care during the year ending 31 March 2009. Adoption, says Bainham (2005, 306),

> ...represents the best solution for long-term care but it is only one of the possible solutions.' The practice from care to adoption was influenced by empirical evidence that many children in long-term care of local authorities could never look forward to the prospect of a permanent home. The Waterhouse Report recommended that the government should promote the use of adoption for 'looked after children'.

At the same time however, there is a concern that adoption may be being used as a means of fast-tracking children already in the care system by providing, perhaps too quickly, a permanent solution. Certainly, a balance must be struck between the policy desire to settle a child permanently too soon, and settling a child too late or not at all.

Lewis (2004) argues that the new emphasis on adoption in preference to care raises in an acute form the issue of the evidence base. Deborah Cullen (2005), of the Legal Group of the British Association for Adoption and Fostering (BAAF) observes that in the last few years there has been an increase in the use of 'freeing applications' 'back to back' with care proceedings. She notes '...from next year on it will be commonplace to have placement order applications brought within care proceedings. For those local authorities and courts familiar with freeing applications running concurrently with care proceedings, it will perhaps be a shock to the system, but for others it will constitute a significant "new approach"'.

10.70 There is also a concern that because adoption is a cheaper option for a local authority this consideration may be given too much weight. In *Re F (Adoption: Welfare of Child: Financial Considerations) (2004)*, because of neglect at home, interim care orders were made in respect of five siblings. They went into two separate foster placements. The local authority decided that the girls should remain with their foster parents long term, and the boys, aged seven, six, and four years old, should be placed for adoption. Adoption by their foster family was not an option since the foster parents were not able to manage without the foster care payments. The local authority argued it could not pay for the fostering placement to continue at the current rate (nearly £131,000 per annum; of which the foster parents received £53,000). The court dismissed the local authority's application for a freeing order and invited the local authority to reconsider its position on funding the children's placement with their current foster parents. It was held that, although as a general principle adoption had more to offer children, and particularly younger children, than long-term foster care, it was not in the interests of these particular children to abandon the known and loving family they were living in and to step into the unknown in pursuit of the benefit of adoption with as yet unidentified adopters. The risks of that course were too great and too likely to materialize, and the boys might never in fact feel the benefits. It was in their best interests to stay where they were, albeit that this could only be a fostering placement.

10.71 Adoption now places the welfare of the child as paramount but what exactly is the welfare of the child? Stability and permanence are emphasized in the legislation, which has become the 'Holy Grail credo', but at exactly what price? And, is it right at a time of developing human rights to brush aside and dispense with the right of the parent to a family life by dispensing with the consent of the parent to adoption if the welfare of the child requires it when that welfare test can be interpreted so broadly? And what value is placed in these considerations on the prospect of rehabilitation with the natural family? If rehabilitation some time in the future was a priority, then fewer children would be put up for adoption.

Can we measure how far stability and permanence in a placement and adoption, versus instability in the interim with the prospect of rehabilitation even in the future, is better for child development long term? As Lewis (2004) writes:

> *Rowe and Lambert's (1973) study of 'children who wait' in care emphasised the importance of rehabilitation with birth families, but also called for a 'revolution' in thinking about the possibility of adoption for older children. Tizard's (1977) research on children adopted from care between the ages of two and seven reported good outcomes compared to those for children who were fostered, sent to residential care or returned to their birth families.*

## Welfare test in adoption: family human rights

10.72 The welfare test under ACA 2002, s 1, is now paramount. The welfare of the child, whatever that is taken to mean, is sufficient to remove a child from its natural parents without their consent.

10.73 But why is it that the child's welfare in the past was only first and not paramount? Hayes and Williams (1999, 333) write, 'The reason why the child's welfare is not paramount is because the welfare test in adoption is bound up with the question whether the objection of a parent to his or her child being adopted can ever be reasonable.' Indeed, the working party, 'Report to Ministers Department of Health and Welsh Office, Review of Adoption Law, Report to Ministers of an Interdepartmental Working Group, A Consultation Document' (1992) recommended that the child's welfare should not be paramount in deciding whether to dispense with the parents' consent to adoption.

10.74 Whilst the elevation of the welfare of the child to 'paramount' under the ACA 2002 silenced those critics who argued that hitherto adoption law was out of line with the UN Convention on the Rights of the Child (UNCRC) 1989, which asserts that states parties permitting adoption are to ensure that the best interests of the child are the paramount consideration, it may now be found that the welfare test for dispensing with parental consent is so broad and vague as to be a hostage to human rights abuses.

> In *Re W (Children) (Care: Interference with Family Life) (2005)*, the parents of twins born in 2000 encountered difficulties in the parenting of their older children, so in February 2004, care orders were made by consent in respect of the twins, which ensured that the twins would remain at home with their parents. The father had alcoholism problems and had failed to attend a local treatment centre. The local authority concluded that the twins could not be safely parented at home. On 25 October, the local authority issued an application to free the twins for adoption. The parents subsequently applied for an injunction under the Human Rights Act 1998, to have the children returned to them. The judge dismissed both the parents' applications and adjourned the application to free the twins for adoption, pending further recommendations by the guardian. The parents appealed. The parents submitted, *inter alia*, that the removal of the twins from their natural home had been draconian, unnecessary, and disproportionate to the concerns ventilated at the earlier meetings, and that, in the circumstances, the judge had failed to have regard to the parents' and children's Convention rights. The appeal was dismissed.

# Debate

10.75 There is a concern that adoption is now becoming an automatic option for local authority when a child is received into care. It is worth reflecting on the duty of local authority to support families in partnership and in voluntary agreements (discussed in Chapter 14 and 15).

10.76 It is also worth reflecting on the financial costs of long-term fostering support, which may provide a route back to rehabilitation with the natural family, compared with adoption. There will certainly also be fall-out from a welfare test which, in prioritizing the welfare of the child, can too readily dispense with parental consent. Courts and local authorities will face a difficult task of not usurping the right of the child or the right of the parent to family life. Consider for instance the following case, which raises the rights of family members to children.

> In *Re C-B (A Child) (Care Proceedings: Human Rights Claim) (2004)*, the proceedings concerned a four year-old child, L. The local authority had initially been fully supportive of the placement of L with his maternal aunt. The local authority's social worker

had filed a statement to that effect on 27 April 2004. However, on 6 May, the local author-ity's fostering panel rejected the aunt and her partner as long-term foster parents of L. On 25 May, the aunt met her legal representatives and counsel took initial instructions. The aunt applied for an adjournment. The judge refused that application, and on 27 May delivered judgment rejecting the aunt's application for a residence order and granting a care order in respect of L in favour of the local authority on the basis of the care plan for adoption.

The aunt appealed against that decision on the grounds that, in the circumstances, the judge's refusal of her application for an adjournment had amounted to a breach of her right to a fair trial pursuant to Art 6 of the ECHR. The appeal was allowed and a retrial directed.

10.77 In this context, it is worth reflecting on the earlier debates prior to 2002 in which, although some were critical of the fact that in adoption law the welfare of the child was not paramount, it was argued that such an anomaly was nevertheless perfectly fair since the parental right should also be considered. These positions may now have some renewed support given that Art 8 (the right to family life) of the ECHR also embraces the right of parents as well as children. There is a concern that adoption law can ride too readily over parental rights if 'the welfare of the child requires it'. The 'if the welfare of the child requires it' threshold is considered to be too general and potentially too draconian when after all adoption is final (see, for discussion of these earlier debates, Bainham, 2005, 291).

## Adoption and the former family

10.78 'A new form of adoption, termed "open adoption", ACA 2002, s 1(4)) is developing where links with the former family are retained' (Cretney and Masson, 2003, 875).

There are different forms of openness eg involvement of the birth parents with the selection of adoptive parents, indirect contact with the child after adoption, contact with the child after adoption and provisions for the discovery of birth parents.

### Contact with parents

10.79 In furthering the objective of contact with natural parents where appropriate, con-sider *Re P (1994)*, where the mother suffered from schizophrenia. The local author-ity applied to free the twins for adoption without the mother's consent. The judge dispensed with the mother's consent but made an order to the mother for contact.

# Contact with siblings

10.80 The ACA 2002 completely reverses the position that pertained in the case below.

> In *Re C (1988)*, an application was made by a foster parent to adopt a girl of 13 in care of the local authority. The girl was in care with her younger brother and she was attached to him. The court took the view that it did not have the power to make a condition of contact with the brother on the adoption order. The House of Lords, however, said that an adoption order could be made with a condition of contact with the younger brother. However, their Lordships re-affirmed that it was usual to have a permanent and final break. Lord Ackner added:
>
> *The court will not, except in the most exceptional case, impose terms or conditions as to access to members of the child's natural family to which the adopting parents do not agree. To do so would be to create a potentially frictional situation which would be hardly likely to safeguard or promote the welfare of the child. Indeed in Re S (a minor) (adopted child: contact) [1999] 1 All ER 648 an application was made by a girl (Y), who was nine and who was acting by her next friend and adoptive mother (Mrs M), for leave to bring proceedings for a contact order under s 8 of the Children Act 1989. The judge said: If I give leave, Y as the applicant would seek an order that she has contact with her half-brother (S), who is seven and was represented before me by the Official Solicitor acting as his guardian ad litem. For the reasons set out in this judgment I refuse such leave.*

Modern thinking on adoption considers contact with siblings, but it seems still to be the exception.

> In *Re R (Adoption: Contact) (2006)*, the mother could not care for the child, and she had been cared for instead by her half sister, who was 17. The child was placed for adoption but her half sister wanted contact. The adoption panel recommended direct contact of three times per year. The half sister considered this insufficient. She was refused leave to apply for a contact order. The court held that contact was unusual. Wall LJ said:
>
> *So contact is more common, but nonetheless the jurisprudence I think is clear. The imposition on prospective adopters of orders for contact with which they are not in agreement is extremely, and remains extremely, unusual.*

# Human rights and former family—identity, discovery and information

10.81 The Registrar General is required to keep records on natural parents so it is possible for the adopted child to trace the original birth registration. Since 1975, 70,000 adults who were adopted in 'out of family' adoptions have received their original birth records. After 1976, adopted adults may have access to this information and those who want such information are provided with counselling, since mothers who were ensured confidentiality may not wish the babies they once placed for adoption, now adults, to come into their lives. Clare Short (discussed above) had indicated that if her son ever wished to contact her, she also desired such a reunion.

10.82    The ACA 2002 provides no absolute right to birth records on the part of the adopted child, however. If there are public policy reasons, the Registrar General can refuse such access, as in the case of the conviction of a son for murder, as in *R v Registrar General, ex parte Smith (1991)*, below.

> Here, the applicant who was 31 was adopted as a baby. He had no knowledge of his parents. He was suffering from a psychotic illness. In 1977 he was convicted of murder and in 1979, killed a fellow prisoner whom he believed was his adoptive mother. In 1987, he instructed solicitors to apply for access to his birth records; his application was refused on public policy grounds. The Divisional Court dismissed his application for judicial review and the Court of Appeal dismissed his appeal.

> In *D v Registrar General (1996)*, the natural mother sought information about the well being of her child who had been adopted and the local authority refused to supply that information. She applied to the Registrar General in order that such information should be provided to her. The test for authorizing such disclosure was that it was of benefit to the adopted person rather than the birth family. The application was dismissed.

The focus of the openness debate in recent years, however, has rested on the child's right to know his or her genetic identity and it is this issue which has driven open adoption in current adoption law and practice.

## Human rights: genetic identity

10.83    It is interesting that, at a time when the family is multifaceted and clearly about relationships rather than blood ties, genetic identity seems to loom large in public policy and law. The Houghton Report considered this to be important in 1972. Human rights legislation and the UNCRC 1989 reinforced the right of a child to know his or her history and biological origins:

> *Article 7: Each child should be registered immediately after birth, and has the right from birth to a name, to acquire a nationality, and as far as possible to know and be cared for by his or her parents.*

> *Article 8: Each child has the right to preserve his or her identity, including nationality, name and family relations as recognised by law, without unlawful interference.*

> *Article 9: Children shall not be separated from their parents against their will, unless competent authorities which are subject to judicial review determine through the applicable legislation and procedures that such separation is necessary for the best interests of the child. All parties to such procedures shall be given an opportunity to participate in the proceedings and to make their views known. A child*

*separated from one or both parents has the right to maintain personal relations and direct contact with both parents on a regular basis, unless this is contrary to the child's best interests. Where separation results from state action such as detention, imprisonment, deportation or exile, the state shall provide essential information about the absent family member's whereabouts to the child or another member of the child's family on request, unless to do so would be detrimental to the child's well being.*

## Human rights and the meaning of family life

10.84 We return once again to *Singh* (discussed in Chapter 9).

In this case the son and his natural parents were born in India. The son's father's cousin adopted the son in India shortly after his birth with the deed of adoption being recognized under Hindu law but not UK law. The son applied to the British High Commission for entry clearance to the UK but his application to join his sponsors (his adoptive parents, who were British citizens) was refused. It was argued on appeal before the adjudicator that this refusal was a breach of Arts 8 and 14. The court held that the adjudicator had been entitled to hold that family life had been established within Art 8(1) and that there had been and was evidence of family life. The appeal was allowed. Dyson LJ, held that family life had been established and referred to the considerable body of Strasbourg opinion. The adjudicator found that family life had been established although the tribunal found it had not because 'the respondent and his sponsors... have not been shown to have created that lasting psychological bond necessary to the existence of family life'. Munby J said:

*We must be cautious before setting too high a benchmark for the existence of family life, certainly where there is the constancy and commitment which these parents have shown to a boy who is emotionally and psychologically their son.*

## Human rights, family life and adoption

10.85 In considering adoption Art 8, family life, is engaged and failure to consider this right will provide a basis for criticism and overruling a decision of the lower court.

In *Re A (Children) (Fact-finding Hearing: Care Order) (2010)*, a mother was in a relationship with an abusive partner who was father to the chidren. The mother agreed to separate from him but was seen with him at a later stage (there was however some dispute as to eye witness identification).

A full care order was made on behalf of the authority and a placement order in respect of the two children. The mother appealed. The Court of Appeal criticized the judge in the court of first instance:

*The failure to mention article 8 of the Convention was flawed. In a case where the care plan led to adoption the full expression of the terms of art 8 had to be explicit in judgment because, ultimately, there could be no greater interference with family life. The judge should have turned his mind to the established attachment to a loving mother who, with targeted assistance, might be able to provide some form of future mothering. Where the positive features of a parents' care had been highlighted, it was only proper that steps be taken to foster and support the positives so that rehabilitation was given a reasonable prospect of success (see [57]–[59], [62] and [64] of the judgment).*

## FURTHER READING

Bainham A, *Children: the Modern Law* (3rd edn, Family Law, 2005)

Bamforth N, 'The Benefits of Marriage in All But Name'? Same-sex Couples and the Civil Partnership Act 2004' [2007] CFLQ 133

Cretney S and Masson J, *Principles of Family Law* (Sweet and Maxwell, 2003)

Cullen, D, 'Adoption—A (Fairly) New Approach' [2005] CFLQ (17) 4

Department of Health, *Adoption: Achieving the Right Balance* (CI (2000), LAC (98)20)

Douglas G, *Adoption: Changing Families, Changing Times* (Routledge, 2003)

Fanon F, *Black Skins, White Masks* (Grove Press, 1967)

Hall A, 'Special Guardianship and Permanency Planning: Unforeseen Consequences and Missed Opportunities' [2008] CFLQ 359

Hayes M and Williams C, *Family Law: Principles, Policy and Practice* (Butterworths, 1999)

Hershman and McFarlane, *Children Act Handbook* (Jordan, 2007)

Hoggett B, *Parents and Children* (4th edn, Sweet and Maxwell, 1993)

Lewis J, 'Adoption: the Nature of Policy Shifts in England and Wales' (2004) 18 International Journal of Law, Policy and the Family 235

Masson J, Norbury D and Chatterton SG, *Mine, Yours or Ours: a Study of Step Parent Adoption* (HMSO, 1983)

*Report of the Departmental Committee on the Adoption of Children* (Home Office, Scottish Education Department) (Cmnd 5107, 1972), The Houghton Report

Tizard B, *Adoption: a Second Chance* (Open Books, 1977)

Triseliotis J, 'Maintaining the Links in Adoption' (1991) British Journal of Social Work 21 401–414.

## SELF-TEST QUESTIONS

1  How different are the children placed for adoption today compared with the children so placed in the 1920s?

2  How far has adoption law changed in response to the needs of children being placed for adoption?

3  Explain the circumstances in which a parent's consent to adoption will be dispensed with. Is the test under the ACA 2002 sufficiently specific? Remembering that '...(It) ought to be recognised by all concerned with adoption cases that once formal consent has been given or perhaps once the child has been placed with adopters, time begins to run against the mother and, as time goes on, it gets progressively more and more difficult for her to show that withdrawal of her consent is reasonable', per Ormrod LJ in *Re H (Infants) (1977)*. To what extent is former case law still of relevance?

4  Has recent adoption practice become overly embroiled in debates about ethnocentricism, thereby leaving children from ethnic minority backgrounds without the prospect of being adopted?

5  What are the main considerations which have resulted in the move from closed to open adoption?

6  There is some concern that adoption provides a fast track for children from the care system. Is there any evidence for this concern?

# 11

# Adolescent rights: autonomy and participation

## SUMMARY

In this chapter, the focus is centred on the child and especially the adolescent's right to self-determination with regard to matters which affect them including their right to participate in the legal process. We consider the several expressions in statute, case law, and also in human rights law which recognize and formalize the right to their self-determination and participation, including the requirement placed on the courts to consider the 'wishes and feelings of the child' in deciding any matter which affects them. Special significance is attached to adolescent self-determination and participation as they inhabit the legal space between childhood and adulthood. In this respect the case of *Gillick* (1986) and the meaning and application for subsequent case law of the principle of '*Gillick* competence' which developed directly from the issues that arose in that case, is explored. The case law demonstrates that the scope for adolescent self-determination and participation in decisions, which affect them, is in practice limited; that the courts have retreated from the principle of giving weight to an adolescent's expressed wishes even where he or she is competent to exercise a choice, and especially so in circumstances where the consequences of that decision are serious and life threatening. The more recent case law which does indeed recognize adolescent competence, suggests that the competent adolescent's full rights to self-determination and participation is only wholeheartedly embraced in trivial matters leaving full determination removed from decision making in the more difficult questions.

# Rights of the child: general principles and sources of law

11.1 To the nineteenth-century legal and public imagining, children had no rights. Children were physically abused by parents, beaten until half-dead and also beaten by those acting on behalf of parents (*R v Hopley* (*1860*)).

11.2 It was not until the latter half of the twentieth century, that 'paternal' and then 'parental' rights over children dwindled (remember *Hewer* in Chapter 9). At the same time as the parental right declined the child's right to self-determination was in the ascendant. Indeed, the idea of children having rights to self-determination and autonomy became a legal and public policy imperative, and an increasingly relevant consideration evident in statute and case law, and in international law.

11.3 There are five sources of law, which enshrine and reflect the recognition of the aspiration of the principle of the child and the adolescent's right to a role in decision making in their own lives.

11.4 First, the Family Law Reform Act 1969 (FLRA 1969), s 8 grants 16 to 17 year-olds the right to consent to his or her own medical treatment:

> *The consent of a minor who has attained the age of sixteen years to any surgical, medical or dental treatment which, in the absence of consent, would constitute a trespass to his person, shall be as effective as it would be if he were of full age; and where a minor has by virtue of this section given an effective consent to any treatment it shall not be necessary to obtain any consent for it from his parent or guardian.*

11.5 Second, the momentous decision in *Gillick* (*1986*) (introduced in Chapter 9 and discussed at some length in this chapter) declared not only that adolescents who have sufficient understanding and maturity to make their own decisions in certain matters should be allowed to do so, but where that decision conflicts with the parental view the adolescent's wish should be considered on equal terms. So controversial was this ruling that some courts have struggled to limit the potential application of *Gillick* to its own facts or else otherwise tried to narrow the ambit of its application to the freedom to consent to treatment but not extended to the freedom to refuse treatment.

11.6 Third, in domestic law, the Children Act 1989, s 1(3)(a) places a duty upon the court and upon the local authority to consider the child's wishes and feelings as part of the consideration of the child's welfare. Section 1(3)(a), in exercising its jurisdiction over any matter relating to the care and upbringing of the child or in relation to the child's property, requires the court, to consider 'the ascertainable wishes and feelings of the child concerned considered in the light of his age.'

11.7 Fourth, by 1989, the United Nations Convention on the Rights of the Child (UNCRC) 1989 defined children's rights to include participation and imposed obligations on member states to implement national laws which enforce these rights. As of November 2009, 194 countries, including all member states of the European Union, had ratified the UNCRC and are obliged under international law to promote the implementation of the rights that are protected. The UNCRC applies to persons under 18 years of age and Art 12(1) asserts:

> *States parties shall assure to the child who is capable of forming his or her own views the right to express those views freely in all matters affecting the child, the views of the child being given due weight in accordance with the age and maturity of the child. (2) For this purpose the child in particular be provided the opportunity to be heard in any judicial and administrative proceedings affecting the child, either directly or through a representative or an appropriate body, in a manner consistent with the procedural rules of national law.*

Article 12(2) is however a conditional provision because the UNCRC is not directly enforceable by the courts. Baroness Hale of Richmond in *R (Williamson) v Secretary of State for Education and Employment (2005)*, said, 'Above all, the state is entitled to give children the protection they are given by an international instrument to which the UK is a party, the United Nations Convention on the Rights of a Child.'

11.8 Other articles of relevance which continue to reflect the significance of an adolescent's emerging self-determination are: Article 16(1) which asserts: 'No child shall be subjected to arbitrary or unlawful interference with his or her privacy, family, home or correspondence, nor to unlawful attacks on his or her honour and reputation.' The right to participation must be read alongside Art 3, of the UNCRC, which provides that all organizations involved with children should work towards what is best for the child. Children's views and the views of adolescents should be taken into account in matters regarding issues within the family, at school, with regard to children's health, and in all aspects of their lives.

> Article 18(1) of the UNCRC provides:

> *States parties shall use their best efforts to ensure recognition of the principle that both parents have common responsibilities for the upbringing and development of the child. Parents or, as the case may be, legal guardians, have the primary responsibility for the upbringing and development of the child. The best interests of the child will be their basic concern.*

11.9 Fifth, the ECHR, although by no means child centred, protects everyone and that includes children and their right to self-determination and participation. Indeed, children are equally entitled to its protection. Art 6 'fair trial' rights guarantees adolescents and children the right to be heard in legal proceedings. (See *Re L (Care: Assessment: Fair Trial (2002))* and *Mabon v Mabon (2005)*.) As MacDonald (2009) notes:

> *The provisions of s 1 of the 1989 Act and the United Nations Convention have a*
> *slightly different emphasis to Arts 6 and 8 of the European Convention. Section 1(3)*
> *(a) of the 1989 Act and Art 12 of the UNCRC emphasise participation of the child in*
> *the decision making process through the articulation and expression of their wishes*
> *and feelings. Arts 6 and 8 emphasise the participation of the child in that decision*
> *making process in broader terms, through the adequate and independent represen-*
> *tation of the child's interests within that process.*

Other rights that are protected include the right to life (Art 2); the right to be free from inhuman and degrading treatment (Art 3); the right to liberty (Art 5); the right to a fair trial (Art 6); the right to family life and privacy (Art 8); the right to religious thought (Art 9); the right to freedom of expression (Art 10); and the right to freedom from discrimination (Art 14).

11.10   The application and enforcement of the adolescent's right to self-determination and participation has been limited, and piecemeal. Curiously in educational matters, often at the heart of a child's life, the child and adolescent's right to self-determination, is virtually suspended, *Gillick* competence is rarely, if ever embraced, even less articulated or considered Fortin on this point asserts:

> *...the principles of education law currently show little appreciation of the matur-*
> *ing child's capacity for taking responsibility for his or her school life or for reaching*
> *important decisions over his or her education....in some respects, education law*
> *seems to have become increasingly blinkered to such an ideal...*
>
> *((2003, p 161), see also Monk)*

11.11   The adolescent's right to determine matters in school has recently become the centre of a contested struggle over school uniform.

> The case of *R (on the application of Begum) v Head Teacher and Governors of Denbigh*
> *High School* has been the subject of numerous legal and academic commentaries. In this
> case Ms Begum, a pupil at Denbigh High School, was refused permission to attend school
> wearing a 'jilbab'—a long sleeved ankle length loose fitting dress. She was sent home and
> requested to return wearing the approved school uniform. She claimed that refusal to allow
> her to wear the jilbab denied her right to manifest her religious beliefs. The House of Lords
> ruled that the school had behaved correctly and her Art 9 rights to freedom of thought, con-
> science and religion had not been breached. Their Lordships were agreed that if there had
> been any interference with her rights, such interference was necessary for the protection of
> the rights of others at the school and especially to protect other young Muslim adolescent
> women from feeling pressurized to wear the jilbab; and not appearing to favour any one
> religion; preserving the multi-cultural mix of the school and avoiding divisiveness.

What was striking about this case is that Shabina Begum was herself the applicant (supported by her brother as next friend) and yet with regard to this matter of what one should wear at school the issue of her rights to choose, her competence was not considered nor indeed was weight placed on the rights of those exercising parental responsibility for her (Edwards 2007).

# Three ages and stages of rights

11.12 Over the last three decades especially (1980–2011), the law has increasingly grappled with adolescents' claims to a right to have their wishes heard and respected in matters which affect them and also to be permitted to participate fully in the legal process, as parties in their own right. Where the child is able to express his or her views then their wishes have been considered, in accordance with the age and development of the child. And so the older and more mature the child, the weightier his or her voice in the matter in question. Children's rights to self-determination are not absolute but incremental. Lord Donaldson in *Re W (1992)* said, 'Adolescence is a period of progressive transition from childhood to adulthood.' The law has acknowledged three ages and stages of rights including the rights of the unborn, of infants (both of which have included rights to protection but not self-determination or participation), and young children, and of adolescents (both of which include rights to protection and also to self-determination and participation). There is no exactitude as to where the law draws the line with regard to the chronological age or stage of development with regard to the particular issue when the child can express a view. The drawing of boundaries is artificial. Mary Douglas captures the artificiality of the legal organization of boundaries when she writes:

> *Over a very large area the law is indifferent to sex. Yet when property rights are transmitted by marriage the question of a legally valid bond becomes a matter of concern. It is no new thing for the law to be drawing the line between the biological and social events, choosing the moment when a foetus is enough of a person to require legal protection, deciding when a marriage has been physically consummated, deciding on the definitions of death, rape, cruelty, indecency, and a standard of living above starvation. At less public and weightier levels the same assessment and drawing of boundaries proceeds through the whole social process. Physical nature is masticated and driven through the cognitive meshes to satisfy social demands for clarity, which compete with logical demands for consistency.*
>
> *(1973, 113)*

# The unborn foetus and 'rights'

11.13 The rights of the foetus to protection has had a chequered and, even now, uncertain status. Whilst a foetus does not have rights in its own name, its right to develop to full capacity is a right protected before birth. And when born and then a person in law, he or she can sue for any injury inflicted whilst in the womb before personhood is acquired. Sir George Baker in *Paton v British Pregnancy Advisory Service Trustees (1979)* articulates what remains the legal position:

> *The foetus cannot, in English law, in my view, have any rights of its own at least until it is born and has a separate existence from the mother. That permeates the whole of the civil law of this country.*

Baroness Hale (when as Brenda Hoggett) wrote:

> *Once the unborn child is capable of being born alive it is an offence intentionally to cause the child's death before he has an existence independent of his mother except where this is done in good faith in order to save the mother's life. This indicates that the mother's life takes priority over the child's and also that doctors may take steps to protect the mother's health even at some risk to the baby provided that there is no intention that the baby should die. Where an unborn child is not capable of being born alive of course the pregnancy may be terminated if the risk to the mother's life or health would be greater in letting it continue: Abortion Act 1967 s 1(1)(a). Neither a married or unmarried father has the right to prevent a mother from having a lawful abortion: Paton v British Pregnancy Advisory Service Trustees (1979)) QB 276, C v S (1988)) QB 135. Otherwise an unborn child is not a person with legal rights and status until he is born (or it now seems, on the point of birth).*
>
> *(1994, 11–12)*

## 'Rights' of young children

11.14   It has been, in recent times, a matter of both public policy and law to protect infants and young children. The question of the young child's right to participate and be consulted, and to speak and be heard, in legal decisions depends on the issue in question. The right to participate also exists in proportionate relationship to the age, understanding, and development of the child. An infant is not able to express his or her wishes and feelings about which parent he wishes to live with or whether to have a transplant operation, although a three year-old child is capable of expressing some view on both matters, but is not capable of assessing what might be in his or her best interests. A 10 year-old, whose parents have separated, is able to express his or her wishes and feelings over whether he or she wishes to live with the mother or father but may not be considered capable of exercising a choice about complex matters.

11.15   The child's wishes and feelings are voiced through the appointment of a children's guardian who represents the child. And in some cases the child or adolescent, if considered competent to do so, may appoint his or her own representative.

11.16   The weight the court will attach to those wishes and feelings will depend upon whether the court considers the wishes and feelings to be truly those held by the child; to what extent it considers the child's expression of wishes and feelings are sentiments a child can hold; and whether those wishes expressed are in the child's best interests.

> In **CDM v CM and others (2003)**, where the resident parent had persuaded the children that the non-resident parent had physically and sexually abused them and also that the paternal grandparents were physical abusers, the court considered that the wishes and feelings of the child, who had expressed a desire not to see the father, were not truly the child's wishes and feelings but the result of the 'residential parent's false and distorted belief system about the non-residential parent, which the children had imbibed'.

11.17 The court in *Re B section 91(14) Order: Duration (2004)*, a case where a nine year-old child did not wish to have contact with his father because of the attitude of his mother and his sisters, the Court of Appeal held:

> *(15) In my judgment, Ms Waddicor has the better of these exchanges. It is very important where a child is effectively denied or inhibited from an ordinary relationship with her father by the determination of her mother to excise the father from her life that the court should never abandon endeavours to right the wrongs within the family dynamics. Certainly His Honour Judge Barratt QC has done all he could in a difficult situation to revive, in an imaginative and sensitive way, a relationship which is in danger of terminal decline. In my judgment, the order that he made simply gives the wrong message. Its justification does not seem to me to flow from the paragraph that I have cited. This is not a case in which the father has in any way abused the family justice system to disturb or undermine the mother's primary care. The judge has specifically found that he has acted responsibly in pursuing his desire for an ordinary relationship with his daughter by contact applications and by ensuring that the mother's endeavours to remove or lessen the use of his name as her name were checked by the court's intervention. The reference to Ms Reddy's report has to be read in the context of the judge's evaluation in para (19), which I have also cited. Ms Reddy seems to have been too quick to criticise the father for his responsibility for court proceedings. The judge, in relation to that, reminded her of the father's right to apply to the court for contact.*

11.18 Having ascertained those genuine wishes, the court will consider how far they should be taken into account in accordance with what the issue in question involves. But no hard and fast rules can be drawn as to how far and to what extent a child should participate in a particular issue, since it is recognized that every child develops intellectually and personally at different rates. Is it possible to set a fixed age with regard to when a child can attend a doctor's surgery or a dentist unaccompanied by a parent and consent to an examination or a dental procedure? In *Suss v Germany (2006)*, a four year-old child expressed a wish not to see her father and the ECHR, following an application by the father that the court's decision had abrogated his right to access and family life, ruled that the child's best interest overrode the applicant's interest.

11.19 In *Re R (No 1) (Inter-Country Adoption) (1999)* (cited in Chapter 10) which involved a ten year-old child, Bracewell J asserted:

> *The wishes and feelings of AM are clear. I am abundantly satisfied that she wants to stay where she is and to be part of her present family where she has put down roots. She has, in effect, voted with her feet...I find that although she wants to keep in touch with her birth family, she would be devastated if she had to return. Her wishes cannot be decisive of outcome because a child of her age and understanding may know what she wants but not necessarily what she needs. However wishes of this intensity must be given due consideration when balancing all the factors...*

In *Re J and K (Abduction: Objections of Child) (2005)*, the mother had two children. One child, who was nearly nine years old, was the son of the mother's husband. The younger child was almost five years old and was the son of a man with whom the mother had cohabited. The mother's second relationship ended and she left the children with her former partner, who arranged for the elder boy to live with his own father, the younger boy remaining in the care of the former partner for a few weeks, until the mother returned and could care for the younger child and at some time later care for the elder boy also. The mother removed the two children from Malta, where they were residing. The Children and Family Court Advisory and Support Service (CAFCASS) reported that the nine year-old did not wish to return to Malta. The court granted the fathers' applications for return of the children, and held that its decision to take account of a child's stated objection to being returned to the state of habitual residence did not relieve the court of the task of deciding, in the discretionary analysis, what weight to afford the objection. In this case, the child's stated objection was to returning to the care of the paternal grandparents, whereas the father had provided an undertaking not to bring the child into contact with the grandparents and thus the weight that would be afforded to the child's objection in the discretionary analysis would take into account all the other factors.

As Baroness Hale observed in *Re D (A Child) (2007)*:

*There is a growing understanding of the importance of listening to the children involved in children's cases. It is the child, more than anyone else, who will have to live with what the court decides. Those who do listen to children understand that they often have a point of view which is quite distinct from that of the person looking after them. They are quite capable of being moral actors in their own right. Just as the adults may have to do what the court decides whether they like it or not, so may the child. But that is no more reason for failing to hear what the child has to say than it is for refusing to hear the parents' views.*

## Adolescents and self-determination

11.20  Whilst the CA 1989, s 1 gives the child a right to a voice, the right of the adolescent, not only to a voice, but to be heard and their wishes acted upon is rather more weighty. A young person achieves majority at 18 years of age. Coming of age is full entry into adulthood, for all purposes. Consider the case below which demonstrates the responsibility of the local authority for providing assistance to children in need.

In *R (on the application of W) v Essex County Council; R (on the application of F) v same; R (on the application of G) v same (2004)*, the claimants were children who had approached the defendant authority for assistance in relation to accommodation. The authority failed to produce initial assessments and each claimant applied for judicial review of that failure. At the hearing, W's effective challenge was to a continuing failure to provide accommodation that the authority by then had acknowledged it was under a duty to provide, and F and G sought to challenge decisions of the authority to provide support and accommodation for them under CA 1989, s 17 rather than s 20.

Munby J, set out the legal framework in respect of such children:

*Section 17(6) empowers the local authority to provide accommodation, but there is no duty to do so under s 17: see R (G) v Barnet London Borough Council (2003) UKHL 57, (2003) 3 WLR 1194. Section 20, in contrast, does in certain circumstances impose a duty to provide accommodation. Section 20 so far as material for present purposes provides as follows:*

*(1) Every local authority shall provide accommodation for any child in need within their area who appears to them to require accommodation as a result of:*

*(a) there being no person who has parental responsibility for him;*

*(b) his being lost or having been abandoned; or*

*(c) the person who has been caring for him being prevented (whether or not permanently, and for whatever reason) from providing him with suitable accommodation or care...*

*(3) Every local authority shall provide accommodation for any child in need within their area who has reached the age of sixteen and whose welfare the authority consider is likely to be seriously prejudiced if they do not provide him with accommodation.*

When it comes to the adolescent right to self-determination the approach of the courts in recent times is summarized by Thorpe LJ in *Mabon v Mabon (2005)*:

*Although the tandem model has many strengths and virtues, at its heart lies the conflict between advancing the welfare of the child and upholding the child's freedom of expression and participation. Unless we in this jurisdiction are to fall out of step with similar societies as they safeguard article 12 rights, we must, in the case of articulate teenagers, accept that the right to freedom of expression and participation outweighs the paternalistic judgment of welfare.*

# Adolescent autonomy—the law

11.21 There are two legal considerations specifically concerned with adolescent autonomy and self-determination.

First, under FLRA 1969, s 8 there is a rebuttable presumption of lack of competence with regard to an adolescent of 16 and 17 years and capacity to consent to treatment. The adolescent, it would seem, can say 'yes' but not 'no' to treatment. It is not a capacity to refuse: see *R (on the application of W) v Essex County Council; R (on the application of F) v same; R (on the application of G) v same (2004)* where the court asserts:

*Section 20(6), as we have seen, requires the local authority to ascertain and give due consideration to the child's wishes regarding the provision of accommodation. Plainly when dealing with 16-year old children, who are likely to have minds of their own and may well be Gillick competent—see Gillick v West Norfolk and Wisbech Area Health Authority (1986) AC 112 (below)— a local authority has to have regard to the realities. In particular, a local authority has to have regard to the reality that young people faced with proffered support packages which are perceived as being unacceptable may well reject the support being offered and simply vote with their feet. A young person may, for example, prefer the financial independence of managing their own benefits rather than living on local authority pocket-money, and for that reason prefer to be accommodated under section 17 rather than under section 20. Similarly, a young person may not wish to be subjected to the more intrusive role which a local authority is likely to need to adopt if the young person is, by reason of being accommodated under section 20, to be treated as a looked after child. There is therefore nothing objectionable in principle to a local authority deciding to accommodate under section 17 rather than under section 20 a young person who would otherwise qualify for accommodation under either section 20(1) or 20(3), provided always, that is, that the young person has been given a genuine choice and has made a fully informed decision. I emphasise these important qualifications because in the nature of things the young people seeking local authority support will often, like W, P, F and G, be vulnerable. Nor, in the nature of things, can one blind oneself to the financial and other incentives that a local authority may have for persuading a young person to accept support under section 17 rather than under section 20.*

11.22 *Gillick* competence applies to adolescent's under the age of 16 years and is relevant to any matter not only those matters involving a medical question.

There are many other situations where the adolescent's wishes will carry considerable weight because of his or her age and understanding of the issues concerned. The law has recognized the importance of the adolescent's views even when they conflict with parents or with other adults who have responsibility for them. Adolescents whom the court consider have reached an age of maturity where their views can be considered may even outweigh the views of the adults responsible for them. Such adolescents are called '*Gillick* competent' (see further discussion in Bridge, 1999).

11.23 As the case law demonstrates, the precise meaning, ambit, and application of *Gillick* competence depends on the facts in each case. Age and participation are not absolute and are treated as incremental by the courts. The adolescent approaching 16 years, is regarded in law quite differently from the adolescent of 12 years of age.

## The *Gillick* competence construct

11.24 In the *Gillick* case, the Department of Health and Social Security (now the Department of Health) issued a notice to all area health authorities detailing guidance on the treatment of young people under 16 years of age seeking contraceptive advice. It was anticipated that where advice involved young children under 16 their parents would attend such consultations and that it would be most unusual to provide contraceptive advice to a young person without parental consent/knowledge. The guidance stated:

> *There is widespread concern about counselling and treatment for children under 16.*
> *Special care is needed not to undermine parental responsibility and family stability.*
> *The Department would therefore hope that in any case where a doctor or other pro-*
> *fessional worker is approached by a person under the age of 16 for advice in these*
> *matters, the doctor, or other professional, will always seek to persuade the child to*
> *involve the parent or guardian (or other person in loco parentis) at the earliest stage*
> *of consultation, and will proceed from the assumption that it would be most unusual*
> *to provide advice about contraception without parental consent.*

The plaintiff, Mrs Victoria Gillick, the mother of five girls and five boys wrote to the local authority asking for an assurance that no contraceptive advice would be given to any of her daughters without her knowledge and consent. She wrote:

> *Concerning the new D.H.S.S. guidelines on the contraceptive and abortion treatment*
> *of children under both the legal and medical age of consent, without the knowledge*
> *or consent of the parents, can I please ask you for a written assurance that in no*
> *circumstances whatsoever will any of my daughters (Beatrice, Hannah, Jessie and*
> *Sarah) be given contraceptive or abortion treatment whilst they are under 16 in any*
> *of the family planning clinics under your control, without my prior knowledge, and*
> *irrefutable evidence of my consent? Also, should any of them seek advice in them,*
> *can I have your assurance that I would be automatically contacted in the interests*
> *of my children's safety and welfare? If you are in any doubt about giving me such*
> *assurances, can I please ask you to seek legal medical advice.*
>
> *Yours faithfully, Mrs. Victoria Gillick.*

The local authority refused to give such assurance. Mrs Gillick initiated an action by writ for a declaration that the guidance giving advice was unlawful, adversely affecting parental responsibility. Woolf J, in the court of first instance, said:

> *The fact that a child is under the age of 16 does not mean automatically that she*
> *cannot give consent to any treatment. Whether or not a child is capable of giving*
> *the necessary consent will depend on the child's maturity and understanding, and*
> *the nature of the consent which is required. The child must be capable of making*
> *a reasonable assessment of the advantages and disadvantages of the treatment*
> *proposed, so the consent if given can be properly and fairly described as true con-*
> *sent...since the interests of parents, I consider, are more accurately described as*
> *responsibilities or duties.*

Mrs Gillick appealed the decision of the lower court to the Court of Appeal. In **Gillick v West Norfolk and Wisbech Area Health Authority and another (1985)** Eveleigh, Fox, and Parker LJJ unanimously reversed the decision of the lower court on the ground that a girl under 16 years of age was incapable of consenting to medical treatment or prohibiting a doctor from seeking the consent of her parents and, as such, the DHSS guidance was contrary to law. In the Court of Appeal, the court considered the relevant authorities including **Agar Ellis, J v C, Hewer** and **Re D**, and also **R v Howes (1860)**, where the question was whether a father was, by habeas corpus, entitled to recover the custody of a child between 15 and 16 notwithstanding that the child did not desire to be in his custody. Cockburn CJ, giving the judgment of the court on the father's application for the return of the child to his custody, said:

> *Now the cases which have been decided on this subject shew that, although a father is entitled to the custody of his children till they attain the age of twenty-one, this Court will not grant a habeas corpus to hand a child which is below that age over to its father, provided that it has attained an age of sufficient discretion to enable it to exercise a wise choice for its own interests. The whole question is, what is that age of discretion? We repudiate utterly, as most dangerous, the notion that any intellectual precocity in an individual female child can hasten the period which appears to have been fixed by statute for the arrival of the age of discretion; for that very precocity, if uncontrolled, might very probably lead to her irreparable injury. The Legislature has given us a guide, which we may safely follow, in pointing out sixteen as the age up to which the father's right to the custody of his female child is to continue; and short of which such a child has no discretion to consent to leaving him.* (our emphasis)

And concluded:

> *We have to decide the case according to law. The relevant authorities have been referred to, and in my judgment they lead to the orders which we propose to make. I do not seek to express my own views on the wider questions which the subject of birth control provokes. I would also emphasise that I do not intend to lay down a rule that in every case, no matter what the question is, no matter who the child is, the parent must be consulted before any important decision can ever be arrived at in relation to the child.* (per Eveleigh LJ)

The DHSS appealed to the House of Lords. The appeal was allowed (Lords Brandon and Templeman dissenting). For the majority, Lords Fraser, Scarman, and Bridge held that legislation indicated that Parliament regarded contraceptive advice and treatment as essentially medical matters and that a girl under 16 years had the legal capacity to consent to medical examination and treatment. The parental right to control a child was a 'dwindling right' which existed only in so far as it was required for the child's benefit and protection and the exercise by a doctor of his clinical judgement as to what he honestly believed to be necessary for the physical, mental, and emotional health of the patient removed him from liability. Lord Scarman said:

> *Parental rights are derived from parental duty...the dwindling right...of a parent yields to the child's right to make his own decisions when he reaches a sufficient understanding and intelligence to be capable of making up his own mind on the matter requiring decision...the underlying principle of the law was exposed by Blackstone and can be seen to have been acknowledged in the case law. It is that parental rights yields to the child's right to make his own decisions when he reaches a sufficient understanding and intelligence to be capable of making up his own mind on the matter requiring decision.*

Lord Fraser said:

> *The Children Act 1975 made sweeping changes to the way in which courts dealt with children. Parker LJ was incorrect in his analysis of the Act...and in particular*

> *it cannot be accepted that the Act gave parents the right to determine the place at which and manner in which (the child's) time is spent. There is a dwindling scale of parental rights from birth to the age of majority.*

It is interesting that Lord Brandon who had championed the rights of the child in *Re D (1984)* dissented and said:

> *The only answer which the law should give to such a threat is, 'Wait till you are 16.' And Lord Templeman known for his famous dissent said "There are many things which a girl under 16 needs to practise but sex is not one of them. Parliament could declare this view to be out of date. But in my opinion the statutory provisions discussed in the speech of noble and learned friend Lord Fraser and the provisions of s 6 of the Sexual Offences Act 1956 indicate that as the law now stands an unmarried girl under 16 is not competent to decided to practise sex and contraception.*

11.25 The case of *Gillick* establishes in law, for the first time, the child's right to make decisions for him or herself as a free standing right, and enshrines in law the importance of considering a child's wishes in accord with intellect and understanding. It is a beacon proclaiming the recognition under certain circumstances of a child's right to self-determination and autonomy, in the interests of the child, for the child, by the child. This places the child in a new subject position in law, a position moving far beyond *J v C* (Chapter 9) where the interests of the child was perceived through the lens of judicial paternalism. *Gillick* represents a revolutionary watershed in establishing for children the recognition of the child's right to autonomy before he or she has attained full age. It has implications for health care professionals and also has implications for patient confidentiality.

The Access to Health Records Act 1990 further complicates the picture in allowing a child under 16, deemed '*Gillick* competent' by a doctor, to veto the parent's access to medical information held by that doctor, even though the parent can consent to treatment which the child cannot veto (Oxford Radcliffe Hospitals Confidentiality guidelines, July 30, 2007 © 2010 Oxford Radcliffe Hospitals NHS Trust).

## Acquiring competence

11.26 Acquiring competence (either as '*Gillick* competent' or else as competent under Family Proceedings Rules, r 9.42 where participation in legal proceedings is the issue in question) is not a fixed or absolute quality. Competence to make a decision with respect to contraceptive treatment may not mean that the same individual would be considered competent to make a decision with regard to refusing a blood transfusion. Competence is situation specific and assessed in the light of particular circumstances. It is not a fixed trait or quality like hearing or sight, which, when you have it, you have it, for all purposes. Nor is it a constant quality which when you have it in relation to a particular aspect it is always in evidence.

11.27 Lord Donaldson in *Re R (A Minor) (Wardship: Medical Treatment) (1992)*, explained the variable and fluid nature of competence which especially arises with regard to an adolescent with psychological issues when he said:

> But, even if she was capable on a good day of a sufficient degree of understanding to meet the Gillick criteria, her mental disability, to the cure or amelioration of which the proposed treatment was directed, was such that on other days she was not only 'Gillick incompetent', but actually sectionable. No adolescent in that situation can be regarded as 'Gillick competent' and the judge was wholly right in so finding in relation to R.

Competent as to what? In this regard, the courts have approached this question in several ways concentrating on: the decision itself, the adolescent's understanding of the decision, the process and procedure involved, the consequences of the decision, the adolescent's understanding of procedures, and the outcome of the decision. Often, the threshold of the test of comprehending the outcome and the procedures involved is set at a higher bar than what might be required of an adult.

11.28 Measuring competence in accordance with the adolescent's understanding of the procedure, medical or legal, has in some cases resulted in the court arriving at a decision that the adolescent is 'not competent'. The US case of *In the matter of Anonymous, a Minor (2001)*, see below, further underscores the fact that, not only in the UK but also in the USA, whilst there is much talk about adolescent autonomy there is far less evidence of the court's honouring and acceding to adolescent self-determination and participation.

An 'unemancipated minor' petitioned the court to review the judgment of the Court of Civil Appeals affirming the trial court's denial of the minor's petition for a waiver of parental consent to an abortion. The law of the State in question provided that:

> A minor who elects not to seek, or does not or cannot for any reason, obtain consent from either of her parents or legal guardian, may petition, on her own behalf, the juvenile court, or the court of equal standing, in the county in which the minor resides or in the county in which the abortion is to be performed for a waiver of the consent requirement of this chapter. Notice by the court to the minor's parents, parent or legal guardian shall not be required or permitted.

> ...The adolescent was 17 years old. She was eight weeks' pregnant and said that her parents would react poorly to the news of her pregnancy. She wanted an abortion....The judge denied the minor's petition for a waiver of parental consent, and the trial judge included the following findings and conclusions:

> [The] petitioner has been denied the opportunity to engage in pre-op counselling with the physician, evaluate the physician or interview and question the physician. Likewise the physician hasn't evaluated petitioner or furnished information to petitioner, so the court finds the petitioner is not mature or well informed and that abortion at this time under the proposed circumstances is contra to her best interests. The proposed provider refused to let petitioner even speak to physician after earlier saying she could...First, she must show that she has obtained information from a health-care provider about the health risks associated with an abortion and that she understands those risks. That would include an understanding of the risks

*associated with the particular stage of the minor's pregnancy... Second, she must show that she understands the alternatives to abortion and their implications. As with any medical procedure, part of making an informed decision is knowing the available alternatives. A minor should be able to demonstrate that she has given thoughtful consideration to her alternatives, including adoption and keeping the child. She should also understand that the law requires the father to assist in the financial support of the child... She should not be required to justify why she prefers abortion above other options, only that she is fully apprised of her options... Third, she must show that she is also aware of the emotional and psychological aspects of undergoing an abortion, which can be significant if not severe for some women. She must also show that she has considered how this decision might affect her family relations. Although the minor need not obtain this information from licensed, professional counsellors, she must show that she has received information about these risks from reliable and informed sources, so that she is aware of and has considered these aspects of the abortion procedure.*

The adolescent was denied an abortion on the grounds that she was denied the opportunity to be fully informed of the procedure and therefore did not understand the procedure.

## Interpreting '*Gillick* competence': age?

11.29 In considering whether a child is *Gillick* competent the courts have taken into account age, understanding, and maturity. However, it does appear that chronological age is the first hurdle which must be negotiated and surpassed before the question of competence can be considered. Consider the cases below which turn on the question of age.

In the case of *Re M (1996)* (where there was conflict between the natural parents and the prospective adoptive parents with regard to whom the child should live) the fact that the child was 10 years of age and not 12 years of age appeared to assume significance in the court's reasoning. Thorpe J (in the court of first instance) ruled that the boy concerned should be returned to South Africa to his biological parents notwithstanding that he had expressed more than a wish to remain in the United Kingdom with his prospective adoptive mother. Thorpe J accepted that if, in two years' time, the boy, who was 10 years of age at the hearing, still wished to remain with the foster parents, his wishes would 'have' to be taken into account (see Welstead, 1996).

11.30 Once the age threshold is met, whatever that might be with regard to any particular issue, *Gillick* competence then requires an assessment of the adolescent's maturity and ability to understand what is involved. Lord Scarman, in *Gillick*, said:

*When applying these conclusions to contraceptive advice and treatment it has to be borne in mind that there is much that has to be understood by a girl under the age of 16 if she is to have legal capacity to consent to such treatment. It is not enough that she should understand the nature of the advice, which is being given: she must also have a sufficient maturity to understand what is involved.*

11.31　The meaning of 'to understand what is involved' is again unclear. In the US abortion case of *In the matter of Anonymous, a Minor (2001)*, cited above, understanding what was involved required an ability to understand the procedure. In *Gillick*, understanding what was involved also required an ability to understand the process and procedure of abortion, the termination of a pregnancy, including the two-stage process which involved the insertion of an extra amniotic catheter, and an intravenous infusion cannula, and the connection of infusions of the abortifacient drugs to the catheter and, if appropriate, to the cannula, and the regulation of those infusions.

11.32　In *Re HB (Abduction: Children's Objections) (1997)*, the adolescent's solicitor formed the view that the adolescent was sufficiently mature to participate in the litigation without the intervention of a next friend or the children's guardian. The court allowed the appeal since the Hague Convention on the Civil Aspects of International Child Abduction 1980, as set out in Sch 1 to the Child Abduction and Custody Act 1985, places an obligation on the court to consider whether the proviso in Art 13 ought to be considered. The proviso allows the court to refuse to order the return of the child if it finds that the child actually objects to be being returned and, importantly, has attained an age and degree of maturity whereby it is appropriate for the court to take account of the child's views. In this case, the court accepted that the child had indeed attained that level of maturity and that the court could not:

> now shut its eyes to the relevance of the objections of a child with sufficient maturity at which it is appropriate for the court to take account of her views. We must, therefore, in the unusual circumstances allow the appeal by the daughter and remit the case to Hale J if available. She will have the task of balancing the objections of the child to returning to Denmark and to her mother against the arguments in favour of return to the country of her habitual residence for a decision to be made by that court.

11.33　Post-*Gillick* case law is characterized by a lack of coherence as to age, maturity, and understanding required to satisfy the competence threshold, as the cases, which follow below, demonstrate. Judges cannot, it would appear, agree to focus and be guided by the overarching principle of the aspiration of adolescent self-determination and autonomy, their decisions instead being frequently influenced by the consequences of the adolescent's wishes and an outcome orientated approach to law.

# Interpreting '*Gillick* competence': only a right to refuse consent?

11.34　The case of *Gillick* dealt specifically with whether an adolescent had the capacity to consent to contraceptive treatment. Since *Gillick* was decided, the courts have debated the question of whether the construct of *Gillick* competence is confined to its own facts of consent to contraceptive treatment and therefore only applicable where the issue relates to an adolescent's capacity to consent to treatment, or whether in fact it is wider than that so that 'if young people have the right to consent to medical treatment, logically they should have the right to refuse treatment' (Cretney and Masson, 2003, 504). There seems to be a universal agreement between family law academics that logic should prevail, and that the ambit of the ruling in *Gillick* should apply both in cases in which the issue raises the matter of consent to the matter in question and also in cases where refusal of consent is in issue.

11.35 However, the courts for some time were tethered by two significant landmark decisions, where Lord Donaldson (then Master of the Rolls), in interpreting Lord Scarman's ruling in *Gillick*, held it to apply only to those cases where the issue in question related to an adolescent's capacity to consent to treatment (see *Re R (A Minor) (Wardship: Medical Treatment) (1991)* and *Re W (A Minor) (Wardship: Medical Treatment) (1992)*), with the result that the application of *Gillick* became extremely restricted.

> In *Re R*, the competence of an adolescent to refuse sedation was in question. The adolescent girl, R, was 15 years and 10 months old. She was on the local authority's at-risk register and was received into voluntary care after a fight with her father. The local authority obtained a place of safety order and an interim care order. She was admitted into an adolescent psychiatric unit where she was sedated from time to time because of her suicidal and volatile behavior. Specialists in the adolescent unit wanted to sedate her in order to treat her because she had psychotic episodes. When she was in a lucid state she objected to the continuation of the medication and doctors feared that if the medication was withdrawn she would return to a psychotic state. R, telephoned her social worker protesting against this continuation of treatment. The local authority decided that they could not give authorization to such treatment under these circumstances and made her a ward of court. In wardship proceedings the court considered: (i) whether the judge had power to override the decision of a ward who was a minor to refuse medication and treatment irrespective of whether the minor was competent to give her consent; and (ii) whether the ward had the requisite capacity to accept or refuse such medication or treatment.
>
> The court decided that although a wardship judge could not override the decision of a ward who had the requisite capacity on the facts the ward did not have that capacity. The Official Solicitor (James Munby QC) as guardian ad litem appealed, contending that if a child had the right to give consent to medical treatment then the parents', and a fortiori the wardship court's right to give or refuse consent terminated.
>
> Lord Donaldson said:
>
> *Consent by itself creates no obligation to treat. It is merely a key, which unlocks a door. Furthermore, whilst in the case of an adult of full capacity there will usually only be one keyholder, namely the patient, in the ordinary family unit where a young child is the patient there will be two key holders, namely the parents, with a several as well as a joint right to turn the key and unlock the door. If the parents disagree, one consenting and the other refusing, the doctor will be presented with a professional and ethical, but not a legal, problem because, if he has the consent*

*of one authorised person, treatment will not without more constitute a trespass or
a criminal assault.*

The court concluded that the **Gillick** competence test was of general importance, but
not decisive. So, an adolescent refusing treatment did not have the ultimate say in the
matter or a right of veto, but their refusal was a factor. Lord Donaldson again said:

> I do not understand Lord Scarman to be saying that, if a child was 'Gillick com-
> petent', to adopt the convenient phrase used in argument, the parents ceased to
> have an independent right of consent, as contrasted with ceasing to have a right of
> determination, or veto... If Lord Scarman intended to go further than this and to say
> that in the case of a 'Gillick competent' child, a parent has no right either to consent
> or to refuse consent, his remarks were obiter... Furthermore, I consider that they
> would have been wrong... One glance at the consequences suffices to show that
> Lord Scarman cannot have been intending to say that the parental right to consent
> terminates with the achievement by the child of 'Gillick competence'.

Farquharson LJ, in his judgment, did not consider that **Gillick** competence was ever
achievable where an adolescent had mental health problems:

> 'Gillick competence' is not open to her... for my part I would find it difficult to import
> the criteria applied in Gillick to the facts of the present case. We are not here solely
> concerned with the developing maturity of a 15-year-old child, but with the impact
> of a mental illness upon her.

R failed the test of competence.

11.36    Later in the case of *Re W (a Minor) (Wardship: Medical Treatment) (1992)* the issue
arose once again.

> In **Re W**, a 16 year-old adolescent girl was suffering from highly advanced anorexia.
> She was transferred against her wishes to a London specialist clinic for the treatment of
> eating disorders. Her medical condition was very serious, she was so thin that her arms
> were encased in plaster to protect them and she was fed with a nasogastric tube. The
> question arose whether, under s 8 of the Family Law Reform Act 1969, such a minor had
> an exclusive right to consent to such treatment and therefore an absolute right to refuse
> medical treatment because no one else would be in a position to consent. An application
> was made under CA 1989, s 100(3), which allows intervention of the inherent jurisdiction
> where there is risk of harm, and allows for the authorization of treatment. W appealed. The
> court exercised its jurisdiction and authorized treatment on the grounds that within one
> week she would suffer irreversible harm. An emergency protection order was also made
> enabling her to be treated in a London hospital.

> But W's anorexia did not arise from a psychological condition of body perception.
> W simply wanted 'out', she wanted to die. As Lord Donaldson said 'Fate has dealt harshly
> with W. She is now aged 16, having been born on 31 March 1976. She has an older sister,
> now aged 18, and a younger brother, now aged 13. In November 1981, when she was 5,
> her father died of a brain tumour and in September 1984, when she was 8, her mother
> died of cancer.' Her short life up until then had been an excoriating series of tragedies. Her
> father had died of a brain tumour in 1981; her mother had died of cancer in 1984 and she

was consequently orphaned and taken into care. In 1989, her foster mother had breast cancer; and in 1990, her grandfather died.

Unlike R, W was considered *Gillick* competent. Thorpe J said she was competent, so did the Court of Appeal. She was, of course, 16 years old and therefore, in accordance with the FLRA 1969, legally compellable, could consent to treatment although could not refuse it. Indeed, Nolan LJ commenting on the effect of this statute in this case made it clear that the 16 and 17 year-old was in possession of 'the same capacity as an adult to surgical, medical or dental treatment'. Lord Donaldson embarked on a new concept this time—the flak jacket! He said:

> There seems to be some confusion in the minds of some as to the purpose of seeking consent from a patient (whether adult or child) or from someone with authority to give that consent on behalf of the patient. It has two purposes, the one clinical and the other legal. The clinical purpose stems from the fact that in many instances the co-operation of the patient and the patient's faith or at least confidence in the efficiency of the treatment is a major factor contributing to the treatment's success. Failure to obtain such consent will not only deprive the patient and the medical staff of this advantage, but will usually make it much more difficult to administer the treatment. I appreciate that this purpose may not be served if consent is given on behalf of, rather than by the patient.... On reflection I regret my use in Re R of the key holder analogy...because keys can lock as well as unlock. I now prefer the analogy of the legal 'flak jacket' which protects from claims by the litigious whether he acquires it from his patient who may be a minor over the age of 16, or a 'Gillick competent' child under that age or from another person having parental responsibilities which include a right to consent to treatment of the minor. Anyone who gives him a flak jacket (i.e. consent) may take it back, but the doctor only needs one and so long as he continues to have one he has the legal right to proceed.

11.37 Lord Donaldson was also mindful to assert that even competent adolescents do not have an exclusive right of veto to determine their own treatment. Indeed, he had said earlier in *R* that *Gillick* competence was not decisive and he showed it, once again, not to be so in *W*.

11.38 So what self-determination, autonomy or participation might a 'competent' adolescent expect to enjoy? Lord Donaldson's interpretation of *Gillick* demonstrated that in *W* it was worth very little.

Competence was forfeited or, at the least, compromised where the adolescent displayed behavioural problems. As Farquharson LJ had said in *R*, that an adolescent displaying behavioural difficulties was, in his view, in fact incompetent by virtue of the psychological difficulties. Lord Donaldson arrived at the same practical outcome in *W*, for although he accepted that she was indeed competent, he went on to say that a feature of anorexia is that it can destroy the ability to make an informed decision. So what was he really saying? On the one hand, he said he found her competent, whilst on the other he was equivocal about whether she was making an informed decision. In any event, he ruled that the court should impose their inherent jurisdiction to overrule her refusal.

The academic fraternity was more that concerned. 'In a remarkable U-turn, the Court of Appeal in *Re R* and *Re W* radically undermined the liberal sentiments expressed only a few years earlier by the House of Lords' (Fortin, 2003, 84). And, in 1992, Gillian Douglas described *Re R* and *Re W* as a 'retreat from Gillick'.

11.39 But in any event how was the weight of the wishes and feelings of the *Gillick* competent adolescent to be distinguished from the child not old enough or not mature enough or not sufficiently understanding of the procedure? This critical distinction has never been really grappled with. Surely the *Gillick* competent adolescent requires a different treatment from the younger counterpart? The courts would no doubt agree with that general principle but to what effect?

So from the subject position of the *Gillick* competent child, what does this status mean for the issue at hand?

## Testing the application of '*Gillick* competence'

11.40 Depending on the particular adolescent, and on the particular issue under determination, the courts seem to reach a decision on whether the child is competent or incompetent working from the consequences of a decision of competence, rather than from competence to consequences.

Adolescents have been deemed incompetent in the following cases.

## Incompetent: refusing to consent to blood products

11.41 When an adolescent refuses life-saving treatment, the court has either regarded that person as incompetent to make such a decision and then ordered the medically prescribed treatment, or, if the adolescent is deemed competent, the court must decide whether to let the adolescent's position on the matter prevail, or else invoke its powers under the inherent jurisdiction/wardship on the grounds that the adolescent will suffer harm if permitted to realize the consequences of his or her decision. In other words self-determination may not be considered in the adolescent's best interests. In practical terms, it may not make a great deal of difference to the adolescent whether a determination of competence or incompetence is made since a status of competence is pretty worthless if the consequences are the same either way and the adolescent's wishes disregarded or overridden.

11.42 From the court's vantage point, a finding of incompetence leaves the court in less of an ethical dilemma and less open to criticism than a finding that an adolescent is *Gillick* competent yet decides to override her wishes. When a *Gillick* competent adolescents wishes are overridden by invoking the inherent jurisdiction/wardship, this practice leads to the criticism that *Gillick* competence is no competence at all!

**Table 11.1** Competence and post-*Gillick* landmark cases

| | | |
|---|---|---|
| **Not competent** | to refuse treatment | **No, to blood**<br>1. Re E (1993)<br>2. Re S (1994/5)<br>3. Re L (1998)<br>4. Re P (2004)<br><br>**No, to organ transplant**<br>1. Re M (1999)<br><br>**No, to sedation**<br>1. Re KW and H (1993)<br>2. Northampton AHA v Official Solicitor (1994)<br><br>**No, to detention**<br>1. R v Kirklees Metropolitan Borough Council, ex parte C (1993)<br><br>**No, to Caesarean**<br>1. A Metropolitan Borough Council v DB (1997) |
| | as to legal procedure | 1. Re S (1993)<br>2. Re C (1994)<br>3. Re H (2000)<br>4. Re N (2003) |
| **Competent—with some reluctance** | Wishes accepted | 1. Re H (1993)<br>2. Re SC (1993)<br>3. Re F (1993)<br>4. Re T (1993)<br>5. Re C (1995) |
| | Wishes overruled— adolescent warded | 1. Re C (1993)<br>2. South Glamorgan v W and B (1993)<br>3. Re C (1997) |
| **Fully competent** | Wishes accepted | 1. Re Roddy (a child) (2004) |
| | Wishes overruled | 2. Re P (2004) |

## A question of Faith—Jehovah's Witness and blood products

11.43 The legal issue of administering life-saving blood products has arisen for consideration in many medical situations involving both adults and children. David Ziebart in a compelling article (see under Further Reading below) raises the issue of Art 9 of the ECHR in this context. Art 9 provides:

*(1) Everyone has the right to freedom of thought, conscience and religion; this right includes freedom to change his religion or belief and freedom, either alone or in community with others and in public or private, to manifest his religion or belief, in worship, teaching, practice and observance*

*(2) Freedom to manifest one's religion or beliefs shall be subject only to such limitations as are prescribed by law and are necessary in a democratic society... for the protection of the rights and freedoms of others.*

Ziebart considers what should be the proper stance of the courts when the ECHR right to manifest a religious belief arises. The viewpoint of the courts is expressed by those who are not Jehovah's Witnesses. Jehovah's Witnesses (JW) regard blood as sacred. It would be interesting to consider how the reflections of Munby J with regard to multi-culture and multi-faith (in *Singh* cited above in Chapter 9) might sit with cases which involve the right to religious belief.

The stance of the courts in such cases has been to make a finding that such adolescents are incompetent. This has allowed the courts in wardship to grant doctors the permission and authority to treat them such that the adolescent patient has been forcibly transfused with blood. However, whilst the courts have purportedly considered competence; whether the adolescent is or is not competent has taken second position to whether the wishes of the adolescent are in his or her best interests.

Consider the four cases below:

In *Re E (a Minor) (Wardship: Medical Treatment) (1993)*, a male adolescent of 15 years and nine months, who was a Jehovah's Witness, refused to consent to a blood transfusion (a decision supported by his parents). He was deemed incompetent, even though Ward J was impressed by E's intelligence and said:

*I find that he has no realisation of the full implications, which lie before him as to the process of dying. He may have some concept of the fact that he will die but as to the manner of his death and to the extent of his and his family's suffering I find he has not the ability to turn his mind to it nor the will to do so. Who can blame him for that?*

In *Re S (a Minor) (Consent to Medical Treatment) (1994)*, a 15 year-old Jehovah's Witness with a rare blood disease (thalassaemia major) refused a blood transfusion (a decision supported by the parents). Johnson J concluded that:

*... whilst as she gave evidence I was so very strongly impressed by her integrity and her commitment, I believe they were the integrity and commitment of a child and*

*not of somebody who was competent to make a decision that she tells me she has made.*

In overriding her wishes, he did so by declaring that she did not understand the implications of refusal, that is the consequence of death, and more specifically the manner of her inevitable death and the pain and distress if treatment were to be discontinued. Johnson J concluded that:

*...an understanding that she will die is not enough. For her decision to carry weight she should have a greater understanding of the manner of the death and pain and the distress.*

In *Re L (1998)*, a 14 year-old girl was in a life-threatening condition following extensive burns. She required medical treatment involving the possibility of a blood transfusion, to which, because she was a Jehovah's Witness, she would not consent. She had already signed an Advanced Medical Directive prohibiting the use of blood. Sir Stephen Brown, P, acknowledged that her religious beliefs were strongly held. He acknowledged that she was 'mature for her age'. Yet, because, said the court, she did not understand death the court declared that she was not *Gillick* competent and ordered the treatment.

In *Re P (Medical Treatment: Best Interests) (2004)*, P (John) a 16 year and 10 month-old Jehovah's Witness had an inherited condition; hypermobility syndrome, which manifests in fragility of blood vessels—bleeding. Symptoms included a tendency to bleed because of the fragility of blood vessels. The adolescent refused treatment. Johnson J said:

*There may be cases as a child approaches the age of 18 when his refusal would be determinative. A court will have to consider whether to override the wishes of the child approaching the age of majority when the likelihood is that all that will have been achieved will have been the deferment of an inevitable death and for a matter of months. Here, however, I am reminded of the words of Nolan LJ (as he then was) in Re W (A Minor) (Medical Treatment: Court's Jurisdiction): 'In general terms the present state of the law is that an individual who has reached the age of 18 is free to do with his life what he wishes, but it is the duty of the court to ensure so far as it can that children survive to attain that age.*

But Johnson J did make an order in the terms sought by the NHS Trust adding the words 'unless no other form of treatment is available'. He did this by considering the interests of P (John) in the widest possible terms, and he did so he said, 'reluctantly'. His reluctance arose because of John's age, his ability to articulate his wishes as John said, 'I am my own person. I have a separate mind. It makes no difference what my parents think. I make my own decisions'. In addition John was 16 years and 10 months at the time of the court hearing and here the FLRA 1969, s 8 was of some general relevance.

In this case the court whilst clearly respectful of the autonomy of a person of his age avoided the *Gillick* competence question, although it can be assumed from what the court said that the court considered him clearly competent although did not indulge in discussions as to whether he understood what was essentially his treatment or the consequences of not having the treatment. A significant break, Justice Johnson who five years earlier had dealt with 15 year-old M (discussed below in the section on transplants) begins to demonstrate that the tendency to allow children autonomy in trivial decision-making but to exclude them from self-determination in more serious questions sometimes with fatal consequences, cannot be sustained. Johnson J expresses himself in *P* as merely 'deferring death', authorizing treatment as a last resort and 'with reluctance'.

Fortin has said, 'case law establishes far less stringent requirements when assessing an adult patient's competence to refuse treatment (than a child). These requirements are difficult to justify on logical grounds to the teenagers themselves' (2003, 133).

## Incompetent: refusing to consent to organ transplant

11.44   In some cases, adolescents who are gravely ill and in need of an organ transplant have decided that they do not want to endure the pain and suffering and refuse to consent to transplant surgery. On 13 November 2008, Hannah Jones, 13 years old, succeeded in the High Court in refusing a transplant. 'I am not a normal thirteen year old I am a very deep thinker. I have had to be with my illness. Its hard to know I am going to die but I know whats best for me' (see *Hannah's Choice* by Kirsty Jones and Hannah Jones, HarperCollins, 2010).

> In *Re M (Child: Refusal of Medical Treatment) (1999)*, a 15 and a half-year-old adolescent was close to death. The court ordered that doctors should be allowed to treat the adolescent with a heart transplant. The doctors applied to the High Court for authorization to carry out the operation. They contacted the judge, Johnson J at home in the evening (as is often the case in such cases which require emergency intervention). The judge then immediately contacted the Official Solicitor at his home. As the Official Solicitor was in London, he was unable, in the time available, to see M himself and to ascertain from M her wishes and to hear representations on behalf of the child. The Official Solicitor appointed a local solicitor, Mr Winter to act as his agent. Mr Winter interviewed M that same evening and his notes contained these reflections from M:
>
> ...*if I don't have the operation I will die. I really don't want a transplant—I am not happy with it—I don't want to die..... If I had the transplant I wouldn't be happy. If I were to die my family would be sad....Death is final—I know I can't change my mind. I don't want to die, but I would rather die than have the transplant and have someone else's heart, I would rather die with 15 years of my own heart. If I had someone else's heart, I would be different from anybody else—being dead would not make me different from anyone else. I would feel different with someone else's heart.*

Johnson J having considered M's wishes and the view of the Official Solicitor that M was overwhelmed by events concluded:

> *Whilst I am very conscious of the gravity of the decision I was making in overriding M's wish, it seemed to me that seeking to achieve what was best for her required me on balance to give the authority that was asked.*

Thus, adolescent *M* was considered incompetent although the court did not expressly say so nor was this expression used by the court. However, the fact that *M* was considered to be 'overwhelmed by her circumstances' weighed heavily, and for all practical purposes she was considered incompetent.

## Incompetent: refusing to consent to medication/sedation

11.45 What if the adolescent's refusal is a refusal to consent to medication? We have already partially addressed this question in respect of the child R (*Re R (a Minor) (Wardship: Medical Treatment) (1992)* which involved the administering of sedation when considering Lord Donaldson's interpretation of *Gillick*.

> In *Northampton AHA v Official Solicitor and the Governors of St Andrews Hospital* (1994) (first reported as *Re K, W and H (Minors) (Medical Treatment) (1993)*) the issue as to whether three adolescents were Gillick competent arose once again for determination. A consultant psychiatrist of the hospital applied for specific issue orders in relation to the future administration of emergency medication to three minor patients. The three patients (two of whom were aged 15, and one of whom was 14 years old) who were admitted were required to consent to the administering of oral or intramuscular tranquillizing treatment should an emergency situation dictate that such medication was necessary. Consent to such medication had been given by all families, in the exercise of their parental responsibility for their offspring, but the adolescents concerned refused consent to such treatment. The consultant psychiatrist applied for specific issue orders (CA 1989, s 8 in relation to the administration of future emergency medication). The first adolescent was diagnosed as suffering from 'unsocialized adolescent conduct disorder' in that she was said to have had an 'extremely disturbed and chaotic adolescence'. In her case no emergency medication had been administered, as it had not been considered necessary. The second adolescent was diagnosed as suffering from 'adolescent conduct disorder,' she too was described as having had an extremely disturbed adolescence and in her case the staff at St Andrew's hospital found it necessary to administer a tranquillizing drug, Droperidol. The third adolescent was diagnosed with suffering from 'bipolar effective disorder' and on the day of her admission was considered to be mentally ill and professional judgement was that her admission could have been secured under the Mental Health Act. She had been prescribed Lithium. In her case, an application was made under the Family Proceedings Rules 1992, r 9.2A(4) to remove the guardian ad litem and an

application under r 9.2A(6): 'Where the court is considering whether to grant leave under paragraph 4 and remove a guardian ad litem it shall grant the leave sought and remove the guardian ad litem if it considers that the minor concerned has sufficient understanding to participate as a party in the proceedings concerned or proposed without a guardian ad litem'. In determination of this issue the guardian was called and asked 'Do you consider that J, do you consider that D, has sufficient understanding to participate in the proceedings concerned without a next friend or guardian ad litem?' Both guardians said 'No'. So, as a result the Official Solicitor acted for all three adolescents. Thorpe J held that **Gillick** competence was a developmental concept. (Note that this is something different from age, and where behavioural problems are presented competence is negated.) The judge, Thorpe J, in the Family Division of the High Court in **K, W and H** held:

*In the instant cases I am in no doubt at all that none of these three is Gillick competent. Even were they Gillick competent, it is manifest that their refusal of consent would not expose Dr Burnett to the risk of criminal or civil proceedings if he proceeded to administer medication in an emergency and in the face of such refusal since in each instance he has parental consent.*

Thorpe J seemed to take the view that behavioural problems negate an adolescent's capacity to make a fully informed decision and he continued:

*I am in no doubt at all that the treatment methods that St Andrews have developed to deal with these extremely difficult and very important cases are not open to reasonable criticism or question, quite apart from a challenge to their legality. Dr Burnett established in evidence the statistics, which show, in relation to the John Clare unit, that of the 67 patients admitted to the unit and carried forward to discharge since January 1989, only 20 received tranquillising medication in emergency situations.*

The case went to the Court of Appeal, on another matter, that of whether Thorpe J was correct in ordering Northampton Health Authority to pay half of the Official Solicitor's costs as he had agreed to act and the adolescents were joined as parties. Sir Thomas Bingham ordered that the Hospital and not the Health Authority should pay half of the Official Solicitor's costs.

## Incompetent: refusing to consent to compulsory detention

11.46    In *R v Kirklees Metropolitan Borough Council Ex Parte C (1993)*, a 12 year-old who was in care was admitted to a mental hospital (St Luke's, Crossland, Huddersfield) by the local authority following violent and self-destructive behaviour: 'breaking windows, deliberately cutting herself with glass and threatening to throw herself out'. Before leaving the assessment centre, W was seen by Mr S, the deputy officer in charge. He explained to W why there was so much concern about her, especially her self-mutilation, and why therefore she would have to go to hospital. He did not consider that she was in a fit state to decide for herself whether she should be admitted. So he gave permission on her behalf, in line with the advice which had been received from Dr G. W was duly admitted at about 1 am on 18 November 1989. The issue was whether the admission was lawful and whether consent had been given. The adolescent applied for judicial review of the local authority's decision on the ground that since there had not been a compulsory admission within the Mental Health Act 1983, and as she was not a person needing treatment for mental disorder under MHA 1983, s 131(1), there was no power under the MHA 1983 nor at common law to arrange for her voluntary admission. The court held that there was nothing at common law to inhibit or restrict the admission of a voluntary patient. The local authority considered she was not *Gillick* competent and the local authority assented on her behalf under s 10 of the Child Care Act 1980: 'they were entitled to conclude that she was not competent, both on account of her age and on account of her general behavioural problems which were being exhibited at that time'.

## Incompetent: refusing to consent to Caesarean section

11.47     In *A Metropolitan Borough Council v DB (1997)*, D was 17 years and one month, pregnant, and a crack-cocaine addict. She had not received any antenatal care until very shortly before the birth of her child. Two days before the birth of her child, D suffered from eclamptic fits resulting from high blood pressure. As a result she was admitted into hospital, later discharging herself. On the day of the birth she was dangerously hypertensive; however she refused any examination and wanted to discharge herself. An application was made by the local authority, supported by her mother to the High Court for D to 'undergo such medical treatment as necessary, whether or not she consented; for reasonable force to be used to transfer D to hospital; and generally to furnish such treatment and nursing care as might be appropriate to ensure that D suffered the least distress and retained the greatest dignity'. As a result of that order a Caesarean was performed on D.

An emergency protection order was made in respect of the newly born child.

The local authority requested leave for D to be placed in secure accommodation, namely the maternity ward of the hospital, and for the order regarding medical treatment to continue. Mr Neisenbaum, the consultant obstetrician and gynaecologist formed the impression that D was a simple soul, possibly with some level of educational handicap, that she was diffident, neglected her appearance, and that her boyfriend encouraged her into prostitution to fuel their drug habits. Mr Neisenbaum was asked to express his views as to her competence and the judge summarized what he had said in this way:

*D is simple. She has some understanding. She does not understand what is being given to her or why. She knows as a fact that if she does not receive drugs she will be ill, but Mr Neisenbaum does not believe that she fully comprehends this.*

Cazalet J in considering whether she was competent applied the test in **Re C Refusal of Medical Treatment (1994)** where Thorpe J approached the question in three stages considering first the ability of the patient to comprehend and retain treatment information, secondly the ability to believe the information, and thirdly weighing the information in the balance to arrive at a choice. Cazalet J was satisfied that D failed at each of the three stages. He went on to say, 'I am satisfied on the evidence now before me that she is clearly not competent within the appropriate test.'

Cazalet J then followed Lord Donaldson in the case of **Re W** and said 'the requirement of her consent to necessary medical treatment in the face of a condition which is life-threatening or is a serious danger to her health carries very limited weight'. Because of her history of absconding from hospital the judge ordered that she be compulsorily detained for a period of seven days in order to enable her to have the treatment she required (see Judith Masson, Maureen Winn Oakley, and Kathy Pick, 'Emergency Protection Orders— Court orders for child protection crises').

## Incompetent as to participation in legal proceedings

11.48 Where the issue in question is not one of consent to medical treatment or to self-determination but one of consent to participate in legal proceedings, the courts, for different reasons, until very recently have been reluctant to accept that an adolescent may be competent. Section 10(8) of CA 1989 provides that leave may only be granted to the child concerned if the court is satisfied that the child has sufficient understanding to make the proposed application. The criteria for non-child applicants under s 10(9) of CA 1989 does not apply when deciding whether to grant a child leave if that child is the subject of the proceedings.

11.49 The test of competency where these circumstances arise is governed by the Family Proceedings Rules 1991, r 9.2A; Family Proceedings Rules 1991 (SI 1991/1247 (L 20)), r 9.2A (as inserted by Family Proceedings (Amendment) Rules 1992 (SI 1992/456 (L 1)), r 9). This rule is outlined by Sir Thomas Bingham in **Re S (A Minor) (Independent Representation) (1993)**. Rule 9.2A applies only to proceedings under the 1989 Act or the inherent jurisdiction of the High Court with regard to minors.

11.50 The rule distinguishes between those cases where a minor wishes to begin or continue with the proceedings without a next friend or to defend proceedings without a guardian ad litem having never had one, and the other situation is where the minor has had a next friend or guardian but wishes to dispense with the guardian or next friend and continue the proceedings without them. In the first situation the minor must be considered to have sufficient understanding to participate, second he must be able to give instructions. Sir Thomas Bingham in referring to the authorities states:

> *We accept that what has come to be known as 'Gillick competence' is the appropriate test in relation to the sufficiency of a child's understanding under the Act and rules. The earlier case law reflects the reluctance with which children's participation in legal proceedings was viewed and does not accord with the sentiments observed by Baroness Hale in Re D (A Child) [2007] 1 AC 619 FLR.*

In *Re C (A Minor) (Care: Child's Wishes) (1993)*, a single parent father of 64 years of age and in poor health was solely responsible for the upbringing of two children, a girl of 13 and a boy of 12 years. The girl was arrested for shoplifting, and she and her friend had reported to the police of incidents, which involved their ill treatment and rape by male friends of her father. The local authority applied to remove her from her father and place her in their care. The court made a care order. The girl wanted to remain with her father and the father appealed. His appeal to the Family Division of the High Court was dismissed. Waite J said that it felt that the father was unable to meet the girl's needs and said:

> *I agree with comments that were made by her guardian ad litem, both in the original report and in evidence on this appeal. Those are to the effect that C is too young to carry the burden of decisions about her own future, and too young to have to bear the weight of responsibility for a parent who lacks authority and plays on her feelings of protectiveness.*

And later Waite J said:

> *She would be sad, of course, but she must learn and be helped to make the best of it.*

Waite J also added that young children should be discouraged from attending High Court appeals since, even where children are competent to assess the situation, it was simply inappropriate. In this case, the adolescent's wishes were overridden because the court considered that the threshold of significant harm had been met. It could be argued that removal of the child was unnecessary and that the local authority could have supported the father in caring for his daughter. Whilst the court considered that 'C is too young to carry the burden of decisions about her future', and that participation in court proceedings should be avoided because 'it undermines the stability and lightness of heart which could be called the natural birthright of every child', the court in another breath were content that she would be 'sad' but would have to get on with it, which is incompatible with their view of 'lightness of heart'.

Again, an unrealistic threshold of understanding has been set which in many cases the adolescent is unable to meet.

11.51  Where competency with regard to participation is concerned age has been considered by the courts to be a central issue. Sir Thomas Bingham in *Re S* did not consider an eleven year-old boy old enough to fully participate.

In *Re S (a Minor) (Independent Representation) (1993)*, in the course of divorce proceedings, the son S, aged 12, asked for leave to make an application for a residence order. S wanted to live with his father. He was fearful that unless he was able to make representations to the court, the court would attach insufficient weight to his wishes. The court refused the application and supported the view of the judge at first instance because S was not considered sufficiently mature enough to understand the legal proceedings and participate as a party. The judge of first instance had refused the application because S's wishes might be the result of influence exerted by the father and refused his application. On appeal, Sir Thomas Bingham MR stated the legal position:

*The proposition that a boy of 11 should be accorded the full rights of a litigant to intervene in a dispute between his parents about the arrangements best suited to promote his welfare (including his emotional, psychological, intellectual and social development) may be surprising to some. But it is said to be justified by the reforms made by the Children Act 1989 in the law and practice relating to children.*

In that case the court was referred to three other cases:

*We have been referred to three recent authorities, which illustrate the way in which the courts have approached the matter. In In re H. (Minors) (unreported), 6 August 1992; Transcript No. 769 of 1992, a case concerning children aged 10 and 7, Butler-Sloss LJ in a judgment with which Kennedy LJ agreed, said: 'I would expect that rule 9.2A would be extremely valuable for the older teenager and is most unlikely to be used in regard to younger children.'*

In *In re T (A Minor) (1993)*, Thorpe J commented, in proceedings launched under rule 9.2A by a 13 year old without a guardian:

*I am bound to say that in an issue of this great complexity, and with a child of only 13 years of age, I doubt whether, on an application for leave, I would have been persuaded that she had sufficient understanding to participate without the aid of a guardian. In a case of this sort, which is referred to the High Court with much complexity and delicacy, I would have certainly regarded the Official Solicitor as the appropriate guardian ad litem...*

In *Re H (A Minor) (Care Proceedings) (1992)* Thorpe J rejected a submission that almost any child of 15 years and eight months must be taken to have sufficient understanding to instruct a solicitor: emotional disturbance may be of such a level 'as to remove the necessary degree of rationality that leads to coherent and consistent instruction'. He went on to say, at p 340:

*Adolescent representation in private proceedings and public proceedings are different for 1991 part 4 care proceedings and part 9 private law cases. In care proceedings the adolescent—if competent—can discharge the guardian ad litem.*

11.52    *Re C (a Minor) (Leave to Seek Section 8 Orders) (1994)*, involved a teenager's application for judicial authority to go on holiday to Bulgaria against her parents' wishes. She was seeking leave under CA 1989, s 10(8) to apply for a specific issue order regarding the holiday and a residence order to confirm the lawfulness of her living with her friend's family instead of her own. She was nearly 15 years of age and was unhappy at home. The court however did not assess her competence, but assessed her on the basis of its perception of the wisdom of exactly what she was asking, and held that it would not be in C's interests to be given leave. Although the court said that if given leave 'C might interpret being given leave as having achieved some advantage against her parents in a situation where she should be dealing directly with them'.

By 2000, the participation of the adolescent in proceedings became increasingly less resisted although children must still pass the test of competency. Where a child is named in an existing contact order, an application may be made by the child without leave as in *Re W (Application for Leave: Whether Necessary) (1996)*.

Although resistance still clearly exists as the following cases demonstrate:

In *Re H (Residence Order: Child's Application for Leave)* (2000), a 12 year-old sought leave to apply for a residence order to reside with the father. He felt that unless he was able to make representations to the court on his own behalf then little weight would be attached to his views. In this case, leave was refused by Johnson J because he considered it disadvantageous in the family situation of a child seeing all the evidence in a case between the parents. He went on: 'there would be the spectre (a word I choose deliberately) of a mother being faced across courtroom by solicitor or counsel acting on behalf of the child she bore'.

In *Re N (Contact: Minor Seeking Leave to Defend and Removal of Guardian) (2003)*, a boy of 11 years and four months wished to remove the guardian ad litem (children's guardian). Coleridge J held:

*I have come to the conclusion that in this particular case and against the background of this particular long and stormy application, L does not have sufficient understanding to participate in the proceedings and give instructions that are fully considered, in the sense of fully considered as to their implications. His wishes and feelings are clear beyond any doubt. That the guardian has communicated those to the court on numerous occasions is also beyond any doubt. He feels that he has not been listened to. What that means in practice, however, of course to an adolescent is that the adults are not doing what he wants. That is very often the state of affairs in applications similar to this.*

The court dismissed the applications by the adolescent for leave to defend the proceedings and for removal of the guardian.

The question of participation in legal proceedings arose *in S (A Child Acting by the Official Solicitor) v Rochdale Metropolitan Borough Council and another (2008)*. However, the question is not merely one of participation but also of representation. Art 6 (3)(c) (ECHR) states that every person under the ECHR has the right 'to represent himself in person or through a representative of their own choice.' This clearly has also been an issue for children who have not wanted the appointment of Family Court Reporters or Children's Guardians.

## '*Gillick* competence'—or simply raising the bar

11.53    Having explored some of the cases where the courts have ruled adolescents to be incompetent, what principles have guided them in arriving at this finding? What degree of adolescent understanding do the courts require in order that adolescents meet the hurdle of competence?

11.54    In the medical cases, e.g. ***Re S (1994)***, we are concerned with the adolescent's understanding of death and serious illness. Yet, the threshold of understanding set by the court, it would seem, is virtually unattainable. But there are further difficulties since the courts consider that those who are dying to be so 'overwhelmed by circumstance', that dying robs them of the ability to make an informed choice and they are therefore considered incompetent.

11.55    In the cases involving anorexia or behavioural problems, the courts have, it would appear, taken the view that competence requires a clean bill of mental health. Again, there is a paradox, since where the adolescent is behaving badly, is out of parental control, is suicidal or volatile, etc, albeit couched in medical jargon, i.e. 'anti-social behaviour disorder', then the adolescent automatically fails the test of competence. It is suggested that a higher threshold of competence is required for the adolescent than for the adult, since a badly behaved, suicidal, volatile 18 year-old would not be considered incompetent merely on the basis of the facts that so readily render the adolescent incompetent.

## '*Gillick* competent' at last!

11.56    But when some adolescents are deemed to be *Gillick* competent, even where this status is achieved, it is not given but always has to be fought for and wrested from the law by the adolescent concerned. And even where competent, there is no absolute right of a competent minor under 16 or an adolescent of 16 to 17 years to refuse treatment or to realize the object of self-determination. *Gillick* competent minors do not stand on the same ground as 'competent' adults, since a finding of competence is not determinative. The court may, and frequently does, override the wishes of the competent adolescent because the decision of the adolescent is not, as the court sees it, best for him or her. And thus their decision-making capacity is subordinated to the nature of the decision itself. The court overrides or trumps the adolescent's wishes by invoking the inherent jurisdiction/wardship jurisdiction.

The court has repeatedly said that, even where the adolescent is competent, he or she does not have the right of veto. So what is the weight that is attached to the adolescent's wishes in any matter for determination and what principles guide the court in such matters?

11.57 The guiding principle is stated by the court in the cases before them that a child's wishes will be considered and that the adolescent's wishes will have greater weight. But inspection of the case law inexorably demonstrates that the weight attached to the adolescent's wishes depends on the issue and the consequences of allowing the adolescent's wishes to prevail. Especially in cases where the adolescent's decision will lead to their own death their power to make that kind of decision is suspended. The court adopts its paternalistic role and acts as it sees fit with regard to what, in its view, is best for the adolescent. Where the adolescent's decision is not likely to have such extreme consequences the court can with greater ease of mind find competence and allow the decision to be realized. Compare the cases here below on procedure with the cases in the next section raising matters of consent to treatment.

> In *Re H (A Minor) (Care Proceedings: Child's Wishes) (1993)*, a 15 and a half year-old male adolescent had been made a ward of court on the application of his parents. His parents and sister went to live in France when H was 14. He stayed in England and lived with the R family. Mr R was later arrested for sexual offences against another boy and the local authority removed H, his parents taking him back to France. He ran away and returned to England and was in the care of another family, wishing to have nothing to do with his own family. He was receiving counselling and had made a suicide attempt. The Official Solicitor was acting as guardian ad litem. The adolescent applied to have him removed (under CA 1989, s 6(7)(b)) and to have his own solicitor, as he did not feel that the Official Solicitor was representing his views. His application was granted and the court said the test was that the court must be satisfied that he had sufficient understanding to participate as a party in the proceedings without a guardian ad litem (give evidence, be cross-examined, etc) and that the test for understanding is that the adolescent must understand what is happening now and what will happen in the future.

Booth J stated, 'This is an exceptional case' (and perhaps took a unique view). But, in the author's view, what is exceptional in this case is the fact that judicial paternalism did not render the adolescent incompetent. What is best for the adolescent, the court said, was not correctly an issue for them:

> *[I]n those circumstances, I am satisfied that H has sufficient understanding to participate as a party in the proceedings and should be permitted to do so. It is not for the court in applying that test to take into account what the court may or may not consider to be in the best interests of the child... I will remove the Official Solicitor and will allow H to instruct his own solicitors but I will invite the Official Solicitor to act as amicus.*

Similarly, in *Re SC (A Minor) (1993)*, an adolescent female aged 15 years who was living in a children's home, wished to apply for a residence order to allow her to live in the home of a long-standing friend. An application under CA 1989, s 10(1)(a)(ii) was transferred to the High Court. The court was satisfied that the adolescent had sufficient understanding to make a s 8 application as required by CA 1989, s 10(8). She was granted leave.

11.58 Consider the factual issues in the following cases.

> In *Re T (Wardship) (1993)*, the court upheld the right of a 13 year-old girl to represent her case, where T had contended on her appeal that once she had satisfied her solicitor that she had the required degree of understanding to give him instructions, she was entitled to make her own judgement as to what those instructions might be.

> In *Re C (Residence: Child's Application for Leave) (1995)*, the child's parents had separated and initially there was an order that she and her brother should live with their mother. In 1992, it was ordered that the child should live with the father. There were contact difficulties and at Christmas 1994 the child (aged 14 years) remained with the mother. The adolescent sought leave to make an application under the CA 1989, s 8, that she be permitted to live with the mother. The court granted the application.

## '*Gillick* competent': overruled in wardship

11.59 When the child is considered competent, his or her wishes may still be overruled. The court in such circumstances will ward an adolescent. This allows the court to act on his or her behalf. It has been said of the wardship jurisdiction that it is a protective cloak, but in the eyes of an adolescent it may well be perceived as a powerful weapon, which inevitably challenges their autonomy and defeats their claim.

> In *South Glamorgan v W and B (1993)*, a 15 year-old adolescent was depressed but refused to undergo psychiatric assessment, which she was permitted to refuse under CA 1989, s 38(6). The court found her to be competent, although it expressed it in the negative ie 'she is not incompetent'; nevertheless they exercised their inherent jurisdiction to overrule her wishes because of her depression. Douglas Brown J, said, 'I am not prepared to find on that evidence that she is "*Gillick* incompetent"'.

> In *Re C (Detention: Medical Treatment) (1997)*, a 16 year-old adolescent girl was suffering from anorexia. She refused recommended treatment and absconded from the clinic. The local authority applied for an order authorizing her detention in the clinic. The court ruled that:

> *that power included the authorisation of her detention in the clinic for the purposes of treatment, and the power to authorise the use of reasonable force if necessary for*

*that purpose. The precedent set in Re W (a minor) (Consent to Medical Treatment)*
*was followed.*

Although C was not in fact deemed incompetent.

11.60   So what exactly would these competent or not incompetent adolescents make of the court's decision to override their wishes and what would they make of their momentous achievement of satisfying the threshold of *Gillick* competence?

Certainly, any adolescent is concerned with consequences and outcomes and the effect of the ruling on his or her conduct in question. The adolescent who achieves competence will not be able to understand the judge who having deemed them competent appears to obstruct the realization of their wishes. As for the judges, their rulings have demonstrated little development of the principle of adolescent self-determination and autonomy. They may have considered the question but they disregard it if they consider that the wishes of the child do not further what they consider to be the child's best interests.

11.61   The dilemma persists. On the one hand the courts have a duty to respect the child and the wishes of the child and even more so the older the child, however where those wishes are considered to conflict with what the court considers is in their best interests and where those wishes amount to harm and especially to significant harm then the competent adolescent is overruled by recourse to the inherent protective jurisdiction of wardship. The courts have said their duty is to keep adolescents alive.

## On the road to adolescent self-determination

11.62   One cannot help drawing the conclusion that the *Gillick* competence principle, the principle of adolescent autonomy provided in the UNCRC and also in CA 1989, s 1(3)(a), have been little realized. Yet, when adolescents run into problems and difficulties in criminal matters, then the criminal law affords them all the autonomy and responsibility in the world.

11.63   Many of the cases that have been considered in this chapter reflect the feeble status accorded to adolescent self-determination. Should judges be concerned about the principle or the consequences? Indeed, is it possible to strip the principle from the case in which it is applied. Can judges put their own opinions of what is best for a child aside and to what extent should they when child law after all makes paramount the welfare principle. Booth J, clearly thought not when stating it was not for the courts, in considering the competence test, to consider whether the issue was one which was in the best interests of the child (*Re H (1993)*). But it is of course 'best interests' which justifies the court in overriding or undermining adolescent autonomy. Is it really worth the paper it was written on?

## Judicial activism

11.64 There is, however, some glimmer of hope for young people which may not be on a too distant horizon, which suggests that some judges are beginning to realize that the days of judicial paternalism, espoused by Lord Donaldson in *Re R* and *Re W* are over, and whether judges like or dislike the consequences and outcomes of the adolescent's right to autonomy and participation in the decisions young people make for themselves, the principle of competence and autonomy must not only be recognized but also applied and respected. This new chapter in the adolescent rights story is emerging in the four cases, which conclude this chapter. Munby J is determined that adolescent rights and autonomy is a principle not merely to be realized but to be defended. Thorpe LJ is of like mind, in defending the importance of legal principle over consequences.

## '*Gillick* competence': it's for real

11.65 Four important cases taken together show a decisive shift towards embracing *Gillick* competence.

> In *Re P (2004)*, a case discussed above, although the judge (Johnson J) did not accede to the adolescent's wishes, nonetheless his judgment and reasoning clearly marks a new way, demonstrating that judges no longer can justify making a decision contrary to a adolescent's wishes merely on the basis of a disagreement with outcomes. To repeat, Johnson J said he reluctantly ordered treatment, whilst recognizing that he was merely deferring death (see Richard Daniel, 'Mature Minors and Consent to Treatment: Time for Change').

> As Johnson J said:

> *In the words of Balcombe LJ in Re W (A Minor) (Medical Treatment: Court's Jurisdiction) (1993): As children approach the age of majority they are increasingly able to take their own decisions concerning their medical treatment...It will normally be in the best interests of a child of sufficient age and understanding to make an informed decision that the court should respect its integrity as a human being and not lightly override its decision on such a personal matter as medical treatment. All the more so if that treatment is invasive.*

> In *Re Roddy (A Child) (Identification: Restriction on Publication) (2004)*, the question arose as to whether Angela, who was 16 years old, was entitled to sell her story to the media. She had been in care, had given her child up for adoption and there was an

injunction preventing publicity made in her favour. She wished to vary that injunction so she could tell her story. The lawyers acting for her couched her case in terms of Arts 8 and 10 of the ECHR, on the basis that a child or an adolescent is equally entitled to protection by the ECHR rights.

Munby J in true Denningesque style so reminiscent of Lord Denning in *Hewer* (see Chapter 9) said:

*We no longer treat our 17-year-old daughters as our Victorian ancestors did, and if we try to do so it is at our—and their—peril...She is what Ward LJ described in Re Z (1996) 2 FCR 164 at 189, (1995) 4 All ER 961 at 984 as a 'competent teenager taking (her) story to the press'. She is, to use the language of Woolf J (as he then was) in Gillick's case (1984) 1 All ER 365 at 373–374, (1984) QB 581 at 596, 'capable of making a reasonable assessment of the advantages and disadvantages' of what is proposed. In my judgment (and I wish to emphasise this) it is the responsibility—it is the duty—of the court not merely to recognise but, as Nolan LJ said, to defend what, if I may respectfully say so, he correctly described as the right of the child who has sufficient understanding to make an informed decision, to make his or her own choice...For, as Balcombe LJ recognised, the court must recognise the child's integrity as a human being. And we do not recognise Angela's dignity and integrity as a human being—we do not respect her rights under arts 8 and 10—unless we acknowledge that it is for her to make her own choice, and not for her parents or a judge or any other public authority to seek to make the choice on her behalf.*

*Mabon v Mabon and others (2005)* raised the issue of the child's right to representation in a private law dispute. The applicants were three boys aged 17, 15, and 13 each of whom wanted their own solicitor and each to be separately represented in their parents' dispute, which involved residence and contact. The judge in the court of first instance found that they failed the test of competence under r 9.2A (6) (Family Proceedings Rules 1991 (SI 1991/1247). His Honour Judge Dixon found that involvement in the proceedings in this way would result it '...unquantifiable emotional damage from contact with the material in this case...' (quoted by Thorpe LJ at para 18). Thorpe LJ in the Court of Appeal said that it was simply unthinkable to exclude young men from knowledge of and participation in legal proceedings that affected them so fundamentally. They had been seen by an experienced family practitioner who had no doubts as to the sufficiency of their understanding: they were educated, articulate and reasonably mature for their respective ages. He said:

*Unless we in this jurisdiction are to fall out of step with similar societies as they safeguard art 12 rights, we must, in the case of articulate teenagers, accept that the right to freedom of expression and participation outweighs the paternalistic judgment of welfare.*

In *Axon v Secretary of State for Health and the Family Planning Association (2006)*, the contest was between the parent and the local health authority, the issue concerned whether the adolescent had the right to determine her contraceptive treatment unimpeded, or with no interference by parental wishes, and in the absence of their knowledge. The matter was the substance of *Gillick* and arguably had already been decided in 1986. However in the case of **Axon** what was new was the advent of the Human Rights Act 1998; the emergence of the right to family life (Art 8), and how broadly that Article could be construed. Mrs Axon, through judicial review, challenged the lawfulness of the 2004 guidance. The new guidance had extended the remit of matters over which a doctor could treat an adolescent patient to include sexually transmitted diseases and abortion; in addition the guidance stated that involving parents would be considered to be the exception. Silber J asserted at para. 86:

*The speeches of Lord Fraser, Lord Scarman and Lord Bridge do not indicate or suggest that their conclusions depended in any way upon the nature of the treatment proposed because the approach in their speeches was and is of general application to all forms of medical advice and treatment.*

The court concluded per Silber J that the parental right to respect for privacy of family life 'dwindles as their child gets older' (para 129). He went on to assert that: '…the parent only retains such rights to family life and to be notified about medical treatment if but only if the young person so wishes'.

And declaring that Art 8 was not engaged, he said:

*A third reason why I do not consider that the 2004 Guidance interferes with any article 8 rights of a parent is that it is established that a child's article 8 rights overrides similar rights of a parent. In Hendriks v The Netherlands (1982) 5 EHRR 223, para 115, the European Commission on Human Rights explained: 'The commission has consistently held that, in assessing the question of whether or not the refusal of the right of access to the non-custodial parent was in conformity with article 8 of the convention, the interests of the child pre-dominate.' 145. Similarly in Yousef v The Netherlands (2002) 36 EHRR 345, para 73, it was said: 'The court reiterates that in judicial decisions where the rights under article 8 of the parents and those of the child are at stake, the child's rights must be the paramount consideration.'*

More recently in *In the Matter of J (Children) (2009)*, the question of the weight to be given to **Gillick** competent children/adolescents who have expressed a specific wish, arose. Two boys who were the subject of a care order: namely S, 16 years of age, and Adam, 14 years of age, applied for permission to appeal the order of His Honour Judge Newton, in which he dismissed their application to discharge a care order made by him in February 2008.

However, this arose out of circumstances where the boys had been deliberately alienated by the father from the mother and where their express wishes were the creation of the manipulation of the father.

# Conclusion

11.66    Of course, the cases of *Roddy* and *Mabon* rest on the right to publicity and private law matters of residence and contact and legal representation; the decisions of the parties involved do not result in any serious harm unlike the cases which involve decisions regarding medical treatment and life and death matters. Johnson J in *P* was dealing with such a life and death case and his judgment clearly reflects his own disquiet with the position of the courts in such cases in enforcing their decision on a recalcitrant adolescent on no other basis than that the decision the adolescent would otherwise wish to make is irreversible and in extremis.

Death is a terrible consequence; the need for contraception for adolescents may be considered an undesirable consequence (certainly Lord Templeman thought so); abortion too may be a terrible consequence. Equally, one might argue that forcible sedation of young people is a terrible consequence. The judge in the court of first instance in *Mabon* considered the process of litigation itself to have terrible consequences.

11.67 What should the law's primary focus be—the empowerment of young people? the protection of their right to autonomy? And what if the exercise of that right positively harms them? Where does the court stand then, does it have a duty to protect them from such harms? Such questions would not be asked of adults. The contemporary vexed moral question is this: on the one hand the courts have a contract with the welfare of the child as paramount principle, so as Nolan LJ in *Re W (A Minor) (Medical Treatment: Court's Jurisdiction) (1993)* said: 'it is the duty of the court to ensure so far as it can that children survive to attain that age (majority)'. On the other, the courts have a contract with the adolescent to respect his or her wishes. Yet the courts will draw a line and suspend the adolescent's right to expression and self-determination if it considers that the adolescent requires protection from him or herself and will not, to use Lord Donaldson's expression, give the adolescent enough rope to hang himself, and will delay death as in E, a Jehovah's witness (*Re E (A Minor) (Wardship: Medical Treatment) (1993)*), who when an adolescent, the court compelled to undergo life-saving treatment amounting to blood transfusion. Ward J, said in his judgment that in later years, E would be likely to 'suffer some diminution in his convictions'. When E reached the age of 18 years, he demonstrated that his convictions were as strong as they had ever been and he exercised his right as a competent adult to refuse treatment. As a result of his refusal he died.

What should the law do? Should it embrace *Gillick* competence and let the living die, or exclude life and death requests from the *Gillick* application? The courts will probably eschew the judgement of Solomon and continue to manipulate the principle and the threshold of competence so as to achieve the most palatable outcome.

We wait and see for the moment when a life and death case comes before the courts to test the limits of judicial decision making in this new era of activism.

## FURTHER READING

Bridge C, 'Religious Beliefs and Teenage Refusal of Medical Treatment' (1999) 62(4) MLR 585

Cretney S and Masson J, *Principles of Family Law* (Sweet and Maxwell, 2003)

Daniel R, 'Mature Minors and Consent to Treatment: Time for Change' International Family Law Journal [2009] IFL 233

Douglas G, 'The Retreat from Gillick' (1992) 55 MLR 569

Douglas M, *Rules and Meanings* (Penguin, 1973)

Fortin J, 'Rights Bought Home for Children' (1999) 62(3) MLR 350

Fortin J, *Childrens' Rights and the Developing Law* (Butterworths, 2003)

Fortin J, 'Children's Rights—Substance or Spin?' September 2006 Fam Law 36 (759)

Fortin J, 'Accommodating Children's Rights in a Post HRA Era' (2006) 69 MLR 299

Hall A, 'Children's Rights, Parents' Wishes and the State: the Medical Treatment of Children' 1 April 2006 Fam Law 36 (317)

Hoggett B, *Parents and Children* (Sweet and Maxwell, 1984)

Houghton-James H, 'Children Divorcing their Parents' (1994) Journal of Family and Social Welfare 185

Jones K and Jones H, *Hannah's Choice* (HarperCollins, 2010)

Longhrey J, 'Can You Keep a Secret? Children, Human Rights, and the Law of Medical Confidentiality' [2008] CFLQ 312

Masson J, Winn Oakley M and Pick K, 'Emergency Protection Orders. Court orders for child protection crises'

Monk D, 'Children's Rights in Education—Making Sense of Contradictions' [2002] CFLQ 45

Murphy T, '*Re CT*: Litigious Mature Minors and Wardship in the 1990s' (1993) 5(4) Journal of Child Law 186

Macdonald A, 'The Child's Voice in Private Law: Loud Enough?' [2009] Fam Law 40

Raitt F, 'Hearing Children in Family Law Proceedings: Can Judges Make a Difference?' [2007] CFLQ 204

Taylor R, 'Reversing the retreat from Gillick? R (Axon) v Secretary of State for Health' (2007) CFLQ 81

Welstead M, 'Children's Rights or Parental Property?' (1996) Denning Law Journal 101

Ziebart D, 'Jehovah's Witnesses—Medical care, minors and the religious rite/right' (2007) Denning Law Journal 219

## SELF-TEST QUESTIONS

1  What issues are raised by the case **In the matter of *J (Children)?***

2  Baroness Hale observed in ***Re D (A Child) (2007)***:

    There is a growing understanding of the importance of listening to the children involved in children's cases. It is the child, more than anyone else, who will have to live with what the court decides. Those who do listen to children understand that they often have a point of view which is quite distinct from that of the person looking after them. They are quite capable of being moral actors in their own right. Just as the adults may have to do what the court decides whether they like it or not, so may the child. But that is no more reason for failing to hear what the child has to say than it is for refusing to hear the parents' views.

    To what extent have the courts embraced the wishes of children and adolescents?

3  What does it mean to be *Gillick* competent? How has this construct been understood and applied? How valid is Fortin's (2003, 87) assertion, '. . . parents and the courts may now exercise a form of "we know best" paternalism which takes little account of the need to respect adolescent capacity for independence'.

4  'The parental right yields to the child's right to make his own decisions when he reaches a sufficient understanding and intelligence to be capable of making up his own mind on the matter requiring decision', *Gillick (1986)*, per Lord Scarman (at 186). How far have the courts honoured the spirit and sentiment of Lord Scarman's ruling in *Gillick*?

5  However sad, tragic, and regrettable death is, do judges have the right to override the wishes of an adolescent whom they have agreed is competent? Should they?

6  Should judges be developing law in accordance with legal principles or is it right that the consequences of decision making should be the judges' primary consideration in approaching the question of adolescent autonomy?

# 12

# Children's welfare and private disputes

**SUMMARY**

In this chapter we consider what orders are available to secure the welfare of the child when parents separate or where they have lived separately, with regard to matters such as with whom a child should live, and the arrangements that the court can make with regard to contact with the non-resident parent and other parties (Children Act (CA) 1989 s 8 residence/contact). We consider the importance the law attaches to preserving contact between child and parent and regulating any change a resident parent or the parent with contact may wish to make in respect of a child's name, place of residence, or any of the myriad of other matters (schooling, circumcision, medical treatment, holidays abroad etc) that may arise relating to the child's upbringing (s 8 specific issue). We consider how the courts deal with contact applications where domestic violence is perpetrated by one parent against the other and where contact under such circumstances might be harmful to the child, and the further support for contact arrangements provided in the Children and Adoption Act 2006. The chapter concludes with a consideration of the problem of child abduction within the jurisdiction and by a parent domiciled in a different country from the parent with care and the role s 8 prohibited steps orders play.

## When parents fall out

12.1 When parents live separately from one another there may be a dispute between them as to where, and with whom, the children of their relationship will live (residence). The mother may want the children to live with her, the father may want the children to live with him. A Jewish mother may want her daughter to go to a Jewish school and her son to prepare and take barmitzvah (as was the case in *Re W (Minors) (1992)*). Differences of habit, taste, political opinion, interests, faith, culture, and background, which seemed so very minor or at the most negotiable between the parties when they were in love, may become major battlegrounds now they have fallen out.

12.2 If the parties form new relationships and new families and remarry, a parent may want to change the child's surname to reflect the newly constituted family's name, and a step-father or step-mother who is now be part of the child's life may want that arrangement to be formalized as for example through or through a parental responsibility order (CA 1989, s 4(1)). Conflict and difference between biological or adoptive parents or those tasked with caring for the child over issues relating to care and upbringing may persist throughout the child's minority.

12.3 Fortunately, for many children, such differences are resolved amicably, between parents and those caring for them, without recourse to the courts (for example, research conducted by Blackwell and Dawe (2003) indicates that only 10 per cent of parents come to court over contact). For such parents/carers, it is just not possible to resolve matters outside the gaze of the court. In some cases, there may be arguments or violence between the parties and the children may become mere pawns in their game of hurting or controlling the other party, or else become a lever in bargaining for other spoils of the marriage, financial or otherwise.

## Someone to fight over me

12.4 The 1970s film *Kramer v Kramer,* starring Dustin Hoffman and Meryl Streep, where a marriage breaks down and a high-pitched custody battle ensues, demonstrates how all too often this fall out can be war, a theme replicated in the film *Losing Isaiah.* In **Beale v Beale (1983)**, the court welfare officer in her report said, 'Gary knows that both parents are fighting over him which, he says, is putting him under a long-term strain; he is trying to be loyal to both parents, but the situation is not doing him any good'. Nor was the situation doing Timothy any good. In *Janos v Janos (1988)*, the court welfare office reported, 'Timothy, reacting to the bonds formed in two opposing directions, is confused. This results in his behaving in a way that is only too familiar to the court'.

12.5 Children become something to fight for. So tragically in August 2010,

> *Theresa Riggi, 46, jumped from the balcony of the Edinburgh house where the bodies of twin boys Augustino and Gianluca, eight, and Cecilia, five, were discovered. It also emerged police had been searching for her after she apparently fled her home in Aberdeenshire with her sons and daughter last month.The tragedy happened just*

*one day after she was ordered to appear in person at the Court of Session. She is currently engaged in a divorce battle with her husband Pasquale, with the future of the children one of the issues between them. (Telegraph 10 August 2010)*

The child at the centre of *Re O (Contact: Withdrawal of Application) (2004)*, poignantly articulated the experience of the custody battlefield: 'its like a war ... you know they are fighting, and they are fighting over me'.

In *Re L (A Child) (Internal Relocation: Shared Residence Order) (2009)*, the judge recognized the battle that so frequently ensues:

*[69] L must therefore be able to appreciate that even though her parents are separated, they have respect for each other. Most disputes about children following parental separation have nothing to do with the children concerned: they are about the parents fighting all over again the battles of the past, and seeking retribution for the supposed ills and injustices inflicted on them during the relationship. This case shows every sign of going that way.*

Likewise *In The Matter of N (A Child) (2009)* the unhappiness of litigation is apparent as Munby J explained:

*2. The proceedings began on 17 October 2003, when N was only 2½ years old, and have continued ever since with unabated vigour. The President of the Family Division recently described the attitude of the parents until July 2008 as "acrimonious, confrontational and emotionally fraught in relation to N's residence and parental contact: see A v G [2009] EWHC 736 (Fam) at para [1]. I see no reason to differ from that assessment, which accords entirely with my own impressions of this unhappy litigation.*

Indeed, as research into the operation of the Family Proceedings Rules 1991, r 9.5 discovered, 'Many contested contact and residence disputes are emotionally abusive to the child but the parents are so caught up in their petty squabbles they don't see that' (Research into the Operation of Rule 9.5 of the Family Proceedings Rules 1991, at http://www.dca.gov.uk/family/familyprocrules_research_3.pdf, p 166.

12.6 In 2002, 30,006 residence and 61,365 orders for contact were granted (*Judicial Statistics* (2003)). This remained about the same in 2005, when 26,523 residence and 60,294 orders for contact were made (*Judicial Statistics* (2005)), and in 2006, 30,035 residence and 62,672 orders for contact were made (*Judicial and Court Statistics* (2006). However, by 2008, whilst orders for residence remained about the same as in previous years at 26,605 contact orders increased to 80,168. By 2009, 28,160 residence orders were made and 91,890 for contact. (*Judicial and Court Statistics* (2008), 2009). See also Butler-Sloss 2001, Pearce et al., 1999. See Table 12.1.

# Partnership principle

12.7 The overarching principle of partnership is central to the Children Act 1989 (CA 1989, s 17) in the resolution of these private conflicts. Partnership is encouraged between divorced/separated spouses and partners based on the experience that if parents/partners can resolve matters amicably then it will be far better for the welfare of the children of those relationships.

12.8 Partnership promotes conciliation and mediation in assisting parties towards agreement on residence and contact matters and to supporting parents towards developing agreements on a voluntary basis without recourse to a court order. The real work for the family lawyer is often less inside the courtroom and more outside, in mediating and negotiating between the parties in accordance with the Family Law Protocol.

## Family Law Protocol

12.9 The Family Law Protocol was first published in March 2002 by the Law Society Family Law Committee. It is intended to (a) develop a conciliatory approach to the resolution of family disputes; (b) to encourage, the narrowing of the issues in dispute; (c) work towards the effective and timely resolution of disputes; (d) minimize any risks to the parties and/or the children; (e) alert the client to treat safety as a primary concern; (f) have regard to the interests of the children and long-term family relationships; and (g) endeavour to ensure that costs are not unreasonably incurred (see Family Law Protocol, 3rd edition). In resolution of private disputes at what is called a 'first directions hearing', the duty of the advocate is to investigate the issues, inquire into the possibility of a settlement, and to give directions to the client (see Hershman and McFarlane, 2007). Directions are instructions given by the court with regard to what the parties or their lawyers need to do before the next court hearing including a timetable for the proceedings. Unless the case is urgent, a request for directions must be made in writing, and filed and served on the other parties, or, if by agreement, made in writing and signed by the parties or their representatives (see http://www.manches.com/practices/family/service.php?id=133).

## Conciliation

12.10 The Principal Registry of the Family Division operates a conciliation scheme (Practice Direction: Custody and Access (1982), as amended in 1992 and 2004 Practice Directions District Judge's Direction: Children-conciliation (12 March 2004)) where district judges may direct a conciliation appointment. Under a District Judge's Direction (Children: Conciliation) (2004), all s 8 applications (residence, contact, specific issue, and prohibited steps) are automatically placed in the conciliation list (and where the child is eight years old or above she/he is encouraged to attend) to allow both parents to see if an agreement can be reached. This discussion is guided by the judge and by an officer from the Children and Family Court

Advisory and Support Service (CAFCASS). No order can be made at the conciliation appointment unless the parents reach an agreement. If conciliation fails, the
judge will give directions for the future conduct of the application. Research shows
that conciliation appointments rose in 2004–2005 to 1,141 from 549 in the previous year. In addition, the Family Proceedings Rules, r 9.5 is being used more and
intractable hostility between parents was listed as being the main reason for such
applications (see Bellamy and Lord, 2003). Research conducted by Roberts and
Hunt (2005) found that 50–95 per cent of mediating parents achieved settlement
(cited in Stevenson, 2006).

# Child welfare: paramount consideration

12.11 In the past when the court considered any aspect relating to the child, the child's
welfare was only one of a number of considerations to which the court should have
regard. So, in the case of *Richards v Richards (1984)*, in a dispute between a married
couple regarding the occupation of the matrimonial home, and where the applicant
had made an application for an ouster injunction to remove the other party, the
House of Lords in its interpretation of the Matrimonial Homes Act 1984 refused
to allow the child's welfare to be placed 'first and paramount' (which in 1984 was
the terminology used by the courts) in its determination of the outcome—instead
ruling that child welfare was only one of a number of factors to which the court
should have regard (see Edwards and Halpern, 1988).

12.12 The CA 1989 resolved the uncertain weight to be accorded to child welfare, once
and for all, and established for the first time that the welfare of the child was 'the
paramount consideration'. The CA 1989, s 1(1) states:

> When the court determines any question with respect to—
>
> (a) the upbringing of a child; or
>
> (b) the administration of a child's property or the application of any income
>     arising from it,
>
> the child's welfare shall be the court's paramount consideration.

At the same time, on 20 November 1989, the United Nations Convention on the
Rights of the Child (UNCRC) 1989, Art 3, established that the best interests of the
child shall be the primary consideration.

12.13 The child's welfare is now at the epicentre of decision-making. Parental conduct
is now irrelevant unless it directly affects the welfare of the child. If the CA 1989
had been in force when *Agar-Ellis (1883)* was decided, Mr Agar-Ellis's children,

especially Harriet, (see Chapter 9) would have being allowed to spend the summer holidays with their mother; their wishes would have been considered, and their welfare would have been the court's paramount consideration.

# Court orders

12.14 The orders under the CA 1989, s 8 which the court can make with regard to the child include:

- **residence**: an order determining where and with whom a child is to live;
- **contact**: an order requiring the parent with residence to allow the person named in the order to have contact with the child;
- **prohibited steps**: an order to prohibit a party from making a particular arrangement, or doing something, which involves the child;
- **specific issue**: an order addressing a particular question regarding upbringing or care which needs the court to resolve.

## Who can apply?

12.15 Section 10(4)(a) of the 1989 Act provides that a parent, guardian, special guardian, step-parent by marriage or civil partnership who has parental responsibility and any person in whose favour a residence order has been made may apply for any of the orders listed above.

However, in the case of a residence only application, in addition, local authority foster parents may apply (s 10(5A)) and also a relative of the child (s 10(5B)) but the child must have been living with the applicant for over a year prior to the application (s 9(3) Adoption and Children Act 2002). Local authorities may not apply for a residence or contact order.

A child may also apply for leave to apply for an order under under s 10(8) which may be granted if the court is satisfied that he or she has sufficient understanding (see s 10(2)(b), (8)). See *Re C (Residence: Child's Application for Leave) (1995)*; *Re J (Leave to Issue Application for a Residence Order) (2002)*. Following the CA 1989, children sought applications because they disagreed with parents and for example wished to reside elsewhere. In view of these applications a Practice Direction: *Children Act 1989: Applications by Children (1993)* was issued which set down provisions for the regulation of such applications, requiring the application for leave to be made in the Family Division of the High Court. In addition, the need for children to have separate representation is recognized in the District Judge's Direction (*Children: Conciliation*) *(2004)*). A child may apply for leave to participate as a party in private law proceedings under the provisions in r 9.2A of the Family Proceedings Rules 1991 but such applications still remain unusual (see Baroness Hale's observations in *Re D* in Chapter 11).

## Welfare checklist: six factors

12.16 Under the CA 1989 s 1(4), when the court is considering any order under s 8 (residence, contact, specific issue, or prohibited steps), and, where:

(a) the court is considering whether to make, vary or discharge a s 8 order, and the making, variation or discharge of the order is opposed by any party to the proceedings; or

(b) the court is considering whether to make, vary or discharge an order under Part IV (care/supervision).

then, the checklist in s 1(3) applies.

However, it would be unlikely that the court, in applying the child's welfare as paramount principle under s 1(1), which it is always required to do, would not consider the checklist factors in some form or another even if the conditions in s 1(4) did not prevail.

12.17 In considering the welfare checklist under s 1(3) a court shall have regard in particular to:

(a) the ascertainable wishes and feelings of the child concerned (considered in the light of his age and understanding) (Gillick);

(b) his physical, emotional and educational needs;

(c) the likely effect on him of any change in his circumstances;

(d) his age, sex, background and any characteristics of his which the court considers relevant;

(e) any harm which he has suffered or is at risk of suffering;

(f) how capable each of his parents, and any other persons in relation to whom the court considers the question to be relevant, is of meeting his needs.

12.18 Whilst the CA 1989 introduces the statutory checklist under s 1(3), no particular outcome is envisaged or indeed can be predicted except in the terms of ensuring that child welfare is paramount. However, some of the presumptions that operated under the old law still remain 'good' practice with regard to interpreting the checklist factors. So, for example, where both parties are making an application for a residence order and where one party is homosexual, on balance it remains debateable whether homosexual parenting is really considered on equal terms with heterosexual parenting.

> In *C v C (A Minor) (Custody: Appeal) (1991)*, the parties married in 1983 and parted in 1984. They had a daughter born in 1983. The father issued a petition for divorce which the wife did not contest. By consent, the mother had care and control of the child with reasonable access to the father. The mother became a prison officer. She then fell in love with a woman prisoner, who was serving a sentence for unlawful wounding and theft, and on the prisoner's release went to live with her, taking her daughter with her. Meanwhile the father remarried. When the daughter was staying with her father and her new step-mother during the half-term holiday in October 1989, the mother and her partner were evicted from their home, and the mother asked the father to look after their daughter for a short period. The father then made an application for custody. The court of first instance awarded custody to the mother forming the view that the fact she was a lesbian made no difference to whether the child visited her mother from time to time or lived with her permanently. The father appealed.
>
> The Court of Appeal allowed the appeal and said:
>
> *The fact that the mother has a lesbian relationship with Ms A does not of itself render her unfit to have the care and control of her child. It is, however, an important factor to be taken into account in deciding which of the alternative homes, which the parents can offer the child is most likely to advance her welfare. The judge did not give proper consideration to this factor. That is why I would allow this appeal and order a rehearing.*

12.19 Since 1991 attitudes to lesbians and homosexuals and their capacity for parenting have changed, but the court may still consider on balance that a child's welfare is best served (where relationships with both parents are equally balanced) in being placed with a heterosexual parent.

## Failure to consider the statutory checklist provides grounds for appeal

12.20 A failure to consider the checklist where the court is required to do so, (i.e. where there is an application to vary, discharge, or challenge an order), may leave a judge's decision open to appeal (CA 1989, s 94). The House of Lords held that the principle adopted by the appellate courts in hearing custody appeals should be to overturn a judge's decision only when the judge in question has 'exceeded the generous ambit within which a reasonable disagreement is possible' (per Lord Fraser in *G v G (1985)*; see also *Re F (A Child) (2009)*). In *Re H (Contact Order) (2010)*, a married couple separated shortly after birth of their disabled child, Z, and the mother became the sole carer. The father applied for contact and at the interim hearing the judge made a shared residence order, involving several periods of contact with the father prior to the final hearing. The mother appealed. The appeal was allowed on the basis that the judge had failed to take account of a number of important factors under the checklist.

12.21 The statutory checklist represents, in fact, those factors which were most commonly taken into account under the old law and now places these six 'good practice' considerations on a statutory footing.

**'The ascertainable wishes and feelings of the child concerned (considered in the light of his age and understanding)'**

12.22 The inclusion of this factor arises from the development in case law following *Gillick* (considered in Chapters 9 and 11) and the responsibilities and obligations of states parties to implement the UNCRC. In *C v Finland (2006)*, the lower court had placed exclusive weight on the children's views.

12.23 The court is especially concerned to ensure that the views they express are indeed their own (see, e.g. *G v L (2010)*, where the court was concerned that the child's perception of his father had been orchestrated and manipulated by the mother, and see later in this chapter alienation factor). In *Williamson v Williamson (1986)*, where the children of 14 and 15 years of age said that they did not wish to live with their mother and 'voted with their feet' by arriving at the home of their father, this was a factor taken into account on appeal, together with the fact that the trial judge had erred in treating the occupation of the former matrimonial home as a relevant consideration on the matters of custody and was not entitled to find that there was a realistic probability that the two girls might change their mind (see also *Re: K (Minors) (1995)*).

> In *Re P (A Minor) (Education) (1992)*, where a 14 year-old boy did not want to attend Stowe School in Buckinghamshire as a boarder, but wanted instead to attend the local secondary school, the Perse school, in Cambridge, the Court of Appeal (per Butler-Sloss LJ) held:
>
> *We are dealing with the welfare of a 14-year-old boy. The courts, over the last few years, have become increasingly aware of the importance of listening to the views of older children and taking into account what children say, not necessarily agreeing with what they want nor, indeed, doing what they want, but paying proper respect to older children who are of an age and the maturity to make their minds up as to what they think is best for them, bearing in mind that older children very often have an appreciation of their own situation which is worthy of consideration by, and the respect of, the adults, and particularly including the courts.*

### 'His physical, educational and emotional needs'

12.24 The physical needs of a child include housing, accommodation, food, other material provisions and resources, and, if disabled, or otherwise a child with special needs, physical, emotional provisions and environment available to him or her. In *Re AR (A Child: Relocation) (2010)* where the court held that A's physical and educational needs would be equally well met in London or Troyes the court found that 'He has a strong emotional need to have a meaningful participation in his upbringing by F; this would be adversely affected were he to be relocated to France' (see also *In the Matter of G (A Child) (2010)* concerning a child with Asperger's syndrome).

12.25 A physically or mentally disabled child or child with special needs has particular needs.

> In *Re M (A Child) (Residence Order) (2003)*, A child, C, aged two years old, had been put under the care of foster parents by the local authority. At an interim hearing, the judge heard evidence that C's natural father and his new partner, L, should not be ruled out as future long term carers of C. A number of reports were compiled. The social worker contended that given the very special needs of C, and the demands that she would place on any parent, it would not be prudent to return her to the care of her father and L in their household which already contained six other children.... At the hearing, the judge concluded that despite those parties' misgivings, he considered that the father and L demonstrably had the capacity to meet C's needs. He therefore ordered the transferral of C from foster care to her father's house under a residence order, supported by a supervision order. The guardian, supported by the local authority, appealed. The appeal would be dismissed.

12.26 Educational needs refers to schooling provision, including type of school, continuity in education, and proximity of school. Emotional needs will raise issues of parenting and especially a child's need for mothering, and will also consider sibling and any other important attachments, such as the extended family.

12.27 A child's emotional needs are still best served by being raised by the mother, known as the 'mother is best' principle. However, where there is a dispute between parents over, say, residence, the idea that 'mother is best' is only a consideration, not a presumption.

> In *Re S (A Minor) (Custody) (1991)*, in an appeal from an order of Johnson J allowing an appeal from a magistrates domestic court (when that court ordered custody to the father and access to the mother), Butler-Sloss LJ in the Court of Appeal allowing the father's appeal and remitting the case to a new bench of justices for a fresh hearing said:
>
> *The welfare of the child is the first and paramount consideration...It used to be thought many years ago that young children should be with their mother, that girls*

*approaching puberty should be with mother and that boys over a certain age should be with father. Such presumptions, if they ever were such, do not in my view, exist today. There are dicta of this court to the effect that it is likely that a young child, particularly perhaps a little girl, would be expected to be with her mother, but that is subject to the overriding factor of the welfare of the child is the paramount consideration... I would just add that it is natural for young children to be with mothers but, where it is in dispute, it is a consideration not a presumption.*

In *Re A (A Minor) (Custody) (1991)*, the couple had six children. The mother developed an interest in the occult and in the paranormal. Four of the children were under 18 years of age and in respect of the children four applications for custody were made. As L was 16 years of age it was agreed that L did not require an order. The judge awarded custody of C and K to the mother and H to the father. The father appealed with regard to K's award of custody to the mother and the appeal was allowed on the basis that 'the judge's erroneous approach, based on his view that this little girl ought naturally to be with her mother, clouded his dispassionate assessment of the two homes'. The court held that there was no presumption that the mother should be the primary carer.

In *Re H (A Minor) (1990)* the court stated:

*it is not a principle but a matter of observation of human nature in the case of (the) upbringing of children of tender years, that given the normal commitment of a father to support the family, the mother, for practical and emotional reasons, is usually the right person to bring up her children.*

12.28 The child's attachment to siblings is also of relevance in the application of the welfare principle, since it is considered undesirable to separate brothers and sisters (see *Bowden v Bowden (1974)*; *Adams v Adams (1984)*). In *C v C (2003)*, Sumner J said, 'It is not usually advisable to separate siblings who are close in age and obviously allied with one another'. Half-sibling attachment was also considered in *Re N-B and others (Children) (Residence: Expert Evidence)*, and in *Re M-H (A Child) (Care Order) (2007)* where the court recognized the advantage of K being brought up with his half-sibling.

### 'The likely effect on him of change in circumstances': status quo

12.29 In *Re B (A Minor) (1983)*, Ormrod LJ said that the fundamental rule of childcare is stability and continuity. The stability or status quo principle continues to be reasserted in deciding where the welfare of the child lies. This principle is illustrated in the two cases below.

In *Allington v Allington (1985)*, for the first 18 months of her life, a baby girl had lived with her parents. The mother then left the home and her baby and went to live with another man. The baby continued to live with the father and spent some time with the mother. The judge awarded care and control to the father. On appeal, this was reversed since the basis of the judge's decision at first instance was that a status quo had been established which should not be altered. On appeal, the court held that, since such a short time had elapsed, there was not really any opportunity for the status quo with the father to have developed and the status quo was actually with the mother.

In *Re M (Residence) (2004)* an Israeli mother and English father who were married, settled in the town where the father had obtained a place at university. After the birth of the second child, the father started full-time work in another town and spent his working week away, spending weekends with the mother and his children. He subsequently found local employment and was able to be with the family during the week and at weekends. Several months later, the mother took the children on holiday to Israel and decided to remain there with the children. The father applied for a court order and the court granted the father custody of the children. The mother appealed. The appeal was allowed and the case remitted to a different judge for a retrial.

In *Re B (A Child) (Residence Order) (2009)*:

*a social care manager in her report, stated that the child was thriving in the grand-mother's care and that 'there [needed] to be compelling reasons to disrupt [the child's] continuity of care and the consistency and predictability that [accompanied] it'. The court, in allowing the appeal ruled that 'The judge had ... erred in allowing the question of the child's so-called right to be raised by his biological parent to define the outcome of the residence debate' and raised concerns that the issue of rights had become a distraction over welfare.*

## 'His age, sex, background and any other characteristic of his which the court considers relevant'

12.30 The age and gender of a child are relevant factors in considering what is in the child's welfare. 'Background and any other characteristic' embraces the characteristic of class, culture, ethnicity, race, language and religion. Class is, and certainly has always been, important.

12.31 The recent patterns of immigration (detailed in Chapter 9) have resulted in a diverse multi-faithed, and multi-cultural society, and in considering the welfare of the child as paramount, these dimensions of faith and culture are some of the more salient factors the court must consider.

### Faith

12.32 Religious faith may be given more or less weight depending on the particular facts of a case. Suhraiya Jivraj and Didi Herman (2009) explore how 'Christian norma-tivity' underlies judicial deployments of 'secularity' in a case study of the way in which judges have considered being Jewish, Muslim, and Sikh, and, in one case, Jain, within a welfare framework.

12.33　As each of the cases below demonstrate, the courts approach issues of religious faith from a position of the importance of religious belief and related practices to the present and future life of the child, depending on the age of the child, the ability of the child to understand religious and related heritage, and the relevance of religion to the child in future life, ie whether the child is likely to be reared in a particular faith or in a secular home. The wishes of the parents in this regard are largely immaterial especially where the child is not likely to be reared in an environment where the faith of the non-resident parent is practiced. Each case turns on its own particular facts—there are no hard and fast rules. Let us begin with the circumcision debate.

> In *Re S (Specific Issue Order: Religion: Circumcision) (2004)*, the parties, a Muslim mother and Hindu father, brought up their children as Hindus 'with Islamic influences'. After the birth of the children, the mother asked the father to convert to Islam, which he was not prepared to do. Instead, with assistance from the mother's family, the father underwent a Muslim ceremony of marriage in which he held himself out, falsely, as a Muslim. After the separation of the mother and father, the mother applied to the court for permission for both children to become practising members of the Islamic faith, and for a specific issue order to allow her son to be circumcised. The father opposed the application for a specific issue order. The court refused the mother's application and held that children of mixed heritage should be allowed to decide for themselves which, if any, religion they wished to follow. Circumcision was not in the son's best interests at present, because it would limit his freedom of choice. The Muslim religion permitted circumcision later, at a time when the son would be old enough to make an informed decision.

Let us now turn to religious education.

> In *Re W (Minors) (1992)*, the mother and her family were Jewish. The father was not. The parents separated, the mother had residence and the father had contact with the children through access. The father sought a specific issue order relating to his daughter's proposed attendance at a Jewish school, to which he objected. He also sought a prohibited steps order in respect of the preparation of his son for barmitzvah.

> In *Re P (A Child) (Residence Order: Child's Welfare) (1999)*, the child was born into an orthodox Jewish family. She was mentally handicapped. The judge found that because of her disability the child was unlikely to have any perception of her religious and cultural heritage so that culture or faith could not be the overwhelming factor nor could it displace other weighty welfare factors, including the exceptional attachment of the child to the foster parents and of them to her and the evidence of the harm to her which a move would cause.

In **Re B and G (Minors) (1985)**, the father was a practicing scientologist, although the mother had broken away from the sect. The Court of Appeal, even though disturbing the status quo principle, as the child had lived with the father, said that the child should be allowed to go abroad and live with the mother clearly considering that a child's best interests would be served by living with the mother in an environment away from scientology.

## 'Any harm which he has suffered or is at risk of suffering'

12.34 This means ill-treatment or the impairment of health or development (CA 1989, s 105(1)) in its very broadest sense. However, the threshold is not set at the level of 'significant harm', which is the threshold required in care proceedings when an application is made for a care or supervision order (discussed in Chapters 14 and 15) and where the harm includes physical, sexual or mental harm or neglect. The threshold, here, in private law proceedings involves 'any' harm. This might include the child's reaction to the father's alleged violence to the mother, as in **Re M (A Minor) (Contact: Conditions) (1994)** or the harm from witnessing the violence of a father to a mother (**Re F (A Child) (Indirect Contact Through Third Party) (2006)**). Indeed, the law has acceded that the harm to a child occasioned by witnessing a father's violence against a mother may in some circumstances satisfy the threshold of significant harm (see ACA 2002, s 120). 'Any' harm might involve a father administering 'a wrong dose of medicine, possibly because of difficulties in appreciating what the label said' (**Re B (Children) (2000)**) or, it might involve the harm that was identified in the following case.

In **Re J (A Child) (2005)** the father was from Saudi Arabia and the mother from Iraq. The mother came to the UK as a student with her son and filed for a divorce.. The father filed an application for a specific issue order requiring the child to be returned to Saudi Arabia. The court decided that the child should remain with the mother. The judge in the Principal Registry held on balance, were it not for one factor, he would have found it in the child's best interests to be returned to Saudi Arabia for his future to be decided 'according to the norms of his own society'. The factor tipping the balance the other way, however, was that the father had raised, albeit subsequently withdrawn, allegations about the mother's association with another man. The judge had heard expert evidence about, among other things, the effect of such allegations in Saudi Arabian society, bound by *Sharia* law, and the consequences for the reputation of the family member about whom the allegations were made. He was 'seriously concerned that an occasion will arise in which (the child's) interests are seriously damaged by a dispute between the parents in which the father deploys complaints of this kind and they have the dramatic effects that they would have in Saudi Arabia' (para 64). Hence, he declined to order that the child be summarily returned to Saudi Arabia. The father appealed and the Court of Appeal reversed the decision. The mother appealed and the House of Lords allowed the appeal and restored the orders made by the trial judge.

### 'How capable each of his parents, and any other person in relation to whom the court considers the question to be relevant, is of meeting his needs'

12.35 When required to make a decision between two parents, the courts will also consider amongst other matters standards of care, material circumstances, geographical location, the character of new partners and the child's relationship with them. With regard to material advantages, in the application of the welfare principle, the courts have accepted that, 'affluence and happiness are not necessarily synonymous' (*Re P (Adoption: Parental Agreement) (1985)*).

> This is how the court approached this welfare checklist factor in *Re B (Children) (2000)*. Hale LJ said:
>
> *But those needs then have to be considered in the light of the sixth factor, factor (f), which is how capable each of the parents (and any other person in relation to whom the court considers the question to be relevant) is of meeting those needs. The court welfare officer had made a bland statement that each parent was so capable. The judge clearly had in mind that this was not a father who had been out at work all day during these children's early years. He had been at home and on any view had played a considerable part in looking after them, although again it is not clear whether he had played the main part at all times, and that might be a factor which requires to be resolved. But there were matters which did have to be looked at. The father himself has difficulties with reading, although he clearly is able to overcome those difficulties in certain circumstances. The father also has physical difficulties, and those again may be thought possible to be overcome, but they are relevant to the capacity of these parents. It is striking when one looks at the response of each parent to the statement of P's special educational needs (and any court considering the capacity of each of these parents to meet those needs will be bound to look at what they had each been saying in statements which had been made on 21 and 20 July 1999 respectively) and the perceptiveness with which they approached those needs.*

Having considered all the factors on the welfare checklist in determining what is best for the welfare of the child, the court must move to the second stage, which is to consider whether it is better to make an order or not to make an order at all.

## 'No order' principle (CA 1989, s 1(5))

12.36 Under the CA 1989, there is a presumption against a court order and s 1(5) provides that a court will only make an order if doing so would be better for the child than making no order at all. The intention is to allow parents to make arrangements for themselves and to preserve joint and several parental responsibility. This is based on the experience that, if at all possible, it is better to support parties towards agreement without interference from the court and is in line with the spirit of partnership, mediation and conciliation.

12.37 However, if parents cannot agree, an order may become inevitable. But disagreement is not the only basis for an order, an order may be needed to confirm and give stability to existing arrangements, to clarify the respective roles of parents, or just to reassure and support the parent with whom the child is living.

12.38 The 'no order' principle places the burden on the person making the application to explain to, and persuade, the court why an order is better than leaving things as they are.

# Orders under the Children Act 1989

## Residence order

12.39 A residence order is an order 'settling the arrangements to be made as to the person with whom a child is to live' (CA 1989, s 8(1)). Residence can be ordered in favour of one party (resident parent) but also in favour of two persons who, eg, do not live together.

12.40 Where a residence order is made in favour of one party, no person may change the child's surname s 13 (1) (a) or remove the child from the jurisdiction for longer than one month. If a residence order is made to a person who does not have parental responsibility, say for example a grandparent, that person will acquire parental responsibility by virtue of the order (s 12(2)) (see *Re M (Sperm Donor Father) (2003)*). Residence orders may be made for a fixed period (s 11(7)(c)) and anyone who is entitled to apply for an order can also apply for a variation or discharge of a residence order (s 8(2)). With regard to the new nomenclature, in *In the Matter of G (A Child) (2008)*, Ward LJ stated:

> *The whole purpose of the Act in getting rid of the concept of custody and access, with concomitant thoughts that they each carry different rights and power and authority and regulation and control, all of that should have been swept away, so that you have an order which conveys no right but simply regulates a factual state of affairs.* (para 18)

## Towards joint residence

12.41 The CA 1989 allows for a joint or shared residence order, such orders are extremely useful in producing a level playing field for partners. Joint residence orders will only be effective where there is a good level of cooperation between the adults concerned. Wilson J in *Re F (Shared Residence Order) (2003)* summed up the aspiration of joint or shared residence and the importance of 'performative' language (see J Austin, 1958) in achieving a specific goal:

> *Speaking for myself, I make no bones about it: to make a shared residence order to reflect the arrangements here chosen by the judge is to choose one label rather than another...But labels can be very important...Indeed, where there is proximity of homes and arrangements between the two parents can be easily facilitated such cases are better suited to joint residency.*

> In *Re A (Children) (Shared Residence) (2003)*, the shared residence order recognized the equal status of both parents. (See also *Re R (Residence: Shared Care: Childrens' Views (2005)*.)However, in *A v A (Shared Residence) (2004)*, where the parents were not working in harmony and were opposed to one another, the case was nevertheless considered suitable for a shared residence order on the basis of the time the children spent in each of the parent's homes and the importance of each home to the children.

> In *P v BW (2003)*, P applied in January 2003 for a joint residence order in respect of his child and for the application to be heard in open court and with a public pronouncement of the judgment. P also applied for a declaration of incompatibility of s 97(2) of the Children Act 1989 with, Art 6 of the ECHR (see also *Re L (A Child) (Internal Relocation: Shared Residence Order) (2009)*).

How shared residence was arranged where to two parents lived in different jurisdictions was considered in *Re G (Leave to Remove) (2007)*, and in *Re H (2010)* following a long litigation history between the parents, the mother sought leave to remove her nine-year-old child to Australia. After a two-day hearing the judge involved in earlier litigation granted permission to relocate.

## Contact order

12.42 A contact order requires the party with residence to allow contact between the child or children in the resident carer's care and the person(s) named in the contact order. CA 1989, s 11(7) allows for the order to contain directions or impose conditions. The Children and Adoption Act 2006 aims to make provision regarding contact with children; to make provision as regards family assistance orders; and to make provision about risk assessments.

12.43 In custody disputes between parents, residence is usually awarded to the mother and contact to the father, although as has already been demonstrated there is no presumption favouring the granting of residence to mothers. Where children are in care (see Chapters 14 and 15), both or one of the parents may have a contact order made in their favour. Contact orders may also be made in respect of other relatives including siblings (*Re S (Contact: Application by sibling) (1999)*—here contact was refused). Or in the case of aunts (in this case the application was refused *Re H (A Minor) (1995)*, or uncles, and grandparents (see *A Local Authority v Y, Z and others (2006)*).

## Whose right—the Strasboug jurisprudence

12.44 Article 9 of the UNCRC asserts that contact is the right of the child. In *M v M (Child: Access) (1973)*, contact was regarded as the right of the child; see also *Re R (1993)*.

12.45 In *Re F* (1995), the court held:

> The starting point always, is that every child has a right to be brought up in the knowledge of his non-custodial parent. This is a right which the courts are determined to preserve'. It is not the right of a parent to contact with the child. However, the approach of the courts is that fathers should only be denied contact in wholly exceptional cases. These exceptional circumstances include domestic violence, illness, criminality, and eccentricity.

At the same time Art 8(1) of the ECHR which upholds the right to privacy and family life, has been successfully invoked in particular circumstances to preserve the right of a parent to contact with a child (see *Re KD (A Minor) (1988)*). This suggests that the parental right to access (now contact) did exist independently of considerations of the child's welfare. In *Kosmopolou v Greece (2004)*, the protection of family life rather than merely the interests of individual parties was an important consideration.

12.46 The views of the child are all important although not always decisive. Although the rights of the child may be paramount in a consideration of family life.

> In *Zawadka v Poland (2005)* and in *Kaleta v Poland (2009)*, the ECtHR held that there had been no violation of Art 8 where the child opposed contact. In *C v Finland (2006)*, the British father's two children had been living with the mother and her partner in Finland, When the mother died custody was awarded to the natural father but the decision was overturned and custody awarded to the child's deceased mother's partner on the basis that it was the clearly stated wish of the children. However, the Supreme Court overturned that decision because a proper balance between the child wishes and the natural father's wishes was not struck and there had been a violation of Art 8.

## Is contact forfeited where a spouse is violent?

12.47 There is considerable evidence that contact with a father who has been violent to the mother is damaging and harmful to the child. For some children, the effects of watching a mother being constantly abused are so great that in protecting the mother, they resort to killing the violent father (see *R v Maw and another (1980)*; *Pearson (1992)*). In *Maw*, Annette and Charlene Maw were sentenced to three years' imprisonment for the manslaughter of their father who was abusing their mother, following pleas of guilty to manslaughter, which were accepted by the prosecution with the approval of the Judge. In some cases the children themselves are murdered. The Women's Aid Federation of England compiled a report on the problem, 'Twenty-Nine Child Homicides: Lessons still to be learnt on domestic violence and child protection' in which 29 children from 13 different families had been murdered by their fathers during contact (see Saunders, 2004). In other cases children are physically or mentally harmed. Notwithstanding, domestic violence has never been a bar to child contact with the violent spouse as was asserted in *Re H (Contact: Domestic Violence) (1998)*, where a recorder's order for contact was upheld. Wall J said:

> As a matter of principle, domestic violence of itself cannot constitute a bar to contact. Each case must inevitably be decided on its own facts. Domestic violence can only be one factor in a very complex equation. There will be contact cases in which it is decisive against contact. There will be others in which it is peripheral.

12.48 However, by 1999, the danger and harm of contact for the child where the father had previously been violent to the mother began to be understood, recognized, and reflected in court decision making.

> In the case of *Re M (Minors) (Contact: Violent Parent) (1999)*, where the mother was subjected to domestic violence and the father had a drink problem, the justices found serious risk of destabilizing the family unit if the father were to be granted direct contact to the children. The justices refused to order contact. The Court of Appeal upheld their decision and reaffirmed what they considered the correct test to be applied in such cases as laid down by Bingham MR in *Re O* (above). Similarly, Hale J, sitting in the Court of Appeal, in *Re D (Contact: Reasons for Refusal) (1997)*, had said:
>
> It is important to bear in mind that the label 'implacable hostility' is sometimes imposed by the law reporters and can be misleading. In some cases the judge or the court finds that the mother's fears, not only for herself but also for the child, are genuine and rationally held.

However, in *Re L, V, M, H (Contact: Domestic Violence) (2000)*, where the fathers' applications for contact had been refused because of their violence to the mothers involved and the risk to the children of physical or emotional harm, the fathers' appeals to the Court of Appeal were dismissed. Although it is to be noted that the Court of Appeal rejected the recommendation of the expert psychiatric evidence against contact in domestic violence cases ruling that domestic violence would only be a factor in their consideration.

The extent to which judges throughout the jurisdiction have been elevating a presumption in favour of a contact order too high or trivializing a history of domestic violence must depend on the judges' interpretation of the principle and the facts of the case. The following cases suggest that domestic violence is still not regarded as a serious matter where contact orders in issue.

> In *Re F (A Child) (Indirect Contact Through Third Party) (2006)*, an order for indirect contact was made between the child and the father even though the father had been violent to the mother and the mother and child had to take on new identities in order for their safety to be safeguarded.
>
> In *H (Contact: Domestic Violence) (2006)*, where a judge had granted contact to a father in the context of domestic violence against the mother, on appeal the Court of Appeal remitted the application for contact to the county court and allowed the appeal on the basis that:
>
> *In the instant case, there were several errors in the later judgment as to his earlier findings of fact. It was wholly unacceptable for the judge to have made only one incomplete and highly selective reference to the judgment in Re L, a seminal decision of the court, in his first judgment, and to have made no reference to it whatsoever in his second judgment... [and his failure to follow the guidance in Re L and to have regard to the Sturge/Glaser report]. The critical area of the guidelines which the judge did not appear to have addressed were 'the capacity of the parent seeking contact to appreciate the effect of past and future violence on the other parent and the children concerned' and 'the attitude of the parent seeking contact to past violent conduct by that parent; and in particular whether that parent has the capacity to change and/or to behave appropriately'. Many of the views expressed by the judge in his May 2005 judgment were partial, distorted, and not based on the evidence. So hostile was the judgment to the mother, and so partial were the judge's findings, that it should be open to another judge on a re-hearing (should he or she deem it appropriate) not to be bound by the findings made by the judge...*
>
> In *Re M (Children) (2009)*, the father applied for contact in a case where there were allegations of domestic violence between the parents; see also *Re E (A Child) (2009)*.

## Contesting an application for contact and 'Implacable hostility' for no good reason

12.49 Over the past two decades, the courts have also made it clear that objections to contact put forward by mothers will rarely succeed.

> In *Re D (A Minor) (Contact: Mother's Hostility) (1993)* the Master of the Rolls, Waite LJ said:
>
> *The courts should not at all readily accept that the child's welfare will be injured by indirect contact.... Neither parent should be encouraged or permitted to think that the more intransigent, the more unreasonable, the more obdurate and the more un-cooperative they are, the more likely they are to get their own way.*
>
> Balcombe LJ in *Re J (A Minor) (Contact) (1994)* similarly remarked:

*I would like to say that judges should be very reluctant to allow the implacable hostility of one parent (usually the parent who has a residence order in his or her favour) to deter them from making a contact order where they believe the child's welfare requires it.*

In *Re P (Minors) (Contact: Parental Hostility) (1997)*, the court summarized the decision in *Re O (Contact: Indirect Contact) (1996)* in the following propositions:

- the welfare of the child is the paramount consideration;
- it is almost always in the interests of a child whose parents are separated that he or she should have contact with a parent with whom the child is not living;
- the court has power to enforce orders for contact, which it should not hesitate to exercise where it judges that it will overall promote the welfare of the child to do so;
- in cases in which, for whatever reason, direct contact cannot for the time being be ordered, it is ordinarily highly desirable that there should be indirect contact.

In such cases the courts will seek to discover whether the child's hostility to contact is genuine or whether it is shaped by the attitude of the mother (see *Re T (Contact: Alienation: Permission to Appeal) (2002)*).

The Children and Adoption Act 2006 gives powers to the courts to enforce contact where it has been ordered by the court and case law has shown that where there is implacable hostility to contact by the residential parent for no good reason then residence may be transferred to the parent with contact as in *Re C (A Child) (2007)*.

In *Nowak v Poland (2006)* the mother refused to facilitate contact between the father and the child. Several attempts were made to facilitate contact. The child began to resist contact. The court refused to impose fines on the mother on the basis that forced contact was not good for the child. The father alleged that failure to facilitate contact was a breach of Art 8. The court held:

*that the obligation to take measures to facilitate contact is not absolute and there was no violation of Art 8. A key consideration was whether the authorities had taken all necessary steps to facilitate contact such as could reasonably be demanded in the special circumstances of the case. There were difficulties in arranging contact due in large measure to animosity between the parents and subsequently to the child's attitude. It was relevant that the father did not seek any contact for about four years.*

The Children and Adoption Act 2006 now makes provision for monitoring contact, including warning notices for failure to comply including (an 'enforcement order') imposing on the person an unpaid work requirement (inserting s 11 I and

11 J) into the CA 1989). In addition, the *Practice Direction (Residence and Contact Orders: Domestic Violence (No 2) (2009)* issues guidance setting out how such cases should be handled.

The Practice Direction states that "before an order for contact is made the court must be satisfied "that the physical and emotional safety of the child and the parent with whom the child is living can, as far as possible, be secured both during and after contact" (Para 26).

## Defined contact

12.50   Under CA 1989, s 11(7), the court can attach conditions to contact. Some parents have defined contact, where contact is confined to times, places, and conditions, etc. Contact directions set out the conditions of contact. Consider the directions set out in *Re H (A Child) (2010)*:

> *[23] The father works fully for one week and has one week off. Therefore when he is not working it is easier for him to have contact than it is during the week that he is working. During the week that he is working I would order two two-hour periods of contact at the contact centre in Manchester, and, in the week that he is not working, I would order on the Saturday and Sunday either two hours if it is possible, or one hour if it is not possible. That would cover the first two weeks from now. Thereafter, I would direct two overnight stays per fortnight with the father staying in Manchester in the circumstances that he has advocated in the argument put before us by Ms Eaton. That would, I think, be between 2pm on one day and 11.30am on the following day, and that order should continue until the full hearing.*

See also *In the Matter of B (A Child) (2009)* and *Re S-R (Jurisdiction) Contact) (2008)*.

> In *Re B (A Child) (Contact: Parent's Liability to Pay Child Support) (2006)* the order for contact dated 5 July 2004 provided, broadly, for L to have contact with the father as follows:
>
> (a) *each alternate weekend, both in term-time and during holidays, from 6:00pm on Friday until Monday morning;*
>
> (b) *each Wednesday evening in term-time until 8:00pm;*
>
> (c) *a fortnight plus one day during each summer holiday;*
>
> (d) *at least two further nights during each summer holiday;*
>
> (e) *a week, plus in alternate years one day, in each October half-term holiday;*
>
> (f) *five nights during each Christmas holiday;*
>
> (g) *two days in each February half-term holiday;*
>
> (h) *a week during each Easter holiday and, in alternate years, one further day; and*
>
> (i) *visiting contact on L's birthday and on Father's Day.*

## Restrictions on contact

12.51 In *Re B (Minors: Access) (1992)* where a father who was socially awkward and suffered from anxiety, and where his eccentric behaviour, e.g. walking along a street with a plastic bag on his head, distressed his children, an application for contact with them was refused. However on appeal, the Court of Appeal said that, 'a father who was genuinely fond of his children, but who exhibited eccentric, bizarre behaviour, capable of baffling or distressing a child, should not be prevented from having defined access to his children'.

In *Re H (Children) (Contact Order) No 2 (2002)*, the father, who had Huntington's Chorea, applied for contact. Direct contact had been withdrawn following his threats to kill himself and the children. The children wanted direct contact with their father.

The judge refused direct contact. On appeal, the Court of Appeal was critical of the judge's failure to analyse the nature of the harm of which the father was capable and also of the judge's rejection of professional recommendations for supervised contact. It allowed the appeal to the limited extent of directing a review of the father's application for direct contact.

In *Re D (Children: Contact Order) (2005)*, where the court found that the parents had failed to protect the children who had suffered numerous incidents of physical harm and accepted that the threshold conditions had been established under CA 1989, s 31, the Court of Appeal granted the father an order for indirect contact.

## Supervised contact

12.52 Some parents/carers will have supervised contact, where contact with the child is supervised by a child contact social worker (contact co-ordinator). David Blunkett, a former Home Secretary, who was blind, was awarded two hours' supervised contact per month with his son. The visits were ordered to take place under the personal supervision of a friend of Ms Quinn (*Blunkett v Quinn (2005)*).

## An order for 'no contact'

12.53 It is unusual for the court to make an order for 'no contact' as the courts recognize the importance for the child of having regular contact with both parents, as has been demonstrated above. In recent years, it has been recognized in public policy and by the courts that in some circumstances contact may be detrimental for the child.

In *Re F (Minors) (Denial of Contact) (1993)*, two boys aged nine and 12 did not wish to have contact with their father after their parents separated. The father was a transsexual. The father then made an application for contact which had to be determined by the court. Contact was refused and the father appealed. The court welfare officer stated in her report, 'I do not believe that access should be denied to (the father); before that ever happens there should be much greater effort at mutual understanding. If the boys are denied contact completely with their father now I believe they will be more damaged in the long term than if work is done helping this family to meet and work something out now.' The judge was not prepared to make any order which would have a coercive effect on the boys or would compel the mother to coerce the boys into contact which they did not want. The Court of Appeal upheld the decision of the lower court.

An order for 'no contact' may also be ordered where the court is attempting to settle a child in a foster placement. In *Re B (Minors) (Termination of Contact: Paramount Consideration) (1993)*, the local authority obtained care orders in respect of two girls born in 1988 and 1990 respectively. The mother hoped for the girls' eventual return to her care. The local authority applied, under CA 1989, s 34(4), for an order authorizing them to refuse to allow contact between the girls and the mother so as to be able to place the girls with prospective adopters. The mother opposed the application but it was granted by the judge.

> *In The Matter of G (A Child) (2010)*, the child was three years of age. The English father had been living in Panama and the Lithuanian mother in England. The mother made allegations of violence and alcohol abuse against the father. An order for no contact with the father and a s 91(14) order was made for five years. In arriving at this decision, the judge had relied on a two-year old social services report stating that contact with the father was impractical because there was no means of monitoring it, although there were no findings of fact. The court held that refusal of all forms of contact was excessive and ordered two years of indirect contact, when the father could then apply for a more direct form of contact (see also the no contact with mother case *Re A (Contact Order)*).

### The problem of alienation

12.54  In such situations of parental acrimony one parent's hostility towards the other may create alienation for the child. HHJ Bellamy notes in *Re S (A Child: Transfer of Residence (2010)* that:

> The concept of alienation as a feature of some high conflict parental disputes may today be regarded as mainstream. Here the courts are concerned that the child's wish for no contact with a parent should not be a posture instigated by the parent with residence. The courts have dealt with such situations by granting contact to the non-resident parent, or where appropriate by transferring residence altogether.

In this case, the father consented to indirect contact only and the child had been deliberately 'alienated' from one parent. S, aged 12, had been the subject of court proceedings and in January 2010 Bellamy J transferred the residence of S to the father. The mother's appeal aagainst this order was dismissed. But at contact sessions with the father S would sit with his head in his lap and fingers in his ears with the result that the father consented to S returning home to the mother under an interim care order. In July 2010 the father abandoned his attempts to enforce the residence order. By consent, it was ordered that there should be a residence order to the mother, a supervision order to the local authority, indirect contact by the provision of school reports and photographs.

## Specific issue order

12.55 A specific issue order empowers the court to give directions for the purpose of determining a specific question, which has arisen with regard to, eg, moving the child to another part of the country, a change of name, immunization, circumcision, holiday or police interviewing of a child, as the cases below reflect.

> In *H-D (Children) (2001)* cited above, where the parents had separated and the mother wanted to move with the children to another part of the country, the father had made an application for a prohibited steps order pending the final decision of residence and contact. The judge accepted undertakings from the mother T.

> The court made an order of residence to the mother, and contact to the father. He also made a specific issue order so that the mother could control the choice of the children's schools (the children concerned were two boys—J who was eight and a half years of age and K who was five years old) because, in his view, she would struggle to keep them at their present school, but he provided that she should give two months' notice to the father if she wanted to change (see *Re J (A Child) (Return to Foreign Jurisdiction: Convention Rights) (2005)*, where the father applied for a specific issue order for the child to be returned to Saudi Arabia and where the order was refused).

> In *Dawson v Wearmouth (1999)*, the question before the court was whether the judge had jurisdiction to make an order specifying the name by which a child should be known. It was held that the surname Wearmouth had been the mother's actual name at the time it was chosen by her, as well as being the surname of Alexander's half-brother and half-sister. It was therefore a logical choice for her to make and could not be criticized as alien simply because it was also the name of the mother's ex-husband. The considerations cited by the judge would apply to virtually every case where the father sought to play a role in the life of his illegitimate child. In the circumstances, the court would decline to make the order sought by the father.

> In *A v Y (Child's Surname) (1999)*, the judge did not consider it in the best interests of the child to attach the father's name alongside the mother's maiden name with regard to the child.

In *Re C (Welfare of Child: Immunisation) (2003)*, the applications concerned two children (from two different families), aged four and 10 years, neither of whom had received any form of immunization against infectious diseases. In each case, the child lived with the mother, who was opposed to immunization, while the non-resident father approved of immunization. Both fathers applied for a declaration requiring immunization. Both mothers argued that immunization involved risks, and that immunization would cause undue distress. One of the mothers argued that the father's application was part of an attempt to exercise control over her. The court held that appropriate immunization was in the best interests of the children (see also *Re B (A Child) (Immunization) (2003)*).

In *Re J (Child's Religious Upbringing and Circumcision) (2000)*, the English mother, a non-practising Christian, met the father, a non-practising Muslim of Turkish origin, whilst on holiday in Turkey in 1992. They married in Turkey and returned to England. Their son, J, was born in March 1994. The parents separated when he was two and a half years old. The child was brought up by the mother. His only contact with Islam was through his father, and he himself did not have any Muslim friends or mix in Muslim circles. When J was five years old, the father applied for a specific issue order that J be circumcised. The judge held that it was not in J's best interests to be circumcised. The father appealed with leave to the Court of Appeal contending, *inter alia*, that the judge confused the child's religion with the child's religious upbringing. The Court of Appeal decided that circumcision was not a matter that one parent could decide upon; it was a matter for both parents and any disagreement should be referred to the court for its determination, each case being decided on its own facts.

In *Chief Constable of Greater Manchester v KI and KW (by their Children's Guardian, CAFCASS Legal), and PN (2007)* twin seven year-olds had witnessed their sister being shot with a gun fired by their 17 year-old brother. Their mother refused consent for them to be interviewed by police. A specific issue order was applied for and granted.

In *J v S (Leave to Remove) (2010)*, the Japanese mother was living in the UK with her children. She was divorced from the father and very unhappy. She wanted to return with the children to Japan. The court granted permission because it was felt her health would suffer if permission was refused. The mother was required to arrange contact and be flexible with regard to the children maintaining contact with the father.

## We're all going on a summer holiday

12.56 Arranging summer holidays for children can be something of a special problem where parties are separated and/or live in separate jurisdictions.

In *Re N (Leave to remove: Holiday) (2006)*, the mother had been refused leave to send her two children of 11 and on a holiday to relatives in Slovakia. The Court of Appeal granted consent but deferred the visit until the following year when the court considered the two children would be better equipped to deal with an unaccompanied flight especially as it also involved a change of plane.

In *M (A Child) (2009)*, an appeal against an order made in September 2009 permitting a father to take a seven year-old child on holiday to France and/or Cameroon was allowed. In this case the mother was concerned that the court should obtain expert evidence on the legal situation in Cameroon (a non-Hague Convention country) and how the child could be recovered in the event that the father retained him there before permission were given. In addition, the mother wanted the father to provide an undertaking to return and effect a notarised agreement in the High Commission of Cameroon in London. However, the notarized agreement anticipated by the judge was not possible, nor was the case adjourned for expert evidence.

There were 3,320 specific issue orders granted in 2005 (*Judicial Statistics* (2005)), 3,824 orders granted in 2006 (*Judicial and Court Statistics* (2006)) and 5,020 in 2009 (*Judicial and Court Statistics* (2009).

## Prohibited steps order

12.57 This is an order made by the court that no step, which could be taken by the parents in meeting their parental responsibility, should be taken without consent of the court. Prohibited steps are modelled on the wardship jurisdiction where the court can require that no important step in the child's life is taken without the consent of the court. The steps must be identified in the order.

12.58 Prohibited steps orders are made where there is a concern that one of the parents may remove the child or children from the jurisdiction. See eg *Re M (A Minor) (Abduction: Consent or Acquiescence) (1998)*; *E v E (Child Abduction: Intolerable Situation) (1998)* and the cases below:

In *Re M and A (Disclosure of Information) (1999)*, the local authority social services department became involved with the family. The children were living with their grandparents. On 9 January 1998, the grandparents issued an application for residence and a prohibited steps order to prevent the mother from removing the children from their care. That application came on for hearing ex parte as a matter of urgency. The judge granted the grandparents leave to apply for the s 8 order, committed the interim residence of both children to the grandparents, made a prohibited steps order, and provided for a further hearing to take place on 2 February 1998.

In *Re L (minors) (Sexual Abuse: Disclosure); Re V (Minors) (Sexual Abuse: Disclosure) (1999)*, there was evidence of an unusual and unhealthy sexual relationship between the child, C, and W. The judge held that W posed a risk of significant harm both to D and C unless some protective measures were kept in place, including a prohibited steps order and retaining the boys' names on the Child Protection Register.

In *Re B (Leave to Remove) (2008)*, the mother sought leave to take her children back to Germany. Whilst it was recognized that refusal would exacerbate the mother's already depressive state the court nevertheless refused because it would result in the father being effectively removed from the children's lives. Permisson to relocate was refused.

In *Re B (Prohibited Steps Order) (2008)*, the English father applied for a prohibited steps order and a residence order, wanting to prevent the mother, who came from Northern Ireland, from taking the child to live in Northern Ireland. Judicial consent was not needed for such a removal, as Northern Ireland was within the UK. The judge prohibited the mother from transferring the child's residence to Northern Ireland, although she was permitted to take him there for holidays. No order was made in relation to residence on the basis that the mother would continue to be the primary carer. The mother appealed, relying on a case that had not been cited to the judge, *Re E (Residence: Imposition of Conditions)*, which stated that, except in exceptional cases, a condition of residence was an unwarranted imposition upon the right of the parent to choose where he or she would live within the UK.

## Statistics

**Table 12.1** Selected Applications (Residence and Contact) made and disposed of, by type, in private law in all tiers of court 1999–2009

| Year | Applications withdrawn | | Orders refused | | Orders of no order | | Orders made | |
|------|-----------|---------|-----------|---------|-----------|---------|-----------|---------|
| | Residence | Contact | Residence | Contact | Residence | Contact | Residence | Contact |
| 2000 | 3078 | 5419 | 491 | 1276 | 941 | 2067 | 25809 | 46070 |
| 2001 | 1983 | 3226 | 282 | 713 | 434 | 1168 | 29546 | 55030 |
| 2002 | 1536 | 2373 | 158 | 518 | 431 | 945 | 30006 | 61356 |
| 2003 | 1654 | 2753 | 202 | 601 | 652 | 1522 | 31966 | 67184 |
| 2004 | 1480 | 2751 | 178 | 504 | 1246 | 3002 | 31878 | 70169 |
| 2005 | 1363 | 2536 | 154 | 495 | 662 | 2381 | 26523 | 60294 |
| 2006 | 1267 | 2165 | 129 | 383 | 431 | 1046 | 30,035 | 62,672 |
| 2007 | 1227 | 2210 | 118 | 402 | 426 | 942 | 25474 | 73267 |
| 2008 | 1223 | 2243 | 126 | 338 | 383 | 828 | 24873 | 76759 |

*Source*: Judicial Statistics for respective years

**Table 12.2** Selected Applications (Prohibited steps and specific issues) made and disposed of, by type, in private law in all tiers of court 1999–2009

| Year | Applications withdrawn | | Orders refused | | Orders of no order | | Orders made | |
|------|------|------|------|------|------|------|------|------|
| | Pro Steps | SIssue | Pro Steps | SIssue | Pro Steps | SIssue | Pro Steps | SIssue |
| 2000 | 580 | 386 | 115 | 91 | 185 | 118 | 5345 | 2457 |
| 2001 | 303 | 289 | 59 | 42 | 67 | 81 | 7343 | 2960 |
| 2002 | 300 | 207 | 40 | 33 | 77 | 67 | 8889 | 2940 |
| 2003 | 380 | 284 | 60 | 24 | 101 | 82 | 9487 | 3142 |
| 2004 | 342 | 334 | 27 | 43 | 216 | 175 | 9556 | 3893 |
| 2005 | 301 | 295 | 55 | 40 | 175 | 142 | 8227 | 3320 |
| 2006 | 364 | 254 | 39 | 35 | 134 | 90 | 9081 | 3824 |
| 2007 | 353 | 266 | 18 | 26 | 97 | 68 | 10594 | 4229 |
| 2008 | 370 | 290 | 39 | 22 | 127 | 69 | 12961 | 4434 |
| 2009 | 410 | 260 | 60 | 20 | 150 | 80 | 14650 | 5020 |

*Source*: Judicial Statistics for respective years

# Child abduction

12.59 When parents fall out and are domiciled in different towns or in different countries, managing residence and contact can be fraught. Whilst there is no requirement regarding restrictions on residence, the court, in exceptional circumstances, has imposed conditions (see *Re S (A Child) (2002)*). In some cases the purpose of the move by the parent with residence may be to exclude the other party from the life of the child, as in *B v B (Residence: Condition Limiting Geographic Area (2004)*, where a condition requiring the mother to live within the M25 was imposed to facilitate contact between the non-resident parent and the child.

Parents may abduct their own children in the absence of and in defiance of court orders. Child abduction is a national and international problem. The Child Abduction Act 1984 was passed to prevent a person from removing a child from within and outside the UK. The Child Abduction and Custody Act 1985 makes further provision and incorporates the Hague Convention, ICA, and European Convention into domestic law. In 2006, Molly Campbell (Misbah Iram Ahmed Rana) was abducted by her father and taken to Pakistan. A Pakistan court ordered her return. However, she appeared on television and in several interviews and made it clear that she had no wish to return to Scotland to be with her mother. Although she loved both her parents, she wanted to live with her father and his family in Pakistan (Grania Langdon-Down, 2006).

There are four areas in which disputes can arise. First, where a child has been taken overseas without the other parent's consent. Second, where a child has been retained in a foreign country following an overseas trip. Third, where there is a risk that a child will be abducted overseas. And fourth where one parent is trying to exercise rights of residence or access in a foreign country.

## International child abduction

12.60 The removal of a child outside the jurisdiction creates much greater problems for discovery and for recovery and return of the child. The National Council for Abducted Children (otherwise known as Reunite) states that approximately 1,200 children are abducted every year. Reunite is a UK charity specializing in international parental child abduction, part-funded by the Department for Constitutional Affairs, the Foreign and Commonwealth Office, and the Home Office. Parents and Abducted Children Together (PACT) is a charity run by Lady Meyer (the two sons of Catherine Meyer, the wife of Sir Christopher Meyer, the former British Ambassador to the USA, were abducted by her former husband, Hans-Peter Volkmann, in 1994. He defied a court order by keeping them in Germany when they went there on holiday without their mother); see http://www.pact-online.org/.

In the jurisdiction of England and Wales, there were 70 judicially ordered returns in 1999 and 2000. In an effort to deal with a global problem, international laws and cross-country cooperation have developed.

## International law

12.61 The UNCRC 1989, Art 11 requires states parties to take measures to prevent the transfer and abduction of children. The Convention also provides for bilateral and multi-lateral agreements.

## The Hague Convention

12.62 Eighty-two contracting states have joined the Hague Convention on the Civil Aspects of International Child Abduction (as per July 2010). The Convention enforces return of abducted children and the Child Abduction and Custody Act 1985 implements the Hague Convention.

> Articles 1–4 of the Hague Convention state:
>
> *[Article 1] The objects of the present Convention are: (a) to secure the prompt return of children wrongfully removed to or retained in any Contracting State; and (b) to ensure that rights of custody and of access under the law of one Contracting State are effectively respected in other Contracting States.*

*[Article 2] Contracting States shall take all appropriate measures to secure within their territories the implementation of the objects of the Convention. For this purpose they shall use the most expeditious procedures available.*

*[Article 3] The removal or the retention of a child is to be considered wrongful where: (a) it is in breach of rights of custody attributed to a person, an institution or any other body, either jointly or alone, under the law of the State in which the child was habitually resident immediately before the removal or retention; and (b) at the time of removal or retention those rights were actually exercised, either jointly or alone, or would have been so exercised but for the removal or retention. The rights of custody mentioned in sub-paragraph a above, may arise in particular by operation of law or by reason of a judicial or administrative decision, or by reason of an agreement having legal effect under the law of that State.*

*[Article 4] The Convention shall apply to any child who was habitually resident in a Contracting State immediately before any breach of custody or access rights. The Convention shall cease to apply when the child attains the age of 16 years.*

## Habitual residence

12.63  A child is wrongfully removed where there is a breach of rights of custody (residence). Rights of custody are determined in accordance with the law of the country where the child is 'habitually resident'. Habitual residence applies where a child has been resident in a country for some time, and a child's habitual residence depends upon the residence of carers or parents and is largely a matter of fact.

> In *Re H (A Minor) (Child Abduction: Mother's Asylum) (2003)*, a mother who kept her son in the UK after being granted asylum on the basis of a 'well founded fear of persecution' was required to allow the father to take her son back to his country of habitual residence on the ground that that would be in the child's best interests (see also *Al-Habtoor v Fotheringham (2001)*).

12.64  Such decisions have presented mothers with an impossible choice, tantamount to enforcing the mother's return to the country of origin if she wishes to remain with her children. If this is a reading of 'best welfare' it seems wholly perverse, where the result must be in many cases to send asylum seekers home. And those who seek asylum on the basis of domestic violence (following *Shah and Islam (1999)*) are placed in a dreadful predicament, one which wholly undermines the Convention on the Status of Refugees 1951.

## Deciding cases between countries within the Hague Convention

12.65  Where abduction occurs in countries which are signatories to the Convention, the Convention applies.

> In *Re P (A Child) (Abduction: Custody Rights) (2005)*, the mother and father were US citizens and 'habitually resident' in New York. The mother was granted sole custody, with

contact to the father. The mother took the child to England. The father claimed that he had not consented to the child's removal, that the removal was in breach of his rights of custody and therefore in breach of Art 3 of the Hague Convention. He invoked Art 12 of the Convention and applied for the child's return.

The court allowed the father's appeal, *inter alia*, as the Hague Convention required the court to give the expression 'rights of custody' an autonomous interpretation; the reference in Art 3 to 'rights of custody' applied to a person under the law of the child's habitual residence and that, accordingly, the court had to order the immediate return of the child to New York under Art 12 of the Convention.

In *Re C (Abduction: Residence and Contact) (2006)*, the mother had abducted the child from the US, brought the child to the UK, concealed her identity, and obtained a new birth certificate. After four years, the child's whereabouts were discovered by the father who made an application under the Hague Convention. However, given that the child had resided for four years in the UK with the mother, the court decided that it was not in the child's best interests to be returned.

In *Re D (A Child) (Abduction: Foreign Custody Rights) (2007)*, the child who was born in Romania had been brought to England by the mother after the parents' divorce, and was eight at the time of the litigation. The court had to consider whether the removal of the child was 'wrongful' under Art 3 of the Convention. The House of Lords considered one had to ask first what rights that person had under the law of the home country, and secondly whether those rights were 'rights of custody' within the Convention. The House of Lords held that the father did not have 'rights of custody' for the purpose of the Convention when the child was removed to the UK in December 2002. The removal was, accordingly, not unlawful.

## Rights of custody

12.66 In *Re D (A Child) (Abduction: Rights of Custody) (2006)*, D's parents had married in Romania where he was born in July 1998. In November 2000, his parents divorced. In December 2002 the mother brought the child to England and his father brought proceedings under the Child Abduction and Custody Act 1985 which gave domestic effect to the Hague Convention Art 3a; Art 15b of the Convention. This provided that prior to the making of an order for the return of a child the judicial authorities could request from the authorities of the state of the habitual residence of the child a determination that the removal or retention had been wrong within the meaning of Art 3. The High Court judge directed that a determination be obtained from the Romanian court pursuant to Art 15. However, the Romanian court held that the father's rights actually did not amount to rights of custody for the purposes of Art 3. On appeal, the court held that, at the relevant time, a divorced non-custodial parent did not have a right of veto of measures taken by the custodial parent relating to the child's person and concluded that the removal of the child by the mother in December 2002 had not been wrongful. The High Court allowed further evidence to be adduced as to Romanian law and the judge then ordered the child's return to Romania. The mother's appeal to the Court of Appeal was unsuccessful and she appealed to the House of Lords.

Baroness Hale asserted:

*The simple question before us is whether A should now be returned to Romania, some three years and ten months after he left. But this depends upon the answers to some more complex questions arising under the Hague Convention. That is in their interests, and those of the applicant, that this be obtained as quickly as possible. It is sad that it took so long in this case, but the Romanian authorities must be mystified indeed that the English courts have ordered the return to Romania of a child whose removal the Romanian final court of appeal has authoritatively and irrevocably determined was not wrongful. [47] For these reasons, essentially the same as those of my noble and learned friends, Lord Hope of Craighead, Lord Carswell and Lord Brown of Eaton-under-Heywood, I would allow this appeal and dismiss the proceedings.*

## Best Interests

12.67   Even where the removal is unlawful the Convention allows under certain 'limited and precise circumstances' for the child not to be returned. See *Re M (Abduction: Zimbabwe) (2007)*, where Baroness Hale said that the welfare of the child would need to be balanced against swift return and respect for one another's judicial processes.

And Art 13 (b) of the Convention states that a child would not be returned if there was a grave risk of physical or psychological harm or of placing the child in an intolerable situation.

Where child who has attained a degree of maturity objects to being returned this is a factor that must be taken into consideration. This is set out by Sir Mark Potter P in *Re M (Abduction: Child's Objections) (2007)*. Where the child has 'settled' in another country the court may be unlikely to order a return although a discretion is still retained (*Cannon v Cannon (2004)*).

## Non-Convention cases

12.68   Where countries are not signatories to the Hague Convention, inter-country cooperation is difficult and outcomes for parents haphazard and unpredictable, with the result that the courts have adopted divergent rules with regard to non-Convention cases.

In *Re J (Child Returned Abroad: Convention Rights) (2005)*, the court said that there was no warrant in statute or authority 'for the principles of the Hague convention to be extended to countries which are not parties to it' (para 22).

The case of *Re E (Abduction: Non-Convention Country) (1999)* concerned the return of children to Sudan after their mother had brought them to England and sought asylum. Thorpe LJ treated a case from a non-Convention country in the same way as if it had been a signatory to the Convention, applying the habitual residence test.

In *B v El-B (Abduction: Sharia Law: Welfare of Child) (2003)*, the key issue was whether the application of *Sharia* law to the custody of children was to be respected by English courts in international child abduction cases or to be considered as potentially in conflict where the fundamental principle that the child's welfare should be protected operated. A Lebanese mother brought the children to England in breach of an order of the Lebanese court. The case was brought under the wardship jurisdiction, as Lebanon was not a signatory to the Hague Convention. The welfare of the child had to be considered in relation to the circumstances. Here, both parents were devout Muslims and this was also the religious and the cultural background of the children. Under Muslim law, the transfer of legal custody of children from mother to father takes place at the ages of seven (for boys) and nine (for girls).

The court found that there was no substance in the suggestion that *Sharia* law was not to be regarded as child-centred. The apparent suggestions in *Re JA (1998)* that welfare was not the test in *Sharia* law needed to be taken in the context of a case where the family had lived in England for substantial periods and where there was expert evidence of harm to the mother and child if return to the United Arab Emirates was ordered. A careful review of the welfare issues might lead to a refusal to return an abducted child in certain cases, but it was not an outright rejection of *Sharia* law.

See *Re E (1999)* and also *Re J (Child Returned Abroad: Convention Rights) (2005)*. For further reading on this complex area of law see Young, 2003.

In *Re T and another (Children) (Abduction: Recognition of Foreign Judgment) (2006)* the Spanish judgment was recognized because, as the court explained, if the court made an order for the return of the children to Spain, it would be failing to give effect to its recognition of the Spanish judgment and thus failing to accord precedence to Brussels IIb [Brussels Convention II] over the Hague Convention in that respect. The primary rationale underlying the Hague Convention was to ensure that decisions as to the welfare of children, and questions where and with which parent they should reside, were taken in the country of the child's habitual residence. The mother had initiated proceedings in Spain, by the time the matter came before the English court the matter would have already been heard before a Spanish court in possession of all the relevant facts as to welfare decisions, and as to the father's removal of the children. The Spanish court had specifically vested interim custody in the father on the basis that the children should continue to reside in England with the father as their main carer, and with appropriate and beneficial educational arrangements, pending a full and final hearing. By virtue of the relevant Spanish law, that interim custody order was not capable of appeal and would remain in place till the resolution of divorce and/or separation proceedings. In those circumstances, if the court was obliged to return the children, it would defeat rather than assist the overall purpose of the Hague Convention. However, by application of the provisions of Brussels II b, such a result was avoided.

In *Re U (Abduction: Nigeria) (2010)*, the mother abducted her children from their home in Nigeria and brought them to England. The mother alleged that she was a victim of domestic violence. Summary return of the children was ordered because it was held that the relevant State within Nigeria had enacted domestic violence legislation and that protection from domestic violence was available. In addition the father was prepared to arrange and pay for separate accommodation and to pre-register a version of his undertakings with the Nigerian court and was also prepared to prepay money to lawyers to represent the mother in Nigerian proceedings.

## Balancing rights: welfare or best interests tests

12.69 The resolution of child abduction has been guided by the principle of the best interests of the child and the paramountcy of the child's welfare, and the best solution is considered to be to return the child to his or her country of residence.

12.70 Whilst the original problem to be combated was the removal of the child from the status quo (habitual residence), this can only be one factor to be considered. The welfare of the child is not always protected by the habitual residence presumption (see *Re C* above). Where the country of origin does not resolve issues of domestic violence and custody in family proceedings by making child welfare paramount considering instead the rather more moveable feast of best interests, then it is not surprising that mothers will take a course of forcible abduction in an effort to resolve custody battles and gain protection from domestic violence.

The balancing exercise involved in these cases where principles are in conflict make for a difficult and uncertain area of law bringing into conflict many good practice principles that have developed in the law.

### FURTHER READING

Bellamy, C, and Lord, G, (2003) reported in 'Research into the Operation of Rule 9.5 of the Family Proceedings Rules 199: Final Report to the Department for Constitutional Affairs' (DCA, 2006)

Blackwell A, and Dawe F, *Non Resident Parent Contact* (Office for National Statistics, 2003)

Craig J, 'Everybody's Business: Applications for Contact Orders by Consent' (2007) Fam Law 37 (26)

Douglas G, Murch M, Miles C and Scanlan L, 'Research into the Operation of Rule 9.5 of the Family Proceedings Rules 1991: Final Report for the Department of Constitutional Affairs' (DCA, 2006)

Edwards S, and Halpern A, 'Conflicting Interests: Protecting Children or Protecting Title to Property' (1988) JSWFL 10(2), 110–124

Gilmore S, 'The Nature, Scope, and Use of the Specific Issue Order' (2004) CFLQ 16 (4), 367

Hershman D and McFarlane A, *The Children Act 2004* (Jordans, 2007)

Hunt J and Roberts C, Family Policy Briefing 4: *Intervening in Litigated Contact: Ideas From Other Jurisdictions* (University of Oxford, 2005)

Kaganas F and Sclater SD, 'Contact Disputes: Narrative Constructions of Good Parents' (2004) 12 (1) *Feminist Legal Studies*

Kaganas F and Sclater SD, 'Contact: Mothers, Welfare and Rights' in A Bainham, B Lindley, M Richards and L Trinder (Eds), *Children and Their Families* (Hart Publishing, 2003)

Langdon-Down G, 'Islamic Family Law;Culture Clash' Law Society Gazette (2006) 103 (48), 14

May V and Smart C, 'Silence In Court?—Hearing Children In Residence And Contact Disputes' (2004) CFLQ 16(3), 305

Pearce J, Davis G and Barron J, 'Love in a Cold Climate: Section 8 Applications under the Children Act' (1999) Fam Law 29 (22)

Saunders H, 'Twenty-Nine Child Homicides: Lessons still to be learnt on domestic violence and child protection' (2004) Women's Aid Federation, England

Stevenson M, 'Compulsory Mediation—A Discussion' (2006) Fam Law 36 (986)

Young J, 'The Constitutional Limits of Judicial Activism: Judicial Conduct of International Relations and Child Abduction' (2003) MLR 66, 823

## SELF-TEST QUESTIONS

1 Given the circumstances of the Hillard family in the film *Mrs Doubtfire* (where the parents separate and the father, Daniel, in an effort to be with his children on a daily basis, dresses as a woman and is employed as the housekeeper in the former matrimonial home), how would a judge have dealt with the issues of residence and contact given that both parents wanted a residence order made in their favour? What weight might the judge have given to Daniel's organization of his son's birthday party when the court considers his parenting skills? Daniel clearly thought 'families need fathers'.

What view might a judge have taken of his bizarre behaviour in cross-dressing in his efforts to see his children?

2  The mother left the matrimonial home and resided at several addresses with the child. She had a series of partners and was living in temporary accommodation. The child was well cared for and settled in the local school. The father, on the other hand, could provide a home for the child as he continued to live in the matrimonial home. The father was also a caring and loving father and, in addition, the paternal grandparents were living nearby with both grandparents being able to provide help and assistance with the daily care of the child. Both mother and father had applied to the court for a residence order. If you were the judge, what factors would you need to take into consideration?

3  Mr and Mrs Khan separated in April 2010. They have one son Ali, aged three. Ali is living with his mother. Mrs Khan is cohabiting with Mr Smith. Mr Khan wants Ali to be circumcised as he believes that is central to his and his child's identity. He also wants to take his son to Pakistan for the summer school holidays to stay with his paternal grandparents. Mr Khan is concerned that Ali is going to be enrolled at a Roman Catholic nursery, he is also concerned that his wife might marry Mr Smith and that Ali might be adopted. You are acting for Mr Khan. What orders might you apply for on his behalf and what principles will guide the court?

4  How have the courts approached the question of habitual residence in abduction cases?

5  What issues are raised by 'implacable hostility' of one party and conversely the problem of alienation with regard to contact arrangements.?

6  When and under what circumstances would a supervised contact order be appropriate?

# 13

# In the child's best interests: the jurisdiction of wardship

**SUMMARY**

In this chapter we consider the protective jurisdiction of wardship, and the interface between wardship and the inherent jurisdiction and the interface between wardship and prohibited steps orders under s 8 Children (CA) Act 1989. We also consider the limitations placed on the wardship jurisdiction by the CA 1989. The principle of 'the best interests of the child' has guided the courts in resolving such matters. We explore the kind of cases and circumstances in which the wardship jurisdiction has been invoked, to include for example where wardship has protected a child from unwanted publicity, to cases where wardship has protected a child from being forced to continue with an unwanted pregnancy. Detailed consideration is given to those cases where the court in wardship has taken a decision with respect to the treatment of a terminally ill or gravely ill child, and where wardship has been used to prevent a competent adolescent from refusing life-saving treatment.

## Defining wardship

### Ancient wardship

13.1 The jurisdiction of wardship is derived from the principle that all subjects owe an allegiance to the Crown and that the Crown as *parens patriae*, protects its subjects, and, has a special obligation to care for those who cannot look after, or make decisions for themselves. This included all infants as well as lunatics. Protection for children was ensured by making them wards of court. Once a child was made a ward of court, the court then became in effect the judicious parent and no decision could be made about the infant child without permission.

13.2 Wardship originated in the Court of Chancery, which had a jurisdiction in equity to protect equity wardship and was described in the sixteenth century as protecting 'all infants, as well as idiots and lunatics'. Until the 1840s, the equitable jurisdiction was largely limited to cases where the ward had property which needed protection.

13.3 The concept of the child's welfare in wardship decisions was then broadened in scope to include the child's 'moral, religious, and physical welfare.' This was established in *Wellesley v Duke of Beaufort (1824–34)*, a case in which the Court of Chancery had jurisdiction to appoint a guardian for infants, being wards of the court, excluding the father; . . . upon evidence that the father was living in a state of adultery, and had encouraged his children in swearing, and keeping low company. It was held a fit case to exercise the power to exclude him from the guardianship.

> Lord Eldon LC summarized the wider purpose of wardship in more modern times:
>
> *the jurisdiction belongs to the King, as parens patriae, having the care of those who are not able to take care of themselves, and is founded on the obvious necessity that the law should place somewhere the care of individuals who cannot take care of themselves, particularly where it is clear that some care should be thrown around them.*

## Modern wardship

13.4 Under modern wardship, the High Court takes responsibility for the child, no order can be made or action taken which affects the child, unless permission is obtained from the court. Once a child is warded, the court has parental responsibility for the child, that responsibility is a continuing one until the order is discharged. Wardship orders can be of several months' or years' duration. In 1989, in *Re A (A Minor)*, the court took the place of 'the parents or guardian' in giving its consent to the caution being issued, when the Crown Prosecution Service decided to administer a verbal caution to a ward of court who had admitted a criminal offence.

> The ambit of modern wardship is enunciated by the Master of the Rolls, Lord Evershed, in *Re Baker (Infants) (1961)*, who said:
>
> *The prerogative right of the Queen, as parens patriae in relation to infants within the realm, is not for all purposes ousted or abrogated as the result of the exercise. But even where a child is made a ward of court by virtue of the Act of 1949, the judge in whom the prerogative power is vested will, acting on familiar principles, not exercise control in relation to duties or discretions clearly vested by statute in the local authority, and may, therefore, and in a case such as the present normally will, order that the child cease to be a ward of court.*

13.5 By 1971, the wardship jurisdiction was transferred from the Chancery Division to the Family Division under the Administration of Justice Act 1970, s 1(2) (see now Supreme Court Act 1981, s 61, Sch 1). Following the CA 1989, the prohibited steps order under CA 1989, s 8 (discussed in Chapter 12) now affords, in certain circumstances, the protection which was formerly provided under wardship, with the result that wardship proceedings are resorted to less frequently. In 1951, there were 71 wardship orders; in 1973, 622, in 1988, 3,704, in 1990, 6,227 wardship orders and in 1991, 4,961 orders.

13.6 Rosie Winterton, MP, in a reply to Mr Vaz, MP, who tabled a Commons question asking for information on the extent of wardship said this:

> The Children Act 1989 came into force on 14 October 1991. Under the Act, the use of wardship by local authorities is severely limited. Leave to make an application for any exercise of the court's inherent jurisdiction must be granted by the High Court. Applications by private individuals are not restricted, but the same results can generally be achieved by obtaining a prohibited steps or specific issue order under s 8 of the Act. Statistics have not been collected since 1991 because the number of wardship orders made has been negligible.
>
> *(16 May 2002, col 837W Hansard)*

According to the Law Reform Commission's Consultation Paper 2006, around 160 individuals come into wardship each year, the number is rising, and the total number of wards is estimated at 2,600 (see 'The Case for Reform', a report by the Law Society's Law Reform Committee, March 2006).

# The jurisdiction of wardship

13.7 The High Court has the power to make certain orders (wardship). An application is provided in accordance with the Family Proceedings Rules 1991 (SI 1991/1247 (L20)):

> 5.1—(1) An application to make a minor a ward of court shall be made by originating summons and, unless the court otherwise directs, the plaintiff shall file an affidavit in support of the application when the originating summons is issued.

## The Official Solicitor

13.8 The Official Solicitor is normally appointed as litigation friend to represent the child's interests in wardship proceedings. In *Supreme Court Practice* (1982) Vol 2, p 987, para 3452A, the following passage details his role:

> The Official Solicitor is a servant of the court and may at any time be called upon by a judge to carry out an investigation or to assist the court to see that justice is done

*between the parties (see Harbin v Masterman (1896) 1 Ch 351, per A L Smith LJ, at p 368, and per Rigby LJ at p 371). He is appointed to act where, if this were not done, there would be a denial or miscarriage of justice.*

In *Re B (A Minor) (Wardship: Guardian Ad Litem) (1989)* the judge concluded that the Official Solicitor had the independent objectivity and expertise to act for children in such cases when the guardian being to close to the action might not possess.

However, the child may wish to have independent representation in appointing his own solicitor to represent his interests. In some cases the child is represented by the guardian ad litem.

# Wardship and the Children Act 1989

## Wardship cannot be invoked by the local authority

13.9    The CA 1989 ended the use of wardship by the local authority s 100(3), unless if, without the intervention of the court, the child would be likely to suffer significant harm (s 100(4)(b)). However, whilst a s 100(4)(b) application is commonly regarded as wardship it is in fact an instance of the exercise of the courts' inherent jurisdiction, since under the CA 1989, s 100(2)(c):

> No court shall exercise the High Court's inherent jurisdiction with respect to children—(c) so as to make a child who is the subject of a care order a ward of court;

> And (3) No application for any exercise of the court's inherent jurisdiction with respect to children may be made by a local authority unless the authority have obtained leave of the court. (4) The court may only grant leave if it is satisfied that—(a) the result which the authority wish to achieve oould not be achieved through the making of any order of a kind to which subsection (5) applies; and (b) there is reasonable cause to believe that if the court's inherent jurisdiction is not exercised with respect to the child he is likely to suffer significant harm.

Local authorities cannot use wardship as an alternative to the statutory care system. The CA 1989 imposes two prohibitions with respect to a child who is in the care of the local authority, subject to a care order. First, no s 8 order other than residence can be made (see s 9(1)) and second a child subject to a care order cannot be made a ward. The CA 1989 provides instead for a prohibited steps order (s 8) where no step can be made about the child's future without leave of the court.

## The inherent jurisdiction

13.10    The inherent jurisdiction provides protection to any individual regardless of age who is incapacitated (see *Re SK*). In the case of *E (By Her Litigation Friend The Official*

*Solicitor) v Channel Four; News International Ltd And St Helens Borough Council (2005)*, Pamela, a 32 year-old woman had a learning disability (mental impairment within the meaning of the Mental Health Act 1983) and additionally had been diagnosed as suffering from dissociative identity disorder (DID). DID manifests as different 'personalities' and in Pamela's case, there were four personalities in addition to Pamela herself: 'Sandra', 'Andrew', 'Margaret', and 'Susan'. In this case, Channel Four television wished to complete and transmit a film they had already started on Pamela and her condition. An application was made under the inherent jurisdiction because it was argued on her behalf by the Official Solicitor and the local authority that she was not able to give her consent. The Official Solicitor and local authority sought an interim injunction. The injunction failed on the basis that her lack of capacity had not been established, although the court recognized that there was a narrow margin and even if it had acceded the incapacity to consent it held that the making of the film was not necessarily against her best interests.

The inherent jurisdiction can also, however, be used in respect of children and CA 1989, s 100(3), applies in accordance with conditions specified in s 100(4)(b), where 'it is likely that the child will suffer significant harm' (as detailed above).

The inherent jurisdiction is exercisable where the child is present in the jurisdiction. In *H v D and others (2007)* an extremely complex inter jurisdictional residence and contact case between the parties, the court made the children wards of court.

Sumner J said:

*It can be exercised irrespective of the proceedings in which the need to protect the children arose. It can be exercised where there are concurrent proceedings in another territorial jurisdiction. It can also be exercised if the child's presence is transient provided there is a good enough reason, such as damage or risk of damage to the child's well-being* (para 57).

*Supporters of a family, made an application in wardship where, in a case reported in the Guardian, (12 October 2005), concerning three Ugandan children, whose mother was deported to Uganda. The Guardian reported that the eldest daughter had said that she was raped, beaten, and tortured in Uganda and reported that the Home Office had said notwithstanding that it could still expel them.*

If the child or adult is however 'habitually resident' in the UK but not within the jurisdiction at the time of the application the inherent jurisdiction may still be exercised. This was the case where a child had been removed by his parents to The Gambia (*Lewisham London Borough Council v D (Criteria for Territorial Jurisdiction in Public Law Proceedings (2008)*).

13.11 So, with regard to minors under 18 years of age, the inherent jurisdiction (provided the conditions above apply) and wardship can both be used depending on the circumstances, and are, for all practical purposes, the same. In *Re Z (1996)*, Ward LJ asserted, 'For all practical purposes the jurisdiction in wardship and the inherent jurisdiction over children is one and the same thing'.

## Who can make an application in wardship?

13.12 Anyone may make an application by originating summons to make a child a ward of court (Supreme Court Act 1981, s 41(2)) including for example, a concerned a health care professional, a relative, neighbour, or friend, an organization, a charitable body, or a solicitor as the examples below demonstrate.

> In *Re D (A Minor) (Wardship: Sterilisation) (1976)*, an application in wardship was made by an educational psychologist. Here, the mother of an 11 year-old handicapped girl was concerned that her daughter, because she was vulnerable and had no understanding of sexual matters, might become pregnant. The mother made arrangements for her daughter to be sterilized. Following an application made by the educational psychologist the girl was made a ward of court. The court ruled against the proposed sterilization finding that it was not in the child's best interests.

> In *B v W (Wardship: Appeal) (1979)*, a grandfather made an application in wardship where there was a conflict between him and the children's mother over whether or not his grandson should go into the grandfather's business or continue in boarding school.

> In *Re A (A Child) (Wardship: Habitual Residence) (2007)*, the father sought political asylum and was granted indefinite leave to remain in the UK. He married and his wife gave birth to a child in the UK. The father took the mother and the child to Kurdistan purportedly for a holiday but the family remained in Kurdistan. The marriage deteriorated and a court in Kurdistan granted custody of the child, A, to the father. The father told the mother she could not see A. The mother left Kurdistan and issued wardship proceedings in respect of A. An issue arose over 'habitual residence'. The court said that the jurisdiction of the court rested on the fact based concept of 'habitual residence' and since the child's habitual residence was Kurdistan then the child should be returned to Kurdistan.

## Who can be warded?

13.13 The jurisdiction of wardship applies to those who are:

- unmarried minors;
- not necessarily British subjects (see, eg, children seeking asylum) see below;
- not necessarily residing in England and Wales (see, eg, a child removed from the jurisdiction by child abduction see previous chapter, and see *Re B* below);
- under 18 years.

In *Re B; RB v FB and MA (Forced Marriage: Wardship Jurisdiction) (2008)*, a 15 year-old girl who was a British National said she wanted to move to Scotland to live with her half-brother as her mother in Pakistan had made arrangements for her to marry in Pakistan. The court said: '... in these very dire circumstances the tentacles of this court should stretch towards Pakistan to rescue the child from the circumstances she found herself in.'

In *R v B (Piara) (2010)*, a mother had arranged for her under age daughter to be married to an adult man. The mother was subsequently sentenced to eight months' imprisonment for inciting a child to engage in sexual activity. She appealed. The appeal was dismissed as the sentence was not excessive.

## No wardship over 18 years

13.14 Whilst a person over the age of 18 years cannot be warded, the inherent jurisdiction (discussed earlier) can be invoked to protect such a person and the importance of this jurisdiction is emphasized in *Re SK* (below).

In *Re SK (An Adult) (Forced Marriage: Appropriate Relief) (2004)*, the question arose as to whether wardship extended to adults who were, through being forced to enter into marriage against their will, deprived of the capacity to make their own decisions, albeit that they were over 18 years of age. Anne-Marie Hutchinson (solicitor) of Dawson, Cornwell, made an application to the court with regard to SK whom Miss Hutchinson feared might be being kept by relatives and family in Bangladesh against her will, and her return to the UK deliberately delayed as part of an attempt to marry her forcibly. The court ruled:

*An adult cannot be made a ward of court but the inherent jurisdiction of the High Court can, in an appropriate case, be relied upon and utilised to provide a remedy. I believe that the inherent jurisdiction now, like wardship... is a sufficiently flexible remedy to evolve in accordance with social needs and social values.*

## Cannot ward before birth

13.15 The concern of health care professionals with regard to the problem of alcohol/drug/ substance addict mothers and the safety of their unborn and newly born babies is an ever-pressing issue. Concern for such babies has resulted in the local authority making an application in wardship to protect the unborn child.

In *Re F (In Utero) (1988)*, the local authority applied ex parte for leave to issue a summons making a foetus a ward of court. The judge held that the court had no wardship jurisdiction over an unborn child. In *Re D (Unborn Baby) (Emergency Protection Order: Future Harm) (2009)* Munby J said:

*6. I am not concerned with the exercise of any jurisdiction directly concerned with the welfare of the child. The child is, as I speak, still en ventre sa mere and, accordingly, no court has jurisdiction to make any order under the Children Act 1989, nor (see In re F (In Utero) [1988] Fam) can the court exercise its inherent or wardship jurisdiction in respect of children.*

In this case the court accepted that in the circumstances it was right for the local authority to conceal from mother the birth plan for the unborn child which involved a plan of immediate removal of the born child into adoption since the mother was a serious danger to children and the following cases were applied: *W v United Kingdom (1988)*; *O (A Child) (Supervision Order: Future Harm), Re*; *C and B (Children) (Care Order: Future Harm), Re (2000)*; *H (A Child) (Interim Care Order), Re (2002)*; *B (Children) (Care: Interference With Family Life, Re) (2003)*.

## No jurisdiction in financial provision

13.16    An application albeit incorrectly was made in the wardship jurisdiction in a case relating to financial provision.

In *W v J (Child: Variation of Financial Provision) (2004)*, the parents were not married. There had been much litigation in relation to their daughter. In the course of this litigation, the child was made a ward of court and an order made by consent set out the amount of periodical payments the father was to make for the child. The mother was seeking a variation in those payments under CA 1989, Sch 1, or under the court's inherent jurisdiction, to cover her estimated legal costs in relation to a forthcoming contested dispute as to residence, leave to remove the child from the jurisdiction, and financial provision for the child. The court dismissed the mother's application and held that the court had no jurisdiction under CA 1989, s 15 and Sch 1 to order one parent to make a payment to the other parent to cover the latter's legal fees in relation to litigation over their child or children.

# Test to be applied in wardship

## Best interests test: golden thread

13.17    In wardship proceedings, the best interests of the child test prevails and not the welfare paramount test. However it is unlikely that in considering the best interests of a child the child's welfare will not be considered as the paramount consideration. The 'best interests test' has been severally articulated as ensuring the welfare of the child and predates the welfare paramount test.

In *Re K (Infants) (1965)*, a case which concerned the disclosure of the guardian ad litem's report in wardship proceedings, Lord Devlin quoted with approval the dictum of Ungoed-Thomas J, the trial judge:

*The jurisdiction regarding wards of court, which is now exercised by the Chancery Division, is an ancient jurisdiction deriving from the prerogative of the Crown as parens patriae. It is not based on the rights of parents, and its primary concern is not to ensure their rights but to ensure the welfare of the children.*

(approved in *Re L (1997)*).

In *Re D (A Minor) (Justices' Decision: Review) (1977)*, Dunn J said of the test: 'the golden thread, which runs through the whole of this court's jurisdiction, the welfare of the child, which is considered in this court first, last and all the time'.

Lord Scarman in *Re E (SA) (A Minor) (Wardship) (1984)* said:

*a court exercising jurisdiction over its ward must never lose sight of a fundamental feature of the jurisdiction that it is exercising, namely that it is exercising a wardship, not an adversarial, jurisdiction. Its duty is not limited to the dispute between the parties: on the contrary, its duty is to act in the way best suited in its judgment to serve the true interest and welfare of the ward. In exercising wardship jurisdiction, the court is a true family court. Its paramount concern is the welfare of its ward.*

## Welfare paramount

13.18 In wardship cases, the terminology of 'best', 'welfare' has been varied and sometimes confusing, 'paramount' is often the language of the wardship court in considering the welfare of the child as eg in *Re F (In Utero) (1988)*, where the court said the 'welfare of the child is the first and paramount consideration in wardship proceedings: see section 1 of the Guardianship of Minors Act 1971'. However, the welfare of the child as paramount is not the test that is applied. This is simply because in wardship, there are not supposed to be any competing interests, thus obviating the need to talk in terms of making the welfare of the child 'paramount.'

As Cross J in *Re B (JA) (an infant) (1965)* described the jurisdiction:

*Wardship proceedings are not like ordinary civil actions. There is no 'lis' (a controversy or dispute; a suit or action at law) between the parties. The plaintiffs are not asserting any rights; they are committing their child to the protection of the court and asking the court to make such order as it thinks fit for her benefit.*

That of course may be true but children who are warded are often warded so as to allow the court to decide matters over which parties are in conflict.

In recent years, the two rather different principles of 'best interests' and 'welfare as paramount' have provoked considerable debate (see Herring, 2008 for a cogent examination of these two principles).

## What kind of cases invoke wardship?

13.19 Wardship is invoked in a very wide range of circumstances and situations where the child requires the protection of the court. The circumstances and cases detailed below demonstrate the very wide ambit of the jurisdiction.

# Children seeking asylum

13.20  A growing number of children arrive in the UK as members of families seeking asylum, and some children arrive on their own, unaccompanied.

## Unaccompanied asylum-seeking children

13.21  In 2006, 3,245 unaccompanied asylum seeking children (UASCs) aged 17 or under applied for asylum in the United Kingdom (*Asylum Statistics United Kingdom 2006*, Kerry Bennett, Tina Heath, Richard Jeffries, 14/07, Home Office Statistical Bulletin, p 11). In 2009, 2,985, UASCs were reported, including 90 from Europe (including 55 from Albania), 45 from Algeria, 225 from Erirtrea, 115 from Somalia, 195 from Iran, 145 from Iraq, 1,525 from Afghanistan, 80 from China, and 100 from Vietnam; see http://www.guardian.co.uk/news/datablog/2010/jun/08/child-asylum-seekers-data-uk#data accessed 10 June 2010 when Home Office figures show there are more than 4,200 UASCs in Britain.

Benjamin Zephaniah, in *Refugee Boy*, speaks poignantly of this predicament:

> My name is Alem Kelo. I live with the Fitzgeralds, my foster family, at 202 Meanly Road, Manor Park, London. I have also lived in Ethiopia and Eritrea. I have spent a few nights in a hotel in Datchet, one night in a children's home in Reading, and for a short while I stayed in a hotel in Forest Gate, which was a bit rough. I have stayed in all these places in the last year. To be really honest I would prefer to live in Africa with my mother and father but they have both been killed and there is a war in my country...I am not a beggar; I am not a bogus.

(at pp 290–291)

13.22  Home Office immigration policy requires the Immigration and Nationality Department to refer all unaccompanied children who apply for asylum to social services. But such children may not be here for long, as the Home Office operates a discretionary leave policy whereby children seeking asylum from so-called 'white list' or 'safe' countries (Albania, Bangladesh, Bulgaria, Jamaica, Macedonia, Moldova, Romania, Serbia, and Montenegro (including Kosovo) and Sri Lanka) are granted 12 months' leave or leave until their 18th birthday (whichever is shorter) unless they qualify for more favourable terms. From 2010, the UK Border Agency is setting up a £4 million 'reintegration centre' in Afghanistan so that it can start deporting the 1,525 unaccompanied child asylum seekers to Kabul from Britain.

13.23  When children arrive unaccompanied they are either taken into care and/or made a ward of court. The charity Barnardo's, reported, 'the majority of authorities have no specific policies to work with unaccompanied children (72 per cent of authorities), they have not included them in their Management Action Plans under the Quality Protects initiative (62 per cent) or in the Department of Health's new assessment frameworks (74 per cent). More than a third of authorities place unaccompanied children outside the responsible borough with very varied levels of support then available' (see http://www.harpweb.org.uk/content.php?section=children&sub=ch19).

In a recent study entitled 'A long way to go' (2007, 5) by Eleanor Stringer and Tris Lumley:

> *Eva was 15 when she was taken from her home in Africa by a family 'friend'....she was taken round different countries in Africa and raped repeatedly. She was taken to London when she was 16 and continued to be sexually exploited. She managed to escape and lived on the streets until a stranger took her to a refuge and she applied for asylum.*

According to figures obtained under the Freedom of Information Act, approximately 1,000 foreign national children were taken into care by local authorities in the eight months between April 2008 and the end of the year.

### Asylum seeking children may be made wards of court

13.24    In *E (By Her Litigation Friend EW) v London Borough of X (2006)*, E obtained a visa and came to the UK with an older sister. The older sister said E was 17 years of age. She arrived in England and lived with a woman she believed to be her mother. By 2004, the relationship had broken down and she then lived with foster parents. The 'mother' wanted to return to Ghana with E, but E refused. She was made a ward of court, and the local authority was ordered to prepare a report under CA 1989, s 37(1). The court held that in the light of the uncertainty as to her present circumstances wardship would not be discharged until her 18th birthday.

13.25    The Home Office claims to detain unaccompanied asylum-seeking children in detention centres only in the most exceptional circumstances, when they arrive in the UK 'out of hours' or where their age is in dispute.

Jamie Beagent, a solicitor with Leigh Day & Co, represented two unaccompanied children seeking asylum in the UK who were detained by the Home Office in an adult detention facility:

> *Mr Justice Owen, sitting in London, ruled that the boys—referred to as I and O—both were now entitled to damages because they were victims of a breach of Home Office policy that requires unaccompanied asylum-seekers under 18 to be put in the care of local authorities, and not sent to detention centres.*
>
> *(Morning Star, 28 May 2005)*

13.26    But asylum-seeking children do not usually succeed with their applications for refugee status. The *Care Matters White Paper* (2007) says:

> *[p]athway planning for [UASC] is concerned with providing them with the skills and services necessary so that they can make a successful transition to adulthood in their*

*home communities. For the small minority whose asylum claim is accepted, their com-*
*munity will be the UK. However, 95% of asylum claims are refused and young people*
*will need to be prepared to be resettled in their countries of origin. Therefore, the path-*
*way planning process must also be relevant to the circumstances and needs of those*
*UASC who will be required to return to their countries of origin (p. 116)*

## The Refugee Convention

13.27  The children must fulfil the conditions set out in para 2 of the Convention and
Protocol relating to the Status of Refugees ((1951) Cmnd 9171 and Cmnd 3906):

> *(2) As a result of events occurring before 1 January 1951 and owing to well-founded*
> *fear of being persecuted for reasons of race, religion, nationality, membership of a*
> *particular social group or political opinion, is outside the country of his nationality and*
> *is unable or, owing to such fear, is unwilling to avail himself of the protection of that*
> *country; or who, not having a nationality and being outside the country of his former*
> *habitual residence as a result of such events, is unable or, owing to such fear, is unwill-*
> *ing to return to it. In the case of a person who has more than one nationality, the term*
> *'the country of his nationality' shall mean each of the countries of which he is a national,*
> *and a person shall not be deemed to be lacking the protection of the country of his*
> *nationality if, without any valid reason based on well-founded fear, he has not availed*
> *himself of the protection of one of the countries of which he is a national.*

In *Fornah v Secretary of State for the Home Department,* (2007), Zainab Esther
Fornah was an unaccompanied minor of 15 years of age when she arrived at Gatwick
airport in March 2003 claiming asylum. As she was a child she was taken into the care of
West Sussex Social Services Child Asylum Team. She had fled Sierra Leone where she
had been captured by rebels, who killed her family, and repeatedly raped her. She did not
want to return to her uncle's village because she feared that she would be forcibly genitally
mutilated since this was the customary practice, from which her father had protected her
when he was alive (see Edwards, 2007).

In *QD (Iraq) v Secretary of State for the Home Department; AH (Iraq) v Secretary*
*of State for the Home Department (2009),* the applications were refused because the
applicants did not meet the threshold of violence suffered that was required.

## Resisting deportation: asylum-seeking children

13.28  In *R (on the application of Ahmadi) v Secretary of State for the Home Department*
*(2002),* the Ahmadi family, who were victims of torture, fled Kabul on the back of a lorry
with their children. They claimed asylum in the UK having travelled via Germany, and having applied for asylum in Germany where their application was refused. Under the Dublin
Convention, the appropriate country in which to make an asylum application is the first
country of arrival, which in this case was Germany. The claimants stated that conditions
in Germany for asylum seekers were so poor that to return them to Germany would be in
breach of Art 3 of the ECHR (inhuman and degrading treatment). They sought refuge in
a mosque in Stourbridge until they were arrested by police for deportation, during which

time the family were kept in detention at Harmondsworth Detention Centre. The children, a daughter aged five and son aged three, were made wards of court and an emergency application was made to Bennett J, in the Family Division, for their release from detention. The family were finally deported to Germany in 2004.

In *R (Anton) v Secretary of State for the Home Department: Re Anton (2005)*, the court refused to grant an injunction which would prevent a child from being deported. Munby J said that the fact that a child was a ward could not limit or confine the powers of the Secretary of State. Although he also made it clear that it had not been fair of the immigration authorities to allow family proceedings due to be heard imminently to be adjourned without informing the parties that removal directions had already been set for before the adjourned date. It was unfair because it must have been obvious that with knowledge of the true facts the other side would never have allowed the hearing to be adjourned (see para [77]). He also granted similar relief in the judicial review proceedings and directed that the family proceedings go for a full hearing.

In *R (On the Application of A) (FC) (Appellant) v London Borough of Croydon (Respondents)* and one other action *R (On the Application of M) (FC) (Appellant) v London Borough of Lambeth (Respondents) (2009)*, and one further action two children arrived unaccompanied in the United Kingdom and claimed asylum. They said that their ages were 15, and 16, respectively; they were referred to the defendant local children's services authorities for assessment, and in both cases the authorities concluded that they were over the age of 18. In consequence, the local authorities were not obliged to accommodate them by s 20(1)(a) of the CA 1989. The claimants sought judicial review of the authorities' decision. The judge rejected the claimants' submission that the question of whether a person was a child or not for the purposes of s 20 was one of precedent fact for the court to determine.

The Court of Appeal dismissed the claimants' appeals and they appealed to the Supreme Court. The Supreme Court considered, *inter alia*, whether the duty imposed by s 20(1) was owed only to a person who appeared to the local authority to be a child, so that the authority's decision could only be challenged on *Wednesbury* principles (see *Associated Provincial Picture Houses Ltd v Wednesbury Corporation (1947)*), or whether the s 20 duty was owed to any person who was in fact a child, so that the court could determine the issue on the balance of probabilities. Lord Hope (P):

*[47] This case raises two distinct issues of general public importance. Their importance extends well beyond the facts of the two cases that are before us. On the one hand there is the question whether the word 'child' in s 20(1) of the Children Act 1989 means, as the Court of Appeal held, a person whom the local authority has reasonable grounds for believing to be a child: [2008] EWCA Civ 1445; [2009] PTSR 1011, paras 30–31; or whether it raises a question of precedent fact which must be determined, if necessary, by a court. On the other there is the question whether a decision that the local authority makes as to whether or not*

*to provide accommodation for a child in need under s 20(1) is a determination of a
"civil right" within the meaning of art 6(1) of the European Convention on Human
Rights...*

*[51] It seems to me that the question whether or not a person is a child for the
purposes of s 20 of the 1989 Act is a question of fact which must ultimately be
decided by the court. The appeals were allowed.*

## Abducted children

13.29   The use of wardship in the prevention of potential child abduction provides a further illustration of the ambit of the wardship jurisdiction. Potential child abduction cases, which are complex, may invoke the wardship jurisdiction rather than protection being pursued under CA 1989, s 8 prohibited steps (see Chapter 12).

13.30   Where there is a dispute between the parties in respect of who should care for the child, the child may be made a ward of court in order to afford the child protection, from the possibility of abduction, and to resolve complex inter-jurisdictional custody battles. Here are some of them.

> In *Re HB (Abduction: Children's Objections) (1997)*, a boy aged 13 and a girl aged 11
> were taken to Denmark in 1989 by their Danish mother when the marriage ran into dif-
> ficulties. They remained there with her and her second husband. The English father also
> remarried. He initiated wardship proceedings, which resulted in 1990 in care and control
> being given to the mother in Denmark, with staying access to the father.

> In *Re H (Child Abduction: Whereabouts Order to Solicitors) (2000)*, on the claim-
> ant's's ex parte application in wardship proceedings, the judge made an order requiring
> the proposed defendant's solicitors to disclose to the claimant''s solicitors any informa-
> tion which they had as to the whereabouts of the proposed defendant, who was missing,
> and the missing child of both parties.

13.31   A child is also made a ward of court to ensure the protection of the child during complex inter-jurisdictional custody battles, particularly where countries have not acceded to the Hague Convention (see *In Re J (A Child) (Custody Rights: Jurisdiction) (2006)*—a Saudi Arabian case; *Re W (A Child) (Abduction: Jurisdiction) (2003)*—a Pakistani case; and *Re H (Abduction: Non-Convention Application) (2006)*—a Dominican case). Consider also the cases below.

> In *Re S (Children) (Abduction: Asylum Appeal) (2002)*, the appellant and respondent
> were the parents of two sons, aged five and three years. The family was from India and
> resided in India until June 2001, when the appellant and her sons came to England for
> a holiday. They stayed with the respondent's family and the appellant then went to live
> with a family friend. The appellant said that the respondent had been violent towards her

and decided not to return to India. The respondent denied the allegations. He issued an originating summons seeking the summary return of the children to India. The children were made wards of court.

*ES v AJ (2010)* turned on the question whether the children were 'habitually resident' in England. The court was satisfied that there was an agreement between the parents to send the twins to Cameroon, The twins were currently habitually resident in Cameroon and so the English court had no jurisdiction and it was decided that the mother could pursue remedy there (see Chapter 12). In *Re S (2010)*, the local authority was concerned that a seven year-old child was being neglected and applied for an emergency protection order. The order was refused. The mother took the child to Spain, where the father lived. Notwithstanding, the local authority continued with an application for care proceedings and the child was made a ward of court, with the requirement that she return to the jurisdiction. The issue was whether the child had lost habitual residence in England when she was removed to Spain.

The court held that the judge was entitled to make the child a ward of court, and to conclude that the CA 1989, s 100(2)(4)(a) applied and that the child was likely to suffer significant harm if the inherent jurisdiction was not exercised.

In *Re T (Wardship: Review of Police Protection Decision) (No 2) (2008)* the child, had been abducted at the age of six months by the father and taken to India for two years, and had been made a ward of court. When the father returned to England with the child, the child was removed from the paternal home and placed in the mother's care. The father was subsequently arrested, and charged with the criminal offence of child abduction (see Chapter 9 and *Re D (1984)*).

## Publicity v a child's right to privacy

13.32 The media is always eager to report stories of interest to the public especially where parents have committed grave criminal offences or where the child is the 'love child' of a public figure or celebrity. The court has the power to protect a child who is a warded from unwanted or harmful publicity by making an order restraining any individual from publishing any details which would enable the identity of the child concerned becoming known. The following cases explore the principles which have guided the court in wardship in its endeavour to protect the child's privacy. It is to be observed that, whilst in earlier cases the court in wardship imposed an outright ban on publishing details potentially harmful to the child, recent case law (see *Re S (A Child) (Identification: Restriction on Publication) (2004)*) balances Art 10 of the ECHR (right to freedom of expression) with the protective purpose of wardship. It would appear that the rights of the child under wardship are not absolute and under certain circumstances Art 10 rights are the weightier.

## Child killers

13.33 Mary Bell and Norma Bell (who were not related) were both accused of murdering Martin Brown, four years of age, and Brian Howe, three years of age, in May and July 1968. Norma Bell was acquitted of the murder and manslaughter of both boys. Mary Bell, however, was found guilty of manslaughter on the grounds of diminished responsibility. At the time of the killings, Mary Bell was 10 years of age. After serving 12 years in a juvenile detention centre, she was released. When she was 24 years old, she gave birth to a baby girl. The birth of Mary Bell's daughter was of considerable interest to the public and therefore attracted media attention. As a result, of this interest an application was made in wardship to ward her daughter (which was granted) and a further injunction granted to prohibit publication of her whereabouts.

> In *X County Council v A (1985)*, the parents of the baby who had been made a ward of court made a successful application by summons in the wardship proceedings for an order restraining the respondents, News Group Newspapers Ltd, by themselves, their servants or agents, from (i) publishing the name or identity of the ward or the parents of the ward or any information which would lead to their identification; (ii) publishing the address, locality, or area of the ward or the parents or any information which could lead to the identification of its location; (iii) publishing the identity, name or address, or any information by which the same could be established, of the ward's maternal grandmother, until the ward reached 18 years of age. A further injunction was granted in 1995 following renewed media interest in Mary Bell and her daughter, who was then an adolescent. Exceptionally, in 2003, an injunction was granted *contra mundum* to protect the anonymity of both Mary Bell and her daughter (see *X (A Woman Formerly Known as Mary Bell) and another v O'Brien and others (2003)*).

## Love child

13.34 Cecil Parkinson, Secretary of State for Trade and Industry (under Margaret Thatcher's government), had a sexual relationship with Sara Keays, his secretary. Their daughter, Flora, was born in 1983, suffering from learning disabilities. Her mother, in pursuit of treatment for her daughter, attended the Peto Institute. Subsequently, a documentary was made of the work of the Institute and Flora was one of the children filmed in the documentary. An injunction was sought to prevent the transmission of the documentary.

> In *Re Z (A Minor) (Freedom of Information) (1995)*, Flora (Z) was made a ward of court and an injunction was granted restraining publication of her identity. Ward LJ said that Cazalet J, who had refused a request by Miss Keays to lift the existing injunction, 'was of the clear view that the welfare of the child would be harmed and not advanced by her being involved in the making and publication of this film'. The Court of Appeal wholeheartedly agreed. Why was there so much interest in this child?

## Victims of child abuse

13.35 In the 1980s an unprecedented number of cases of child sexual abuse were diagnosed in Middlesbrough, Cleveland (discussed further in Chapters 14 and 15). Sixty-seven of the 125 children who were diagnosed as having been sexually abused between February and July of 1987 were made wards of court.

> In *Re X, Y and Z (Wardship: Disclosure of Material) (1992)*, a newspaper made an application for leave (1) to have access to wardship files relating to certain wards or ex-wards; and (2) to disclose documents for the purposes of a libel suit in which the newspaper was the defendant and in which two paediatricians were the plaintiffs. The two doctors sued for libel, following the publication in the newspaper of two articles accusing the doctors of incompetent and irresponsible promulgation of unsound techniques, in particular reflex and dilation, which were used as diagnostic indicators in the investigation of child sexual abuse and which subsequently led to children being removed from their families. The newspaper pleaded justification, relying on a number of case histories including the *X, Y and Z* children. The court held, on the basis of the authorities, that the privilege of confidentiality in wardship proceedings was that of the court, not the child, and the court had a dispensing power to authorize publication in particular instances, having regard to the welfare of the child, and the public interest in the due administration of the wardship jurisdiction, in accordance with its parental functions. The injury to the wardship jurisdiction, having regard to its parental role, was likely to be substantial. The application, therefore, failed and the originating summons was dismissed.

## Child victims of disasters

13.36 On 23 May 1987, the *Daily Mail* newspaper published an article, which had referred to a ward of court. The ward, L, aged 12 years, had been a passenger on the Herald of Free Enterprise when the ferry sank off Zeebrugge. L lost her parents and a grandmother when the ferry sank. The funeral of the child's parents and grandmother took place on 22 May. The article described the events at the funeral and referred to L by name and also to the fact that she was a ward of court. The question arose as to whether, as a ward of court, the newspaper, in disclosing the name of the child, was in contempt. Booth J found that the newspaper had not committed a contempt of court, since the article complimented L on her courage, and it did not contain inaccurate information (*The Times*, 4 July 1987).

## Balance of rights: freedom of information and children's rights and wardship

13.37 By the end of the 1990s, and with the introduction of the Human Rights Act 1998 (HRA 1998), challenges were made by invoking the right to freedom of information in resisting such injunctions. As the cases on injunctions restraining publication considered below demonstrate, in recent years, with the impact of the HRA 1998, the child's right to privacy has been held not to be absolute.

In *R v Central Independent Television plc (1994)* in a case where a mother was concerned that a television programme on sexual abuse would lead to the identification of her son as a victim Waite LJ said:

*No child, simply by virtue of being a child, is entitled to a right of privacy or confidentiality. That is as true of a ward of court (or child in respect of whom the inherent jurisdiction is otherwise invoked) as of any other child. Any element of confidentiality concerning a child in respect of whom the court's jurisdiction is invoked belongs not to the child but to the court. It is imposed to protect the proper functioning of the court's own jurisdiction, and will not be imposed to any further extent than is necessary to afford that protection.*

However, in *Re X (A Child) (Injunctions Restraining Publication) (2001)*, where X, a four year-old black African child had been living with white European foster carers and had developed a strong attachment to them and also had a relationship with the Y family, who were of the same ethnic origin, the local authority care plan proposed that X should be placed with the Y family with a view to adoption. The judge found that in the long term, the Y family would be better able to meet the issues that might arise during X's childhood as 'a black girl in a predominantly white society', and made the care order. Newspaper interest in the matter followed and an injunction against publicity was granted. Associated Newspapers Ltd brought an application to vary or discharge the injunction, as it was their contention that it was in the public interest that the story be published and also that the injunction was a breach of the right to freedom of expression in accordance with Art 10 of the ECHR. The court held that any restraints on freedom of expression called for the most careful scrutiny.

However, in *Re S (A Child) (Identification: Restrictions on Publication) (2004)*, the court held that there was a legitimate public interest in publishing information about a criminal trial. In this case, a parent was charged with the murder of her son. The judge found that death had been caused by salt poisoning administered by his mother, who was subsequently indicted for murder. An application in wardship was made to restrict reporting of the criminal trial by prohibiting identification of both the defendant and victim in order to protect the privacy of the surviving child. The House of Lords held:

*While art 8(1) of the Convention was engaged, and none of the factors in art 8(2) justified the interference, the nature of the relief sought, being the grant of an injunction beyond the scope of CYPA 1933, s 39, the remedy provided by Parliament to protect juveniles directly affected by criminal proceedings, was a step too far. The interference with art 8 rights, however distressing for the child, was not of the same order when compared with cases of juveniles who were directly involved in criminal trials. The rights under art 10 of the Convention, by contemporaneous reporting of criminal trials in progress, promoted the values of the rule of law. The consequence of the grant of the proposed injunction would be that informed debate about criminal justice would suffer. The judge had been correct, given the weight traditionally given to the importance of open reporting in criminal proceedings, in carrying out the balance required by the Convention, to begin by acknowledging the force of the argument under art 10 before considering whether the right of the child under art 8 was sufficient to outweigh it. The appeal would, accordingly, be dismissed.*

At the criminal trial of the mother, who was convicted of manslaughter and sentenced to five years' imprisonment (The *Guardian*, 25 February 2005) it was discovered that the mother had put 18 teaspoons of salt into two drip milk bottles stored in the ward kitchen at Great Ormond Street Children's Hospital in London.

However, the case of **Re W (Children) (Identification: Restriction on Publication) (2005)** was distinguished from **Re S (2004)** above, where the children's mother suffered from HIV and was awaiting sentence in respect of her guilty plea to a charge under the Offences against the Person Act 1861, s 20 (grievous bodily harm) of knowingly infecting the father with HIV. The court took the view that, since in these unusual and exceptional circumstances, knowledge about the mother's HIV status would impact on the children's care, the children's rights under Art 8 of the ECHR (right to respect for private and family life) outweighed, in these particular circumstances, the newspaper's rights under Art 10 (freedom of expression) to publish details of the case.

## Orphaned

13.38 Paula Yates' death left her four year-old daughter, Tiger Lily, orphaned since the child's natural father Michael Hutchence had died some years previously. Tiger Lily's paternal grandparents in Australia wanted to have care of her, whilst Bob Geldof, the former husband of the child's mother, who had custody of their three daughters, wanted to care for Tiger Lily in a family with her half-sisters. Tiger Lily was made a ward of court and custody was resolved some time later in favour of Bob Geldof.

The surviving child of Nicole Smith, who committed suicide in 2007, was warded. The courts subsequently determined the care and custody of this child in favour of the biological father.

## Wardship and medical intervention

### Reproduction, abortion, sterilization

#### Abortion

13.39 In **Re P (A Minor) (1986)**, a 15 year-old girl wanted an abortion; her mother was opposed to it. The local authority made an application in wardship. The girl had already given birth to a child when she was 13 years old. The court held that the girl could have an abortion and applied the welfare of the girl as the paramount consideration in the court's decision. The parent's objection to the abortion and offer to care for the current child were factors taken into consideration but the court held that such factors could not weigh in balancing the needs of the ward and the dangers to her mental health if such a termination were to be refused.

## Sterilization

13.40 Sterilization raises many moral and ethical questions, especially where the minor concerned is mentally vulnerable. The court in wardship has authorized sterilization in several cases where the adolescent was unable to understand sexual relations and pregnancy and childbirth. Consider the four cases below:

> In *Re M (A Minor) (Wardship: Sterilization) (1988)*, the local authority made an application in wardship for leave to carry out a sterilization operation on a 17 year-old girl. The girl was physically normal but had a mental age of five or six years. The court authorized the surgery.

> In *Re B (A Minor) (Wardship: Sterilisation) (1988)*, the court ruled in favour of sterilization in a case where, a local authority, had the care of the adolescent girl. In *Re P (A Minor) (Wardship: Sterilization) (1989)*, the mother made a successful application for her daughter, who had the intellectual development of a six-year-old child but was 17 years old, to be sterilized. However, Heilbron J in *Re D (A Minor) (Wardship) (1976)*, did not authorize sterilization as the child would be able at some point to make an informed decision. She described as 'a basic human right... the right of a woman to reproduce'.

# Life and death matters

## One life, one death

13.41 The decision in *Re A (Conjoined Twins: Medical Treatment) (No 2) (2001)* was a matter for the court in wardship concerning twins joined at birth. In order that one twin might have the possibility of life, the other would die in an operation to separate them.

Jodie and Mary were born in August 2000, and were ischiopagus (joined at part of the pelvis) tetrapus (with four legs). They each had their own brain, heart, lungs, liver, and kidneys, although Mary's brain, heart, and lungs were defective. One 'crucial anatomical fact' was that the arterial circulation ran from Jodie to Mary. Because of the defects in Mary's vital organs already identified, she was not capable of independent existence, but if there were an elective separation, the prognosis for Jodie would be for at least a reasonable quality of life. If the twins were not separated, Jodie's heart would fail within a matter of months through the strains imposed on it. It was accepted that separation entailed rapid death for Mary (see Burnet, 2001).

The court held that it was necessary to operate in order to save the life of one child where the death of both was imminent, knowing that the separation would result in the death of the weaker child.

13.42 We saw in Chapter 12 how wardship is used to protect adolescents from the consequences of taking life-ending decisions when refusing blood products or donated organs. Wardship is also invoked where babies and young children are not competent to make medical decisions for themselves and where parents, in exercising parental responsibility, wish to make a decision which is contrary to the views of the hospital or medical professionals, or indeed where medical professionals wish to pursue a course of 'treatment' with which the courts might disagree. Where babies and young children are terminally ill or are so sick that they are unlikely to live for even a short while, decisions must be made with regard to their ongoing medical care, including decisions regarding how to feed, medicate, provide pain relief, ventilate or resuscitate, the infant or young child. In addition, a decision may need to be taken with regard to authorize a heart, heart and lung, or liver transplant for a child (see Michalowski, 1997).

13.43 Loving parents may reach a decision to consent to resuscitating a child or consenting to an organ transplant in treating the child to live. Loving parents may equally reach a decision that they do not wish their child to be resuscitated, or to receive a donated organ, since in their view it is kinder to 'treat' the child by allowing him or her to die with medication to alleviate pain. Downie (2000) notes that the courts tend to give more weight to parental objections where the treatment proposed is experimental—that is, when the prognosis which the treatment offers is uncertain. The enormity of these life and death decisions is self-evident. The courts step in where doctors and parents cannot agree, or when doctors and parents agree and fear criminal prosecution. Doctors caring for very sick children work with the 'sword of Damocles' over their head, fearing criminal prosecution. Such was the predicament of Dr Leonard Arthur, who was described as 'letting' a very sick baby die and faced a criminal prosecution for murder.

In *R v Arthur (1981)*, Dr Leonard Arthur was indicted for the murder of John Pearson, a charge that was dropped and attempted murder substituted. John Pearson was born on 28 June 1981 and was suffering from Down's Syndrome as well as other related disabilities and conditions. His parents did not want him to live. Dr Arthur prescribed 'nursing care only' and doses of dihydrocodeine to sedate the baby, who died three days later. The jury found Dr Arthur not guilty.

## The power of language

13.44 Ivan Illich, in *Medical Nemesis* (London, 1975), his celebrated critique of the institution of modern medicine, pronounced that, 'the medical establishment has become a major threat to health'. Very sick babies and very sick adults are being kept alive and life is being prolonged. If life is prolonged, what is the quality of that life, and if that life merely prolongs suffering and nothing more, what is the moral basis for prolongation as against letting an individual die without further suffering? The ethics of what is being done is justified or else condemned by and through the use of language and rhetoric which is performative (see Searle, 1969; Austin, 1958) that is, when a word is spoken or written it becomes a relational entity; and words are used to justify and condone a behavior or act or otherwise condemn the decision or action that is being taken. The words themselves have a force and signify and give permission for, or else prohibit, the action.

13.45 Over the years, the language and words used in such cases has straddled the two positions of (a) 'letting a child live' or 'letting a child die', and then has moved to express these two positions as (b) 'treatment to live' and 'treatment to die', in an attempt to inscribe 'treatment to die' formerly expressed as 'letting a child die' with a positive inflection rather than an act of omission. More recently, the medical approach has now centred not on the outcome of treatment with regard to life or death outcomes but instead focused on the medical objective of (c) easing of suffering as the primary focus.

## Palliative care for children

13.46 On palliative care:

> *1,100 children die each year from conditions for which there is no reasonable hope of cure: 40% from cancers, 20% from heart disease, and 40% from other life-limiting conditions.*
>
> *(see http://www.helpthehospices.org.uk/clip/index.htm)*

## What should be the primary objective, to ease suffering, or to prolong life?

13.47 The notion of letting a baby or child die is antipathetic to the entire purpose of the medical imperative of treating to live. Conventional medical care, as Dame Cicely Saunders, the founder of the Hospice movement, pointed out, was ill-equipped to deal with the need to care for the dying and how that might best be accomplished in accordance with the needs of the patient.

# 'Live or let die'

13.48    In *Re B (1982)*, a baby was born with Down's Syndrome, duodenal atresia, and intestinal blockage. The parents thought it kinder to 'let her die'. Doctors, fearing criminal prosecution, given the *Arthur* case cited above, contacted the local authority, who made her a ward of court. The court refused to consent to the treatment to live. But on appeal (in the light of the *Arthur* case) the Court of Appeal authorized surgery since it said she should not be (in the performative utterance of the court) 'condemned to die'.

However, as the cases below demonstrate, each case seems to turn on its own particular facts, since suffering, prognosis of duration of life, and quality of life for the child do not constitute a precise science. In addition, the question of prolonging life or allowing a child to die is a decision which may carry a criminal as well as a moral liability.

Lord Goff of Chieveley said, in *Airedale NHS Trust v Bland (1993)*:

*I agree (with Professor Glanville Williams) that the doctor's conduct in discontinuing life support can properly be categorized as an omission. It is true it may be difficult to describe what the doctor actually does as an omission, for example where he takes some positive step to bring the life support to an end. But discontinuation of life support is, for present purposes, no different from not initiating it in the first place. In each case the doctor is simply allowing his patient to die in the sense that he is desisting from taking a step which might, in certain circumstances, prevent his patient from dying as a result of his pre-existing condition...*

But as the court said in *An NHS Trust v MB (A Child Represented by CAFCASS as Guardian ad Litem) (2006)*:

*'For every case and every child is unique, and this case concerns M alone.'*

# 'Treat to ease pain and suffering'

13.49    The case of *Re C (A Minor) (Wardship: Medical Treatment) (1989)*, reflects the use of language, which embodies a moral position that letting a child die, is indeed a positive act involving treatment of the child and is not a negative act as the Court of Appeal in *Re B* (above) considered it to be. The shift from considering consequences of life and death to considering the suffering of the child is reflected in the much-publicized and controversial case of Baby C (*Re C (A Minor) (Wardship: Medical Treatment) (1989)*), where the court considered the case from a perspective of the importance of treatment to ease pain and suffering rather than to prolong life.

C was made a ward of court shortly after her birth because the local authority's social services department considered that her parents would have great difficulty in looking after her. Where a ward of court was terminally ill, the court would authorize treatment which would relieve the ward's suffering during the remainder of his or her life but would accept the opinions of the medical staff looking after the ward if they decided that the aim of nursing care should be to ease the ward's suffering rather than achieve a short prolongation of life, and in such circumstances it would be inappropriate to include in the court's directions any specific instructions as to how the ward was to be treated.

Giving judgment in the appeal brought by the Official Solicitor, Lord Donaldson, Master of the Rolls, said 'Baby C is dying. Nothing that the court can do, or the doctors, can alter that fact'. Lord Donaldson said that Ward J had 'failed to express himself with his usual felicity', when he said in the course of his judgment that leave would be given to 'treat the ward to die'. 'No one would uphold such a phrase', Lord Donaldson said. The amended judgment said that Baby C who was born with severe hydrocephalus, should be treated 'in such a way that she may end her life and die peacefully with the greatest dignity and the least pain, suffering and distress'.

In *Re J (A Minor) (Wardship: Medical Treatment) (1991)* the court made an order that a premature 27-week baby born as a result of an accident which resulted in brain damage, blindness, paralysis, and epilepsy, should be treated with antibiotics if he developed a chest infection but not reventilated unless doctors deemed appropriate. Where a ward of court suffered from physical disabilities so grave that his life would from his point of view be so intolerable if he were to continue living that he would choose to die if he were in a position to make a sound judgment, the court could direct that treatment without which death would ensue from natural causes need not be given to the ward to prolong his life, even though he was neither on the point of death nor dying. Lord Donaldson said:

*Again I have to cavil at the use of such an expression as 'condemn to die' and 'the child must live' in Templeman LJ's judgment, which, be it noted, was not a reserved judgment. 'Thou shalt not kill' is an absolute commandment in this context. But, to quote the well-known phrase of Arthur Hugh Clough in The Latest Decalogue, in this context it is permissible to add 'but need'st not strive officiously to keep alive'. The decision on life and death must and does remain in other hands. What doctors and the court have to decide is whether, in the best interests of the child patient, a particular decision as to medical treatment should be taken which as a side effect will render death more or less likely. This is not a matter of semantics.*

In *Re J (A Minor) (Child in Care: Medical Treatment) (1993)*, as a result of serious head injuries sustained when he was one month old, J, who was born in January 1991, became profoundly mentally and physically handicapped, suffering from microcephaly, cerebral palsy, cortical blindness, severe epilepsy, and requiring to be fed by a nasogastric tube. The local authority shared parental responsibility under a care order. The judge directed that if J were to suffer a life-threatening event while in the health authority's care and the required drugs and equipment were or could reasonably be made available, the health authority should cause such measures (including artificial ventilation) to be applied so long as they were capable of prolonging his life. The health authority appealed. The Court of Appeal, allowing the appeal, held that in the exercise of its inherent jurisdiction the court would not order a medical practitioner to treat his patient in a manner contrary to his clinical judgement. Accordingly, the order would be set aside.

13.50 Subsequent cases law may not have used the phrase 'treat to die' because of its performative implications, the language of treatment to ease pain and suffering is less controversial even though death follows from high doses of pain relief.

## Intolerable life as a guide to best interests

13.51 In the following case, the parents opposed the medical opinion that the child should not be resuscitated 'in the event of a respiratory crisis'. However, since resuscitation is considered more invasive than feeding and drug treatment, a higher level of justification for resuscitation is required and in considering this question the court approached its task by considering the course of action from the child's vantage point or subject position:

> In *Re Wyatt (A Child) (Medical Treatment: Parents' Consent) (2004); Portsmouth NHS Trust v Wyatt and Wyatt, Southampton NHS Trust Intervening (2004)*, C, who was 11 months old, was born at 26 weeks' gestation and weighing 458g (approximately one pound). She suffered from, *inter alia*, poor kidney function and respiratory difficulties and had required ventilation for most of her first three months of life. She had also suffered severe brain damage. The damage to her kidney function and respiratory system was probably irreparable. The damage to her brain was certain and irreversible. The medical evidence indicated that she could feel pain and distress and that it was unlikely, although not impossible, that she experienced pleasure. To supply C with the necessary supplemental oxygen her head was covered with a transparent plastic box. When removed from the box she generally became distressed and turned blue. In July 2004 she contracted an infection, which had led to a deterioration of her condition. The realistic prognosis for her survival for a further 12 months was 5%. The unanimous medical opinion was that it was not in C's best interests to artificially ventilate her in the future. The applicant NHS Trust sought a declaration, which would, in essence, permit them to discontinue invasive and aggressive treatment of C. The parents believed it was their duty to maintain C's life, as she was not yet ready to die. They also believed that they had experienced C's reacting to them. The court ruled that further aggressive treatment, even if necessary to prolong C's life, was not in her best interests. The concept of best interests had to be given a generous interpretation. The infinite variety of the human condition never ceased to surprise and it was that fact which defeated any attempt to be more precise in a definition of best interests. Moreover, the concept of 'intolerable to that child' should not be seen as a gloss on, much less a supplementary test to best interests. It was, however, a valuable guide

in the search for best interests in this type of case. Both the quality of life and its toler-
ability had strong subjective elements to them. The test was not whether life would be
tolerable to the decider but whether the child in question, if capable of exercising sound
judgment, would consider the life intolerable. Given C's age, the key to any decision was
the quality of her sensory faculties. The medical evidence established that she had no
sense of sight or sound and was effectively without volition. Considering all the relevant
factors, including the sanctity of life, the principles of the right of self-determination and
respect for the dignity of the individual, the views of the parties, and taking account of the
evidence, further aggressive and invasive treatment would be intolerable to C and such
treatment would not be in her best interests. Accordingly, a declaration in similar terms to
that contended for by the applicant NHS Trust was granted.

In *A NHS Trust v MB (2006)*, the child of 18 months suffered from severe spinal muscular
atrophy, which was incurable and degenerative. The trust caring for the child was, like
the trust in the case above, concerned about whether the child's life had become intolerable. The parents opposed any discontinuation of ventilation. The medical witnesses
were unanimous that it was in MB's best interests to withdraw treatment. The consultant
intensivist said it was difficult to assess whether the child was in pain, the neurologist
said he was not happy about subjecting MB to further pain and discomfort. The father
did not want resuscitation in the event of heart failure. The mother wanted resuscitation.
Determining the meaning of 'intolerable' and whether the baby's life was intolerable was
difficult for medical witnesses to determine and there was no consensus as to whether the
baby's life was intolerable. The judge decided that it was not in the child's best interests
to discontinue ventilation although it held that it was in the child's best interest to withhold
procedures that went beyond ventilation including CPR (cardio-vascular resuscitation).

Where the medical professionals and both parents agree with the proposed course
of action the decision for the court is less problematic.

In *K (A Minor) (2006)* where a five and a half month-old child was suffering from congenital myontonica dystrophy and in care of the local authority, the NHS Trust made an
application to the court to remove the feeding tube and move to a regime of palliative
care to allow the child to die peacefully. The parents both approved of what the doctors
proposed as did the child's guardian. Sir Mark Potter (P) granted the declaration to allow
her to die peacefully, saying it would 'not only be a mercy, but it is in her best interests' and
illustrated how like sand in the wind 'bests interests' is hard to define.

In applying the 'best interests' test the court said:

*Dame Elizabeth Butler-Sloss P made clear in Re S (Adult Patient: Sterilisation)
(2001) Fam 15 at 30E, (2000) 3 WLR 1288, (2000) 2 FCR 452: at p 28 that the principle
of the 'best interests' of the patient as applied by the court extends beyond the
considerations governing the propriety and advisability of medical treatment
developed in the Bolam Case (1957) 2 All ER 118, (1957) 1 WLR 582 and 'The judicial*

*decision will incorporate broader ethical, social, moral and welfare considerations'. As stated by Hedley J in Portsmouth NHS Trust v Wyatt (2004) EWHC 2247 (Fam), (2005) 1 FLR 21 at para 23, 84 BMLR 206:Best interests must be given a generous interpretation. As Dame Elizabeth Butler-Sloss P said in Re A (Male Sterilisation) (2000) 1 FLR 549 at 555:...best interests encompasses medical, emotional and all other welfare issues....The infinite variety of the human condition never ceases to surprise and it is that fact that defeats any attempt to be more precise in the definition of best interest.*

# Transplant or die

13.52   As already suggested, where the treatment proposed involves an organ transplant, the courts have tended to give less weight to any presumption of treatment to live. As Butler-Sloss LJ recognized: 'But to prolong life.... is not the sole objective of the court' (*Re T (A Minor) (Wardship: Medical Treatment) (1997)*; see also Pedain, 1995).

> In *Re T (A Minor) (1997)* T was born with a life-threatening liver defect and a transplant was required. His parents, who had gone with him to live and work abroad, were both health care professionals with experience in the care of young, sick children. They did not wish T to undergo transplant surgery and refused their consent to an operation should a suitable liver become available. The doctors who had treated T in England were of the opinion that his parents were not acting in his best interests and referred the matter to the relevant local authority, which applied under CA 1989, s 100(3) for the court to exercise its inherent wardship jurisdiction. The judge held that the mother's refusal to accept the unanimous advice of the doctors and her refusal to consent to the operation was not the conduct of a reasonable parent and he ordered that T be returned to the jurisdiction within 21 days to be assessed for transplant surgery. On appeal by the mother, the court said that: 'it was in his best interests to require his future treatment to be left in the hands of his parents'. Accordingly, the judge's order was set aside.
>
> Roch J said this:
>
> *This brings me face to face with the problem of formulating the critical equation. In truth it cannot be done with mathematical or any precision. There is without doubt a very strong presumption in favour of a course of action which will prolong life, but, even excepting the 'cabbage' case to which special considerations may well apply, it is not irrebuttable... The presumption in favour of the sustaining of life is not irrebuttable and perhaps has less weight where the issue is whether to prolong or not to prolong life by means of organ transplantation. I agree that this appeal should be allowed.*
>
> The Court of Appeal, disagreeing with the judge of first instance, said that the decision was the action of a reasonable parent, although reasonableness or unreasonableness was not the primary issue. The primary issue was the welfare of the child.

# Human rights and treatment

13.53 Whilst in recent years the courts have focused in these cases on the objective of easing the suffering of the child and reflect a child-centredness in that the court itself tries to situate itself in the position of the sick child, increasingly human rights have become engaged, especially ECHR Art 2 'right to life' claims. Health authorities, not wishing to fall foul of the law, are increasingly making applications to the court for authorization of a proposed course of treatment, which will ease suffering and allow the child to die, as the two cases below demonstrate.

In *A National Health Service Trust v D (2000)*, a child was born prematurely with serious disabilities, including a chronic, irreversible, and worsening lung disease, heart failure, hepatic and renal dysfunction, and severe developmental delay. In June 2000, the applicant applied for a declaration that, in the event of any future respiratory and/or cardiac failure or arrest, the child should not be resuscitated but should be given palliative care to ease suffering and 'to permit his life to end peacefully and with dignity'. In this case, the parents opposed the application, contending that it was premature.

The court held that, having regard to:

*the minimal quality of life, the short life span left, the irreversible and worsening lung condition, any possible very limited short-term extension that mechanical ventilation might give him had to be weighed, from his assumed standpoint, against the increasing pain and suffering caused by further mechanical ventilation.*

The court referred to the 'palliative treatment' proposed as being in the best interests of the child, adding that such a declaration did not disclose any breach of the ECHR: there could be no infringement of Art 2 because the treatment as advised was in the best interests of the child, and Art 3, which required that a person was not subjected to inhuman or degrading treatment, included the right to die with dignity.

Similarly, in *Re L (Medical Treatment: Benefit) (2004)*, two National Health Service Trusts applied for a declaration about the future care of a nine month-old baby, following disagreements between the Trusts and the baby's mother over his future care. The baby was born with Edward's Syndrome, a genetic disorder that caused him to suffer multiple heart defects, chronic respiratory failure, gastroesophageal reflux, severe developmental delay, epilepsy, and hypertonia. The baby's condition was incurable and he was unlikely to survive beyond a year. Any treatment given would be palliative, not curative. The mother contended that the baby had not deteriorated to the extent set out in the medical reports and that the medical profession was giving up too soon. The Trusts sought a declaration that it would be lawful not to provide further aggressive treatment, either by artificial – ventilation or by cardiac massage. The court granted a declaration as to artificial ventilation.

13.54 Wardship will continue to impose itself as an important jurisdiction with the best interests of the child at heart. The case of *A National Health Trust* (above) indicates that the modern subject position of the court in wardship is to place itself in the position of the child in determining where the best interests of the child lie. Hence in such cases, discussions of whether the child's life is painful or intolerable now become relevant. This suggests a departure from the earlier position in wardship where the court stood in the place of the judicious parent and in a default position that prolongation of life was the correct course. It is established that the doctor will not be forced to treat against his judgement and conscience. Doctors now seem increasingly unwilling to accede to pressure.

# Reform

13.55 The Law Reform Commission recently recommended the abolition of the wardship jurisdiction and its replacement with a new Public Guardianship system.

## FURTHER READING

Bainham A, *Children: the Modern Law* (Family Law, 2005)

Burnet D, 'Case Commentary: Conjoined Twins, Sanctity and Quality of Life, and Invention the Mother of Necessity' (2001) CFLQ 13 (1), 91

Downie A, 'The Autonomy of Parents' (2000) CFLQ 12 (2), 197

Fortin J, *Children's Rights and the Developing Law* (Butterworths, 2003)

Heath T and Jeffries R, *Asylum Statistics: United Kingdom* (Home Office, 23 August 2005)

Herring J, *Family Law* (Longmans, 2008)

Illich I, *Medical Nemesis* (Boyars, 1975)

Michalowski S, 'Case Commentary: Is it in the Best Interests of a Child to have a Life-saving Liver Transplantation?' (1997) CFLQ 9 (2), 179

Mitchell J, 'Whatever Happened to Wardship?' Part 1 (2001) Fam Law (February), Part 2 (2001) Fam Law (March)

Morris A, 'Selective Treatment of Irreversibly Impaired Infants: Decision-Making at the Threshold' (2009) Med Law Rev 17, 347

Pedain A, 'Doctors, Patients and the Courts, legitimising restrictions on the continued provision of lifespan maximising treatments for severely handicapped non-dying babies' (2005) CFLQ 17 (4), 535

Searle JR, *Speech Acts: an Essay in the Philosophy of Language* (Cambridge University Press, 1969, 1999)

Stringer E and Lumley T, *A long way to go* (New Philanthropy Capital, 2007)

Taylor R, 'Case Commentary: **Re S (A Child) (Identification: Restrictions on Publication) and A Local Authority** v W: children's privacy and press freedom in criminal cases' (2006) CFLQ 18 (2), 269

Zephaniah B, *Refugee Boy* (Bloomsbury Press, 2001)

## SELF-TEST QUESTIONS

1 'Contrary to fears which were expressed before the Children Act 1989 came into force, wardship remains vigorously alive...wardship remains an important last resort in a variety of situations where a child's welfare requires the intervention of the High Court' (Mitchell, 2001). Discuss, with reference to case law, the range of circumstances in which wardship provides important protection for children.

2 Trina is eighteen months old, and has a rare condition known as dilated cardiomyopathy. She will need a heart transplant before she is three years of age, otherwise she will die. Her parents, Mr and Mrs Mort, do not want her to have the operation as her brother Malcolm, also has the condition and had a heart transplant. Sadly, he had a stroke following surgery and is now severely mentally handicapped. The doctors want to support the parents. Advise the doctors and the parents.

3 'Wardship is where the court assumes responsibility for the welfare of a child and exercises parental responsibility. Only the High Court can order that the child be made or cease to be a ward of court. Under the Children Act, the use of wardship by local authorities is severely limited and leave to make an application for any exercise of the court's inherent jurisdiction must be granted by the High Court' (*Judicial Statistics 1997,* 52). How has the Children Act 1989 affected the wardship jurisdiction?

4 Mrs Fox has completed a term of imprisonment for child cruelty on her young daughter who was four years of age. She is due to be released and plans to reside in the former matrimonial home in a small village in London Brooke. The Rix family adopted her daughter whilst the mother was in prison. The *London Brooke Herald* wants to run her release from prison as the lead story. Her daughter, Mary Ellen, is 12 years of age. What course of action, if any, is open to the Rix's?

5 Consider with reference to decided cases the way in which the courts have balanced the rights of the press versus the right of the child to privacy.

6 'With the advent of the Children Act 1989 the wardship jurisdiction is redundant'. Discuss?

# 14

# Child protection: the public law procedure

**SUMMARY**

In this chapter we explore the sexual, physical, emotional abuse and neglect of children, and the steps taken by the local authority to protect the child. Local authority intervention is mandated by law where there is a suspicion of 'significant harm'. The Children Act 1989 establishes procedures for the investigation and effective prevention of child abuse including setting up a care conference, placing a child on the child 'at risk' register, and the emergency measures which authorize the immediate removal of a child from the home and also the human rights issues which are posed by ex parte removal of children. We explore the role of expert opinion in the determination of non-accidental injury and consider the problem of flawed findings made by experts for children and their families, and also evidential issues around the disclosures made by parents and the right of a parent to privilege against self-incrimination.

## What is child abuse?

14.1 In 2004, in the USA, Joel Steinberg was released from prison after serving 17 years for the manslaughter of his six year-old adopted daughter, Lisa. Joel Steinberg was was a highly successful lawyer, middle class, and privileged, but with a crack cocaine addiction. Child abuse is not, as is so often assumed, confined to families in poor, run-down neighbourhoods.

14.2   In 2000, in the UK, Victoria Climbié, eight years old, died of starvation, hypothermia, neglect, and abuse at the hands of her great-aunt and her aunt's partner. Lord Laming opened the Victoria Climbié Inquiry Report (2003) with these words:

> *During this gruelling Inquiry our increasing familiarity with the suffering experienced by Victoria did not make it easier to endure. I will not dwell on it. Suffice to say that at the end Victoria spent the cold winter months, bound hand and foot, in an unheated bathroom, lying in the cold bath in a plastic bag in her own urine and faeces and having to eat what food she could get by pressing her face onto the plate of whatever was put in the bath beside her. Little wonder that at the time of her last admission to hospital her body temperature was so low it did not register on a standard thermometer and her legs could not be straightened. So in a few months this once lively, bright and energetic child had been reduced to a bruised, deformed and malnourished state in which her life ebbed away because of the total collapse of her body systems. As the very experienced pathologist Dr Carey told us: 'All non-accidental injuries to children are awful and difficult for everybody to deal with, but in terms of the nature and extent of the injury and the almost systematic nature of the inflicted injury, I certainly regard this as the worst I have ever dealt with, and just about the worst I have ever heard of'.*

The Climbié Inquiry Report made 18 recommendations including: (rec 8) the need to establish reliable ways of assessing the needs and circumstances of children in their area, with particular reference to the needs of children who may be at risk of deliberate harm; (rec 10) the need for government inspectorates to inspect both the quality of the services delivered, and also the effectiveness of the inter-agency arrangements for the provision of services to children and families; (rec 11) the need for government to review the law regarding the registration of private foster carers; (rec 13) the need to prescribe a clear step-by-step guide on how to manage a case through either a CA 1989, s 17 or a s 47 track, with built-in systems for case monitoring and review.

14.3   Gillian Shepherd MP reported in the House of Commons on another child death:

> *Lauren Wright my constituent, died from a blow to her abdomen, with extreme bruising all over her body, on 6 May 2000, two days before the date of the case conference that Norfolk social services had finally organised to discuss her plight. From her birth she had been known to Hertfordshire social services. She was known to Norfolk social services for the three years before her death. For the 16 months before she died she was at primary school—a two-teacher, 29-pupil primary school in which she could hardly get lost. During that time, aged six, she lost four stone in weight. She was seen by a community paediatrician and a general practitioner, and again by a paediatrician just a couple of months before she died. She was visited by social workers. Too late they alerted the area child protection committee, and too late the case conference was finally convened for a date after her death.*
>
> *The real concerns about this case are that Lauren's treatment at the hands of her stepmother, who was eventually convicted of her manslaughter, took place in public,*

*observed by the local community, and under the supervision of doctors, social work-ers and teachers. Trial evidence revealed that the stepmother was seen hitting the child and screaming abuse at her; that she fed her pepper sandwiches; that she put bugs from the garden in her food; and that she turned off the taps so tightly that the child could not get a drink of water.*

*Lauren's class teacher said at the trial that she saw marks on Lauren:*

*lots of times, often she was covered with lots of small bruises and with major bruises about once a month. These included black eyes, bruising on her face and scratches across her back. As I said, at the time of her death, she weighed little more than two stone. In the words of her head teacher, her physical deterioration had been 'appar-ent for at least five months before she died'.*

*(16 Jul 2003: Column 379, Hansard)*

On 3rd August 2007, Baby P died from multiple bruising and a broken back and ribs (which were perpetrated by Tracey Connelly, 28, and her partner Steven Barker, 33), 'Baby P was known to the social services for many months... he was said to have been visited on sixty occasions by health care and social work professionals and was also on the child at risk register' (*The Times*, 12 November 2008). The circumstances are a mirror image of the circumstances surrounding the death of Maria Colwell in 1974. On the night of 6 January 1973 she was wheeled in a pram to the local hospital with internal injuries and brain damage . She died shorly after admission.

A report in *The Times* (1 February 2010) states that 'More than 8,000 children have been taken into care in the year since the Baby P tragedy came to light, up more than 40 per cent on 2008.'

And in 2010, Simon and Susan Moody were jailed for neglecting their eight year-old daughter who was found hanged in her bedroom in which she was kept locked in for 14 hours a day. Charlotte Avenall, however, had been known to the social ser-vices for several years (28 July 2010). Tracey Sutherland was found guilty of child neglect of her 13 month-old son (21 April 2010). We might ask what impact then has Lord Laming's report on Victoria Climbié had in preventing child abuse?

## Changing perceptions of abuse

14.4 In the nineteenth century, physical abuse of children was extremely common, and there were no laws to protect them. Cretney and Masson (2003, 712) write, some-what provocatively, that, 'child maltreatment is a socially constructed phenomenon which reflects the values and opinions of a particular culture at a particular time'.

In the nineteenth century, a parent or person acting for the parent could moderately chas-tise a child. In *R v Hopley (1860)*, Mr Hopley, a schoolmaster at a school in Eastbourne, wrote to the father of one of the boys at the school seeking the father's permission to chastise the boy and, as he stated in his letter to the father, he asked if he might 'continue it at intervals, even if he held out for hours'. The father replied stating, 'I do not wish to interfere with your plan'. The schoolmaster did just that, beating him for hours, until eventually the child died. The court had to decide whether the beating was excessive, since only moderate chastisement was permissible. The jury found Hopley guilty. He was sentenced to four years' imprisonment.

14.5 Indeed, it was not until 1961, a century after the ***Hopley*** case, that health care professionals recognized and acceded that child abuse occurred within the family. Henry Kemp coined the term 'battered child syndrome' after seeing children in accident and emergency departments with unexplained 'accidental' injuries.

14.6 The law was slow to condemn and regulate certain aspects of violence. By 1998, following the decision in *A* (below), parents could no longer beat or cane their children, or authorize someone else to do so.

> In *A v United Kingdom (1998)*, A was caned by his stepfather, S. The step father was prosecuted in criminal proceedings and acquitted of assault causing actual bodily harm. The European Court of Human Rights held that failure to criminalize such behaviour violated A's right not to be subjected to inhuman or degrading punishment.

By 2004, the Children Act 2004 criminalized such conduct in s 58 as follows:

*Reasonable punishment*

*(1) In relation to any offence specified in subsection (2), battery of a child cannot be justified on the ground that it constituted reasonable punishment.*

*(2) The offences referred to in subsection (1) are—*

*(a) an offence under section 18 or 20 of the Offences against the Person Act 1861 (wounding and causing grievous bodily harm);*

*(b) an offence under section 47 of that Act (assault occasioning actual bodily harm);*

*(c) an offence under section 1 of the Children and Young Persons Act 1933 (cruelty to persons under 16).*

*(3) Battery of a child causing actual bodily harm to the child cannot be justified in any civil proceedings on the ground that it constituted reasonable punishment.*

*(4) For the purposes of subsection (3) 'actual bodily harm' has the same meaning as it has for the purposes of section 47 of the Offences against the Person Act 1861.*

*(5) In section 1 of the Children and Young Persons Act 1933, omit subsection (7).*

14.7 On 8 June 2005, the Council of Europe delivered a ruling banning smacking in the home. The European Committee of Social Rights upheld complaints against corporal punishment in Ireland, Greece, and Belgium. In 2003, a ban was introduced stating that a childminder 'shall not give corporal punishment to a child for whom he acts as a child minder or provides day care' (see the Day Care and Child Minding (National Standards) (England) Regulations 2003 (SI 2003/1996), reg 5).

14.8    However, in *R (on the application of Williamson and others) v Secretary of State for Education and Employment and others (2005)*, the claimants were teachers and parents of children at Christian independent schools who brought proceedings for judicial review to challenge the lawfulness of the ruling that teachers could not stand in the place of parents and administer physical punishment to children who misbehaved (see Chapter 12). Lord Nicholls reiterated the legal position:

> *Punishment of a child which caused 'actual bodily harm' cannot be justified, either in civil proceedings or in respect of certain criminal offences, on the ground that it constituted reasonable punishment: s 58 of the CA 2004. Thus, to be lawful, corporal punishment administered by a parent must stop short of causing actual bodily harm.*

# Physical abuse (non-accidental injury)

14.9  What exactly is physical abuse? Signs of physical abuse include for example bruising, black eyes, grazing, burns, blindness, deafness, paralysis, fracture, subdural haematoma, and retinal haemorrhaging. It is the task of forensic expert opinion to determine whether the cause of these injuries is accidental or deliberate. An injured child may come to the attention of the police and/or local authority (both of whom have a statutory duty to protect and investigate) as a result of a referral from a doctor or teacher (who have a statutory duty to report any concerns). Perpetrators of abuse routinely deny responsibility for the injuries, claiming that such injuries are accidental, so the task of child protection involves a careful piecing together of evidence of injury and other relevant information which goes towards establishing causation in the determination of how the child has been harmed.

# Sexual abuse

14.10  Sexual abuse includes a wide range of conduct, from indecent touching of a child, the rape of a child to forcing a child to watch pornography or forcing a child into prostitution. Sexual abuse of children like physical abuse, but more so, until very recently was thought not to exist. If professionals in Cleveland were criticized for being overzealous, at least the public were made aware that child sexual abuse did in fact occur, that the perpetrators were not strangers but family members, that boys were almost as much at risk as girls, and that anal rape of young children, as well as vaginal rape of girls, formed part of this pattern of abuse. So what happened in Cleveland?:

> *In total 125 children were diagnosed as having been sexually abused between February and July 1987 in Middlesbrough General Hospital: 66 children became wards of court. In the wardship cases, 27 were dewarded and went home with the proceedings dismissed; 24 went home on conditions as to medical examination of the children, and two went home on interim care orders. Nine children who were wards of court remain in care of the County Council and away from families. Of those not made wards of court, 27 were the subject of place of safety orders. In all, 21 children remain in care. We understand that out of the 121 children 98 are at home.*
>
> *(Cleveland Inquiry (1988, 12))*

14.11     In *Re W (Children) (Threshold Criteria: Parental Concessions) (2001)*, the local authority initiated care proceedings in relation to three boys aged 15, 12, and 11 years because of: (i) their poor physical presentation; (ii) non-intentional physical injuries; (iii) sexualized behaviour, including masturbation and simulated sex, in particular inappropriate sexualized behaviour by one of the boys towards his mother which took place during a supervised contact visit in full view of his father and social worker; and (iv) allegations of sexual abuse, in particular against their father.

In *Re D (Children: Contact Order) (2005)*, the local authority commenced care and adoption proceedings in relation to four children, S, aged 16, I , aged 11, L, aged 7, and T, aged 4, where:

> *it was alleged by the authority that both parents had subjected S, L and L to repeated acts of sexual abuse including sexual intercourse, indecent touching, oral sex, exposure to pornography, exposure to an adult sex object, participation in a sex game involving family members removing all of their clothing, sexual activity between the adults in the children's presence and sexual abuse of one child in the presence of one or more of the other children; that S had sexually abused his sisters, L and L, and that the parents had failed to protect them from such abuse; that the children had suffered numerous incidents of physical harm through a combination of physical assault, neglectful parenting and inter-sibling aggression; that the children had suffered emotional harm by reason of all the above, and through exposure to adult conflict.*

In both these two cases, the judge found that the threshold criteria in the CA 1989, s 31 was satisfied.

# Emotional abuse

14.12 Emotional abuse is often very difficult to define. To professionals of the twenty-first century, a class action of emotional abuse could be brought against the nineteenth-century parent. The aloof, emotional, cold, and clinical parent may be just as guilty of emotional abuse as an overbearing and domineering parent. Emotional abuse often arises in a context of cruelty and unkindness, ranging from belittlement and humiliation of a child to making a child feel hopeless, unworthy, and unwanted. Telling a child that he or she will never amount to anything, that he is useless, ridiculing the child, controlling the child in everything he does, blaming the child for every mishap. Isolation, cutting the child off from friends and other family members. Inconsistency in attending to the child's needs, denigrating the child and then telling the child that he really is loved in order to lock him into a hopeless dependency and confusion. Placing expectations which are too high for the child's developmental capabilities and thereby diminishing his confidence and self-esteem, are all examples of emotional abuse, as is unfairness in discipline and punishment and unequal treatment of siblings, bullying and scape-goating, threats of violence, and attempts to frighten the child with homelessness especially at times like Christmas.

14.13 The law now concedes that a child witness of domestic violence between parents can suffer immeasurable harm and such harm may amount to the threshold standard of 'significant harm' (see ACA 2002, s 120).

> In *Bassett v Bassett (1975)*, Cumming-Bruce LJ acknowledged:
>
> *Where there are children whom the mother is looking after, a major consideration must be to relieve them of the psychological stresses and strains imposed by the friction between their parents, as the long-term effect upon a child is liable to be of the utmost gravity.*

14.14 The signs and symptoms of emotional abuse manifest in low self-esteem, a lack of confidence, fearfulness, self-deprecation, nervousness, speech disorders and other physical and mental disorders, and attempted suicide by a desperately unhappy and unloved child or adolescent.

> In *Re G (Emotional Harm) (1999)*, the court dismissed the mother's appeal against the care order in respect of her two children since there was sufficient evidence of emotional harm to the children in the form of the children's disturbed behaviour, and of their emotional instability, and inconsistent parenting within the home.
>
> In *Re S and A (children) (Care Orders: Threshold Criteria) (2001)*, S and A, were taken into care. The judge found that they were suffering from emotional harm. The mother had been married four times. In 1995, she commenced a relationship with A's father. That relationship ended before the birth of A. The mother said that her last three relationships were characterized by violence. At one point, to escape the violence she had to leave the home and take refuge in local authority bed and breakfast accommodation. She suffered from depression and at one point took an overdose. As a result, the children experienced six different moves into alternative care. An expert assessment of child S found him to be

unhappy and disorientated by the chaotic home arrangements. An expert assessment of the mother considered that she would need several years of therapy before she herself would be able to cope with adequately caring for her children following the violence she had experienced.

In *Re E (Care Proceedings: Social Work Practice) (2000)*, Bracewell J made care orders in respect of four children:

*After a 12 day hearing I have found threshold criteria established under s 31 of the Children Act 1989 in respect of three children, E aged 16, P aged 15 and I aged 3. A substantial part of the history in evidence has concerned two older children, F who is now 24, and D, who died aged 16 in 1997. I have found that over a period of some 20 years the four oldest children in this family have been successively emotionally, physically and sexually abused. The documentation on this family is massive. I have been concerned with 12 lever arch files consisting of some 6,000 pages of core material, but the total social work files cover a period from 1979 when F was placed on the child protection register and the files occupy a height in excess of four feet. Since 1979 there has been a history of social work intervention accompanied by failure by the family to co-operate with professionals. The children have been in and out of care, have been placed on and removed from the child protection register, files have been opened and closed. The four children in turn have each exhibited remarkably similar characteristics of serious sexualised behaviour, emotional disturbance, anti-social conduct, difficulties in school, suicidal tendencies and serial rejection by the parents.*

# Neglect

14.15 This involves a failure to provide the physical necessities of life, including failure to provide medical care, adequate nourishment, shelter and care. Signs of neglect include children who are inadequately or improperly clothed, unkempt, unwashed, are hungry and tired. It can include parents/carers leaving children unsupervised at weekends and during school holidays. Such situations often occur where there is an introduction of a new partner. And whilst no one factor in itself constitutes neglect, 'more than any single form of abuse, the detection and diagnosis of neglect is dependent on establishing the importance and collation of sometimes small, apparently undramatic single pieces of factual information which, when seen together are of considerable significance' (Lyon et al., 2003, 87).

14.16 Where there is a finding of neglect, children are frequently made the subject of a care order (see, e.g. *Re G and R* in Chapter 15). In the more extreme cases of neglect, local authority intervention is often too late and children die.

Paul Bridge was 15 months old when he died on 7 March 1993. The inquiry, by the Bridge Child Care Consultancy Service, reported that Paul was found dead in a pool of urine.

Photographs showed burns over most of his body caused by urine and septicaemia. The Bridge Child Care Development Service (1995), *Paul: Death Through Neglect:*

*In 1980 the eldest child was described by a health visitor as 'grossly overweight'—a sign of neglect. At school, the children were ostracised for being dirty, and other parents provided clothes. The family also consistently failed to keep hospital or doctors' appointments. On one occasion the mother and some of the children were seen begging by a school nurse. On another occasion school staff took food to the family because of concern.*

*(Independent, 2 March 2005)*

14.17　Emotional abuse may involve leaving children to fend for themselves. In 2004, a mother was sent to prison for six months after leaving her two children, aged 12 and six, 'home alone' while she went on holiday to Spain. She also pleaded guilty to leaving them for long periods at night while she went out to work as a barmaid at a private members' club (*Birmingham Post*, 18 December 2004). Angela Frankham was sentenced to five months' imprisonment for child cruelty as she left her three year-old girl locked up in a garage whilst she went out to work (*Guardian*, 20 July 2000).

## Failure to protect

### Facts and figures about child abuse

14.18　The NSPCC reports that a significant minority of children suffer serious abuse or neglect

- 7 per cent of children experienced serious physical abuse at the hands of their parents or carers during childhood.

- 1 per cent of children experienced sexual abuse by a parent or carer and another 3 per cent by another relative during childhood.

- 11 per cent of children experienced sexual abuse by people known but unrelated to them. 5 per cent of children experienced sexual abuse by an adult stranger or someone they had just met.

- 6 per cent of children experienced serious absence of care at home during childhood.

- 6 per cent of children experienced frequent and severe emotional maltreatment during childhood.

- 16 per cent of children experienced serious maltreatment by parents, of whom one third experienced more than one type of maltreatment.

- http://www.nspcc.org.uk/news-and-views/media-centre/key-information-for-journalists/facts-and-figures/Facts-and-figures_wda73664.html

# The law

14.19 Both international law and domestic law protect children from abuse. The United Nations Convention on the Rights of the Child (UNCRC 1989) states in Art 3(2): 'States Parties undertake to ensure the child such protection and care as is necessary for his or her well-being, taking into account the rights and duties of his or her parents, legal guardians, or other individuals legally responsible for him or her'. Art 6(1) and (2) provides, '(1) States Parties recognise that every child has an inherent right to life. (2) States Parties shall ensure to the maximum extent possible the survival and development of the child'. Principle 9 of the Declaration of the Rights of the Child states, 'The child shall be protected against all forms of neglect, cruelty and exploitation'. The HRA 1998, incorporating the ECHR, provides protection for everyone, including children. Art 2 provides that 'everyone's right to life should be protected by law', and Art 3 provides 'no one shall be subjected to torture, or to inhuman or degrading treatment or punishment'. Whilst both these rights have been mentioned in previous chapters, they have a particular relevance in this chapter and Chapter 15.

# Significant harm

14.20 A finding of non-accidental injury in a case where the local authority is seeking to make a care order in respect of a child who is suffering or likely to suffer significant harm is referred to as a CA 1989, s 31 finding. Here, the court must be satisfied that the child is suffering or likely to suffer 'significant harm'. This term has a specific legal meaning discussed in some detail below with regard to procedure and also in Chapter 15 with regard to how the courts have interpreted the term. Whilst the CA 1989 itself does not define 'child abuse', it defines 'harm'. Under s 31(9)(b):

> 'Harm' means ill-treatment or the impairment of health or development including, for example, impairment suffered from seeing or hearing the ill-treatment of another. 'Development' means physical, intellectual, emotional, social or behavioural development. 'Health' means physical or mental and 'ill treatment' includes sexual abuse and forms of ill treatment, which are not physical.

14.21 The CA 1989 specifies two thresholds of harm: s 1(3)(a) identifies 'any harm the child is at risk of suffering' (discussed above in Chapter 12), while in ss 31 and 47 (discussed below), 'significant harm' is the threshold of harm required before the local authority initiates a care investigation and it is this threshold that is required before the court will make a care or supervision order.

# The investigative process

## Reporting suspicions: referral

14.22 Any individual can report to the local authority their suspicions and concerns for the safety of a child. The local authority in which the child resides is responsible for the child.

> In *Re C (Responsible Authority) (2005)*, where the children were placed on the CAR (child at risk register) and then into foster care, the paternal grandparents later offered to care for the children. After an authority assessment the children moved to live with the grandparents in a different local authority area. The mother later withdrew her consent and the issue which fell to be decided was which of the two local authorities were responsible. The court held that the new authority was the responsible authority, as the children had resided in the new authority area for 11 months.

Neighbours had reported their concerns to social services when they saw Victoria Climbié prior to her death. Gibbons, et al (1995) in a research study found that 23 per cent of referrals to the local authority came from educational professionals, 17 per cent from health professionals, 17 per cent from neighbours and family friends, 13 per cent from social services, 12 per cent from police, 6 per cent were anonymously reported, and 'others' reported in 12 per cent of cases. Once a case is reported to the local authority or to the police, the matter must be investigated. However, in the cases of Victoria Climbié and Lauren Wright, to name only two of many cases, the local authority failed to investigate. In 2003, there were 570,220 referrals of children to local authority social services departments in England (DfES, 2004), and 572,700 in 2004 (DfES (2005)). There were 547,000 referrals to social services departments in the year ending 31 March 2009.

14.23 The local authority decides whether to take no action or to undertake an initial assessment, the latter involves obtaining reports and interviewing family members, this should be completed within seven days of the date of the referral. At the conclusion of this initial assessment a determination of whether the child is a child in need is made. A plan will then be devised which identifies the services the child requires. This is followed by a case conference to decide whether to initiate a s 47 CA 1989 inquiry and make a core assessment (see below).

## Local authority duty (s 47)

14.24 Whilst 'significant harm' is the threshold for commencing an investigation, factual evidence of 'significant harm' does not have to be proved, since reasonable suspicion of 'significant harm' is sufficient. The local authority in whose area a child lives or is found has a duty under CA 1989, s 47 to investigate when such a suspicion is raised. Section 47 provides:

*(1) Where a local authority is informed that a child who lives, or is found, in its area:*

*(i) is the subject of an emergency protection order; or*

*(ii) is in police protection or*

*has reasonable cause to suspect that a child who lives, or is found, in its area, is suffering, or is likely to suffer, significant harm.*

The threshold is articulated by Charles J, in *A v General Medical Council and another (2004):*

*The above-mentioned trigger for the duty imposed by s 47 namely 'reasonable cause to suspect' is lower than the trigger for other provisions (eg, ss 31, 38, 44, 46). This reflects the purpose of the duty imposed by s 47. That duty is to make enquiries to enable properly informed decisions to be made. In my judgment this trigger also informs persons other than the local authority as to circumstances, which may warrant them taking steps in connection with the care and welfare of a child.*

In *Re S (Sexual Abuse Allegations: Local Authority Response) (2001)*, the court held that even where a suspected perpetrator had been acquitted in a criminal trial, the local authority was still entitled to make a finding of significant harm and take whatever protective measures they considered necessary. Here, a consultant gynaecologist formed a relationship with a woman who had a 12 year-old daughter. Later, in January 1999, he was arrested and charged with indecent assault on the girl and found not guilty. The first and second defendants formed the view that the girl's allegations were highly credible and that the child was at risk. The claimant sought judicial review of the respective decisions of the first and second defendants on the basis that they had not applied their statutory duties correctly. The claim for judicial review was dismissed and the court held that each of the defendants acted lawfully in the assessment of risk since they were not required to make a finding on the balance of probabilities as to past conduct before assessing risk.

14.25 Approximately 65,000 children were the subject of s 47 investigations in England in the year to 31 March 2003. Over half this number (37,400) were the subject of an initial child protection conference during that year (DfES, 2004). Approximately 72,100 children were the subject of s 47 enquiries in 2005. Over half this number (38,500) were the subject of an initial child protection conference during that year (DfES, 2005). An estimated 71,800 children were the subject of s 47 enquiries in 2006 (NSPCC).

14.26 Following this decision a core assessment will be conducted which must be completed within 35 days of the initial assessment. At the conclusion of this, it will be decided whether to convene a child protection conference.

## Local authority failings

14.27    In *Mairs v Secretary of State for Education and Skills (2005)*, the court found that
there was a failure to hold a child protection conference in respect of Victoria Climbié.

In September 2002, a disciplinary hearing was convened in relation to Ms Mairs, which
she declined to attend. The hearing concluded by dismissing her for gross misconduct.
That misconduct included, among other things, a conceded failure to provide management direction to social workers managed by her. An aspect of the gross misconduct
found proved was that she failed to act upon knowledge in relation to Victoria Climbié that
(it was concluded) that she had gained on 15 November 1999 at a supervision session
with Lisa Arthurworrey. 'It was also found that she had misled the Part 8 Inquiry by denying this knowledge (which had resulted in that Inquiry accepting that she was 'unaware
of the allegations until after (Victoria's) death')' (see also *Westminster City Council v R,
B and S (2005)*).

## Court ordered investigation: s 37 directions

14.28    In private law family proceedings where, for example, the parties are applying for
s 8 CA 1989 orders of residence, contact, specific issue, or prohibited steps orders
(discussed in Chapter 12), the court may direct the local authority to investigate
the child's circumstances if there are concerns regarding welfare. Section 37(1)(2)
provides:

> *Where, in any family proceedings in which a question arises with respect to the
> welfare of the child, it appears to the court that it may be appropriate for a care or
> supervision order to be made with respect to him, the court may direct the appropri-
> ate authority to undertake an investigation of the child's circumstances (2) Where
> the court gives a direction under this section the local authority concerned shall,
> when undertaking the investigation, consider whether they should- (a) apply for a
> care order or for a supervision order with respect to a child; (b) provide services or
> assistance for the child or his family; or (c) take any other action with respect to the
> child.*

In *Re CE (Section 37 Direction) (1995)*, CE, aged 14 years, left home to live with her boyfriend at his parents' home. CE's parents made an application to the Family Proceedings
Court for a residence order in respect of CE. The district judge made an order under
CA 1989, s 37(1) directing the local authority to investigate CE's circumstances and to
produce a report within three weeks. Wall J (per curiam), said that the court should not
order a local authority to conduct a s 37 investigation unless it appeared that it might be
appropriate to make a public law order. In purely private law proceedings, any investigation required should be conducted by other means.

In *Re L (Section 37 Direction) (1999)*, a girl, aged six, was cared for from birth by her
maternal grandmother. The judge had made a number of directions, one being a direction

for a s 37 investigation which was the subject of the application for leave to appeal by the maternal grandmother. The court held that, in making the s 37 direction in reliance upon some evidence regarding the mother on the basis that it might eventually justify a care or supervision order, the judge had been wrong, since the evidence in the case was nowhere near the threshold at which public law powers could be invoked. It was plain that the court should not order the local authority to conduct a s 37 investigation unless it appeared that it might be appropriate to make a public law order.

In *Re F (Family Proceedings: Section 37 Investigations) (2006)*, where the children no longer wanted to see their mother, a position supported by the father, who was considered to be in complete subjugation to their views and their reaction and attitude to their mother (in which he was complicit). This all caused the boys emotional harm which was likely to be significant. Whilst the children were not to be removed from the father's care, a s 37 direction was required unless the father would give his consent to the children being seen by a psychiatrist as the court needed to know what the boys were thinking, how they were performing at school, and whether they needed therapy.

(See also *C v C (Children) (Investigation of Circumstances) (2005)*.)

## Child protection register

14.29 When a child has been referred to the local authority, the first stage of the investigative process involves checking the Child at Risk Register to discover whether a child or member of the family is registered and, if registered, to consider the nature of the concerns with regard to any particular child. It is to be noted that the Whittaker/Askew children mentioned above were not registered on the child at risk register. In 2006, there were 569,300 referrals (NSPCC).

14.30 For the purposes of registration, 'risk' falls into four categories (cf *Working Together* (1991, para 6.40)):

- neglect;
- physical injury;
- emotional injury; and
- sexual abuse.

14.31 The number of children registered on the 'at risk' register has declined since 1989, when there were 41,200 children on Child Protection Registers in England; dropping in 1991, to 32,500; and in 1994, 34,900 (*Children Act Report 1993* (DOH, 1995) 2, Table 3.4). Registrations have further declined in recent years to 34,220 in 2000; 30,020 in 2001; 25,700 in 2002; and 26,600 in 2003 (DfES, 2005, Table 3c). This suggests that there is less willingness to report than hitherto or else that the threshold of the risk factors has been raised.

14.32 In England alone children were registered as at risk of harm under the following categories:

| | |
|---|---|
| Neglect: | 12,600 (41%) |
| Physical abuse: | 5,700 (18%) |
| Emotional abuse: | 5,600 (18%) |
| Sexual abuse: | 2,800 (9%) |
| Mixed categories: | 4,300 (14%) |

(*Source for 2003/2004 DfES (2005)* Statistics of Education: Referrals, Assessments and Children and Young People on Child Protection Registers: Year Ending 31 March 2004. For 2010 see NSPCC figures and, as they represent a new method of data collection, should be treated with caution.).

14.33 Once a child is placed on a Child Protection Register, following a risk assessment, when and under what circumstances can the child be removed from the register?

In *R v Kent County Council, ex parte B (1996)*, a father made an application for judicial review to have his elder son removed from the Child Protection Register. The child's name was placed on the register because the local authority had some concerns regarding emotional abuse with regard to the child. The local authority originally involved was Kent County Council, and it was their decisions and procedures, which the father sought to challenge. The father and his family moved to Yorkshire and, consequently, the child was removed from the Kent 'at risk' register and placed on the register of the relevant authority in Yorkshire. Later, the child was removed from the 'at risk' register. The father felt aggrieved about what had happened and renewed his application notwithstanding that the relevant decisions had become academic. The matter, which the local authority had to consider, was emotional abuse. The court said:

*Questions of this kind give rise to strong passions, as has been recognised in the courts on a number of occasions. Parents, quite understandably, consider that they are being criticised or accused. They feel strongly about the implications of having one of their children placed on the at risk register. Therefore they understandably take an active part in the proceedings and assessments which lead up to the child being placed on an at risk register and, in some cases, they thereafter pursue their own perception of the situation in the courts.*

This was recognized by the Court of Appeal in the case of *R v Harrow London Borough, ex parte D (1990)* in the judgment of Butler-Sloss LJ. To which Douglas Brown J in the case of *R v Kent County Council, ex parte B* refers:

*In coming to its decision, the local authority is exercising a most important public function which can have serious consequences for the child and the alleged abuser (and) it would also seem that the recourse to judicial review is likely to be, and undoubtedly ought to be, rare. Local authorities have laid on them by Parliament the specific duty of protection of children in their area. The case conference has a duty to make an assessment as to abuse and the abuser, if sufficient information is*

*available. Of its nature, the mechanism of the case conference leading to the deci-*
*sion to place names on the register, and the decision-making process, is unstruc-*
*tured and informal.*

Butler-Sloss LJ points out that it is not a judicial process, and in refusing the applications said:

*In proceedings in which the child is the subject, his or her welfare is paramount.*
*In balancing adequate protection to the child and fairness to an adult, the interest*
*of an adult may have to be placed second to the needs of the child. All concerned*
*in this difficult and delicate area should be allowed to perform their task without*
*looking over their shoulder all the time for the possible intervention of the court.*
*The important power of the court to intervene should be kept very much in reserve,*
*perhaps confined to the exceptional case which involves a point of principle which*
*needs to be resolved, not only for the individual case but cases in general, so as to*
*establish that they are not being conducted in an unsatisfactory manner. In a normal*
*case where criticism is made of some individual aspect of procedure, which does*
*not raise any point of principle, leave should be refused.*

It is to be noted that the same reasoning informs the approach of the courts to interim care orders where in *D v Bury Metropolitan Borough Council; H v Bury Metropolitan Council (2006)* it was held that a local authority investigating the possibility of child abuse did not owe a duty of care to the parents of the child the only duty owed was to carry out its plans for child protection in a professional manner.

## Child protection conference

14.34 Investigations of child abuse require professionals to work together and to convene a child protection conference (by day 22 or within 15 days of the last strategy discussion). The object of the child protection conference is to decide whether or not there is any foundation for the reasonable suspicion of significant harm, which resulted in the original referral. At the child protection conference, all relevant parties are required to be present. This includes doctors, social workers, teachers, and other professionals involved with the child. Parents are also encouraged to be present. The participation of parents is important, as, prior to the CA 1989, parents were excluded and not properly informed, and their exclusion was one of the criticisms made in the Butler-Sloss Report on the Cleveland Inquiry.

14.35 Following the CA 1989, procedures were put in place which ensured the inclusion of parents in the process of child protection. However, parents may be reluctant to cooperate since it is they who are suspected of perpetrating injuries against the child. Under such circumstances, where parents resist and challenge the investigation the presence of parents at such conferences may not be helpful.

14.36 The only decision which the child protection conference can make, is whether the child should be placed on, or removed from, the Child at Risk Register.

14.37 The test for convening a child protection conference is established in *R (on the application of Redmond) and others v Health Service Commissioner (2004)*, where Henriques J, cites the evidence of a principal family support and child protection adviser, stated, 'The test for a child protection conference is "is the child at continuing risk of significant harm?"'

14.38 Where a child protection conference has indicated that court proceedings should be initiated, and an application for a care or supervision order made, CA 1989, s 31(9) gives the local authority this power.

## Care plans

14.39 There is a duty placed on the local authority to prepare a care plan in respect of a child to ensure that the future plans for the child are clearly considered, planned and communicated to all those involved, in order to achieve the objectives of the Protocol for Judicial Case Management in Public Law Children Act Cases June 2003 (Hershman and McFarlane, 2007) See also *Practice Direction (Public Law Proceedings) (Guide to Case Management): April 2010*.

The key objective of the Protocol is to avoid delay. Yet, as has been reported:

> *The average care case lasts for almost a year. This is a year in which the child is left uncertain as to his or her future, is often moved between several temporary care arrangements, and the family and public agencies are left engaged in protracted and complex legal wranglings. Though a fair and effective process must intervene before a child is taken from its parents, we believe it is essential that unnecessary delay is eliminated and that better outcomes for children are families are thereby achieved. This protocol sets a guideline of 40 weeks for the conclusion of care cases.' It sets out a timetable for the several hearings and applications and directions involved in such cases. One of the obligations placed on local authority is to devise and present a care plan. The Social Services Assessment and Care Planning Aide-Memoire sets out a timetable, which a referral (above triggers) followed by a decision not to take any action or else to undertake an initial assessment.*

> *(http://www.i-law.com/ilaw/doc/view.htm?id=163927)*

Consider the cases of *Re S (Minors) (Care Order: Implementation of Care Plan); Re W (Minors) (Care Order: Adequacy of Care Plan) (2002)*. In the first case, the judge made final care orders in respect of two children but the local authority failed to implement the care plan, which included working with the mother with a view to reuniting her with her children. The mother appealed on the ground that the judge should have made an interim care order. In the second case, the judge made final care orders in respect of two boys even though the care plan for their immediate future, including placement, was far from certain, because he was satisfied that it would be impossible for them to return to live with their parents at that time. The parents appealed on the ground that the judge should have refrained from making a final care order until the uncertainties had been resolved. The Court of Appeal heard both appeals together, dismissing the appeal in the first case and substituting an interim care order in the second case. The court, however, regarded elements in the way care orders were made and implemented as incompatible with the rights of parents and children under Arts 6(1) and 8 of the ECHR.

# Orders during the preliminary stage

14.40 Following a CA 1989, s 47 investigation, the local authority may decide that there are no further concerns in respect of the child and thus no further investigation or intervention necessary. This being the case they must, in accordance with s 47(7), decide whether it would be appropriate to review the case at a later date, and if they so decide then to fix a date for that review.

14.41 However, where there is 'reasonable cause to suspect that a child is suffering or is likely to suffer significant harm' three orders may be applied for:

- an emergency protection order (s 44(1));
- a child assessment order (s 43(1));
- police protection order (s 46).

## Emergency protection order

14.42 Anyone can apply for an emergency protection order (EPO). The grounds for an EPO are that the child is likely to suffer significant harm if he or she is not removed (s 44(1)(a)(i)), or if he or she does not remain in a place in which he or she is accommodated (s 44(1)(a)(ii)), or enquiries are being frustrated (s 44(1)(b)).

14.43 The court may order on an application without notice—an EPO ex parte (s 44(1)). As Davis (2007) notes, 'Inevitably, EPO applications usually proceed on the evidence of the local authority alone; even if the parents are present, their chances of presenting an opposing case are severely limited (the Masson et al study found an active contest in only 7 out of 60 cases where parents were notified)'.

> In *Re M (Care Proceedings: Judicial Review) (2003)*, Munby J said that an EPO required 'exceptional justification' and such an order is only appropriate 'if immediate separation is essential to secure the child's safety; (and that) "imminent danger" must be "actually established" '.

Munby J, later, in *X Council v B (Emergency Protection Orders) (2005)*, said, 'an EPO summarily removing a child from his parents, is a terrible and drastic remedy' and went on to review of the law and practice relating to EPOs.

He said:

*(i) An EPO, summarily removing a child from his parents, is a 'draconian' and 'extremely harsh' measure, requiring 'exceptional justification' and 'extraordinarily compelling reasons'. Such an order should not be made unless the FPC is satisfied that it is both necessary and proportionate and that no other less radical form of order will achieve the essential end of promoting the welfare of the child. Separation is only to be contemplated if immediate separation is essential to secure the child's safety: 'imminent danger' must be 'actually established'. (ii) Both the local authority which seeks and the FPC which makes an EPO assume a heavy burden of responsibility. It is important that both the local authority and the FPC approach every application for an EPO with an anxious awareness of the extreme gravity of the relief being sought and a scrupulous regard for the European Convention rights of both the child and the parents. (iii) Any order must provide for the least interventionist solution consistent with the preservation of the child's immediate safety.*

The Munby principles were then applied in *Re X (Emergency Protection Orders) (2006)*. In this particular case the parents were unstable, the father was suicidal and the mother drew attention to the child and to herself by inventing the child's illness. There was no suggestion at the case conference that the child should be removed from the care of the parents, either immediately or at all. Yet, on a later date, the social worker and team manager decided that the child should be removed immediately and applied to the court for an EPO, by making misleading statements to the court. The court granted an EPO and the child was removed from her mother's care by four uniformed police and social workers from the hospital. After one year in care the local authority abandoned its reliance on any allegation of sexual abuse or induced or fabricated illness, basing their application instead on emotional abuse. The court did not find the threshold met.

McFarlane J reiterated the 14 principles and guidance laid down by Munby J, and added:

*... it is the duty of the applicant for an EPO to ensure that the X Council v B guidance is brought to the court's attention of the bench; (c) mere lack of information or a need for assessment can never of themselves establish the existence of a genuine emergency sufficient to justify an EPO.... (d) evidence given to the justices should come from the best available source. In most cases this will be from the social worker with direct knowledge of the case; (e) where there has been a case conference with respect to the child, the most recent case conference minutes should be produced to the court; (f) where the application is made without notice, if possible the applicant should be represented by a lawyer, whose duties will include ensuring that the court understands the legal criteria required both for an EPO and for an application without notice; (g) the applicant must ensure that as full a note as possible of the hearing is prepared and given to the child's parents at the earliest possible opportunity; (h) unless it is impossible to do so, every without notice hearing should*

*either be tape-recorded or be recorded in writing by a full note being taken by a
dedicated note taker who has no other role (such as clerk) to play in the hearing; (i)
when the matter is before the court at the first 'on notice' hearing, the court should
ensure that the parents have received a copy of the clerk's notes of the EPO hearing together with a copy of any material submitted to the court and a copy of the
justices' reasons; (j) cases of emotional abuse will rarely, if ever, warrant an EPO, let
alone an application without notice; (k) cases of sexual abuse where the allegations
are inchoate and non-specific, and where there is no evidence of immediate risk of
harm to the child, will rarely warrant an EPO.*

See also *Webster and another v Norfolk County Council and others; Re Webster
(Children)(2009)* where such orders were made and the court later decided there
was no basis for the orders.

14.44  Whilst anyone can apply for an EPO, research over the last 10 years shows those
applicants have been the NSPCC or the local authority. Importantly and uniquely,
hearsay evidence, such as the evidence of a police officer to the effect that a child
told him that she had been abused, even though normally excluded, is permissible
(the Civil Evidence Act 1968 allows the use of hearsay although the use of hearsay
is not admissible in all children cases).

14.45  The child must normally be allowed to return home the moment that it appears to
the applicant that it is safe to do so (s 44(10), (11)). The EPO confers on the applicant
parental responsibility for the duration of the order. Contact with parents may be
maintained, although this is subject to the court's power to give a direction. Under s
44(6), where the court orders an EPO it may also give directions for other assessments
to be made, including medical, psychological, and social work reports. The court may
give directions for contact under s 44(6)(a), and medical and psychiatric assessment
under s 44(6)(b). Alternatively, the court may prohibit contact altogether.

In *Re A (A Child) (Mental Health of Mother) (2001)*, the mother, who was of Caribbean
origin, arrived in the UK from Holland on the day that her baby was due to be born. Due
to concerns about the mother's mental health, the mother and baby V were admitted to
a residential unit for a psychiatric assessment of the mother and an assessment of the
mother's parenting skills. The local authority applied for an EPO when the mother left
the unit. She was certified as incapable of managing her affairs and her daughter was
removed from her care and placed with foster parents whilst the authority brought care
proceedings.

14.46  The decision is final and there is no right of appeal.

In *Re M (Care Proceedings: Judicial Review) (2003)* above, Munby J held that judicial
review was not appropriate to challenge a local authority's decision to make an application for an EPO.

### Ex parte orders and human rights

14.47 Because of the draconian effect of an EPO on parents, and potentially on the child, in that it removes a child from the parents' care without any advance warning, and in the absence of allowing them to be heard before so doing, recent litigation has centred on the human rights issues involved with regard to the parental right to a fair hearing (Art 6 of the ECHR) and the need to balance the rights of the child and the family rights of parents (Art 8).

> In *X Council v B (Emergency Protection Orders) (2005)* cited above, Munby J outlined the interrelationship of parents' and children's rights in these orders:
>
> *Where the application for an EPO is made ex parte (without notice) the burden on the local authority is even heavier. In the first place, the local authority must make out a compelling case for applying without first giving the parents notice. As I have already observed, the Strasbourg court accepts that there may be situations justifying an ex parte application. Thus in P, C and S v United Kingdom (2002) 35 EHRR 31, (2002) 2 FLR 631 the court specifically held (at para 127) that the local authority could not be criticized for using the ex parte procedure, and in Covezzi and Morselli v Italy (2003) 38 EHRR 28 the challenge failed, even though the application had been made without notification to the parents. But in Venema v The Netherlands (2003) 1 FLR 552, where the order was made without notification to the parents, and without there having been any discussion with the parents, this lack of involvement was held (see paras (98)–(99)) to have been a breach of Art 8, the parents having been presented with 'a fait accomplis without sufficient justification'. Likewise, in Haase v Germany (2004) 2 FLR 39, where there had been an ex parte application, the court held (see paras (96)–(105) that there had in all the circumstances been a breach of Art 8. In particular it held (at para (99) that there had been no urgency so as to justify the making of an ex parte order.*

### Contact and Emergency Protection Order

14.48 In *Kirklees Metropolitan District Council v S (Contact to Newborn Babies) (2006)*, the court had ordered daily contact where the mother, a drug addict, had her newly born baby removed from her care. Following an EPO, the mother was to have daily-supervised contact when the EPO expired, and an ICO (Interim Care Order) for eight days was put in place. Munby J said:

> *If a baby is to be removed from his mother, one would normally expect arrangements to be made by the local authority to facilitate contact on a regular and generous basis. It is a dreadful thing to take a baby away from his mother: dreadful for the mother, dreadful for the father and dreadful for the baby. If the state, in the guise of a local authority, seeks to intervene so drastically in a family's life—and at a time when ex hypothesi its case against the parents has not yet even been established— then the very least the state can do is to make generous arrangements for contact. And those arrangements must be driven by the needs of the family, not stunted by lack of resources. Typically, if this is what the parents want, one will be looking to contact most days of the week and for lengthy periods. And local authorities must*

*be sensitive to the wishes of a mother who wants to breast-feed, and must make*
*suitable arrangements to enable her to do so—and when I say 'breast-feed', I mean*
*just that, I do not mean merely bottle-feeding expressed breast milk. Nothing less*
*will meet the imperative demands of the European Convention. Contact two or three*
*times a week for a couple of hours a time is simply not enough if parents reasonably*
*want more.*

The local authority appealed against the order for daily contact. Bodey J in the Family Division dismissed the appeal.

## Police removal

14.49 In ensuring the protection of children, a police officer may remove a child, under CA 1989, s 46(1), for 72 hours. In protecting children, the use of police protection is common practice.

14.50 One study found that in 39 out of 86 families where EPOs were made, the child had already been taken into police protection (Masson, 2005). Police protection is a vital aspect of child protection as Masson observes: 'Court processes were insufficiently responsive to be relied on in "real emergencies" and largely unavailable out of office hours. This was tolerated because police protection powers could be used to solve the problem' (2005, 96).

> In *A v East Sussex County Council and Chief Constable of Sussex Police (2010)*, the mother sought damages under the Human Rights Act 1998, s 7, against the local authority and the police. The court held that the judge was entitled to conclude that the decision to remove the child was justified and that in the circumstances it was impractical to convene a family proceedings court.

## Child assessment order

14.51 Once an investigation has commenced, it will be necessary to gather all the evidence with regard to the concern and suspicion that the child is suffering from significant harm, including medical, psychological, psychiatric, educational, and any other relevant information. In cases where the child is of a young age, it is for the parent with parental responsibility to give consent to medical assessments being carried out on their child. Where those with parental responsibility refuse to consent, it will be necessary for an application to be made for a child assessment order (CAO) so that such investigations can be carried out (s 43(1)). Of course, the child may refuse to consent (and is entitled to do so if he or she is *Gillick* competent (see above, s 43(8) and 44(7), if '*Gillick* competent' under FPR, r 92A, the child may refuse to consent to such investigations and/or interviews being carried out,such a refusal will frustrate the investigation (see The Department of Health publication

*The Children Act 1989 Guidance and Regulations Vol 1 Court Orders* (HMSO, 1991) para 4.8).

14.52 A CAO is an order of short duration (seven days), which allows for the necessary assessments of the child to be carried out. A local authority or the NSPCC may apply for an order. Unlike an EPO, this order cannot be made ex parte. The applicant must take such steps as are practicable to ensure that the child, his or her parents, and anyone else with parental responsibility, are given notice.

14.53 The court, in considering whether to grant such an order, must also consider whether it ought to make an EPO rather than a CAO (s 43(4)(b)). In practice, CAOs are rare, possibly because, where the parents are refusing to cooperate, it is considered wiser and safer for the child concerned to make an EPO which can also have court directed assessment attached. Most assessments of children are undertaken with parental consent or, more accurately, without parental opposition.

14.54 An EPO operates by removing the child from the home, although in the case of a CAO, removal from the home for an overnight stay is rare (s 43(9)).

## Exclusion order provision

14.55 The CA 1989 made no provision for removing the suspect abuser from the family home and so the solution to child protection rested with the removal of children from their home. This practice was widely criticized. In 1992, the Law Commission considered the removal of the suspected abuser in their report, *Family Law, Domestic Violence and Occupation of the Family Home*, recommending a short-term ouster order with the power to attach a power of arrest (paras 6.15–6.22):

> There are obviously cases where a child needs immediate and guaranteed protection from risk of serious harm, which can only be given by removal from home. There are other cases where instant removal is not obviously the answer, but there are serious concerns and it is difficult to know whether the trauma to the child of a hasty or unjustified removal will be greater than the hazards of leaving him at home pending further investigations. Sudden removal from home, whatever its deficiencies, always carries some risk to the child's welfare, varying with the age of the child and how the removal is done.
>
> *(para 6.16)*

14.56 The Family Law Act 1996, s 52, Sch 6, para 3, and Sch 6, para 1, introduced amendments to the CA 1989 which provided for the removal of an alleged abuser from the home under an exclusion order, where the courts had granted an EPO (CA 1989, s 44A) or an interim care order (s 38A). The court may also accept undertakings from the suspect in respect of the exclusion requirement for EPOs (s 44B) and interim care orders (s 38B).

The new exclusion provision has been little used, perhaps because of real problems with its effectiveness. The duration of an exclusion order is limited to 15 days, after which the abuser will be allowed to return. (See *Practice Direction: Children Act 1989: Exclusion Requirement) (1998)*, under which the court may attach a power of arrest to an exclusion order.) Furthermore, an exclusion order can only be made where '2b...that another person living in the dwelling—house (whether the parent of the child or some other person)—(i) is able and willing to give to the child the care which it would be reasonable to expect a parent to give him, and (ii) consents to the inclusion of the exclusion requirement.' This condition obviously totally undermines the purpose of the order and defeats the application. It is inconsistent with thinking on domestic violence in holding the other party to ransom by sacrificing the protection of children on their compromised consent or assent. Moreover, the Department for Constitutional Affairs collects no figures on the number of such applications. This of itself ensures that the operation and use of this provision cannot be monitored or evaluated and suggests that the government may not be wholly serious about these provisions either.

> Consider the case of *W v Middlesbrough Borough Council (Exclusion Order Evidence) (2000)*. The court stated:
>
> *The object of serving a statement of the evidence relied upon by an applicant seeking to exclude a person from the family home was to ensure that the relevant party was made aware of the evidence upon which the exclusion requirement had been based. It was essential that the statement not only should set out the factual material clearly but also had to contain reference to the evidence supporting the relevant provisions of the CA 1989.*
>
> Cazalet J, sitting in the Family Division, so held when allowing an appeal against the decision of Teesside Family Proceedings Court on 6 March 2000 whereby the appellant father, W, was committed to two months' imprisonment suspended for six months for breach of an exclusion order with power of arrest attached, which was attached to and formed part of an interim care order made by the same court on 4 February 2000 in respect of three children, on the grounds that it was manifestly excessive in the light of the change of circumstances since the order was made.

## Interim orders

14.57 Following the initial investigations, a local authority will then need to assess whether an application for the long-term care of the child concerned is required. Meanwhile, an interim care order may be made. An application made by the local authority for care/supervision is considered a last resort; by this time, any vestiges of partnership between the parents and the local authority have often broken down, parents are either not cooperating with the local authority or else refuse to accept the threshold findings. Where the local authority is intent on making an application for a care or supervision order (CA 1989, s 37(2)(a)), an interim order under s 38(1) will usually be made in the first instance. This is because there may be several hearings as the local authority presents its evidence, and parties are provided with the opportunity to present their evidence in reply.

14.58 The court must usually appoint a children's guardian to represent the child. Most are qualified social workers. The role of the children's guardian is detailed in *Oxfordshire County Council v P (1995)*. Section 38(1) provides:

> *(1) Where—(a) in any proceedings on an application for a care order or supervision order, the proceedings are adjourned . . . the court may make an interim care order or an interim supervision order with respect to the child concerned.*

> *(2) A court shall not make an interim care order or interim supervision order under this section unless it is satisfied that there are reasonable grounds for believing that the circumstances with respect to the child are as mentioned in section 31(2).*

> At the interim stage in *Re F (Care Proceedings: Interim Care Order) (2009)* a mother's fifth and sixth children were newborn twins. The mother's previous four children were involved in care proceedings. Care proceedings were issued in respect of the twins. An application for interim care order was refused and the parent's application for leave to instruct an independent social worker was granted. The parents appealed on the basis that they would provide good standards of interim care and that without an independent social worker they would have no prospect of success at trial. The Appeal was allowed and it was held that the court should not at interim stage decide issues being prepared for trial and separation was only to be ordered if the child's safety demanded immediate separation (Family Law Brief (2010)).

# Partnership

14.59 CA 1989, s 17(1)(b) emphasizes the ideology of partnership, where:

> *It shall be the general duty of every local authority . . . (a) to safeguard and promote the welfare of children within their area who are in need; and (b) so far as is consistent with that duty, to promote the upbringing of such children by their families.*

Section 37(2)(b) provides that:

> *Where the court gives a direction under this section the local authority concerned shall, when undertaking the investigation, consider whether they should provide assistance or services for the child or his family.*

The partnership concept developed partially in response to the overwhelming public concern over the methods employed by local authority following Cleveland, where children were removed in dawn raids from homes and parents were not consulted prior to or at the point of removal, nor kept informed months and, in some cases, even years afterwards (see the Butler-Sloss *Report of the Inquiry into Child Abuse in Cleveland* and the review of Cleveland in Edwards, 1996). The idea of partnership also developed out of the idea that cooperation between parents and the local authority, and a principle of non-intervention, could protect children and so it was anticipated that arrangements for child protection may be made with parents on a voluntary basis (CA 1989, s 20).

14.60 There is a wealth of evidence which points to the fact that there is really little or not enough support given to families that need it. Fortin (1998) argues that research suggests that children are not receiving the assistance they need within the home.

14.61 Partnership and support services that might make a real difference are expensive and there is no guarantee that there will be an outcome of real difference at the end. The preferred local authority route is not support services but child protection, through the removal of the child and placement with foster carers.

## Evidential questions

### Experts

14.62 In the investigation of a child's injury, the evidence of the medical expert (paediatrician, neurologist, etc) is pivotal in determining causation. Expert medical evidence is opinion evidence and, as such, the medical expert, presents his clinical findings, forms an assessment and may also express an opinion on the issues in the case which may also include the ultimate issue. However, no fact finder is bound by such opinion, and it is for the judge as fact finder to decide particular issues in his or her finding of fact.

14.63 In many cases, evidence of causation may be overwhelming, as was apparent in the death of Victoria Climbié. In many other cases, there will be a contest between the experts as to causation as, for example, in the case of the expert called on behalf of the local authority and the expert called on behalf of the parents. In 'Shaken Baby Syndrome' and 'Sudden Infant Death Syndrome' cases, experts for the local authority may attribute the injuries sustained to violent deliberate shaking, or deliberate injury, whilst experts for the parents may attribute the injuries to accident. In the trial of Sally Clark, a mother charged and convicted with the murder of her own baby, (conviction quashed on appeal) the experts were in conflict:

> *In relation to the statistical evidence the defence relied on CONI figures (as opposed to the CESDI figures relied on by the prosecution) and Professor Berry's evidence that the risks were inherently greater in a family that had already had a SIDS death.*
>
> *(R v Clark (2000))*

In some cases, medical opinion, at one time accepted and relied upon, may at a later date be suspect or wholly discredited. In 1987, in Middlesbrough, Cleveland, an unprecedented number of young children were diagnosed by paediatricians as having suffered from child sexual (anal) abuse. In arriving at this finding, the anal dilation or dilatation test was used as a diagnostic indicator to determine whether child sexual abuse had occurred. Dr Marietta Higgs diagnosed anal rape in a large number of children. Higgs relied largely, but not exclusively, on the anal dilatation test. Children who had been admitted into hospital were anally examined and this test (which depended on reflex dilation of the anal sphincter when the buttocks near the anus were pressed) was used to make a finding of sexual abuse. As a result, a significant number of children were removed from their homes under EPOs (formerly place of safety orders).

More recently, there has been controversy over the meaning of findings of the presence of subdural haematoma and retinal haemorrhaging which has been regarded as the diagnostic indicator in infants and young children who manifest physical injuries some injuries resulting in death.

14.64　By 2000, however, such injuries of subdural haematoma and retinal haemorrhaging were being considered symptomatic of deliberately inflicted injury. As a result many parents were convicted in the criminal courts of abuse including murder and manslaughter where children had died, and parallel care proceedings in the civil courts resulted in abused children and other children of the family being placed into care and also placed for adoption.

### The trouble with experts or the trouble with knowledge

14.65　However, in 2004–5, following further ongoing research into the causes of subdural haematoma and retinal haemorrhaging it was conceded that the medical opinion upon which the courts had relied in several of these earlier cases was flawed. As a result successful appeals in the criminal courts followed, including the case of Sally Clark, a solicitor accused of killing her two infant boys (*Clark (Sally) (2003)*). (Sadly, in 2007 Sally Clark went on to take her own life because of the trauma of losing her sons and being unjustly accused and imprisoned until her release in 2006.) In July 2005, the Court of Appeal in *Rock, Harris, Faulder (2005)* quashed further convictions in similar cases. A further 79 or so criminal cases were then reviewed. In addition, several hundred care proceedings cases where children have been removed from parents following such expert evidence are also being reviewed. On 14 July 2005, Sir Roy Meadow, who had been the prosecution medical expert in many of these cases, was struck off the medical register by the General Medical Council for gross professional misconduct (*Telegraph*, 16 July 2005). On 26 October 2006, whilst he was reinstated, his theories were not. All this had led to difficulty in finding medical experts willing to give evidence in care proceedings cases.

> In *Re A and D (Non-Accidental Injury: Subdural Haematomas) (2002)*, a baby was admitted to hospital, suffering from convulsions. Upon clinical examination, the boy presented with two acute subdural haematomas, a fresh haemorrhage, and bilateral retinal haemorrhages. The paediatrician concluded that the injury appeared to be non-accidental and was probably caused by shaking. The parents replied that the injury to the baby might be the result of rough play. Seven consultants submitted reports and six gave oral evidence. Although the court found that the CA 1989, s 31 threshold conditions had been met, Dame Elizabeth Butler-Sloss said, 'the courts must be careful not to jump to conclusions, nor to accept too readily the diagnosis of non-accidental injury in "brain injury" cases'.

> Dame Elizabeth Butler-Sloss, when President of the Family Division, in a later case stressed the need for caution and careful analysis of findings in SBS cases:

> *The cause of an injury or an episode that could not be explained scientifically remained equivocal; recurrence was not in itself probative; particular caution was necessary in any case where the medical experts disagreed; the court always had to be on guard against the over-dogmatic expert; and the judge in care proceedings should never forget that today's medical certainty might be discarded by the next generation of experts.*

> *(Re U (A Child); Re B (A Child) (Serious Injury: Standard of Proof) (2004))*

14.66 Experts are placed under a duty to inform the solicitor of any conflicting findings which controverts their own:

> *If an expert has carried out experiments or tests which tend to disprove or cast doubt on the opinion he is expressing (or knows that such experiments or tests have been carried out in his laboratory), he is under a clear obligation to bring the records of such experiments and tests to the attention of the solicitor instructing him (so that it may be disclosed to the other party) or to the expert advising the other party directly (Ward (1993) 1 WLR 619). In Clark (2003) EWCA Crim 1020,........ a forensic patholo-gist, in breach of normal practice, had omitted from his autopsy report and had failed to disclose the fact that, in the case of one of the infants, following microbiological examination of certain bodily fluids, a form of bacteria which in some parts of the body can prove lethal had been isolated.*

> *(Blackstone's Criminal Practice 2010)*

## Flawed expert opinion—probability and injury—miscarriages of justice

14.67 In these SBS cases, some experts relied on a balderized version of probability theory, and drew conclusions based more on intuitive heuristics than hard evidence, in advancing their claims and so called findings on causation. Put simply they said that since the chances of two cot deaths/unexplained deaths occurring in a family was remote then the only explanation was that the injuries were deliberately inflicted. Sir Roy Meadow, the prosecution's medical expert, when giving evidence in the *Sally Clark* case, said **'one cot death in a family is a tragedy, two is suspicious and three is murder'**. In that case, he said that the chances of there being two innocent cot deaths in any one family were in excess of one in 73 million. (He reached this figure by multiplying the statistical chance of one cot death (one in 8,600) again by 8,600 to accommodate two cot deaths; a statistic he has since accepted is flawed.) Looking at Meadow's statistical hyperbole from another angle: if he concluded as he did that the chance of two cot deaths occurring was one in 73 million, given that the population of the UK is 67 million, that would mean that Sally Clark was the only mother who had two children who had died in this way. Yet, Sally Clark herself knew of 40 other families who shared the same experience.

> In *R v Cannings (2004)*, the appellant was convicted of the murder of two of her four children who had died aged seven weeks and 17 weeks. The Crown's case depended on expert evidence, which again relied heavily on a truncated version of probability theory. But it was not reliance on flawed probability theory alone which presented as the only error in the case. Where there are two deaths in the family, the defence make an application to sever the indictment, that is, to try each case separately. A decision to sever the indictment rests with the judge who, in exercising his discretion, will consider whether the facts in the two deaths are sufficiently similar and whether the probative value exceeds the prejudicial effect in refusing an application.

Both the convictions of Clark and Cannings were subsequently quashed when the probability theory of chance put at 1:73 million became wholly discredited (see Mansfield, 2010, 53).

14.68 In addition, fresh medical evidence on SBS emerged, establishing that sudden infant death may be the result of a range of other factors, including a gene, and that injuries observed in SBS cases may be occasioned by very little force ('a head rocking back and forth') and that such injuries may be the result of the birthing process itself.

### Undoing earlier decisions on the basis of fresh medical evidence

14.69 In *Norfolk County Council v C (2007)*, in care proceedings it was found that that non-accidental injuries had been caused to a child. The child and two siblings were placed in care and subsequently adopted. A further sibling was born, and the local authority commenced care proceedings in respect of this fourth child. After the parents and the child underwent a successful residential assessment the local authority sought permission to withdraw the application in respect of the fourth child. Further medical evidence had been obtained in respect of the injured child: this would form the basis of an appeal to the Court of Appeal in respect of the earlier orders made in connection with the first three children.

### Undoing decisions in care and adoption proceedings

14.70 However not all decisions can be undone. Many children were taken into care, adopted and parents convicted following the flawed evidence on SBS and SIDS AS Mansfield writes with regard to the case of the Webster family whose child was adopted following a presumption made by the local authority of abuse by them against their child.

> *The court was unable to undo the formality of the adoption orders and observed that if there is a lesson to be learned from the case it is the need to obtain second opinions on injuries to children at the earliest opportunity, particularly in cases where, as here, the fault was unusual.*
>
> *(Mansfield, 2010, 53)*

## Protecting parents—the right not to self-incriminate

14.71 On the other hand there is a need also to protect parents. The CA 1989, s 1 places the welfare of the child as the court's paramount consideration when determining any question concerning the upbringing of the child. Parliament decided that the public importance of child protection inquiries and the need to discover the truth about causation override the private right to claim privilege, such that in proceedings under Parts IV (care and supervision) and V (child protection) of the CA 1989, witnesses can be compelled to give self-incriminating evidence. CA 1989, s 98:

> (1) In any proceedings in which a court is hearing an application for an order under Part IV or V, no person shall be excused from—
>
> (a) giving evidence on any matter; or answering any question put to him in the course of his giving evidence, on the ground that doing so might incriminate him or his spouse of an offence.

The rationale behind this abrogation of the self-incrimination privilege, in this particular statutory exemption, is the paramount public importance of child protection, the need to determine causation and make an accurate assessment of the cause of the harm to a child. Parents can be compelled to give evidence at any stage of the care proceedings and Hale LJ (as she then was) in *Re Y and K (Split Hearing: Evidence) (2003)* sets out the current position:

> *We are glad, therefore, to have the opportunity today of clarifying the situation. Parents can be compelled to give evidence in care proceedings; they have no right to refuse to do so; they cannot even refuse to answer questions, which might incriminate them. The position is no different in a split hearing from that in any other hearing in care proceedings. If the parents themselves do not wish to give evidence on their own behalf there is,*

*of course, no property in a witness. They can nevertheless be called by another party if it is thought fit to do so, and the most appropriate person normally to do so would be the guardian acting on behalf of the child.*

However, as Edwards (2005) argues:

*The rich evidential jewel of 'frankness' in civil courts in child protection proceedings is currently under siege. Its object to discover causation rather than attribute blame, is being thwarted, when self-incriminating statements made in care proceedings are disclosed to the police. Following the rulings authorising disclosure in Re L (a minor) (Police Investigation: Privilege) (1996) 1 FLR 731, HL and Re EC (Disclosure of Material) (1996) 2 FLR 725, CA, (sub nom Re C), the preservation of the principle of encouraging frankness through promising confidentiality is being compromised with the result that parents/carers are now less likely than ever to assist those involved in child protection in the discovery of causation. Legal practitioners are obliged to advise their clients that what they say in confidence to third parties and in oral evidence in care proceedings can no longer assure confidentiality. When the police make applications for disclosure of confidential incriminating documents and/or transcripts, the civil court, in making child welfare paramount, routinely grants the application, leaving it to the criminal courts to 'shut the stable door' and develop a jurisprudence with regard to the obligation to ensure a fair trial in their exercise of discretion regarding exclusionary evidence. It is the concern of this author that where the prosecution have the advantage of access to, and use of, admissions made in other proceedings, the equality of arms principle is stacked in the prosecutor's favour at the pre-trial and trial stages.*

*The Family Proceedings (Amendment No 4) Rules 2005 (SI 2005/1976) have extended the parties permitted to have access to documents, information and findings at the welfare and threshold stages of care proceedings. The response to the consultation paper which preceded these new rules (Disclosure of information in family proceedings cases involving children: response to the public consultation, Cm 6623 (TSO, 2005)) set out to try to achieve a balance between, 'allowing legitimate access to information to those who need it... against the need not to discourage those giving evidence or statements from full and frank disclosure.'*

In ***Reading Borough Council v D and Others (2006)***, the chief constable applied to the court for clarification regarding what use the police could make of five documents, including those written by a consultant neurosurgeon, a consultant paediatric radiologist, an undated and unsigned statement from the father, a signed statement from the father, and an undated and unsigned statement from the mother, which were handed to police by a social worker involved in care proceedings. The father, in a police interview, admitted and then retracted an admission, that he was using violence on one of his children, E (E, C, D being the subject of the proceedings). Mr Justice Sumner outlined the new procedure as he explained, the text, summary of the judgment or part of the judgment can be disclosed if disclosure is for the purpose of a criminal investigation. However, this promises to raise issues of child protection and issues of human rights and fair trial where there are parallel care and criminal proceedings.

Consider the following cases:

In *Re U (Care Proceedings: Criminal Conviction: Refusal to Give Evidence) (2006)*, two children, M and H were the subject of care proceedings, their sister having died at the age of three months, following a post mortem which disclosed a long catalogue of injuries. Both parents denied inflicting any injuries. Shortly after the death of this child, M and H were fostered. In January, both parents were charged with murder. Whilst in custody awaiting trial, the mother, SB was interviewed and said that SU, the father had inflicted the injuries and had also abused her. And at the father's trial she was a key witness for the prosecution. The father was convicted of murder and appealed. Pending the criminal appeal, the hearing with regard to care proceedings came before Holman J, and the father on advice of his solicitor pending the criminal appeal refused to give evidence (see also *Re X Children (2007)*).

However this discourse on the balance of parental rights and child rights remains unfinished.

## Which perpetrator—deliberate harm: which parent?

14.72    Further evidential problems arise in determining which out of two or more persons is the perpetrator. In the case of **Lancashire Country Council v A (2000)**, significant harm was found due to absence of proper parental care. In this case, however, it could not be established which of the two parents or the childminder had inflicted the harm, since all three of them strenuously denied harming the child. The baby sustained serious head injuries. The local authority commenced care proceedings. The judge held that for the purposes of s 31(2)(b)(i), he had to be satisfied that the significant harm was 'attributable to the care given to the child by the parent'. The judge was unable to conclude that the harm was attributable to either of the parents and dismissed the application. The Court of Appeal held that the 'attributable' condition in s 31(2)(b)(i) was satisfied if the harm was attributable to an absence of proper care and reversed the judge's decision. A's parents appealed to the House of Lords, who dismissed the appeal.

Whilst the decision in the case above was no doubt the correct one with regard to protecting the child in the future, it presents a dilemma for the many working parents who may be innocent of committing abuse but who may lose the care of their children under similar circumstances.

In *Re K (Care: Threshold Criteria) (2006)*, two children, X and Y were the subject of applications by the local authority for care orders. Y had suffered hypoxic-ischaemic damage to the brain following suffocation and the judge said:

*Suffice it to say at this stage that [Y] had suffered hypoxic ischaemic damage to the brain which was very extensive. He had an epileptic seizure which lasted for over 20 hours. The prognosis is that he will have motor disability cerebral palsy; he will have speech and hearing difficulties; he is blind, and is unlikely to recover vision. He will thus have continuing and significant disability. In plain terms, he has suffered a devastating injury which is lifelong in its consequences.*

The primary question was how had that injury occurred. Was it accidental or was it attributable to Y's parents or to one of his parents? The judge was clear that one of the parents was responsible but could not say which one. A care order was granted in respect of Y. X had not been injured, the local authority sought a care order on other grounds relating to the effect on the child of witnessing domestic violence and other factors including the mother's chaotic lifestyle. In respect of this child, X, the judge did not find that the threshold conditions were met. On appeal the court found that in respect of X the judge's findings were faulty as insufficient weight had been attached to the factors of concerns submitted on behalf of the local authority and especially that the judge had compartmentalized the two children and did not consider the likely suffering to a child where the finding was that other child had been deliberately harmed by at least one of the two parents. The court allowed the appeal of the local authority.

14.73 The question of which parent? poses a problem for a successful prosecution in the criminal law and until recently if it could not be proved which of the two parents harmed the child then neither could be convicted (see *Lane and Lane (1985)*, see also Law Commission Report on *Non Accidental Injury* (Law Com No 282, 2003). The new provision in the Domestic Violence, Crime and Victims Act 2004, s 5 creates a new manslaughter offence of 'causing or allowing the death of a child or vulnerable adult' which intends to resolve the difficulty of securing convictions and will ensure that whether causing the death can be proven the fact of allowing the death will be sufficient to convict (see Edwards, 2006 for a discussion of this provision).

## Evidential issues and the child giving evidence

14.74 In *Re W (Children) (Care Proceedings: Evidence) (2010)*, the court said this:

*The family court would have to be realistic in evaluating how effective it could be in maximising the advantage while minimising the harm; what was important was that the questions which challenged the child's account were fairly put to the child so that she could answer them, not that counsel should be able to question her directly. The essential test was whether justice could be done to all the parties without further questioning of the child; the consequence of the balancing exercise, if the court was called upon to do it, would usually be that the additional benefits to the court's task in calling the child did not outweigh the additional harm that it would do to the child. In the instant case, the question of whether the child should give evidence at the hearing would be remitted to the judge for determination in the light of the instant judgment (see [22]–[32], [35], below).*

(See also *Re S-B (Children) (Non-Accidental Injury) (2009)*).

# Family rights issues and the childcare process

14.75 Whilst parental rights over children in the form of the proprietorial rights witnessed in *Agar-Ellis* (detailed in Chapter 9) are certainly dead, parents do retain
some vestiges of rights, particularly insofar as care procedures in care investigations
and proceedings are concerned. These rights are the parents' human rights and
'family rights', which may engage ECHR, Art 8 (the right to family life) or indeed
any of the other Convention rights. It will be a matter for the courts to determine
how these Convention rights will be construed and will come to shape domestic
child law. Clearly, Art 8 will serve as much as a check on local authority procedures
and the courts in respect of the parental right as it will to protect child welfare. (See,
for an in-depth discussion of rights discourse and the child versus parental rights,
Herring, 2004, 351.)

> In *KA v Finland (2003)*, the correctness of local authority procedure and processes and
> the parental right to family life in the future fell to be determined. The court held:
>
> *For the purposes of art 8(2) of the European Convention for the Protection of Human
> Rights and Fundamental Freedoms 1950, any order related to the public care of a
> child had to be capable of convincing an objective observer that the measure was
> based on a careful and unprejudiced assessment of all the evidence on file, with
> the distinct reasons for the care measure stated explicitly and therefore there had
> been a violation of art 8 as a result of the authorities' failure to take sufficient steps
> directed toward a possible reunification of the applicant and his children, which
> began with an assessment of the evidence which in his view showed an improve-
> ment of his condition in late 1993.*

## Cuts to legal aids and human rights challenges to representation

14.76 By 2010 the family justice system faced its greatest crisis and family law provision
was drastically cut. The first problem is that fewer law firms have been awarded
legal aid contracts and the amount of money available for representation in each
family case has been capped. This is the result of the tendering exercise introduced
by the government in January 2010. N 1,300 firms secured legal, out of 2,400
applications. To date (October 2010) the Legal Services Committee has received
approximately 900 appeals across all civil tenders. Dr Debora Price and Anne
Laybourne of King's College London's King's Institute for the Study of Public
Policy, conducted a study and found that in a 'week in the life' study, over 5,000
cases were being undertaken by more than 1,600 barristers in the third week of

October 2008. The report's findings published before the savage cuts in January 2010 include analysis of:

- The role that legal aid and the current 'graduated fee' system plays in the income and function of the family Bar, and the way in which barristers and sets of chambers adapted to the major legal aid changes introduced in 2001
- The specialization undertaken within the family Bar including the split between legal aid and privately funded work
- The breakdown of the family Bar by gender and ethnic group, and respective average incomes.
- Quantification of the workload and the emotional impact of cases, and an assessment of the drivers of case complexity.

In October 2010, the Law Society called upon the Legal Services Commission to extend existing family contracts until April 2012 following the High Courts' decision to quash the outcome of the family tender round for new legal aid contracts. Mr Justice Moses quashed the contracts in four categories of practice, family, housing and family, children only, and child abduction.

14.77 Secondly the fees cuts for family cases in my view violate the United Kingdom's positive obligations under the Convention. Local authorities have a duty to pursue cases where children appear to be at risk (DCA and DfES, *Review of the Child Care Proceedings System in England and Wales* Cm 6591 (TSO, 2006), at p 32). It may be difficult for subsequent cases to conclude as Pitchford J concluded in *R (on the application of Hillingdon London Borough Council and others) v The Lord Chancellor and another (2008)* that, 'Access to justice for vulnerable children is not in the process put at risk. In my judgment, upon the evidence we have considered, there is no such risk' (at para 114).

As I have written elsewhere 'The recent increase in court fees will no doubt deter local authorities from issuing proceedings' (see also Welbourne, 2008). If Michael Mansfield QC (2010), is right when he says that the *Webster* case (2009) (reported in this chapter and Chapter 10) demonstrated the importance of the need to obtain a second opinion, second opinions simply will not be affordable.

This crisis seemed to fall on deaf ears until 21 October 2010 when the government announced that court fees in child care proceedings will no longer be abolished in April 2011 as had been previously planned. In March 2010 the Justice Minister had announced that the court fees charged to local authorities for care and supervision proceedings would be abolished. On 1 May 2008 court fees in public law family proceedings increased from £150 to £5,225 for a fully contested court case.

Lord Laming's report on the protection of children in England, concluded that the increase in fees would deter local authorities from bringing proceedings. At last someone is listening, I think!.

## FURTHER READING

Butler-Sloss E, *Report of the Inquiry into Child Abuse in Cleveland* (Cm 412, 1988)

Cretney S and Masson J, *Principles of Family Law* (Sweet and Maxwell, 2003)

Davis L, 'Protecting Children in an Emergency—Getting the Balance Right' (2007) Fam Law 37 (728)

Department for Education and Skills, *Statistics of Education: Referrals, Assessments and Children and Young People on Child Protection Registers: Year ending 31 March 2003* (The Stationery Office, 2004)

Department for Education and Skills, *Statistics of Education: Referrals, Assessments and Children and Young People on Child Protection Registers: Year ending 31 March 2004* (The Stationery Office, 2005)

Department of Health, *Working Together* (DOH, 1991), para 6.40

Edwards S, *Sex and Gender in the Legal Process* (Blackstone, 1996)

Edwards S, 'Sealing One's Own Fate: Disclosure of Documents in Care Proceedings—on the Trail to the Abrogation of a Fair Trial? (2005) CFLQ 17(1) 13

Edwards S, 'Disclosure: sacrificing the privilege of self-incrimination for the greater good of child protection?' Fam Law (2007) 37 (510)

Edwards S, 'Child Protection: Trapped in the Middle of the Edge' [2009] Fam Law 220

Gibbons J, Gallagher B, Bell C and Gordon D, *Development after Physical Abuse in Early Childhood: a Follow-up Study of Children on Protection Registers* (HMSO, 1995)

Herring J, *Family Law* (2nd and 3rd edns, Pearson Longman, 2004, 2007)

Lord Laming, *The Victoria Climbie Inquiry Report of Lord Laming* (January 2003)

Lyon C, Cobley C, Petrie S and Reid C, *Child Abuse* (3rd edn, Family Law, 2003)

Mansfield M, *Memoirs of a Radical Lawyer* (Bloomsbury, 2010)

Masson J, 'Emergency Intervention to Protect Children: Using and Avoiding Legal Controls' (2005) CFLQ 17 (1) 75

## SELF-TEST QUESTIONS

1   Mrs Murray has telephoned the local authority social services department because she is concerned about the girl who lives next door, Sophie, who is nine years old and looks tired, unkempt, unwell, and undernourished. She is a timorous child and always

asks Mrs Murray for food or drink and calls round in the early evening saying she if frightened of being alone in the house after dark. Sophie's parents are never at home during the day or early evening always returning home late after 11.00 pm. Sophie also says to her neighbours, 'You won't hurt me, will you?' What should the local authority do after the conclusion of Mrs Murray's telephone call?

2  Three siblings, aged from five to 11 years, all attending the same primary school, have been reported by the head teacher to the local authority social services department. The children are unwashed, arriving at school always late and hungry and tired. All three children have head lice and two are being treated for scabies (a parasitic infestation of the skin, which causes them to scratch). They are in poor health with persistent coughs and colds. Their attention span in lessons is short and all three are well behind attainment levels in reading and writing for children of their age. Advise the local authority.

3  To what extent is the parental right to a fair hearing (Art 6 of the ECHR) and the need to balance the rights of the child and the family rights of parents (Art 8) relevant considerations when making an EPO?

4  Edwards (2005) argues:

'The rich evidential jewel of "frankness" in civil courts in child protection proceedings is currently under siege'.

Discuss with reference to the self-incrimination privilege in care proceedings.

5  What have constituted the main areas of dispute in recent years between medical experts in child abuse cases?

6  Do parents have a right to a residential assessment when they are contesting care order applications?

# 15

# Protecting children from 'significant harm': constructing the law

**SUMMARY**

In this chapter, we consider how the courts in child protection proceedings have interpreted the law with regard to the meaning of 'significant harm' in making a finding of causation and also in deciding whether to make an interim or a final order for care or supervision. We explore the burden and the standard of proof, and, in cases of sexual abuse following *Re H and R (1996)* explore the relevance of the hypothetical probability of the allegation occurring to the reasoning in the particular case. We consider especially the case of *Re B (Children) (Sexual Abuse: Standard of Proof) (2008)*, and assess to what extent this House of Lords decision has destabilized the authority of the House of Lords decision in *Re H and R (1996)*, and reasserted the balance of probability as the standard of proof in care proceedings involving allegations of sexual abuse. Finally, we consider the impact of human rights law on local authority liability to protect the child from abuse, and on child protection generally.

## Threshold finding of 'significant harm'

15.1 Once a childcare investigation has been initiated and the local authority makes an application for a care or a supervision order, the court, having considered all the evidence, must first make a finding regarding whether there is evidence of 'significant harm' having occurred or else likely to occur. This is a finding of causation and is called the threshold test or threshold finding. Under the Children Act (CA) 1989, s 31(2)(a), before the court makes an order to protect a child from abuse/neglect, the court must be satisfied on the civil standard of proof, that is, on the balance of probabilities (i) that the child 'is suffering, or is likely to suffer, significant harm' and [that] the harm or likelihood of harm, is attributable to (s 31(2)(b)(i)) the care given to the child, or likely to be given to him if the order were not made, not being what it would be reasonable to expect a parent to give him; or (ii) the child is beyond parental control.

15.2 In making this determination, the court will consider evidence from the local authority or the National Society for Prevention of Cruelty to Children (NSPCC) who brings the application, from the parents or carers who contest the application, and from the children's guardian who represents the child. In these proceedings the court will also receive expert evidence from experts with regard to the allegations made. If a finding of significant harm is made at this fact finding stage, the court will then go on to consider whether to make an order or whether, in applying the non-interventionist presumption, it is better for the welfare of the child not to make an order at all (CA 1989, s 1(5)). If, having decided to make an order, the court must then determine whether any additional order, for example, residence or contact with family members (CA 1989, s 8) should also be considered.

## Split hearings

15.3 Most applications proceed as split hearings (see .g *Re B (Split Hearing: Jurisdiction) (2000)*; *Re O and another (Children) (Non-accidental Injury) (2003)*; *Re B (children) (Non-accidental Injury) (2003)*; *Re Y and another (Children) Ccare Proceedings: Split Hearing) (2003)*; *Re E (Children) (2001)*; *Re G (A Child) (Care Order: Threshold Criteria) (2001)*) which means that the court considers separately the factual matters, that is, the evidence from the local authority which supports their case and the evidence from the suspect abuser(s) which refutes the allegations before going on to consider whether to make any order or no order at all (see Practice Direction (2002)).

> In *Re S (Care Proceedings: Split Hearing) (1996)*, Bracewell J said that, 'it was desirable to consider the factual threshold at an early stage'. Hale LJ, in *Re G (A Child) (Care Order: Threshold Criteria) (2001)*, emphasized the importance of split hearings:
>
> *Split hearings like this can be very useful when there are early decisions which can be made about factual disputes, for example as to the causation of a child's injuries. Once that has been done, assessments can be made in the light of those findings and this often produces acceptance, understanding and movement on the part of*

*those who will be involved in the child's future. In my experience the later hearing, if that takes place, can often be quite short. But the early hearing has to be early, not many months into the case, and it has to be clearly focused.*

However, even where a fact-finding hearing is dispensed with, for whatever reason, the courts have made it clear that the evidence to establish causation will still need to be considered at some point. In **Re F-H (Dispensing With Fact-Finding Hearing) (2008)**, the judge said this:

*The fact that certain material need not be considered before a conclusion is reached that the court has the power to make a care order in no way supports a conclusion that it does not need to be considered before deciding whether the optimim out-come for the children is to make such an order (para 28).*

## The burden of proof

15.4 The burden of proof is on the local authority to establish to the standard of the balance of probabilities that the child 'is suffering or likely to suffer significant harm'.

Wall LJ in **Re K (Care: Threshold Criteria) (2006),** asserted:

*The burden of establishing the threshold criteria lies of course on the local authority, and the reason for a split hearing is frequently that the facts on which the threshold criteria depend are disputed by the parents, and if resolved in the parents' favour would bring the proceedings to an end.*

## What does 'significant harm' mean?

15.5 Under the CA 1989, s 31(2)(b), the harm, or likelihood of harm must be 'significant'.

In the previous chapter, we have already explored the more likely forms of abuse (physical, sexual, emotional, and neglect), which may constitute the threshold of harm required to satisfy a finding of 'significant harm'. Sir Stephen Brown, in **Newham London Borough Council v AG (1993)**, emphasized that the wording of the Act was not intended to be unduly restrictive and warned against an over legalistic interpretation of s 31(2). For example, in **Re M Minors (Children) (Repatriated Orphans) (2002)**, the court considered that forcing a young person to marry constituted significant harm. Singer J said, 'both abduction and imposed marriage are child abuse'.

15.6 The CA 1989 offers no definition of 'significant' ie the 'degree' of harm. However, the *Review of Child Care Law* (DHSS, 1985), para 5.15 considered that having decided what might be reasonable it would be necessary to show a 'substantial deficit'.

In *Humberside County Council v B (1993)*, Booth J accepted the local authority's submission that a dictionary definition should be used. The result was that the definition of 'significant' turned upon (1) whether the harm was 'considerable, noteworthy or important', and (2) that the harm should also be considered in the context of the child's future.

Significant harm might be found where the parents have learning difficulties which result in parenting deficiencies, although in *Re L Children (2006)*, the parents learning difficulties were not in themselves sufficient justification for finding the threshold criteria to be satisfied. Significant harm might also be found where, for example, a father is violent to the mother and the mother is unable to prevent the children from witnessing the violence.

In *Local Authority v M, F and M&M (2009)*, there were allegations of violence by the mother against the father which included, strangulation, assaults with a screwdriver, boiling water and petrol, false imprisonment, threats to kill the mother and the child and the kidnap of a child. The father had threatened the mother in letters sent from prison, and the father's family had found out where the mother was living, and had made additional threats. The local authority issued care proceedings the real purpose of which was to assess the mother's ability to remain separate from the father. The mother made an application to prevent the father being informed of the proceedings (although as he had parental responsibility he had a right to this information) the mother also applied to the court to discharge him as a party. However, the local authority opposed her application, on the basis that it needed information from the father and his family. The starting points were (i) that the father should be entitled to participate in the case, and (ii) that the children and mother should not be put at risk of serious harm by the conduct of the proceedings. The father, even from prison, represented a real and substantial risk to the children and the mother; only his exclusion from the proceedings would realistically achieve the objective of protecting the mother and children. The court considered that although extensive redaction of documents was possible, the risk of accidental disclosure of a crucial piece of information would be high. Given that the father had shown no interest in making any contact with the children, and that any order to discharge him from the proceedings was to be kept under review, the father would be discharged as a party. The court was wholly not persuaded that discharging the father and directing that the fact of the proceedings not be disclosed to him would significantly inhibit the authority in the assessment they were undertaking (see Bridge, 2010).

## Satisfying the threshold

15.7    In *Re CL v East Riding Yorkshire Council, MB and BL (A Child) (2006)*, it was held that in a finding of accidental injury, such a finding was not sufficient to satisfy the threshold criteria. In this case, the judge had been wrong to find that the threshold criteria had been met. However, where accidental injuries amounted to a failure to protect a child such a finding would be relevant to the threshold criteria because it could be evidence of a failure on the part of the parents to adequately care for the child (s 31(2)(b)(i)).

## Objective and subjective tests

15.8 How is 'significant harm' measured or assessed? In attempting to measure whether a standard of care is substandard or defective or whether the health and development of a child is inadequate both an objective and a subjective assessment of harm is made. The objective test relies on evidence of the nature and extent of harm. So, indecently touching a child is, of its very nature, 'significant,' and breaking a child's arm is, by its very seriousness, significant. For example, in *Re W (A Child) (Care Proceedings) (2007)*, Wall LJ said:

> We have to say, however, that in the overall context of the issues raised in this case, we do not think that, of itself a single blow by the father (or even more than one blow) would be sufficient to satisfy the threshold criteria under the first limb of CA 1989, section 31).

The subjective test by contrast relies on the effect and impact of the harm on the individual child concerned. Thus, harm may be considered 'significant' if the child is deeply affected by what has happened whereas another child may not be affected to such a degree.

15.9 This objective/subjective formulation is indicated in the *Guidance to the Act* (DOH, 1991), where significant harm may be established from 'the seriousness of the harm or in the implications of it', adding that it will be a 'finding of fact for the court' (para 3.19).

## How is the objective test of 'significant harm' measured?

15.10 The 'similar child' comparator test has been used both explicitly and implicitly to measure whether there has been harm. In assessing the harm to a child the court will consider evidence which evaluates what standards of care, physical, emotional, etc one might expect a reasonable parent to give a child and in examining this issue would compare the child who is the subject of the investigation with other children of a similar background, age and gender according to their particular health and development. Where ill-health or developmental impairment is being assessed, then a minimum standard of physical development and health expected of an average child of a given age and sex is taken as the starting point.

15.11 The guidance offered in the CA 1989, s 31(10) states:

> Where the question of whether harm suffered by a child is significant turns on the child's health or development, his health or development shall be compared with that which could reasonably be expected of a similar child.

The *Review of Child Care Law* (1985) states:

*having set an acceptable standard of upbringing for the child, it should be necessary to show some substantial deficit in that standard. Minor shortcomings in the health and care provided or minor defects in physical, psychological or social development should not give rise to any compulsory intervention unless they are having, or likely to have, serious and lasting effects upon the child.*

*(para 15(15))*

15.12 Expert evidence will be called to address the issue of what would be expected of a similar child with regard to the particular factor being compared, for example weight, general standard of health, physical or intellectual development.

In *Re O (A Minor) (Care Order: Education Procedure) (1992)*, a young girl had been truanting from school. The local authority justified their application for a care order under s 31(1)(a), rather than an education supervision order, on the basis that what could be achieved by an education supervision order had already been unsuccessful. But had O suffered significant harm? That judgment could only properly be made by comparison with a similar child. Ewbank J held that a similar child was:

*In my judgment, in the context of this type, a child of equivalent intellectual and social development, who has gone to school, and not merely an average child who may or may not be at school. In fact what one has to ask oneself is whether this child suffered significant harm by not going to school. The answer in my judgment, as in the magistrates' judgment, is obvious.*

*(at 12)*

Jane Fortin (1998) is critical about the reasoning in this particular case. She asserts that it does not appear that there was in fact any real attempt to consider evidence about the progress of a similar child. Indeed, the evidence provided by the guardian ad litem and the evidence of the educational psychologist made no comparison with a similar child ie a 15 year-old girl who had not attended school. In fact, the educational psychologist said:

*O is a girl of average general ability; she has a good vocabulary; she reads novels for pleasure; her writing is neat and legible, spelling good; she writes at a good speed; her mental arithmetic ability is slightly below average for her age, which probably reflects missing school; she is numerate and has no specific difficulty with mathematics.*

However, the wording of the section is 'reasonably expected of a similar child' and guidance from the DHSS *Review of Child Care Law* indicates that the deficit has to be substantial.

The following two cases illustrate how the courts might use this comparator.

In *Re C (A Minor) (Care: Child's Wishes) (1993)*, Waite J upheld the findings of the justices, who concluded:

*we have considered whether the grounds under s 31 have been met. We find that the child has been suffering from significant harm and that her development has been impaired and her health has suffered compared with a similar child of her age and similar background and this harm or likelihood of harm is attributable to the care given to the child in the past and likely to be given to her in the future if an order were not made.*

The expert evidence reported in this case amounted to a finding of a failure to thrive emotionally. C's physical development was also a source of medical concern.

In *Re W (A Minor) (Interim Care Order) (1994)*, the court said:

*Much of the evidence is concerned with the alleged fact that the child's weight has both fluctuated and not increased as might be expected with a normal healthy child of his age. The court relied on this evidence in making an interim care order.*

Often there is no need for a comparator since the evidence is indisputable as in the case of Victoria Climbié (see Chapter 14):

*When Victoria was admitted to the North Middlesex Hospital on the evening of 24 February 2000, she was desperately ill. She was bruised, deformed and malnourished. Her temperature was so low it could not be recorded on the hospital's standard thermometer. Dr Lesley Alsford, the consultant responsible for Victoria's care on that occasion, said, 'I had never seen a case like it before. It is the worst case of child abuse and neglect that I have ever seen'.*

*(Laming Report, para 1.5)*

## Similar children: similar to whom?

15.13 Where there is evidence of failure to thrive, etc, this may be evidence of neglect and of an inability or failure to adequately parent. Comparisons are rightly made with the development of a child of the same sex, age, etc and with other families. But, in cases like *O*, a finding is about making as judgement. As Baroness Hale said in *Re B (2008)* with reference to the judge, 'He is not allowed to sit on the fence. He has to find for one side or the other'. Sometimes making a judgement is easy where the evidence is overwhelming, but this is not always the case. And in making a judgement about whether a hypothetical standard of care is met for example and judgements about physical and emotional development, there is a case for arguing that a subjective judgement may seep into that assessment, and an idealized template of child development and attainment, of family life, and of parenting may be set as an absolute yardstick by which other cases may be measured. Consider for example that some local authorities are applying for and being granted care orders on the basis of neglect in respect of children who are considered seriously overweight (morbidly obese) (*The Times*, 13 July 2007). See the children of a 23 stone mother who were taken into care (22 October 2009, *Daily Mail*). How prescriptive or flexible should the courts be in setting parameters of adequacy, inadequacy, and harm?

15.14 Channer and Parton (1990, 105) raise their concerns about where we draw the boundary line in this assessment of what is normal and what is harmful. They ask, 'Is it possible to judge absolute standards of family care and functioning while also understanding the different approaches to rearing children within different cultures?' Michael Freeman (1993) asks whether the hypothetical reasonable parent has to be located within the dominant white English Christian culture. Bainham (2005, 500) queries whether:

> ...it is legitimate to go beyond the inherent characteristics of the child and explore his cultural or social background is more debatable and [this] has given rise to an apparent difference of opinion between the Lord Chancellor and the Department of Health, and certainly between academic commentators. One view is that cultural pluralism or relativity ought to be relevant, especially since the legislation has an ideological commitment to this. According to this view, 'Muslim children, Rastafarian children, the children of Hasidic Jews may be different and have different needs from children brought up in the indigenous, white, nominally Christian culture.

In the multi-cultural society of 2011 such questions are even more pertinent. On the other hand, what degree of allowance from the norm, if any, should be made for culture, class, or any kind of difference in accommodating pluralism? Since the purpose of child protection in care proceedings is to determine a minimal standard of care which a child must receive in ensuring his or her proper development, then, can we justify any flexibility at all?

15.15 In *Re H (Minors) (Wardship: Cultural Background) (1987)*, a Vietnamese mother's chastisement practice was judged against minimal standards of childcare. The court said it, 'must consider the case against the reasonable objective standards of the culture in which the children have hitherto been brought up, so long as these do not conflict with our minimal acceptable standards of child care in England' (discussed in detail in Chapter 9).

In *R v Adesanya (1974)* (see Poulter, S. 1998) where a mother had made tribal markings on a son's face,

Mrs Adesanya's main line of defence was that she had merely inflicted authentic tribal markings on her sons face to ensure cultural identity. Judge King Hamilton QC said that 'Nigerian custom' (Mrs Adesanya was Yoruba) was no defence to the charge of assault occasioning bodily harm, and he imposed a suspended sentence (see Renteln 2005).

15.16 But it is clear that judgements are indeed made on the basis of class, culture, race, and ethnicity. Cobley and Sanders (2003, 107) found that doctors were less likely to make referrals to social services in relation to children of middle-class parents.

# Standard of care given by the reasonable parent

15.17 This provides for circumstances where the child may suffer significant harm because the child is beyond parental control or where parents themselves are ill or disabled, or are lacking in caring skills and unable to adequately parent, not circumstances where parents have deliberately harmed children in their care. Here, a judgement is made about what is the line over which poor parenting becomes inadequate or defective parenting. The capability of parents to adequately parent can be further assessed following a residential assessment of the family under CA 1989, s 38(6) which gives parents the opportunity to demonstrate that their parenting is adequate.

## Observing the standard of care: s 38(6) residential assessments

15.18 As both parties—the child and the suspect abusers—are entitled to a fair hearing, this means that the parties about whom allegations are made should be permitted to submit assessments of their ability to parent. It is a matter for the judge to order/grant permission for such assessments (see eg *Re L (Care: Assessment: Fair Trial)*, *Re L (Children) (Threshold Criteria) (2006)*; *Re L and H (2007)*).

> In *Re G (Interim Care Order: Residential Assessment) (2006)*, the mother had two children, J and R, born in 1996 and 1998 respectively, by two different fathers. R died of multiple, non-accidental injuries which the judge held could have been caused by either of R's parents. The local authority had brought care proceedings in respect of J, who was placed with his father. In 2003 the mother had a third child, E, by a different father. The local authority initiated care proceedings in respect of her. The court made a s 38(6) order to allow for a six- to eight-week period of in-patient assessment of E and her parents, and an extension of the residential assessment was applied for. The local authority refused to fund it. The judge held that he had no power under s 36(8) to direct the local authority to do so because what was proposed was therapy rather than assessment. The Court of Appeal allowed the mother's appeal and reversed the judge's decision on the ground that the essential question should always be whether what was sought could broadly be classified as an assessment to enable the court to obtain the information necessary for its own decision.

15.19 However, there is clearly a balance to be struck and in *Re J (Care Assessment: Fair Trial) (2006)*, Munby J said of the precepts in *Re L (2006)*:

> *In particular it gives us the opportunity to stress that, although any actual infringement of parental human rights in the course of care proceedings, far from being*

*brushed under the carpet, must in court be rooted out and exposed, the precepts must not be used as a bandwagon, to be drawn across the tracks of the case and to de-rail the proceedings from their prompt travel towards the necessary conclusions referable to, and in the interests of, the child. No doubt it is a difficult balance for trial judges to strike; but we here will support those who deal robustly with suggestions of such minor non-compliance with the precepts commended by Munby J as could never sensibly be translated into an infringement of human rights. The precepts in Re L should not be used as a bandwagon to derail care proceedings from their prompt travel towards necessary conclusion in the interests of child protection.*

(See also *In the Matter of B (Children) (2010)*.)

15.20 Even where parents are trying to do all they can to provide good parenting, they may find that their children are taken into care (see *Re C (Child's Wishes) (1993)*). In this case a single parent father who was elderly and in poor health was responsible for the upbringing of his 13 year-old daughter and 12 year-old son and was considered unable to provide adequate care. In *Re W (Minors: Sexual Abuse Standard of Proof) (1994)*, the mother was considered to be incapable of adequately caring for her children because she had the mental capacity of a ten year-old child. See also the case below.

> In *Re C (A Minor) (1995)*, Ward LJ said:
>
> *This very sad case concerns S. S is just four years old having been born on 6 August 1991. Her parents were sadly unable to look after her properly because they have various difficulties. S's mother is slightly disabled from looking after her and her father suffers from manic depression and is likewise subject to low stress tolerance levels. That caused the grandparents, who appear before us today, a great deal of anxiety... In the early part of 1993, when S was about 18 months, there were the beginnings of real worry that S was not developing as she should....I find that it is attributable to the care given to S by her grandparents, not being what it would be reasonable to expect a parent to give. The threshold criteria are therefore met and I go on to consider what, if any, order is necessary to promote S's welfare.*

# Present and future harm: a temporal question

15.21 The disjunctive wording 'is suffering' or 'is likely to suffer' allows for the making of a care order not only when a child is suffering harm in the present but also where a child is likely to suffer harm in the future. Prior to the CA 1989, before a care order was made proof of present harm was required. Whilst under the old system the courts could consider future risk to a child, no order could be made solely on this basis (*Essex County Council v TLR and KBR (Minors) (1978)*). In accordance with the Children and Young Persons Act 1969, s 1(2) a juvenile court could make a care order in respect of a child or young person (ie a person under 17) if it was satisfied that any of certain specified conditions are satisfied in respect of him.

15.22 The problem, under the earlier legislation was that where future risk was apprehended, little could be done to protect the child. Jasmine Beckford and Kimberly Carlisle were two of many children who died following professionals' failure to exchange and act on relevant information (see Edwards, 1996). Their deaths and the deaths of other children in similar circumstances led to the second limb of CA 1989, s 31 which allows for a pre-emptive strike ie the removal of a child where it is considered that the child is likely to suffer harm in the future.

## 'Is suffering'

15.23 An issue for the courts has been at what point in time is the harm to have occurred from which protection is needed and significant harm established? It is now settled law following *Re M (A Minor) (Care Order: Threshold Conditions) (1994)* that the relevant time for 'is suffering' is at the date when the local authority initiates the investigation and not the time at which the court makes an order. Lord Mackay said:

> .... There is nothing in s 31(2), which, in my opinion, requires that the conditions to be satisfied are to be dissociated from the time of the making of the application by the local authority. I would conclude that the natural construction of the conditions in s 31(2) is that where, at the time the application is to be disposed of, there are in place arrangements for the protection of the child by the local authority on an interim basis, which protection has been continuously in place for some time, the relevant date with respect to which the court must be satisfied is the date at which the local authority initiated the procedure for protection under the Act from which these arrangements follow. If, after a local authority had initiated protective arrangements, the need for these had terminated because the child's welfare had been satisfactorily provided for otherwise, in any subsequent proceedings it would not be possible to found jurisdiction on the situation at the time of initiation of these arrangements.

In this case, the father had murdered the mother when the child was four months old. The mother's cousin later applied for a s 8 CA residence order in respect of the child. The father and the guardian ad litem appealed against the decision and supported the making of a care order. The original order of Bracewell J followed the reasoning in *Northamptonshire County Council v S (1993)* and applied the test to the period immediately before the local authority initiated the process of protecting the child. The Court of Appeal in substituting a residence order in favour of the mother's cousin held that the harm must be suffered at the relevant time the court makes its decision and not at the time the local authority commences proceedings. This reasoning was, as has been demonstrated above, rejected by the House of Lords.

### Is suffering—suspicion is not enough

15.24 In assessing present harm suspicion is not enough to find the threshold test met. And, it can be observed that where the allegation is one of sexual abuse the court reluctantly finds the allegations proven often preferring to find that where such allegations are made then emotional abuse or neglect is the ground for making the order.

### Is suffering—Physical abuse

15.25    In *Re B (Children) (2006)*, supervision orders were made in respect of three children following a finding with regard to one of them (J) of bilateral subdural haemorrhages. These injuries had been discovered following the child J being accidentally dropped at a wedding party on 6 November 2004 by a guest who had been holding the child. However, examination of the child (MRI) on 10 and 11 November disclosed injuries, said the expert, of more than two weeks' duration. In the Plymouth County Court on 24 June 2005, HHJ Tyzack QC found that: '... on a balance of probability, on a date unknown but two–three weeks before 10.11.04, either the mother or the father (but likely to be the mother) caused [J] to suffer bilateral subdural haemorrhages probably by shaking her on one occasion. The retinal haemorrhages probably occurred at the same time.' The Court of Appeal, Longmore LJ (in agreement with Laws LJ and Ward LJ) asserted:

> *In these circumstances, while it is perfectly possible to acknowledge there may be suspicion, I cannot think it was right for the judge, with respect, to have found on the balance of probabilities that J was non-accidentally injured while in the control of her parents. The evidence does just not have that degree of cogency which is required to overcome the unlikelihood of the serious allegation that is being made, to adapt the words of Ungoed-Thomas J, approved by Lord Nicholls in Re H [1996] AC 563 at 586H, [1996] 1 All ER 1, [1996] 1 FCR 509. As Lord Nicholls also said, a judicial suspicion is not a proper factual basis on which the court's jurisdiction can be exercised '...because that is no more than a judicial state of uncertainty about whether or not an event happened;...*

### Is suffering—Sexual abuse

15.26    Where sexual abuse is alleged as having occurred the courts seem reluctant to make a finding of sexual abuse instead finding emotional abuse or neglect, this has repercussions for the later work to be undertaken with the family.

> In *Re W (A Child) (Care Proceedings) (2007)*, W who was two years of age was taken into care. Experts concluded that she had been 'grossly anally abused'. W was freed for adoption. The mother appealed against the care order and the case was remitted for a rehearing where the judge found, *inter alia*, that W had not suffered sexual abuse although found that there was a failure on the part of the mother to protect W (s 31(2)(b)(i)). He made a care order and the mother appealed on the basis that if the judge had failed to find that there was evidence of sexual abuse how could he go on to find that she had failed to protect. In this case the appeal was allowed and remitted for a rehearing.

## Future suffering: 'likely to suffer'—General principles

15.27    CA 1989, s 31(2) provides protection against harm in the future. Such applications are made in order to protect other siblings in the family where a funding of significant harm has been made in respect of another sibling.

> The relevant time question fell once again to be decided in *Southwark London Borough Council v B (1998)*, a case which turned on the whether the child was 'likely to suffer.'

Counsel for the mother contended that the relevant time for consideration of this was at the date of the hearing. The court held that the House of Lords decision in *Re M (1994)*:

*applied to both limbs of the threshold criteria, and the relevant date in respect of both actual harm and the likelihood of harm was the date upon which the local authority initiated protective arrangements for the relevant child, so long as such protective arrangements had been continuously in place from the time of such intervention and initiation until disposal of the case by the court.*

Finally laying to rest the temporal question of relevant time with regard to both limbs of CA 1989, s 31.

### Retrospectivism

15.28 The principle that suffering in the past is a guide to the future was asserted in *Re B (A Minor) (Care Order: Criteria) (1993)*. Douglas Brown J said 'The court is not confined, in my judgment, to conditions obtaining at the date of the hearing in determining this question'.

### Prospectivism

15.29 In *Re H (A Minor) (Section 37 Direction) (1993)*, Scott Baker J emphasized that: *the likelihood of harm is not confined to present or near future but applies to the ability of a parent or carer to meet the emotional needs of a child in the years ahead. I am not limited ... to looking at the past and immediate future. If a court concludes that a parent, or a carer, is likely to be unable to meet the emotional needs of a child in the future—even if years hence—my view is that the condition in s 31(2) would probably be met.*

In *Newham London Borough Council v Attorney General (1993)*, where the child was cared for by the grandmother because of the mental illness of the mother, Sir Stephen Brown P argued that 'likely' did not have to be strictly construed:

*Clearly that is not the meaning, which could or should be given to the term 'likely to suffer'. The court is not applying a test to events which have happened in the past and deciding on the evidence, on the balance of probabilities, which is the stand- ard of civil proof, whether such an event has in fact happened. That is not what is involved in this case ... you can prove that a past event has happened.*

He continued by quoting, with approval, Lord Reid in *Davies v Taylor (1974)* where Lord Reid said:

*but you cannot prove that a future event will happen and I do not think that the law is so foolish as to suppose that you can. All that you can do is to evaluate the chance. Sometimes it is virtually 100% sometimes virtually nil. But often it is somewhere in between.' The court in Newham concluded that 'in looking to the future the court has to assess the risk. Is this child likely to suffer significant harm?*

## Evaluating the future risk of harm

15.30 In evaluating the risk of harm the courts are more willing to make a finding of emotional harm and reluctant to make a finding of sexual harm when future risk is being assessed.

*Re G and R (1995)* concerned a number of children from various families where the local authority alleged that the families had been involved in a paedophile ring. In the G family, in respect of siblings D, K, and L, the local authority made care applications. D, the court found, had been smacked, and this the court found sufficient for a care order. The step-father appealed; the court could find no fault with the finding of the court of first instance. K was neglected on 10 occasions and admitted to the Accident and Emergency Department; there was evidence of inadequate parenting but no evidence of cruelty. The threshold conditions were satisfied for inadequate parenting and a care order was made on the basis of the possibility of further sexual abuse., With regard to sexual abuse in respect of L who was not suffering harm but was considered likely to suffer because of the evidence relating to K, the mother and step-father appealed on the basis of the judge's finding of significant harm in the future. Physical or sexual abuse was not made out in L and K's case, and poor parenting was the basis for the order.

In *Re H and R (1995)*, a step-father was acquitted in criminal proceedings of the rape of one of his step-children D1. The local authority applied for a care order in respect of the remaining siblings D2, D3, and D4 as they were at risk of harm in the future. The Court of Appeal found that since it had not been proven that the step-father had sexually abused the step-daughter in the criminal proceedings, there were no grounds upon which to find that the remaining children were likely to suffer significant harm in the future.

The Court of Appeal had held that the standard of proof in sexual abuse cases involved a two-stage test: first, the standard was beyond the mere balance of probabilities, and secondly, that there was a real possibility that the child would suffer significant harm and not the threshold of more likely than not (Sir Stephen Brown P and Millett LJ; Kennedy LJ dissenting).

Nottinghamshire County Council appealed to the House of Lords, Lord Nicholls asserted:

*In my view, therefore, the context shows that in s 31(2)(a) 'likely' is being used in the sense of a real possibility, a possibility that cannot sensibly be ignored having regard to the nature and gravity of the feared harm in the particular case. By parity of reasoning the expression 'likely to suffer significant harm' bears the same meaning elsewhere in the Act: for instance, in ss 43, 44 and 46. 'Likely' also bears a similar meaning, for a similar reason, in the requirement in s 31(2)(b) that the harm or likelihood of harm must be attributable to the care given to the child or 'likely' to be given him if the order were not made. Although the result is much the same, this does not mean that where a serious allegation is in issue the standard of proof required is higher. It means only that the inherent probability or improbability of an event is itself a matter to be taken into account when weighing the probabilities and deciding whether, on balance, the event occurred. The more improbable the event, the stronger must be the evidence that it did occur before, on the balance of probability, its occurrence will be established (Lord Browne-Wilkinson and Lord Lloyd dissenting).*

Lord Browne-Wilkinson in his dissenting judgment said this:

*Where I part company is in thinking that the facts relevant to an assessment of risk ('is likely to suffer...harm') are not the same as the facts relevant to a decision that harm is in fact being suffered. In order to be satisfied that an event has occurred or is occurring the evidence has to show on the balance of probabilities that such an event did occur or is occurring. But in order to be satisfied that there is a risk of such an occurrence, the ambit of the relevant facts is in my view wider. The combined effect of a number of factors which suggest that a state of affairs, though not proved to exist, may well exist is the normal basis for the assessment of future risk. To be satisfied of the existence of a risk does not require proof of the occurrence of past historical events but proof of facts, which are relevant to the making of a prognosis.*

Lord Browne-Wilkinson referred to the findings of the judge in the criminal trial who said:

*I cannot be sure to the requisite high standard of proof [the criminal standard of beyond reasonable doubt] that [D1's] allegations are true...This is far from saying that I am satisfied the child's complaints are untrue. I do not brush them aside as the jury seem to have done. I am, at least, more than a little suspicious that [Mr R] has abused her as she says. If it were relevant, I would be prepared to hold that there is a real possibility that her statement and her evidence are true. Nor has [Mr R] by his evidence and demeanour, not only throughout the hearing but the whole of this matter, done anything to dispel those suspicions.*

Lord Browne-Wilkinson then said:

*that conclusion that there was a real possibility that the evidence of D1 was true was a finding of fact based on evidence and the micro facts that he had found. It was not a mere suspicion as to the risk that Mr R was an abuser: it was a finding of risk. My Lords, I am anxious that the decision of the House in this case may establish the law in an unworkable form to the detriment of many children at risk.*

## Probability theory in *Re H and R*

15.31 Lord Nicholls' commentaries on hypothetical child sexual abuse and probability are reminiscent of the nineteenth-century disbelief in the existence of sexual abuse against children. Lord Nicholls in *Re H and R* relies on Ungoed-Thomas J, who summarized the position in *Re Dellow's Will Trusts (1964)*: 'The more serious the allegation, the more cogent is the evidence required to overcome the unlikelihood of what is alleged and thus to prove it' (this case concerned the issue of whether a wife who killed her husband was entitled to benefit from his will).

## The problem with *Re H and R* and assessing evidence

15.32 Four premises, elevated to 'articles of faith' followed the House of Lords in *Re H and R*. They are, firstly, the more serious an alleged incident the more evidence is required to prove it. Secondly, '...the more improbable the event, the stronger must be the evidence that it did occur' (at 17). (Here, there is some conflation between the use of the words 'serious' and 'improbable'.) Thirdly, '... the probability standard can accommodate one's instinctive feeling that even in civil proceedings a court should be more sure before finding serious allegations proved than when deciding less serious or trivial matters' (at 17). Fourthly, '... the more serious the allegation the less likely it is that the event occurred...' (at 17) which is a variant of the first and the second. The flaw in the reasoning is this.

There is a misconception that there is a sliding scale in volume of evidence required which depends on the seriousness of what is being alleged; the belief that improbable events require more evidence; the arrogation of instinct to the level of a rule of law or somewhere approximately a legal rule, and the opinion that serious incidents are less likely to occur. *Re H and R*'s legacy has beleaguered the area of child protection by promulgating as truth a visceral disbelief in the possibility of child sexual abuse. *Re H and R*'s legacy also required a consideration of the 'inherent probability' by the court which meant, as Lord Nicholls asserted, 'The inherent probability or improbability of an event is itself a matter to be taken into account when weighing the probabilities and deciding whether, on balance, the event occurred' (at 17).

# After *Re H and R*—assessing future harm

15.33    In *Re M and R (Minors) (Sexual Abuse: Expert Evidence) (1996)*, R, one of six children, alleged that he and several of the other children had been sexually abused by their mother and two men. The four younger children were placed with foster parents pending the local authority's application for full care orders. The judge considered medical evidence, video-recorded interviews with the children, and the expert evidence of two child psychiatrists. The judge concluded that, although the balance of the psychiatric evidence was unanimously to the effect that sexual abuse had probably occurred, he was not satisfied on the balance of probabilities that the allegations of sexual abuse were proved. He was, however, satisfied that the threshold criteria in CA 1989, s 31 were met in respect of emotional abuse and made interim care orders, after having regard to the welfare principle in CA 1989, s 1. The local authority, supported by the guardian ad litem, appealed, contending principally that the judge, having found that there was a real possibility that sexual abuse had occurred, had erred in law in not taking into account the allegations of sexual abuse in his assessment of the welfare of the children.

The Court of Appeal held:

*When assessing under s 1(3)(e) of the 1989 Act whether a child was at risk of suffering harm, the court could have regard only to any harm that the child had suffered or was at risk of suffering if it was satisfied on the balance of probabilities that such harm or risk of harm (ie a real possibility of future harm) in fact existed.*

In *Re C and B (Children) (Care Order: Future Harm) (2001)*, a case in which no sexual allegations were made, the outcome was somewhat different. Here, care orders were made under s 31(2) on the basis that K had suffered actual harm to her intellectual and emotional development, and the likelihood of such harm occurring to CM in the future. In 1998, the mother gave birth to a son, J. The social worker concluded that, although there was no evidence that J was currently suffering any harm, 'it was highly likely that [J] will suffer similar significant harm as his sisters in the future'. The local authority applied for, and was granted, an interim care order in relation to him, and he was removed from his parents when he was 10 months old. In 1999, the mother gave birth to the youngest child, C, and the local authority obtained an emergency protection order in respect of him the same day. The parents appealed. The appeal in relation to J and C was allowed; their care orders were set aside, and the case remitted to a High Court judge for reconsideration.

## Determining whether a child is 'likely to suffer' is like dancing on the head of a pin

15.34    In *Re T (Abuse: Standard of Proof) (2004)*, a 20 month-old child was admitted to hospital with a perineal tear. Subsequent investigation under general anaesthetic revealed anal fissures, the hymen was intact and there was no injury to the upper vagina. As a result, the children were voluntarily accommodated by the maternal grandparents and interim care orders were made. One of the paediatricians changed his opinion of the injuries due to different sets of photographs being submitted and the result of the non-disclosure of crucial photographic evidence. The judge, His Honour Judge Wade did not regard the threshold conditions satisfied, the local authority appealed and the appeal was allowed.

Dame Elizabeth Butler-Sloss said,

> *So it may very well be that, in looking at these more recent dicta one is somewhat (as Miss Ball counsel for the mother in Re ET (Serious injuries: Standard of Proof) 2004 2 FLR 1205) put it) dancing on the head of a pin' (cited in Re U and Re B (2004) and Re T). In Re T (2004) para 27, 'I don't agree that the issue is one of dancing on the head of a pin which would suggest that the efforts to define likely and probably are matters which cannot be decided with any exactitude'.*

The sexual abuse allegation cases above do suggest the reluctance of the courts to find on the balance of probabilities that sexual abuse is likely to occur.

It was easier to decide this non sexual case: In *Local Authority v C (E and another intervening) (2004)*, the court took the view that the child was likely to suffer significant harm as both his parents believed he had been conceived as a result of a miracle birth and were determined in continuing in this delusion. The parents had been unable to have children. They had joined a religious group whose beliefs embraced traditional African custom and Christian belief. One of this group's beliefs was in the power of divine intervention to facilitate miracle births. Whilst all medical tests confirmed that the mother was not pregnant she continued to believe she was and went to Kenya, where she met a man who she thought was a doctor. He told her she was 12 months' pregnant. During some procedure she was tricked into believing she had given birth to a child, G, who she brought to England.

# Burden of proof—from *Re H and R* to *Re B*

15.35 Putting evidence of significant harm to proof, requires providing proof to the civil standard, that is, on the balance of probabilities—or proving a real possibility (*Re H (minors) (Sexual Abuse: Standard of Proof) (1996)*; *Re B (Children) (Sexual Abuse: Standard of Proof) (2008)*). Since *Re H and R*, and indeed prior to this case, where sexual allegations formed the basis of the evidence it was thought that the standard of proof, because of the seriousness of a finding of sexual abuse was so devastating to the alleged abuser that the standard of proof in these particular circumstances was in fact higher than on the balance of probabilities.

15.36 The burden is on the local authority to prove its case since it is the local authority who bring it. The principle of the balance of probabilities as the standard of proof in civil cases as set out in *Re H and R* by Lord Nicholls has been considered in subsequent dicta.

> In *Re T (Abuse: Standard of Proof) (2004)*, the court said the test set out by Lord Nicholls in *Re H* had not been varied nor adjusted by the dicta of Lord Bingham of Cornhill in *B v Chief Constable of Avon and Somerset Constabulary* or Lord Steyn in *R (McCann and others) v Crown Court at Manchester*; or that in *Clingham v Kensington and Chelsea Royal London Borough Council*. Lady Butler-Sloss in *Re T* held:
>
> *I understand that in many applications for care orders counsel are now submitting that the correct approach to the standard of proof is to treat the distinction between criminal and civil standards as 'largely illusory'. In my judgment, this approach is mistaken. The standard of proof to be applied in Children Act cases is the balance of probabilities and the approach to these difficult cases was set out by Lord Nicholls of Birkenhead in his speech in Re H (Minors) (Sexual Abuse: Standard of Proof) (1996). That test has not been varied nor adjusted by the dicta of Lord Bingham of Cornhill nor of Lord Steyn who were considering applications made under a different statute. There would appear to be no good reason to leap across a division between crime and preventative measures taken to restrain defendants for the benefit of the community and wholly different considerations of child protection and child welfare, nor to apply the reasoning in R (McCann and Others) v Crown Court at Manchester;*

*Clingham v Kensington and Chelsea Royal London Borough Council (2002) UKHL 39, (2002) 3 WLR 1313, (2002) UKHRR 1286 to public, or indeed to private, law cases concerning children. The strict rules of evidence applicable in a criminal trial, which is adversarial in nature, are to be contrasted with the partly inquisitorial approach of the court dealing with children cases in which the rules of evidence are considerably relaxed. In my judgment, therefore, Bodey J applied the incorrect standard of proof in the case of Re ET (Serious Injuries: Standard of Proof), Note (2003) 2 FLR 1205.*

She went on to criticize the judge in *Re T* (above) for eliding the distinction between care proceedings and criminal proceedings in considering the allegations of sexual abuse, and for failing to distinguish between the different functions of the judge and the medical experts. Quoting from Thorpe LJ in *Re B (Non Accidental Injury) (2002)*, who said, 'The expert of ultimate referral was there to guide the judge as to the relevant medical and scientific knowledge, inevitably expressing himself in different language. The judge's function was a very different one. He had to consider the question posed by s 31 of the Children Act . . .' she then said, 'His approach to the medical evidence fell into the error of requiring a standard equal to the criminal standard of proof. At different stages of the judgment he referred to "it is difficult to be dogmatic and absolutely certain", "degrees of certainty" or "degree of certainty" and "lack of certainty" ' *(T (2004))*.

15.37 The standard of proof in *Re H and R* was affirmed by the Court of Appeal in *Re U (Serious Injury: Standard of Proof) (2004); Re B (2004)* and *Re B (2008)*.

In *Re B (2008)*, the House of Lords dismissed an appeal by two children, N, a girl aged nine, and A, a boy aged six, through their guardian. The judge made interim care orders in respect of R (a step daughter) as well as N and A, on the basis of a plan to remove them all from their mother (Mrs B) and place them with Mr B at his parents' home. R had alleged that Mr B had sexually abused her and hit her with a belt. The judge could not make a finding on whether R had been abused, and was subsequently criticized by the House of Lords for 'sitting on the fence.'

Lady Hale follows Lord Lloyd in *Re H and R* who said:

*Where it is claimed that the child has suffered or is suffering significant harm the standard of proof is the simple balance of probabilities, no matter how serious the underlying allegation' (at 13, para 2). Lord Hoffmann said in Re B , 'I think that the time has come to say, once and for all, that there is only one civil standard of proof and that is proof that the fact in issue more probably occurred than not (para 13).*

## *Re B (2008)*—closing the lid on some of the reasoning in *Re H and R*

15.38 *Re B (2008)* has certainly put firmly aside some of the postures of belief and disbelief and instinct, placing them firmly and properly outside the law. Lady Hale in *Re B* severs seriousness from probability and echoes Lord Lloyd's dissent in

*Re H and R* when he said that, '…..the subsection (s 31) does not require a degree of probability commensurate with the seriousness of the allegation.' Lady Hale says, 'As to the seriousness of the allegation, there is no logical or necessary connection between seriousness and probability' (para 72) Lord Hoffman in agreement with Lady Hale said, 'Some confusion has however been caused by dicta which suggest that the standard of proof may vary with the gravity of the misconduct alleged or even the seriousness of the consequences for the person concerned'(para 5). Lady Hale concludes offering sound advice,

> My Lords, Lord Lloyd's prediction proved only too correct. Lord Nicholls's nuanced explanation left room for the nostrum, 'the more serious the allegation, the more cogent the evidence needed to prove it', to take hold and be repeated time and time again in fact-finding hearings in care proceedings…It is time for us to loosen its grip and give it its quietus…(para 64).

Lord Hoffmann, in *Re B*, though embracing the rejection of some of the reasoning in *Re H and R*, says, 'If a child alleges sexual abuse by a parent, it is common sense to start with the assumption that most parents do not abuse their children'. Further, Lord Hoffman, whilst not supporting the relevance of instinct as endorsed by Lord Nicholls in *Re H and R*, instead instates common sense as of relevance and the term common sense has given a legitimacy to disbelief.

There is further the survival of the attention to be given to 'inherent probabilities'. Lady Hale said this, 'The inherent probabilities are simply something to be taken into account, where relevant, in deciding where the truth lies' (para 70). Leaving 'inherent probabilities' as a matter 'to be taken into account, where relevant' keeps the back door open for common sense and instinct to foment and enter.

Hayes (2008), points out, that *Re B* is not stripped entirely of all assumptions, as inherent probability is not totally disbanded and the use of the term 'common sense' makes the application of 'instinct' more palatable. I agree with Hayes that the improbability /probability of an event will still be considered of relevance. It is incorrect to regard inherent probabilities as a 'factor' to be taken into account. It is certainly not relevant to truth. Where I depart from Hayes is when he argues that, 'The effect of the House of Lords ruling in *Re B* is that it is wrong to assume that a serious allegation must be supported by cogent evidence'. However, *Re B* does not completely purge the fallacies from *Re H and R*'s legacy.

# Where are we now?

## Proof and general allegations

15.39    A significant step forward in child protection in sexual abuse case was made in *P (A Child) (2010)*. Here, the court concluded that it is open to a judge conducting a fact finding hearing to make a finding in general terms that it is probable a party has behaved towards and touched a child in an inappropriate sexual manner. This decision is important as it provides protection for children where it is not possible to make a finding on each allegation but as in this case the allegations and description of events made by the child to the foster carer were considered so alien to a child of such tender years that the only conclusion that could be drawn was that such events had in fact happened.

E (three years of age)and D (six years of age) , are daughters of RP and LJ. The girls were then placed in foster care and E, began to say worrying things suggestive of inappropriate sexual activity by the father. The father denied any inappropriate behaviour. Whilst the trial judge acknowledged a question mark over the accuracy of the memory of a child of her age he found the father untruthful in his explanations for missed contact which raised issues of his credibility as a witness. The judge found certain descriptions made by E aged three alien to a child of her age who had not been exposed to inappropriate sexual activity. And he said that to ignore this evidence would be shutting one's eyes to the obvious.

However, he could not make specific findings concluding that the father had been guilty of sexually inappropriate behaviour involving E without being able to say with any confidence that it was more than sexually motivated touching...On appeal it was argued on behalf of RJ that if the evidence was not good enough to warrant any specific finding the judge could not then, on precisely the same evidence, damn the father in generalized terms.

The Court of Appeal dismissed the appeal unanimously and said:

*31. Some of what [E] says may have an innocent explanation. Evidence of her apparently 'masturbating' would have no probative value on its own. Equally, evidence of her 'trying to wee like Daddy' should not be held against [the father]. I accept that [the father] would have several innocent reasons for touching [E] in the vaginal area. He has proffered explanations for some of what has been described. But why would [E] allege not only that her father had 'played' with her vagina but that he 'touched' her vagina 'with his bum' which in this context must surely mean his penis 'and it hurt' if that is quite untrue? Why would she say her father had 'licked' her vagina, and put his fingers in her vagina, if he had not? Even more worryingly, where has she got this concept of Daddy's 'bum' (I presume penis) 'coming out oh his house to say hello [E] I love you'? The obvious adult interpretation is that this is her father with an erection. These are descriptions that would be alien to a child of this age who had not been exposed to inappropriate sexual activity.*

*32. To ignore this evidence and say that it amounts to nothing probative would, in my judgment, be shutting one's eyes to the obvious (Lord Justice Thorpe). There is no foundation for the suggestion that this was a mere expression of judicial suspicion and dismissed the appeal.*

## Orders refused

15.40 Where there is no finding of harm, the court will refuse the application, although the court may make an interim care order to allow for further assessments to be made (***Re M (ICO: Removal) (2005)***).

In *Re H (A Child) (Interim Care Order) (2002)*, Thorpe LJ said

*that the decision taken by the court on an interim care order application must necessarily be limited to issues that cannot await the fixture and must not extend to issues that are being prepared for determination at that fixture.*

However, refusals, however, are rare. The more recent position is this. In 2004, of 7,796 care orders made, 11 were refused. In 2006, 7,222 care orders were made, 12 were refused and 289 orders of 'no order' were made. Looking to supervision orders in 2004, 3,012 supervision orders were made, one was refused. In 2006, 3,223 supervision orders were made, one was refused and 25 orders of 'no order' were made. (See *Judicial Statistics* 2004, *Judicial and Court Statistics* 2006 (see Table 15.1 below).)

## Orders withdrawn

15.41 In 2004, 380 care order and 59 supervision order applications were withdrawn. In 2005, 307 care and 52 supervision applications were withdrawn. An application may be withdrawn only with leave of the court (FPR 1991 r 4.45) (see *Judicial Statistics* 2004, 2005; see Table 15.1 below). It is difficult to draw any certain

**Table 15.1** Applications made and disposed of by type in public law in all tiers of court 1997–2009

| Year | Applications made | | Applications withdrawn | | Orders refused | | Orders of no order | | Orders made | |
|------|------|------|------|------|------|------|------|------|------|------|
| | Care | Sup. | Care | Sup. | Care | Sup. | Care | Sup. | Care | Sup. |
| 1997 | N/a | N/a | | | | | | | 4985 | 1201 |
| 1999 | N/a | N/a | 288 | 106 | 28 | 57 | 95 | 24 | 4124 | 787 |
| 2000 | N/a | N/a | 459 | 74 | 26 | 1 | 177 | 10 | 6298 | 784 |
| 2001 | N/a | N/a | 355 | 60 | 15 | 0 | 164 | 13 | 5984 | 1466 |
| 2002 | N/a | N/a | 304 | 24 | 27 | 1 | 185 | 17 | 6335 | 1538 |
| 2003 | N/a | N/a | 433 | 71 | 26 | 1 | 257 | 50 | 7387 | 2383 |
| 2004 | N/a | N/a | 380 | 59 | 11 | 1 | 306 | 30 | 7796 | 3012 |
| 2005 | 13498 | 897 | 307 | 52 | 15 | 0 | 250 | 10 | 7051 | 2641 |
| 2006 | 13421 | 938 | 325 | 47 | 12 | 1 | 289 | 25 | 7222 | 3223 |
| 2007 | 13717 | 1069 | 336 | 96 | 23 | 1 | 290 | 35 | 7264 | 3095 |
| 2008 | 11790 | 730 | 298 | 56 | 20 | 4 | 245 | 27 | 7077 | 3663 |
| 2009 | 17090 | 950 | 270 | 10 | 20 | — | 230 | 10 | 5720 | 2780 |

*Source*: Judicial Statistics for the respective years

conclusions from these refusals and withdrawals. However withdrawals are costly and Coventry City Council, where the council had commenced a care proceedings application which the court said had fallen below accepted standards, were ordered to pay £100,000 in court costs (*Coventry City Council v X, Y and Z (Care Proceedings: Costs: Identification of Local Authority) (2010)*).

> In *WSCC v M and others (2010)*, there was a cessation of the proceedings. In this case the court reports:
>
> *There are currently four children involved in these proceedings: W aged 14, X aged 12, Y aged 9 and Z who will soon be 5 and is the only girl in the family. It will, however, be necessary to mention two other children in this judgment: U aged 18 and who has long since been adopted elsewhere and V aged 16 who is in long term foster care. There are three adult parties in this case: F who is the father of Y and Z but has also acted in that role for W and X; M who is the mother of U, V, W, X and Z; and SM who is the mother of Y. F and M had been in a relationship for some time but married on 6th June 2009. There are three other adults (all former partners of M) who will be mentioned: P (now deceased) was the father of U, Q who is the father of V, W and X, and R; neither R nor Q have taken any part in these proceedings. It will be convenient in this judgment, however, to refer to M as 'the mother' and F as 'the father'.*
>
> *8. The mother's relationship with P began when they were respectively aged 15 and 18. It was a stormy relationship characterised by domestic violence which resulted in U being removed (in the event permanently) and made the subject of a care order on 3rd June 1992. The mother then had a relationship with Q which was also characterised by domestic violence; indeed in 1997 Q served a short prison sentence for making threats to kill the mother. V was not an easy child and there was frequent involvement from a London local authority. Between 2001 and 2003 the mother was in a relationship with R which ended because R's violence extended to W and X. The mother was involved in further care proceedings which culminated on 11th June 2004 with a care order in respect of V and supervision orders in respect of W and X. thereafter the mother moved, began a relationship with the father and they now reside in the area of the applicant local authority.*
>
> The court concluded that 'their welfare will be promoted by the cessation of proceedings.'

15.42 *Re H and R* may have deterred local authorities from making child care applications in anything other than what they perceive to be watertight cases.

> In *Re N (Leave to Withdraw: Care Proceedings) (2000)*, the local authority applied for care proceedings to be withdrawn where their involvement with the family had resulted from health and behavioural problems of the second and third children who had been born of different fathers. They were placed with foster parents, where they flourished and wished to stay. Full psychiatric assessment of both parents demonstrated that their care of the baby (who was not the subject of the application) was exemplary. The local authority sought leave to withdraw its application for a care order under the Family

Proceedings Rules 1991, r 4.5(1). The parents supported the application to withdraw, relying upon Art 8(1) of the ECHR. The court held that under the second limb of CA 1989, s 31 (likely to suffer) the court was also concerned with the immediate future and the capacity of parents to provide appropriate care throughout childhood and therefore the court refused the application to withdraw. (For a case where application to withdraw was granted see *London Borough of Southwark v B (1993); R v Birmingham Juvenile Court, ex parte G and others (Minors); R v Birmingham Juvenile Court, ex parte R (A Minor) (1990)*).

## 'No order' presumption (CA 1989, s 1(5))

15.43   As in private proceedings, similarly here in public proceedings, the court must decide, once the threshold has been met, whether it is better to make an order for the child than not to make an order at all (see *Re G (Children) (Residence Order: No Order Principle) (2006)*).

15.44   As Freeman (1993), writes (at 29), 'A court which is satisfied that the condition is met needs also to be satisfied that the care order will be better for the child than making no order: s 1(5)'. The court will be required to apply the CA 1989, s 1(3) checklist and the range of powers available to the court, including s 8 orders. In consideration of whether to make an order or not, the court must place the child's welfare as the paramount consideration (s 1(1)).

In *Northamptonshire County Council v S and others (1993)*, Ewbank J's interpretation of s 1(5) described the correct procedure as:

*The fact that the threshold test is met does not mean that the family proceedings court has to make a court order...the justices have the choice once the threshold conditions are met of making a care order, of making a supervision order, or of making any other order under the Children Act 1989.*

The burden is on the local authority who brings the application to explain to the court why an order for care or supervision is better than leaving things as they are. The *Children Act Report* (DHSS, 1985) para 15.24, stated that this will require 'positive proof that a care or supervision order will result in [the child's] needs being met or at least better catered for, and further that intervention will not do more overall harm than good'.

15.45   In the early days, it would appear that judges (*Kent County Council v C (1993)*), considered the 'no order' principle only where there was a contest (*Re M*). The importance of the two-stage process was enunciated in *Re CH (Care or Interim Care Order) (1998)*.

In *Re K (Supervision Orders) (1999)*, the mother's fourth child died when he was one month old. The local authority commenced proceedings in respect of the three surviving children. The local authority and the parents had reached a sensible agreement, which clearly protected the children. Once the threshold criteria were satisfied, in considering whether to make a supervision order or no order in accordance with CA 1989, s 1(5) there had to be something in the making or operation of a supervision order which made it better for the children for it to be made. It would be wrong to make a supervision order where the duties imposed on the local authority under Part III of the 1989 Act to provide services for children and their families would be sufficient to meet the children's needs, as the court should start with a preference for the less interventionist approach rather than the more interventionist approach.

The conclusion was that that a supervision order was better for the children than no order at all.

# Evaluating child protection

## Parental co-operation or contest: how important is this for the outcome?

15.46   Parental co-operation with the local authority throughout the investigation has a significant impact on the outcome (disposal) of the case and in influencing the courts in their decision whether to make a final order or no order at all. The Department of Health (1991), para 3.61, suggests that the conditions where no order will be made are those where 'the prognosis for change is reasonable and parents show a willingness to co-operate with voluntary arrangements'. However, it can never be right for example that parental willingness to co-operate should prejudice risk assessment and child safety.

## The balancing exercise at the heart of civil law

15.47       In *Re M (A Minor) (Application No 2) (1994)*, there was evidence of both neglect and physical abuse; the child had a duodenal haematoma; was underweight, emaciated, and there was evidence of multiple bruising to the shins, knees, buttocks, face, chest and back, which the mother and boyfriend denied causing. The local authority applied for a care order subject to the child residing with the maternal grandparents. The judge found that the child was likely to suffer significant harm although the judge was not prepared to find that the mother or boyfriend had beaten or starved the child. The judge refused the care order of the local authority and refused the residence order sought by the maternal grandparents and granted the mother's application for a residence order and made it subject to a condition that she continue to reside at the home of the boyfriend's parents. In considering s 1(5), he concluded that he would 'give the parents a chance', and the child was returned to the mother. This was even though the child had told her foster mother, 'On Christmas Day I could not finish my dinner. Daddy started kicking me and punching—then Mummy'. The Court of Appeal could find no fault with the judge's handling of the case and the appeal was dismissed.

# Disposal: making a care or supervision order

## Care order

15.48 A care order may be made to foster parents or to a relative. In fact as Eddon (2006) notes:

> *Something like 70% of children who become involved in care proceedings do not return home. Instead, the court approves a plan for permanent care outside the immediate family. Increasingly, such children either are placed with members of the extended family such as grandparents (kinship care) or remain permanently with their existing short-term foster carers. Kinship care placements can in turn be implemented under the terms of a care order, a residence order or a special guardianship order.*

## Supervision order

15.49 Alternatively, the court may make a supervision order (CA 1989, s 31(1)(b)), which places a child under the supervision of a local authority supervisor who may be a social worker or probation officer. The duty of the supervisor is 'to advise, assist and befriend' the child. It is to be noted, however, that the order is to give the opportunity to the local authority of monitoring the welfare of the child. Whilst the order allows the local authority access to the child so that the relevant checks can be made, the order does not allow for the parents to have conditions imposed upon them. This may seem strange, when after all the primary object of the order is to monitor the care parents are giving the child.

15.50 Indeed, the Short Committee recommended that the supervisor have greater powers to impose conditions on children and parents. Whilst conditions have been incorporated into the CA 1989, there are problems since parental responsibility does not lie with the local authority. With this order, as with the care order, again there are a number of placement options, although the child is placed usually at home or with those exercising parental responsibility. Thus, such orders may also be accompanied by a residence order to the person who is looking after the child. Thus, where a child is being abused in the immediate family, the court may make a supervision order, which allows for local authority supervision and also a residence order for example, to the maternal grandmother. (In March 1993, as few as 40 supervision orders carried a residence requirement (*Children Looked After by Local Authorities* (DOH, 1993 47).) Both a care and a supervision order may be made in relation to a child who has reached the age of 17 years (see *Re B (Children) (2006)*; *Re C-G (Children) (2006)* or re an interim supervision order, see *M (A Child) (2006)*).

## When care? When supervision?

15.51   In *Re B (Care or Supervision Order) (1996)*, Holman J laid down the principles to be applied when making this determination:

> *On the choice between a care order or a supervision order there are now a number of authorities. It is now clear that it can be appropriate to make a full care order even though all parties, including the guardian ad litem and the court itself, agree that the child should not in fact be removed from the daily care of living with its parents; and the local authority only wish and propose that there should be a supervision order. However, it is also clear and obvious that a care order is a stronger and more serious order to make. A care order rather than a supervision order should only be made if the stronger order is necessary for the proper protection of the child... There is a fundamental difference between these two orders. In the one case it is the local authority, which has to undertake the safeguarding of the child, in the other case it is the mother. (at 698)*

In *Re O (Supervision Order) (2001)*, 'A supervision order was proportionate to the risk'. The length of the supervision order is normally one year but can be extended but cannot be extended beyond three years. A care order lasts until the child is 18 unless it is brought to an end.

## The trend in orders: 1990–2010

15.52   Since the CA 1989, the number of care orders made has increased. In 1997, 4,985 care orders were granted; in 1999, 4,124; in 2004, they had risen to 7,796 and 7,222 in 2006. In 1997, 1,201 supervision orders were granted; this compares with 787 in 1999; 2,641 in 2005 and 3,223 in 2006 (*Judicial Statistics* for 1999–2005 and *Judicial and Court Statistics* 2006). Although in 2009, 5,720 were recorded (*Judicial Court Statistics*, Ministry of Justice, 2009).

## Commentary

15.53   In recent years it has been surmized that the tragic death of Baby P may have resulted in a greater diligence with regard to child protection. However, whilst the statistics show a rise in orders it may be the result of a greater willingness of local authorities to pursue applications.

> *From 11th–30th November 2007 there were a total of 365 care order applications received by Cafcass. By contrast, 11th-30th November 2008 saw a total of 449 care*

*order applications filed, an increase of 37% over the previous twenty day period and an increase of 23% over 11th-30th November 2007. Throughout 2009 Cafcass has received its highest ever level of demand for work relating to s31 applications, peaking at 784 requests in June 2009, an increase of 113% compared to the June 2008 figure (368) and an increase of 52% compared to the June 2007 total (514). Between April and September 2009, Cafcass received an average of 706 new s31 applications per month. See also the impact of the Public Law Outline in April 2008.' (See Cafcass 'The Baby Peter effect and the increase in s31 care order applications Elizabeth Hall / Jonathon Guy November 2009) http://www.cafcass.gov.uk/pdf/Baby%20peter%20 summary%20report%20FINAL%202%20Dec.pdf.*

But by 2009/2010, the Ministry of Justice figures for April to June 2010 reveal that public law applications are down compared with the same period for 2009, 6,100 children involved in public law applications compared with 6,600 in the same quarter in 2009, although Cafcass reports a rise in care applications between April–August 2010.

## Voluntary agreement (CA 1989, s 20)

15.54 Many children who are the subject of child protection enquiries do not become involved in the legal proceedings detailed above. Many children who leave home for a period of time are accommodated by foster parents or other family members (see Child Protection: Messages from Research 1995 at p 56). The number of children looked after by voluntary agreement represented 29 per cent of all final orders granted as at March 1991, 32 per cent in 1992, and 37 per cent in 1993. The CA 1989 has at its heart the principle of partnership. The Act introduced the provision of support services under Part III of the Act.

# Child protection and public authority liability

15.55 Where a local authority fails to protect a child in its care can they be held liable for this failure? The relevance of Art 3 (inhuman and degrading treatment) of the ECHR has been recently tested in cases where violence is directed towards children, thereby establishing the liability of local authorities.

15.56 **Osman v United Kingdom (1999)** has important implications for child protection and suggests that local authorities have a positive obligation to protect the lives of children known to them in accordance with Art 2, the right to life obligation. Art 2 of the ECHR is an inalienable right from which no State can derogate. The European Commission has established that it requires the State not only to refrain from taking life intentionally, but to take appropriate steps to safeguard life (**X v United Kingdom (1979)**). It is in this second aspect—the role of the State in taking appropriate steps to safeguard life—that the effectiveness of public authorities to safeguard the lives of children subject to or under threat of abuse and harm is directly relevant. Any failure to safeguard life on the part of the State, which includes public authorities eg police, emergency services, and prosecutors, may constitute a breach of Art 2.

> The ambit of this duty for the police has been prescribed in *Osman v United Kingdom (1999)*. This case involved a male teacher who was obsessed with a boy pupil. He made persistent threats, committed criminal damage and harassment over a period of time, which culminated in the murder of one person and serious injury of another. The European Court of Human Rights found that none of the incidents leading to the murder of the victim in themselves presented a life-threatening situation, and thus in these particular circumstances there was no infringement of Art 2. However, the Court did examine and consider the scope and meaning of the 'right to life' and established as a general rule that the police have a positive duty to protect the 'right to life' and also have a duty to prevent and suppress offences against the person. This duty was qualified by a requirement on the applicant to prove that the police authority under investigation for potential breach of Art 2 'knew or ought to have known of a real and immediate risk to the life of the person from the criminal acts of another'. The court said:

> *the State's obligation in this respect extends beyond its primary duty to secure the right to life by putting in place effective criminal law provisions to deter the commission of offences against the person, backed up by law-enforcement machinery for the prevention, suppression and sanctioning of breaches of such provisions.... [It] may also imply in certain well-defined circumstances a positive obligation on the authorities to take preventive operational measures to protect an individual whose life is at risk from the criminal acts of another individual.*

> *(at 115)*

> The duty placed upon public authorities to protect life is, however, not absolute but qualified:

> *not every claimed risk to life can entail for the authorities a Convention requirement to take operational measures to prevent that risk from materialising. [I]t must be established to [its] satisfaction that the authorities knew or ought to have known at the time of the existence of a real and immediate risk to the life of an identified individual or individuals from the criminal acts of a third party and that they failed to take measures within the scope of their powers which, judged reasonable, might have been expected to avoid that risk.*

> *(at 116)*

15.57 The *Osman* case has specific implications, especially for police and other public authorities such as emergency services, where harm to children is characterized by repeat victimization, and thus any failure by public authorities to act will inevitably raise the question of how far an authority knew or ought to have known of the risk to the victim. It is worth noting too that the *Osman* case also established that the standard of failure of a public authority to perceive the risk to an individual does not have to come up to that of gross negligence or wilful disregard (see also *R (Plymouth City Council) v HM Coroner for the County of Devon and Secretary of State for Education and Skills (2005)*).

In *D v East Berkshire Community Health NHS Trust and others MAK and another v Dewsbury Healthcare NHS Trust and another RK and another v Oldham NHS Trust and another (2005)*, the House of Lords considered whether a duty of care was owed by healthcare professionals or social workers to parents. The appeals were dismissed. In the words of Lord Nicholls,

*the law has moved on since the decision of your Lordships' House in X (Minors) v Bedfordshire County Council [1995]. There the House held it was not just and equitable to impose a common law duty on local authorities in respect of their performance of their statutory duties to protect children. Later cases, mentioned by my noble and learned friend, Lord Bingham of Cornhill, have shown that this proposition is stated too broadly. Local authorities may owe common law duties to children in the exercise of their child protection duties'. [But in this case he held]:*

*In my view the Court of Appeal reached the right conclusion on the issue arising in the present cases. Ultimately the factor which persuades me that, at common law, interference with family life does not justify according a suspected parent a higher level of protection than other suspected perpetrators is the factor conveniently labelled "conflict of interest". A doctor is obliged to act in the best interests of his patient. In these cases the child is his patient. The doctor is charged with the protection of the child, not with the protection of the parent. The best interests of a child and his parent normally march hand-in-hand. But when considering whether something does not feel "quite right", a doctor must be able to act single-mindedly in the interests of the child. He ought not to have at the back of his mind an awareness that if his doubts about intentional injury or sexual abuse prove unfounded he may be exposed to claims by a distressed parent.*

*Although suspected abusers deserve not to be unjustly accused or suspected of abuse on little evidence, the protection of children remains paramount.*

In *Z v United Kingdom (2001)*, the children were subject to neglect and brought an action against the local author for failure to protect. The neglect included starvation, living in filthy conditions, and sleeping on urine-soaked mattresses. The children scavenged in bins for food, soiled their pants, smeared excrement on the windows of their bedroom and their mattresses were sodden with urine. Despite several meetings with social services over a period and a case conference, no steps were taken to remove the children from their carers. Full care orders were eventually made in 1993, six years after the family were first reported to the social services. The four siblings all lodged a complaint with the European Court of Human Rights invoking Arts 3, 6, 8, and 13 of the ECHR, alleging, *inter alia*, that the local authority had failed to protect them from inhuman and degrading treatment (Art 3), that their respect for family life had been breached (Art 8), that they had been denied access to court (Art 6), and that they had not been afforded any effective remedy for the damage suffered (Art 13). The Official Solicitor, as next friend for the children, commenced proceedings against the local authority claiming damages for negligence and/or breach of statutory duty. The Court held that there was a contravention of Art 3 in that the local authority had failed to protect the applicants from serious long-term neglect and abuse (see also *E and others v United Kingdom (2003)*).

# Human rights and care proceedings

15.58    In care proceedings several human rights issues are raised. And this question is to be considered alongside the human rights issues raised in Chapter 14. Proportionality is an important overriding principle and was so held in *Re W Removal (2005)*, where the court held that the parents must issue a human rights challenge prior to removal not as a reaction to removal. Procedural fairness was considered in *Re J (Care Assessment: Fair Trial) (2006)*. And *Re L (Care Assessments: Fair trial) (2002)* raises the need for parents to be involved, full notes to be taken, parents and the right to make representations and be permitted to attend (Art 6).

With regard to Art 8 rights the following principles have been established. In *Hokkanen v Finland (1995)*, a fair balance had to be struck between the interests of the child remaining in public care and the interests of the parents. In *K and T v Finland (2001)* and *P, C, and S v UK (2002)*, taking newborn babies into care violated Art 8. As Justice Munby in *Bury MBC v D (2009)* articulates:

> 7. It is elementary that under Article 8 of the Convention parents have a right to be fully involved in the planning by public authorities of public authority intervention in the lives of their family and their children, whether before, during or after care proceedings, the emphasis for present circumstances obviously being upon that element of the obligation under Article 8 which arises before the commencement of the proceedings. I need not rehearse the authorities in detail. It suffices to refer to such cases as W v United Kingdom (1988) 10 EHRR 29 at paras [63]–[64], McMichael v United Kingdom (1995) 20 EHRR 205 at para [87] and Re G (Care: Challenge to Local Authority's Decision) [2003] EWHC 551 (Fam), [2003] 2 FLR 42, at paras [30]-[31], [35]-[36].

## FURTHER READING

Bainham A, *Children: The Modern Law* (Family Law, 2005)

Bridge C, 'Case Reports: Family Proceedings' [2010] Fam Law 236

Butler Sloss, *Report of the Inquiry into Child Abuse in Cleveland* (Cm 412, 1988)

Channer Y and Parton N, 'Racism, Cultural Relativism and Child Protection' in *Taking Child Abuse Seriously* (Violence against Children Study Group, Routledge, 1990)

Cobley C, and Sanders T, 'Shaken baby syndrome child protection issues when children sustain a subdural haemorrhage' (2003) 25 Journal of Social Welfare and Family Law 101–19

Department of Health and Social Security, *Review of Child Care Law* (DHSS, 1985), para 5.15

Department of Health, *The Children Act 1989: Guidance and Regulations*, vol 1: *Court Orders* (HMSO, 1991)

Edwards S, *Sex and Gender in the Legal Process* (Blackstone, 1996)

Edwards S, 'The Domestic Violence Crime and Victims Act 2004' (2006) Denning Law Journal 243–260

Eddon G, 'Placing Children with Family members' (2006) Fam Law 36 (949)

Fortin J, 'Significant Harm Revisited' (1998) Journal of Child Law 4 (151)

Freeman MDA, 'Legislating for Child Abuse: the Children Act and Significant Harm' in Levy A, (ed), *Refocus on Child Abuse* (Hawksmere, 1993), 18–41

HMSO, *Child Protection; Messages from Research* (HMSO, 1995)

Lord Laming, *The Victoria Climbie Inquiry Report of Lord Laming* (January 2003)

Poulter S, *Ethnicity, Law and Human Rights: The English Experience* (Oxford University Press, 1998)

Renteln A, 'The Use and Abuse of the Cultural Defense' (2005) 20(1) Canadian Journal of Law and Society 47–67.

Walker A, *The Colour Purple* (Women's Press, 1983, reprinted 1998)

Welbourne P,' Safeguarding children on the edge of care: policy for keeping children safe after the Review of the Child Care Proceedings System, Care Matters and the Carter Review of Legal Aid' [2008] CFLQ 335

## SELF-TEST QUESTIONS

1  Jane Fortin has argued in *Children's Rights and the Developing Law* (2003) at 474, that *'Re H* has created an evidential straight-jacket for local authorities'. If this is true to what extent has the dicta in **Re B (2008)** released its restraint?

2  How useful is Lord Nicholls' formulation in **Re H and R** of the standard of proof and the question of probability in assessing the likelihood of sexual abuse happening in the future in assisting the court in arriving at a threshold finding? Discuss with reference to relevant dicta.

3 What is the burden and standard of proof in cases of physical abuse, sexual abuse, emotional abuse, or neglect? Discuss with reference to past and present case law.

4 Can there ever be one normative standard of parenting below which it must be found that significant harm has occurred or is likely to occur or must each case be looked at on its facts and by taking into account the social and cultural context?

5 How useful is the hypothetical comparator test in establishing whether a child has suffered 'significant harm'? How is it used in deciding such cases?

6 What problems are posed for the determination of care proceedings where experts are in disagreement with regard to causation?

# 16

# Financial provision for children

## SUMMARY

In this chapter we consider the legal mechanisms which ensure the financial support for the child and examine the two systems of financial provision. The responsibility for child support rests with the parents of the child and two systems of financial support have developed over the years in this regard. First, there is the State system of support whereby through the provision of welfare benefits known as 'income support for children' or more recently as child support a child may receive some level of income. However this operates in conjunction, where there is some income, with requiring the absent parent to make his or her financial contribution to the upbringing of a child. Second, parents may negotiate their financial responsibility through the private arrangements made by the courts under the Matrimonial Causes Act—MCA 1973 and the Children Act 1989. However, the enforcement of child payments, that is, making parents pay, through both systems has always been problematic especially where the absent parent—usually the father—defaults and fails to make financial provision. In recent years the enforcement provision has been strengthened.

The first system provides for child support through a State-sponsored agency, the Child Support Agency. In recent times there has been a shift away from State-sponsored support for the child to enforcing parental responsibility even if the level of financial support is nominal only. We consider how far the Child Support Act 1991 and 1995 has obviated the need for parents to go to court to recover child maintenance where the parent with care is reliant on a spouse's/non-resident parent's contribution to maintaining the child in their care, and whether the Child Support Act 1991 and its Agency improved the financial position and financial security of children. We also examine the new provisions under the reformed legislation of the Child Maintenance and Other Payments Act 2008.

Second, we consider the workings of the law relating to private arrangements for child maintenance (Domestic Proceedings and Magistrates' Courts Act 1978, Matrimonial Causes Act 1973, Children Act 1989, s 15 and Sch 1). This pertains in the rather more wealthy arrangements where there is sufficient income to provide more than adequately for the child.

# Child support obligation—sources of law

16.1 There are several sources of law that establish the importance of ensuring financial provision for children of the family.

## UNCRC 1989

16.2 Article 27(4) of the UNCRC 1989 mandates child maintenance and support:

*States Parties shall take all appropriate measures to secure the recovery of maintenance for the child from the parents or other persons having financial responsibility for the child, both within the State Party and from abroad. In particular, where the person having financial responsibility for the child lives in a State different from that of the child, States Parties shall promote the accession to international agreements or the conclusion of such agreements, as well as the making of other appropriate arrangements.*

## The Child Support Act 1991

16.3 With regard to domestic legislation the Child Support Act 1991 (CSA 1991) mandates financial maintenance for children by requiring the biological/ adoptive parents of a child (both the parent with residence and the absent/non-resident parent) to meet their respective responsibilities. It establishes a State mechanism to assist in enforcing that obligation, and in addition it provides a system of penalties for those who fail to comply. This enforcement objective was furthered in the Child Maintenance and Other Payments Act 2008.

### The background to the Child Support Act 1991

16.4 The background to the CSA 1991 is found in the White Paper *'Children Come First'* (1990). The White Paper reported, that many absent fathers made no provision for their families, and it was this failure that the government sought to address. An equally important motivation for the legislation was that the cost to the public purse of child maintenance, that is, State benefit otherwise known as child support or income support, was a cost that the State was no longer prepared to shoulder. The government's objective, therefore, was to transfer, wherever possible, the responsibility of the financial burden of child maintenance, onto the absent or non-resident parent by creating an enforcement mechanism to recover maintenance. Felicity Kaganas, and Christine Piper note that Edwards and Halpern with a 'cynical eye'

> saw [the government move as an] unsuccessful attempt to introduce equality between parents. They maintained that the Children Act 1989, along with the Child Support Act 1991 and the Criminal Justice Act 1991, included provisions designed as mechanisms to restructure thinking on parental responsibility so as to legitimate a reduction in state support for members of the family.

16.5 The cost of child maintenance had certainly grown in the years preceding the CSA 1991 as a result of the increasing number of children dependent on State welfare following the rise in divorce and a rise in one-parent families as a result of women deciding against marriage. Consider, for example, that in 1978, there were 142,726 divorce decrees (absolute), compared with 152,139 in 1988, and 153,689 in 2004, although falling to 142,393 in 2005 and 133,157 in 2006. The number of children of divorcing parents also marginally fell due to the reduction in number of children in the contemporary family, numbering some 159,403 in 1981, decreasing to 150,129 in 1998, and in 2003 there were 153,500 children under 16 years of divorcing parents. The Office of Population and Census Surveys reported that, in 1989, 27 per cent of children born were born to unmarried mothers, whereas in 2002, 40 per cent of births were outside marriage (see *Married or Not*).

## Recovery of maintenance prior to the Child Support Act 1991

16.6 Research conducted by Edwards and Halpern (1990) during the period immediately prior to the CSA 1991 discovered that, even in those cases where a maintenance order was made by the courts in favour of a dependent child, the financial reality of those orders was that many were made for nominal sums of as little as £1 per year. The nominal order was put in place to ensure that whilst the absent parent had no resources to provide for his child at the time of making the order, it allowed for a reconsideration of the order at a later date should the absent parents circumstances improve. They found that 'only 26.5 per cent of dependent children under 16, and only 18 per cent of children under 18 and over 16 receive an order for maintenance' (1990, 75).

They also found that 50 per cent of all orders made actually went unpaid. Significantly, 61 per cent of non-payers cleared their arrears once enforcement proceedings were commenced, whilst in the remaining 39 per cent of cases, orders could not be enforced because there were obvious financial difficulties or the ex-spouse was untraceable. Edwards and Halpern pioneered important research in this field exposing the ineffectiveness of the pre-1991 system of child maintenance (see Edwards and Halpern (1990) and Edwards, Halpern and Gould (1991)).

### Duty to maintain: Child Support Act 1991

16.7 CSA 1991, s 1(1) provides that 'each parent of a qualifying child is responsible for maintaining him'. Section 1(2) states:

> *a non-resident parent shall be taken to have met his responsibility to maintain any qualifying child of his by making periodical payments of maintenance with respect to the child of such amount, and at such intervals, as may be determined in accordance with the provisions of this Act.*

A resident parent is the parent with care (the natural or adoptive parent or person who in accordance with the Human Fertilisation and Embryology Act 1990, s 30 becomes the parent) Human Fertilisation and Embryology Act 1990 2006. The non-resident parent is the parent who does not have the day-to-day care of the child (CSA 1991, s 3(2)). A 'qualifying child' for the purpose of the CSA 1991 is a child where one or both of the biological parents are absent parents (s 3(1)). A child is a person under 16 years or else under 19 years if in full-time education (see Child and Boden (1996) for an interesting discussion).

16.8 Wikeley (2006) criticizes the primacy accorded to the genetic link between parent and child—'qualifying child'—at the heart of the duty to maintain embodied in the CSA 1991. He argues that the CSA's insistence on genetic parentage reflects in an 'atavistic way' the concerns of the nineteenth century Poor Laws and the Bastardy Laws. He contends that the genetic link between parent and child actually no longer fits into the reality of parenthood in the contemporary family. In furthering this argument he cites the way in which the genetic link argument is flawed in that it ignores scientific advances with regard to IVF, and that private law arrangements for financial provision of children under the Matrimonial Causes Act 1984, s 25 have already made provision for step-children and other children of the family to be maintained by a non-biologically related parent, which suggests that the new State law has not kept abreast with the social reality of children within a family.

16.9 One might ask whether the Child Maintenance and Other Payments Act 2008 (see later) has solved this conflict of legal approach with the social reality. It states,

> *for s 55 of the Child Support Act 1991 (c. 48) substitute—'55 Meaning of 'child' (1) In this Act, 'child' means (subject to subsection (2)) a person who a) has not attained the age of 16, or b) has not attained the age of 20 and satisfies such conditions as may be prescribed.*

But note that even the reformed legislation still fails to accommodate the social reality of family life as this section is merely to be read alongside s 1(1) of the CSA 1991 which underscores the role of biological/adoptive parents.

### The Common law duty to maintain—Biological fathers

16.10 Despite its shortcomings the CSA 1991, for the first time, placed the responsibility to maintain the child on both biological parents regardless of their marital status. In this regard it strove to bring about equality between both biological parents with regard to their duty to maintain the child regardless of their marital status, whether married, or unmarried, separated, divorced, living together, or living apart. This was not the situation at common law, and it is worth spending some time reflecting on that position. At common law, the legal duty to maintain was placed on the biological father to maintain only his legitimate children (children born within marriage) and on the mother to maintain her illegitimate children (children born outside marriage). Of course, in reality mothers were left to financially fend for both illegitimate and legitimate children in the event of separation.

16.11 The Matrimonial Causes Act 1857, s 35 provided that on dissolution of marriage, the court could make an order against the father as it deemed just and proper with respect to the 'custody, maintenance and education' of children.

> In *Thomasset v Thomasset (1894)*, the court affirmed that it had the power to make orders in respect of the custody, maintenance, and education of children during the whole period of their infancy until they attained the age of 21 years.

> In *Leadbeater v Leadbeater (1985)*, in a complex marital breakdown where the wife had applied for maintenance from her second husband for her children from a former marriage the court held that the maintenance of the wife's two children was the primary obligation of their natural father.

*Exceptional circumstances—the mother*

16.12 However, the court, in certain circumstances, might require a wife to make financial provision for a child or even a husband.

> In *March v March and Palumbo (1861–1873)*, the court made an order for the benefit of both a child of the marriage and the husband. On the dissolution of a marriage, following the wife's adultery, the court made an order directing the trustees of a marriage settlement to pay to the husband £200 pounds per year for the maintenance and education of the child of the marriage.

> In *Moy v Moy and White (1961)* following divorce from the wife the husband, applied for an order under the Matrimonial Causes Act 1950, s 24 (1) that a settlement should be made of a part of the wife's property for the benefit of the child of the marriage. A settlement of £8,000 (i.e. a quarter) of the wife's property would be ordered to be made for the primary benefit of the child of the marriage.

*The illegitimate child*

16.13 Where the child was illegitimate (the parents being unmarried), it remained the mother's responsibility to financially provide for the child, although a mother could try to pursue the biological father through the courts to try and recover child maintenance regardless of the legitimacy of the child. Women, throughout history, have been presented with the unenviable choice of pursuing fathers for child maintenance through the courts, both for their legitimate and illegitimate children, or else face destitution and poverty. For mothers, so destitute, their only recourse, until the last century, was to subject themselves to the mercy of the parish which meant that they would have to go into an adult workhouse (essentially no more than a shelter) and be separated from their children, who would be cared for in a workhouse for children. In both, conditions of life were subsistence. From 1733, the Bastardy Act ordered that fathers of illegitimate children should be committed to jail unless they made arrangements to indemnify the parish (who were responsible for the so called workhouses) for the upkeep of their child. In 1871, the Bastardy Laws (Amendment) Act gave the mother of an illegitimate child the right to apply to a court for a maintenance order against the father of the child.

> In *Ward v Byham (1956)*, the unmarried cohabiting biological parents of a child separated. Denning LJ reaffirmed the respective legal position of the biological parents, where the mother brought a claim for the sum of £1 a week in respect of the maintenance of her illegitimate child: 'By statute the mother of an illegitimate child was bound to maintain it, whereas the father is under no such obligation' (see National Assistance Act 1948, s 42).

16.14 It was against this background of nominal orders and non-payment that the CSA 1991 was enacted and the Child Support Agency (CS Agency) (the mechanism for collection and enforcement of child payment) was established. As Bird (1996, 1) writes:

> *Before 1990, the idea that the courts were not the appropriate forum for decisions as in child maintenance when the parents could not agree would have seemed foreign to most lawyers...maintenance of children was regarded as a branch of family law which naturally fell within the jurisdiction of the courts, and there were few who thought that it should be removed into some free-standing system. Nevertheless, this is what the 1991 Act attempted to achieve.*

## Who is a child of the family?—Child Support Act 1991

16.15 As monogamous marriage provided the legal template for marriage, it was not only the child of an unmarried couple that the law refused to recognize and thereby protect with regard to maintenance, but also a child of a polygamous (and presumably bigamous) union was not recognized.

16.16 Under the Child Support Act 1991:

> 3.—(1) A child is a 'qualifying child' if—
>
> > (a) one of his parents is, in relation to him, an absent parent [3a non-resident parent]; or

(b) *both of his parents are, in relation to him, absent parents [3non-resident parents].*

(2) *The parent of any child is [6 a 'non-resident parent'], in relation to him, if–*

(a) *that parent is not living in the same household with the child; and*

(b) *the child has his home with a person who is, in relation to him, a person with care.*

(3) *A person is a 'person with care', in relation to any child, if he is a person–*

(a) *with whom the child has his home;*

(b) *who usually provides day to day care for the child (whether exclusively or in conjunction with any other person); and*

(c) *who does not fall within a prescribed category of person.*

(4) *The Secretary of State shall not, under subsection (3)(c), prescribe as a category–*

(a) *parents;*

(b) *guardians;*

(c) *persons in whose favour residence orders under section 8 of the Children Act 1989 are in force;*

(d) *in Scotland, persons having the right of custody of a child.*

(5) *For the purposes of this Act there may be more than one person with care in relation to the same qualifying child.*

(6) *Periodical payments which are required to be paid in accordance with a maintenance assessment [1maintenance calculation] are referred to in this Act as 'child support maintenance'.*

## What of children of the polygamous union?

16.17 Fathers who entered into a polygamous marriage, as in the case of *Sowa v Sowa (1961)* were not under an obligation to maintain even if the family was domiciled in the UK, demonstrating that the validity of the marriage union under UK law was placed above biological paternity in the duty to maintain the children. In this case, the parties were both Ghanayan, and domiciled in Ghana. They were both members of the tribe of Ga. In September 1955, the husband became engaged to the wife in Ghana; in October, the husband left Ghana to come to England and in November, a marriage by proxy, according to the customs of the tribe of Ga, was performed; it was a valid marriage contracted in Ghana. In January 1956, the wife came to England and lived with the husband in Liverpool. Two years later she left him. She made a complaint to the magistrates' court that her husband had deserted her, the complaint was found proved, and she was granted the custody of the child and the husband ordered to pay £4 10s a week for the wife and 30s a week for the child. The husband appealed against that order. The court allowed the appeal and set aside the order, as it had no jurisdiction with regard to what was not a lawful marriage.

16.18 However that position changed with Child Support, SI 1992/1815 where 'family' is defined as—

> (a) a married or unmarried couple (including the members of a polygamous marriage) and any child or children living with them for whom at least one member of that couple has day to day care...

It is generally thought there are fewer than 1,000 legally recognised polygamous marriages within the UK.

Polygamous marriages which take place in another country may be recognised as being valid. In a written answer on 23 April 2008, Lord Hunt of Kings Heath, then Parliamentary Under-Secretary of State at the Ministry of Justice, said:

> For a polygamous marriage to be considered valid in the UK, the parties must be domiciled in a country where polygamous marriage is permitted, and must have entered into the marriage in that country. Provided the parties follow the necessary requirements under the law of the country in question, the marriage would be recognised in England and Wales. The law is drafted thus because the Government have no desire forcibly to sever relationships that have been lawfully contracted in other jurisdictions. This should not, however, be construed as government approval of polygamous marriage. The Government do not support polygamous marriage and support the law that prohibits parties from contracting polygamous marriages in this jurisdiction.

> It is also 'possible to apply for maintenance for any children under the facilities available for the provision of maintenance through the Child Maintenance and Enforcement Commission (CMEC). It is also possible for a parent, or special guardian of a child, to apply to court under Schedule 1 of the Children Act 1989 for an order requiring one or both parents of a child to make payments or transfer property for the benefit of a child...A former partner from a polygamous relationship can apply for maintenance for any children from the polygamous relationship involved under the Child Support Acts and capital provision for the benefit of children may be sought under Schedule 1 of the Children Act 1989 following a breakdown in the relationship'. (See Polygamy Standard Note SN/HA/5051 23 June 2009 Catherine Fairbairn Home Affairs Section, http://www.parliament.uk/briefingpapers/commons/lib/research/briefings/snha-05051.pdf accessed 26 October 2010)

### What of children of the civil partnership union?

16.19 And following the Civil Partnership Act 2005, a 'child of the family' will be a child within a civil partnership family. As Bamforth writes:

> The meaning of 'family life' was addressed in Secretary of State for Work and Pensions v M, which concerned the basis on which child maintenance payments were calculated under the Child Support Act 1991 and accompanying secondary legislation. The claimant argued that a parent who now lived with a same-sex partner was assessed less generously than a parent who lived with an opposite-sex partner, and that this difference fell foul of Article 14 coupled with the 'family life' limb of Article 8. Since the majority judgments placed considerable weight on the Strasbourg 'margin of appreciation' and four of the five judgments differed about how the Strasbourg Court

*would now interpret 'family life', the decision offers an ambiguous, but probably dis-*
*couraging, message to those concerned to challenge the marriage/civil partnership*
*distinction. Turning first to the ambit of 'family life', Lord Nicholls was confident that*
*the Estevez exclusion of same-sex couples from this limb of Article 8 still applied,*
*and asserted that since signatory States enjoyed a wide margin of appreciation in*
*this area, '[f]or the time being the respect accorded' to same-sex relationships was a*
*matter for them. Article 14 was thus not engaged. Lord Mance also invoked Estevez*
*and the wide 'margin', but was far less categorical in that he linked the existence of*
*the wide 'margin' to the time period 'very shortly before the period relevant to the*
*present appeal'. While the claimant's same-sex relationship did not fall within the*
*ambit of family life at that time, Lord Mance had 'little doubt' that were a similar ques-*
*tion to arise based on contemporary circumstances, it 'could well be regarded, in*
*both Strasbourg and the United Kingdom, as involving family life for the purposes of*
*[A]rticle 8. at para [152].*

## Child Support Act 1991—maintaining the child, working together with State support

16.20   Where a child is born to a married or unmarried couple, and the resident parent (usually the mother) is without independent means of support and is in need
of income support both for herself and for the child, before the State will assist
the resident parent with financial support for the child, the resident parent must
apply to the Child Support Agency under the CSA 1991, s 4(1) for a maintenance
assessment. This is an assessment based on the needs of the child and the respective incomes of the parties. The qualifying child, the non-resident parent, or the
parent with care, may apply. Usually, it is the mother who is in receipt of income
support/family credit who applies for a maintenance assessment. The applicant for a
maintenance assessment is required to provide all the necessary information to the
Secretary of State. This includes financial information as well as naming the father,
so as to enable the CS Agency to trace the non-resident (absent) parent—indeed,
naming the non-resident parent is a precondition of receiving benefit.

16.21   CSA 1991, s 6(1)(b) requires the parent of a qualifying child to authorize the
Secretary of State to take action to recover child maintenance via the CS Agency.
Under s 6(10), this obligation to disclose the name and details of the non-resident
parent may be waived by statutory instrument in certain prescribed circumstances
(discussed below). This section is now repealed under the Child Maintenance and
Other Payments Act 2008.

16.22   The procedure for obtaining payment from the non-resident parent is outlined
in *Secretary of State for Social Security v Harmon; Same v Carter; Same v Cocks*
*(1999)*:

*Once an effective application for child support maintenance has been made, the pro-
cedure is for the Secretary of State to give notice of the application to the absent
parent and send him a maintenance inquiry form. The absent parent is required
to complete the form and return it to the Secretary of State. If he does so within
4 weeks, the effective date (which is the date from which his liability, if any, to pay child
support maintenance runs) is 8 weeks after the receipt of the maintenance inquiry
form. If he fails to complete and return the form within the 4 weeks, then the effective
date is the date on which he received the form. Thus he has an incentive to complete
and return the form within the time limited, since this delays the date from which he
can be required to pay child support maintenance.*

# Whose child is it anyway? Paternity

16.23    Under the CSA 1991 only the biological parents have a duty to maintain the child.
Determining who is the natural or biological father often requires proof of paternity, as absent fathers may dispute paternity. It has not been possible until recently,
with scientific advances, to establish paternity with any degree of certainty. The
motivation to establish or disavow the genetic link with a child, for the purpose
of the CSA 1991 at least, has been a financial one. For the resident parent in need
of financial support from the non-resident parent establishing paternity is crucial,
whilst for the person names as the father by the resident parent a blood test which
disproves paternity is the only way in which financial responsibility can be avoided.
Wikeley (2006) examines the centrality that paternity testing has had, not on
parental responsibility, nor parenthood, but on the legal obligation to pay for the
child. Wikeley shows that, for example, 200,000 cases each year involve a denial
of paternity. Of those 20,000 are subject to testing and in 2,000 cases the denial of
paternity is upheld (2001 figures).

16.24    Under CSA 1991, s 27, an application can be made for declaration of paternity.
'Paternity suits', as they are often called, have become of enormous public interest,
especially where celebrities are involved, where so often their denials of paternity
are exposed as lies by the unassailable truth of DNA findings.

## Test to be applied in blood testing orders

16.25    The test to be applied when the court is considering whether to make a blood testing order is that of 'best interests of the child' and not the 'welfare of the child as
paramount'. In the past, however, the court would not order a paternity test unless
it was solely for the child's benefit.

So in *H v H (1966)*, the court held that, assuming that there is power in the court to order
a child to submit to a blood test when such a course seems to be likely to be to the

advantage of the child, or possibly when it is necessary for the determination of some issue properly before the court where the child's interest is paramount (though the court would probably require a prima facie case for doubting paternity to be established before taking such a course), a child will not be ordered to submit to a blood test where to do so would not be in any way to the advantage of the child, as where the avowed purpose is to provide an argument for the mitigation of the husband's liability to maintain the child or the child's mother.

In *Re L (An Infant) (1968)*, the wife, husband, and third party cited wished to know who was the child's natural father. They were willing to undergo blood tests and also wished for the child's blood to be tested. The Official Solicitor, as guardian ad item of the child, refused consent to the child's blood being tested. Ormrod J made an order directing the Official Solicitor to arrange for the child to be blood-grouped, subject to the wife, husband and other party cited first submitting themselves to be blood-grouped. This decision was upheld on appeal.

In *Re T (A Child) (DNA Tests: Paternity) (2001)*, a child was looked after by the mother. The mother and husband were unable to conceive and so the mother had sexual relations with the applicant and other men in order to become pregnant. The applicant sought blood and DNA tests to determine the paternity of the child. The mother refused her consent to the tests. The court held that for the purposes of an application for blood tests in respect of a child, the relevant test was not the welfare of the child as paramount; the relevant test was what was in the best interests of the child. The court held that it was important to consider the interests of the child as well as the interests of the adult parties, since competing human rights principles were at stake as between Art 8, the right to family life, and the right to know one's genetic family, and the rights of the child.

In *Re L (Family Proceedings Court) (Appeal: Jurisdiction) (2005)*, the mother divorced and applied to the CS Agency for a child support maintenance assessment. The husband accepted that he was the father and made payments for two years. He later said that he thought he was not the father, although the mother said that he was the child's father. The court made a declaration of non-parentage under FLA 1986, s 55A(1).

In this case, the child herself wanted to resolve the issue of who was her genetic father and applied for permission to appeal the declaration out of time, alleging breaches of her rights under Art 6 (right to fair trial) and Art 8 (family life and knowledge) of the ECHR. The court allowed the appeal and set aside the order of the Family Proceedings Court, transferring the child's proposed s 55A proceedings to the county court and giving directions in respect of DNA tests.

The 'best interests' test displaces the 'welfare paramount' test because of the human rights issues around paternity, including the competing rights of parents and putative parents to know the genetic origins of the children for whom they are responsible or about whom they wish to know, and the right of the child to know his or her genetic heritage.

## Presumption of paternity

16.26 Since the introduction of the Child Support, Pensions and Social Security Act 2000 (CSPSSA 2000), s 15, the CSA may now automatically assume the non-resident parent to be the father of a child if, 'he was married to the mother at some stage between conception and birth; he is registered as the father; or he refuses to take scientific (for example DNA) tests' (s 83, making insertions into Part III of the Family Law Act 1986). All three conditions are contentious and paternity cannot be presumed. First, being married to the mother between conception and birth no longer leads to a foregone conclusion that the husband is the father. Second, whilst registration on the birth certificate is probably the most reliable it is not a certainty of paternity. Third, a refusal to take a scientific test may in fact indicate that the person so refusing is not the biological father but there may also be reasons why a biological father might refuse. Where a non-biological father refuses to take a blood test, it may be that he wishes to continue acting in the capacity of father and in the belief that he is the father which may indeed be in the best interests of the child in his care and the family.

## Damages for deceit

16.27   In *P v B (Paternity: Damages for Deceit) (2001)*, the matter before the court was whether there was an action in tort for damages where a mother had deceived a man into believing that he was the father of the child. It had been determined that the man was not the father of the child. The court held that the tort of deceit applied as between a cohabiting couple. The claim for damages could proceed to trial, although the court warned that it did not follow from this that any of the special damages claimed for, *inter alia*, payments made by him in respect of a child amounting to some £90,000 were recoverable, even if liability was established.

In *A v B (2007)*, where a mother made fraudulent representations that the claimant was the child's father and where the claimant had provided financial support for the mother and the child the court held that the claimant was entitled to general damages and special damages for money spent on the mother but not for money that benefited the child.

### Whose child is it?—non-paternity issues

16.28    In *T v B* (2010), the respondent—a female—had lived with the female applicant but not in a legal civil partnership. The applicant became pregnant by artificial insemination after a joint application by the parties in 2000 a child was born. The question arose whether the respondent was a parent under Sch 1 of the Children Act 1989 so that the court had jurisdiction to make an order against her for financial relief. The court conducted that while the respondent was a parent of the child as identified in *Re G (2006)* (namely as a social and psychological parent) it was held that the word 'parent' in Sch 1 means legal parent and that it is for the legislature to determine who should be liable to financial claims for the benefit of children and the extent to which it includes those who are not the legal parents of children but are either to be treated as parents or are otherwise to be made liable.

# Enforcing maintenance requirement and non-disclosure

16.29 As noted, under the CSA 1991 women were required to disclose information regarding the non-resident parent. Many women, for a variety of understandable reasons, do not want to set a process in motion that will lead to the tracing of the whereabouts of the absent/non-resident biological father. Some women never had a relationship with the non-resident father where the child was conceived following a 'one night stand' or a brief encounter. Other women may not wish to disclose such details because they are the victims of domestic violence or sexual abuse and fear that the non-resident father in discovering their whereabouts will further harass, intimidate and threaten violence or commit violence. Under the 1991 Act it was the case that if they refused they would have imposed a reduced benefit direction. This notorious s 46 has now been repealed in the Child Maintenance and Other Payments Act 2008.

16.30 Formerly however, CSA 1991, s 46(3) gave authorization for the disclosure requirement to be waived if there were 'reasonable grounds' for believing that compliance would lead to a risk to the claimant or the child. In consideration of this, the CS Agency officer was required to consider the welfare of the child under s 2:

> *whether, having regard to any reasons given by the parent, there are reasonable grounds for believing that, if she were to be required to comply, there would be a risk of her or any children living with her suffering harm or undue distress as a result of complying.*

If there were no such 'reasonable grounds', penalties could be imposed on women who refused to name the non-resident father. Such penalties were in the form of a reduced benefit direction under s 46(5) in accordance with a direction binding on the adjudication officer in s 46(10)(b) which stated:

> *that the amount payable by way of any relevant benefit to, or in respect of, the parent concerned be reduced by such amount, and for such a period, as may be prescribed.*

A reduced benefit direction had the effect of reducing by an amount equal to 40 per cent of the personal allowance, the income support/job seekers allowance otherwise payable to the parent with care.

## Refusing to name: what constituted reasonable grounds?

16.31 What has amounted to reasonable grounds, and what has the CS Agency considered to constitute harm and undue distress? Bird in 1996 was correct when he predicted that the following situations would justify the child support assessment officer in deciding not to proceed with a reduced benefit direction:

(a)  the parent has been the victim of rape;

(b)  the absent parent has sexually assaulted the child living in the household of the parent with care;

(c)  the child was conceived as a result of incest;

(d)  the absent parent is a celebrity and unwelcome publicity might result which would be adverse to the welfare of the parent and child (*Re Z (1996)*).

## Blood test refusal penalties

16.32 Penalties were also imposed on women who refused to consent to undergo the blood test to establish paternity. CSA 1991, s 46(1)(c) provided for a reduced benefit direction where a woman, 'having been treated as having applied for a maintenance calculation under section 6, refuses to take a scientific test within the meaning of section 27(A)'. However, as with disclosure of the whereabouts of the non-resident parent, if there are reasonable grounds for believing that if she took the test, 'there would be a risk of her, or any children living with her, suffering harm or undue distress as a result of his taking such action, or her complying or taking the test', then a reduced benefit direction may not be imposed (s 46(3)(c)).

## Enforcement: reduced benefit directions

16.33 Decisions of Social Security Commissioners indicated that the child support officer must consider the mother's reasons for refusing to divulge the father's identity very carefully before making a reduced benefit direction. CSA 1991, s 2 requires the child support officer to 'have regard to the welfare of any child likely to be affected by his decision'.

16.34 As stated above one of the most controversial aspects of the legislation was the requirement that the resident parent must disclose details of the non-resident parent as a condition of receiving benefit and s 46 provided that, in certain circumstances, the resident parent would not be denied child support if she refused to make such a disclosure. In the first three years of the operation of the CSA 1991 'good cause' for non-disclosure was an issue in 15 per cent of cases, disclosure exemptions were approved in 110,000 cases and in 50,000 cases reduced benefit directions were imposed. Statistics produced by One Parent Families—Scotland showed that, up to August 1995, nearly 90,000 single mothers were exempted and an estimated 20,000 to 30,000 reduced benefit penalties were imposed. Reduced benefit directions data was also requested more recently by Earl Russell (3 April 2000, col WA135, 1996) in response to a question tabled in the House of Lords. Earl Russell also asked the government:

> *What is the incidence among parents with care, who have been subject to a reduced benefit direction, of (a) theft; (b) prostitution; (c) serious illness; and (d) disappearance from government records, and what proportion of parents with care who have been subject to a reduced benefit direction, and have subsequently agreed to co-operate, have been victims of domestic violence?*

The information he requested was not available but the nature of the question of itself clearly reflects a concern that denial of full benefit imposes such economic hardship that those subject to it may be propelled into crime and also that a major disincentive to cooperation is the experience of domestic violence.

The Child Support Agency Standards Committee, Annual Report, 2003/2004 Executive Summary para 2.1 states:

> *In line with last year's exercise, 100 cases were randomly selected and monitored from decisions made by Jobcentre Plus, between the 4th February and the 26th May 2003...the Monitoring and Guidance Unit examined 50 cases where Good Cause was accepted and 50 cases where a Reduced Benefit Direction Decision was imposed. From 3rd March 2003, a further consideration for the Good Cause Decision-Maker to consider is whether a Good Cause Decision should be reviewed. Section 46 of the Child Support Act 1991 (as amended by the Child Support, Pensions and Social Security Act 2000), provides that Good Cause Decision-Makers set a date in the future to reconsider the Good Cause decision. Physical abuse was the reason in the majority of cases, although many cases were a combination of physical, verbal and emotional abuse.*

(See also *Secretary of State for Work and Pensions v Roach (2006)*.)

16.35 The result of the unsatisfactory situation pertaining above is that the Child Maintenance and Other Payments Bill 2006 (Child Maintenance and Other Payments Act 2008) repeals s 46—reduced benefit direction.

## Parental responsibility as a 'trade-off'

16.36 Absent fathers who have been pursued for maintenance and have made maintenance payments for the upkeep of their children have regarded contact as a right which follows automatically. But making maintenance payments and fulfilling the statutory obligation to maintain does not grant the payer any automatic entitlement to parental responsibility rights as, for example, access to or contact with the child concerned.

> In *R v Halifax Justices ex parte Woolverton (1981)*, the husband fell into arrears with maintenance payments; the husband sought to get the arrears remitted because obstacles were put in his way by the wife with regard to access. The court held that it was wrong to order remission of arrears of child maintenance as a penalty to the wife for failing to allow access.

At the same time where a father does not pay child support this does not automatically disqualify him from parental responsibility rights/duties or access/contact with the child (*Re H (Parental Responsibility: Maintenance) (1996)*).

16.37 In addition, there is a further issue with regard to the maintenance requirement where, for example, the child is staying with the non-resident parent and the non-resident parent is paying maintenance for the child with regard to the time spent and the deduction of the maintenance payment. The Court of Appeal, in *Re B (Contact: Child Support) (2006)*, decided this vexed and ongoing question.

> The parents had one daughter aged 11 who lived with her mother after the relationship broke down. There was ongoing contact litigation between the parties with regard to exactly how much contact the father should have. The daughter expressed her wish to have less contact time with the father and in March 2006 the court reduced that to 93 nights per year. The father saw this reduced staying contact as an attempt to increase the father's child support liability and in effect the father received no discount on his child support liability for the staying contact of 93 days annually. If the father had been assessed under the new scheme he would have received some recognition for the staying contact. As this case was decided under the old scheme staying contact results in a reduction in child support liability where there is staying contact for at least 104 nights a year, whereas under the new scheme it is 52 nights.

Mummery and Wilson LJJ, held that the level—quantum—of child support liability was not a relevant factor in determining the amount—time—of appropriate contact (see Gilmore (2007) for+ further discussion on this case).

# How much is a child worth?
# The maintenance formula

16.38 The CSPSSA 2000 has introduced a simplified formula for maintenance assessment based on three considerations: first, the non-resident carer's income, secondly, the number of children in the family, and thirdly whether they live in a household with other children. The basic rate of child maintenance is assessed as a percentage of the non-resident parent's net income of at least £200: 15 per cent for one child, 20 per cent for two, and 25 per cent for three or more children with a reduced rate for those who earn less that £200. The CSPSSA 2000 also introduced the option of making a driving disqualification order. However Pirrie (2002) warns:

> Unfortunately, the new CSPSSA 2000 does not produce a new and comprehensive scheme. Instead, it is an Act that amends the 1991 Act so that it is really 'the 1991 Act as amended' that remains the framework for the legislation.

> *(at 196)*

Wikeley (2006) analyses the early years of the CS Agency, together with the need to make changes to the formula for assessment and modifications to the formulae. These included: a reduction in the carer component of the maintenance requirement, adjustments to the protected income formulae, adjustments in the formula to accommodate the costs of high travel to work, a broad brush approach to take account of capital and property settlements, full allowance in exempt income for the housing costs of new partners and stepchildren, followed by departure directions.

This formula is further simplified by the Child Maintenance and Other Payments Act 2008 s 16.

# Evaluation of the Child Support Act 1991

16.39 How far and to what extent has the post-CSA 1991 situation addressed these criticisms and resolved these problems? Has it taken children out of poverty? Halpern, Edwards, and Gould (1990) write:

> We believe that it makes little sense to make orders for financial support which are unlikely to be paid or which are paid with considerable difficulty... A clear social policy which seeks to address the poor economic position of women on divorce, guided by the recognition that it is the product of their position within the family and the social

*structure, would do more to alleviate the problems of divorced mothers and children than anything else. Social policy could now recognise that the best way to protect children of the divorced is not to force mothers to remain at home caring for children whilst reliant on a mixture of state support, maintenance and part time earnings, but to actively encourage mothers into employment.*

16.40 Has the CSA 1991 put children first, or is there evidence that it has put the tax-payer first? The Act and its Schedules have been criticized for not being intelligible. In *Re C (1994)* the court said:

> The Child Support Act 1991 provides that, each parent of a qualifying child is respon-sible for maintaining him at a rate fixed by mathematically obtuse calculations in innu-merable unintelligible Schedules.

The new Act of 2008 proposes a more simplified formula.

16.41 Is the enforcement mechanism effective? During 1993, 5,954 applications to have maintenance orders registered in magistrates' courts were granted in county courts, 24 per cent less than in 1992. In addition, 2,782 attachment of earnings orders were made compared with 2,553 in 1992. Bird had this to say (1996, 2):

> More significantly, a series of both official and independent reports began to highlight serious deficiencies in the performance of the Child Support Agency, and hardships, which resulted from the rigid interpretation of the formulae. A pattern emerged of critical Select Committee Reports every Autumn, followed by amended Regulations the following Spring. The Child Support Agency failed to meet its performance targets for 1993/94, the Select Committee Report published in November 1994 was highly critical; the Ombudsman Report revealed serious misadministration.

16.42 Where all else fails with regard to retrieval of maintenance, the non-payer may be committed to prison for contempt, the CS Agency having enhanced enforcement powers. In 2005, there were 640 applications made for attachments of earnings orders on maintenance orders and 623 orders made compared with 156 in 2000, whilst 1,033 maintenance orders in the magistrate's courts were registered, com-pared with 1,070 so registered in 2000.

16.43 The CSPSSA 2000, s 17 amends CSA 1991, s 39(a) and provides for driving disqualification:

> (2) An application under this section is for whichever the court considers appro-priate in all the circumstances of—
>
> (a) the issue of a warrant committing the liable person to prison; or
>
> (b) an order for him to be disqualified from holding or obtaining a driving licence.
>
> (3) On any such application the court shall (in the presence of the liable person) inquire as to—
>
> (a) whether he needs a driving licence to earn his living;

> *(b) his means; and*
>
> *(c) whether there has been wilful refusal or culpable neglect on his part.*
>
> *(4) The Secretary of State may make representations to the court as to whether he thinks it more appropriate to commit the liable person to prison or to disqualify him from holding or obtaining a driving licence; and the liable person may reply to those representations.*

The controversial disqualification from driving as the ultimate sanction for those in arrears, or for failing to pay on the basis of 'wilful refusal or culpable neglect' has been a sanction rarely imposed by the courts. Wikeley (2006) writes that in first five years since the bringing into force of the CSPSSA 2000, as few as 11 driving licences were removed and 63 suspended disqualification orders were made. Nonetheless, the threat of the sanction may have acted as a Draconian sword of Damocles.

## The Child Support Agency fiasco

16.44 On 9 September 2005, Frank Field announced that the CS Agency was in meltdown. Despite the avowed objective of the CSA 1991 of 'children come first', the new system has not been able to deliver a service to children: there are substantial delays with the delay in forwarding cash to single parents lengthening from an average 12 to 15 weeks in 2003 to an estimated 15 to 22 weeks in 2004; children remain in poverty: only 61,000 of the 478,000 parents who had applied for support since the introduction of the computer system in 2002 (supposedly to improve the efficiency of the CS Agency) had received any money at all 18 months later in 2004. In fact, it would seem that the CSA 1991 has made matters worse for children.

> Jane Fortin writes:
>
> *The irony is that, for many children in families dependent on income support, the intervention of the Child Support Agency has made their life worse. In some cases, intervention of the agency has exacerbated the relationship of their parents and rendered their fathers less ready to visit them.*
>
> *(at 244)*

## Human rights and child support under the 1991 Act

16.45 The total disarray and fiasco of the CSA 1991 and the CS Agency, not surprisingly, resulted in an application, amongst others, by a mother testing whether in fact the CSA 1991 was human rights compliant, since she was excluded from access to the court in her efforts over a long period to get the non-resident parent to pay what he owed, that is to effect the order made in favour of the child in her care.

> In *R (Kehoe) v Secretary of State for Work and Pensions (2004)*, the mother sought a declaration that the provisions of the CSA 1991 were incompatible with Art 6 of the ECHR because they had the effect of denying a parent access to court in connection with disputes as to whether the non-resident parent had paid or ought to pay the sums due under a maintenance assessment, or as to the manner in which the maintenance assessment should be enforced. She sought a further declaration that delay on the part of the CS Agency constituted a breach of her Art 6 rights, and claimed damages under the Human Rights Act 1998, s 7. The Secretary of State appealed against the judge's finding that the mother's inability personally to enforce arrears of maintenance engaged her Art 6 rights. The mother cross-appealed against the judge's conclusion that the scheme under the CSA 1991 was compliant with Art 6 of the ECHR. The court allowed the Secretary of State's appeal, dismissing the mother's cross-appeal (see Wikeley (1995) for a detailed discussion of this decision).

16.46 Wikeley (2006) concludes that children have a right to child support and that it is incumbent on the government, as expressed in Treaty obligations, to develop a system that is effective. He argues, too, that higher child support liabilities have a beneficial effect not just on children's material well being but on their 'post separation cognitive development' (p 473). Children's material and psychological well-being depends upon an adequate and effective system of financial provision.

> In *Rowley v Secretary of State for Work and Pensions (2007)*, the mother made an application to the CS Agency for child maintenance for her three children from their non-resident father under CSA 1991, s 4. The mother and the children claimed that the CS Agency (i) delayed in carrying out the maintenance assessment; (ii) obtained inadequate information on which to base the assessment; (iii) made interim and final assessments that were wrong; (iv) delayed in enforcing the assessments; and (v) delayed in dealing with the claimants' appeal against the assessment. They claimed damages in negligence in respect of these failings. The claim was originally struck out on the basis that a common law duty of care owed to the claimants by the Secretary of State would be inconsistent with the statutory scheme created by the CSA 1991. The claimants appealed.
>
> The question of law was whether or not the Secretary of State owed a duty of care to the claimants. The claimants argued that when the CS Agency responds to an application under the statutory scheme there is an assumption of responsibility by the Secretary of State sufficient to give rise to a duty of care.
>
> The appeals were dismissed.
>
> The court held that there was no common law duty of care owed by the Secretary of State to avoid personal injury.

# Reform—child maintenance and other payments

## The Bill

16.47 The White Paper, *A New System of Child Maintenance* (2006) claimed to put forward a new and radical scheme to that which already existed and proposed a new formula for assessment, a new system for appeals and departures from the formula, and extensions to the existing system of enforcement. This was followed by the publication of the Child Maintenance and Other Payments Bill on 6 June 2007.

16.48 The Bill proposed to establish a new child maintenance delivery organization—the Child Maintenance and Enforcement Commission—to simplify how child maintenance is calculated, and to introduce tougher enforcement powers to collect arrears, for example Clause 46 included the ability to impose a curfew on a non-resident parent, which would be monitored electronically; and to remove a person's passport. Most importantly the reduced benefit s 46 was to be abolished. And existing parents with care whose application for child maintenance was made under s 6 (and was therefore compulsory) would have a choice of withdrawing from the statutory scheme should they wish to do so.

## The Child Maintenance and Other Payments Act 2008

16.49 Under this new Act the CS Agency is replaced by the Child Maintenance and Enforcement Commission, CMEC. Part of the draconian and punitive side of the former CS Agency will be removed as parents, may, if they wish, seek an assessment and no parent is placed under a duty to apply for child support. The role of the new Agency is to facilitate child support. Although at the time of writing there are proposals afoot to scrap the CMEC. Nonetheless, encouraging the payment of maintenance and compliance is a central objective. Wikeley suggests that it is 'carrots and sticks.':

> *The main carrot is the increased maintenance disregard for PWCs who are on means–tested benefits. The sticks are a whole new range of weapons which have been added to the Commission's collection and enforcement armoury. At the time of writing most of these latter measures have yet to be brought into force and are expected to come into operation between 2009 and 2011.*

But that does not mean that there is an absence of enforcement mechanism and the CMEC will have the following penalties available to them: including curfew orders, removal of travel documents, driving disqualification, and imprisonment.

It remains to be seen whether the swinging back somewhat of the pendulum will mean that the system becomes ineffective because of a too light touch on the question of maintenance payments for children (see Fotheringham, 2010).

## Private and public provision in the same purse

16.50 By 2006, the CS Agency had already been described as being in 'meltdown,' declared a 'fiasco', and described as a 'shambles'. In addition, resident and non-resident parents made a series of legal challenges against the agency whom they considered had failed to recover payments from absent parents (see *R (on the application of Kehoe) v Secretary of State for Work and Pensions (2005)*—in this case Mrs Kehoe was owed £17,000 in unrecovered maintenance).

16.51 In addition, the the courts came to assess what finances/assets were available to be divided between the parties on the break-up of a marriage, in cases where the family might also depend on the State, some judgments reflected the view that the court, in reaching a decision as to settlement, could take into account the State benefits that would be paid to the spouse on divorce in assessing the income of each of the parties.

16.52 In *Delaney v Delaney (1990)*, the Court of Appeal held that where the wife was entitled to family credit and the husband had only very limited resources, even when taking into account the contribution made by his girlfriend, the court was entitled to 'have regard to the fact that in proper cases social security benefits are available to the wife and children of the marriage'. Thus the court took these benefits into account when determining the assets of the respective parties (this was not the view taken in the CSA 1991). It was also not the general principle established in *Barnes v Barnes (1972)* and furthered in *Shallow v Shallow (1978)*, which stated that where a wife receives or could receive income support or family credit, this entitlement should, in most cases, be ignored when assessing the father/husband's obligation to maintain.

## Unpicking orders made prior to 1991

16.53 In *Crozier v Crozier (1994)*, the parties were divorced in 1988. A consent order was made in 1989 whereby the father transferred his interest in the former matrimonial home, which at that time had an equity of £16,000, to the mother in exchange for an assurance that he would have a no maintenance liability to the wife and a no maintenance liability for the child of the family both now and in the future. The order provided:

*this order is intended to effect full and final settlement of all financial and property claims arising between the parties from the breakdown of the marriage whether present or future, save for child maintenance.*

However, in March 1993, proceedings were brought by the Department of Social Security under the Social Security Administration Act 1992, s 106, requiring the father to contribute to the child's maintenance. The father was subsequently ordered to pay £4 per week under liable relative legislation. The father applied to have the consent order that was made prior to the CSA 1991 set aside. The court held that, although harsh, the consent order could not be set aside. Mr Crozier felt he was being required to pay twice over.

In *Farley v Secretary of State for Work and Pensions (2006)*, on 15 July 2003, an officer acting on behalf of the Secretary of State for Work and Pensions laid a complaint before the North Somerset magistrates' court that the amount of £32,639.94 was due from Mr Alec Farley by way of payments of child support. Mr Farley was required to show cause why a liability order should not be made under s 33. Apparently Mr Farley was self-employed, so there was no prospect of recovering payments under a deduction from earnings order.

Before the magistrates Mr Farley accepted that the amounts of maintenance set out in three maintenance assessments, dated 28 November 2002, 29 November 2002, and 3 December 2002, were outstanding and unpaid. These amounts totalled £32,639.94. Mr Farley's case before the magistrates was that these three maintenance assessments were not lawfully made. And that s 4(10) precluded an application for a maintenance assessment under s 4 if there was in existence a written maintenance agreement made before 5 April 1993.

The House resolved the matter in this way:

*My conclusion, therefore, is that section 33(4) precludes the justices from investigating whether a maintenance assessment, or maintenance calculation in the current terminology, is a nullity. That has been the position ever since section 33 was enacted in 1991. Such an investigation is a matter to be pursued today through the statutory appeal structure. I would allow this appeal. I would set aside the order of the Court of Appeal of 22 June 2005 insofar as it granted relief on Mr Farley's application for judicial review. I would dismiss this judicial review application and declare that the decisions of the magistrates and Keith J were correct in law.*

# The private arena of child support

16.54 The private law mechanisms for child support have also had a chequered history. Neville Brown asserted in 1968, that 'the law of maintenance has become a treacherous quagmire'. Part of the quagmire to which Brown referred was that there were two systems of maintenance, one in the divorce courts and the other in the magistrates' matrimonial jurisdiction. The failure of the system of private maintenance to recover monies from non-resident fathers for child support, and the divorce explosion in the 1960s, together with the rise in childbirth amongst unmarried and divorced women with their dependent children created an exponential rise of dependency on the State. With the advent of the CS Agency following the CSA 1991 it was envisaged that there would be a residual role for the courts in respect of those parents not in receipt of State benefit and therefore not mandated to go through the CS Agency with regard to an assessment of child maintenance. Indeed, in the early days after the CSA 1991, John Dewar argued in 1992 that with the introduction of the Act, it seemed unlikely that MCA 1973, ss 23–25 would survive for much longer.

However, the MCA 1973 has survived.

# Matrimonial Causes Act 1973, ss 23–25

16.55 In accordance with the Matrimonial and Family Proceedings Act 1984 (MFPA 1984), the MCA 1973 was amended in two significant ways; first, in the event of divorce, the court should give first consideration to the welfare of a minor or any child of the family when making financial arrangements.

Section 25 provides that 'it shall be the duty of the court' when deciding whether, and in what manner to exercise powers including those referred to above to have regard to 'all the circumstances of the case, first consideration being given to the welfare, while a minor, of any child of the family who has not attained the age of eighteen'.

Note the meaning of 'first' in *Suter* below and secondly, the court should try to achieve a 'clean break' between the parties in respect of financial settlement. In 1984, 148,501 children under the age of 16 years were children of divorcing parents (compared to 153,500 in 2003), therefore potentially there was a lot of work for court-based ancillary relief for children. The MCA 1973, as amended, provided for the following orders to be made: capital lump sum, matrimonial property, orders for weekly periodical payments for a wife (two types, fixed term/periodical payments), orders for weekly periodical payments for a child. After 1984, in line with the clean break principle, there was a decline in periodical payments to wives and a move to lump sum settlements.

> In **S v S (1986)**, the husband, Ringo Starr, the Beatles drummer, was extremely wealthy, and the court had to decide whether to grant the variation application by Starr (Starkey) in making a once and for all capital settlement. The court did so, ending the wife's periodical payments of £70,000 per annum, substituting a capital lump sum. The clean break was to be achieved by considering earning capacity and the steps each party should/could take to acquire this. This soon became a controversial issue, as often scant regard was paid

to the reality of a wife who had not worked and instead had cared for a family, who was unable or less able to provide a prospective employer with skills, experience, qualifications, and therefore whose position in the labour market was not a strong one. Further, the 'clean break' could not be affected where there were children whose material welfare was affected by the material well-being of the resident parent.

It became apparent that maintenance for children could not be considered in isolation from maintenance payments and/or other financial settlement on the resident parent. Indeed, financial provision for children was enmeshed with financial provision for the carer.

## A roof over the child's head

16.56 The courts have always been determined, wherever possible, to provide a roof over a child's head. For many years, where the wife had custody of the children, the commonest type of order made, was the *Mesher* order where the matrimonial property could not be sold until the children reached the age of 17 years, thus ensuring that children had security and their housing needs addressed with a roof over their heads.

16.57 As *Halsburys* (5:316) notes:

> Mesher (Mesher v Mesher and Hall (1973)), and Martin (Martin v Martin (1977)) orders are orders made originally in respect of matrimonial proceedings, but which are presumably also applicable in respect of civil partnership proceedings, which take effect as trusts under which the sale of a property is deferred until certain events occur or by way of charges over the property, where the realisation of the charge is postponed until the happening of those events. Under the terms of a Mesher order the sale is postponed, or realisation of the charge is deferred, until the death or remarriage of the party in occupation, the youngest child of the family attaining a certain age or ceasing full-time secondary or tertiary education, whichever is the later, or further order of the court ( Mesher v Mesher and Hall (1973). See eg Alonso v Alonso (1974) ;Browne (formerly Pritchard) v Pritchard(1975), CA; Drinkwater v Drinkwater (1984) ) and under the terms of a Martin order the sale is postponed, or realisation of the charge is deferred, until the death or remarriage of the party in occupation, such earlier date as he or she ceases to live at the property, or further order of the court.

The divorce settlement in ***Radmacher and Granatino (2010)*** includes a provision that a property settled in favour of the ex spouse should revert to the children now 11 years and seven years when they reach the age of 22 years. This decision allows children to visit the non-resident carer and have stays with the non-resident carer in comfort and ease with a view to facilitate contact rather than cushion, in this case, the adjustment of the non-carer to a reduced standard of living. The court said: '[16] The award should make provision for the husband's role as the father of the two children, but should not otherwise make provision for his own long term needs'.

16.58 When the MFPA 1984 was introduced, *Mesher* orders declined as it controverted the clean break principle between the parties, although frequently the courts would make a Mesher order transferring the matrimonial home to the carer spouse as a 'trade-off' against her making any future claim to periodical payments and/or capital settlement.

> In *Mortimer v Mortimer-Griffin (1986)*, the marriage had lasted 10 years. The husband had become unemployed. The wife lived in the former matrimonial home with their 24 year-old daughter. At first instance, a Mesher order was made giving the husband 40 per cent of the value of the house when sold. The Court of Appeal ruled that the husband should receive an immediate lump sum of £2,500, and the house be transferred to the wife outright.

> In *B v B (Mesher Order) (2003)*, following a marriage of under one year and one child born of the union, the deputy district judge ordered periodical payments for the wife and for the child, and ordered a lump sum so that the wife could house herself and the child. The judge did not make a Mesher order (upheld by the Court of Appeal) because the judge explained, 'it would leave the wife in fear of observation by the husband to see whether he could realise his charge'. The husband appealed to reduce the periodical payment quantum to limit the wife's payments to a fixed term and contended that there should have been a Mesher order.

> In *E v E (2006)*, where the parents were divorced and a joint residence order was made in favour of the parents, the financial proposal apparently agreed between the parties at the time was that there should be 'a *Mesher v Mesher* order in favour of the parent who remained in the residential home with the children'.

## The Children Act 1989

16.59 In accordance with the Children Act 1989 Sch 1, the court may make an order:

> *In the case of an application to the High Court or a county court, the court may make one or more of the following orders:*
>
> (a) *an order requiring either or both parents of a child to make to the applicant for the benefit of the child, or to make to the child himself, such periodical payments, for such term, as may be specified in the order;*
>
> (b) *an order requiring either or both parents of a child to secure to the applicant for the benefit of the child, or to secure to the child himself, such periodical payments, for such term, as may be so specified;*
>
> (c) *an order requiring either, or both parents of a child to pay to the applicant for the benefit of the child, or to pay to the child himself such lump sum as may be so specified;*
>
> (d) *an order requiring a settlement to be made for the benefit of the child, and to the satisfaction of the court, of property to which either parent is entitled (either in possession or in reversion) and which is specified in the order;*

*(e) an order requiring either or both parents of a child to transfer to the applicant for the benefit of the child or to transfer to the child himself such property to which the parent is, or the parents are, entitled (either in possession or in reversion) as may be specified in the order.*

16.60 In *CF v KM (2010)*, a jurisdictional issue on appeal arose as to whether the court has power, where a child maintenance calculation below the maximum assessment is in place, to make a payment for the benefit of the child in respect of legal fees of Sch 1 of the Children Act 1989 proceedings and/or other proceedings (s 8 proceedings). The court held that it does have jurisdiction.

## Child maintenance and the wealthy

16.61 However, the principles guiding the courts where there are very large sums of money involved have been lacking in precision and consistency. In *J v C (Child: Financial Provision) (1998)* it was held that 'a child is entitled to be brought up in circumstances which bear some sort of relationship with the father's current resources and standard of living'. Some guidance is offered in *Halsburys* 7, (4) (546):

> The approach of a court in determining cases where the financial resources are substantial is to start by deciding on an appropriate home for the child, then decide the cost of equipping and furnishing that home and finally the appropriate budget that the mother reasonably requires: see Re P (child: financial provision) supra at [45] per Thorpe LJ. A decision to make a lump sum order must be reasoned and based on findings of fact as to the capital resources of the party against whom the order is made: Re C (a minor) (financial provision: lump sum order) [1994] 2 FCR 1122, [1995] 1 FLR 925. See also K v H (financial provision for child) [1993] 1 FCR 683, sub nom K v H (child maintenance) [1993] 2 FLR 61 (court must have regard to child's financial needs).

However, the precise proportion is left open.

16.62 Where there are substantial sums of money it is assumed that such large sums, as they provide more than adequately for children perhaps, should not be interfered with. Although the courts have applied a construct of 'reasonable'. In *Miller v Miller; McFarlane v McFarlane (2006)*:

> [86]The district judge concluded that £60,000 a year for the children's maintenance was reasonable and that the appropriate award for the wife was £250,000 a year.' However, where there are limited fund children's financial support will fall somewhere between the maintenance payments made by the absent parent to be topped up where necessary by state support. Enforced by the CMRA which is at the moment of writing undergoing reform.

See also *McFarlane v McFarlane; Parlour v Parlour (2004)*. And also note that orders for children are made until further order least the circumstances of the absent parent changes.

In *Hvorostovsky v Hvorostovsky (2009)*, the wife returned to the court with regard to maintenance for herself and the children because of the increased earning capacity of the former husband—a leading world class baritone. On appeal the court held:

*[28] The judge's order of £12,500 per child appears to me to be low. We do not know and cannot now extrapolate what figure 'the judge put on indirect childrens' expenditure, that is to say all the costs of home, household and holidays born by the primary career. As a generality £12,500 seems to me a low figure given the extent of the father's income and the high standard of living that all his dependents enjoy. However it seems that both counsel directed their submissions to one global target. Neither called evidence that would enable the level of child periodical payments to be more profoundly assessed. When we enquired whether the twins have holidays and other staying contact with the father, neither counsel offered an answer.*

*... [34] Having regard to the need for proportionality, I would increase the wife's periodical payments ordered to £140,000 per annum and the child orders to £15,000 per annum. The overall gain for the wife in this appeal will then be £25,000 per annum or twice the judge's allowance for generosity.*

16.63   However, Lord Justice Thorpe in 2009 recognized this: 'There have, during the past generation, been radical statutory innovations, mostly with very poor outcome, for child maintenance but I exclude them from my territory'. A final word should be said about the new Child Maintenance Enforcement Commission, which is now to be abolished before it has even been properly established and whose decisions are already subject to legal challenge (see *PB v Child Maintenance and Enforcement Commission (2009)*; *Child Maintenance Enforcement Commission v Forrest (2010)*).

We watch this complex and rapidly developing area of law with considerable interest and apprehension.

## FURTHER READING

Bird J, *Child Maintenance* (3rd edn, Family Law, 1996)

Brown LN, 'Maintenance and Esoterism' (1968) 31 MLR 31 (121)

Childs M and Boden R, 'Paying for Procreation: Child Support Arrangements in the UK' (1996) Feminist Legal Studies 4 (2) 131

DHSS White Paper, *Children Come First* (Cmnd 1264, 1990)

Edwards S and Halpern A, 'Regional "Injustice" Financial Provision on Divorce' (1990) Journal of Social Welfare Law 71

Edwards S, Halpern A, and Gould C, 'The Continuing Saga of Maintaining the Family after Divorce [1990] Family Law 31–35

Edwards S, and Halpern, A, 'Parental Responsibility: An Instrument of Social Policy' [1992] Fam Law 113

Fotheringham J, 'In Practice: Child Support: New Powers for CMEC' [2010] Fam Law 849

Gilmore S, '*Re B (Contact: Child Support)*—horses and carts: contact and child support' [2007] CFLQ 357

Kaganas, F and Piper, C 'Shared parenting —a 70% solution? [2002] CFLQ 365

MacCormick N, 'Children's Rights: A Test-Case for theories of Right' in N MacCormick, *Legal Right and Social Democracy: Essays in Legal and Political Philosophy* (Clarendon Press, Oxford 1982)

*Married or not in Britain today, key facts, key trends,* One Plus One.org.uk

Pirrie J, 'Child Support Update, Part 1' (2002) Fam Law 195

*The Rt Hon Lord Justice Thorpe* 'London—The Divorce Capital of the World' [2009] Fam Law 21

Wikeley N, 'Kehoe v Secretary of State for Work and Pensions: No Redress when the Child Support Agency Fails to Deliver' (1995) CFLQ 17(1) 113

Wikeley N, *Child Support Law and Policy* (Oxford, Portland, Oregon, Hart Publishing 2006)

*Wikeley N,* 'Child Support: Carrots and Sticks' [2008] Fam Law 1102

## SELF-TEST QUESTIONS

1 John Dewar argued that with the introduction of the CSA 1991, it seemed unlikely that the MCA 1973, ss 23–25 could survive for much longer without a root and branch reappraisal. Evaluate this prediction by considering the principles, which apply to both of the aforementioned statutes and examine the relevant case law.

2 The CSA 1991 was introduced to revolutionize the system in the UK for providing financial maintenance for children by requiring the biological/adoptive parents of a child (both the parent with residence and the absent /non resident parent) to meet their respective responsibilities, and by setting up a State mechanism to enforce their obligation, and also by providing a system of penalties for those who fail to comply. Has it? What were the major benefits, if any, to children arising from the CS Agency?

3 What are the problems for mothers who have experienced domestic violence in the requirement that naming the non-resident father is a precondition of receiving benefit? And to what extent have these problems led to the provision in the 2008 Act abolishing this direction?

4 What is the basis for the presumption of paternity in the CSPSSA 2000, s 15?

5  John Eekelaar argued: 'when circumstances allow it, the main objective of the courts, and also of most care giving parents, is to retain the house for the children. The rest of the package is fashioned to achieve that purpose. Under the [Child Support Act 1991] the child support element is fixed; it may not then be possible to fashion the package so as to prevent the homelessness of the children'. Discuss.

6  What is the logic behind the thinking that places the resident parent as central in disclosing details of the non-resident parent for the purpose of child support but, as *Kehoe* demonstrates, denies the resident party the right to participate in the proceedings for enforcement? Has that logic now been set aside?

# Index